W9-BKU-035

NEW BOOK
NO REFUND IF REMOVED
B 63.00

Fourth Edition

Drugs and Human Behavior

David M. Grilly
Cleveland State University

SUFFOLK UNIVERSITY
MILDRED F. SAWYER LIBRARY.
8 ASHBURTON PLACE
BOSTON. MA 02108

Allyn and Bacon
Boston • London • Toronto • Sydney • Tokyo • Singapore

Executive Editor: Carolyn O. Merrill
Editorial Assistant: Jonathan Bender
Marketing Manager: Caroline Croley
Editorial-Production Administrator: Annette Joseph
Editorial-Production Coordinator: Holly Crawford
Editorial-Production Service: Colophon
Composition Buyer: Linda Cox
Electronic Art and Composition: Omegatype Typography, Inc.
Manufacturing Buyer: JoAnne Sweeney
Cover Administrator: Kristina Mose-Libon
Cover Designer: Joel Gendron

Copyright © 2002, 1998, 1994, 1989 by Allyn & Bacon
A Pearson Education Company
75 Arlington Street, Suite 300
Boston, MA 02116

Internet: www.ablongman.com

All rights reserved. No part of the material protected by this copyright notice may be reproduced or utilized in any form or by any means, electronic or mechanical, including photocopying, recording, or by any information storage and retrieval system, without written permission from the copyright owner.

Between the time Website information is gathered and then published, it is not unusual for some sites to have closed. Also, the transcription of URLs can result in unintended typographical errors. The publisher would appreciate notification where these occur so that they may be corrected in subsequent editions. Thank you.

Library of Congress Cataloging-in-Publication Data
Grilly, David M.
  Drugs and human behavior / David M. Grilly.—4th ed.
    p. cm.
  Includes bibliographical references and index.
  ISBN 0-205-31831-2 (alk. paper)
    1. Psychopharmacology.   I. Title.

RM315 .G75 2001
615'.78—dc21
                            2001022022

Printed in the United States of America
10 9 8 7 6 5 4 3   RRD-VA 06 05 04 03 02

To my wife, Debra,
for her patience and support

Contents

Preface

It is a very rare person who does not, at some time or another, use a psychoactive drug—that is, a drug that alters psychological processes such as mood, thought, and behavior. In fact, some drugs, such as caffeine, nicotine, and alcohol, are so common in our society that we usually do not even think of them as drugs. Although the use of psychoactive drugs has a long history, the actual systematic study of the relationships between drugs and psychological processes—psychopharmacology—is quite new. Therefore, our knowledge about psychoactive drugs is relatively limited. This is rather unfortunate because their use is pervasive in most Western cultures, particularly our own. Drugs are used in a wide variety of social, recreational, and therapeutic settings.

The purpose of this book is to introduce the student to the field of psychopharmacology, with special emphasis on the relationships between drugs, their mechanisms of action in the nervous system, and human behavior. For most students, this book will be their first exposure to this diverse field. The text is written for the psychology student who wishes to go into some field of research associated with drugs or into clinical areas where the persons they deal with are taking psychoactive medications or using psychoactive drugs recreationally, and perhaps abusing them. It is also written for nursing students, who will be observing patients who are prescribed psychoactive medication; chemistry students, who may be interested in going into pharmacy; biology students, who may enter the field of medicine and eventually prescribe a number of psychoactive medications for their patients; and any other students interested in the fascinating relationships among drugs, the brain, emotions, mental activities, and behavior.

Because psychopharmacology involves biological functions, chemical reactions, physics, and psychological processes, ideally students reading this book will already have a basic familiarity with each of these areas. The text is not written for the specialist. Therefore, the use of esoteric and specialized jargon to describe the effects of drugs and the psychiatric and psychological conditions they induce or alleviate has been minimized. Key pharmacological terms are set in boldface type and defined the first time they appear. Other scientific and clinical terms that could impede the student's understanding of certain principles are italicized and defined. All definitions in this text are from the following sources: *Stedman's Medical Dictionary,* 25th Edition; *Dictionary of Psychology,* 2nd Edition, by A. S. Reber; *Mosby's Medical and Nursing Dictionary;* and *Webster's Deluxe Unabridged Dictionary,* 2nd Edition. The descriptions and classifications of mental disorders are roughly based on those described in the *Diagnostic and Statistical Manual of Mental Disorders,* 4th Edition (DSM-IV), published by the American Psychiatric Association in 1994.

It is hoped that the information contained in this book will enable the student to appreciate more fully why people use drugs and what the consequences of that use might be. Chapter 1 deals briefly with the field of psychopharmacology from a historical perspective. Chapters 2 and 3 acquaint the student with the principles and mechanisms behind the actions of drugs that can be generalized to all drugs, including those affecting mood, mental functions, and behavior. Chapters 4 and 5 review the nervous system, through which psychoactive drugs induce their effects. All thoughts, emotions, and behaviors are the result of electrical and biochemical activities taking place in the nervous system, and drugs that affect these psychological variables do so by disturbing or altering these activities. Without an understanding of the basic mechanisms behind these electrical and biochemical events, it will be very difficult for the student to appreciate and understand why psychoactive drugs do what they do. These first five chapters contain definitions of psychopharmacological terms and describe concepts necessary for understanding the processes and actions of the drugs to be discussed in the remaining chapters.

Chapter 6 discusses the general processes behind drug tolerance, drug abuse, and drug dependence. Chapters 7 through 11 classify, describe, and discuss the actions and effects of drugs commonly used in our culture for social and recreational purposes, often leading to drug abuse and dependence. Many of these drugs have been or still are being used in a medical or psychiatric context, but their present impact on our society is due primarily to their use in nonmedical settings. These are the drugs with which the students themselves may have direct contact.

Chapters 12 through 14 describe and discuss the actions and effects of drugs used primarily in the treatment of medical and emotional disturbances. Although these drugs are used in a medical context, many students in psychology, biology, chemistry, and nursing will go on to specialize in clinical fields where the patient population has been prescribed such medications. In order to deal fully with the needs of their clients, these clinicians should be aware of what these drugs are capable of doing, what their side effects are, and why they are being prescribed. Even students who do not become clinicians should be aware of these properties because there is a strong likelihood that they will have friends or family members who do use these drugs.

I would like to thank the many students I have taught over the years who have provided the inspiration behind this book and whose comments and suggestions on the previous editions led to considerable modification in the content of the present edition. I am most indebted to Barb Simon, Jody Pickle, and Rachel Wolf for their assistance in putting the second, third, and fourth editions together and making them more readable from the standpoint of the student. Finally, I would like to thank the reviewers for the present edition—Lee Bakner, Linfield College; Jeffrey S. Mogil, University of Illinois; Kim Roberts, Sacramento State University; Thomas F. Sawyer, North Central College; and Brent C. White, Centre College—and also my colleagues, listed here, who read and commented on previous editions. Their comments were invaluable. They include Lisa Baker, Western Michigan University; Robert W. Bell, Texas Tech University; John Broida, University of Southern Maine; Mark Masaki, Youngstown State University; Helen M. Murphy, John Carroll University; Gaylord Ellison, University of California, Los Angeles; Dennis Glanzman, Arizona State University; Carol van Hartesveldt, University of Florida, Gainesville; Keith Jacobs, Loyola University, New Orleans; and W. Jeffrey Wilson, Purdue University at Fort Wayne.

Chapter *1*

Psychopharmacology in Perspective

The use of drugs that alter brain function and behavior is ubiquitous, with considerable ramifications for individuals and society. For example, seven of the 10 leading causes of disability in the United States either involve disorders that drugs are commonly used to treat (major depression, schizophrenia, manic depressive illness, obsessive-compulsive disorder, dementia, and degenerative CNS disorders) or involve alcohol or other drug use disorders (Hyman, 2000). **Psychopharmacology** is the discipline that attempts to systematically study the effects of drugs on behavior, cognitive functioning, and emotions. Drugs that alter behavior, cognitive functioning, or emotions are called **psychoactive** or **psychotropic drugs.** The term *psychopharmacology* is a combination of the terms *psychology* and *pharmacology,* which refer, respectively, to the study of the variables affecting behavior and the study of the effects of drugs on biological systems. Originally the word *psyche* referred to the soul, but lately it has been used to refer to the mind—an abstract concept commonly used to represent the totality of hypothesized mental processes and acts that serve as explanatory devices for psychological data. *Pharmakos* originally meant scapegoat; a pharmakos was a person who was sacrificed as a remedy for whatever maladies another person might have been experiencing. For obvious reasons, there were few volunteers for the position, but I suppose that the procedure worked in roughly a third of the cases—about the same success rate one might get nowadays using a placebo. Later on, around 600 B.C., the term came to refer to a medicine, drug, or poison. Presently, the term *drug* is used in a much more general way to denote chemicals that alter the normal biological functions of the body.

Psychoactive drugs are chemicals that induce psychological effects by altering the normal biochemical reactions that take place in the nervous system. A drug's chemical structure, how much of the drug is taken, how long it has been since it was taken, and how frequently it is taken are important factors that will be discussed in relation to the drug experience. In addition, three other ingredients in the drug experience should always be kept in mind: the **set** (the psychological makeup and the expectations of the individual taking the drug), the **setting** (the social and physical environment in which the drug is taken), and the individual's unique biochemical makeup (Wallace & Fisher, 1999). Factors such as the physical setting and the person's body chemistry, attitudes, emotional state, and previous drug experiences all interact with the drug to alter the person's level of awareness, mood, thought processes, and behavior. These factors should always be taken into consideration in any attempt to describe the effects of a particular psychoactive drug.

A drug should not be viewed as simply bad or good. Consideration must be given to how much is taken, what it is taken for, and in what context it is taken. For example, heroin can be a very effective drug in the treatment of pain in terminally ill cancer patients, and cocaine is a very effective local anesthetic for use in certain kinds of surgery. However, when injected in unknown quantities for their euphoric properties, these drugs can lead to dependence, economic and social disaster, incarceration, toxic reactions, and death.

A Historical Overview of Psychopharmacology

Ancient records indicate that human beings have been using drugs to alter mood and behavior for a long time. (For fascinating and more detailed discussion of this topic, see Brecher, 1972; Caldwell, 1978; and Szasz, 1974.) Considering the thousands of plants available that contain psychoactive substances and the likelihood that our ancestors were just as curious and willing to experiment on themselves as some people are today, this information should not come as any surprise. Substances that can induce mystical experiences and hallucinations are found in cannabis and in numerous herbs, mushrooms, and cacti, all of which grow throughout the world.

For example, in order to enhance their ferociousness, early Viking warriors were said to ingest the mushroom *Amanita muscaria,* which is capable of inducing gaiety, exuberance, and berserk behavior—a term derived from their name, the Berserkers. Some Native American Indians have used the peyote cactus, which contains the hallucinogen (hallucination-producing substance) mescaline, in their religious ceremonies for centuries. (Their use of peyote for this purpose was legal until 1990, when a U.S. Supreme Court ruling made it illegal. It was returned to legal status in 1993 when Congress passed the Religious Freedom Restoration Act, but the Act was subsequently ruled unconstitutional by the U.S. Supreme Court in 1997.) Archaeological findings of "mushroom stones" in Guatemala indicate that a sophisticated mushroom cult existed there some 3,500 years ago. Early Spanish chroniclers wrote of their opposition to the Aztecs' ceremonial eating of the diabolical mushroom *teonanacatl* (food of the gods) for purposes of divination, prophecy, and worship. It is likely that these mushrooms contained the hallucinogenic substances psilocybin and psilocin. Cannabis, which we now call marijuana, was first used more than 4,000 years ago, primarily for its medical value in treating a number of different ailments.

Opium poppies, which contain the narcotics morphine and codeine, were probably used by the ancient Sumerians in Mesopotamia almost 7,000 years ago. Substances that effectively suppress manic symptoms can be found in rauwolfia, a plant common to the Himalayas. Substances that elevate mood and reduce fatigue are found in many plants. For centuries South American Indians have chewed the coca leaf, which contains small amounts of the drug cocaine, to alleviate fatigue, elevate mood, and reduce hunger, and archaeological evidence suggests that early humans may have used coca as far back as 3000 B.C.

The use of tea as a pleasurable stimulant began about A.D. 600 in China. An intoxicating beverage made from coffee beans was introduced to the Arabians in the thirteenth century. Numerous other plants containing caffeine or similar-acting substances have been used by ancient cultures in Mexico, South America, and Africa, among many others. The use of nicotine-containing tobacco by Native Americans goes back at least 2,200 years.

In ceremonies during medieval times, witches used various herbs (such as mandrake, henbane, and belladonna) containing scopolamine, hyoscyamine, and atropine to induce hallucinations and the sensation of flying. They also may have thrown in a few toads, whose sweat glands contain the hallucinogenic drug bufotenine, one of the few psychoactive drugs of animal origin. Physicians during this and later periods used the same substances as sleep inducers and analgesics, as well as for other purposes.

Except perhaps for caffeine, the most common psychoactive substance used around the world today is alcohol, and it has been available for thousands of years. There is hardly a culture, primitive or advanced, that does not value its peculiar properties. Alcohol is a simple product of fermentation, which occurs when certain yeasts, molds, and bacteria act upon sugar in a variety of fruits and which is easily produced both accidentally and purposefully. The earliest records of purposeful alcohol production were left by the Egyptians more than 5,500 years ago, and there is physical evidence that wine was being produced in what is now western Iran 2,000 years before this.

Every culture that we are aware of has used a plant or plants with psychoactive properties at one time or another. In their experimentation over the centuries, human beings must have eaten, drunk, smoked, or rubbed on their bodies thousands of substances. They found that some of these substances nourished them, while others made them ill or killed them, relieved their psychological or physical discomforts, or had extraordinary and incomprehensible effects on mood, consciousness, or behavior.

Even nonhuman animals have been observed to seek out substances with mood-altering properties (Siegel, 1989). Elephants, chimpanzees, baboons, and horses have been noted to prefer water containing a small percentage of alcohol over pure water. Some birds prefer fermented berries over unfermented berries. Goats nibble coffee berries; some species of bees guzzle stupefying nectars of specialized flowers; llamas chew coca leaves (which contain cocaine); and some species of ants maintain "herds" of beetles, apparently for their intoxicating secretions. These observations have led Siegel to propose the intriguing—and controversial—hypothesis that intoxication is a universal "fourth drive," as natural as the innate drives of hunger, thirst, and sex.

Predecessors to Modern Pharmacotherapies

During the 1800s a number of psychoactive drugs were isolated or distilled from plants or developed from nonplant sources. Morphine was isolated from opium in 1805 and was viewed as a most effective treatment for periodic insanity. Cocaine was extracted from the coca leaf in 1857 and was suggested as a potential treatment for depression. Bromine, discovered in 1826, and chloral, discovered in 1832, were used as sedatives and sleep-inducing agents. The anesthetic gases chloroform and nitrous oxide were suggested as potential treatments for insanity. Compounds such as cannabis, hemlock, strychnine, and *Datura stramonium*—used for centuries to treat a variety of disorders—were still viewed as valuable psychiatric tools, although we realize today that they probably did more harm than good. The first phenothiazine (a type of antipsychotic discussed in Chapter 12), methylene blue, was developed in 1883. A few years later, it was reported to have calming effects on manic and hallucinating patients. Despite its apparent effectiveness, it would take another 50 years before the closely related compound chlorpromazine would revolutionize the treatment of the severely mentally disturbed. Drug-induced sleep therapy, where emotionally disturbed patients were kept unconscious for several days, became popular toward the end of the nineteenth century.

It was during the 1800s that investigations of the formal relationships between drug variables and psychological processes, particularly those involved in mental illness, began. The first of these investigations was probably that conducted by Jacques-Joseph Moreau de Tours, a highly respected physician in France. In the mid-1800s he published a book, for which he is most noted, called *Hashish and Mental Illness*. After taking a hashish-laced concoction (hashish is a concentrated form of marijuana) on numerous occasions and observing others who volunteered to ingest his concoction, he compared the drug-induced symptoms with the mental symptoms that occur spontaneously in psychoses. Moreau was one of the first to emphasize that the person's particular or immediate context greatly influenced both the quality and intensity of the drug experience. He also observed the effects of hashish on some of his patients with mental disorders and suggested that hashish-induced excitement may be beneficial in treating depressed patients. He reported that some depressed individuals, after taking his hashish concoction, chatted, laughed, and acted silly all evening. Unfortunately, however, those effects were transitory, and the patients relapsed. He also found that occasionally manic patients improved after taking hashish.

Moreau also studied the psychoactive effects of opiates, nitrous oxide, and a number of sedative-hypnotic drugs. Unfortunately, his work in this area went largely unrecognized by his contemporaries, but shortly after *Hashish and Mental Illness* was published, a few American psychiatrists who read of his work tried cannabis preparations in the treatment of insanity. Despite the lack of recognition during his time, today some people view Moreau as the first psychopharmacologist.

However, the very first book in modern experimental psychopharmacology, as well as the first book solely devoted to drugs and animal behavior, was published in 1826 by A. P. Charvel, a young medical student (Siegel, 1989). Charvel studied the effects of opium on a variety of animals, including water beetles, crayfish, snails, fish, toads, birds, and various mammals (including himself and other medical students). Like Moreau, Charvel discovered that a drug's effects depend on numerous factors, such as the individual's history, tolerance to the drug, dose, and method of administration. But like the observations of Moreau, Charvel's discoveries were largely ignored by his contemporaries.

During the late 1800s and early 1900s, some of the most famous early psychologists were also some of the first to explore systematically the relationship between various drugs and psychological variables. Early in his career, Sigmund Freud spent three years investigating the effects of cocaine on fatigue, depression, strength, and morphine addiction, among other things. In many of these studies, he was the test subject. Until recently, many of the most comprehensive, up-to-date descriptions of cocaine's effects were contained in Freud's

25-page essay "Über Coca" (On Coca), published in 1884. However, a growing number of reports critical of cocaine at that time, as well as Freud's own dismal failure in treating a good friend's morphine addiction with cocaine (the friend turned from morphine to heavy cocaine use), led him to direct his scientific interests into very different areas. However, Freud retained an interest in drugs and behavior throughout his lifetime. Curiously, although Freud was able to give up cocaine, apparently with very little discomfort, he remained a nicotine addict who chain-smoked cigars despite suffering from angina (chest pain) and having had multiple operations for oral cancer (Brecher, 1972). Even the man who discovered the ego-defense mechanism of denial was unable to avoid its consequences.

Ivan Pavlov, best known for his work in the conditioning of reflexes, attempted to treat schizophrenics by using some of his conditioning techniques and inducing long periods of sleep with bromides. However, it is doubtful that he was very successful with this technique, because bromides tend to accumulate in the body and can reach levels that can induce toxic symptoms such as headache, sedation, violent delirium, mental confusion, and gastric distress. In some cases, these symptoms are very similar to those of a psychosis. Pavlov's work in the area of conditioning reflexes led some of his colleagues to use drugs like morphine as potential stimuli for the induction of new reflexes. These researchers probably did not realize just how important the Pavlovian process is in what we now refer to as drug dependence.

William James, the first American-born psychologist, wrote about some of his fascinating experiences while under the influence of nitrous oxide, sometimes known as "laughing gas" (Leavitt, 1982). He found that consciousness, in which he was very interested, could be profoundly altered by nitrous oxide, although not necessarily for the better. It seems that while he was under the influence of nitrous oxide (the effects last but a few minutes), he was capable of very mystic revelations. Unfortunately, though, he could never remember what the revelations were when the effects wore off. It is reported that upon one occasion while under the influence he was able to quickly jot down one of these profundities. It read

> *Hogamous, higamous*
> *Man is polygamous*
> *Higamous, hogamous*
> *Woman is monogamous.*
> (Gibbons & Connelly, 1970, p. 77)

The first half of the twentieth century was accompanied by the synthesis or clinical use of a wide variety of new psychoactive substances with potential therapeutic value. Barbiturates were introduced in 1903 and helped sustain interest in sleep therapy for various mental ailments. Amphetamine, first synthesized in the 1800s, came into clinical use in 1927 in the treatment of narcolepsy and mild depressive states. Albert Hofmann first synthesized lysergic diethylamide (LSD) in 1938. Five years later, when he accidentally ingested LSD during one of his experiments, he discovered that it was one of the most potent psychoactive substances known to humankind. LSD would be used a few years later as a psychedelic (mind-manifesting) adjunct to psychotherapy and as a means of inducing what many people believed to be a model psychosis.

The Psychopharmacological Revolution

Despite the extensive history of drug use and these early investigations, there was no real interest in studying drugs and their influence on cognition, emotions, and behavior until the middle of the twentieth century. During the 1950s, a drug used in France as a preanesthetic was tested on some schizophrenic patients and was found to induce a dramatic reduction in their symptoms. Previously, many different drugs had been used in treating schizophrenia; all of these simply put the patients to sleep or made them so drowsy or sedated that they could not do anything. This particular drug, however, did more than simply calm the patients; it worked by reducing the core symptoms of the disorder. The drug was known as chlorpromazine, and, as we will see shortly, it was this discovery that led to the formation of the formal and distinct discipline known as psychopharmacology.

One of the first antihistamines was developed in 1937. Although antihistamines were initially used in the treatment of allergies, their sedative properties, viewed by those taking them for allergic conditions as an undesirable side effect, were suspected as being beneficial in the treatment of other clinical conditions. The antihistamine promethazine was introduced in 1949 as an adjunct to surgery. It was found to reduce surgical shock, to calm patients both before and after major surgery, and to reduce the emotional suffering associated with surgery. A year later it was used by a psychiatrist in the treatment of schizophrenia, primarily for its hypnotic effects. Although promethazine calmed his patients, the psychiatrist apparently saw it as just another sedative. In the same year another psychiatrist noted similar calming effects in schizophrenic patients with a related compound, but the manufacturer was not interested in developing such a drug. However, reports of these effects in surgical patients and schizophrenics eventually led to the evaluation and development of compounds with similar structures with even more specific actions.

One of these compounds, initially called 4560 RP, was found to have some interesting pharmacological properties (Mitchell, 1993). It had minimal antihistaminic action, but it reduced both sympathetic and parasympathetic activity, abolished conditioned reflexes, and had a host of other desirable properties. In clinical trials it abolished preoperative anxiety, reduced surgical stress, and eliminated the postoperative consequences of stress. Here was a drug that could turn off the world and its harrowing stress without inebriating the patient or putting the patient to sleep. The surgeon who attempted these clinical tests closed his report with the suggestion that 4560 RP, now called chlorpromazine, be used in treating psychiatric conditions. The first report on chlorpromazine treatment of psychosis was published in France in 1952. In 1953 chlorpromazine was tried more extensively in psychiatric wards in Paris.

It could be said that at that time chlorpromazine started the pharmacological revolution in psychiatry. Although it did not cure mania and schizophrenia, chlorpromazine did suspend their symptoms with great efficacy and much less toxicity than any previous drug. Chlorpromazine was used immediately in Italy and Switzerland, and shortly thereafter in the United States. Its use spread to England and South America in 1954 and to Australia, Japan, and the Soviet Union in 1955. Its trade name in Europe was Largactil, because of its *large* spectrum of therapeutic *acti*vity. In the United States it was marketed as Thorazine, perhaps after the powerful god of thunder, Thor (although this derivation is purely speculative).

The pharmacological revolution expanded. Between 1952 and 1954, chlorpromazine monopolized drug therapy for all mental diseases. It stirred the ambitions of drug manufacturers and researchers. New drugs were developed, and drugs that had been abandoned were clinically tested again. In India as early as 1931 it was suggested that the rauwolfia plant, which contains reserpine, had some beneficial effects in the treatment of mental disorders, but it was not introduced to the Western world until 1954. Meprobamate, the first of the so-called anxiolytics (anxiety reducers), was first used clinically in 1955 and became as popular for the treatment of neuroses as chlorpromazine was for psychoses. The treatment of depression with the first of the monoamine oxidase inhibitors (iproniazide) became acceptable in 1957, five years after its antidepressant action was noted in tuberculosis patients who were administered the drug for its antituberculosis properties. A drug developed in 1948, with properties that did not generate any enthusiasm on the part of its manufacturer, was again tested clinically in 1957 because of its molecular resemblance to chlorpromazine. Unlike the phenothiazines, however, the drug was relatively ineffective in quieting agitated psychotic patients. Instead, it seemed to have remarkable mood-lifting properties in severely depressed patients. Thus was born the first tricyclic antidepressant, imipramine (Tofranil).

The enthusiasm created by chlorpromazine led to one oversight with respect to a drug that would later take the place of chlorpromazine as one of the most valuable treatments for cyclical mood disorders. As early as 1870, it was suggested that, in one of its salt forms, lithium, an alkali metal, had mood-altering effects. It wasn't until 1949, however, that the Australian psychiatrist John Cade discovered, quite fortuitously, that lithium had profound mood-stabilizing effects in manic patients. Despite verification of his findings in studies conducted one or two years later, the vast majority of psychiatric practitioners remained unimpressed with his findings. Lithium was believed to be too toxic. It also had minimal marketability because it was unpatentable as a natural substance. In addition, chlorpromazine suppressed the symptoms of mania much more quickly than lithium did and had a much lower potential for toxicity. It took almost 10 years for the medical community, at least in the United States, to recognize the true value of lithium and to rectify the oversight.

LSD research advanced because of chlorpromazine and the interest stimulated between brain biochemistry and psychosis. Because chlorpromazine could readily block the effects of LSD, it made research and psychotherapy with LSD safer. LSD psychosis became the model with which other potential antipsychotic drugs could be tested, and with LSD inducing a model psychosis, it became a tool in exploring the etiology (the science of causes or origins of diseases) of schizophrenia. However, we now know that the LSD psychosis is considerably different from the psychoses that occur naturally in humans.

Beginning in the early 1950s, a multitude of drugs were developed that revolutionized the treatment of major mental and emotional illnesses. Despite the increase in the number of diagnosed schizophrenic patients due to the growth in the general population, the number of schizophrenic patients hospitalized in the United States has dropped from around 600,000 in 1954 to less than 200,000 today. The goal of the community mental health movement—to deinstitutionalize patients and allow them to function successfully in the community—became a reality. Many patients who were totally refractory to behavioral therapy and psychotherapies became more amenable to these treatments with these drugs. The new pharmacotherapies also encouraged practitioners to become more rigorous in their diagnoses. The drugs stimulated interest in the relationships between brain biochemistry and behavior.

Since the 1950s psychopharmacologists have made great strides in understanding and treating virtually every affliction of the human mind. Many, if not most, mental disorders are now viewed as having a biochemical basis and can often be treated as such. (It should not be inferred from this statement that environmental events such as stress, conflict, and inappropriate parental activities are not important factors in these biochemical disturbances or that psychologically based therapies are inappropriate in treating many forms of mental dysfunctions. We will leave these issues for others to discuss in textbooks more suited for those purposes.)

With new techniques, such as magnetic resonance imaging, computerized axial tomography, and positron emission tomography, researchers are now able to look at the machinery and workings of the living brain. Molecular biologists are even beginning to relate abnormal behavior to specific parts of chromosomes. The specific actions of new drugs like clozapine (Clozaril), risperidone (Risperdal), fluoxetine (Prozac), and buspirone (BuSpar) are giving us a better understanding of the relationship between moods and feelings, and the action of specific chemicals in the brain. Drugs with greater degrees of specificity and effectiveness have been developed for treating schizophrenia and depression. Symptoms of disorders such as Tourette's syndrome, panic and phobic disorders, and obsessive-compulsive disorder, which were previously treated with ineffective psychoanalytic talk therapy, can now be reduced or eliminated with newly developed drugs. Different methods of delivering old drugs, like morphine, into the body have been developed that have enhanced their effectiveness or reduced their side effects. More information about these drugs, disorders, mechanisms of action, and methods will be presented in subsequent chapters.

Unfortunately, however, psychotherapeutic drugs do not cure mental disorders or suppress their symptoms in all individuals. Sometimes they cause toxic or irreversible side effects. The potential for such side effects brings out a number of ethical questions about the right of a society to control the behavior of individuals with substances that might do them harm. Although drugs allow patients to leave hospitals, the communities to which the patients return are often poorly prepared to provide continuing care. In other cases practitioners rely solely on medications to deal with their patients' problems, without looking into other psychological or socioeconomical interventions that might be available and beneficial for their patients. In spite of the fact that the prognosis for mentally and emotionally ill people is much better now than it was 45 years ago, we as a society must continue searching for drugs with greater specificity and for other interventions that will help us deal with these problems and allow these individuals to lead happier and more productive lives.

Recreational and Social Drug Use

Many individuals who exhibit the normal range of moods, emotions, cognitive activity, and behavior willingly administer drugs to themselves to alter their emotional experiences, consciousness, or behavior in recreational, social, or religious settings. Such phenomena are of particular interest to psychopharmacologists. Very few individuals in modern cultures do not, at some time or another, use a psychoactive drug for such a purpose. Even caffeine, nicotine, and alcohol, which we often do not even think of as drugs, are psychoactive drugs. In many cases, taking these drugs is explicitly (in advertisements) or implicitly indicated as having positive or beneficial effects. For example, smoking cigarettes and drinking alcohol are often portrayed in fiction as beneficial tools for coping with emotionally stressful situations (Kushnir, 1986). As a whole the mass media reflect the national culture and have conditioned Americans to accept drug use as part of daily life (Gitlin, 1990). (With all the references to drugs—many of them uncritical, to say the least—it is reasonable that questions should be raised about the media's contributions to drug use.)

In the 1990s, national surveys indicated that approximately two-thirds of Americans over the age of 12 drank alcoholic beverages, with an annual per capita consumption of 24.8 gallons of beer, 2.8 gallons of wine, and 1.6 gallons of spirits (a total of 2.2 gallons of pure ethyl alcohol). According to estimates from the United States Department of Agriculture and the Centers for Disease Control and Prevention, in 1998 25 percent of adult Americans were cigarette smokers who smoked 458 packs of cigarettes per year; the good news is that these figures were down from 42 percent smokers who smoked 512 packs per year in the mid 1960s—the peak years for cigarette sales and use in the United States (Achievements, 1999).

The average American adult consumes approximately 100 grams of caffeine a year; most of this amount comes from drinking coffee or tea, but in young adults up to 50 percent of dietary caffeine may come from soft drinks (Barone & Roberts, 1996).

In addition to these socially accepted drugs—caffeine, nicotine, and alcohol—Americans are heavy consumers of numerous illicit substances. Because of its nature, the extent of illicit drug use in the United States is difficult to estimate, but it is clearly pervasive. Estimates from the office of National Drug Control Policy indicate that, during the mid-1990s, approximately $57 billion was spent every year on illicit drugs in the United States. Approximately 12 percent was for marijuana and hashish; almost two-thirds was for cocaine; and just over 20 percent was for narcotics or other illicit drugs, such as black-market amphetamines and barbiturates and illicitly manufactured hallucinogens.

Statistics from the National Household Survey on Drug Abuse (a large nationwide survey conducted yearly by the federal government since 1971) indicate that in the late-1990s approximately one-third of Americans over the age of 12 had used an illicit drug at least once; 23 percent had used one or more illicit drugs during the previous year; and 7 percent were current users of one or more illicit drugs. Marijuana was the most popular illicit drug used, with one-third of the sample having used it at least once and almost 9 percent using it in the past year. (In 1984 the National Organization for the Reform of Marijuana Laws [NORML] estimated that marijuana was the number-two cash crop in the United States— behind corn and ahead of soybeans. In 1987, NORML estimated it was the number-one cash crop.) However, for those individuals under the age of 18, for whom alcoholic beverages and tobacco would be considered illicit substances, marijuana use ranked third behind alcohol (first) and tobacco (second).

During the 1990s, the estimated number of Americans using cocaine has consistently been around 2.5 million for occasional use, 1.5 million for current use, and a little over 0.5 million for heavy use. Estimates of lifetime heroin use have generally remained at around 2 million since 1979, and current users number between 100,000 and 200,000. Approximately the same number currently use hallucinogens or inhalants.

Clearly those who engage in recreational or social use of drugs may eventually cause functional or physical damage to themselves or others around them. For as long as humankind has been using drugs for such purposes, there have been concerns over drug abuse and attempts to restrict it (Szasz, 1974). As far back as 2000 B.C., an Egyptian priest attempted to proselytize alcohol users, suggesting that they were degraded like the beasts. In the seventeenth century a prince in England paid money to people to denounce coffee drinkers, and the Russian tsar executed those found to possess tobacco (after torturing them into divulging the names of their suppliers). A similar penalty was levied by the sultan of the Ottoman Empire.

In 1736 the Gin Act of England was passed, making alcohol so expensive that the poor could not use it excessively. Note that whiskey, which only the rich could afford, was not included in this act. In 1792 the first prohibitory laws against opium in China went into effect; the punishment for possession was strangulation. Similar draconian attempts to reduce drug use have been made around the world. The United States passed the Harrison Narcotic Act in 1914 and the Marijuana Tax Act in 1937, among others, which basically outlawed the nonmedical (or untaxed) possession or sale of a number of drugs, including opium, morphine, heroin, and marijuana. In addition, prohibition of alcoholic beverages was in effect in the United States from 1920 to 1933. In 1921 cigarettes were illegal in 14 states.

Unfortunately, however, drug use did not decline in most cases (Brecher, 1972). One of the fundamental reasons restrictions have failed is that it is not clear to many users why they must stop using the drugs, since they feel their drug consumption affects only themselves. Society as a whole might agree that there are certain forms of drug consumption that should be avoided and that can be called drug abuse, but there is no universal agreement as to what these are. The criteria for what constitutes drug abuse are heavily dependent on one's culture and the time period. Generally, the term *drug abuse* refers to the self-administration of any drug in a manner that deviates from the approved medical or societal patterns within a given culture. A more operational definition might be the use of any drug that causes functional or structural damage to the users or to others, or that results in the users' inability to voluntarily control their social or drug-taking behavior. Unfortunately, human beings are excellent at self-deception and rarely recognize instances in their own lives when these criteria apply.

Thus it is clear that psychotropic drugs are used widely in a nonmedical context and that this use is fraught with many problems. The National Institute on Drug Abuse and the National Institute on Alcohol Abuse and Alcoholism estimated that the annual cost to U.S. society of substance abuse reached $231.9 billion in 1995, with alcohol abuse alone accounting for $166.5 billion. In addition to the cost of treatment (24 percent of the total), these figures include costs related to lost productivity, law enforcement, crime, traffic accidents, and fires. Cigarette smoking is the leading cause of lung cancer and a key component of other cancers, cardiovascular disease, and other disorders, which end up shortening the lives of more than 400,000 Americans every year. About three-fourths of poisoning deaths in 1995 were caused by drugs, with opiates and cocaine accounting for the majority of these deaths (Fingerhut & Cox, 1998). Drug Abuse Warning Network (DAWN) records indicate that there were more than 550,000 drug-related hospital emergency department episodes in the United States in 1999.

Use of other psychotropic drugs, and the rapid development of new ones, can only worsen the situation. The question frequently asked is, What can be done about it? Some people rely on the legislative process, whereby certain drug-taking practices are declared illegal. Unfortunately, though, history reveals that the legislative approach has rarely had much impact on these practices except to make them less safe than they were originally, and it has numerous other repercussions.

Since the passage of the Harrison Narcotic Act in 1914, the United States has engaged in a war on drug abuse. This and subsequent legislation have done little to dampen the desire for or use of drugs (Marshall, 1988). Traditionally, around 70 percent of the money appropriated for drug control has gone toward interdiction of supply, and only 30 percent has gone toward manipulating the demand for drugs (Jarvik, 1990). Because of difficulties in smuggling and concealment of drugs, less bulky, more potent drugs became preferred (e.g., heroin instead of morphine or opium), and more hazardous methods of administering drugs came into use (e.g., injecting or smoking instead of oral administration). Drug prices skyrocketed, and drug quality declined. Sellers willing to take high risks for lucrative financial gain began to engage in violence to settle disputes over drug trading, and users began committing crimes to help finance their drug purchases. In response, federal antidrug expenditures continued to grow (e.g., from around $130 million in 1970 to around $18 billion in 2000), with most of this directed toward catching and jailing drug law violators. Collectively, federal, state, and local governments spent around $40 billion per year to reduce illegal drug use and trafficking and to deal with their consequences.

Drug control policies bear primary responsibility for the quadrupling of the national prison population since 1980 and a soaring incarceration rate, the highest among Western democracies. According to retired General Barry McCaffrey, director of the Office of National Drug Control Policy under the Clinton administration, the nation's war on drugs has propelled the creation of a vast "drug gulag." At the present time, more people are sent to prison in the United States for nonviolent drug offenses than for crimes of violence. Throughout the 1990s, more than 100,000 drug offenders were sent to prison annually. More than 1.5 million prison admissions on drug charges have occurred since 1980. The rate at which drug offenders are incarcerated has increased ninefold. The rate of incarceration has been particularly devastating to the African American community. Research by the Human Rights Watch organization shows that Blacks comprise 63 percent and Whites 37 percent of all drug offenders admitted to state prisons, even though federal surveys and other data show clearly that this racial disparity bears scant relation to racial differences in drug offending (Human Rights Watch, 2000). There are, for example, five times more White drug users than Black. Relative to population, Black men are admitted to state prisons on drug charges at a rate that is 13.4 times greater than that of White men. In large part because of the extraordinary racial disparities in incarceration for drug offenses, Blacks are incarcerated for all offenses at 8.2 times the rate of Whites. One in every 20 Black men over the age of 18 in the United States is in state or federal prison, compared to one in 180 White men. Meanwhile, prisons are so overcrowded that convicts often have to be released early to make room for new arrivals. Despite these efforts, the illicit drug business has continued to grow.

In recognition of these phenomena, a number of political and academic leaders began to raise a provocative alternative—drug legalization. They argued that the cheapest and cleanest way to reduce drug-related crime and the hazards of drugs of unknown quality and quantity would be to do away with the laws that make drug use a crime. Their assumption was that society would be better off if it did not stand in the way of the drug users and their habit. Less tax money would be needed for interdiction, prosecution, and imprisonment of illicit drug suppliers; in fact, legalization could enhance tax revenues. Users would not be submitted to the hazards of unknown drug quality or quantity or the disastrous consequences of imprisonment. Violent crimes against property and people would be significantly reduced. Urban street gangs and organized crime, now sustained by the illegal drug trade, would be severely weakened.

Critics of this idea (Jarvik, 1990; Goldstein & Kalant, 1990) were quick to point out that it would likely have some potentially disastrous outcomes. It would probably increase the number of new addicts. Some drugs, such as cocaine and phencyclidine (PCP), have properties that are potentially hazardous to users and society no matter how they are used. Other drugs would likely be developed that produce faster and more intense effects, and thus be more addictive, than currently available ones. Finally, even with legalization, there would have to be age restrictions, as with alcohol, for legally obtaining drugs; consequently, there would still be a group of individuals for which a black market would likely exist. So, at the present time, in the United States we are at a stalemate, with minimal prospects for moving away from the criminalization approaches for dealing with drug abuse.

Although we have little empirical evidence for what would happen if all drugs were decriminalized and regulated, much like alcohol presently is in the United States, we do have evidence on what might happen if marijuana were to be decriminalized (Zimmer & Morgan, 1997). The Netherlands' policy regarding marijuana is the least punitive in Europe. Although technically illegal, for over 20 years Dutch citizens over the age of 18 have not been prosecuted for buying and using small amounts of marijuana and hashish in government-regulated coffee shops. In contrast, in the 1990s almost one in five prisoners in U.S. federal prisons were there for marijuana sales or possession, and in some states the incarceration rate was considerably higher. However, surveys of drug use in these two countries in the 1990s indicate that use of marijuana and most other illegal drugs is similar for most age groups, and lower in young adolescents in the Netherlands than in the United States (Smart & Ogborne, 2000; Zimmer & Morgan, 1997). The prevalence of cannabis use in the Netherlands is also similar to that of other European countries, including those with much harsher prohibition policies. Furthermore, in the 1970s, the penalties for marijuana offenses were reduced in the United States, with some states instituting what amounts to de facto decriminalization, with possession of small amounts of marijuana being a minor misdemeanor punished with a fine. Interestingly, according to national surveys, the lifetime prevalence of marijuana/hashish use in the United States by individuals under the age of 25 decreased dramatically from the late 1970s until the early 1990s.

A number of other countries have been using, or are beginning to experiment with, drug decriminalization approaches. For example, in 1994 the German Supreme Court overturned federal laws banning possession of cannabis (marijuana) in small quantities for personal use. Previously, sale or possession of cannabis in Germany carried a maximum five-year prison term, with no distinctions made between traffickers and individuals who smoked an occasional "joint." Over the past several years, the Swiss government has been trying a number of approaches to deal with heroin abuse (Nadelmann, 1995). In the early 1990s, the Swiss first tried establishing a "Needle Park" in Zurich—an open drug scene where people could use drugs without being arrested—but the scene grew unmanageable, and it was closed down in 1992. A second attempt faced similar problems and was shut down in 1995.

However, the Swiss idea of prescribing heroin to addicts in hopes of reducing both their criminal activity and their risk of spreading AIDS and other diseases took off in 1991, after the International Narcotics Control Board—a United Nations organization that oversees international antidrug treaties—was convinced that the Swiss innovation was experimental, which is permitted under these treaties, rather than a shift in policy (Nadelmann, 1995). Their experiments with heroin prescriptions (which, as discussed in Chapter 10, are variations of the approach used in the United Kingdom for almost three decades) started in January 1994 with various programs being conducted, although most provide supplemental doses of oral methadone, psychological counseling, and other assistance. Some are located in cities, others in towns. Some provide just one drug, while others offer a choice. Some allow addicts to vary their dose each day, while others work with addicts to establish a stable dosage level. One program is primarily for women. Another program permits addicts to take heroin-injected cigarettes home.

The Swiss experiments are designed to answer a host of questions about how to deal with heroin abuse. For instance, can addicts stabilize their drug use if they are assured of a legal, safe, and stable source of heroin? Can they hold steady jobs? Do they stop using illegal heroin or cut back on the use of other illegal drugs? Do they commit fewer crimes? Are they healthier and less likely to contract HIV? Are they less likely to overdose? In 1994 the Social Welfare Department in Zurich issued some preliminary findings related to some of these questions: (1) heroin prescription is feasible and has produced no black market in diverted heroin; (2) the health of addicts in the programs clearly improved; and (3) heroin per se causes very few, if any, problems when used in a controlled fashion and administered in hygienic conditions. Program administrators also found little support for the widespread belief that addicts' cravings for heroin are insatiable, as addicts offered practically unlimited amounts of heroin soon realized that the maximum doses provided less of a "flash" than lower doses and cut back their dosage levels accordingly. However, it was also concluded that heroin prescription alone cannot solve the problems that led to the heroin addiction in the first place.

Officials in other countries—for instance, the Netherlands, Austria, and Germany—are either conducting or contemplating similar heroin prescription programs. These approaches fit with a strategy many countries have pursued since the mid-1980s, that is, tough police measures against drug dealers and a "harm reduction" approach toward users (Nadelmann, 1995). For example, making sterile syringes more available through needle-exchange programs, selling needles in pharmacies and vending machines, and creating legal "injection rooms," where addicts can inject heroin in a regulated, sanitary environment, epitomize the harm reduction philosophy. Numerous studies have shown that these approaches are effective in reducing the spread of AIDS and drug-risk behaviors without increasing illicit drug injection rates (Durante et al., 1995; Nadelmann, 1995; Paone et al., 1995). In the United States, many states and municipalities have acted to improve access to sterile syringes through syringe-exchange programs and by allowing pharmacies and clinics to dispense needles without prescriptions (Lerner, 2000). However, the possession, distribution, and sale of syringes remains a criminal offense in much of the country, and the federal government—while officially acknowledging the efficacy of such programs—prohibits the use of its funds for syringe-exchange programs.

For a number of years, drug legislation in the Netherlands has been directed primarily toward reducing the risks of drug use for the individual users as well as society in general

(National Drug Monitor, 2000). Although harm to society is taken into consideration, a great effort is made to prevent criminal prosecution from being more damaging to the individual drug user than the relevant drug itself. For example, the Dutch distinguish between the market for "soft" drugs (cannabis products, such as hashish and marijuana) and the market for "harder" drugs (such as heroin and cocaine). This policy allows for some limited freedom for the retail trade—typically in so-called coffee shops—and the possession of small quantities of cannabis products for individual (not minors') consumption, while at the same time trying to combat the hard-drug trade in every possible way. The point of these innovations is not to coddle drug users, but to reduce the human and economic costs of drug use—costs paid not only by users but also by nonusers through increased health-care, justice, and law-enforcement expenditures (Nadelmann, 1995).

One approach in dealing with illicit drug use that has not been particularly fruitful has been to tell exaggerated stories about the potentially harmful effects of particular drugs. For example, in the 1930s authorities indicated that even occasional use of marijuana commonly led to permanent insanity, excessive violence, criminal activities, and sexual depravity. Such stories are quickly recognized by the potential drug users for their hypocrisy and misrepresentation, and, before long, warnings about any drugs are no longer heeded, no matter what the truth is (Newcomb & Bentler, 1989).

The National Institute on Drug Abuse has estimated that for every dollar spent on drug use prevention, communities can save four to five dollars in costs for drug abuse treatment and counseling. However, it is likely that truly effective prevention efforts will require numerous (and in many cases, politically difficult) strategies and approaches. Because use of alcohol and tobacco by adolescents has been so strongly associated with the subsequent use of illegal drugs (e.g., marijuana, cocaine, heroin), and because alcohol and tobacco themselves may produce more adverse consequences than many illegal drugs, approaches focusing on the demand for and acceptability of these substances may be the most fruitful approach to decreasing all forms of drug abuse (Goldstein & Kalant, 1990; Jarvik, 1990; Mosher, 1990; Wallack & Corbett, 1990). For example, we could (1) increase the price of alcohol and tobacco through taxes; (2) be more careful in monitoring age restrictions on their purchase; (3) increase restrictions on their use in public settings; (4) provide alternative forms of recreation; (5) make drug abuse treatment more accessible; (6) increase public warnings of their negative health consequences (e.g., by providing more noticeable warning labels on these products); (7) decrease their promotion through advertising; (8) reduce modeling of their use in television and films; (9) enhance the civil liability of producers and suppliers for harm caused to users; and (10) decrease their general availability (e.g., sell them through special outlets rather than grocery stores).

Numerous studies have noted that each of these approaches, by itself, has a small impact on alcohol and tobacco use. For example, numerous lines of research have indicated that for every 10 percent increase in the price of cigarettes, there is an approximately 3 percent to 5 percent reduction in the demand for cigarettes by adults, and research indicates that youths may be more price sensitive than adults (Chaloupka & Grossman, 1996; Harris & Chan, 1999). There is also recent evidence that states with more extensive tobacco control policies have significantly lower youth smoking rates (Luke et al., 2000). If all of these approaches were combined, it is likely that they would have a much greater impact than they have had in the past. Unfortunately, drug prevention programs targeted at young people, which have attempted to provide correct information on the long-term consequences of drug use, provide general skills useful in resisting drugs, or provide peer models of not using drugs, have produced minimal benefits in altering drug-taking patterns of behavior (Dukes et al., 1997; Ellickson & Bell, 1990; Lynam et al., 1999).

Several of these approaches have recently been implemented, or are likely to be implemented, particularly with respect to tobacco since the Food and Drug Administration (FDA) officially determined in 1996 that tobacco was a nicotine delivery system and that tobacco companies intended to provide nicotine to satisfy users' addiction. This intention would have allowed the FDA to regulate cigarettes under the Federal Food, Drug, and Cosmetic Act, which considers a product a drug if the vendor intends it to be one (Kessler et al., 1996). The FDA subsequently issued a number of rules to curb the use of tobacco by youths. Among these were the following: (1) vending-machine sales would be allowed only in adults-only areas; (2) tobacco-product billboard ads would be banned within 1,000 feet of schools and playgrounds; (3) color imagery would be allowed in tobacco ads only in adults-only areas, providing the image couldn't be seen from outside and couldn't be removed easily, (4) tobacco ads wouldn't be placed in publications with a significant youth readership, (5) brand-name tobacco sponsorship of sporting events (or individuals, teams, or cars in sporting events) would be banned; and (6) publicity items such as hats and T-shirts bearing tobacco product names and logos would be banned. In addition, the FDA began discussions with tobacco companies to fund an education campaign regarding the health hazards of tobacco.

In 1997 the tobacco industry essentially conceded the FDA's authority over tobacco products and agreed to a settlement that went well beyond the FDA's rules attempting to reduce youth access to tobacco products and tobacco marketing. For example, the industry accepted even further constraints on tobacco advertising, agreed to replace health warnings on tobacco product packages with more specific, detailed, prominently displayed warnings (for example, Cigarettes are Addictive, Cigarettes Cause Cancer, Smoking Can Kill You), and agreed to provide funds for tobacco cessation programs and devices for those who want to quit. These concessions by the tobacco industry are quite remarkable considering that over the years there have been numerous attempts to curtail the positive image of tobacco and alcohol use by the mass media and to increase the knowledge of their harmful consequences. However, the hundreds of billions of dollars a year earned by the tobacco and alcohol industries is a tremendous incentive for them to fight most of these proposals with every legal recourse available to them, which until recently they have done fairly successfully.

In March 2000, the U.S. Supreme Court, despite its acknowledgment that "tobacco alone kills more Americans annually than AIDS, alcohol, car accidents, homicides, suicides, illegal drugs and fire combined," ruled that the FDA did not have the power to regulate the manufacture and sale of tobacco products. Concluding that Congress never intended tobacco products to be treated as drugs under the Food, Drug and Cosmetic Act, the Court ruled that the Clinton administration exceeded its authority when it announced new anti-smoking regulations designed to protect the nation's youth. A primary argument against allowing the FDA to regulate tobacco products was the fact that, as an agency whose primary responsibility is to determine the efficacy and safety of drug products, it would almost automatically require the FDA to ban them from the market entirely as dangerous drugs. However, the ruling did not shield the tobacco industry from huge money judgments in the trial courts, which at this point amounted to $246 billion to settle lawsuits filed by the states, and in all likelihood the industry will continue to adhere to its original concessions to prevent Congress from enacting legislation that might force them to make further concessions.

Despite the often glaring headlines in the media about the increasing incidence of illicit drug use in this country, national surveys have indicated that illicit drug use is considerably lower now than it was in the late 1970s, the peak years of illicit drug use in the United States. An estimated 14.8 million Americans were current users of illicit drugs in 1999, meaning they used an illicit drug at least once in the prior 30 days (National Household Survey on Drug Abuse, 1999). By comparison, the number of current illicit drug users was at its highest level in 1979, when the estimate was 25 million. From 1979 to 1999 the rate of illicit drug use remained fairly constant for individuals 35 and older, decreased for 12- to 17-year-olds until 1992 and then increased, increased for 26- to 34-year-olds until 1985 and then decreased, and decreased dramatically for 18- to 25-year-olds until 1992 and then gradually increased. Trends for use of marijuana, by far the most commonly used illicit substance if one excludes the use of alcohol and nicotine by minors, were similar to the trends for any illicit use. There were no significant changes between 1998 and 1999 for any age group, but there was an increasing trend for use since 1997 among young adults and a decreasing trend since 1997 for youths aged 12 to 17 years.

The incidence of use of other illicit drugs generally is too low to register clear trends in surveys, although use of hallucinogens appears to have peaked between 1975 and 1980 and then gradually declined. Estimates of heroin incidence have been subject to wide variability and usually have not shown any clear trend, although there was an increase in the number of first-time users of heroin in the late 1990s. Most of these young initiates took heroin by way of smoking, sniffing, or snorting rather than by injection because of the increased availability of higher grades of heroin, which allowed these routes of administration to produce desirable effects at a low cost. Use of cocaine rose rapidly in the 1970s, reaching a peak in 1979. It then remained relatively stable until 1985, at which point use declined, from 5.8 million users in 1985 to 1.7 million users in 1999. On the other hand, the proportion of frequent users has remained basically unchanged between 500,000 and 700,000 since 1985, and the number of emergency room episodes related to cocaine use increased dramatically from 1985 to 1989, most likely as a consequence of cocaine being marketed and administered in a form called **crack** (DAWN Survey, 1996).

Alcohol is the most commonly used illegal drug for individuals under the age of 21, and its use by high school students also declined from the late 1970s to the early 1990s, at which point there has been a trend toward increased drinking by this group up to the late 1990s (Monitoring the Future Survey, 1999). Use of cigarettes (technically an illicit substance for individuals under the age of 18) by high school students also reached its peak in the late 1970s, declined until the early 1980s, and stayed fairly constant until the early 1990s, when adolescent use began to increase, primarily among Whites.

The general trend toward increased use of illicit drugs by youths from the early to late 1990s appears to be coupled with their decreased perception of the negative consequences of drug use (Monitoring the Future Survey, 1999). Unfortunately, these perceptions are inconsistent with the increase in the number of drug-related emergency department episodes reported across the nation in the 1990s (DAWN Survey, 1996). Whether these trends will continue remains to be seen. (The statistics in this section are provided by surveys that are notorious for their methodological inadequacies, but likely reflect trends in drug use in the United States over the past 25 years.)

The approach to drug abuse taken in this book is an educational one. In order to combat drug abuse, people need to be educated as to what drugs are and what their effects are. People should know under which circumstances drugs may be beneficial and under which they may be detrimental. The information given must have validity and must not be hypocritical. A person sipping on a martini cannot give a very convincing argument against marijuana use. Unfortunately, as just discussed, information alone will not necessarily stop, or even decrease, drug use. But it is hoped that individuals reading this book will adopt safer drug-taking practices, at the very least.

Websites for Further Information

This National Clearinghouse for Alcohol and Drug Information website provides information on drug abuse prevention, treatment, education, research, survey databases, resources, and so on:

>   http://www.health.org/index.htm

The Substance Abuse and Mental Health Services Administration website, providing information from the National Household Survey on Drug Abuse:

>   http://www.samhsa.gov/

Information from the Monitoring the Future Survey, which is an ongoing survey of the incidence of drug use, behaviors, attitudes, and values of American secondary school students, college students, and young adults:

>   http://monitoringthefuture.org/

Information on D.A.R.E.—Drug Abuse Resistance Education:

>   http://www.dare-america.com/ (proponent site for D.A.R.E.)
>   http://drcnet.org/DARE/index.html (site critical of D.A.R.E.)

Sites devoted to the topic of harm reduction as an approach to dealing with drug use and abuse:

>   http://www.cts.com/crash/habtsmrt/harm.html
>   http://www.ccsa.ca/harmred.htm
>   http://www.realsolutions.org/donoharm.htm
>   http://www.lindesmith.org/

General information sites on federal government drug policies:

>   http://www.druglibrary.org/
>   http://www.whitehousedrugpolicy.gov/
>   http://www.ncjrs.org/drgsdoc.htm

These are a sampling of the many sites that have sprung up that are critical of U.S. drug control policy:

>   http://www.november.org/index.html
>   http://metalab.unc.edu/warstop/warstop.html
>   http://www.soros.org/lindesmith/index.html
>   http://www.csdp.org/
>   http://www.drugsense.org/
>   http://www.drcnet.org/
>   http://www.dpf.org/

Bibliography

Achievements in Public Health, 1900–1999: Tobacco use- United States, 1900-1999. (1999, November 5). *CDC Morbidity and Mortality Weekly Report, 48,* 986–993.

Barone, J. J., & Roberts, H. R. (1996). Caffeine consumption. *Food and Chemical Toxicology, 34,* 119–129.

Brecher, E. M. (Ed.). (1972). *Licit and illicit drugs.* Boston: Little, Brown.

Caldwell, A. E. (1978). History of psychopharmacology. In W. G. Clark & J. Del Giudice (Eds.), *Principles of psychopharmacology* (pp. 9–40). New York: Academic Press.

Chaloupka, F. J., & Grossman, M. (1996). *Price, tobacco control policies and youth smoking.* (Working Paper 5740). Cambridge, MA: National Bureau of Economic Research.

DAWN Survey. (1996). Highlights. <http://www.health.org/govstudy/AR017/> (2000, October 23)

Dukes, R. L., Stein, J. A., & Ullman, J. B. (1997). Long-term impact of Drug Abuse Resistance Education (D.A.R.E.): Results of a 6-year follow-up. *Evaluation Review, 21,* 483–500.

Durante, A. J., Hart, G. J., Brady, A. R., et al. (1995). The Health of the Nation target on syringe sharing: A role for routine surveillance in assessing progress and targeting interventions. *Addiction, 90,* 1389–1396.

Ellickson, P. L., & Bell, R. M. (1990). Drug prevention in junior high: A multi-site longitudinal test. *Science, 247,* 1299–1305.

Fingerhut, L. A., & Cox, C. S. (1998). Poisoning mortality, 1985–1995. *Public Health Reports, 113,* 218–233.

Gibbons, D., & Connelly, J. (Eds.). (1970). *Selected readings in psychology* (p. 77). St. Louis: Mosby.

Gitlin, T. (1990). On drugs and mass media in America's consumer society. In H. Resnick (Ed.), *Youth and drugs: Society's mixed messages* (pp. 31–52). Rockville, MD: U.S. Department of Health and Human Services.

Goldstein, A., & Kalant, H. (1990). Drug policy: Striking the right balance. *Science, 249,* 1513–1521.

Harris, J. E., & Chan, S. W. (1999). The continuum-of-addiction: Cigarette smoking in relation to price among Americans aged 15–29. *Health Economics, 8,* 81–86.

Human Rights Watch. (2000). Punishment and prejudice: Racial disparities in the war on drugs. <http://www.hrw.org/reports/2000/usa/> (2000, October 23).

Hyman, S. (2000). The NIMH perspective: Next steps in schizophrenia research. *Society of Biological Psychiatry, 47,* 1–7.

Jarvik, M. E. (1990). The drug dilemma: Manipulating the demand. *Science, 250,* 387–392.

Kessler, D. A., Witt, A. M., Barnett, P. S., et al. (1996). The Food and Drug Administration's regulation of tobacco products. *The New England Journal of Medicine, 335,* 988–994.

Kushnir, T. (1986). Smoking and drinking as psychological tools in stressful social situations: Assumptions of fiction writers. *International Journal of the Addictions, 21,* 1119–1123.

Leavitt, F. (1982). *Drugs and behavior.* New York: John Wiley & Sons.

Lerner, S. (2000, May 17–23). Legal needles. *The Village Voice* <http://www.villagevoice.com/issues/0020/ lerner.shtml> (2000, October 23).

Luke, D. A., Stamatakis, K. A., & Brownson, R. C. (2000). State youth-access tobacco control policies and youth smoking behavior in the United States. *American Journal of Preventative Medicine, 19,* 180–187.

Lynam, D. R., Milich, R., Zimmerman, R., et al. (1999). Project DARE: No effects at 10-year follow-up. *Journal of Consulting and Clinical Psychology, 67,* 590–593.

Marshall, E. (1988). Flying blind in the war on drugs. *Science, 240,* 1605–1607.

Mitchell, P. (1993). Chlorpromazine turns forty. *Psychopharmacology Bulletin, 29,* 341–344.

Monitoring the Future Survey. (1999). Drug trends in 1999 are mixed. <http://monitoringthefuture.org/data/99data.html#1999-drugs> (2000, October 23).

Mosher, J. F. (1990). Drug availability in a public health perspective. In H. Resnick (Ed.), *Youth and drugs: Society's mixed messages* (pp. 129–168). Rockville, MD: U.S. Department of Health and Human Services.

Nadelmann, E. A. (1995, July 10). Switzerland's heroin experiment. *The National Review,* 46–47.

National Drug Monitor. (2000). Drug policy. <http://www.trimbos.nl/indexuk.html> (2000, October 23).

National Household Survey on Drug Abuse. (1999). National estimates of drug abuse. <http://www.health.org/govstudy/bkd376/Chapter2.htm#> (2000, October 23).

Newcomb, M. D., & Bentler, P. M. (1989). Substance use and abuse among children and teenagers. *American Psychologist, 44,* 242–248.

Paone, D., Des Jarlais, D. C., Gangloff, R., & Milliken, J. (1995). Syringe exchange: HIV prevention, key findings, and future directions. *International Journal of the Addictions, 30,* 1647–1683.

Siegel, R. K. (1989). *Intoxication.* New York: Pocket Books.

Smart, R. G., & Ogborne, A. C. (2000). Drug use and drinking among students in 36 countries. *Addictive Behaviors, 25,* 455–460.

Szasz, T. (1974). *Ceremonial chemistry.* New York: Anchor Press/Doubleday.

Wallace, B., & Fisher, L. E. (1999). *Consciousness and behavior* (4th ed.). Boston: Allyn & Bacon.

Wallack, L., & Corbett, K. (1990). Illicit drug, tobacco, and alcohol use among youth: Trends and promising approaches in prevention. In H. Resnick (Ed.), *Youth and drugs: Society's mixed messages* (pp. 5–30). Rockville, MD: U.S. Department of Health and Human Services.

Zimmer, L., & Morgan, J. P. (1997). *Marijuana myths, marijuana facts.* New York: The Lindesmith Center.

C h a p t e r 2

Basic Principles
of Pharmacology

Before getting into the "psycho" part of psychopharmacology, it might be useful to become familiar first with the "pharmaco" part—that is, the drug component. There are some basic pharmacological principles that all drugs share and that influence the action of psychotropic drugs. This chapter will briefly describe these principles and define many terms that will be used in subsequent chapters.

The first term that should be defined is **drug.** This might appear to be a simple task, but in fact there is no legal or commonly accepted definition of the word *drug.* As indicated in Chapter 1, a drug originally referred to any substance used in chemistry or medical practice. Gradually, the term was restricted to any agent used in medicine or any ingredient in medicines. Today many people use the term as a synonym for a narcotic agent or illicit substance. None of these definitions is of much value. Each one defines the term in a highly restrictive way, defines it by using a synonym that itself is undefined, or fails to define it in terms of function.

What is a drug then? In general, it is a chemical that affects one or more biological processes. However, not all chemicals that affect biological processes are considered drugs. Substances that are commonly used for nutritional purposes, such as salt, water, proteins, fats, carbohydrates, vitamins, and minerals, are not generally considered drugs, because they are necessary for carrying out the normal biological functions of the body. However, certain vitamins and minerals that might be found in our diet, if isolated and used in certain quantities, might also be thought of as drugs.

Recently, a related issue has come up regarding the status of "dietary supplements," which have developed into a multibillion dollar industry. Unlike food additives and drugs that are subjected to strict premarket tests for safety and effectiveness, because of the 1994 Dietary Supplement Health and Education Act, products labeled "dietary supplement" may enter the market untested, and the Food and Drug Administration (FDA) cannot restrict the use of such supplements unless substantial harm has been proven (Chang, 2000). One of the most popular of these "supplements" is St. John's wort, which has become phenomenally successful as an herbal antidepressant. Not only is there documented evidence for its effectiveness in the treatment of mild to moderate cases of depression, but there is also considerable evidence for its interacting with a variety of medications in adverse ways (Ernst, 1999). These properties indicate that, pharmacologically, one or more ingredients in St. John's wort would be considered a drug, but until there is legislation to change its status, the FDA cannot regulate it as a drug.

What about nicotine? Is it a drug? For decades, virtually all of the individuals working in the field of pharmacology and related disciplines have viewed nicotine as a drug. Furthermore, to those trying to quit cigarettes, it seemed obvious that nicotine is an addictive drug. But in the mid-1990s, governmental hearings were held to determine whether scientific evidence supported these assumptions. The reason: If the FDA could prove that tobacco companies intended for cigarettes to provide nicotine to satisfy an addiction, the FDA would have the right to regulate cigarettes under the Federal Food, Drug, and Cosmetic Act, which considers a product to be a drug if the vendor intends it to be one (Kessler et al., 1996). However, as indicated in Chapter 1, in spite of the general acknowledgment by virtually everyone that the tobacco companies knew nicotine was addictive and that they manipulated the nicotine levels in cigarettes to enhance the tobacco users' "enjoyment," the U.S. Supreme Court eventually ruled against allowing the FDA to regulate tobacco products. But this decision was made on the basis of political and legal considerations and not on the basis of pharmacological principles, which would indicate that nicotine is a drug. A similar issue revolves around alcohol (ethanol). The manufacturers of alcoholic beverages (and perhaps their consumers) would prefer not to view alcohol as a drug. It certainly contains calories, but I doubt that it is consumed by humans for its nutritional value. Thus, ethanol should be considered a drug in that it disrupts the normal biological activities of the body.

Chemicals originating or produced within an organism that are used to carry out the normal biological functions in the body are not usually thought of as drugs. Such chemicals are referred to as *endogenous* substances, as opposed to drugs, which are *exogenous* substances. However, biochemists and neuroscientists have isolated a variety of substances found to be important in the functions of the body, have extracted or synthesized them, and have administered them in purified form to reverse neurological deficits. The use of L-dopa, a chemical necessary for the production of an important brain chemical, in the treatment of Parkinson's disease is one example, and it is viewed as a drug.

Although chemicals used in the normal biological processes of the body are generally not viewed as drugs, one may ask what is considered normal. As an example, consider aspirin, which is an effective treatment for several kinds of pain. It is believed that most of its action is due to its ability to inhibit the activity of prostaglandins, a class of chemicals found throughout the body that play a vital role in almost every life process, including respiration, reproduction, and circulation. Unfortunately, their presence can also be painful, presumably because they induce swelling of the sensory nerve tips responsible for detecting painful stimuli. If one thinks of the pain as the result of excessive prostaglandin activity, is this considered an abnormal condition that is restored to normal with a chemical, or is it a normal condition that is altered through the action of aspirin?

From a pharmacological perspective, it seems most appropriate to define a **drug** as a nonfood chemical that alters one or more normal biological processes in living organisms. It is this perspective that is taken in this book. However, as already noted, there are several potential exceptions to this definition.

Aside from the actual molecular structure of a drug, the most important factors in determining a drug's effect are the concentration of the drug at its site(s) of action and the rate of accumulation there. These factors, in turn, can be affected by many other factors, most commonly the drug **dose**—that is, the quantity of drug administered at one time. Often, particularly under experimental conditions in psychopharmacology, drug dose is expressed in terms of unit of drug per unit of body weight of the organism, such as milligrams per kilogram (mg/kg). (Drug **dosage** refers to administrations of the drug per unit of time, such as 10 mg/kg four times a day for three days.) That is, we would clearly expect 10 mg of a drug to result in much higher concentrations in a rat than in a human, and therefore to be capable of exerting a much greater effect in that rat than in the human. Unfortunately, equivalent units of drug per unit of body weight do not usually translate into equivalent effects, either across species or within species. As we will see, there can be large differences in the rate and degree of a drug's absorption, distribution, metabolization, and excretion across species and in different ages. Also, animal species differ with respect to the amounts of tissue for drug storage. The fact that drugs are not generally dispersed evenly throughout the body and are usually taken up in tissues other than the site of drug action can affect the drug's action.

Drugs and Receptors

Pharmacodynamics refers to the biochemical and physiological effects of drugs and their mechanisms of action (Ross, 1996). The vast majority of drugs act at very specific sites throughout the body, referred to as *receptors*. These are fairly large molecules (usually protein) which comprise the sites where biologically active chemicals of the body, often called **ligands,** induce their effects. (Most of the ligands you are probably familiar with are hormones, such as insulin, testosterone, estrogen, and adrenaline. Later you will become familiar with the ligands known as neurotransmitters, neurohormones, and neuromodulators.) When a chemical occupies a receptor, it is referred to as being "bound" to it. If the receptor then starts some biological activity, it is said to be "activated." In most cases, binding is temporary, or reversible, and when the chemical leaves the receptor, it is said to "dissociate" from the receptor. **Affinity** refers to the capacity of a compound to maintain contact with or be bound to a receptor. **Intrinsic activity** refers to the relative capability of a compound to activate the receptor after being bound to it. Further details on receptor activation in the nervous system and its relationship to pharmacodynamics will be provided in Chapter 4. However, it should be noted that each neuroactive ligand in the nervous system generally has several different types of receptors on which it acts, each with their own separate function. Drugs vary considerably in terms of which of the receptors for each neuroactive ligand they bind to or act on. As we will see shortly, drugs may mimic the actions of a particular ligand at one or more of its receptor types and may have no actions or act in an opposing fashion at others.

Agonists are compounds with both an affinity for and a capability of activating a receptor. If the compound activating the receptor is endogenous (naturally synthesized in the body), it is called a ligand. If it is exogenous (produced outside the body), it is a drug. Both ligands and some drugs can be called agonists. In some cases, drugs do not combine directly with a receptor, but enhance the amount of the endogenous ligands available for the receptor. In such situations, the drug may be referred to as an **indirect agonist.** Some drugs exert their effects by blocking the action of agonists and are thus called **antagonists;** different types of antagonists will be discussed later in this chapter. **Partial agonists** are drugs that display intermediate effectiveness in receptor activation between the effectiveness of a full agonist and an antagonist. A partial agonist may actually have a greater affinity for a particular receptor than a full agonist. However, because it cannot achieve the maximal response of the full agonist at those receptors, it may act as an antagonist to the full agonist. This is because it reduces the receptors' accessibility to the full agonist.

In addition to the preceding classifications, a complicated and sometimes contradictory nomenclature has arisen to describe the effects of some classes of drugs, for example, opiates and benzodiazepines, That is, drugs may produce complex patterns of response, which has led to the terms **inverse agonist** and **mixed agonist–antagonist** (Kenakin, 1987). Specifically, an inverse agonist is defined as a drug that appears to act through the same receptor as an agonist but produces effects opposite to those of the agonist; thus, it can also be viewed as a type of agonist (e.g., see p. 152). Most notably, a mixed agonist–antagonist is evidenced when a drug acts as an agonist by itself, but blocks the activity of another agonist in the same system (e.g., see p. 243). Functionally, mixed agonist–antagonists and partial agonists have similar properties; that is, by themselves they exert agonist effects but are capable of reducing the effects of full agonists in the same system. The basic difference appears to be that a partial agonist works on the same receptors as a full agonist, but because of its lower maximal effect and its ability to reduce the full agonist's access to those receptors, the maximal effect of the full agonist is reduced if the two are given together. In contrast, a mixed agonist–antagonist may be a full agonist at one type of receptor and a complete antagonist at another type of receptor; thus, when combined with a full agonist that activates both types of receptors, the mixed agonist–antagonist blocks some of the effects that would normally occur with the full agonist alone.

Although these scenarios are indeed confusing, the overall picture is not likely to become clearer until we get a better understanding of how receptors and their ligands interact to alter biological systems. For example, one view of the receptor is that it consists of one element comprising a "binding" site and another element comprising an "effector" site (Cooper et al., 1996). This model very easily handles cases in which a drug with a molecular structure compatible with both sites is an agonist and a drug with a structure compatible only with the binding site prevents the agonist from binding and thus prevents its action; that is, the latter drug acts as an antagonist. However, this model has difficulties in explaining some phenomena, most notably inverse agonism and mixed agonism–antagonism. Another model proposes that receptors exist in an active and an inactive configuration, each of which is capable of combining with a drug molecule. Thus, whether a drug acts as an antagonist or agonist will be determined by the ratio of the drug's affinity for the two configurations. For example, a drug may have a higher affinity for the active configuration than the inactive configuration, so that at low concentrations the drug acts as an agonist. However, at higher concentrations the drug may combine with the inactive configuration, preventing the receptor from attaining its active configuration, so that the drug acts as an antagonist. These and other models of receptors are at present purely conjectural and subject to modification as we gain more information on receptor structure–activity relationships.

It is likely that a critical number of receptors of some specific type have to be occupied by an agonist before a biological response can begin to occur and that once all receptors or a certain minimal number are occupied no further increase in biological activity is possible. This hypothesis accounts for the typically nonlinear relationship between drug dose and drug effect. An agonist with high intrinsic activity causes a maximal response by activating proportionately fewer receptors. An agonist with low instrinsic activity may fail to elicit a maximal response compared with compounds with higher intrinsic activity.

The interaction between ligands (or drugs, since they operate in much the same way) and receptors is much like that between keys and locks. Just as one may have many keys and many locks, the body has many ligands and many receptors. Not all keys (ligands) fit all locks (receptors), but some keys may fit in several different locks, although one may have to wiggle the key a lot in some cases in order to get it into the lock. It could be said that the keys have different affinities for each lock; in some cases there is no fit at all, in others the fit is poor but adequate, and in others the fit is very good.

Continuing this analogy, note that each lock (receptor) and key (ligand) combination serves a different function; one key may unlock your car door, another may turn on the ignition, another opens your front door, another opens your safe-deposit box, and so on. It could be said that each key has intrinsic activity at its respective lock. However, have you ever driven a car with separate keys for the door and the ignition? If so, have you ever stuck the ignition key in the door lock or vice versa? It fit fine, but you could not turn the key (activate the receptor). The same thing happens with ligands and receptors. Thus, a key may have an affinity for a lock but have no effect on it—that is, no intrinsic activity. As is the case with affinity, a key's intrinsic activity may be high, low, or absent; that is, it may open (activate) the lock easily, with difficulty, or not at all.

There are a few basic differences between the ligand–receptor relationship and the key–lock relationship. First, although the receptor fit may be determined by a ligand's molecular shape—that is, the arrangement of its atoms—it may also be determined by the position of the molecule's positive and negative electrical charges. Second, there is no human hand guiding the ligand into the receptor; except for the differential electrical charges on the ligands that allow proper alignment with their receptors, ligands run into receptors pretty much randomly. Therefore, whether ligands come in contact with their receptors or not is heavily dependent on the concentration of the ligands and the number of receptors available.

By the mid-1990s approximately 300 types of receptor molecules had been identified and shown to exist in the human brain (Sedvall & Farde, 1995). Many of these belong to families that share a great deal of similarity in their protein structure; in some cases their functions are very similar, whereas in others their functions are very different. We know very little about their anatomical distribution and even less about their physiological role in psychological activities. This has hampered our ability to develop drugs that have highly specific actions and provide the types of effects we want without disabling side effects. Only in the last decade or so have neuroscientists and pharmaceutical companies been able to generate new compounds with considerably more selectivity in their actions than the therapeutic drugs discovered—through serendipity—in the past.

Due to a growing body of evidence that variable drug responsiveness is caused by polymorphisms (variations) within multiple genes—protein products of which are involved in critical metabolic and/or physiologic pathways relevant for drug action—two new interrelated disciplines have evolved (Rioux, 2000). **Pharmacogenetics** is the study of the impact of heritable traits on pharmacology and toxicology. An extension of pharmacogenetics is the discovery that genetic polymorphisms have the potential to affect a drug's action. The interplay of genotype and drug efficacy has been defined as **pharmacogenomics**. However, the two terms—*pharmacogenetics* and *pharmacogenomics*—are often used interchangeably. For most drugs, variations in patient response have, until recently, been considered a result of pharmacokinetic factors (discussed in Chapter 3) rather than pharmacodynamic differences. However, it now appears that pharmacodynamic variability in humans is substantial and may be more pronounced than pharmacokinetic variability. These rapidly expanding fields have led to the hope that, within a few years, prospective genotyping will lead to patients being prescribed drugs that are both safer and more effective ("the right drug for the right patient," or personalized medicine).

Dose–Response Relationships

From the previous discussion, you learned that a drug's actions depend on the amount of drug available, which, in turn, is dependent on the dose of drug given (Ross, 1996). The usual way of discussing a drug's action is in terms of the **dose–response function,** which expresses the relationship between the dose administered and the response observed. Dose–response functions are determined by taking groups of individuals, which represent a certain population that one is interested in, administering each group a different amount of the drug in question, waiting a sufficient length of time for the drug to act, and assessing the degree of effect or the number of individuals displaying a specified effect of the drug.

For purposes of comparison, one group is administered a substance without any physiological effects, called a **placebo,** instead of the drug, because many individuals display physical or psychological symptoms if they expect to receive a drug (Rudorfer, 1993). In animals, a placebo generally consists of **saline** solution (water containing the same amount of sodium chloride as is normally found in the body). In some cases—for instance, with humans who may be knowledgeable about some of the characteristics of a drug they are reportedly taking—it is advisable to administer an **active placebo.** This is a substance that mimics some of the noticeable physiological characteristics of the drug being evaluated but without the effects on the brain that the researcher is interested in. As a final control measure, a **double-blind procedure** is used, whereby neither the subject nor the person administering the preparation knows whether it is a drug or a placebo.

Though proper experimental drug protocols require the use of a placebo, in clinical trials in which a drug is being evaluated for its effectiveness in relieving the symptoms of a particular disorder, the use of a placebo may be unethical or impractical. For example, if a drug is being evaluated for its antidepressant properties, it may be unethical to give depressed patients a placebo when there are drugs currently in use that have a 50 percent to 60 percent effectiveness rate. If these patients do not show symptom remission and they attempt or commit suicide or feel even more hopeless than they did before the treatment, the researchers might be held morally, if not legally, responsible. Fortunately, there is little, if any, evidence that the use of placebo control groups in psychiatric drug research is associated with an increased risk of harm (Leber, 2000). It is also understandable why some patients are reluctant to participate in such a trial when they know they might be part of a control group that receives an inactive substance. Thus, it may be necessary for those who are placed in a control group to receive a substance that has a medically accepted level of effectiveness. The effectiveness of the experimental drug would then be compared with that of the control drug. Unfortunately, this procedure makes it more difficult to establish the experimental drug's true level of effectiveness, because it is often easier to obtain results indicating that there is no difference between two treatments when they are in fact different, than it is to demonstrate that they are different. (See Leber [2000] and Miller [2000] for a more complete discussion of this issue.)

For illustrative purposes, Figure 2–1 shows several idealized dose–response functions for some of the effects of the drug *d*-amphetamine that have occurred in laboratory rats. In Figure 2–1(a), we can see that as the dose of amphetamine administered increases, the percentage of time that the rats exhibit stereotypy (a repetitive, ritualistic, or compulsive set of behaviors, such as moving the head back and forth repetitively or gnawing at nonexistent objects) also increases.

In Figure 2–1(b), which expresses the relationship between the dose of amphetamine and the generalized locomotor activity of rats, we see that activity tends to increase with increases in amphetamine dose up to a point. With larger doses of amphetamine, activity appears to be less and less apparent, and with a sufficiently large dose of amphetamine, activity may actually occur at lower levels than with no drug at all (depicted as 0 mg/kg). Such functions are often called *biphasic* or *curvilinear.* For example, it is not unusual to find that some drugs used in the treatment of mental illness display a curvilinear relationship between their concentration levels in the blood plasma (which is dependent on drug dosage but is a better predictor of a drug's effects) and clinical improvement (Preskorn et al., 1988; Van Putten et al., 1988). In this case, the optimal therapeutic effect in the patients can be obtained when the concentration levels in the plasma are in a certain range, known as the **therapeutic window;** levels below and above the window are associated with poorer outcomes.

For the many drugs with a therapeutic threshold or range of effective drug levels, knowledge of these drugs' **plasma half-lives**—that is, the time it takes to eliminate half the drug from the bloodstream—can help to predict desirable drug doses and intervals between administrations (Benet et al., 1996). For example, the antidepressant drug Prozac has a long plasma half-life of 1 to 3 days. Thus it may only need to be taken once a day to maintain plasma levels within the therapeutic window. If administered more frequently or in too large a dose, the plasma levels may progressively increase and exceed the therapeutic window; then it may induce toxic effects or side effects that decrease the overall well-being of the patient.

In Figure 2–1(c), we see that the effect of amphetamine on schedule-controlled behavior (that is, operant responses whose rate of occurrence is determined by the schedule of reinforcement) is quite complex. The effect depends on the dose of amphetamine and the normal rate of response without the drug (Seiden & Dykstra, 1977). That is, responses that occur at a fairly high rate to begin with become relatively less frequent with increasingly larger doses of amphetamine, whereas responses that occur somewhat infrequently become relatively more frequent with low to moderate doses of amphetamine, and then decrease with high doses of amphetamine. In the figure, condition *i* might occur if there were no reinforcement provided; condition *ii* might occur if responses were only reinforced if the animal spaced its responses with some minimum interval (such as 10 seconds) between them; condition *iii*

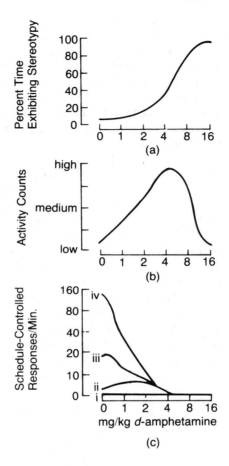

FIGURE 2–1 Various relationships
between the dose of *d*-amphetamine
and its behavioral effects in rats.

might occur if responses were reinforced after variable periods of time had elapsed; and condition *iv* might occur if responses were reinforced after a specified number of responses had occurred. In each of these cases, the direction of amphetamine's effect at each dose—that is, whether there is a relative increase or decrease in the response frequency—depends on the normal rate of responding that occurs without the drug.

In summary, several observations may be made regarding dose–response relationships:

1. One cannot say what effect a drug will have unless one specifies what the dose of the drug is (and in what species).
2. There may be many different dose–response functions for any particular drug, depending upon the type of response monitored.
3. There is no "typical" dose–response function.
4. Larger doses of a drug do not necessarily mean a greater magnitude of response.

It should also be mentioned that there are two general types of dose–response functions, one describing the degree or magnitude of a specified response and another describing the percentage of organisms displaying a specified response.

Despite these difficulties in characterizing dose–response functions, let us look at some "typical" dose–response functions, shown in Figure 2–2, and discuss their various attributes. First, note that there are some doses that do not induce any noticeable effects. The arrow at point *a* indicates the **threshold dose** (or minimally effective dose), which is the dose just large enough to produce a detectable change in the response. The arrow at point *b* indicates the **maximum (or maximal) response,** which is the greatest degree of a given response that can be achieved with that drug. The maximal response is not necessarily produced by the largest effective dose of a drug, because at higher doses some agents (such as nicotine) antagonize the response brought about at lower doses, and some agents (such as amphetamine) induce effects that may compete with, interfere with, or suppress the behavior noted at lower doses. The arrow at point *c* depicts the **median effective dose,** which is the dose of the drug that produces a desired, and generally therapeutic, effect in 50 percent of the individuals tested. It is abbreviated **ED50.** If you draw a perpendicular line up from the ED50 to where it intersects the dose–response function, and then horizontally over to the response axis, it intersects with the 50th percentile—that is, the point at which 50 percent of the population is affected. Other EDs can be specified for a drug, but in practice such levels are rarely specified. For example, the ED5 would indicate the dose effective in 5 percent of the population. At this point it should be mentioned that because drugs are often used in different therapeutic contexts, a drug may have several ED50s. For instance, a barbiturate may have one ED50 for its sedative effects, another for its sleep-inducing effects, and another for its anesthetic actions.

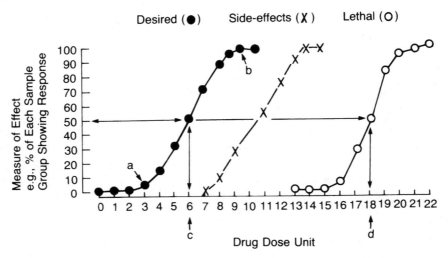

FIGURE 2–2   Stylized dose–response functions depicting (*a*) the threshold dose, (*b*) maximal (desired) response, (*c*) the ED50 of the drug, and (*d*) the LD50 of the drug.

All drugs can have lethal consequences, and clearly there is a relationship between the dose of a drug and lethality. Just as the ED50 for a drug can be specified, so can the **median lethal dose,** or **LD50** (indicated by the arrow at point *d* in the figure). The LD50 is the dose that causes death in 50 percent of the population. Therapeutically speaking, one hopes that the LD50 for a drug is considerably larger than its ED50. In fact, a drug's relative margin of safety, called the **therapeutic index,** is often specified in terms of the drug's LD50 relative to its ED50. It is determined by simply dividing the LD50 by the ED50. For the hypothetical drug in Figure 2–2, the ED50 is 6 units and the LD50 is 18 units, so the drug's therapeutic index is 3. A drug with a therapeutic index of around 100—that is, where the LD50 is 100 times larger than the ED50—is generally considered safe, whereas a drug with a therapeutic index under 10 is generally considered quite hazardous. Unfortunately, though, the therapeutic index is a very gross measure of a drug's potential hazards, because many drugs have side effects, some of which may be very disabling, which can occur at doses much lower than the LD50. Also, one drug may have a considerably higher therapeutic index than another drug, but may have certain properties that increase the likelihood of the individual self-administering lethal amounts. For example, a person taking a drug that induces euphoria or mental confusion could accidentally take too large a dose.

By its very definition, the ED100 of a therapeutic drug would be most likely to exhibit positive effects in the greatest number of patients. However, the **maximum efficacy** of a drug is sometimes determined by other factors, such as side effects, which limit the largest amount of the drug that can be given to a patient. For example, in Figure 2–2, note that the ED100, which is about 9 units, produces side effects in about 30 percent of the subjects. With some drugs, variability in response from one patient to another is small, while in others it is very large, requiring each patient to be individually "titrated." (Most commonly, the variability is large when the slope of the dose–response function is steep.) Those individuals who overrespond to the ED50 of a drug are called **hyperreactors;** those who underrespond are called **hyporeactors.** The term **idiosyncrasy** is used to describe an unexpected response or unusual effect of a drug, such as drowsiness induced by amphetamine. The response may be independent of dose, and it implies more than just a hyper- or hyporesponsiveness.

The dose–response function can be used to illustrate a number of other concepts in pharmacology. Figure 2–3 depicts the dose–response functions for several analgesic drugs. Note that the doses of heroin needed to achieve analgesia are smaller than the doses of morphine needed to induce equivalent degrees of analgesia, which, in turn, are smaller than the doses of aspirin needed. The differences depicted reflect differences in the drugs' **potency,** which simply refers to the relative pharmacological activity of a compound or the relative ability of a drug to produce a particular effect. Drug potency is generally determined on the basis of the dose of the drug (or better yet, the plasma concentration of the drug) needed to produce that effect. It is not synonymous with a drug's lethality or **toxicity** (a drug's ability to damage biological systems) unless these are the specific effects in which one is interested. The lower the dose or concentration of the drug needed to produce a given effect, the more potent the drug. Therefore, heroin is considered to be the most potent of the three drugs in inducing analgesia.

The potency of a drug is really of little clinical importance as long as the required dose can be given conveniently—unless an increase in potency is associated with a decrease in undesirable side effects or with an increase in the maximal response achieved. Although heroin is more potent than morphine in inducing analgesia, morphine is capable of achieving the

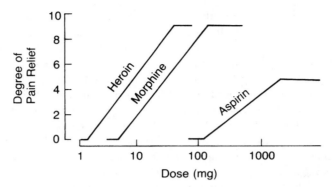

FIGURE 2–3 Dose–response relationships for aspirin, morphine, and heroin with respect to their relative potencies in reducing moderately severe pain, with 0 indicating no pain relief and 10 indicating complete absence of pain.

same maximal degree of pain relief as heroin. In fact, the clinical profiles of the two drugs are so similar that there is little reason to recommend one over the other. On the other hand, heroin and morphine not only are more potent than aspirin, but also are capable of achieving a higher maximal effect. Thus, they are said to have a greater **efficacy** or to be more **efficacious**—terms that refer to the degree to which a drug is able to induce a given desirable effect.

A drug's efficacy may be measured in terms of its relative ability to achieve some specified maximal effect. Thus, in terms of reducing pain, for example, a strong opiate agonist would have maximal efficacy, a partial opiate agonist would have weak efficacy, and an opiate antagonist would have no efficacy. However, with respect to a drug's therapeutic effectiveness, or **clinical efficacy,** the use of the term *efficacy* can be confusing at times, because in the latter instance there are a number of potential parameters involved: (1) the percentage of patients exhibiting symptom relief; (2) the magnitude or degree of the desired effects; and (3) time factors, such as how quickly or long the drug effects are displayed and how soon it takes for symptom relief to occur after the treatment regimen begins. A drug's clinical efficacy may also be influenced by the number or severity of side effects that add to the patients' discomfort and potentially reduce compliance in taking the drug.

The steepness of the slope of a dose–response function (or concentration–effect curve), other than indicating the range of clinically effective doses, generally has more theoretical than practical usefulness (Nies & Spielberg, 1996). The slope and the shape of the curve can be useful in determining the mechanism of action of a drug and drug binding to its receptors. For example, these may be useful in determining whether an antagonist of a drug acts through a competitive or noncompetitive mechanism (to be discussed shortly).

When discussing the dose–response function for any drug, one must take into consideration the route of administration, the time since the drug was administered, and the number and spacing of drug exposures. As we will see in Chapter 3, a given amount of a drug can have very different effects, in terms of intensity and duration, when administered orally versus intravenously. Once a drug has been administered, the type of effect and the magnitude of a given effect will vary across time because the concentration of a drug is rarely sufficient to exert much of an effect if the time period is too short or too long. Thus time–response curves are often graphed in much the same way that dose–response functions are graphed.

Finally, if a drug is administered on more than one occasion, a number of changes in the response to the drug may occur. The drug may accumulate in the body and produce greater and greater effects. In many cases, particularly with drugs used to treat mental and emotional disturbances, it may take several days or weeks of continued exposure before the beneficial effects of the drug are evidenced. In some cases, an enhanced response to a drug may occur because of previous exposure, but the drug is given at intervals far enough apart that the response cannot be attributed to drug accumulation. This effect, found with a variety of drugs, including amphetamine, cocaine, marijuana, antipsychotics, antidepressants, and antianxiety drugs, is known as **sensitization** (Ross, 1996). However, in most cases, effects noted with initial drug exposures are no longer evidenced or are greatly reduced after chronic use—a phenomenon referred to as **tolerance,** which will be discussed in Chapter 6.

Drug Interactions

Sometimes the potency of a drug is reduced in the presence of another drug, and sometimes it is enhanced. The situation in which the response to one drug is decreased in the presence of another drug is referred to as **antagonism.** The opposite situation is referred to as **synergism,** whereby doses of two drugs taken together produce a greater effect than either drug dose produces alone.

Various forms of antagonism and synergism for several hypothetical drugs are depicted in Figure 2–4. In the figure, note that while drugs *A, B,* and *D* are all effective in inducing sleep, drug *A* is most potent, whereas drugs *C* and *E* are incapable of inducing sleep at any dose. The *A + B, A + D, A + E, A + C,* and *B + C* dose–response functions show what may happen to the dose–response functions for drugs *A* and *B* when various doses of these drugs are combined with a given dose of the other drugs.

There are two basic types of antagonism: **pharmacological** and **physiological.** A **pharmacological antagonist** is a drug that has a definite affinity for a receptor but has little or no

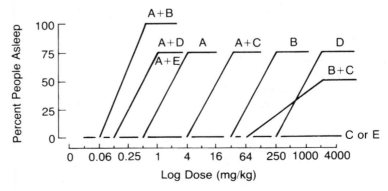

FIGURE 2–4   Dose–response function for drugs *A, B, C, D,* and *E* when administered alone and in various combinations.

intrinsic activity after being bound to it. In the case of **pharmacological antagonism**—that is, when a pharmacological antagonist is in combination with a receptor—an agonist cannot bind to and activate that receptor. If the antagonist is capable of dissociating from the receptor, so that there is "competition" between the antagonist and agonist for the receptor, it is referred to as **competitive antagonism.** In Figure 2–4 the shift to the right (without change in the slope or maximal response) in the dose–response function for *A* in the presence of 500 mg/kg of *C* (*A* + *C* function) would indicate that *C* is a competitive antagonist of *A*. If the antagonist is incapable of being dissociated or displaced from the receptor, the relationship is referred to as **noncompetitive antagonism.** In Figure 2–4 the shift to the right in the dose–response function of *B,* and the lower maximal response achieved in the presence of 500 mg/kg of *C* (*B* + *C* function), would indicate that *C* is a noncompetitive antagonist of B.

In both cases, in the presence of a given dose of the antagonist, the agonist's potency is reduced, as reflected in the agonist's dose–response function being shifted to the right. However, in competitive antagonism, since the number of receptors available does not change, the agonist's original maximal effect can still be achieved, assuming a large enough dose of the agonist is administered. In noncompetitive antagonism, the number of available receptors declines. Thus, the maximal effect achievable decreases, and the slope of the agonist's dose–response function is likely to be shallower.

Physiological antagonism is a form of drug interaction in which two drugs (they may be either pharmacological agonists or pharmacological antagonists) act at two different kinds of receptors—that is, receptors whose biological actions oppose each other. For example, a drug may activate receptors that cause the heart to beat faster. Another drug may activate receptors that cause the heart to beat more slowly. Upon exposure to the first drug, the heart would speed up. Upon exposure to the second drug, the heart rate would return to normal levels; that is, the effects of the first drug would be counteracted (antagonized) by the second. Functionally, an inverse agonist is the same as a physiological antagonist, except that with the inverse agonist the receptor involved appears to be the same type that is activated by an agonist.

There are also several kinds of synergism, two of which are **addition** and **potentiation.** In the case of addition, two drugs produce the same overt effect, and the effect of the two drugs taken together is the sum of their individual effects. In Figure 2–4 the dose–response function for *A* in the presence of 500 mg/kg of *D* (*A* + *D* function) would suggest that addition is involved, since *D* by itself is capable of inducing the same degree of effect as *A* and the maximal response to *A* was unchanged in the presence of *D*. For instance, two beers and two glasses of wine lead to greater intoxication than do two beers alone or two glasses of wine alone. Alcohol and barbiturates—two drugs that have similar sedative–hypnotic properties—also have an additive effect when used together.

Potentiation is most clearly illustrated when two drugs, only one of which produces a given effect, in combination induce effects that are greater than that achieved with the active drug. The greater effect could be evidenced as an increase in the potency (i.e., a leftward shift in the dose–response function) or an increase in the maximal efficacy of the active drug. For example, the shift to the left in the dose–response function for *A* in the presence of 500 mg/kg of *E* (*A* + *E* function) would indicate that *E* potentiates the effects of *A,* since *E* was incapable of inducing any effect by itself.

If two drugs are each capable of inducing the same overt effect (as is the case with drugs *A* and *B* in Figure 2–4), it is often difficult to distinguish whether addition or potentiation is occurring when the drugs are combined. For this reason, one often hears on the one hand that alcohol potentiates the effects of antianxiety agents, and on the other that their effects are additive. In general, however, potentiation is indicated if the maximal effect of two drugs together is greater than the maximal effect achieved with either drug alone or if the slope of the dose-response function for one drug is steeper when that drug is combined with the other drug. For example, in Figure 2–4 the greater maximal response and shift to the left of the dose–response function for *A* in the presence of 64 mg/kg of *B* (*A* + *B* function) would indicate that *B* potentiates the effects of *A*.

Although some readers may find the concepts of potentiation and addition fairly easy to grasp, others have trouble with them—particularly with respect to drugs having a similar spectrum of effects. Perhaps an illustration will clarify matters. If 100 people drink 200 ml of ethanol in an hour, probably none of them will die, unless, of course, they go out and try to drive a vehicle under the influence of this amount of alcohol. However, if they drink an additional 100 ml of ethanol, for a total of 300 ml (about a fifth of 80-proof whiskey) in an hour, 10 of those people may die. If those 100 people drink 600 ml of ethanol in an hour—double the 300 ml—the number of people who die will not be 20, or double the deaths, but will be closer to 90. In other words, doubling the dose of alcohol that produces a given effect does not necessarily double the magnitude of the effect.

Now let's assume that, although drinking 200 ml of ethanol does not kill anybody, drinking 350 ml of ethanol is capable of killing 40 percent of the people in the sample. Furthermore, assume that 50 mg of Valium produces the same effects as 150 ml of ethanol. If 100 people were to take 50 mg of Valium along with 200 ml of ethanol, and 40 people died, it would be an illustration of addition. That is, the effects of 150 ml of ethanol plus the effects of 200 ml of ethanol equal the effects of 350 ml of ethanol, or 40 deaths; the effects of 150 ml of ethanol equal the effects of 50 mg of Valium; therefore, the effects of 50 mg of Valium plus the effects of 200 ml of ethanol equal the effects of 350 ml of ethanol, or 40 deaths, if the effects are additive. It would only be a case of potentiation if more than 40 people died. However, because neither 50 mg of Valium nor 200 ml of ethanol are lethal by themselves, and because their combination results in a sizable number of deaths, many people might assume that they potentiate each other.

Thus, to summarize, in order to determine whether the combination of two drugs that are capable of inducing the same effects involves addition or potentiation, one must do all three of the following:

1. establish what the dose–response functions for the drugs are separately;
2. establish what the minimally effective doses of the two drugs are; and
3. determine whether the combination of these two doses results in an effect greater than that achieved by simply doubling the minimally effective dose of one of the drugs.

If the effect with the drug combination exceeds the effect of simply doubling the minimally effective dose of one of the drugs, it would indicate potentiation. If the effect of the drug combination and the effect created by doubling the minimally effective dose of one of the drugs are comparable, then you have addition. Since this three-step procedure is rarely followed, there generally are confusing differences in terminology used by different sources in distinguishing whether drugs like alcohol, "minor" and "major" tranquilizers, sleeping aids, and antidepressants induce additive or potentiating effects.

Antagonistic and synergistic effects are only some of the potential results of combining drugs. Drugs typically interact in inexplicable ways, and the more drugs given, the more complex the situation becomes. Therefore, generally speaking, the fewer the drugs given, the better. Nevertheless, it is not uncommon to see a schizophrenic treated with two or more antipsychotic drugs, despite the admonitions of most experts. The patient may also be prescribed an antidepressant (also contraindicated in most cases), drugs to counteract the motor disturbances induced by the antipsychotic, and a muscle relaxant. With such chemical "salads," it is almost impossible to predict what the outcome will be. Unfortunately, people who see different physicians for different problems sometimes do not inform their physicians of all the drugs they are currently taking, or their physicians may not be aware of certain drug interactions, and the patients end up taking combinations in which the drugs negate or amplify each other or induce idiosyncratic reactions. For example, the cardiac damage associated with the popular 1990s' appetite-suppressant drug combination called "fen-phen," which led to the recall of Redux (dexfenfluramine) from the market, may well have been the result of one of the unappreciated properties of the other ingredient (phentermine) in the combination (Ulus et al., 2000). Similarly, recreational drugs with very different biochemical properties—for example, alcohol and cocaine, alcohol and nicotine, or cocaine and heroin—are commonly combined to produce complex mixtures of synergistic and antagonistic actions and effects. Few empirical studies specifically concerned with these drug combinations have been published (Dial, 1992; Kerr et al., 1991).

There are also notable examples of herbal medications—which, as indicated earlier in this chapter, are not regulated by the FDA or Drug Enforcement Agency because they are not legally viewed as drugs—interacting with a variety of pharmaceutical and recreational drugs to mimic, magnify, or oppose their effects. For example, plausible cases of psychoactive drug–herb interactions include a cluster of unpleasant symptoms called "serotonin syndrome" in patients who mix St. John's wort with certain antidepressant medications; induction of mania in depressed patients who mix antidepressants with ginseng; worsening of motor disturbances with antipsychotic drugs and betel nut; and hypertension with antidepressants and yohimbine (Fugh-Berman, 2000). Thus, it is clear that health-care practitioners should caution patients against mixing herbs with pharmaceutical drugs. Just because something is natural doesn't mean it's safe.

Websites for Further Information

This website lists a variety of medical dictionaries that provide information on drug and medical terminology:

http://www.1000dictionaries.com/medical_dictionaries_1.html

Medical dictionaries that define most psychopharmacological terms:

http://webmd.lycos.com/content/asset/unknown
http://my.webmd.com/index

Site providing information on the affinity of drugs and ligands for hundreds of receptors:

http://PDSP.cwru.edu/PDSP.asp

Bibliography

Benet, L. Z., Kroetz, D. L., & Sheiner, L. B. (1996). Pharmacokinetics: Mechanisms of drug action and the relationship between drug concentration and effect. In A. G. Gilman, L. S. Goodman, J. G. Hardman, L. E. Limbird, P. B. Molinoff, & R. W. Ruddon (Eds.), *The pharmacological basis of therapeutics* (pp. 3–27). New York: McGraw-Hill.

Chang, J. (2000). Medicinal herbs: Drugs or dietary supplements? *Biochemical Pharmacology, 59,* 211–219.

Cooper, J. R., Bloom, F. E., & Roth, R. H. (1996). *The biochemical basis of neuropharmacology,* 7th ed. New York: Oxford University Press.

Dial, J. (1992). The interaction of alcohol and cocaine: A review. *Psychobiology, 20,* 179–184.

Ernst, E. (1999). Second thoughts about safety of St. John's wort. *The Lancet, 354,* 2014–2016.

Fugh-Berman, A. (2000). Herb–drug interactions. *The Lancet, 355,* 134–138.

Kenakin, T. (1987). Agonists, partial agonists, antagonists, inverse agonists and agonist/antagonists? *Trends in the Pharmacological Sciences, 8,* 423–426.

Kerr, J. S., Sherwood, N., & Hindmarch, I. (1991). Separate and combined effects of the social drugs on psychomotor performance. *Psychopharmacology, 104,* 113–119.

Kessler, D. A., Witt, A. M., Barnett, P. S., et al. (1996). The Food and Drug Administration's regulation of tobacco products. *The New England Journal of Medicine, 335,* 988–994.

Leber, P. (2000). The use of placebo control groups in the assessment of psychiatric drugs: An historical context. *Biological Psychiatry, 47,* 699–706.

Miller, F. G. (2000). Placebo-controlled trials in psychiatric research: An ethical perspective. *Biological Psychiatry, 47,* 707–716.

Nies, A. S., & Spielberg, S. P. (1996). Principles of therapeutics. In A. G. Gilman, L.S. Goodman, J. G. Hardman, L. E. Limbird, P. B. Molinoff, & R. W. Ruddon (Eds.), *The pharmacological basis of therapeutics* (pp. 43–62). New York: McGraw-Hill.

Preskorn, S. H., Weller, E., Jerkovich, G., et al. (1988). Depression in children: Concentration-dependent CNS toxicity of tricyclic antidepressants. *Psychopharmacology Bulletin, 24,* 140–142.

Rioux, P. P. (2000). Clinical trials in pharmacogenetics and pharmacogenomics: Methods and applications. *American Journal of Health-System Pharmacy, 57,* 887–898.

Ross, E. M. (1996). Pharmacodynamics: Mechanisms of drug action and the relationship between drug concentration and effect. In A. G. Gilman, L. S. Goodman, J. G. Hardman, L. E. Limbird, P. B. Molinoff, & R. W. Ruddon (Eds.), *The pharmacological basis of therapeutics* (pp. 29–41). New York: McGraw-Hill.

Rudorfer, M. V. (1993). Challenges in medication clinical trials. *Psychopharmacology Bulletin, 29,* 35–44.

Sedvall, G., & Farde, L. (1995). Chemical brain anatomy in schizophrenia. *Lancet, 346,* 743–749.

Seiden, L. S., & Dykstra, L. A. (1977). *Psychopharmacology: A biochemical and behavioral approach.* New York: Van Nostrand Reinhold.

Ulus, I. H., Maher, T. J., & Wurtman, R. J. (2000). Characterization of phentermine and related compounds as monoamine oxidase (MAO) inhibitors. *Biochemical Pharmacology, 59,* 1611–1621.

Van Putten, T., Marder, S. R., Mintz, J., & Poland, R. E. (1988). Haloperidol plasma levels and clinical response: A therapeutic window relationship. *Psychopharmacology Bulletin, 24,* 172–175.

Chapter *3*

Pharmacokinetics

The effects of a particular drug on an organism depend heavily on the rate of accumulation and the concentration of the drug at its sites of action and the duration of contact at those sites. These are a function not only of the amount of drug administered but also of its **pharmacokinetics.** This term refers to the dynamic processes involved in the movement of drugs within biological systems with respect to the drug's absorption, distribution, binding or localization in tissues, metabolic alterations, and excretion from the body (see Benet et al., 1996, for a complete discussion of this area). Whereas the field of pharmacodynamics discussed in the last chapter is primarily concerned with what a drug does to the body, the field of pharmacokinetics is primarily concerned with what the body does to the drug; together these determine the type, degree, and duration of a drug's effects. Differences among organisms in their pharmacokinetics, due to genetic differences, the presence of other drugs, disease, and physiological and psychological status, can result in 5- to 20-fold differences (these are ballpark figures) in their reactions to a given amount of drug within species, and 20- to 100-fold differences in their reactions across species (Gillette et al., 1985). In some cases, a drug may not have the effect, at any dose, in one organism that it may have in another organism.

Drug Absorption

In order for drugs to reach their sites of action, they must first pass through several biological membranes, as diagrammed in Figure 3–1. The type and number of these membranes depend upon the drug's site(s) of action (in the case of psychotropic drugs, this would be the nervous system) and the route of administration. For example, for an orally administered drug to exert an action on the brain, it must pass through a variety of biological membranes before it can reach the cells of the brain that are responsible for the drug's psychoactive properties. Several factors, such as the salt form of the drug, the particle size of the dosage form, and the suspending agent used, can affect the degree of absorption. Differences in these factors may account for why generic drugs, which are chemically identical to brand-name drugs, may occasionally not act like their brand-name counterparts; however, this appears to be a very rare situation.

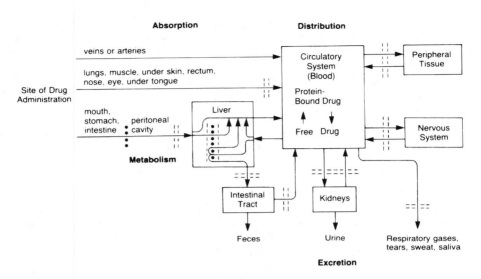

FIGURE 3–1   Summary diagram illustrating the major pharmacokinetic factors that influence the onset, duration, and intensity of psychoactive drug effects. Lipid membranes that must be crossed are indicated by ⦙. Enzymes that are capable of metabolizing drugs are indicated by ⫶. From the site of administration, drugs must cross one or more lipid membranes in order to be absorbed into the circulatory system (unless injected directly into the blood supply). In addition, drugs taken orally or injected into the peritoneal cavity initially pass through the liver, where they may be structurally altered (metabolism) prior to entering the blood. Once in the blood supply, the free, unbound drug molecules—those not bound to plasma proteins—will be distributed to various organs (including the brain, liver, kidney, and adipose tissue) and then redistributed to other organs and tissues by the blood. At some point, an equilibrium is often established whereby the relative concentration of drug in tissue and blood is maintained at a constant level (the blood-to-tissue ratio varies depending on the tissue and whether there are specific binding sites for the drug). Metabolism of drugs may occur in many tissues, but most metabolism occurs in the liver. From the liver, drugs or their metabolites may then reenter the blood supply or may be absorbed into the bile, which eventually ends up in the intestinal tract. From the intestinal tract, drugs or their metabolites may be eliminated in feces or reabsorbed into the circulatory system. Water-soluble drugs or metabolites enter the kidneys and are excreted in urine. If they are still lipid-soluble, they will be reabsorbed into the circulatory system. A small (generally negligible) amount of drugs may be eliminated via the lungs, sweat, tears, saliva, or mother's milk. (See text for further details.)

One of the most fundamental factors affecting the passage of molecules from one side of a membrane to the other is the relative concentration of the molecule on the two sides. The greater the differential concentration of the molecules on the two sides, the more readily the molecules will diffuse from the site of higher concentration to the site of lower concentration. However, because biological membranes consist of lipid materials (i.e., a group of fats and fatlike substances), the most important factor in a drug's ability to pass through these membranes is its **lipid-solubility** (also known as lipophilicity)—that is, its capability of being dissolved in fat. In general, as a drug's lipid-solubility increases (up to a point), the better the absorption from the blood, the more it will accumulate in tissues outside the blood, and the faster it can get into the brain to exert psychoactive effects (although penetration into the brain may decrease if its lipophilicity is too high) (Panchagnula & Thomas, 2000). Although very small water-soluble molecules and *ions* (positively or negatively charged particles) can diffuse through small aqueous channels located in the membranes, most drug molecules are too large to cross membranes in this manner and must diffuse through the substance of the membrane.

In order to dissolve in plasma and be effectively transported by the bloodstream, drugs must also be somewhat soluble in water. For these reasons, most drugs that are effective psychoactive agents are soluble to some extent in both oil and water. However, the relative solubility in each medium is a major factor in a drug's ability to get into the brain. To determine this relative affinity, a drug is often added to a mixture of water and refined olive oil. The mixture is shaken violently for a few seconds and then spun around to separate the oil and water. The drug concentration in the oil is divided by its concentration in the water. This figure is referred to as the drug's **oil/water partition coefficient.** The greater the drug's oil/water partition coefficient, the more easily the drug molecule can passively penetrate a lipoidal membrane, if other factors are held constant (Oldendorf & Dewhurst, 1978). For example, the differences in onset, intensity, and duration of the three analgesics morphine, meperidine (Demerol), and fentanyl (Sublimaze) are largely due to differences in their partition coefficients (van den Hoogen & Colpaert, 1987); that is, morphine's lower partition coefficient results in a slower onset of analgesia and less intensity, but a longer duration of action than fentanyl. A lower partition coefficient also increases the difference between a drug's ED50 when the drug is administered systemically—that is, into the general circulatory system—and its ED50 when it is administered directly into the brain. (See the next section for discussion of routes of administration.)

As stated earlier, two of the most important factors in a drug's effects are its concentration and its rate of accumulation at the site(s) of action. These, in turn, are heavily dependent on its concentration in the blood plasma (unless it is directly introduced into those sites), which is dependent on the drug's access to the blood, which is heavily influenced by the route of administration.

Routes of Administration

The most common route of drug administration is through the mouth (**per os** or P.O.) so that it is absorbed in various parts of the gastrointestinal (G.I.) tract. Rectal administration (through the rectal mucosa) may serve as an alternative *enteral* (within the intestine) route for drugs destroyed in the stomach or small intestine. The P.O. route is generally the safest, cheapest, and most convenient way of administering drugs. However, several factors can influence absorption of drugs from the G.I. tract, which can greatly alter the rate of drug accumulation, its concentration, and its duration at the site(s) of action.

Most drugs are thought to penetrate the G.I. mucosa by a process of passive diffusion, which in turn is limited mostly by the drug's lipid-solubility. Many drugs are weak bases (alkaloids) or weak acids, and this alkalinity or acidity often results in their being *ionized* (a state in which an atom or molecule has a net electrical charge). Such ionization reduces their solubility in cellular membranes, because proteins embedded in these membranes have a mixture of positive and negative charges that tend to repel charged particles. Therefore, to facilitate their absorption, such drugs are commonly administered in the form of a *salt*, a compound formed by the combination of a *base* (often a negatively charged ion, or *anion*) and an *acid* (often a positively charged ion, or *cation*). However, because the components of a salt dissociate in a solution, the drug may exist as both the nonionized and ionized species. Since the nonionized form is more lipid-soluble than the ionized form, the proportion of nonionized to ionized drug molecules present in a given area is important for drug absorption.

The pH of the local area determines the ratio of ionized to nonionized drug in that area. Solutions with a pH of 7.0 are neutral; those with a pH of less than 7.0 are acid; and those with a pH of greater than 7.0 are basic. Weak acids, like aspirin, are less ionized in an acid medium and are therefore more lipid-soluble through the stomach, with a pH of less than 3. Alkaloids like heroin, morphine, and cocaine are poorly absorbed from the stomach. On the other hand, further down the G.I. tract, in the small intestine, where the contents are nearly neutral or slightly alkaline, the environment favors the absorption of weak bases.

However, local pH is only one factor influencing drug absorption. This explains why the greater surface area of the small intestine, combined with a longer duration of drug contact, favors drug absorption there. This is the reason why people get intoxicated faster with carbonated alcoholic drinks; the carbonation forces the alcohol quickly out of the stomach and into the small intestine, where it is absorbed more rapidly. Some drugs are poorly absorbed from any part of the G.I. tract because even in their nonionized state they have low lipid-solubility. Neutral drugs, like alcohol, are readily absorbed all along the G.I. tract.

Other major factors in the absorption of drugs in the G.I. tract include the concentration of the drug, the rate of movement of the contents through the tract, G.I. blood flow, digestive secretions, and G.I. contents. The higher the concentration of the drug, the easier it is for the drug to diffuse passively across the intestinal cell membranes. The effect of the movement of the contents through the G.I. tract would depend on where the drug is best absorbed; for example, rapid emptying of the stomach would decrease the rate of absorption of weak acids, like aspirin. Rapid movement through the intestine could decrease the amount of drug absorbed because of a shorter duration of contact (or because the drug is a weak acid). Slow movement through the intestines would generally favor drug absorption, due to better contact with the absorbing cells lining the intestine. Because intestinal blood carries drugs away from the intestine and maintains a concentration gradient conducive to drug absorption, increasing or decreasing blood flow would increase or decrease, respectively, drug absorption. Digestive secretions can inactivate some drugs or alter intestinal pH and drug ionization. Finally, the contents of the G.I. tract (that is, food) can bind to the drug or dilute it so that it is slowly absorbed.

From this discussion we see that although the oral route is the safest way to administer drugs, it also has several disadvantages:

1. Drugs taken orally are absorbed more slowly than drugs taken by most other routes, so the oral route is usually not good in emergencies.
2. Patients need to be conscious, because otherwise they might choke to death if the drug is given orally.
3. Because of the slow rate of absorption, concentrations of drugs given orally may not even reach levels sufficient to induce noticeable effects.
4. Drug absorption is much more variable with the oral route because of the constantly changing conditions of the G.I. tract.
5. Some substances are very irritating and may produce nausea and vomiting if given orally, unless they are given with food.

Conversely, the introduction of a drug directly into the blood, most commonly done through **intravenous (I.V.) injection,** results in very rapid onset of drug action and relatively intense effects. For example, the time it takes a drug to circulate between the vein of the forearm and the brain is less than 15 seconds. An amount of drug (such as heroin) that may exert minimal effects when administered P.O. may be extremely toxic when administered intravenously. Although fine adjustments in drug dosage are possible with the I.V. route (important in barbiturate anesthesia), if overdosage does occur, little can be done about it, unless a specific antagonist for the drug is readily available. Drugs injected I.V. must also be in solution or microsuspension and must have an aqueous vehicle. For example, injecting illicit drugs such as heroin or cocaine that are diluted with talc, which does not dissolve in water, may eventually clog the capillaries in organs with high blood flow—for instance, the lungs, kidneys, and brain—and cause organ failure. Repeated injections can lead to clot formation, vessel irritation, or vessel collapse. Finally, there is a high incidence of allergic reaction, pronounced cardiovascular action, and side effects with this route.

In addition to the P.O. and I.V. routes, there are several alternative ways of determining and controlling the intensity and duration of drug action. Because of the relatively good blood supply surrounding muscles, **intramuscular (I.M.) injection** generally results in a more rapid absorption than does the P.O. route. Drugs dissolved in an aqueous vehicle are more rapidly absorbed through the I.M. route than when dissolved or suspended in oil.

Because the lining of the inside of the lungs provides a large surface area in close proximity to many blood vessels, **drug inhalation** leads to rapid onset of drug action and intense effects. This route eliminates drug loss through first-pass metabolism by the liver (discussed shortly). However, irritants or oils can cause pneumonia, and long-term consequences, such as cancer associated with cigarette smoking, often occur with this route.

The injection of a drug underneath the skin into the tissue between the skin and muscle (that is, into the body fat) is referred to as **subcutaneous (S.C.) drug injection.** Because of the relatively poor blood supply in fatty tissue, this method can be used with nonirritating substances to produce fairly slow and even absorption. The rate of absorption can be controlled through the form of the drug. For instance, it can be in aqueous solution, promoting fast absorption; in suspension, promoting somewhat slower absorption; or in solid form, such as a pellet, allowing for very slow absorption.

Sublingual or **buccal administration** (through the oral mucosa under the tongue or between the cheek and gum) may be used with drugs that are destroyed in the stomach or intestines, such as nitroglycerin and nicotine. Other, but rarely used, routes of administration are **intraarterial administration** (generally very hazardous because the drug is so concentrated); bone marrow administration (used, for example, in an infant, or when the veins are collapsed); rubbing drugs over a large surface area of the skin (although normal skin is an effective barrier to drug absorption); application of drugs to the mucous membranes of the nose (**intranasal administration**), vagina, or urethra; and administration through the eye. **Intrathecal administration,** or injection of the drug into the subdural spaces of the spinal cord (for example, spinal anesthesia), and **intracerebroventricular injection,** or injection into the ventricular spaces of the brain, may be used to bypass the blood–brain barrier, which will be discussed shortly. Although rarely used in humans, injection of drugs into the abdominal cavity (peritoneum), called **intraperitoneal injection,** is commonly used with small animals such as mice and rats. Absorption by this route is somewhat faster and more uniform than with oral administration, and the drug is not affected by enzymes in the stomach or intestines.

The increasing awareness that drug-release patterns (continuous versus pulsatile) significantly affect therapeutic responses has led to research aimed at creating new drug delivery systems (Langer, 1990). For example, several experimental approaches have been developed that facilitate a drug's ability to cross the blood–brain barrier—for example, by rendering it more lipid-soluble or coupling it to a molecule that has a specific transport mechanism. Controlled-release systems have been developed that are even better than older "sustained-release" or "slow-release" preparations in maintaining drug plasma levels in the desired therapeutic range. Theoretically such preparations should have advantages such as reduction in the frequency of drug administration, maintenance of a therapeutic effect overnight, and decreased incidence or intensity of undesired effects through the elimination of the peaks in drug concentration, which often occur with immediate-release forms. However, there are some potential drawbacks of such preparations. Variability among patients, in terms of the systemic concentration of the drug that is achieved, is generally greater for controlled-release than for immediate-release dosage forms. In some cases, this type of preparation may fail, and "dose-dumping" with resultant toxicity can occur, since the total dose of the drug ingested at one time may be several times the amount contained in immediate-release forms (Benet et al., 1996).

Although the skin is often considered a barrier to all agents, including drugs, several transdermal delivery systems have been developed to allow clinically relevant doses of drugs to penetrate the skin—for example, scopolamine-containing patches to prevent nausea associated with motion sickness and nicotine-containing patches to alleviate nicotine withdrawal. Transdermal drug delivery is a useful alternative to conventional routes of administration because it avoids degradation in the G.I. tract and first pass metabolism (discussed shortly), allows steady or time varying controlled delivery, and improves patient compliance. However, very few drugs, particularly charged or large molecules such as peptides, can be administered transdermally due to the low permeability of the skin. Chemical and physical means to promote transdermal transport have been explored to expand the range of drugs that can be delivered in this fashion. For example, *electroporation,* which involves the intermittent application of short, high voltage pulses (e.g., 150 volts for several milliseconds) to the skin, has been shown to substantially increase the transport of macro-molecules across the skin (Lombry et al., 2000). However, these techniques are still in the exploratory stages with respect to their clinical usefulness.

Until recently, dosage forms of a drug, primarily with oral forms of poorly soluble and slowly absorbed drugs, from different pharmaceutical companies or from different lots of preparations from a single manufacturer, were sometimes not equivalent in terms of their rate of absorption or *bioavailability,* that is, the fraction of drug administered that is actually absorbed into the systemic circulation (Benet et al., 1996). These differences—those be-tween "brand-name" and "generic" drugs—occurred because of differences in crystal form, particle size, or other physical characteristics of the drugs. These factors can affect disinte-gration of a drug preparation and dissolution of the drug and thus the rate and extent of drug absorption. However, with strengthened FDA regulatory requirements, there are very few documented cases in which pharmaceutical equivalents of approved drug products exhibit differences in bioequivalence.

Drug Distribution

After a drug enters the bloodstream, it passes through various body compartments and is distributed throughout the body. Because of binding or dissolving in fat, most drugs accu-mulate in various tissues, often not at their sites of action. These sites of accumulation are often where the drug causes toxicity—for example, the liver and kidneys. These sites may also serve as storage depots within the body where the drug is in dynamic equilibrium with the free drug. The same factors that are involved in drug absorption determine whether and how a drug is accumulated or stored once it is in the body.

Drugs may bind to plasma proteins, which may be important drug storage depots. Dif-ferent drugs that are bound strongly to blood plasma proteins can compete for the same binding sites, such that the use of one drug can displace another drug from them. For ex-ample, several drugs used to treat mental illness can displace the anticoagulant warfarin (used in the treatment of some cardiovascular problems) from its plasma binding sites. The high concentration of free warfarin can, in turn, prevent the normal blood-clotting process and produce unexpected internal bleeding.

One type of tissue in which there is a great deal of drug accumulation is adipose tissue (fat), which makes up approximately 18 percent to 28 percent of the body. Most psychotro-pic drugs are particularly prone to accumulating in adipose tissue because of their relatively high lipid solubility. Most drugs stored in human fat cause no overt symptoms unless the sub-ject undergoes a rapid period of fat utilization, due to starvation or extreme dieting. The short duration of the action of some drugs, or the prolonged duration of others, can be explained on the basis of fat storage. For example, the drug thiopental (an ultrashort-acting drug used in anesthesia) is very lipid-soluble. When injected intravenously, it rapidly enters the brain, leaving a relatively small concentration in the plasma. Thus, the onset of its effects is very rapid, occurring within approximately 10 to 15 seconds. However, the drug is then taken up into skeletal muscle tissue and begins to leave the brain. The drug then enters fat tissue and remains there for some time. As a result, the intensity of the drug's effects is reduced fairly rapidly, but some small, residual effect of the drug may be experienced for many hours.

Because men and women generally differ in the proportion and distribution of their muscle and fat, the intensity and duration of drug action may differ between the sexes. For example, because women's bodies average a lower total water content (54 percent for females versus 60 percent for males) and a higher total fat content (28 percent versus 18 percent), peak plasma levels of alcohol (a water-soluble drug) tend to be higher in women. This difference occurs even if alcohol consumption is comparable with respect to total body weight (Schenker & Speeg, 1990). As a result, women may be more susceptible than men to the adverse effects of alcohol, particularly liver damage (discussed in Chapter 8).

The importance of fat in the effects of psychotropic drugs is also illustrated when patients who receive narcotic analgesics to relieve their pain do not achieve adequate plasma levels because the needles used to inject the drugs are often too short to get past the large padding of fat in the gluteus maximus (the buttocks).

To summarize, the dynamics involved in the distribution of a drug in the body depend on the lipid solubility of the drug, how lipoidal the tissue is, the blood flow through the tissue, the mass of the tissue, and the concentration gradient of the drug between the plasma and the tissue. A drug's pharmacokinetics may also depend on the species, sex, or, as we shall see, the age of the organism.

Some drugs can exert indirect influence on psychological processes. For example, a drug that paralyzes the muscles may induce emotional discomfort. However, in order to exert direct psychological effects, a drug must penetrate into the central nervous system (CNS). The entrance of drug molecules into the CNS and the cerebrospinal fluid (CSF) is a special aspect of cellular penetration.

Considering the fact that the brain comprises only about 2 percent of the body's entire mass but receives approximately 20 percent of the blood flow from the heart, we would expect a relatively large amount of a drug to enter the brain. However, the brain has evolved a way of preventing most nonnutritive substances from entering it and affecting nervous tissue. This is generally referred to as the **blood–brain barrier (BBB)** and is a vital source of stability, as well as a defense. For example, after a meal, blood concentrations of numerous chemicals can rise sharply and could be very disruptive of brain functions if it were not for the BBB, which protects the brain against such fluctuations. The rate of entry of potentially abusable drugs into the brain, which can affect their rate of receptor occupancy, plays a significant role in their abuse liability; the faster the drug penetrates the BBB, the greater the likelihood of its being abused (Stathis et al., 1995).

The BBB is actually a feature of the physical structure of the capillaries supplying blood to brain tissue. Figure 3–2(a) shows the structural relationship between brain capillaries, astrocytes, and neurons. *Astrocytes* are cells whose long processes (extensions) make contact with several other types of brain cells. The astrocyte processes touch neurons and the ependymal cells that line the ventricles, which are spaces at the center of the brain. In addition, each brain capillary is typically in contact with several astrocytes. Astrocytes are members of the largest class of brain cells, the glial cells. Although their function is not yet fully understood, they may influence capillary permeability to drugs.

There is a very lipid sheath made up of extensions of "glial feet" from nearby astrocytes that surrounds the brain capillaries; as shown in Figure 3–2(b), astrocyte foot processes almost completely surround the brain capillary. Because of this relation, it was once thought that the astrocytes formed the BBB. Although the latter may be a factor, it is now

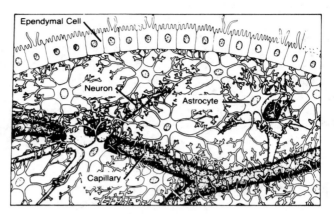

(a) Structural relationship between brain capillaries, astrocytes, and neurons.

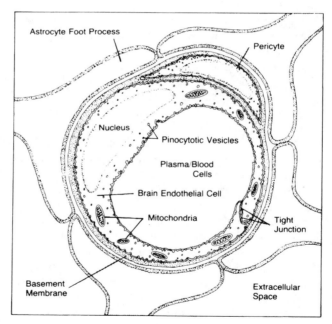

(b) Cross section of a brain capillary.

FIGURE 3–2   Schematic of the structural basis of the blood–brain barrier.

(From "The blood–brain barrier" by G. W. Goldstein and A. L. Betz, *Scientific American, 255,* 76. By permission of the artist, Patricia J. Wynne.)

known that it is the peculiar characteristics of the capillary endothelial cells that constitute the primary barrier to drugs and other chemicals that are potentially toxic to the brain. Unlike the cells of the capillaries elsewhere in the body, brain capillaries are made up of lipid endothelial cells that are packed tightly together. Furthermore, ordinary capillaries in the body have apertures, like small pores, through which drug molecules can pass. Brain capillaries have very few of these apertures.

Thus, in order for a drug to get to CNS nerve cells (neurons), it must be (a) lipid-soluble to some degree or (b) compatible with one of the several *carrier-mediated* or *active transport systems* developed in the capillary and astrocyte cells (Pardridge, 1999). Endothelial cells selectively transport nutrients into the brain, and their many mitochondria probably provide energy for transport. Active transport systems are systems in which ions or molecules are able to attach themselves to proteins embedded in the cell membrane. The proteins then transport the ions or molecules across the membrane through an energy-consuming process—a process that occurs at the expense of metabolic breakdown processes occurring within the cell. Apparently, these active transport systems have evolved in such a way that nutritive but nonlipid substances, such as glucose, vitamins, and minerals, can get into the brain. There are also carrier-mediated transport systems, which do not involve energy utilization, that can facilitate the diffusion of compounds across biological membranes. For example, minute invaginations may form in the surface of cell membranes and close to form fluid-filled vesicles, known as *pinocytotic vesicles,* which then migrate across the membrane and spill their contents on the other side. In contrast to other organs, in which such vesicles may provide relatively unselective transport across the capillary wall, the endothelial cells of the brain's capillaries have few pinocytotic vesicles. Although rare, there are some drugs that penetrate the BBB by way of these two types of transport systems.

The BBB is not completely impermeable to chemicals that do not possess the characteristics just described. The capillaries atop the brain stem where the vomiting center is located are permeable to chemicals because the neurons there must monitor the blood for deadly poisons, detection of which induces vomiting. Also, the BBB may temporarily break down as a result of injury (e.g., a blow to the head or a stroke) or illness (e.g., meningitis), thus allowing chemicals to penetrate it. Such penetrability could be beneficial or detrimental to the person, depending on whether a specific chemical is wanted in the brain or not.

Other factors limiting drug penetration in the CNS involve protein binding and degree of ionization. Drugs that are highly bound to plasma proteins are less likely to penetrate the BBB, because only free drug molecules can pass through. Drugs that are weak acids—that is, are highly ionized at the pH of blood plasma, which is approximately 7.4—are less likely to enter the CNS, because their lipid solubility is low.

Metabolism

Once a drug has been introduced into the body, it generally undergoes several chemical changes before it is eliminated from the body. The term **metabolism** (also known as **biotransformation**) refers to any process resulting in any chemical change in the drug in the body. This chemical change may result in the drug molecule becoming more active, less active, or unchanged in terms of its activity at its binding sites, so metabolism does not mean inactivation (Hoyumpa & Schenker, 1982). When complex chemical compounds are metabolized, or broken down, into simpler ones, the term *catabolism* is sometimes used; the reverse process is *anabolism.* It should be noted that drugs may be affected by all three types of metabolization. For example, codeine is transformed into the inactive codeine glucuronide, the more active molecule morphine, and the equally active compound norcodeine. The duration of action, or the drug's qualitative effects, may depend on which of these types of transformations is most rapid. Since the termination of a drug's action also is dependent to some extent on its being excreted from the body, metabolization of the drug into a more water-soluble compound generally must take place.

The fact that a drug may have several active metabolites is one reason why there are so many drugs of the same type and action on the market. That is, once a drug has been patented, the pharmaceutical company maintains the sole right to manufacture that drug for many years. However, if another company can determine that one of the drug's metabolites is also active, it can patent and market it. Pharmaceutical companies are also attempting to modify drugs into "prodrugs," inert substances converted by the body's own chemistry into active compounds, whenever the parent compound is hard to take or absorb or is slow to accumulate in target tissues (Hiller, 1991).

Many types of metabolic processes affect drugs in the body, and many drugs go through several metabolic changes before they are eliminated from the body. The major metabolic processes are *cleavage* reactions (the splitting of the molecule into two or more simpler molecules), *oxidation* (combining the molecule with oxygen or increasing the electropositive charge of the molecule through the loss of hydrogen or of one or more electrons), *conjugation* (the combining of the molecule with glucuronic or sulfuric acid), and *reduction* (the opposite of oxidation, in which the molecule becomes more negatively charged by gaining one or more electrons). Nearly all tissues of the body are capable of carrying out some type of drug metabolic activity. The most active tissues are generally those involved in the excretion of drugs, particularly the liver, kidneys, lungs, and G.I. tract. Within the cells of these tissues, the different subcellular parts carry out different metabolic activities.

It should be pointed out that some drugs are excreted intact, with only minimal metabolic transformation. This appears to be the case with the active ingredients of *Amanita muscaria,* a mushroom that is toxic and lethal in large enough quantities, but hallucinogenic in smaller quantities, which are passed into the urine and excreted. Siberian tribespeople, for whom the mushroom is quite a treat, take advantage of this fact by recycling the drug. (The recycling process they use and how they discovered it will be left to your imagination!)

As stated earlier, psychotropic drugs are generally lipid-soluble. Before there is any significant elimination of them from the body, they must become more water-soluble, because the excretion of drugs and their metabolites by way of the kidneys into the urine is, by far, the most important in terms of volume. Also, with the exception of the removal of volatile substances through the lungs, other excreta, like feces and perspiration, are aqueous in nature.

Drugs administered orally must initially pass through portions of the G.I. tract, where various enzymes may metabolize them. After the drug molecules cross the membranes of the cells in the G.I. tract, they move into a blood circulation system that goes directly to the liver before getting into the blood that supplies the body and brain. Thus, the molecules can be further metabolized in the liver—that is, the hepatic system (see Figure 3–1). It is for this reason that plasma or brain concentrations of drugs administered in this fashion are generally lower than those of drugs administered through other routes—a phenomenon known as **first-pass metabolism.** For example, blood ethanol levels are approximately 60 percent lower following oral administration than following I.V. administration if ethanol is given after a meal, and approximately 20 percent lower if given after overnight fasting (DiPadova et al., 1987). For most drugs, first-pass metabolism is primarily hepatic, although for some drugs, notably ethanol, it occurs predominantly at an upper G.I. site (Frezza et al., 1990).

By far, the organ most responsible for metabolizing drugs is the liver. Within the membranes of the primary liver cells exists a large complex of *enzymes.* (Enzymes are proteins secreted by cells that act as a catalyst to induce chemical changes in other substances, but which themselves are unchanged in the process.) These particular liver enzymes—technically the *hepatic microsomal enzyme system*—have apparently been developed through millions of years of evolution in order to deal with toxic substances that animals may be exposed to in their food and other environmental pollutants (Guengerich, 1993). Because the actions of these enzymes are nonspecific in nature—that is, they may act on many different types of substances—they also metabolize drugs. To differentiate between these enzymes and a multitude of others in the body, I will refer to these as *cytochrome P450 enzymes* (a name derived from one of their physical properties displayed during one of their chemical reactions). Although found in high concentrations in the liver, the enzymes of this large family are found in virtually every type of cell in the body.

As blood passes through the liver, drugs diffuse into the liver cells and are acted on by P450 enzymes. The metabolites (or, in some cases, the unchanged drugs) then diffuse back into the plasma or are secreted into the bile. Metabolites that are in the plasma and are sufficiently water-soluble are excreted primarily in the urine. If they are not sufficiently water-soluble, they may undergo further metabolization in the liver. Metabolites in the bile are delivered into the intestines. If they are water-soluble, they are excreted in the feces. However, if they are still lipid-soluble, they may be reabsorbed from the intestines to undergo further metabolization.

In most cases, the rate of drug metabolization is proportional to the plasma concentration of the drug (in log units), a relationship that is referred to as **first-order kinetics.** Some drugs exhibit **zero-order kinetics;** that is, they are metabolized at a fairly constant rate regardless of the amount taken—for example, ethanol (the alcohol we drink) (Ritchie, 1985) and certain antidepressants taken in very large doses (Jarvis, 1991). The rate is also dependent upon the concentration of P450 enzymes in the liver. This level can be elevated—in some cases several times over—with continuous exposure to certain drugs, which activate the genes regulating the synthesis of P450 proteins, although the process generally takes several days or weeks. This is an important factor in many cases of drug tolerance, in which the effects of a given amount of a drug are decreased because of previous exposure to the drug. For example, long-term exposure to alcohol can induce a 30 percent elevation in the amount of P450 enzymes of the liver, and barbiturates can elevate these levels to five times that of the normal level. Since all psychotropic medications (except lithium) are metabolized by these enzymes, their plasma levels can be considerably reduced due to this factor (Shoaf & Linnoila, 1991).

In fact, chronic use of most drugs that depress brain functions (such as sedatives) tend to induce higher levels of the P450 enzymes. Such effects are not restricted to sedative-type drugs. Tobacco smoking, for example, can enhance the metabolism and elimination from the body of many psychotropics (e.g., antipsychotics, antidepressants, and caffeine) because of its ability to enhance the hepatic microsomal enzyme system (Shoaf & Linnoila, 1991).

Drugs can also inhibit the metabolization of other drugs through various mechanisms. Some drugs, including estrogens (female hormones) in oral contraceptives, have been suggested to reduce the level of enzymes (Benet et al., 1996). Other drugs, including Antabuse, a drug used in the treatment of alcoholism, may combine with the active sites of the enzyme complex and prevent them from being available for metabolizing other drugs. Alcohol normally undergoes several metabolic changes. It first changes into acetaldehyde, which is fairly toxic. Normally, acetaldehyde is metabolized into nontoxic acetic acid. However, Antabuse competes for the enzyme that changes acetaldehyde into acetic acid. Thus, if the person who is taking Antabuse drinks alcohol, acetaldehyde levels build up and cause the person to become nauseated and to throw up. Supposedly the alcoholics' knowledge of these consequences prevents them from drinking alcohol. Finally, one drug may inhibit the metabolization of another because the two drugs share a common metabolic pathway. For example, higher-than-normal brain levels of barbiturates and other sedative–hypnotics may occur if accompanied by alcohol intake because the enzymes are busy metabolizing the alcohol (Hoyumpa & Schenker, 1982). Since the biotransformation of most psychotropics involves the same type of P450 enzymes, this phenomenon is responsible for the increased blood levels and potentially serious drug interactions that occur with a wide variety of antipsychotics, antidepressants, and anxiolytics that are often combined in the treatment of mental illness (Lin et al., 1996).

Not only can a drug influence the rate of metabolizing other drugs, but also the presence of one drug may alter the types of metabolites formed from another drug. A notable example occurs when the liver enzymes, in the presence of alcohol, convert cocaine into cocaethylene, a metabolite that appears to be synergistic with cocaine in terms of its reward properties as well as its toxicity (Farre et al., 1993).

Because there are vast differences in the ways in which different species metabolize drugs, it is very difficult to predict the response of humans to drugs on the basis of the response of other animals. For example, only around 50 of the approximately 750 varieties of P450 enzymes identified so far in mammals and other animal species are believed to exist in humans (Lewis, 2000). In humans it is now recognized that there are marked between- and within-race variations in the level of drug-metabolizing enzymes and the rates of metabolizing drugs, and perhaps as much as 50 percent of this variation is due to genetics (Reed & Hanna, 1986). Indeed, one of the more striking observations of recent studies is that an individual's response to a particular drug is partly a consequence of the number of active P450 enzymes in that individual's body, with, in some cases, a 50-fold range in enzyme activity (Guengerich, 1993). In a few people—perhaps up to 10 percent of the population—particular enzymes may be effectively missing. This is a likely factor in why there is often a lack of correlation between the dosages of drugs used in the treatment of mental illness and their therapeutic response, why there are differences in the side effects experienced, and why ethnic and racial groups often differ in terms of their response (Jeste et al., 1996; Matsuda et al., 1996; Risby, 1996).

P450 enzymes can activate (e.g., codeine to morphine via the CYP2D6 enzyme) or deactivate (e.g., nicotine to cotinine via the CYP2A6 enzyme) drugs of abuse; thus, pharmacogenetic variations in the patterns of metabolism among individuals can also modulate the risk of drug dependence (Sellers & Tyndale, 2000). For example, individuals with gene mutations that result in little or no activity of the CYP2D6 enzyme may have less risk of dependence on oral opiates (e.g. codeine, oxycodone, and hydrocodone) because of lower levels of metabolites (e.g. morphine, oxymorphone, and hydromorphone) with greater psychoactivity, and individuals with genetically deficient CYP2A6 nicotine metabolism may smoke fewer cigarettes and be able to quit more easily because they achieve toxic levels of nicotine quite readily.

Age may also be a factor in drug metabolization, because older people tend to lose their ability to produce many of these enzymes, making them particularly susceptible to the toxic effects of drugs. In the developing fetus and in newborn infants, in which drugs are metabolized chiefly in the liver, the activity and concentration of many metabolizing enzymes is less than in adults, prolonging and exaggerating drug effects (Ramirez, 1989). Children do not have a full complement of these enzymes until they are a year or two old.

Other important factors in drug metabolization are nutrition and disease (Hoyumpa & Schenker, 1982). For example, in animals, blood alcohol concentration has been found to be lowered and alcohol clearance from the body accelerated with high-carbohydrate (such as simple sugar) diets, whereas alcohol concentration is increased and clearance is reduced with low-carbohydrate diets (Rao et al., 1986). In the initial stages of starvation, drug metabolization may be enhanced, whereas in later stages it will be reduced. Severe liver diseases, such as cirrhosis, obstructive jaundice, and hepatitis, can significantly reduce the ability of the organism to metabolize drugs. The ability of skid-row alcoholics to get drunk on as little as a half pint of wine—what some people might refer to as reverse tolerance—is probably due to both nutritional deficiencies and disease (Wilson et al., 1986).

Very little work has been done on human sex differences in metabolizing drugs. Although some studies have concluded that gender differences are not very significant for most drugs (Dawkins & Potter, 1991), other studies have indicated that there may be notable differences in the ways in which men and women metabolize some drugs. One study indicated that the blood levels of alcohol in women were significantly higher than in men who had been given the same amount of alcohol (relative to their body weights), because women exhibit lower gastric first-pass metabolism of alcohol (Frezza et al., 1990). Other studies have indicated that premenopausal women tend to metabolize some antianxiety, antidepressant, and antipsychotic drugs more slowly than men do (Kando et al., 1995). Therefore, premenopausal women are prone to accumulate higher, and potentially more dangerous, levels of these drugs with repeated administrations. Although some gender differences in metabolism may result from hormonal differences, suggesting that they may not occur when comparing postmenopausal women with men of comparable age, the fact that there are gender differences in body composition, weight, and ratio of fat to total body water that may affect pharmacokinetic processes other than metabolism makes such a suggestion very tentative.

Drug Excretion

The liver excretes drugs into the bile by a secretory process. Highly water-soluble metabolites are not reabsorbed and are removed from the body by way of the feces. However, renal (kidney) excretion of drugs—primarily their metabolites—is the primary way in which they are removed from the body. Excretion of drugs by way of sweat, tears, and saliva is quantitatively unimportant. Excretion of drugs in breast milk may also occur, but this is important not because of the amounts eliminated but because the excreted drugs may be potential sources of unwanted pharmacological effects in nursing infants. For example, the breast milk of women who smoke smells like cigarettes, and the breast-fed babies of these women may learn to like the taste of tobacco this way and may be more likely to smoke when they grow up (Mennella & Beauchamp, 1998).

Because of their lipid-solubility, psychotropic drugs are always excreted slowly in their active forms. To a great extent, the metabolites' rate of excretion depends on their lipid-solubility, on whether they are actively secreted (as opposed to passively diffused) into the urine by the kidney cells, and on their pH and the pH of the urine. For example, an increase in the urinary pH (that is, a decrease in acidity) enhances the excretion of a weak organic acid, like aspirin, but reduces the rate of excretion of a weak base, like morphine. Therefore, the rate of excretion of certain acidic drugs can be enhanced by alkalinization of the urine—for example, with bicarbonate of soda (Alka-Seltzer)—while the excretion of alkaline drugs can be enhanced by acidification—for example, with vitamin C. This is called "ion-trapping." It should be noted that urine is usually acid, although it may not be if a person's drinking water is highly alkaline.

Like metabolism, renal function and, therefore, ability to excrete drugs, varies considerably with age. Fetal excretion of most drugs, via the placenta and fetal urine, is delayed. Excretion through urine increases to maximal levels in humans between the ages of 5 and 10. Renal functioning then declines somewhat, tends to stabilize between the ages of 10 and 40, and then begins to decline thereafter. Thus the plasma half-life of most drugs progressively increases from childhood to old age (Geller, 1991). (See Chapter 14 for further discussion of pharmacokinetics of the elderly.)

Implications of Pharmacokinetics in the Fetus and Neonate

One can make an argument that adults who take drugs are doing so by choice and that they are responsible for whatever consequences a drug may have on their body. Unfortunately, the developing fetus or newborn of a woman who takes psychotropic drugs does not have that choice. As many as 80 percent of all pregnant women take prescribed drugs, and up to 35 percent take psychotropic drugs, none of which have been proved safe for use during pregnancy (Kerns, 1986). In one large-scale survey, approximately 11 percent of the urine samples of women presenting for delivery in California hospitals in 1992 tested positive for at least one drug (e.g., alcohol, nicotine, cannabinoids, benzodiazepines, opiates, cocaine) (Vega et al., 1993). This estimate of drug use by pregnant women is only for very recent use, since the detection period for most of these drugs is less than two weeks.

The tissue through which most psychotropic drugs can easily pass, and which expectant parents should be fully aware of, is the *placenta*. This tissue is specialized to allow transport of oxygen, nutrients, and waste between the woman and the fetus, but it is no different from other cell membranes in its general permeability to drugs. In fact, drugs can cross the placenta, nearly always through passive diffusion, even more easily than they can penetrate the BBB in the adult brain. Therefore, any psychoactive drug can pass through the placenta and accumulate in the developing fetus in significant quantities. Passive diffusion through the placenta is dependent upon characteristics of the drug (such as molecular size, lipid-solubility, and so on), drug concentration, and duration of exposure.

In a fetus, a greater proportion of blood flow is distributed to its brain than is the case in adults. Combined with the less-developed BBB of the fetus and fewer plasma proteins for drug binding, this greater flow leads to more rapid and complete drug exposure of the fetal brain. Furthermore, with greater cerebral blood flow, a less-developed BBB, fewer protein-binding molecules, a lower level of hepatic metabolizing enzymes, and slower drug excretion, the fetus and newborn are much more susceptible to the potential toxic effects of drugs than adults are (Kerns, 1986; Guyon, 1989). This lesson was most agonizingly learned more than 30 years ago when a large number of women who had been taking a mild sedative called thalidomide during their pregnancy gave birth to infants with missing or malformed limbs.

The risks to the fetus include **teratogenic effects** (abnormal development), long-term behavioral effects, and direct toxic effects. Teratogenic effects may be apparent immediately and result in spontaneous abortion, malformation, or altered fetal growth, or they may be delayed and not measurable or manifested for years after birth. The majority of drugs of abuse, including alcohol, nicotine, marijuana, cocaine, and opiates, have been found to impair fetal growth, resulting in lower birth weights and shorter gestational periods (Kaye et al., 1989; Zuckerman et al., 1989). Low birth weight, coupled with exposure to socially disadvantaged environments, has been found to be associated with long-lasting and clinically significant attention problems in children (Breslau & Chilcoat, 2000; Johnson & Breslau, 2000).

In addition to obvious physical abnormalities, psychotropic drugs can disturb nerve cell proliferation, differentiation, and neurotransmitter concentrations. Disruptions in psychomotor activity, behavioral development, and performance may occur. For example, in humans, alcohol, opiates, and some anticonvulsants are well-established behavioral teratogens, producing disturbances of arousal and motor coordination, specific learning disabilities, and mental retardation.

Whether subtle or transient, behavioral effects may still cause problems. Subtle ones may only be evidenced if the infant is exposed to certain environments, such as an impoverished one. Transient ones, like neonatal withdrawal symptoms when drug exposure ceases at birth, can disrupt early mother–infant interactions and bonding, which can lead to long-term consequences for the child's psychological development.

Unfortunately, some emotional or mental disorders require that the pregnant female be maintained on medication in order to protect the fetus. For example, an actively psychotic, manic, or severely depressed female may engage in activities that would endanger the fetus. An epileptic fit, with the likelihood of experiencing seizures, has a significant potential for fetal damage. Fortunately, most studies indicate that the majority of psychotropic drugs used to treat these disorders have minimal teratogenic potential (Hawkins, 1989). Problems with medications that have some teratogenic potential (e.g., lithium and anticonvulsants) can be minimized by reducing dosage or eliminating drug treatment during the first trimester or by taking other precautions. (See Elia et al., 1987, and Hawkins, 1989, for a more complete description of potential teratogenic effects of specific psychotherapeutic drugs.)

Websites for Further Information

Sites providing information on the pharmacokinetics of drugs:

http://www.pharminfo.com/
http://www.infodrug.com

Sites providing information on the blood–brain barrier:

http://faculty.washington.edu/chudler/bbb.html
http://www.sfn.org/briefings/blood-brain.html

Bibliography

Benet, L. Z., Kroetz, D. L., & Sheiner, L. B. (1996). Pharmacokinetics: The dynamics of drug absorption, distribution, and elimination. In A. G. Gilman, L. S. Goodman, J. G. Harman, L. E. Limbard, P. B. Molinoff, & R. W. Ruddon (Eds.), *The pharmacological basis of therapeutics* (pp. 3–27). New York: McGraw-Hill.

Breslau, N., & Chilcoat, H. D. (2000). Psychiatric sequelae of low birth weight at 11 years of age. *Biological Psychiatry, 47,* 1005–1011.

Dawkins, K., & Potter, W. Z. (1991). Gender differences in pharmacokinetics and pharmacodynamics of psychotropics: Focus on women. *Psychopharmacology Bulletin, 27,* 417–426.

DiPadova, D., Worner, T. M., Julkunen, R. J. K., & Lieber, C. S. (1987). Effects of fasting and chronic alcohol consumption on the first-pass metabolism of ethanol. *Gastroenterology, 92,* 1169–1173.

Elia, J., Katz, I. R., & Simpson, G. (1987). Teratogenicity of psychotherapeutic medications. *Psychopharmacology Bulletin, 23,* 531–586.

Farre, M., de la Torre, R., Llorente, M., et al. (1993). Alcohol and cocaine interactions in humans. *Journal of Pharmacology & Experimental Therapeutics, 266,* 1364–1373.

Frezza, M., Di Padova, C., Pozzato, G., et al. (1990). High blood alcohol levels in women. *New England Journal of Medicine, 322,* 95–99.

Geller, B. (1991). Psychopharmacology of children and adolescents: Pharmacokinetics and relationships of plasma/serum levels to response. *Psychopharmacology Bulletin, 27,* 401–410.

Gillette, J., Weisburger, E. K., Kraybill, H., & Kelsey, M. (1985). Strategies for determining the mechanisms of toxicity. *Clinical Toxicology, 23,* 1–78.

Goldstein, G. W., & Betz, A. L. (1986). The blood-brain barrier. *Scientific American, 255,* 74–83.

Guengerich, F. P. (1993). Cytochrome P450 Enzymes: They defend the body against environmental pollutants, detoxify drugs and synthesize several important signaling molecules. *American Scientist, 81,* 440–447.

Guyon, G. (1989). Pharmacokinetic considerations in neonatal drug therapy. *Neonatal Network, 7,* 9–12.

Hawkins, D. F. (1989). Drugs used to treat medical disorders in pregnancy and fetal abnormalities. In E. M. Scarpelli & E. V. Cosmi (Eds.), *Reviews in perinatal medicine* (pp. 91–131). New York: Alan R. Liss.

Hiller, S. (1991). A better way to make the medicine go down. *Science, 253,* 1095–1096.

Hoyumpa, A. M., & Schenker, S. (1982). Major drug interactions: Effect of liver disease, alcohol, and malnutrition. *Annual Review of Medicine, 33,* 113–149.

Jarvis, M. R. (1991). Clinical pharmacokinetics of tricyclic antidepressant overdose. *Psychopharmacology Bulletin, 27,* 541–550.

Jeste, D. V., Lindamer, L. A., Evans, J., & Lacro, J. P. (1996). Relationship of ethnicity to schizophrenia and pharmacology of neuroleptics. *Psychopharmacology Bulletin, 32,* 244–251.

Johnson, E. O., & Breslau, N. (2000). Increased risk of learning disabilities in low birth weight boys at age 11 years. *Biological Psychiatry, 47,* 490–500.

Kando, J. C., Yonkers, K. A., & Cole, J. O. (1995). Gender as a risk factor for adverse events to medications. *Drugs, 50,* 1–6.

Kaye, K., Elkind, L., Goldberg, D., & Tytun, A. (1989). Birth outcomes for infants of drug abusing mothers. *New York State Journal of Medicine, 89,* 256–261.

Kerns, L. L. (1986). Treatment of mental disorders in pregnancy. *Journal of Nervous and Mental Disease, 174,* 652–659.

Langer, R. (1990). New methods of drug delivery. *Science, 249,* 1527–1533.

Lewis, D. F. V. (2000). On the recognition of mammalian microsomal cytochrome P450 substrates and their characteristics. *Biochemical Pharmacology, 60,* 293–306.

Lin, K., Poland, R. E., Wan, Y. Y., et al. (1996). The evolving science of pharmacogenetics: Clinical and ethnic perspectives. *Psychopharmacology Bulletin, 32,* 205–217.

Lombry, C., Dujardin, N., & Preat, V. (2000). Transdermal delivery of macromolecules using skin electroporation. *Pharmaceutical Research, 17,* 32–37.

Matsuda, K. T., Cho, M., Lin, K., et al. (1996). Clozapine dosage, serum levels, efficacy and side-effect profiles: A comparison of Korean-American and caucasian patients. *Psychopharmacology Bulletin, 32,* 253–257.

Mennella, J. A., Beauchamp, G. K. (1998). Smoking and the flavor of breast milk. *New England Journal of Medicine, 339,* 1559–1560.

Oldendorf, W. H., & Dewhurst, W. G. (1978). The blood-brain barrier and psychotropic drugs. In W. G. Clark & J. D. Giudice (Eds.), *Principles of psychopharmacology* (pp. 183–192). New York: Academic Press.

Panchagnula, R., & Thomas, N. S. (2000). Biopharmaceutics and pharmacokinetics in drug research. *International Journal of Pharmaceutics, 201,* 131–150.

Pardridge, W. M. (1999). Blood-brain barrier biology and methodology. *Journal of NeuroVirology, 5,* 556–569.

Ramirez, A. (1989). The neonate's unique response to drugs: Unraveling the causes of drug iatrogenesis. *Neonatal Network, 7,* 45–49.

Rao, G. A., Larkin, E. C., & Derr, R. F. (1986). Biologic effects of chronic ethanol consumption related to a deficient intake of carbohydrates. *Alcohol and Alcoholism, 21,* 369–373.

Reed, T. E., & Hanna, J. M. (1986). Between- and within-race variation in acute cardiovascular responses to alcohol: Evidence for genetic determination in normal males in three races. *Behavioral Genetics, 16,* 585–598.

Risby, E. D. (1996). Ethnic considerations in the pharmacotherapy of mood disorders. *Psychopharmacology Bulletin, 32,* 231–234.

Ritchie, J. M. (1985). The aliphatic alcohols. In A. G. Gilman, L. S. Goodman, T. W. Rall, & F. Murad (Eds.), *The pharmacological basis of therapeutics* (pp. 372–386). New York: Macmillan.

Schenker, S., & Speeg, K. V. (1990). The risk of alcohol intake in men and women. *New England Journal of Medicine, 322,* 127–129.

Sellers, E. M., & Tyndale, R. F. (2000). Mimicking gene defects to treat drug dependence. *Annals of the New York Academy of Sciences, 909,* 233–246.

Shoaf, S. E., & Linnoila, M. (1991). Interaction of ethanol and smoking on the pharmacokinetics and pharmacodynamics of psychotropic medications. *Psychopharmacology Bulletin, 27,* 577–609.

Stathis, M., Scheffel, U., Lever, S. Z., et al. (1995). Rate of binding of various inhibitors at the dopamine transporter in vivo. *Psychopharmacology, 119,* 376–384.

van den Hoogen, R. H. W. M., & Colpaert, F. C. (1987). Epidural and subcutaneous morphine, meperidine (pethidine), fentanyl and sufentanil in the rat: Analgesia and other in vivo pharmacologic effects. *Anesthesiology, 66,* 186–194.

Vega, W. A., Kolody, B., Hwang, J., & Noble, A. (1993). Prevalence and magnitude of perinatal substance exposures in California. *The New England Journal of Medicine, 329,* 850–854.

Wilson, J. S., Korsten, M. A., & Lieber, C. S. (1986). The combined effects of protein deficiency and chronic ethanol administration on rat ethanol metabolism. *Hepatology, 6,* 823–829.

Zuckerman, B., Frank, D. A., Hingson, R., et al. (1989). Effects of maternal marijuana and cocaine use on fetal growth. *New England Journal of Medicine, 320,* 762–768.

Chapter 4

Conduction
and Neurotransmission

All thoughts, emotions, and behaviors come about because of biochemical and electrochemical processes that take place in specialized cells in the nervous system called *neurons*. Drugs that affect these psychological variables do so because they alter these biochemical and electrochemical processes. Therefore, in order for the student to appreciate how psychotropic drugs work and what their short- and long-term consequences are, he or she should be familiar with these basic processes. The purpose of this chapter is to describe the biochemical and electrochemical activities that neuroscientists believe take place in the nervous system, and how they are related to psychotropic drug action.

Many of the descriptions that follow are theoretical in nature, rather than factual, because they deal with what goes on in the *central nervous system* (comprised of the brain and the spinal cord), or CNS. The neurons of the CNS are packed together so tightly and their functions are so interrelated that it is extremely difficult to say precisely what happens in the CNS, whether it is with respect to the normal activities taking place there or with respect to drug action. Neurons are also mixed in with numerous other nonneuronal cellular elements called *neuroglia, glia,* or *astrocytes,* which serve important metabolic and supportive functions. Therefore, much of the evidence for the activities of these cells is based on what has been demonstrated to occur in neurons of the *peripheral nervous system,* or PNS (made up of all neurons outside the brain and spinal cord), which are much easier to isolate and manipulate. However, most evidence suggests that the neurons and the interactions among them in the two systems are very similar, so in most cases information about one should provide us with a reasonably good idea of what goes on in the other.

It has been estimated that the human nervous system contains approximately 85 billion neurons (Williams & Herrup, 1988). To illustrate how enormous this number is, if you were to lose 100,000 neurons a day for 70 years, you would still have around 82 billion left. (Although several recent findings have invalidated the long-standing position that CNS neurons do not regenerate in the adult mammalian brain, the importance of long-term, regular cellular self-renewal in the CNS is still uncertain [Gage, 2000]). So, just in terms of sheer numbers, the CNS is a very complex system. Neurons comprise a communication network in which the information is analogous to codes made up of on and off signals, which correspond to the two drastically different states between which neurons are capable of rapidly alternating. Neurons are specialized to perform different functions. For example, some communicate between the senses and the nervous system, some communicate between neurons within the nervous system, and some communicate between the nervous system and the organs of the body, such as the heart, blood vessels, and muscles. However, they all appear to work in basically the same fashion (Stevens, 1979).

Two basic processes are involved in the communication network: *conduction,* which refers to changes within a neuron that allow the information to be transmitted from one part of the neuron to another part; and *neurotransmission,* which refers to changes that take place within one neuron because of the release of biologically active chemicals from adjacent neurons (Stevens, 1979). Conduction is basically an electrochemical process that is "all or none." Neurotransmission is basically a chemical process and may be "graded." Psychotropic drugs are simply chemicals that alter the normal processes of conduction, neurotransmission, or both. However, before we get into a description of these processes, the primary parts of the neuron that are instrumental in the processes must be identified.

The Neuron

Figure 4–1 depicts a stylized neuron and parts of other neurons that interact with it. Note that each neuron in the figure has numerous excitatory (E) and inhibitory (I) inputs or synapses, which regulate the frequency of action potentials (discussed in the next section) produced by them. The large arrows indicate the direction of information flow.

The main body of the neuron is called its *soma,* parts of which serve integrative functions in the communication of information. Extensions from the soma are termed *dendrites* and *axons.* Normally, there are many dendrites extending from the soma, which serve as receivers of information from other neurons, and one axon, which serves as the pathway over which signals pass from the soma to other neurons. Thus, in a sense, information flows from dendrite to soma to axon. Dendrites tend to be relatively short, but axons can be quite long. For instance, a spinal motor neuron may have an axon several feet long, although they too may be quite short in CNS neurons. The enlarged region where the axon emerges from the soma is called the *axon hillock.* A short distance from their origin, many axons have a coating called the *myelin sheath,* which is analogous to the insulation on a wire. Gaps in the myelin sheath, where the axon comes into direct contact with the extracellular fluid, are called the *nodes of Ranvier.* The presence of these gaps allows for an increase in the rate of conduction down the axon. Conduction in nonmyelinated axons tends to be rather slow. Near its end, the axon branches, and at the tip of each branch is an enlargement called a *terminal button,* which will be referred to hereafter as an *axon terminal.* Chemicals found within the axon terminal can be released into an exceedingly small gap between the neurons, called a *synaptic cleft,* allowing the neuron to affect the excitability of adjacent neurons. The region itself is called a *synapse,* and it consists of the presynaptic membrane of the axon terminal, the cleft, and the postsynaptic membrane of the "target" neuron.

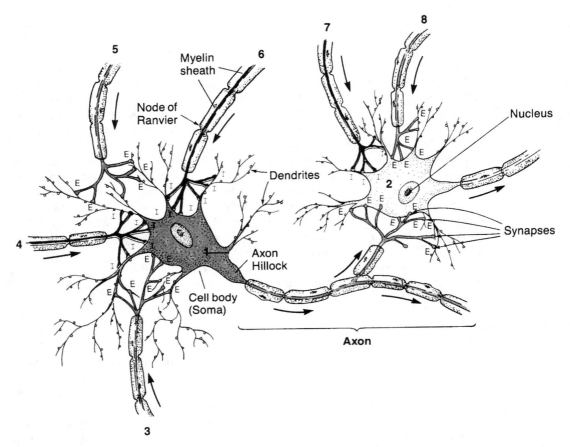

FIGURE 4–1 Schematic of the major parts of two CNS interneurons (1 and 2), depicting the relationship between them and the axons and terminals of other neurons (3–8). (Adapted from Carlson, 1988.)

Conduction

As with all body cells, neurons consist of a cell membrane filled with fluid, within which are subcellular structures that sustain the cell and help carry out its particular function. There is also fluid surrounding neurons (extracellular fluid), from which the cells take up oxygen, various nutrients, and, if present, drugs. Waste products and drug metabolites are discharged in this fluid. In the intra- and extracellular fluids are different concentrations of negatively and positively charged ions. The four primary ions important for conduction are sodium (designated as Na^+, where the Na is the abbreviation for the sodium atom and the $^+$ stands for the positive charge the atom possesses), potassium (K^+), chloride (Cl^-), and large negatively charged protein molecules (which will be designated as A^- because the general term for a negatively charged particle is *anion*). A fifth ion (Ca^{++}, a calcium ion with two positive charges) is also involved, as it appears to be involved in the permeability of Na^+ ions through *sodium channels* in the neuronal membrane. As you might guess, the extracellular fluid is quite similar to the environment in which organisms originally evolved—that is, seawater made up of Na^+ and Cl^- ions and water.

There are two primary forces that influence the concentrations of these ions across neuronal membranes. A *concentration gradient* force refers to the fact that when there are different concentrations of molecules on the two sides of the membrane, they travel from the high-concentration region to the low-concentration region. *Electrostatic pressure* refers to the force exerted by the attraction of oppositely charged ions or by the repulsion of similarly charged ions. As was mentioned earlier, neurons can be in one of two states. One state is called the resting state, although the term "resting" is not really appropriate because the cell is actually expending a considerable amount of energy maintaining this state. In this state, there is a much higher concentration of negatively charged ions on the inside of the cell membrane than on the outside of the membrane, as shown in Figure 4–2. In the figure, the size of the symbol for the various ions indicates their relative abilities to cross the cell membrane by way of the channels located in the membrane, with the smaller ions depicted moving more freely across the membrane. Also shown are examples of two of the primary forces maintaining these ion distributions: 1 shows a potassium ion (K^+) being "pulled" out of the cell because of concentration gradient pressure and "pulled" in because of electrostatic pressure; 2 shows a chloride ion (Cl^-) being "pulled" into the cell because of concentration gradient pressure and "pushed" out because of electrostatic pressure; 3 shows a sodium ion (Na^+) being "pulled" into the cell by both electrostatic and concentration gradient pressure. Not shown is the sodium–potassium pump, which is another major factor in maintaining these ion concentrations. Note that the large negatively charged protein ions are clustered close to the inside membrane, and the positively charged sodium ions are clustered close to the outside of the membrane. The close proximity of these two ions on the two sides of the cell membrane and their attraction for each other produces a considerable amount of pressure (voltage potential) at the membrane.

In the resting state, the cell is referred to as being *polarized*. In the other state, in which there is a rapid exchange of ions across the neuron membrane, the cell is referred to as being *depolarized*, a process resulting in what will be called an *action potential*. (The term "depolarized," which might suggest a loss of potential, is a misnomer; as we shall see, the depolarized state is actually a reversal in polarity.)

The neuron is analogous to a tiny biological battery with positive poles outside the cell and negative poles inside the cell. At rest, the neuron normally maintains an *electrical potential* (electrical pressure measured in volts) of approximately 70 millivolts (mV). Since the inside of the cell membrane is negative relative to the outside of the cell membrane, it is conventional to refer to this voltage potential as –70 mV. (The resting potential of individual neurons varies between –60 and –90 mV, but –70 mV will be used here as a ballpark figure for purposes of discussion.) The cell membrane is a protein and lipid barrier that contains small pores or channels. The differential concentration of ions is believed to be due to the different capabilities of the ions to pass freely through these pores of the cell membrane, where K^+ and Cl^- diffuse freely through them, Na^+ diffuses through with difficulty, and the protein ions essentially do not diffuse through them at all. This phenomenon is referred to as *selective permeability*. The differential permeability of the cell membrane to these ions

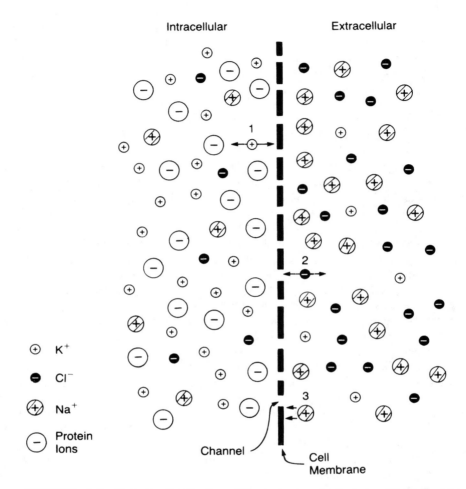

FIGURE 4–2 Relative distribution of the major ions in the intracellular (inside) and extracellular (outside) fluids of a neuron under resting conditions.

is believed to be due to their relative sizes: Na⁺ ions are approximately 50 percent larger in diameter (in water) than K⁺ and Cl⁻ ions.

In addition to concentration gradient and electrostatic forces, the concentration of the different ions under resting conditions is determined by what is referred to as *sodium–potassium pumps* embedded in neuronal membranes. These are energy-dependent pumps responsible for the active transport of both Na⁺ out of the cell and K⁺ into the cell. (They are termed *energy-dependent* because they derive their energy from metabolic processes in the interior of the cell.) The concentration gradient would normally result in equal concentrations of the ions on both sides of the neuron membrane. However, because of the A⁻ ions retained inside, the Cl⁻ ions are repelled through the membrane (remember, like charges repel, opposite charges attract), so the net effect is a greater concentration of Cl⁻ ions outside the neuron. Conversely, the K$^+$ and Na$^+$ ions are "pulled" inside because of the A$^-$ ions. However, there is a greater concentration of K$^+$ inside and a greater concentration of Na$^+$ outside because of the sodium–potassium pumps. The sodium–potassium pump is more effective in transporting Na$^+$ than K$^+$; for every three Na$^+$ ions pumped out, two K$^+$ ions are pumped in. This is another process allowing the inside of the cell membrane to be negative relative to the outside.

As long as the cell membrane of the neuron remains undisturbed, the resting potential remains at approximately –70 mV. However, all of this changes if for some reason the voltage potential shifts approximately 10 mV toward 0—that is, goes to –60 mV. This point is referred to as the *threshold potential*. As soon as this threshold potential is reached, it triggers a rapid sequence of events lasting about 4 milliseconds (ms), which is referred to as an *action potential*. It is also common to say that the neuron "fires" when this happens. During this sequence, the electrical potential is reversed, going from –70 mV to approximately +30 mV, and then returns to the original electrical potential, with an actual overshoot of the –70 mV level (approximately –80 mV) before the final resting potential is reachieved. This sequence of events and the resulting changes in electrical potential are summarized graphically in Figure 4–3.

In most excitable cells, the action potential consists of three phases, each resulting from shifts in voltage that selectively open ion channels and allow ions to flow across the cell membrane (Catterall, 1988). Because these channels open and close as a result of shifts

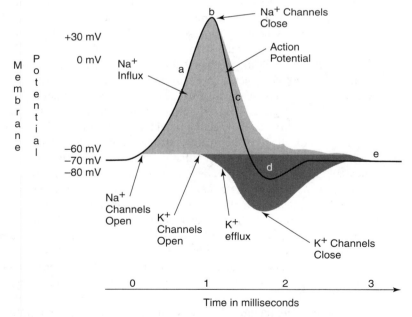

FIGURE 4–3   The action potential depicted here is the result of the rapid exchange of sodium (Na$^+$) and potassium (K$^+$) ions across the neuron cell membrane. (See text for explanation of the dynamics occurring at points *a–e*.)

in membrane voltage potential, they are referred to as *voltage-sensitive* or *voltage-gated channels.* During the first phase, there is a rapid flow of Na^+ into the neuron mediated by voltage-sensitive Na^+ channels that cause depolarization (point *a* in Figure 4–3). In the second phase, the neuron remains depolarized because of inward movement of Ca^{++} ions through voltage-sensitive Ca^{++} channels. The Ca^{++} entering the neuron serves a variety of biochemical functions—for example, activating release of neurotransmitters from the neuron. In the third phase, the action potential is terminated by activation of voltage-sensitive K^+ channels that mediate outward movement of K^+ ions, which *repolarize* the neuron (point *b* in the figure). The K^+ ions (repelled by the Na^+ ions) flow so rapidly outside the cell (point *c* in the figure) that there is an overshoot of K^+ ions, and the electrical potential at that part of the cell becomes even more negative than the normal resting potential (point *d* in the figure). This event is referred to as *hyperpolarization.* Finally, the –70 mV resting potential is reachieved as the sodium–potassium pump works to pump Na^+ ions out of and K^+ ions back into the cell (point *e* in the figure).

The point of origin of what has just been described generally is the region where the axon emerges from the cell body, called the axon hillock. The axon hillock may be viewed as a decision-maker regarding the production of action potentials, since it is the region where the integration of all the inputs to the cell occurs (some of which are inhibitory and some of which are excitatory). With all of this activity, depolarization of adjacent regions (at the nodes of Ranvier in myelinated axons) occurs, and the same sequence that was just described occurs, resulting in what is termed *propagation* of the impulse down the axon, eventually reaching the axon terminals. Once the action potential reaches the axon terminals, it initiates a whole different sequence of events, which will be described in detail shortly. The propagation of the action potential down the axon takes place without a change in the action potential's magnitude; that is, the changes in ionic exchange are the same from beginning to end. However, the rate of propagation depends directly upon the size of the axon and the thickness of the myelin sheath: the larger the fiber and the thicker the sheath, the faster the propagation. It should be added that only a small amount of the available ions are exchanged during a single action potential, so thousands of action potentials in succession do not radically alter the relative concentrations of ions inside and outside the cell.

The excitability of a neuron—that is, its ability to initiate an action potential as a result of an outside stimulus—is dependent upon the degree of polarization when stimulation is applied. If the cell is hyperpolarized (the resting potential moves further from the threshold), it is less excitable; if it is slightly depolarized (between –70 and –60 mV), it is more excitable. Its excitability is also dependent upon whether an action potential has already occurred. Immediately following the action potential, there is a *refractory period* of a millisecond or two, during which no new action potential is generated. During the last part of the refractory period, an action potential can be triggered, but only if the stimulus is much stronger than normal. The cell is also less excitable during phase *d,* a form of hyperpolarization.

To summarize, the prevailing view of how neurons function in the CNS is that miniature synaptic potentials are initiated in the soma or the dendrites, where they propagate passively to the soma, at which time they summate, for instance, at the axon hillock. If the summated potentials result in a large enough membrane depolarization, an action potential is initiated and propagated down the axon to its many terminals. (Normally this action potential goes from cell body to axon terminal, but under abnormal conditions, such as epilepsy, it can backfire—that is, originate in the axon terminals and get propagated to the cell body. Also, backpropagation of action potentials initiated in the axon back to the soma and the dendrites occurs in many neurons to varying degrees, which may convey the activity level of the neuron to dendritic synapses and may be involved in the induction of some forms of synaptic growth or alterations [Hausser et al., 2000]. Another role of this back-propagation is to trigger dendritic release of neurotransmitters, which could then activate autoreceptors [discussed shortly] on the somatodendritic regions of the neuron that reduce the excitability of the neuron. However, these complex processes will be left to more expert authors to deal with.) The information is actually in the form of shifts in the electrical potential in the different parts of the cell due to the opening and then closing of Na^+ channels. The regulation of the density of Na^+ channels in the neuronal membranes of the dendrites, soma, axon, and terminals may be an important determinant of their different functional roles in the process.

How do drugs fit into this picture? First of all, they can affect the properties of the membrane itself. For example, phenytoin (Dilantan), one of the most common drugs used in the treatment of epilepsy (see Chapter 14), has a variety of neuronal membrane-stabilizing properties (Pincus & Kiss, 1986). These properties decrease the Na^+ flow during the resting and action potentials, thus reducing the cell's excitability, and decrease the outward flow of K^+ during the action potential, thus increasing the duration of the refractory period. In addition, phenytoin decreases the flow of Ca^{++} ions into the axon terminals, thus decreasing the depolarization-linked release of several types of neurotransmitters (see the next section).

Ethanol and general anesthetics—including volatile solvents found in glue, industrial solvents, aerosol sprays (such as toluene, acetone, benzene, hexane, and ether)—have been shown to indirectly perturb lipid bilayers of neuronal membranes and alter the neuronal ion channels that play a role in axonal conduction. However, these actions only occur at very high doses that are probably not relevant for explaining their psychopharmacological effects (Franks & Lieb, 1994).

The second way in which drugs can affect conduction is by altering the structure or function of sodium channels located in the axonal membranes. **Local anesthetics** (drugs that block sensation from a specific part of the body) act by blocking voltage-gated sodium channels in neuronal membranes (Ragsdale et al., 1994). For example, one of cocaine's clinical uses is that of a local anesthetic, which in the PNS is the result of its ability to occupy sodium channels, preventing the influx of Na^+, and thereby preventing the triggering and conduction of an action potential (VanDyke & Byck, 1982). This action prevents any sensory information from reaching the CNS. There has been considerable debate over whether these properties are involved in cocaine's effects on mood and mental functions—that is, its CNS effects. Most of the evidence points to cocaine having an entirely different mechanism of action in the CNS.

Third, drugs can alter the balance of ions on the two sides of the membrane. For example, lithium is a small, positively charged ion (Li^+). Studies have indicated that when Na^+ and K^+ are deficient outside neurons, Li^+ substitutes for K^+ and is pumped inside. When Na^+ and K^+ are deficient inside the cell, Li^+ substitutes for Na^+ and is pumped outside the cell (Tosteson, 1981). The ramifications of these actions are still not understood, but they may have something to do with the ability of lithium salts to stabilize mood.

Neurotransmission

This chapter began with a discussion of the process of conduction where the action potential first begins—in the region of the axon hillock. Yet how does the neuron "know" when to generate an action potential? The process actually begins at the dendrites and the soma of the cell in areas that come into very close contact with parts (predominantly axon terminals) of other neurons. A single neuron may receive inputs from thousands of connections on its cell body and dendrites—some excitatory and some inhibitory. It is at these sites that chemicals released at these junctions, referred to earlier as synapses, cause very small, localized fluctuations in the electrical potential of the neuron. It is this process to which we now turn. (More extensive details of this process can be found in Bloom, 1996, and Lefkowitz et al., 1996.)

Getting information across the synapse was once believed to be due to an electrochemical process like conduction, similar to a spark crossing the gap between two electrical wires. While some neurons in the human brain may be electrically coupled in this way, the extent of such coupling appears to be quite limited. We now believe that the vast majority of neurons are coupled through a chemical process (actually a multitude of chemical processes) referred to as *neurotransmission,* which is perhaps even more complicated than the process of conduction. Although some drugs can affect conduction, as I just discussed, most psychotropic drugs appear to induce their effects by altering the neurotransmission process. Therefore, I will discuss the events that theoretically take place in this process in some detail. The word "theoretically" was used because we are dealing with an immensely large and complicated system, the CNS, whose workings are largely inferred from what is known about the PNS. (It should be noted that astrocytes, which until recently were considered to have only supportive functions in the adult nervous system, have been shown to have transmissive properties [Nedergaard, 1994]. In other words, they possess functional neurotransmitter receptors and are capable of direct signaling to neurons. However, most of the research on the biomechanics of information processing and on psychotropic drug action has focused on neuronal activities. Thus, I will focus on the neuron as the primary unit of the communication network of the nervous system.)

Figure 4–4 displays in highly simplified form the basic steps in neurotransmission. On one side of the synapse is an axon terminal, containing enzymes used to synthesize the active neurotransmitter molecules, the neurotransmitter substance, and small granular spheres called *vesicles,* which store and release the neurotransmitters. (Because a number of dilated regions of an axon may make functional contact with parts of other neurons before the ultimate termination, the term "axon terminal" connotes a functional transmitting site rather than the end of the axon.) Terminals also contain small specialized subcellular parts, called *organelles,* serving individual functions. One type of organelles are the *mitochondria,* some of which have an important function in the regulation of the overall amount of certain neurotransmitters in the terminal. The membrane of the axon terminal at the synaptic cleft is referred to as the *presynaptic membrane.*

On the other side of the cleft is the *postsynaptic membrane.* This membrane may be part of a dendrite, soma, or axon terminal of another neuron, or it may be part of a nonnervous system cell under neuronal control, such as a contractile (muscle) cell. The synapses of these four different junctions are called, respectively, axodendritic, axosomatic, axoaxonal, and

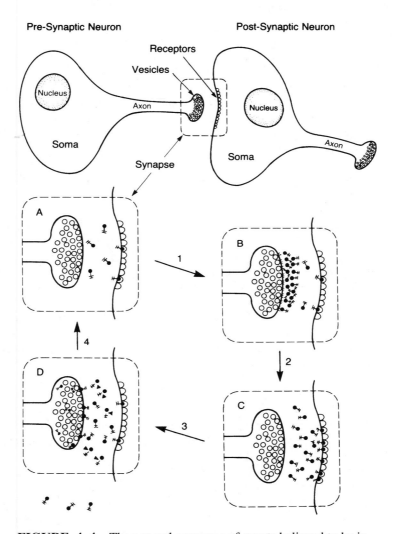

FIGURE 4–4 The general sequence of events believed to be involved in neurotransmission. (*A*) Between impulses only small amounts of transmitter (symbolized by ⊷) leak through the presynaptic membrane, and very few postsynaptic receptors are activated. (*B*) An action potential arrives and causes release of transmitters into the cleft. (*C*) Transmitters diffuse through aqueous material of cleft and bind to postsynaptic receptors. At excitatory synapses, postsynaptic membrane potential is reduced (that is, goes toward threshold potential); at inhibitory synapses, it is increased (that is, becomes more negative). (*D*) Transmitters dissociate from receptors and then diffuse throughout extracellular fluid, undergo reuptake, or are inactivated by enzymes (symbolized by ▲).

neuromuscular synapses. It is not clear how these synapses differ in terms of the processes involved in neurotransmission, so for our purposes, unless stated otherwise, we will assume that the functions are basically the same in all of them, at least with respect to presynaptic activity. Synapses between dendrites of neurons (dendro-dendritic synapses) have been identified in the CNS, but the neurotransmission processes involved at these synapses are still very speculative. In most instances, synaptic transmission involves the passage of chemicals across the synaptic cleft to an adjacent neuron. The transmitters then bind to *postsynaptic receptors* embedded in the membrane of the receiving (target) cell. These receptors then open ion channels to allow the flow of ions across the membrane to alter the excitability of the target neuron. Depending on the types of ions—negatively or positively charged—that are allowed to pass through ion channels in the membrane, the excitability of the target neuron may increase or decrease.

For neurotransmission to occur, the active neurotransmitter substances must be synthesized, which occurs more or less continuously depending on the neuron's activity level. In many cases this process requires a series of enzymatically induced changes in chemicals obtained in our food that take place in our body. Because these chemicals come before the neurotransmitter, they are referred to as *precursors*. Neurotransmitter synthesis generally takes place in various parts of the neuron, such as the cell body and the axon terminal, where precursor molecules called *amino acids* (organic acids with a nitrogen atom combined with one or more hydrogen atoms, such as NH_2) are transported across the BBB and then taken up from the extracellular fluid. If synthesized in a part of the neuron other than the axon terminal, the neurotransmitter is transported down the axon until it reaches the terminal. Transmitter synthesis takes place continuously, and the rate of synthesis is often inversely related to intracellular concentrations of the transmitter (i.e., the more transmitter used, the lower the concentration inside the neuron, and the higher the rate of synthesis), as well as by the amount of synthesis of enzymes and precursor molecules. The speed with which a neurotransmitter is used and replenished is sometimes referred to as *turnover rate*.

Transmitters are found in heavy concentrations in the axon terminals. The heaviest concentrations are found in the synaptic vesicles, which appear to serve several functions. First, they serve as storage depots for future use in neurotransmission. Second, they serve to protect the transmitters from further changes by enzymes in the terminal that can make them chemically inactive (that is, no longer able to induce biological changes at the postsynaptic membrane). Third, it has long been thought that vesicles that are in direct contact with the presynaptic membrane serve an active role in neurotransmission by fusing with the neuronal membrane and releasing their contents into the synaptic cleft when an action potential arrives at the terminal. More recent evidence suggests, however, that at least with one type of neuron (neurons releasing acetylcholine), the neurotransmitter molecules are more readily released from the cytoplasm of the terminal rather than from the vesicles (Dunant & Israel, 1985). Whether this occurs with other types of neurons remains to be determined.

Although we generally talk about neurotransmitters as being released primarily from axon terminals, neurotransmitters are found throughout a neuron and may be released from sites other than the neuron's terminals, thus potentially influencing nearby neurons or itself (Cooper et al., 1996). For example, one of the actions of amphetamine is to enhance the release of dopamine from dopaminergic neurons—from both their axon terminals and at somatodendritic sites. The dopamine then activates the neurons' autoreceptors—located on the somatodendritic membrane—which subsequently inhibits the firing of the dopaminergic neurons and reduces the amount of dopamine released from their axon terminals.

For many years it was believed that each neuron released only one type of neurotransmitter, but recent evidence indicates that many neurons simultaneously release more than one chemical that can serve as a transmitter or play a modulating role in the activity of postsynaptic cells (Bartfai et al., 1988; Sulzer et al., 1998). In many cases the different neurotransmitters—that is, *cotransmitters*—in an axon terminal are stored in different types of vesicles, which in turn may release their contents at different frequencies of stimulation. Thus, there is the possibility of pharmacologically manipulating one type of vesicle population without affecting the other.

Present theory has it that when an action potential arrives, it allows calcium ions (Ca^{++}) to enter the axonal cytoplasm through voltage-sensitive Ca^{++} channels and promote the fusion of vesicles with the presynaptic membrane (Ghosh & Greenberg, 1995). Only those vesicles close to the membrane fuse with it, while other vesicles seem to be held in reserve some distance away. The contents of the fused vesicles, including the transmitter(s), enzymes, and other proteins, are then discharged into the cleft. (As mentioned previously, an alternative is for cytoplasmic transmitter substances to be released.) All of this takes place very quickly—that is, approximately 1 ms for the Ca^{++} spike and 0.3 to 2 ms for synaptic vesicle exocytosis (Kasai, 1999).

Once released into the synaptic cleft, the transmitters passively diffuse through the aqueous material to the postsynaptic membrane, are briefly bound to receptors, and alter cellular functions of the receiving cell. Although the activity of transmitters may be terminated by their diffusing away from the synapse, in order to provide a short, discrete signal to the postsynaptic neuron, under most conditions the action of transmitters is terminated by their being enzymatically degraded or by undergoing a process called *reuptake.* In the case of reuptake, the transmitters are actively taken back up into the neurons that released them or into other neurons or glia (the nonneuronal supportive cells of the nervous system) through membrane transporter proteins via an energy-dependent "pump" mechanism. The neuron is then ready to start the process all over again. With some transmitters, all three processes take place, but in others, the metabolites of the degradation process go through reuptake for later resynthesis into active transmitters. Transmitters that have undergone reuptake by the neuron may be rebound to vesicles for use again at a later time.

Once a neurotransmitter molecule binds to a receptor on the postsynaptic cell, the receptor briefly initiates a chain of events that allows ion channels to open up (Sakmann, 1992). This allows ions to flow across the postsynaptic membrane, generating a change in postsynaptic membrane potential. The size, duration, and direction of this ion flow, as well as the nature of the ions traversing the postsynaptic membrane, determine whether this response will either activate voltage-sensitive ion channels and initiate action potentials or instead reduce the cell's electrical activity.

It should be noted that the term *receptor* is often used in a general sense to refer to a protein complex (made up of several subunits) that not only contains a number of binding sites for drugs and neuroactive ligands, but may also form an ion channel, whose opening or closing is modulated by the actions of those compounds (Figure 4–5) (Miller, 1998). Also, consistent with the evidence that there may be several cotransmitters released at synapses is

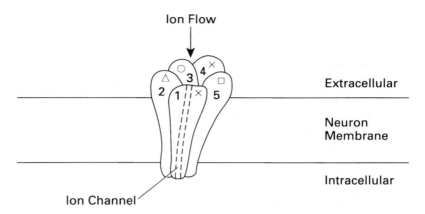

FIGURE 4–5   Model of a fast-receptor–ion-channel complex. It is made up of a protein with five different subunits (labeled 1–5) that form an ion channel in the middle. Each subunit is shown to have different receptor binding sites (indicated by x, ○, △, and □) for different ligands (neuro-transmitters). Depending on which site or sites are occupied, ligand or drug binding may result in ion channel opening directly, thus allowing selected ions to flow into the cell, may facilitate channel opening by another ligand, may inhibit channel opening, or may close the channel after it opens. (Note: other combinations are possible, and ion flow may be in the opposite direction.)

evidence that different types of receptors may be co-localized at many synapses (Bloom, 1996).

At the present time it appears that there are two general classes of receptors, "fast" and "slow" (Cooper et al., 1996). *Fast receptors* or *ionotropic receptors* are directly linked to an ion channel and are responsible for responses that last, at most, tens of milliseconds (see Figure 4–5) (Miller, 1998). In contrast, *slow receptors* or *metabotropic receptors* (Figure 4–6) are responsible for slower and longer-lasting responses, lasting hundreds of milliseconds to tens of seconds, that are generally modulatory; that is, they either dampen or enhance the signal that acts on fast receptors. Slow receptors are coupled to a class of proteins, called G proteins, which in turn are directly coupled to ion channels or linked to what are termed *second-messenger systems.* That is, receptor-ligand binding appears to activate specific enzymes in the target cell membrane that convert energy-carrier molecules into small molecules called nucleotides inside the target cell (Enna & Karbon, 1987). The nucleotides then serve as *secondary messengers,* which trigger the cell's internal machinery, leading to a momentary opening up of ion channels in the neuronal membrane. Two well-researched enzymes involved in this process are adenylate cyclase, which converts adenosine triphosphate (ATP) into cyclic adenosine monophosphate (cAMP), and guanylate cyclase, which converts guanosine triphosphate (GTP) into cyclic guanosine monophosphate (cGMP); cAMP and cGMP then serve as the secondary messengers.

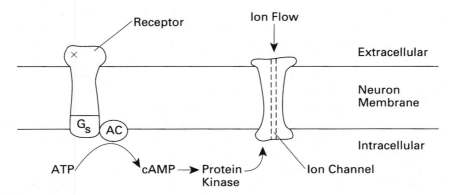

FIGURE 4–6   Model of one type of slow receptor. A ligand (the primary messenger) binds to the receptor site (*x*), which activates adenylate cyclase (*AC*) via the stimulatory G protein (G_s), which forms cAMP, which activates protein kinase (both of which can be viewed as secondary messengers), which opens the ion channel and allows ions to flow into the cell (or out of the cell).

It is unknown to what extent receptor activation leads to the formation of secondary messengers in CNS neurons or how many of these messengers exist. Also, some receptors may be involved in the inhibition of the enzymes responsible for secondary messenger formation (Cooper et al., 1996). Unfortunately, this lack of knowledge complicates our attempt to understand what is going on in the nervous system, since some neurotransmitters may inhibit a secondary messenger system via one type of receptor and activate it via another type of receptor. (For example, see the discussion in Chapter 12 regarding the major types of receptors for dopamine.) However, this apparent contradiction does explain how the same neurotransmitter may have excitatory actions in one area and inhibitory actions in another.

In many cases, the actions of a neurotransmitter or its cotransmitters at different receptors on the same cell are synergistic (Bartfai et al., 1988; Jonas et al., 1998). For example, one cotransmitter may block or slow down the enzymatic degradation of a more active cotransmitter or may change the affinity for or the number of functional receptors available for another cotransmitter. One transmitter can exert a fast-onset, short-duration action and another can exert a slow-onset, long-duration action. In some cases coexisting and core-leased neurotransmitters may induce apparently opposite signals; for example, one may activate a secondary messenger system and the other may subsequently inhibit it, producing a sharp, well-defined signal.

In any case, receptor activation allows for negatively or positively charged ions on the two sides of the membrane to pass through the membrane (Nicoll, 1988). Since these channels open as a function of a chain of biochemical events triggered by receptor activation, they are often referred to as *chemically sensitive* or *chemically gated channels*. (This terminology distinguishes these channels from the voltage-sensitive channels referred to earlier in the discussion of the conduction process.)

Chemically gated channels that allow Na^+ or Ca^{++} to enter the cell cause a small momentary decrease in polarization. This shifts the electrical potential more toward threshold and thus makes the receiving cell more excitable. When this shift occurs, the voltage change is referred to as an *excitatory postsynaptic potential* or EPSP. Conversely, channels that allow Cl^- to enter the cell or K^+ to leave the cell cause a small momentary increase in polarization, called *hyperpolarization.* This shifts the electrical potential away from the threshold, making the receiving cell less excitable, and the voltage change is referred to as an *inhibitory postsynaptic potential* or IPSP.

Each CNS neuron generally has thousands of synapses, some of them excitatory and some of them inhibitory. A neuron's excitability is determined by the algebraic sum of IPSPs and EPSPs, which, as mentioned earlier, can last from several milliseconds to several seconds (Sakmann, 1992).

The influences of EPSPs and IPSPs on neuronal activity are shown graphically in Figure 4–7. Sites 1 and 2 are at the postsynaptic membrane of an excitatory (*B*) synapse and an inhibitory (*C*) synapse, respectively. (Of the typical CNS interneuron's several thousand such synapses, only two are shown here.) Site 3 is located in the region where the axon emerges from neuron *A*'s cell body. Site 4 is located in the axon of neuron *A*. Variations in electrical potential at sites 1 (EPSPs) and 2 (IPSPs) are quite small, are unidirectional, and occur a millisecond or two after the arrival of action potentials at the presynaptic axon terminals at *B* and *C*. Variations at site 3 are somewhat larger and are bidirectional. (Fluctuations at site 3 do not necessarily coincide with fluctuations at sites 1 and 2, since the voltage potential at site 3 is a summation of fluctuations at hundreds of such sites.) Variations at site 4 are relatively large, with the largest shifts (the action potentials created in *A*) coinciding with the shifts at site 3 that reach the –60 mV threshold potential.

In addition to there being many putative neurotransmitters, virtually all neurotransmitters have at least two distinct receptor subtypes coupled to different ion channels on different cells or even the same cell, and each may have several functions. For example, a neurotransmitter may activate fast receptors at low concentrations and slow receptors at higher concentrations (Nicoll, 1988).

The fact that there are different receptors for the same transmitter may explain why a particular transmitter may be inhibitory in one part of the nervous system (that is, its release causes the receiving neuron to become hyperpolarized) and excitatory (causing depolarization) in another part (Cooper et al., 1996). As more and more receptor subtypes become identified, the selectivity of drug action can be greatly enhanced. Future drugs can be designed to fit only a single receptor subtype, which could then reduce or eliminate the side effects that limit the usefulness of currently employed drugs.

Autoreceptors and Presynaptic Receptors

In addition to the several types of postsynaptic receptors, there is considerable evidence that there are receptors on neurons that are activated by the very neurotransmitters they release (Carlsson, 1987). Thus, they are sometimes called *autoreceptors.* These receptors appear to be located in regions of the neuron outside of synapses. Thus, these receptors most likely are activated under conditions in which there is a relatively high concentration of extracellular neurotransmitter. They appear to perform an "inhibitory feedback" function; that is, when activated, they decrease the neuron's physiological activity or decrease the synthesis or release

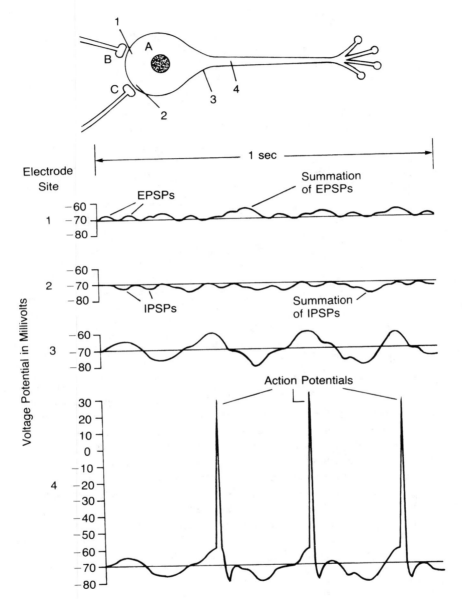

FIGURE 4–7 Variations in electrical potential at the cell membrane of a neuron (*A*) as a function of where the recording electrode is located.

of its neurotransmitters, which then reduces the influence of the neuron on its target cells' activity. Some neurons have autoreceptors located on their cell bodies or dendrites (Figure 4–8). These appear to play a role in the modulation of the physiological activity of these neurons, such as their rate of firing. For instance, when these neurons become active, their dendrites,

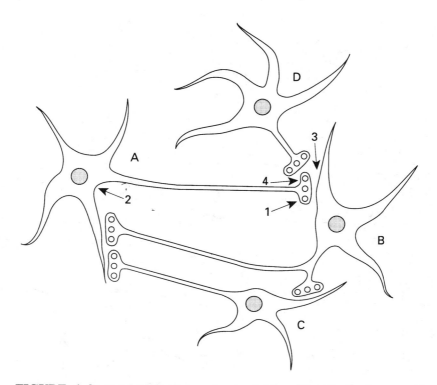

FIGURE 4–8   Schematic of several potential "negative-feedback systems" through which a neuron's activity may be modulated. Depicted are three different receptor sites for the transmitter released from neuron *A*. Autoreceptor activation at site 1 (on *A*'s axon terminals) reduces neuron *A*'s transmitter synthesis or release, whereas autoreceptor activation at site 2 (on *A*'s cell body or dendrites) reduces neuron *A*'s physiological activity, for example, by hyperpolarizing the cell. Postsynaptic receptor activation at site 3 alters neuron *B*'s activity. In turn, axons from neurons *B* or *C* may form a "collateral negative-feedback loop," which modulates neuron *A*'s physiological activity. Finally, neuron *D* may modulate neuron *A*'s ability to release its neurotransmitters by releasing its own neurotransmitters and activating heteroreceptors on *A*'s axon terminals at site 4 (an example of an axoaxonal synapse).

as well as their axon terminals, release transmitters. These transmitters then stimulate autoreceptors located on these same dendrites, which decrease neural firing by producing hyperpolarization and prevent these neurons from becoming too active. Thus, drug agonists at these autoreceptors would exert an inhibitory effect on the neurons, while drug antagonists at these autoreceptors would exert an excitatory effect.

Autoreceptors may also be localized on the axon terminals of some neurons. These appear to modulate the rate of both transmitter biosynthesis and action potential–induced transmitter release, although these two functions may be mediated via different autoreceptor subtypes. In general, it appears that autoreceptors localized on different parts of the neuron act synergistically. Their stimulation reduces the overall influence of the neuron on its target postsynaptic cells, while their blockade enhances its influence on the postsynaptic cells.

Several drugs alter neurotransmission because of their high affinity for these autoreceptors. For example, clonidine is a drug that works by activating (thus, it is an agonist) specific autoreceptors for noradrenaline, thus reducing the amount of noradrenaline released into the synapse. This property makes clonidine a potentially useful drug in a variety of clinical and research settings. For example, it can reduce blood pressure and alleviate some narcotic and alcohol withdrawal symptoms (Svensson, 1986).

The presence or absence of autoreceptors on neurons containing the same neurotransmitter may be an important factor in their differential sensitivity to certain types of drugs and to the development of drug tolerance with chronic drug exposure (discussed in Chapter 6). Drug-induced modifications in autoreceptors may also be responsible for the delayed therapeutic effects shown to numerous drugs (e.g., antidepressants and antipsychotics), that require chronic exposure in order to be effective.

A neuron's activity may also be modulated by *collateral feedback mechanisms* via other neurons. In such cases, the activity of one neuron on another is modulated via collateral axons, which form a kind of negative-feedback loop (see Figure 4–8).

As was just discussed, autoreceptors may play a role in neurotransmitter release. Unlike the all-or-none process of conduction, the process of releasing transmitters from the terminal appears to be graded, in that the amount of transmitter released is dependent on the ability of Ca^{++} ions to enter the terminal when the action potential arrives (Cooper et al., 1996). The greater the flow of Ca^{++} into the terminal, the greater the quantity of neurotransmitter released. The flow of Ca^{++} may be affected because of activation of the neuron's autoreceptors or because of activation of *heteroreceptors,* which are a class of presynaptic receptors activated by transmitters originating from a different neuron (that is, activity at an axoaxonal synapse such as depicted in Figures 4–8 and 4–9). Both autoreceptors and heteroreceptors are often referred to as *presynaptic receptors* because they are located on the axon terminals and affect the amount of neurotransmitter released from those terminals. (It should be noted that heteroreceptors, from the perspective of the neuron whose transmitters activate them, are postsynaptic receptors.) It is likely that both autoreceptors and heteroreceptors are of the slow type. In both cases, the presumed activity decreases Ca^{++} flow into the axon terminal, thereby decreasing the amount of transmitter released from the terminal when an action potential arrives (Wu & Saggau, 1997). However, in some cases, activity at axoaxonal synapses (shown in Figure 4–8, in which axon terminal *D* might synapse with axon terminal *A,* which synapses with dendrite *B*) may enhance transmitter release (from axon terminal *A*) by prolonging depolarization when an action potential arrives.

To summarize, very small electrical potential changes in the dendrites, caused by activity at the synapses, are graded and represent the sum of the contributions of multiple synaptic inputs. Some of them are inhibitory and some of them are excitatory. The summed potentials reach the soma and are modulated by additional synaptic inputs directly to the soma, where there may be enough sodium channels for action potentials to be initiated there. However, in many neurons, a high density of sodium channels at the axon hillock

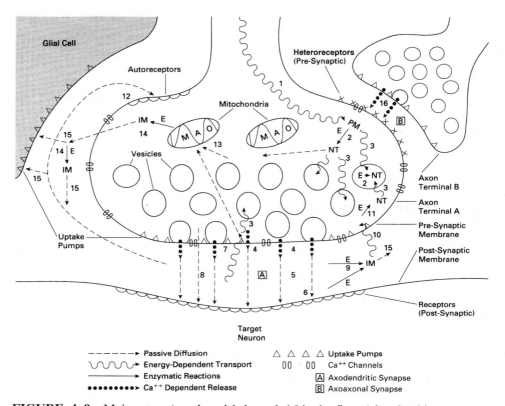

FIGURE 4–9 Major steps (numbered 1 through 16 in the figure) involved in neuro-transmission that are often altered by psychotropic drugs. See text for a discussion of each of these steps.

reduces the threshold for the generation of action potentials, so this initial segment acts as a summation point for the graded potentials from both the dendrites and the soma. In any case, once the threshold potential of the neuron is reached, an action potential is created and propagated down the axon to the axon terminals, which then release the neurotransmitters stored there, and so on and so on and so on.

Figure 4–9 combines all the processes discussed in this chapter that are involved in neurotransmission and that are often altered by psychotropic drugs. Synapse *A* depicts an axodendritic synapse consisting of axon terminal *A* and a postsynaptic membrane of a target neuron's dendrite. Synapse *B* depicts an axoaxonal synapse consisting of axon terminal *B* and a portion of axon terminal *A*'s membrane.

In step 1, precursors (PM) to neurotransmitters (NT) obtained from one's diet must cross the blood–brain barrier, be taken into the neuron, and be transported to the axon terminal. Drugs that are precursors to neurotransmitters found to be deficient in some neurological diseases—for example, Parkinson's disease and Alzheimer's disease—have been used to lessen the symptoms of these diseases.

In step 2, the active neurotransmitter is synthesized from the precursors by way of enzymes (E) located in the axon terminal. Often the synthesis process involves several stages and enzymes and is modulated by step 12. A variety of drugs are available that enhance or reduce these metabolic activities and thus increase or decrease the level of neurotransmitter available for use.

Step 3 depicts the uptake of neurotransmitter molecules or precursors into the synaptic vesicles. Reserpine, a drug originally used to treat extremely agitated patients, prevents several kinds of neurotransmitters from binding to vesicles. This action leaves these neurotransmitters "unprotected" so that they are metabolically inactivated at a higher than normal rate (via step 13). This discovery led to early hypotheses on the biochemical basis of some mood disorders.

Step 4 depicts the entry of Ca^{++} into the axon terminal when an action potential arrives. This results in neurotransmitter release into the synaptic cleft. In some cases, neurotransmitters are released from the vesicles, and, in others, they are released from the cytoplasm. A variety of drugs affect this process either directly, by blocking Ca^{++} ion channels, or indirectly, by activating autoreceptors (step 12) or presynaptic receptors (step 16) that affect Ca^{++} ion channel opening.

Step 5 depicts the passive diffusion of neurotransmitters across the synaptic cleft—a step that drugs rarely alter directly.

Step 6 depicts the binding to and activation of receptors on the postsynaptic membrane of a target neuron, which then results in ion channel opening and a shift in the target neuron membrane's voltage potential. Many drugs discussed in upcoming chapters alter this step because of their agonist or antagonist properties.

Step 7 depicts the reuptake of neurotransmitter back into the axon terminal—a primary mechanism for terminating many neurotransmitters' actions. Cocaine, amphetamine, and some antidepressant drugs inhibit the reuptake of several kinds of neurotransmitters and thus indirectly enhance the amount of neurotransmitter molecules available for receptor binding.

Step 8 indicates that between action potentials some spontaneous leakage of unbound neurotransmitter through the presynaptic membrane can occur. This is one of several processes altered by psychostimulants like amphetamine.

Step 9 indicates the extraneuronal enzymatic alteration of neurotransmitter into inactive metabolites (IM)—another common mechanism for terminating neurotransmitter activity. Some drugs that may potentially reduce the symptoms of Alzheimer's disease alter this step.

Step 10 indicates that some neurotransmitter metabolites may also undergo reuptake so that they can be resynthesized into the active neurotransmitter molecules again (step 11).

Step 12 indicates that neurotransmitters may diffuse through the extracellular fluid and bind to autoreceptors on the axon terminal or other parts of the neuron (not shown), which, when activated, inhibit synthesis or release of neurotransmitters. Most of the drugs that affect step 6 also affect this step.

Step 13 indicates that enzymatic alteration of neurotransmitters into inactive metabolites may also occur intraneuronally when the neurotransmitter is not bound to vesicles. Inhibition of one type of these intraneuronal enzymes, MAO, is believed to be the primary mechanism of action of some types of antidepressant drugs, because this allows neurotransmitter levels to build up in neurons that are deficient in the neurotransmitter.

Step 14 indicates that neurotransmitters may undergo several metabolic alterations, either intraneuronally or extraneuronally. Step 15 indicates that neurotransmitters or their metabolites may also undergo uptake into nonneuronal glial cells or may diffuse through the cerebrospinal fluid to possibly act at sites far removed from their release site. Drugs affecting other steps are also likely to alter steps 14 and 15.

Step 16 depicts the modulating influence of one neurotransmitter on another's activity via an axoaxonal synapse. In this situation the amount of neurotransmitter released from axon terminal *A* can be reduced or enhanced (by altering step 4) through the activity of neurotransmitters released from axon terminal *B* that bind to heteroreceptors on axon terminal *A*. (From the perspective of axon terminal *A,* these are presynaptic receptors, but from the perspective of axon terminal *B,* they are postsynaptic receptors.) A variety of drugs, most notably nicotine, which increases transmitter release, and opiates like morphine, which inhibit transmitter release, are believed to act at this step.

As one might expect, each of these steps interacts in an extremely complicated fashion, so that it is very difficult to determine what the overall consequences of a particular drug's actions might be. Thus, for example, a drug that simply reduces a particular neurotransmitter's reuptake can have far-reaching consequences. This action could increase the number of neurotransmitter molecules available for acting at postsynaptic receptors. On the other hand, it could also increase the number of neurotransmitter molecules acting at autoreceptors. If this results in the decrease in the synthesis or release of the neurotransmitter, it could actually decrease the number of neurotransmitter molecules available for acting at postsynaptic receptors.

This picture will likely be further muddied when you get to subsequent chapters and find out that the number or the sensitivity of various kinds of receptors can change with chronic drug exposure. To reiterate, any drug action, no matter how simple, initiates a cascade of events—some of which eventually are reflected in behavioral effects. Which of these processes are most relevant for the behavioral effects is as yet largely a matter of speculation.

Nonsynaptic Diffusion Neurotransmission

For decades it has been standard to describe neurotransmission as involving a communication system between neuronal membranes that are very close together, for example, at synapses. However, there is accumulating evidence that chemical transmission can occur among neurons that are relatively far apart—a form of intercellular communication called *volume distribution* or *nonsynaptic diffusion neurotransmission,* in which transmitters released from some neurons diffuse in a three-dimensional fashion within the extracellular or cerebrospinal fluid (ECF, CSF) of the brain and interact with receptors that are located relatively long distances away (Agnati et al., 1995). This type of far-reaching communication in the brain is analogous to that in the peripheral endocrine system, in which the signal (neurotransmitter or hormone), once released by the source cell, diffuses in the neighboring ECF, enters a specialized fluid compartment (CSF and blood, respectively) in which it is moved by convection forces, and finally diffuses into the ECF around the target cell and acts on receptors there. This phenomenon explains a long-standing puzzle as to why so often there is no obvious spatial correspondence between the sites of transmitter storage and sites of receptor concentration in the brain. It also accounts for the differential affinities of receptors for some transmitters. For example, with volume transmission, receptor affinity is typically high, whereas with synaptic transmission, receptor affinity is typically low, because high-affinity receptors would be easily saturated in a synapse. Many of the monoamine, amino acid, and neuropeptide transmitters discussed in the next chapter appear to work via volume transmission, as well as by synaptic transmission.

Volume transmission is likely to be involved in psychological processes that are mass-sustained functions (for example, mood, pain, hunger, sleep) as opposed to those that require synaptic activity, in which there is a need for clearly defined onset and offset of signals of short duration (that is, visual perception or fine motor movements). Thus, disorders of mood and other psychiatric disorders may be disorders involving nonsynaptic diffusion neurotransmission (Bach-y-Rita, 1994), and drugs, like Prozac, that are effective in their treatment may work because of their ability to alter this type of neurotransmission.

The process of neurotransmission is exceedingly complex—considerably more complicated than it was thought to be just 5 or 10 years ago. We now recognize the fact that each axon terminal may release one, two, three, or even four different neuroactive chemicals, depending on how frequently the neuron fires. We now know that each of these chemicals generally has more than one type of postsynaptic receptor, presynaptic receptor, or autoreceptor to act on. Some of these receptors induce rapid but short-lived actions on cells, whereas others induce slower-onset and longer actions. Thus, the nervous system is capable of considerably more complex signals than we ever imagined. This makes our understanding of how our nervous system works even more difficult than ever. But these new findings do suggest that we will be able to pharmacologically manipulate mood, cognitive functions, and behavior in much more selective ways than ever before—to the point of being able to enhance psychological processes or alleviate dysfunctional ones without inducing the often uncomfortable and sometimes debilitating side effects that present psychotropic drugs induce.

With new techniques, neuroscientists are having a field day discovering, identifying, cloning, sequencing, and so forth, novel receptors, transporters, and neuroactive chemicals in the nervous system. Their discoveries leave the rest of us wondering what all those chemicals are doing there. Do they all have any functional or physiological significance? Or are some of them the "garbage" left over from our ancient ancestors, who might have had some use for them, but that are no longer necessary? As yet, nobody really knows. It seems the more we study the brain, the more complicated it becomes.

Websites for Further Information

Sites providing general information on neuroscience:

http://faculty.washington.edu/chudler/neurok.html
http://www.sfn.org/
http://www.neuropsychologycentral.com/index.html

Site relevant to axonal and synaptic transmission:

http://faculty.washington.edu/chudler/introb.html

Anatomy of memory site offers brain anatomy tutorials, micrographs of tissue slices, virtual reality models of dendrites:

http://synapses.bu.edu/index.asp

Wander around the brain, using images found at the Harvard Whole Brain Atlas site:

http://www.med.harvard.edu/AANLIB/home.html

Site aimed at generating public interested in brain research; includes book reviews, illusions, brain anatomy drawings, descriptions of brain-related disorders:

http://www.brainconnection.com

Site about brain abnormalities:

http://www.sfn.org/briefings/

Bibliography

Agnati, L. F., Zoll, M., Stromberg, I., & Fuxe, K. (1995). Intercellular communication in the brain: Wiring versus volume transmission. *Neuroscience, 69,* 711–726.

Bach-y-Rita, P. (1994). Psychopharmacologic drugs: Mechanisms of action. *Science, 264,* 640–641.

Bartfai, T., Iverfeldt, K., & Fisone, G. (1988). Regulation of the release of coexisting neurotransmitters. *Annual Review of Pharmacology and Toxicology, 28,* 285–310.

Bloom, F. E. (1996). Neurotransmission and the central nervous system. In A. G. Gilman, L. S. Goodman, J. G. Hardman, L. E. Limbard, P. B. Molinoff, & R. W. Ruddon (Eds.), *The pharmacological basis of therapeutics* (pp. 267–293). New York: McGraw-Hill.

Carlson, N. R. (1988). *Foundations of physiological psychology.* Boston: Allyn & Bacon.

Carlsson, A. (1987). Perspectives on the discovery of central monoaminergic neurotransmission. *Annual Review of Neuroscience, 10,* 19–40.

Catterall, W. A. (1988). Structure and function of voltage-sensitive ion channels. *Science, 242,* 50–61.

Cooper, J. R., Bloom, F. E., & Roth, R. H. (1996). *The biochemical basis of neuropharmacology,* 7th ed. New York: Oxford Press.

Dunant, Y., & Israel, M. (1985). The release of acetylcholine. *Scientific American, 252,* 58–66.

Enna, S. J., & Karbon, E. W. (1987). Receptor regulation: Evidence for a relationship between phospholipid metabolism and neurotransmitter receptor-mediated cAMP formation in the brain. *Trends in the Pharmacological Sciences Reviews, 8,* 21–24.

Franks, N. P., & Lieb, W. R. (1994). Molecular and cellular mechanisms of general anaesthesia. *Nature, 367,* 607–614.

Gage, F. H. (2000). Mammalian neural stem cells. *Science, 287,* 1433–1438.

Ghosh, A., & Greenberg, M. E. (1995). Calcium signaling in neurons: Molecular mechanisms and cellular consequences. *Science, 268,* 239–246.

Hausser, M., Spruston, N., & Stuart, G. J. (2000). Diversity and dynamics of dendritic signaling. *Science, 290,* 739–744.

Jonas, P., Bischofberger, J., & Sandkuhler, J. (1998). Corelease of two fast neurotransmitters at a central synapse. *Science, 281,* 419–424.

Kasai, H. (1999). Comparative biology of Ca2+ dependent exocytosis: Implications of kinetic diversity for secretory function. *Trends in Neurosciences, 22,* 88–93.

Lefkowitz, R. J., Hoffman, B. B., & Taylor, P. (1996). Neurotransmission: The autonomic and somatic motor nervous system. In A. G. Gilman, L. S. Goodman, J. G. Hardman, L. E. Limbard, P. B. Molinoff, & R. W. Ruddon (Eds.), *The pharmacological basis of therapeutics* (pp. 105–139). New York: McGraw-Hill.

Miller, C. (1998). Glutamate receptor activation: A four-step program. *Science, 280,* 1547–1548.

Nedergaard, M. (1994). Direct signaling from astrocytes to neurons in cultures of mammalian brain cells. *Science, 263,* 1768–1772.

Nicoll, R. A. (1988). The coupling of neurotransmitter receptors to ion channels in the brain. *Science, 241,* 545–551.

Pincus, J. H., & Kiss, A. (1986). Phenytoin reduces early acetylcholine release after depolarization. *Brain Research, 397,* 103–107.

Ragsdale, D. S., McPhee, J. C., Scheuer, T., & Catterall, W. A. (1994). Molecular determinants of state-dependent block of Na$^+$ channels by local anesthetics. *Science, 265,* 1724–1728.

Sakmann, B. (1992). Elementary steps in synaptic transmission revealed by currents through single ion channels. *Science, 256,* 503–512.

Stevens, C. F. (1979). The neuron. *Scientific American, 241,* 54–65.

Sulzer, D., Joyce, M. P., Lin, L, et al. (1998). Dopamine neurons make glutamatergic synapses *in vitro. The Journal of Neuroscience, 18,* 4588–4602.

Svensson, T. H. (1986). Clonidine in abstinence reactions: Basic mechanisms. *Acta Psychiatrica Scandinavica, 73,* 19–42.

Tosteson, D. C. (1981). Lithium and mania. *Scientific American, 244,* 164–174.

VanDyke, C. & Byck, R. (1982). Cocaine. *Scientific American, 246,* 128–141.

Williams, R. W., & Herrup, K. (1988). The control of neuron number. *Annual Review of Neuroscience, 11,* 423–453.

Wu, L-G., & Saggau, P. (1997). Presynaptic inhibition of elicited neurotransmitter release. *Trends in the Neurosciences, 20,* 204–212.

Chapter 5

Neuroactive Ligands and the Nervous System

There are literally hundreds of neuroactive chemicals found in and among the billions of cells making up the brain. Some of them appear to exert actions of very short duration (for example, a few milliseconds), while others appear to exert actions of relatively long duration (for example, several seconds or minutes). Some travel very short distances from the cells in which they originate, and others travel relatively long distances. Some exert an action by themselves, while others appear to exert an action only in the presence of other endogenous chemicals. Specific neuroactive ligands are highly localized in some areas of the brain, while others are distributed widely throughout the nervous system.

The nervous system itself has a variety of highly interrelated subsystems, all of which allow us to engage in extremely complex psychological activities, such as thinking, planning, learning, speaking, experiencing emotions, preparing the body for action, and so on. By interacting with the natural neuroactive ligands in various areas of the brain, drugs can shift normal psychological activities carried out by the brain into abnormal ones and, in some cases, can serve to normalize abnormal psychological activities. The purpose of this chapter is to familiarize you with some of the more important ligands found in the nervous system and to review briefly some of the major subsystems of the nervous system, so that you can get a better understanding of how psychotropic drugs act and why they induce the effects they do.

Neurotransmitters, Neuromodulators, and Neurohormones

Neurotransmitters are commonly viewed as chemicals that are located in specific regions of neurons, are released under specific stimulation, act on a specific set of receptors, and induce short-duration changes in membrane potentials. Closely related to neurotransmitters are *neurohormones*. These are chemicals that are synthesized in one area of the nervous system, are released into circulation, travel to some site that is distant from the release site, and then produce some effect on the brain or body. It is not clear just how far apart the release and receptor sites must be before the status of a chemical changes from that of a neurotransmitter to that of a neurohormone. Furthermore, there are chemicals that have some of the characteristics of neurotransmitters or neurohormones, but by themselves have no intrinsic activity except in the presence of other synaptic activity. These are referred to as *neuromodulators* because they modify responses to other transmitters presynaptically or postsynaptically while not showing any direct shifts in membrane potential or conductance when tested for actions on their own. For example, a neuromodulator may induce a change in the binding of a neurotransmitter to its receptor, or it can act through secondary messengers to modulate neural responses to a neurotransmitter (Kow & Pfaff, 1988).

To further confuse matters, a chemical that appears to play the role of a neurotransmitter in one area of the nervous system may play the role of a neuromodulator or neurohormone somewhere else in the body (Cooper et al., 1996). Because of this potential confusion and because, in a way, neurotransmitters, neurohormones, and neuromodulators are all involved in chemical communication among neurons, throughout this text we will simply refer to them all collectively as neurotransmitters. On occasion, when it is important to distinguish a more specific role for a neuroactive ligand, we will apply the more specific term.

Finally, there are numerous chemicals that play an indirect role in these processes. Some of these are precursors, while others are enzymes involved in the synthesis or breakdown of neuroactive chemicals. Others may be the remnants of the active chemicals that have been inactivated through metabolic processes, but which may still influence neurotransmission because their presence reduces the access of the active chemicals to their receptors.

Hundreds of chemicals in the nervous system have been identified as either being or having the potential to be neurotransmitters (or neuromodulators). They range in structural complexity from molecules of two atoms—for example, simple gases such as nitric oxide (NO) and carbon monoxide (CO)—to molecules comprising hundreds of atoms. The major chemical classes of transmitters are *amines* (molecules with a group consisting of one nitrogen atom in combination with one or more hydrogen atoms), amino acids, and *peptides* (molecules made up of two or more amino acids). With respect to the CNS, most of these chemicals have yet to meet several criteria that would definitely indicate their roles as neurotransmitters. In order for a chemical to be designated as a neurotransmitter,

1. *it should be found in presynaptic neurons;*
2. *enzymes necessary for its synthesis must also be present in the neuron;*
3. *there should be a mechanism for terminating its action;*
4. *its direct application to the postsynaptic neuron should be equivalent to stimulation of the presynaptic neuron;*
5. *when the presynaptic neuron is stimulated, the synaptic cleft should contain the neurotransmitter;*
6. *drugs interfering with the synthesis or reaction at the postsynaptic membrane should block the effects of presynaptic neuronal stimulation; and*
7. *drugs blocking the actions of the inactivating enzyme should prolong the transmitter's actions (Cooper et al., 1996).*

Though most of the chemicals to be discussed here satisfy one or more of these criteria, only acetylcholine and norepinephrine in the peripheral nervous system satisfy all of them.

Virtually every drug that alters psychological function does so by interacting with one or more neurotransmitter systems in the brain. Drugs have been shown to alter the synthesis, storage, release, enzymatic inactivation, and reuptake of the neurotransmitters. Many drugs either mimic (that is, they are agonists) or block (that is, they are antagonists) specific neurotransmitters at their receptors, both presynaptic and postsynaptic.

The fact that a drug can act on both presynaptic and postsynaptic receptors can cause considerable confusion as to what behavioral effects the drug will have. If, for example, the drug mimics the neurotransmitter at its postsynaptic receptors, it will enhance the neurotransmitter's ability to alter activity of the postsynaptic, or receiving, cell. If the drug mimics the action of the neurotransmitter at its autoreceptors and inhibits the release of the neurotransmitter, it will reduce the neurotransmitter's ability to alter the activity of the postsynaptic cell. (It may help to refer back to Figures 4–8 and 4–9.)

The situation is even more complicated if a drug mimics a neurotransmitter at both its autoreceptors and its postsynaptic receptors, but has a greater affinity for its autoreceptors—a situation that is not uncommon. In such cases, the drug may reduce the neurotransmitter's action at postsynaptic receptors when administered in low doses (because activation of the autoreceptors decreases the amount of endogenous neurotransmitter available for activating the postsynaptic receptors), but it may activate the transmitter's postsynaptic receptors when administered in higher doses. In such cases, even though there is less endogenous transmitter available for the receptors, the drug takes its place so that there is more postsynaptic receptor activation than might occur normally with the transmitter alone (Skirboll et al., 1979).

Although the preceding scenario is indeed confusing, it does give promise for the development of more specific-acting therapeutic drugs in the near future. One of the primary problems we currently have with respect to drugs is their relative lack of specificity, which can result in dependence and side effects that may, in the long run, be worse for patients than the condition they took the drug to counteract.

To summarize, a psychoactive drug can alter any number of the processes involved in the communication system I have just described. It can

1. increase or decrease the rate of synthesizing one or more neurotransmitters.
2. increase or decrease the amount of neurotransmitter released.
3. enhance or prevent the storage of neurotransmitter.
4. increase or decrease a neurotransmitter's rate of metabolic breakdown.
5. bind to the presynaptic or postsynaptic receptors for the neurotransmitter and, depending on whether or not the drug activates the receptor, it can accentuate or blunt the neurotransmitter's effects.
6. reduce or enhance the neurotransmitter's reuptake.
7. serve as a **neurotoxin** or **neurotoxic agent,** a substance that causes the destruction of neural tissue.

Specific Neurotransmitters

There are many putative neurotransmitters. As we see in Figure 5–1, GABA, aspartate, and glutamate are amino acids believed to serve a neurotransmitter role. Serotonin is shown to be

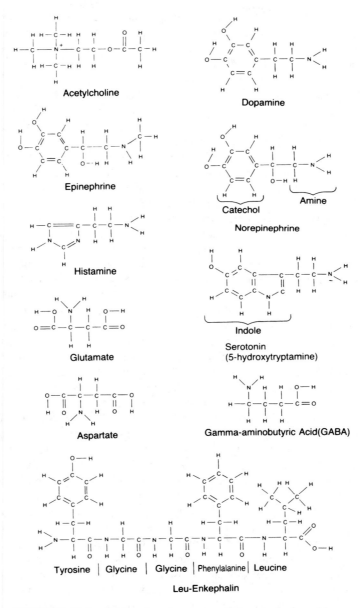

FIGURE 5–1   Molecular structures of chemicals found in the mammalian nervous system that are believed to serve either a neurotransmitter or neuromodulatory role. The symbols stand for atoms: C, carbon; H, hydrogen; O, oxygen; and N, nitrogen. A single bond between atoms is indicated by –, and a double bond by =.

composed of an indole nucleus and an amine; norepinephrine is shown to be composed of a catechol nucleus and an amine. Leu-enkephalin is shown to be composed of a string of amino acids; that is, it is a peptide. Histamine is generally found in non-CNS cells made up of connective tissue (mast cells). It is also found in the brain. Although it shares a molecular similarity to the monoamines (norepinephrine, dopamine, serotonin), and blocking its action with antihistamines produces substantial CNS actions such as drowsiness and hunger, the role of histamine in brain function is still very speculative. However, these are only a few that we know much about with respect to drug action, and even in these cases there is a great deal of speculation. Some of these will be described briefly here in terms of some of their properties, and they will be discussed with respect to drug actions later in this book. During this discussion, you should keep in mind that each neuron releases a specific type (or types) of neurotransmitter. In some cases, two or more substances may be released, each substance playing a different role in synaptic transmission (Bartfai et al., 1988). However, neurons are generally referred to by the neurotransmitter that is released that plays the most predominant role in the process. Such terms are commonly formed by adding the suffix "ergic" to a root designating the neurotransmitter. For example, adrenergic neurons are those that release adrenaline or noradrenaline, noradrenergic neurons release noradrenaline, dopaminergic neurons release dopamine, cholinergic neurons release acetylcholine, and so forth.

Acetylcholine (Ach) was the first transmitter to meet all of the criteria listed at the beginning of the preceding section (Taylor, 1985). It is found in various parts of the PNS and numerous areas of the CNS. It has excitatory properties in the PNS (it depolarizes the membrane of target cells), whereas in the CNS it can have either excitatory or inhibitory influences on neurons, depending on the area being monitored. It is one of the transmitters that undergoes inactivation in the cleft by way of an enzyme. In this case the enzyme is acetylcholinesterase. (Whenever a chemical name ends with "ase," it is an enzyme.) Reuptake then occurs with one of the metabolites (choline).

Cholinergic neurons are found in many different areas of the nervous system, and it is likely that they play a role in a multitude of psychological activities (Blusztajn, 1998). In the CNS, Ach is particularly important in memory functions. Alzheimer's disease, which results in severe memory loss, is due to the destruction of a relatively small portion of Ach-containing neurons. Drugs that block Ach in the brain (anticholinergics) profoundly reduce the ability to form new memories. On the other hand, drugs that enhance Ach activity may be useful in alleviating some types of memory dysfunctions. Ach is probably involved in certain forms of aggression and grand mal seizures, since both have been noted to occur when there is excessive Ach activity. Excessive Ach activity, when coupled with low norepinephrine activity (discussed below), has been suggested to be a factor in certain kinds of depression as well. Cholinergic mechanisms play an important role in the initiation and maintenance of REM sleep (see Chapter 8). Since abnormalities in REM sleep are found in clinical disorders such as major depression, narcolepsy, obsessive–compulsive disorder, and some forms of schizophrenia (all discussed in later chapters), it is possible that abnormal activation of central cholinergic mechanisms may be involved in these disorders (Shiromani et al., 1987).

Ach also plays numerous roles in the PNS. It is released from the preganglionic nerve endings of both the parasympathetic and the sympathetic nervous systems (these will be briefly discussed a little later on), the postganglionic nerve endings of the parasympathetic nervous system, and the nerve endings at neuromuscular synapses. Many of the peripheral side effects of drugs used for the treatment of mental illness are attributed to the reduction of Ach activity at some of these synapses.

Ach has two primary types of receptors, referred to as *muscarinic* and *nicotinic* because the former are easily activated by the drug muscarine (that is, like Ach, it is an agonist at these receptors) and the latter by nicotine. These drugs exert only minimal influence on the opposite receptors. Evidence suggests that there are several subtypes of these receptors, differing in terms of where they are found, what types of drugs are agonists and antagonists for them, and their functions. For example, at least one of the nicotinic Ach receptors is a "fast" receptor, whereas all the muscarinic Ach receptors are "slow" receptors (Cooper et al., 1996).

In addition to nicotine and muscarine, some other drugs known to alter cholinergic functioning are curare, which blocks Ach at neuromuscular synapses; atropine and a number of older antidepressants, which block Ach at muscarinic receptors; and physostigmine, which enhances cholinergic activity at both nicotinic and muscarinic sites by inhibiting acetylcholinesterase. A number of "nerve gases" induce toxicity by irreversibly inhibiting acetylcholinesterase and dramatically elevating Ach levels (Cooper et al., 1996).

Norepinephrine (NE, also known as *noradrenaline*) was the second neurotransmitter to be identified as such by neuroscientists (Weiner, 1985). It has a major influence on both the PNS and the CNS. On peripheral cells it has a depolarizing action; that is, it is excitatory. In the CNS, it appears to be predominantly inhibitory with respect to its target neurons, although this may be the case only when the organism is in a quiet environment. With sudden changes in environment, such as a noise, NE activity at its target neurons may enhance their physiological activity (Olpe et al., 1983). Approximately 95 percent of released NE undergoes reuptake, and the remaining 5 percent undergoes enzymatic inactivation through the action of the extraneuronal enzyme COMT, which stands for catechol *O*-methyltransferase. NE that is not bound to vesicles can also be changed into an inactive metabolite intraneuronally by *MAO* (*monoamine oxidase*).

The NE metabolites produced through COMT and MAO activity are different. The former are referred to as *O-methylated metabolites* (because a methyl group, CH_3, is attached to an oxygen atom of the molecule), and the latter are referred to as *deaminated metabolites* (because the amine group, NH_2, is removed). This topic needs to be mentioned here because researchers have attempted to measure their relative amounts in the CNS to provide clues to disorders, such as manic depression, and drug effects that may be mediated by NE activity. However, as one gets away from the actual sites of NE activity, the metabolites are further metabolized into a common metabolite. That is, *O*-methylated metabolites get deaminated when they come into contact with MAO, and deaminated metabolites get *O*-methylated when they come into contact with COMT. Therefore, measuring urinary metabolites of NE, or any other neurotransmitter, is not particularly useful in determining CNS NE activity.

While the brain content of NE is exceedingly small relative to other putative transmitters, it appears to play a crucial role in arousal and mood, where decreased NE activity is associated with low arousal and depressed activity, and high levels are associated with excitement and increased motor activity. In conjunction with these CNS properties, during acute stress or excitement, NE is released by the postganglionic nerve endings of the sympathetic nervous system.

NE also has two primary types of receptors, with at least two subtypes for each. These are designated as *alpha₁*, *alpha₂*, *beta₁*, and *beta₂* receptors, and all are slow receptors (Cooper et al., 1996). Stimulation of alpha₁ receptors, which are postsynaptic receptors, generally produces an excitatory effect on the target organ, whereas stimulation of beta receptors depresses ongoing functions (except at the heart). Receptors of the alpha₂ type are predominantly autoreceptors on presynaptic axon terminals (although they may also have postsynaptic functions), such that their activation produces effects opposite to those induced by alpha₁ receptor activation. Some beta₂ receptors also appear to be autoreceptors, but these tend to facilitate NE release.

Epinephrine (Epi, also known as *adrenaline*), is closely related to NE, in both structure and function in the PNS. The structural similarity comes about because NE is the immediate precursor to Epi. Their functional similarity comes about because during times of acute stress, when the organism is frightened or must be ready to fight or flee (the *fight-flight-fright* syndrome), Epi is released from the adrenal gland into the bloodstream and is taken to NE sites of action in the sympathetic nervous system, where it is an agonist. In this context, Epi may be viewed more as a neurohormone than as a neurotransmitter. Because Epi is found in very small amounts in the brain, our understanding of Epi's role in CNS functions is very limited. It may be a factor in the control of neuroendocrine function and blood pressure (Cooper et al., 1996).

Closely related to NE and Epi is the transmitter *dopamine* (DA), and it is often found to be co-localized with other neurotransmitters and neuropeptides. While it appears to serve its own transmitter role in some neurons, DA is also the immediate precursor to NE in those neurons where NE is the transmitter. (Because NE, Epi, and DA molecules have two common parts—a "catechol" nucleus and an amine group [NH_2]—they are often referred to as *catecholamines*.) Dopamine's and NE's actions are terminated in the same way; most DA undergoes reuptake, and some undergoes COMT transformation. Intraneuronal metabolization by way of MAO may also occur with DA.

At least two families of DA receptors have been identified, with a major distinguishing feature being that the D_1-like family activates secondary messenger systems that stimulate adenylate cyclase, while the D_2-like family activates secondary messenger systems that inhibit adenylate cyclase (Nicola et al., 2000). The D_1-like family includes the major subtypes designated as D_1 and D_5, and the D_2-like family includes the major subtypes designated as D_2, D_3, and D_4 (a confusing numbering system based on the order of discovery of subtypes of DA receptors that for many years had simply been designated as D_1 and D_2 receptors). In most cases these receptors are segregated on neurons, suggesting that they act independently of each other, whereas in some neurons they coexist, suggesting that they work in conjunction with each other.

While the action of DA appears inhibitory on some neurons and excitatory on others, most recent evidence suggests that the net effect of DA acting on D_1 receptors may be to enhance the activity of cells that receive highly convergent excitatory input while decreasing both background activity and the activity in cells receiving less temporally coherent inputs. This would result in focusing in the specific ensembles of neurons that are receiving the greatest, and presumably most important, inputs from other brain regions (Nicola et al., 2000). Several lines of evidence suggest that some D_2-like receptors serve as postsynaptic receptors, whereas others serve as autoreceptors that reduce neuronal excitability by hyperpolarizing DA neurons, inhibit DA synthesis, or inhibit the stimulation-dependent quantity of DA released (Pothos et al., 1998).

Like NE, DA comprises a relatively small proportion of putative neurotransmitters in the brain, but it appears to exert profound influence on many emotional, mental, and motor functions, as well as drug-induced effects. In many cases, DA appears to play a modulatory role in behavior, with its effects dependent on slow, sustained DA secretion—referred to as *tonic* release—which is relatively independent of nerve impulse patterns (McGinty & Szymusiak, 1988). In other dopaminergic tracts, DA release is very much dependent on nerve impulse pattern and frequency—referred to as *phasic* release.

Dopaminergic modulation of neural activity in the prefrontal cortex is essential for working memory, which is required for guiding actions according to a behavioral plan or goal, focusing attention on goal-relevant objects in the environment, and protecting goal-related behavior against interfering stimuli or behavioral tendencies (Durstewitz et al., 1999). Working memory deficits may be observed with both sub- and supranormal DA receptor stimulation, which can occur with dopaminergic antagonists and agonists, respectively. Dopamine activity in the prefrontal cortex and the nucleus accumbens is a critical component of primary reward, both natural (e.g., food, sex) and drug-induced (e.g., cocaine, amphetamine, alcohol) (Wise, 1998).

An overactive DA system, because of overly sensitive receptors, too many receptors, too much DA release, or too little DA reuptake, has been suggested to be the cause of many symptoms of most cases of schizophrenia, whereas the destruction of a small subset of DA-containing neurons in the brain is responsible for Parkinson's disease. DA neurons have also been suggested to be involved in tic and movement disorders, such as Huntington's chorea and Gilles de la Tourette's syndrome; affective disorders; hyperactivity in children and adults; and long-lasting motor disturbances associated with prolonged use of antipsychotics. Each of these will be discussed later on.

The catecholamines are believed to mediate the mood-altering qualities of a variety of drugs, such as drugs of abuse. Commonly used drugs that directly alter catecholaminergic activity include cocaine and amphetamine, which enhance NE and DA release or inhibit their reuptake; a number of antidepressant drugs, which inhibit their reuptake or prevent their intraneuronal metabolic breakdown; and a number of antipsychotic drugs, which block NE and DA receptors.

Structured somewhat along the lines of the catecholamines just described is a neurotransmitter called *serotonin*. Its more technical name is *5-hydroxytryptamine* or 5-HT. (It would be nice if all neuroscientists could agree on one term for these chemicals so we would not have to learn so many names for the same thing, but unfortunately that is not the case.) It also consists of one amine group attached to what is referred to as an indole nucleus. (Because their structures contain one amine group, 5-HT and the catecholamines are often referred to as *monoamines*.) Termination of 5-HT action appears to be entirely through reuptake.

Over a dozen distinct subtypes of 5-HT receptors have been identified in the mammalian nervous system, and they have been classified in terms of families (designated by a number) and subtypes within families (designated by a letter), for example, 5-HT$_{1A}$, 5-HT$_{1B}$, 5-HT$_{1D}$, 5-HT$_{2A}$, 5-HT$_{2b}$, 5-HT$_3$, 5-HT$_4$, 5-HT$_5$ (Hoyer et al., 1994; Sandou & Hen, 1994). This group of receptors is by far the largest of all neurotransmitter receptors identified at this point, perhaps because the primordial 5-HT receptor may be more than 750 million years old and evolved not only into the variety of receptors for serotonin, but also into most of the receptors for the other biogenic amines, such as Ach, DA, Epi, and NE (Peroutka, 1995). There is evidence that 5-HT receptors serve as autoreceptors on somatodendritic 5-HT neurons (e.g., 5-HT$_{1A}$) that inhibit these neurons from firing, autoreceptors on 5-HT axon terminals (e.g., 5-HT$_{1B}$, 5-HT$_{1D}$) that inhibit 5-HT release, heteroreceptors on non-5-HT neuron terminals that modulate release of other neurotransmitters (e.g., 5-HT$_{1B}$ and 5-HT$_{1D}$ inhibit glutamate, acetylcholine, noradrenaline; 5-HT$_3$ facilitates dopamine release), and postsynaptic receptors (e.g., 5-HT$_{2A}$, 5-HT$_{2B}$) mediating neuroexcitation, as well as inhibition. With the exception of the ionotropic/fast 5-HT$_3$ receptor, all of the 5-HT receptors appear to be metabotropic/slow receptors (G-protein–coupled receptors).

It is clear that serotonergic systems play a role in a wide variety of functions in the CNS (they also have some PNS activity, for example, regulating contractions of various blood vessels), and have been implicated in the modulation of numerous psychological processes—for example, sexual activity, mood, degree of pain sensitivity, aggression, sleep, and mental disorders (Cooper et al., 1996). Commonly used drugs that directly alter serotonergic activity include cocaine, which inhibits 5-HT reuptake; a number of antidepressant drugs, which inhibit 5-HT reuptake or prevent its intraneuronal metabolic breakdown; a number of antipsychotic drugs, which block a variety of 5-HT receptors; and hallucinogenic drugs like LSD and mescaline, which simultaneously act as agonists and antagonists at a variety of 5-HT receptor subtypes.

In addition to its role as a neurotransmitter, serotonin may play a vital role in learning, because it has been shown to strengthen the synapses formed between neurons (of mollusks) that have been grown in cultures (i.e., two or three neurons that have been removed from the animal and grown in a medium of molluscan fluids and factors), much as it does between neurons in the intact animal after a learning session (Barinaga, 1990).

Though amino acids are often intermediary substances in the metabolic synthesis of the types of neurotransmitters just described, many also fulfill several of the criteria for being neurotransmitters themselves. In fact, in sheer quantity, amino acids are probably the major neurotransmitters in the mammalian CNS (Cooper et al., 1996). Some amino acids are excitatory (e.g., glutamate, aspartate); that is, they depolarize neurons. Others are inhibitory (e.g., GABA, glycine, taurine, alanine); that is, they hyperpolarize neurons. Perhaps the most widespread inhibitory neurons in the CNS utilize GABA (gamma-aminobutyric acid) as a neurotransmitter or cotransmitter. Almost every major division of the brain and spinal cord includes some of them. There appear to be at least two functionally distinct types of GABA receptors (both of which can be broken down into further subtypes). GABA$_A$ receptors are fast receptors directly associated with a Cl$^-$ ion channel whose activation induces hyperpolarization. GABA$_B$ receptors are slow receptors coupled to secondary messenger systems that either enhance K$^+$ flow out of neurons, which hyperpolarizes them, or decrease Ca^{++} flow into neurons, which at presynaptic receptors reduces transmitter release (Cooper et al., 1996). Enhancing the activity of GABA at its GABA$_A$ receptor complex is a major common pathway for a diversity of drugs with sedative and sleep-inducing properties—for example, alcohol, diazepam (Valium), and barbiturates.

Several receptors for the excitatory amino acids have been identified—for example, NMDA, AMPA, kainate (ionotropic/fast receptors named after the drugs used initially to identify them) and mGluRs (metabotropic glutamate receptors), each with a number of subtypes (Cooper et al., 1996). Although it is still too early to speculate much on their functional significance or properties, a great deal of interest has been generated over the NMDA receptor. First, it is an unusual receptor, in that ion channel activation requires not only binding of synaptically released glutamate, but also simultaneous depolarization of the surrounding postsynaptic membrane, which may be achieved by activation of AMPA/kainate receptors at nearby synapses from inputs from different neurons (Bloom, 1996). Thus, NMDA receptors may function as "coincidence detectors," being activated only when there is a simultaneous firing of two or more neurons, which may account for these receptors' involvement in what is termed *LTP* (for "long-term potentiation"). LTP refers to long-lasting changes in a neuron's excitability and has been proposed as a cellular model for some forms of learning and memory.

Second, the NMDA receptor has been linked to a number of brain disorders—for example, epilepsy, Parkinson's disease, Alzheimer's disease, Huntington's chorea, AIDS dementia—that may be due to neurotoxicity resulting from excess excitatory amino acid activity associated with low blood sugar or low oxygen levels, seizures, and other disturbances (Olney, 1990). Because NMDA ion channels are selective for Ca^{++} (as well as Na^+), it may be possible to prevent many of these brain disorders through the use of calcium channel blockers. The ion channel regulated by NMDA receptors also appears to be one of the sites of action of phencyclidine, which can produce symptoms identical to schizophrenia, suggesting that NMDA receptors play a role in this disease as well.

A variety of *peptides,* or strings of amino acids, have neuroactive properties. These peptides, with names like Substance P, vasoactive intestinal peptide (VIP), neuropeptide Y (NPY), somatostatin, cholecystokinin, vasopressin, oxytocin, neurotensin, and enkephalin, have a wide variety of ill-defined and poorly documented CNS functions, quite often because they coexist with the "classic" neurotransmitters in neurons and modulate their function (Bloom, 1996). Because linear chains of amino acids can assume many conformations at their receptors, it has been difficult to define the sequence and the binding relationships that are critical for their activity as well as to develop synthetic agonists or antagonists that will interact with specific receptors for peptides. Peptides may serve as neurotransmitters, in which they generally act slowly, with actions that may last 2 to 3 minutes, or as neuromodulators, in which they generally act even more slowly, with actions lasting 45 minutes or longer (Kow & Pfaff, 1988).

Unlike most other neurotransmitters, peptide transmitters do not appear to be inactivated by any specific reuptake mechanisms, but are enzymatically inactivated by various peptidases and are dissipated by diffusion (Lefkowitz et al., 1996). Several important peptides that have created considerable interest in the field over the past 20 years are called *endorphins,* which stands for *endo*genous m*orphine*-like substances. This class of peptides appears to serve as prototype neuromodulators; that is, they may not serve as transmitters in the traditional sense but may modulate the activity of the transmitters. The term *endorphin* is used in two different contexts. In one it refers specifically to endogenous peptides with opiate-like properties found primarily in the pituitary, but also found throughout the various parts of the body. This usage contrasts with the term *enkephalin* (in the head), which refers to a number of endogenous peptides with opiate-like properties found in the CNS. In the other context, *endorphin* is a general term encompassing all endorphin and enkephalin molecules in the body (in most cases, this is how they will be referred to throughout this text).

There has been considerable speculation that endorphins are involved in a wide variety of processes and activities, including pain perception, attention, primary reward, crying, laughing, thrills from music, acupuncture, placebos, stress reactions, depression, compulsive gambling, aerobics, masochism, massage, labor and delivery, appetite, immunity, near-death experiences, and playing with pets (Hopson, 1988). For example, studies on maternal calming of infants have shown that certain substances, milk and sucrose among them, cause the release of endorphins in infants, which, in turn, is manifested in increased pain tolerance, decreased vocalization, decreased activity, reduced heart rate, and bringing the hand to the mouth (Blass, 1992). The effects of narcotics such as morphine and heroin are due to their agonist activity at endorphin receptors. Several subtypes of endorphin receptors (most of them slow receptors) have been identified and will be discussed in Chapter 10. However, one disappointment in the field of opioid peptide research has been its inability to fulfill its promise of providing much insight into the nature of drug dependence, because there is little evidence, despite numerous attempts, that there is a significant change in the concentrations of any of the opioid peptides or their receptors following chronic exposure to dependence-inducing drugs like morphine (Cooper et al., 1996).

The majority of this section has focused on the neurotransmitter systems that most likely mediate the psychological effects of psychotropic drugs, because these systems play such a generalized role in the way we process information, in our readiness to respond to the external environment, and in our emotions and motivational states (Panksepp, 1986). In very general terms, we can say that the cholinergic system is an action system in the brain (in both motor and sensory-processing terms) that helps elaborate the ability to focus on the environment and achieve a coherent behavioral response to it. Practically every type of motivated and emotional behavior is affected by alterations in serotonergic and noradrenergic activity. They exert a direct influence on attentional processes, and hence affect learning and memory formation. Dopaminergic systems mediate a generalized ability for response initiation, having perhaps a more specific role in triggering instinctual processes related to positive and negative incentives. Most motivated and emotive behaviors, ranging from feeding to aggression, are also affected by alterations in GABA activity. Finally, the global function of opioid systems appears to be one of counteracting any major perturbation of physiological homeostasis (i.e., stress). However, as the preceding account should indicate, virtually every psychobehavioral process is mediated by more than one brain area and more than one neurochemical system and affected by drugs with very different mechanisms of action (Panksepp, 1986).

Neurotransmitters and Diet

Neurotransmitters (and other neuroactive substances) and their precursors are chemical substances that are essentially nutrients obtained in the food we eat. In most cases, it is the precursors that are likely to be found in the diet, since most neurotransmitters are unable to cross the blood–brain barrier. One of the most common precursors to a variety of neuroactive ligands is glucose, which follows a number of metabolic pathways to form ligands such as aspartate, glutamate, GABA, and Ach (Cooper et al., 1996). A variety of amino acids making up proteins also serve as transmitters or transmitter precursors. For example, tryptophan, an amino acid found in protein-rich foods like dairy products, meat, fish, and poultry, is a precursor of the neurotransmitter serotonin. (Tryptophan is one of eight essential amino acids, so-called because our bodies cannot synthesize them; they must be obtained from our diet.) Tyrosine, a precursor of dopamine, norepinephrine, and epinephrine, is another amino acid found in proteins. Choline, the precursor of Ach, is a component of the lecithin found in egg yolks, soy products, and liver. Therefore, it makes sense that altering one's diet can give rise to important changes in the chemical composition within the brain and can modify brain function and alter mood and behavior in specific ways (Wurtman, 1982).

For example, loading up on protein-rich foods might be expected to enhance the brain's production of serotonin, which is believed to promote relaxation and hasten the onset of sleep (Radulovacki, 1982). It has been suggested that people who have trouble sleeping should drink warm milk, which contains high levels of tryptophan, before bedtime. Protein-rich foods might also be expected to elevate levels of NE, believed necessary for positive mood states. Loading up on lecithin-containing foods may be beneficial in cognitive and memory disorders such as Alzheimer's disease, which have been associated with Ach deficiencies.

Unfortunately, however, it is not that simple. Numerous biochemical processes must follow in sequence if the consumption of a meal rich in a particular nutrient is to increase the synthesis of a neurotransmitter in the brain (Wurtman, 1982). First, there must be a significant elevation of the plasma level of the nutrient; in some cases, the level of a nutrient in the plasma is regulated by inhibitory feedback mechanisms. Second, the nutrient's concentration in the brain must vary with the plasma concentration; that is, the nutrient must be able to penetrate the blood–brain barrier. Third, the transport system involved in the nutrient's movement between the plasma and the brain must not be easily saturated with the nutrient or other nutrients that compete for the same transport system. Fourth, the enzymes necessary for the conversion of the precursor into the neurotransmitter in the brain must not be easily saturable. Fifth, these enzymes must not be susceptible to negative-feedback inhibition when the intracellular levels of the neurotransmitter rise.

In many cases, not all of these requirements can be fulfilled simultaneously. For example, in the case of tryptophan, you might think that a high-protein meal would make you drowsy. However, high-protein foods contain several amino acids, not just tryptophan, and they all compete for the same transporter molecules in the blood–brain barrier. Because tryptophan occurs in food in relatively small quantities, it does not have much of a chance of getting into the brain if all one eats is protein. If one eats food with carbohydrates (for example, sweets, bread, pasta, potatoes), which stimulate the production of insulin, all the other amino acids can get drawn out of the blood while having little effect on tryptophan blood levels. Thus, if one consumes carbohydrates a few hours before or after a protein-containing meal, brain concentrations of tryptophan and serotonin synthesis may increase (Fernstrom & Fernstrom, 1995). In fact, many of the behavioral effects that have been attributed to eating carbohydrates may be due to the ability of carbohydrates to enhance the influx of tryptophan into the brain (Spring et al., 1987).

In general, single meals, depending on their protein content, can rapidly influence uptake of the aromatic amino acids (tryptophan, tyrosine, phenylalanine) into the brain and, as a result, directly modify their conversion to neurotransmitters and influence brain function. On the other hand, the acidic amino acids glutamate and aspartate, which are neurotransmitters themselves, do not have ready access to the brain from the circulation. As a result, the ingestion of proteins, which are naturally rich in glutamate and aspartate, has no effect on the level of the acidic amino acids in the brain. Furthermore, despite claims that the food additives monosodium glutamate and aspartame (an artificial sweetener containing aspartate) may raise the level of acidic amino acids in the brain and modify its functions or even cause neuronal damage, a substantial body of published evidence clearly indicates that the brain is not affected by ingestion of aspartame and is affected by glutamate only when it is administered alone in extremely large doses (Fernstrom, 1994).

Because various nutrients in food interact in such complicated ways, most of which are not well understood, it is very difficult to predict in advance what a particular nutrient or combination of foods will do with respect to mood and behavior. In most studies showing links between diet and behavior in human beings, the effects have been subtle, in comparison with a multitude of other factors influencing mood and behavior. Furthermore, the relationships may depend on the age of the individual, the time of day the nutrient or food is consumed, individual genetic variations, or whether the individual is normal or mood-depressed (Christensen & Redig, 1993).

Structures and Subsystems of the Nervous System

Moods, thoughts, and behavior do not come about through the activity of single neurons, nor are the actions of drugs due to their actions at single neurons. Neurons make up a number of structures and subsystems of the nervous system, which have different functions and involve different neurotransmitters, which in turn are affected by drugs. Some of these will be briefly described here; they will be discussed with respect to drug action at later points in this book.

Peripheral Nervous System

The *peripheral nervous system* (PNS) is composed of all nervous tissue outside of the spinal cord and the brain. The PNS can be differentiated into nerves (bundles of axons outside the CNS) serving sensory functions (for example, allowing light, sound, and chemicals from the environment to impact on the CNS) and motor functions (such as allowing the CNS to induce changes in bodily functions). *Motor nerves* are further differentiated into the *somatic nervous system,* which controls skeletal muscles, and the *autonomic nervous system,* which controls smooth and cardiac muscle activity and several glands, including the adrenal glands, salivary glands, and sweat glands. Virtually all of these organs are innervated (connected to nerves) by two opposing systems within the autonomic nervous system. One is called the *parasympathetic nervous system,* which is responsible for controlling vegetative, restorative, and energy-saving processes. It is particularly active in calm situations. The other is called the *sympathetic nervous system,* which is responsible for preparing the body for dealing with situations requiring fighting or fleeing, or times when the organism is frightened (the *fight-flight-fright* system). It is particularly active during times of acute stress and excitement. Drugs whose actions mimic those associated with sympathetic activity are often referred to as **sympathomimetics,** and those whose actions mimic parasympathetic activity are referred to as **parasympathomimetics.** Table 5–1 indicates the major activities carried out by the sympathetic and parasympathetic nerve fibers comprising the autonomic nervous system.

TABLE 5–1   Effect of Activity of Autonomic Nerve Fibers

Organ	Sympathetic	Parasympathetic
Adrenal medulla	Secretion of epinephrine and norepinephrine	
Bladder	Inhibition of contraction	Contraction
Blood vessels		
Abdomen	Constriction	
Muscles	Dilation	Constriction
Skin	Constriction or dilation	Dilation
Heart	Faster rate of contraction	Slower rate of contraction
Intestines	Decreased activity	Increased activity
Lacrimal glands	Secretion of tears	
Liver	Release of glucose	
Lungs	Dilation of bronchi	Constriction of bronchi
Penis	Ejaculation	Erection
Pupil of eye	Dilation	Constriction
Salivary glands	Secretion of thick, viscous saliva	Secretion of thin enzyme-rich saliva
Sweat glands	Secretion of sweat	
Vagina	Orgasm	Secretion of lubricating fluid

The axons from both the parasympathetic and sympathetic systems that originate from neurons in the spinal cord and brain are referred to as *preganglionic fibers,* and they release the neurotransmitter acetylcholine. The target neurons for these fibers are clustered together in groups of cell bodies called *ganglia* (a *ganglion* is a grouping of neuron cell bodies outside the CNS). The receptors on the target neurons are those I referred to a little earlier as nicotinic receptors. The axons that originate from these ganglionic cells and connect with, or innervate, the organs are referred to as *postganglionic fibers.* Postganglionic axons of the sympathetic system release norepinephrine, which activates three different types of receptors (alpha$_1$, alpha$_2$, and beta$_2$) in the membranes of target organ cells. Postganglionic axons of the parasympathetic system release Ach, which activates muscarinic receptors in the target organ cells. Because NE activates receptors in the sympathetic part of the PNS, and Ach activates receptors in the parasympathetic part of the PNS, the functions of these two neurotransmitters are generally in opposition in the PNS (Weiner & Taylor, 1985). An exception is the case in which activation of Ach receptors in the adrenal gland results in the release of epinephrine, a neurohormone that enhances sympathetic activity.

The relatively high degree of localization of noradrenergic and cholinergic nerve fibers and several types of receptors for NE and Ach in the PNS has allowed neuroscientists to assess neurotransmission processes and drug actions in a fairly specific manner. This has led them to develop models of what is happening with respect to these processes and actions in the brain, where neurons of various types are tightly packed together and are difficult to

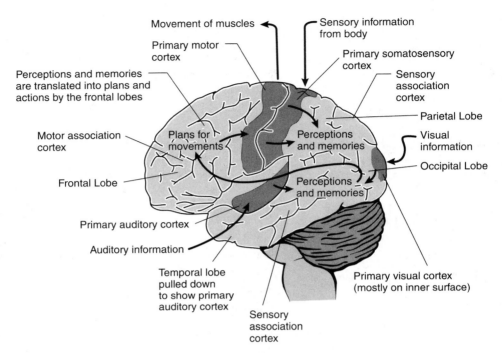

Movement of muscles

Sensory information
from body

Primary motor
cortex

Primary somatosensory
cortex

Perceptions and memories
are translated into plans and
actions by the frontal lobes

Sensory
association
cortex

Parietal Lobe

Motor association
cortex

Plans for
movements

Perceptions
and memories

Visual
information

Occipital Lobe

Frontal Lobe

Perceptions
and memories

Primary auditory cortex

Auditory information

Temporal lobe
pulled down
to show primary
auditory cortex

Primary visual cortex
(mostly on inner surface)

Sensory
association
cortex

FIGURE 5–2   The human cerebral cortex: structures and functions.

isolate. In fact, much of what is thought to go on in the synapses in the CNS is based on studies conducted on the PNS, on the assumption that the two operate in basically the same fashion.

Central Nervous System

The *central nervous system,* or CNS, is comprised of the brain and spinal cord. The top portion of the brain is actually comprised of two semisymmetrical halves called the *cerebral hemispheres.* The outer surface of these is called the *cerebral cortex,* shown in Figure 5–2, and it is composed of several densely packed layers of neuron cell bodies. Certain parts of the cortex are called *sensory projection areas* because these are areas of the cortex where the information from the senses is processed. The *temporal lobes* contain the primary receiving area for auditory information and visual recognition. The *parietal lobes* are the primary receiving area for bodily sensations and are involved in spatial perception. The *occipital lobes* are the primary receiving area for visual information.

The cortex in the *frontal lobes* allows us to ascribe meaning to the incoming stimuli initially processed in the sensory projection areas. It is essential for higher order thought processing, such as synthetic reasoning and abstract thought, and it allows us to organize events from independent places and times and to make plans. The cortex comprising the back part of the frontal lobe, called the *motor projection area,* allows us to act voluntarily on these higher level processes; that is, it is from this region that directives that ultimately go to the muscles are issued.

Finally, while the two hemispheres are viewed as specializing in processing different kinds of information—for example, language in the left and visual-spatial in the right— they are connected by some 200 million nerve axons collectively referred to as the *corpus callosum,* which allows them to communicate with one another.

Considering the variety of functions carried out by these portions of the brain, it should not be surprising that a vast mixture of neurotransmitters and other biologically active chemicals are found in these regions. It should also come as no surprise that we know relatively little about the complex drug interactions that take place in these regions. Any drug affecting these regions is going to have a multiplicity of effects on perceptual and cognitive functions.

Figure 5–3 shows parts of the brain below the cerebral hemispheres and some important subcortical structures comprising the limbic system and the basal ganglia. The *medulla* controls vital reflex functions such as respiration, heartbeat, and blood pressure. The *pons* connects higher brain centers with the cerebellum and, along with the medulla, contains most of the cell bodies of the reticular activating system (discussed later in this section). In these regions of the brain, relatively high concentrations of catecholamines, serotonin, and enkephalins have been noted. The *cerebellum* controls automatic skeletal motor activities and coordinates balance and the body's movements. Collectively, the medulla, pons, and cerebellum are often referred to as the *hindbrain.*

The *midbrain* contains primitive centers for auditory and visual processing. It is also important for the perception of pain, a function that is consistent with the high concentrations of enkephalins found there. The midbrain also contains dopaminergic neurons, whose axons project into areas in the frontal cortex and the basal ganglia (see the last paragraph of this section), which have been suggested to be involved in disorders such as schizophrenia and Parkinson's disease (discussed in Chapters 12 and 14). The *thalamus* is the great "relay" station in the brain, in that it relays incoming sensory information to the appropriate areas of the cortex, as well as relaying information from higher regions of the brain to lower ones. It also appears to play a part in regulating the overall level of excitability of cortical neurons. Several lines of research implicate dysfunction in the thalamus in the pathophysiology of schizophrenia (Andreasen et al., 1999).

The *limbic system* is a conglomeration of diverse structures in the cerebral hemispheres where a large number of circuits relating to different functions come together. It is thought to play a key role in the cognitive arousal of emotion and the formation of memory (McGinty & Szymusiak, 1988). The primary reward and punishment centers are believed to exist in this diffuse system, since mild electrical stimulation applied to various limbic regions can serve as very effective reinforcement for instrumental responding in animals, whereas electrical stimulation in other regions appears to be highly aversive. Limbic structures may also be involved in many mood and thought disorders in humans, since electrical stimulation and lesions in various areas of the limbic system have been found to induce paranoid ideation (characterized by suspiciousness and beliefs that one is being plotted against and persecuted), depersonalization (feelings of strangeness and an unreality of experience), perceptual distortions or hallucinations (compelling perceptual experiences without the presence of a physical stimulus), catatonia (immobility), thought disturbances, and mood and emotional disturbances.

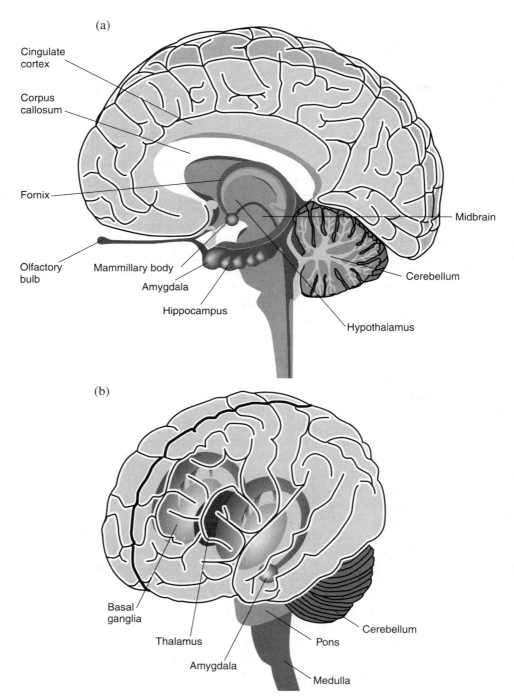

(a)

Cingulate cortex

Corpus callosum

Fornix

Midbrain

Olfactory bulb

Mammillary body

Amygdala

Cerebellum

Hippocampus

Hypothalamus

(b)

Basal ganglia

Thalamus

Cerebellum

Pons

Amygdala

Medulla

FIGURE 5–3   (a) The major components of the limbic system. (b) The location of the basal ganglia and the thalamus.

Some parts of the limbic system are critically important for certain kinds of learning and memory formation—for example, the *hippocampus*. Others are critically involved in mood, emotionality, and emotional expressions—for example, the *amygdala* and *cingulate gyrus*. Neuroimaging studies of individuals with major depressive disorders have identified abnormalities of resting blood flow and glucose metabolism in the amygdala and in prefrontal cortical areas that are extensively connected with the amygdala (Drevets, 1999). In patients with hereditary depressive disorders, parts of the cingulate cortex have been shown in magnetic resonance imaging and post mortem histopathological studies to have reduced grey matter volume and reduced glial cell numbers. The *nucleus accumbens* controls feelings of pleasure and is a primary site responsible for the addictive properties of most drugs of abuse, which either directly or indirectly enhance the release of dopamine into this region (Wise, 1998). Relatively heavy concentrations of catecholamines (primarily norepinephrine), GABA, serotonin, and enkephalins have been found in the limbic system. However, to say that any of these are the major neurotransmitters of this system would be misleading, as there are more than 20 different neurotransmitters or modulators found in the hippocampus alone (Nicoll, 1988).

The *hypothalamus* participates in the regulation of the expression of basic drive states—such as hunger, thirst, sex, and aggression—and body temperature, and it exerts major control over the autonomic nervous system. It is also the nervous system's way of mediating control over the endocrine system, because it has numerous neuronal connections and hormones that can influence the activity of the pituitary gland, whose hormones control numerous functions of the other endocrine glands of the body. As is the case with the limbic system, heavy concentrations of catecholamines and enkephalins are found in the hypothalamus. Thus, drugs that alter activity at catecholamine receptors (such as cocaine, amphetamine, and chlorpromazine) or enkephalin receptors (such as morphine and heroin) profoundly influence mood, emotion, emotional reaction, and primary drive.

The *reticular activating system,* or RAS, shown in Figure 5–4, is comprised of a diffuse network of neurons whose cell bodies originate in the pons and medulla—the midbrain *raphe nuclei* and *locus ceruleus*—and send axons (ascending and descending) to most regions of the brain and spinal cord. The RAS participates in a wide variety of psychological processes, ranging from sleep to perception to mood to our ability to associate events (McGinty & Szymusiak, 1988). It may be thought of as setting "brain tone," by regulating mood and the responsiveness of target neurons to incoming stimulation from the senses or to internally produced stimuli (that is, mental activity). The ascending RAS regulates the level of alertness and screening of information—that is, attentional processes—by filtering out unimportant sensory information and allowing important information to reach higher brain centers for further processing. These functions also suggest that thought and perceptual disturbances may be the result of malfunctions in the RAS.

Although several types of neurons play roles in this system, serotonergic and noradrenergic neurons appear to be particularly important (Rosenzweig et al., 1996). The raphe nuclei neurons, which are serotonergic, play a prominent role in the control of pain suppression, sleep, aggression, and emotion. The locus ceruleus neurons, which are noradrenergic, function to maintain emotion and regulate REM (rapid eye movement) sleep—a state of sleep in which the brain is aroused, dreaming occurs, and the skeletal muscles are temporarily paralyzed. Curiously, it is during REM sleep that these serotonergic and noradrenergic neurons cease firing almost completely, suggesting that dreams may come about because of the loss

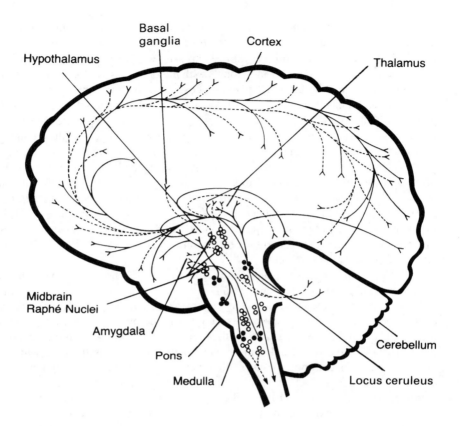

Basal
ganglia   Cortex

Hypothalamus   Thalamus

Midbrain
Raphé Nuclei

Amygdala

Pons   Cerebellum

Medulla   Locus ceruleus

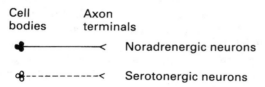

Cell   Axon
bodies   terminals

●————————<   Noradrenergic neurons

☆- - - - - - - - - -<   Serotonergic neurons

FIGURE 5–4   Stylized schematic of the reticular activating system (RAS),
comprised predominantly of serotonergic and noradrenergic cells and axon
fibers (although other neurons, such as adrenergic cells, play a role in the
RAS). Note that both types of fibers are very diffusely distributed and greatly
overlap. They differ, however, in the details of distribution and target cells
they innervate.

of control over higher cortical centers. On the other hand, because of the strong relationship
between the activity of serotonergic neurons and the body's motor activity—these neurons are
most active just before or during gross motor activity—it has been hypothesized that the primary function of the brain serotonin system is to prime and facilitate gross motor output (Jacobs, 1994). At the same time, the system inhibits sensory-information processing while

coordinating autonomic and neuroendocrine functions with the specific demands of the motor activity. The influence of noradrenergic RAS neurons is primarily inhibitory with respect to their target neurons if the organism is in a vegetative state or if there is little environmental stimulation. However, with sudden changes in environmental stimulation, the activity of the target neurons may actually be enhanced (McGinty & Szymusiak, 1988).

Acetylcholine and glutamate are two other neurotransmitters that play a pivotal role in the RAS (Steriade, 1996). For example, brief stimulation of brain-stem cholinergic nuclei enhances the likelihood of thalamic and cortical responses to an incoming message, and potentiates the excitability of thalamic neuronal targets for up to 4 minutes, but does not disrupt the local inhibitory processes required for processing the information analytically. Stimulation of these nuclei also gives rise to the same sharp brain potentials (called PGO spikes) that are characteristic signs of REM sleep.

Along with the descending RAS, numerous brain structures, including the motor cortex and cerebellum, are involved in regulating the activity of motor neurons that control the skeletal muscles. One group of these brain structures comprises the *basal ganglia* (actually this is a misnomer, since ganglia are located *outside* the CNS), located just above and to the side of the thalamus (see Figure 5–3). This group of structures collects inputs from the entire cortex and sends processed information through other parts of the basal ganglia to areas of the frontal cortex that have been implicated in motor planning and execution. These circuits are modulated by the *nigrostriatal* tract, a dopaminergic input system coming from a midbrain area called the *substantia nigra,* which degenerates in Parkinson's disease. The basal ganglia serve in the regulation of slow, voluntary, smooth movement of different speeds, which can be modified by sensory feedback while the movement is occurring. Loss of dopaminergic input to the basal ganglia leads to progressive deterioration of walking, standing, and many other postures and movements involving the body as a whole. Excessive dopaminergic input may result in repetitive or stereotypic movements. Several side effects of dopamine-blocking drugs used to treat schizophrenia arise from disturbances in the basal ganglia.

Until recently, the basal ganglia were thought to be simply involved in motor execution, but evidence suggests that they may participate in motor planning or predictive control, motor sequencing, motor learning, and action repertoires involving motivational and cognitive drive (Graybiel et al., 1994). Disturbances in the basal ganglia may contribute to some of the symptoms of schizophrenia, because schizophrenic patients often show unusual body postures and mannerisms in addition to other abnormal movements, and some metabolic disorders that destroy basal ganglia sites as the result of excessive calcium activity result in symptoms resembling those of schizophrenia (Rosenzweig et al., 1996). There is also evidence that schizophrenics have abnormally high levels of the dopamine D_4 receptor subtype in this area of the brain. As discussed in Chapter 12, it is this subtype of DA receptor that may be particularly relevant in producing some of the symptoms of schizophrenia.

Drugs, the Nervous System, and Behavior: A Perspective

This chapter has dealt very briefly with a number of complex processes through which drugs may act to bring about alterations in mood, emotions, cognitions, and behavior. In some cases, the processes involve molecular activities; in other cases, they involve cellular or multicellular activities and functions in the nervous system. Understanding drug action at these levels is important. However, one of the greatest challenges for neuroscientists is to be able to translate the actions of a drug at the subcellular, cellular, or multicellular level into an understanding of its actions at the psychological level. At present, it is a challenge with which we only vaguely know how to deal.

To illustrate the difficulty in making direct connections between any particular drug action on a neurotransmitter system and a specific type of behavior, consider two studies investigating the influence of serotonergic (5-HT) systems on aggression. One group of investigators bred mutant mice lacking 5-HT$_{1B}$ receptors, observed their mice to engage in excessive aggressive behavior, and claimed that their results supported several studies revealing "an association between aggressive behavior and a reduction in the activity of the serotonergic system" (Saudou et al., 1994). (Curiously, these investigators acknowledged that there is considerable evidence that 5-HT$_{1B}$ receptors are expressed on nerve terminals and inhibit 5-HT release. Wouldn't knocking out the 5-HT$_{1B}$ receptors result in the release of excessive amounts of 5-HT rather than reducing it?) A second group of investigators bred mutant mice lacking in monoamine oxidase B (MAO-B), which resulted in abnormally high levels of serotonin (and noradrenaline), and observed their mice to exhibit excessive aggression (Cases et al., 1995). So which is it? Is aggressive behavior related to high or low levels of serotonin? And if serotonin is involved, which system? Is serotonin associated with aggression or with some other factor that may influence aggression? Maybe these mutant mice were all deficient in fear—another psychological construct hypothesized to be associated with abnormal serotonergic functioning (Chen et al., 1994). Could it be that the mice in these studies were more aggressive because they lacked fear? Or could it be that any number of insults to the developing brain compromise its functioning so that maladaptive social behavior results? Similar questions can be raised with respect to drugs that act on serotonergic systems.

In conclusion, we may be able to determine that a drug activates, or excites, a specific set of receptors, which in turn opens ion channels, which allows negatively charged ions to flow inward, which hyperpolarizes the cell, which decreases its rate of firing, and so on. As impressive as such knowledge might be, it would have little value in leading us to an understanding of how that drug brings about changes in mood, emotion, or cognitive functioning. That is, there is no reason to assume that such a drug action at the cellular level will depress mood or slow one's thought (Cooper et al., 1996). The fact is there are a multitude of intermediate steps between the cellular activities of the nervous system and the behavior, emotions, and thoughts evidenced in the intact organism. While we may discuss neurotransmitter effects as excitatory or inhibitory, it should be made clear that these effects are on neuron membrane potentials, not on behavior. Conversely, when we say an organism has become aroused or excited, we must not confuse this state with alterations in membrane potentials.

For example, what does it mean to become excited? Personally, when I sink a crucial 30-foot putt on the last hole of a golf match, I get excited. I yell and throw my fist into the air, my heart pounds, my blood pressure shoots up, and I breathe heavily. However, when a neuron gets excited, it means something entirely different. It means that the electrical gradient that is present between the inside and the outside of the cell has been reduced to the point at which it is no longer sufficient to keep the Na$^+$ channels closed, which then initiates a whole chain of biochemical events. Is this what we mean when we say the CNS is excited? Probably not. The CNS is a collection of around 85 billion cells, with perhaps 600 trillion connections among them. It is certainly not the case that most or all fire simultaneously or that all the synapses are filled with neurotransmitters. That would be chaos. (This issue will be discussed more fully in the context of drugs with stimulant or depressant properties in Chapter 7.)

Websites for Further Information

Information on the structure of the nervous system:

http://faculty.washington.edu/chudler/nsdivide.html

For some basics on the functional organization of the cerebral cortex, see:

http://faculty.washington.edu/chudler/functional.html

For some basics on the organization of the autonomic nervous system, see:

http://faculty.washington.edu/chudler/auto.html

Information on neuroscience:

http://faculty.washington.edu/chudler/neurok.html

Information on brain abnormalities:

http://www.sfn.org/briefings/

Useful information about the field of neuropsychology:

http://www.neuropsychologycentral.com/index.html

Anatomy of memory site offers brain anatomy tutorials, micrographs of tissue slices, and virtual reality models of dendrites:

http://synapses.bu.edu/index.asp

Wander around the brain, using images found at the Harvard Whole Brain Atlas site:

http://www.med.harvard.edu/AANLIB/home.html

A site aimed at generating public interest in brain research; includes book reviews, illusions, brain anatomy drawings, and descriptions of brain-related disorders:

http://www.brainconnection.com

Bibliography

Andreasen, N. C., Nopoulos, P., O'Leary, D.S., et al. (1999). Defining the phenotype of schizophrenia: Cognitive dysmetria and its neural mechanisms. *Biological Psychiatry, 46,* 908–920.

Barinaga, M. (1990). The high culture of neuroscience. *Science, 250,* 206–207.

Bartfai, T., Iverfeldt, K., & Fisone, G. (1988). Regulation of the release of coexisting neurotransmitters. *An-nual Review of Pharmacology and Toxicology, 28,* 285–310.

Blass, E. M. (1992). The ontogeny of motivation: Opioid bases of energy conservation and lasting affective change in rat and human infants. *Current Directions in Psychological Science, 1,* 116–120.

Bloom, F. E. (1996). Neurotransmission and the central nervous system. In A. G. Gilman, L. S. Goodman,

J. G. Hardman, L. E. Limbard, P. B. Molinoff, & R. W. Ruddon (Eds.), *The pharmacological basis of therapeutics* (pp. 267–293). New York: McGraw-Hill.

Blusztajn, J. K. (1998). Choline, a vital amine. *Science, 281,* 794–795.

Cases, O., Seif, I., Grimsby, J., Gaspar, P., et al. (1995). Aggressive behavior and altered amounts of brain serotonin and norepinephrine in mice lacking MAOA. *Science, 268* 1763–1766.

Chen, C., Rainnie, D. G., Greene, R. W., & Tonegawa, S. (1994). Abnormal fear response and aggressive behavior in mutant mice deficient for alpha-calcium-calmodulin kinase II. *Science, 266,* 291–294.

Christensen, L., & Redig, C. (1993). Effect of meal composition on mood. *Behavioral Neuroscience, 107,* 346–353.

Cooper, J. R., Bloom, F. E., & Roth, R. H. (1996). *The biochemical basis of neuropharmacology,* 7th ed. New York: Oxford University Press.

Drevets, W. C. (1999). Prefrontal cortical-amygdalar metabolism in major depression. *Annals of the New York Academy of Sciences, 877,* 614–637.

Durstewitz, D., Kelc, M., & Gunturkun, O. (1999). A neurocomputational theory of the dopaminergic modulation of working memory functions. *Journal of Neuroscience, 19,* 2807–2822.

Fernstrom, J. D. (1994). Dietary amino acids and brain function. *Journal of the American Dietetic Association, 94,* 71–77.

Fernstrom, M. H., & Fernstrom, J. D. (1995) Brain tryptophan concentrations and serotonin synthesis remain responsive to food consumption after the ingestion of sequential meals. *American Journal of Clinical Nutrition, 61,* 312–319.

Graybiel, A. M., Aosaki, T., Flaherty, A. W., & Kimura, M. (1994). The basal ganglia and adaptive motor control. *Science, 265,* 1826–1831.

Hopson, J. L. (1988, July/August). A pleasurable chemistry. *Psychology Today,* pp. 29–33.

Hoyer, D., Clarke, D. E., Fozard, J. R., et al. (1994). International union of pharmocology classification of receptors for 5-Hydroxytryptamine (Serotonin). *Pharmacological Reviews, 46,* 157–203.

Jacobs, B. L. (1994). Serotonin, motor activity and depression-related disorders. *American Scientist, 82,* 456–463.

Kow, L. M., & Pfaff, D. W. (1988). Neuromodulatory actions of peptides. *Annual Review of Pharmacology and Toxicology, 28,* 163–188.

Lefkowitz, R. J., Hoffman, B. B., & Taylor, P. (1996). Neurotransmission: The autonomic and somatic motor nervous systems. In A. G. Gilman, L. S. Goodman, J. G. Hardman, L. E. Limbard, P. B. Molinoff, & R. W. Ruddon (Eds.), *The pharmocological basis of therapeutics* (pp. 105–139). New York: McGraw-Hill.

McGinty, D., & Szymusiak, R. (1988). Neuronal unit activity patterns in behaving animals: Brainstem and limbic system. *Annual Review of Psychology, 39,* 135–168.

Nicola, S. M., Surmeier, D. J., & Malenka, R. C. (2000). Dopaminergic modulation of neuronal excitability in the striatum and nucleus accumbens. *Annual Review of Neuroscience, 23,* 185–215.

Nicoll, R. A. (1988). The coupling of neurotransmitter receptors to ion channels in the brain. *Science, 241,* 545–551.

Olney, J. W. (1990). Excitotoxic amino acids and neuropsychiatric disorders. *Annual Review of Pharmacology and Toxicology, 30,* 47–71.

Olpe, H. R., Jones, R. S. G., & Steinmann, M. W. (1983). The locus coeruleus: Actions of psychoactive drugs. *Experientia, 39,* 242–249.

Panksepp, J. (1986). The neurochemistry of behavior. *Annual Review of Psychology, 37,* 77–107.

Peroutka, S. J. (1995). 5-HT receptors: Past, present and future. *Trends in Neuroscience, 18,* 68–69.

Pothos, E. N., Przedborski, S., Davila, V., et al. (1998). D-like dopamine autoreceptor activation reduces quantal size in pc12 cells. *Journal of Neuroscience, 18,* 5575–5585.

Radulovacki, M. (1982). L-tryptophan's effects on brain chemistry and sleep in cats and rats: A review. *Neuroscience and Biobehavioral Reviews, 6,* 421–428.

Rosenzweig, M. R., Leiman, A. L., & Breedlove, S. M. (1996). *Biological Psychology.* Sunderland, MA: Sinauer Associates, Inc.

Saudou, F., & Hen, R. (1994). 5-Hydroxytryptamine receptor subtypes in vertebrates and invertebrates. *Neurochemistry International, 25,* 503–532.

Saudou, F., Amara, D. A., Dierich, A., et al. (1994). Enhanced aggressive behavior in mice lacking 5-HT1B receptor. *Science, 265,* 1875–1878.

Shiromani, P. J., Gillin, J. C., & Henriksen, S. J. (1987). Acetylcholine and the regulation of REM sleep: Basic mechanisms and clinical implications for affective illness and narcolepsy. *Annual Review of Pharmacology and Toxicology, 27,* 137–156.

Skirboll, L. R., Grace, A. A., & Bunney, B. S. (1979). Dopamine auto- and postsynaptic receptors: Electrophysiological evidence for differential sensitivity to dopamine agonists. *Science, 206,* 80–82.

Spring, B., Chiodo, J., & Bowen, D. J. (1987). Carbohydrates, tryptophan, and behavior: A methodological review. *Psychological Bulletin, 102,* 234–256.

Steriade, M. (1996). Arousal: Revisiting the reticular activating system. *Science, 272,* 225–226.

Taylor, P. (1985). Cholinergic agonists. In A. G. Gilman, L. S. Goodman, T. W. Rall, & F. Murad (Eds.), *The pharmacological basis of therapeutics* (pp. 100–109). New York: Macmillan.

Weiner, N. (1985). Norepinephrine, epinephrine, and the sympathomimetic amines. In A. G. Gilman, L. S. Goodman, T. W. Rall, & F. Murad (Eds.), *The pharmacological basis of therapeutics* (pp. 145–180). New York: Macmillan.

Weiner, N., & Taylor, P. (1985). Neurohumoral transmission: The autonomic and somatic motor nervous systems. In A. G. Gilman, L. S. Goodman, T. W. Rall, & F. Murad (Eds.), *The pharmacological basis of therapeutics* (pp. 66–99). New York: Macmillan.

Wise, R. A. (1998). Drug-activation of brain reward pathways. *Drug and Alcohol Dependence, 51,* 13–22.

Wurtman, R. J. (1982). Nutrients that modify brain function. *Scientific American, 246,* 50–59.

C h a p t e r **6**

Tolerance
and Dependence

Now that you are familiar with some of the basic principles behind drug action and the theoretical processes involved with conduction, neurotransmission, and brain function, two phenomena that can have a profound influence on drug action and drug abuse may be discussed. These are drug tolerance and drug dependence, which in some cases are related. These phenomena are important theoretically because they tell us something about the mechanism of drug action. Perhaps more important is the fact that, although the processes resulting in tolerance and dependence may not be directly detrimental to the organism, their occurrence may result in severe repercussions for the individual and society.

What Is Tolerance?

Drug tolerance (hereafter referred to as **tolerance**) occurs when there is decreased susceptibility (or diminished response) to the effects of a given amount of drug as a result of previous exposure, typically caused by repeated exposures to the drug. This implies that increasingly larger doses of the drug are required to induce the same behavioral effect, although in some cases tolerance can be so dramatic that no amount of drug is capable of inducing its original effects. Tolerance due to drug exposure is different from so-called genetic or dispositional tolerance, whereby an individual may not be affected by the drug as much as other individuals are because of genetic or dispositional factors. For example, recent evidence suggests that some individuals predisposed to alcoholism metabolize alcohol at a faster rate than those not predisposed to alcoholism, even if they have not been exposed to alcohol before. This characteristic would allow such persons to consume quantities of alcohol much larger than normal before becoming intoxicated.

Although tolerance generally requires several drug exposures before it is evidenced, there is a special case of tolerance in which a noticeable decrease in the organism's sensitivity to the drug occurs over a very short period of time—on the order of a few hours. This is referred to as **tachyphylaxis** or **acute tolerance.** In this form of tolerance, the same amount of drug administered on two separate occasions a couple of hours apart may induce greater effects with the first dose than with the second dose. Tachyphylaxis is also evident when the behavioral or physiological effects of a given dose of a drug dissipate at a faster rate than the rate at which the drug is eliminated from the brain (through catabolization or excretion). For example, a person may experience much greater effects of alcohol as the alcohol is accumulating in the brain than an hour or so later when it is being eliminated from the brain, despite the fact that at the two points in time the brain has the same concentration of alcohol in it (see Figure 8–1).

Between **Cross-tolerance** refers to the phenomenon in which the development of tolerance to one type of drug results in decreased sensitivity to the effects of another type of drug. For example, a heavy drinker who has developed tolerance to alcohol's sleep-inducing properties may not even get sleepy when given a dose of a barbiturate that normally induces sleep in other individuals.

While tolerance per se is not a particularly large problem, it can have severe repercussions. First, most psychoactive drugs we take in our culture are not especially harmful in and of themselves when taken in reasonable quantities with sufficient time between administrations. However, once tolerance to a drug's effects develops, larger and more frequent doses that do become toxic are often administered. Second, tolerance to the effects of drugs does not develop uniformly; that is, some effects may show profound tolerance, whereas others may show little or no tolerance. This is a distinct problem with alcohol and many sedative–hypnotic drugs, where the beneficial or recreational effects of the drugs may show considerable tolerance, but little tolerance develops to the lethal effects of these drugs (O'Brien, 1996). In effect, with this type of tolerance, the therapeutic index for these drugs gets smaller and smaller. With other drugs, tolerance to the desirable effects of a drug may occur while the person actually becomes more sensitive to the side effects of the drug. For example, the ability of amphetamine to induce euphoria decreases with regular use, but the ability for amphetamine to induce psychotic-like effects may actually increase with regular use of large doses. Finally, tolerance is of concern because many of the mechanisms resulting in tolerance contribute to a person's compulsion to take a drug with loss of control over drug intake—that is, drug addiction (Koob, 1996).

Tolerance Mechanisms

There are three distinct types of drug tolerance: **pharmacokinetic tolerance, pharmacodynamic tolerance** (also called **functional** or **nonassociative tolerance**), and **context-specific tolerance** (also called **behavioral, learned,** or **associative tolerance**). Pharmacokinetic and pharmacodynamic forms of tolerance are produced by exposure to high concentrations of a drug, generally with a certain minimum amount of exposure time required, and are not affected by environmental or behavioral manipulations of the organism. Context-specific tolerance is very sensitive to behavioral and environmental manipulations and involves learning and memory. What follows is a description of the various processes that are involved in these three forms of drug tolerance.

Mechanisms of Pharmacokinetic and Pharmacodynamic Tolerance

The most prominent mechanism behind pharmacokinetic tolerance has already been discussed. It involves the ability of the liver to synthesize more drug-metabolizing enzymes than normal when exposed to a drug (O'Brien, 1996). Generally, this process requires several exposures to the drug for some length of time. Once this repeated exposure has taken place, the liver can metabolize the drug at a faster rate than it could previously, thereby decreasing its duration of action. However, the peak intensity of the drug's action may not be reduced very much through this mechanism if it is administered through a route other than oral, because the drug must first pass through the liver before it can be metabolized. This mechanism is also responsible for some cross-tolerance between drugs, since the actions of the drug-metabolizing enzymes are not specific to one particular drug. (This form of tolerance is sometimes referred to as metabolic, or dispositional, tolerance by other authors. However, at the beginning of this chapter, I used the term *dispositional tolerance* to refer to a type of genetically based tolerance that is unrelated to previous drug exposures. Therefore, if you run across this term in other sources, look at the context in which it is used to determine what the author means by it.)

One rather novel explanation for drug tolerance was that something akin to an immune reaction occurred (Cochin, 1970). The drug molecules would be the antigen to which the organism would develop antibodies. This explanation for tolerance was originally invoked to explain how rats, whose mothers were made physically dependent on narcotics and then withdrawn from the drug several weeks before becoming impregnated (so that no drug molecules were present), were more resistant to the effects of morphine than rats whose mothers had not been exposed to narcotics. Presumably, the antibodies formed in the mothers crossed over the placenta into the fetuses, so that when they were later grown and given morphine the antibodies reduced the drug's effectiveness. This mechanism would account for the persistence of some kinds of tolerance for long periods of time and would account for some forms of cross-tolerance. Whether this happens in the body under normal circumstances is unknown. By themselves, most drug molecules are too small to trigger antibody formation, but it is theoretically possible for a drug molecule to bind to some type of tissue and form a complex large enough to trigger an immune reaction to it. This type of strategy—generating an active immunization to cocaine with a stable cocaine conjugate—has been proposed as a means of blocking the action of cocaine by preventing it from entering the CNS (Carrera et al., 1995).

Tolerance to a drug may also develop because the drug's pharmacodynamic properties lead to a depletion of neurotransmitters critical to the drug's effects. That is, some drugs (such as amphetamine and cocaine) act by augmenting a specific type of neurotransmitter activity because they enhance the transmitters' release or inhibit their reuptake and increase the transmitters' access to receptors. However, the drug's actions may lead to a depletion of the transmitters (Gold & Dackis, 1984), either because the transmitters are used faster than they can be replenished or because the actual synthesis of the transmitters is decreased (perhaps because of excessive activity at autoreceptors). Therefore, with fewer transmitter molecules available, a larger drug dose must be administered. If this cycle continues long enough, this form of tolerance can lead to the drug's becoming completely ineffective, regardless of the dose administered. A drug's ability to deplete neurotransmitters can also be a factor in some forms of cross-tolerance. For example, one drug may act by enhancing the transmitters' release, and another may act by reducing the transmitters' reuptake. With either drug, depletion of the transmitters will reduce the effects of the drug. Finally, depletion of neurotransmitters can lead to the person experiencing symptoms that are the opposite of those he or she experienced with the drug; that is, where the drug initially induced its effects by amplifying a neurotransmitter's activity on its target neurons, absence of the drug results in a reduction in the neurotransmitter's activity on its target neurons (Gold & Dackis, 1984).

Another possible tolerance mechanism involves the drug's occupation and saturation of receptor sites, whereby the drug molecules exert their action at the time of occupation of receptor sites (Cochin, 1970). However, once binding occurs, the drug no longer exerts an effect other than preventing the initiation of a new response by other drug molecules combining with the receptor. For example, nicotine is an agonist at nicotinic receptors for Ach, which results in membrane depolarization. However, because nicotine disassociates from the Ach receptor rather slowly, the cell remains depolarized, and a new action potential cannot be initiated until the nicotine is removed from the receptors. Thus, large doses of nicotine may actually exert an antagonistic action at Ach receptors (after the initial agonistic action).

There appear to be several mechanisms for tolerance involving cellular adaptations related to *homeostasis* (the processes that maintain a state of equilibrium in the body with respect to various functions and to the chemical compositions of the fluids and tissues) (Koob, 1996). Lately, a great deal of consideration has been given to homeostatic adaptations taking place in the neuronal membranes or neuronal receptors. For example, as mentioned in Chapter 4, alcohol increases the fluidity of neuronal membranes, possibly leading to the neurons' decreased ability to generate and propagate action potentials. However, the membrane's rigid characteristics return rather quickly (within a few hours), in spite of the fact that brain levels of alcohol are maintained (Chin & Goldstein, 1977). This phenomenon, although clearly a potential factor in tachyphylaxis, is still being explored as a possible factor in long-term tolerance and physical dependence.

Drug-induced alterations in the sensitivity of receptors in neuronal membranes have also been identified by recent research, and it is likely that homeostatic processes are involved. The alterations may reflect either qualitative changes in the neurotransmitters' receptor configuration or changes in the actual number of receptors, which, in turn, affect the transmitters' binding or intrinsic activity (Lefkowitz et al., 1989). It has been suggested that the ability of agonists and antagonists to bind to neuronal receptors is altered when drug exposure exceeds several hours. In many cases, continuous exposure to drugs that mimic or amplify the action of neurotransmitters at their receptors tends to decrease receptor activity through processes referred to as **down-regulation** and **desensitization** (Ross, 1996). Down-regulation refers to a decrease in the number of functional receptors available for activation, whereas desensitization refers to a decrease in the receptors' ability to elicit cellular changes upon activation but no change in receptor number. In contrast, continuous exposure to drugs that act as antagonists or dampen the action of neurotransmitters at receptors tends to increase receptor activity, as if there were more receptors, which may involve **up-regulation** or **sensitization** of receptors—that is, processes that are just the reverse of down-regulation and desensitization.

According to this model of tolerance, with fewer receptors with which the drug molecules or transmitter can interact, higher doses of the agonist must be administered so that the original effect can be induced. This dosage increase, of course, may decrease the receptor population further, so that successively higher doses of the agonist are needed to activate the increasingly smaller population of receptors. With drug antagonists, the reverse process may occur; that is, with a greater population of receptors, higher doses of the antagonist are needed to block them. This model of drug tolerance has great appeal because it explains cross-tolerance between different classes of drugs and because it makes a direct connection between tolerance and physical dependence. Figure 6–1 graphically displays in a step-by-step fashion these theoretical processes for both drug antagonists, seen in Figure 6–1(a), and agonists, in Figure 6–1(b).

If, for example, the actions of drug A are due to its ability to block the postsynaptic receptors for neurotransmitter B, and this blockade is maintained for several hours, the population of postsynaptic receptors may increase. With more receptors available for activation by neurotransmitter B, a greater dose of drug A will be needed in order to block a sufficient number of receptors to bring about the original drug effects; that is, tolerance occurs. Now if the actions of drug C are due to its ability to block the release of neurotransmitter B, and drug C is substituted for drug A, drug C's effects will also be decreased. Conversely, if drug A is not given, there will be more than the normal population of receptors for neurotransmitter B to activate, and effects directly opposite of those induced by the drug—that is, withdrawal effects—will occur.

For how long must exposure to a drug occur for the receptor population to change? Studies with a variety of drugs suggest that several hours of continuous exposure to high drug concentrations may be sufficient to induce significant alterations in many hormone and neurotransmitter receptors (Nathanson, 1987). This time period may be linked to the approximate "lifetime" for a receptor. For example, the receptor for the hormone insulin has been estimated to have a half-life of between 7 and 12 hours in different cell types, which is shortened by exposure of the cell to the insulin ligand; that is, receptor down-regulation occurs (Rosen, 1987). Other receptors may have considerably longer half-lives. For example, adrenergic receptors have been shown to have half-lives greater than 20 hours (Mahan et al., 1987). Nevertheless, agonist exposure markedly shortens their half-life. Thus, we can speculate that the lifetime of a receptor is reduced when extensively activated, and increased when activation is prevented. Furthermore, the number of receptors gradually returns to normal values, after the drug is removed, on a time course that depends on many factors. For example, when some muscarinic receptors are down-regulated with exposure to cholinergic agonists, it appears that they must first be newly synthesized from proteins and then slowly converted to physiologically functional forms before normal cholinergic activity returns (Nathanson, 1987).

In a fashion similar to receptor up-regulation, studies have begun to provide evidence that certain intracellular proteins associated with second-messenger systems may show adaptive up-regulation following chronic drug administration (Self & Nestler, 1995). These molecular adaptations have also been shown to contribute to the increase in activity of the neurons utilizing these second-messenger systems upon drug cessation, which produces many of the physical withdrawal symptoms characteristic of drug dependence.

A final pharmacodynamic-related hypothesis to be discussed in this section involves opiate tolerance and dependence, but a similar process may also apply to other drugs. This

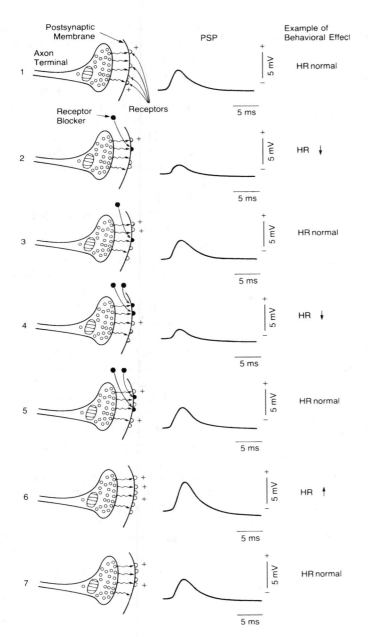

FIGURE 6–1(a) Model for drug tolerance involving alterations in neurotransmitter (NT) receptor population on postsynaptic membrane, how these might affect the magnitude (in mV) of an excitatory postsynaptic potential (PSP), and how the behavioral effect or effector organ activity, e.g., heart rate (HR), may be altered. (1) Normal NT release (with action potential), receptor activation (receptors activated indicated by +), PSP, and HR. (2) Drug antagonist blocks receptors, decreases PSP, and lowers HR. (3) Receptor population increases, so despite drug blockade of other receptors, normal PSP is created, and HR is normal. (4) Drug dose is increased so that more receptors are occupied and blocked; PSP is reduced and HR decreases. (5) Receptor population increases further; PSP and HR return to normal. (6) Drug not given; with greater number of receptors available, NT has increased probability of activating more of them, which results in greater PSP than normal and an exaggerated behavioral effect (i.e., HR elevation). (7) With no further drug exposure, receptor population, PSP, and effector organ activity eventually return to normal.

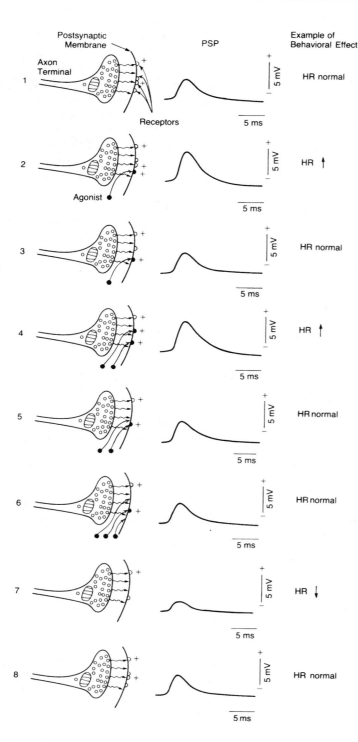

FIGURE 6–1(b) The same model for drug tolerance depicted in Figure 6–1(a), except the drug is an agonist. (1) Normal NT release, receptor activation, PSP, and HR. (2) Drug agonist activates additional receptors, increases PSP, and increases HR. (3) Receptor population decreases, so despite subsequent exposure to the original concentration of the drug, normal PSP is created, and HR is normal. (4) Drug dose is increased so that more receptors are occupied and activated; PSP is enhanced and HR increases. (5) Receptor population decreases further, so that despite the presence of the drug molecules, the PSP and HR are maintained at normal levels. (6) Receptor population is at minimal levels, so that even though the concentration of the drug may be increased with larger doses, no further amplification of the PSP is possible, and HR stays at normal levels. (7) Drug is eliminated from the body; with smaller numbers of receptors now available, NT has decreased probability of activating those that remain, which results in smaller PSP than normal and reduced behavioral activity (i.e., HR declines). (8) with no further drug exposure, receptor population, PSP, and effector organ activity eventually return to normal.

hypothesis proposes that the brain synthesizes and secretes neuropeptides, which we could call anti-opioid peptides, that act as part of a homeostatic system to attenuate the effects of endogenous opioid peptides, as well as exogenous opiates such as morphine (Rothman, 1992). Upon administration of an opiate, the anti-opioid peptides are released, which then attenuate the effects of the opiate—that is, they induce tolerance. As the opiate dosage is increased, more anti-opioid peptides are released. Then, upon cessation of opiate adminis-tration, or with the administration of an opiate antagonist, there would be a relative excess of the anti-opioid peptides, which could partially contribute to withdrawal symptoms.

All the pharmacokinetic and pharmacodynamic mechanisms resulting in tolerance that I have just described are purely physiological mechanisms because they are due to drug-induced changes in cellular enzymes, membranes, or receptors, which then decrease the abil-ity of the drug to induce its effects. The rate at which tolerance develops is dependent upon drug dosage and the time between doses; the larger the dose and the shorter the time between doses, the more rapidly tolerance would be expected to develop. Furthermore, there is a threshold dose for each drug below which tolerance would not be expected to occur.

Mechanisms of Context-Specific Tolerance

Although there is a great deal of research support for many of the pharmacokinetic and phar-macodynamic models of tolerance, there has been increasing recognition that many forms of drug tolerance come about because of learning processes and behavioral adaptations that may occur in the presence of the drug and that are highly task- or situation-specific. Such tolerance is called **context-specific tolerance.** Several mechanisms through which this form of tolerance can develop have been proposed.

The term **context-specific** or **behavioral tolerance** is applied when an organism is ex-posed to a drug in one context, displays tolerance to the drug in that context, but then loses the tolerance when it is exposed to the drug in another context. The most common processes involved in this form of tolerance are *habituation, Pavlovian conditioning,* and *instrumental conditioning.*

Habituation is perhaps the most fundamental of these. When an organism is first exposed to a novel stimulus, the stimulus often induces a reaction. A *stimulus* is any event—external or internal—that is capable of activating receptors in one of the senses. A *response* is any mea-surable reaction in an organism, such as skeletal, smooth, and cardiac muscle contractions; glandular secretions and excretions; neurotransmitter release; EEG pattern changes; or emo-tional reactions. When the stimulus is presented repeatedly to an organism without variation, there generally is a decrease in the magnitude of the reaction to the stimulus, a phenomenon referred to as habituation. (As noted later in this chapter, habituation is sometimes used in the field of drug abuse as a synonym for psychological dependence, or the process of forming a drug habit, which is very different from the process being described here.)

By definition, psychotropic drugs have both stimulus and response-eliciting properties. When a psychotropic drug is first administered to an organism, it introduces the organism to a new stimulus complex and, much like a novel sound or visual stimulus, it may interrupt or alter ongoing behavior. However, after repeated exposures to the drug-induced stimulus complex with no further consequences, behavior is going to be less and less affected. This is habituation; it is also a form of tolerance (Kesner & Cook, 1983). Evidence that the decreased sensitivity to the drug is due to habituation, and not to pharmacodynamic mechanisms, is provided when the organism is subsequently given the drug in a different environment and the drug again induces a reaction (Baker & Tiffany, 1985).

The preceding discussion does not explain what happens physiologically (psychologists are just now beginning to delineate what the physiological mechanisms are behind habituation in simple organisms like marine mollusks), but this description does place drugs in the same domain as that involving the effect of external stimuli on behavior. The difference is that with drugs, internal stimuli are involved.

It has been proposed that Pavlovian conditioning is another process through which behavioral tolerance develops (Stewart & Eikelboom, 1987). Most of you have probably heard or read about how the Russian physiologist Ivan Pavlov conditioned dogs to salivate to tones or lights when these stimuli were paired with food. However, you probably remember little else about this form of conditioning and were not particularly impressed with the process in terms of its potential impact on you and other people around you. However, this process may be a factor in developing tolerance, and it can have a profound impact with respect to the induction of psychological dependence on drugs. In some cases, it can induce conditioned reactions that appear to be similar to the abstinence symptoms associated with physical dependence. Because of its potential role in the areas of tolerance and dependence, this process will be explored in some detail here.

Pavlovian conditioning begins when an organism is exposed to a stimulus that automatically (i.e., innately) elicits one or more reactions in the organism. The stimulus is called an *unconditioned stimulus* (UCS) and the responses it elicits are called *unconditioned responses* (UCRs). Examples of these stimulus–response cause-and-effect relationships, called reflexes, are the withdrawal of your hand (UCR) from a hot stove (UCS), the elicitation of tears (UCR) by onion fumes (UCS), sneezing (UCR) elicited by pepper in the nose (UCS), bronchial constriction (UCR) elicited by pollen (UCS), and increased heart rate, blood pressure, and sweating, and fright (UCRs) elicited by a loud, unexpected sound (UCS). Because psychotropic drugs induce a number of automatic reactions, they also constitute unconditional stimuli. Thus, we can say that administration of morphine (UCS) elicits, among other reactions, constriction of the pupils, drying up of secretions, constipation, respiratory depression, analgesia, and euphoria, as UCRs. As another example, nicotine (UCS) elicits increased heart rate and blood pressure, and altered cortical arousal (UCRs).

When a stimulus that generally does not produce much of a reaction by itself occurs prior to a UCS so that it reliably signals or predicts the occurrence of the UCS, conditioning may take place. We recognize that conditioning has occurred when the signal stimulus begins to elicit its own responses, which in many (but not all) cases resemble the UCRs elicited by the UCS. Because the new responses' occurrences are conditional upon the stimulus being paired with the UCS, they are termed *conditioned responses* (CR), and the stimulus now eliciting them is termed a *conditioned stimulus* (CS).

In most cases CRs elicited by a CS prepare the organism for dealing with the impending UCS (Holland, 1984; Hollis, 1984; Lennartz & Weinberger, 1992). For example, if food is put in the mouth, it is a UCS for salivation (UCR). Because one sees the food before it enters the mouth, the sight of food is a signal for food entering the mouth. Thus, the sight of food becomes a CS that elicits salivation, which serves a function—in this case to enhance the digestion and chewability of the food. However, food (the UCS) may also decrease hunger (a UCR) because it satisfies a bodily need. In contrast, the sight of food may actually increase hunger (a CR)—in this case to produce incentive motivation so the person will approach and consume the food.

Some CRs are very general preparatory responses, for example, "get-ready-for-something-important-to-happen" responses such as fear, increased heart rate, blood pressure, and respiration; whereas, others are very specific, for example, the "get-ready-to-get-hit-in-the-eye" response of an eye blink. Depending on a number of factors too complicated to discuss here (many of which we simply don't understand), some CRs may appear to be similar to the UCRs provoked by UCSs, whereas other CRs appear to be very different from the UCRs—even opposite in their direction.

In the same fashion, signals for impending drug actions come to elicit CRs that prepare the body for the impending drug actions. Unfortunately, as we shall see, some of these CRs may, in the long run, actually be maladaptive for the person—for example, creating a conditioned incentive motivational state that leads the person to take the drug more and more frequently and in larger and larger amounts.

It appears that a wide variety of external stimuli (for instance, the smell of a "joint" or the sight of a syringe), as well as internal stimuli (those of an emotional state such as depression or anxiety, for example), can take on the properties of a CS. The number of pairings of a CS with a UCS that are required for conditioning to take place are dependent on many factors, but to some extent the species' particular characteristics play a role. For example, rats can associate a novel taste with nausea after only one exposure, even if there is a gap of several hours between experiencing the novel taste and receiving the nausea-inducing stimulus. Chickens, on the other hand, do not appear to associate these events, even after many pairings. Birds can associate novel visual stimuli with sickness after only a few pairings, whereas rats do not appear to do so even after many pairings of these events. I mention these esoteric little facts because, in a similar fashion, humans may vary in their tendency to associate certain events with the drug effects they experience. Therefore, they may vary in their tendency to experience conditioned reactions that play a role in their becoming psychologically dependent on the drug.

How can Pavlovian conditioned responses play a role in many types of tolerance phenomena? In most of the studies that have dealt with this question, animals were exposed to a drug like morphine or alcohol (UCS) on several occasions in a specific environmental context (CS) (Hinson & Siegel, 1982). Some of the animals were then given a behavioral test following exposure to the drug in this same (CS) environmental context, while the other animals were given the same drug dose but were tested in a different context (no CS). Usually, the animals tested in the no-CS context exhibited larger drug effects than the animals tested in the CS context. One explanation is that in the CS environment a CR was elicited that was opposite to the drug-induced effects (UCRs); thus it was termed a *compensatory CR*. The net outcome was that the effectiveness of the drug (UCS) appeared to be reduced. However, in the no-CS context, there would be no compensatory CR to counteract the drug-induced UCR. The interesting implication of these studies is that if the organism is exposed to the CS, but without the drug being given, a compensatory CR should occur. Such a reaction would appear withdrawal-like. However, in the few cases in which attempts have been made to directly observe compensatory-type CRs under laboratory conditions (that is, when the organism is exposed to the CS without the drug UCS being present), they appear weak and extinguish rapidly, if they occur at all (Tiffany et al., 1983; Sobrero & Bouton, 1989). Because the withdrawal symptoms associated with chronic use of many drugs are often quite severe and persist for several days, it is likely that other mechanisms, which may act synergistically with compensatory CRs, are involved in their production. In any case, compensatory CRs may be a factor in drug tolerance and drug dependence. As will be discussed later on, other types of CRs may also be involved in producing drug dependence.

A third behavioral mechanism through which drug tolerance can develop is *instrumental conditioning* (Ferraro, 1976). Whereas Pavlovian conditioning occurs without the organism necessarily doing anything—that is, the process occurs by the simple pairing of two different types of stimuli—instrumental conditioning begins with responses that are originally emitted without any apparent stimulus needed to produce them. The form and frequency of their subsequent occurrence are then altered depending upon the consequences of those responses. (The term *instrumental* is used to indicate that the behavior is instrumental or necessary for the conditioning process to occur. Common examples of instrumental behaviors are those involved in driving a car, hitting a golf ball, lighting a cigarette, snorting cocaine, and writing a letter.) These consequences are generally referred to as reinforcers and punishers. Stimuli that follow behavior and subsequently increase the probability of occurrence of that behavior in similar settings are termed *reinforcers.* Stimuli that follow behavior and decrease the probability of occurrence of that behavior in similar settings are called *punishers.*

Reinforcers can be either primary or secondary. Primary reinforcers are stimuli that either reduce physiological needs or have inherent hedonic properties (for example, food, sex, and water). Secondary (also called conditioned) reinforcers are stimuli that predict or are associated with the increased probability of obtaining primary reinforcers (for instance, getting money increases one's chances of obtaining food, sex, and water). Drug-taking behavior is instrumental behavior. Drugs may have primary reinforcing value, and the environmental context cues in the presence of which the drugs are taken may become secondary reinforcers. Therefore, it should be obvious that instrumental conditioning plays a role in drug dependence and, as will now be discussed, in the development of tolerance to drugs.

Drugs that affect performance may also affect the organism's ongoing behavior and the contingencies of reinforcement and punishment, thereby bringing instrumental conditioning processes into the picture (Ferraro, 1976). In most cases the introduction of a psychotropic drug will interfere with the ability of the organism to maintain control over its reinforcement and punishment. For example, people who drive a car well without drugs may find themselves, under the influence of a few drinks, crossing median lines, hitting curbs, being honked at, running red lights, or getting into an accident. In other words, the drug is detrimental to the relationship between the behavior of driving and its consequences. However, with more and more exposure to this set of circumstances, these same people may learn how to compensate for these detrimental effects. For example, they may learn to look at the speedometer more frequently, keep a greater distance between themselves and other cars, and make adjustments in simple motor skills.

This learning model for tolerance applies to all drugs that affect behavior, and there are a number of implications for this form of tolerance (Ferraro, 1976). First, in order for it to occur, the organism must perform the task under the influence of the drug; that is, if two identical organisms are given identical doses of the drug on several occasions, only the organism performing a specific task under the influence of the drug will develop tolerance through this process. In this case, if the organism that had been given the drug without exposure to the task were subsequently given the drug, and then it attempted to perform the task, the effects initially induced in the other organism would be evident.

Second, the tolerance developed in this fashion should be task-specific. In other words, learning to compensate for the detrimental effects of alcohol on driving will probably not alter alcohol's detrimental effects on typing, because the two tasks require entirely different psychomotor skills and involve different consequences. However, should two tasks involve similar components, tolerance developed in one should generalize to the other. For example, the development of compensatory responses allowing one to maintain one's balance on a bicycle when intoxicated with alcohol should transfer when the person attempts to ride a motorcycle under the influence of alcohol.

Third, while drug-induced detriments in performance will result in tolerance, alterations in the organism's behavior that do not hinder its ability to achieve reinforcement (or escape or avoid aversive events) will not show tolerance, because with the latter effects there is nothing for which the organism must learn to compensate. The same principle applies if the drug facilitates performance.

Fourth, the rate of tolerance development should be a function of the difficulty of the task or the availability of compensatory responses. That is, just as in learning how to do any task, the fewer components there are to learn, the faster one learns how to perform the task properly.

Fifth, once compensatory responses are learned under the influence of a drug, they should be available for use over relatively long periods of time without further exposure to the drug or the task. This would be expected simply because learning is generally defined as a relatively permanent change in behavioral potential as a function of practice or experience. What is learned should not dissipate simply through disuse or time, although, of course, forgetting may occur.

Finally, behavioral tolerance established to one drug should transfer to other drug states that produce similar behavioral effects because of either stimulus or response generalization. For example, while alcohol and marijuana may have quite dissimilar pharmacological actions in the CNS, the effects of low doses of alcohol and marijuana may be sufficiently similar that behavioral tolerance developed to one may generalize to the other.

Tolerance due to the development of instrumental compensatory responses that counteract a drug's effects has been demonstrated to occur with a variety of psychotropic drugs, including amphetamine, cocaine, morphine, alcohol, and barbiturates. Interestingly, the compensatory responses need not be overtly behavioral; they can also be cognitive. For example, it has been shown that tolerance to some of alcohol's behaviorally disruptive properties is facilitated even in persons who merely mentally rehearsed performing a task while under the influence of alcohol (Sdao-Jarvie & Vogel-Sprott, 1986).

It should be added that learning has also been suggested to be a process by which increased drug sensitivity with previous exposure can come about (a phenomenon referred to earlier as *reverse tolerance* or sensitization). For example, marijuana has the reputation of not inducing much of an effect the first time a person tries it, but with more exposure to the drug the person begins to experience more of an effect from the same amount. Similar statements have been made by cocaine users. It has been suggested that low doses of these drugs do not induce particularly noticeable effects in the user, but that with continued usage the person learns to recognize the effects that have been labeled by users as pleasurable. It is also possible, through Pavlovian conditioning, that CRs, which are like the UCRs produced by the drug, summate with the drug-induced effects to induce a larger overall subjective effect.

Clearly there are many mechanisms through which drug tolerance occurs. No single mechanism can account for all the phenomena associated with tolerance—particularly the fact that some drug effects dissipate with successive drug exposures, while others remain unchanged or increase in magnitude. We have discussed tolerance in two main frameworks: learning models and pharmacological models. Yet, from a reductionistic perspective, both pharmacological and learned forms of tolerance may come about because of the same physiological mechanisms. Learning models simply emphasize the stimulus context, the task requirements, and the behavioral effects of drugs as factors in tolerance development. Pharmacological models emphasize the drug concentration and time between drug exposures as the primary factors in tolerance development.

What Is Dependence?

Like tolerance, drug dependence per se may not be detrimental to an individual or society, but once it occurs, it may lead the individual to do things that are behaviorally maladaptive, physiologically hazardous, or socially unacceptable. **Drug dependence** is a general term indicating that a person's drug use has led to the user's experiencing uncontrollable and unpleasant mood states that in turn lead the user to use the drug compulsively despite obvious adverse consequences. This is distinguished from **drug abuse,** which commonly refers simply to a person's recurrent or continued use of drugs in doses or ways that result in adverse consequences (Newcomb & Bentler, 1989). However, the functional distinction between drug abuse and drug dependence is generally more quantitative than it is qualitative—that is, a matter of degree rather than kind (Feingold & Rounsaville, 1995).

To a certain extent, the consequences of drug dependence are sometimes related to the laws and social norms of one's culture (Brecher, 1972). For example, because of laws limiting heroin's availability, one can argue that the consequences of heroin dependency in the United States are much more severe for the dependent person than they might be without those laws. (This topic was discussed earlier in Chapter 1 and will be discussed further in Chapter 10.) The point is, we are all dependent upon numerous substances and activities (food, water, sex, and so forth), but we do not normally think of these dependencies as problems unless we are deprived of them.

There are two basic forms of drug dependence: psychological (or psychic) dependence and physical (or physiological) dependence. Neither of these is particularly easy to define, and it is sometimes difficult to distinguish between the two, not only because the symptoms associated with them can be confused, but also because the two often occur together. **Psychological dependence** refers to a strong compulsion or desire to experience the effects of a drug because it produces pleasure or reduces psychic discomfort. This type of dependence can be termed **primary psychological dependence** in order to distinguish it from the secondary form to be discussed shortly. Generally it leads to regular or continuous administration of the drug, so that taking the drug becomes habitual. Because of these characteristics, some authors in the area of drug abuse refer to psychological dependence as habituation. However, since this term can be confused with the phenomenon of habituation described earlier in this chapter, I do not view it as an appropriate term.

In a sense, psychological dependence is the counterpart to context-specific tolerance because the affective states underlying it are heavily influenced by the context the person is in and because it is primarily the result of learning and memory processes. Similarly, physiological dependence is the counterpart to pharmacodynamic tolerance because some of the mechanisms behind the latter are the likely causes of the manifestations of physiological dependence.

Psychological dependence comes about because drug-taking behavior is regularly followed by the rewarding effects of a drug. Human beings self-administer nonprescribed drugs for a variety of purposes, for example, to enhance mood or some aspect of performance, to cope with adverse or stressful situations, to socialize, to conform, or to expand experiential awareness (Cooper, 1994; Simons et al., 2000). Some of these motives (e.g., social motives) appear to have little or no association with excessive drug use or drug-related problems, whereas others (e.g., enhancement and coping motives), have been shown to be predictive of excessive use and problems.

At a more primitive level, virtually all recreational and abuse-prone drugs appear to derive some of their rewarding properties by directly or indirectly activating brain reward circuits—the same brain system that ordinarily plays a role in providing feelings of pleasure—like sex or chocolate or falling in love (Nestler, 1996). The key primary reward system is the *mesolimbic dopamine system,* which connects structures high in the brain, especially the orbitofrontal cortex, in the prefrontal area behind the forehead, with the amygdala in the brain's center and with the nucleus accumbens (Koob, 1996). The latter is a structure that in animal research has proved to be a major site of activity in addiction (Wise, 1998). The ultimate source of the dopaminergic input into these areas is called the *ventral tegmental area,* located in the midbrain.

This complex reward system in the brain was initially discovered over 40 years ago when studies indicated that animals would engage in various behaviors (for instance, pressing a lever) if these behaviors resulted in the delivery of a mild electrical current to some areas in the brain but not others (Olds & Milner, 1954). Virtually all abuse-prone drugs, including widely disparate pharmacologically acting drugs like morphine, cocaine, alcohol, and marijuana, have been found to enhance brain stimulation reward or lower brain reward thresholds in these circuits (Wise, 1998). Animals will also work for microinjections of most of these drugs into these reward circuits but not other brain areas. Finally, virtually all abusable drugs enhance basal neuronal firing or basal neurotransmitter release in these reward circuits (Gardner & Lowinson, 1991).

While there is widespread acceptance of the view that augmented dopamine release in the nucleus accumbens is a major mediator of the primary rewarding properties of drugs of abuse, there is considerable evidence that conflicts with this view. For example, the benzodiazepines, which have strong abuse liability, have been shown to reduce dopamine levels in the nucleus accumbens (Motzo et al., 1997). On the other hand, several different stressful stimuli, including tail pinch, foot shock, immobilization, and anxiety-provoking drugs, have been shown to increase dopamine release in the nucleus accumbens (Sokolowski et al., 1998; Gray et al., 1997). Thus, the specific role of the nucleus accumbens and dopamine in the dependence liability of drugs remains unclear. It may simply be that the dopamine signal serves to draw attention to significant events of all sorts, including those produced by a wide variety of abused psychoactive drugs.

Thus, while a surge of dopamine in the nucleus accumbens may reinforce drug-seeking behavior by capturing the brain's attention, other neurotransmitter systems probably are equally important in producing stable changes in the brain that lead to compulsive drug-seeking (Wickelgren, 1998). For example, glutamate, the major excitatory amino acid neurotransmitter in the CNS, appears to play a critical role in drug craving. Research has shown that blocking glutamate transmission prevents behavioral sensitization to repeated doses of cocaine in the rat. Also, acamprosate, a drug that blocks the ability of glutamate to stimulate electrical activity in the cortex of rats, has been shown to decrease the craving for alcohol in alcoholic patients (Dahchour & De Witte, 2000). On the other hand, drugs that mimic glutamate action at one of its receptors have been shown to reinstate previously extinguished cocaine-seeking behavior in rats (see how drug-seeking in animals is demonstrated below), which suggests that the rats were craving cocaine (Cornish et al., 1999). Also, the degree of cocaine craving in human cocaine abusers watching films displaying cocaine-associated stimuli has been shown to parallel the intensity of neural activity in the frontal cortex and the amygdala (Grant et al., 1996), areas that release glutamate in the nucleus accumbens. Thus, it appears that brain structures that mediate learning and memory functions and that greatly depend on glutamate seem to play a role in the cravings elicited by conditioned stimuli.

How does one go about determining whether a drug has reinforcing properties prior to its compulsive use by humans? A common laboratory technique used to assess the psychological dependence liability of a drug, removed from social, cultural, or expectancy factors, involves determining whether or not nonhumans (for example, monkeys or rats) will self-administer the drug. Typically, the procedure entails a small catheter (tube) being permanently implanted in a laboratory animal. The catheter goes directly into the blood going into the heart and is connected to a pump outside the animal. The animal can activate the pump, and thus self-administer a dose of the drug, by performing some learned behavioral response, like pressing a lever. The dependence liability of the drug is determined by how frequently the animal responds when the drug is injected versus when an inert substance is injected. Animals will readily perform the response in order to administer most drugs that are abused by humans. For example, morphine, heroin, cocaine, and amphetamine, drugs that can induce a strong psychological dependence in humans, are very readily self-administered by rats and monkeys with this procedure, but caffeine, which is not readily abused by humans, is not reliably self-administered by animals (Woods, 1978). This technique is not an infallible approach to determining the potential dependence liability of a drug, because some drugs that may induce psychological dependence in humans are not self-administered by nonhumans—for example, LSD.

Although drug self-administration studies with nonhumans most commonly employ the I.V. route of administration, other routes of administration have been used to demonstrate drug self-administration in nonhumans. Even the oral route can be used, although it is a bit more difficult to establish drug-reinforced responding due primarily to the aversive taste of many drugs and the delayed onset of CNS effects (Macenski & Meisch, 1994).

This technique is also useful in illustrating how habitual drug taking can become. Monkeys allowed to administer morphine in this fashion eventually develop stable patterns of responding so that the amount of morphine administered on a daily basis is fairly constant. In other words, while they can self-administer as much morphine as they wish, they stabilize at an amount considerably below that which they could receive (this phenomenon has been shown not to be due to the animal's becoming so intoxicated that it cannot perform the response). However, if the monkey is administered the amount of morphine that it normally stabilizes on without having to do anything, it will continue to respond and administer even more morphine (Leavitt, 1982).

Physical (or physiological) dependence is said to occur when a state, termed an **abstinence syndrome,** characterized by physical disturbances develops when the administration of a drug is suspended after prolonged use or its actions are terminated by the administration of a specific antagonist. In almost all cases, the effects of withdrawal are the opposite of the direct effects induced by the drug (O'Brien, 1996). Thus, for example, withdrawal from barbiturates, which normally exert a calming, sleep-inducing, anticonvulsant action, is characterized by anxiety, inability to sleep, and convulsions (which can be lethal). Withdrawal from opiates, which cause constipation, dry up the nasal passages, induce sleep, reduce sex drive, and reduce pain (among many other effects), is characterized by diarrhea, runny nose, inability to sleep, spontaneous ejaculations (men) or orgasms (women), and hypersensitivity to pain.

The duration and intensity of an abstinence syndrome are also highly correlated with the duration and intensity of a drug's direct effects (Figure 6–2). For example, a drug with a short plasma half-life (say, 4 hours) will likely induce a relatively intense but short-lasting behavioral effect. If given infrequently, cessation of its use will not likely result in abstinence symptoms. However, if taken frequently, so that the CNS is continuously exposed to the drug, its withdrawal will likely result in a relatively intense abstinence syndrome that dissipates fairly quickly (that is, over a few days). Conversely, a drug with a long plasma half-life (say, 24 hours) will likely induce relatively weak but long-lasting behavioral effects. If taken frequently enough so that the CNS is continuously exposed to the drug, its withdrawal is likely to result in a relatively weak abstinence syndrome that dissipates slowly (that is, over a few weeks). Also, as one might expect, the more frequently a drug is administered and the greater the dose, the more extensive the abstinence syndrome will be (Okamoto et al., 1986).

In Figure 6–2, we see that in case A, with a short-acting drug administered at spaced intervals, there is likely to be no pharmacodynamic tolerance and no withdrawal. In case B, in which a short-acting drug is administered at a constant dosage and at closely spaced intervals, there is likely to be pharmacodynamic tolerance and a mild, but short-lasting, abstinence syndrome. In case C, in which the short-acting drug is administered at closely spaced intervals and the dose is increased (indicated by *X*), there is likely to be a relatively more intense and longer-lasting abstinence syndrome than in case B. In case D, with a longer-lasting drug administered at spaced intervals, pharmacodynamic tolerance will not be readily apparent, and the abstinence syndrome (if evident at all) will be mild. In case E, in which the longer-lasting drug is administered at more closely spaced intervals, pharmacodynamic

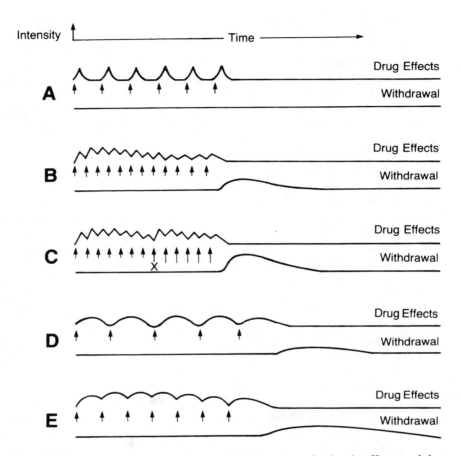

FIGURE 6–2   Relationships between the intensity of a drug's effects and the intensity of the abstinence syndrome when the drug is no longer administered. The arrows indicate when the drug is administered.

tolerance and the abstinence syndrome will be somewhat more apparent than in case D. Furthermore, while the abstinence syndrome in case E may be less severe than in case C, it is likely to be more protracted.

In most cases, abstinence symptoms are not typically displayed unless the individual has consumed the drug for several days or weeks at high dosage levels that would normally induce tolerance to the drug's effects. However, with sufficiently high dosages, signs of abstinence may occur within a relatively short span of time—that is, following high drug concentrations for 12 hours or so. For example, behavioral studies have shown that a single dose of morphine, if large enough to maintain morphine concentrations in the rat for approximately 12 hours, can increase the perceived intensity of mild shock (indicative of a withdrawal-like increase in pain perception) 24 to 72 hours later (Grilly & Gowans, 1986). On a more personal level, if you have ever had an alcohol hangover (which may very likely constitute a mini-withdrawal syndrome), it is probably because you drank sufficient amounts of alcohol to maintain significant brain concentrations of alcohol for at least 12 hours. If you drink enough alcohol to become legally intoxicated in most states—0.10 percent blood alcohol content—it takes approximately 7 hours to eliminate it from your body. (A 0.10 percent blood alcohol content means that in every 1,000 ml of blood there is 1 ml of pure ethanol.) Therefore, if you experience a hangover after a night of drinking, it is likely that you were well over the legal limit by the time you finished drinking.

If a person becomes physically dependent on a drug, a second form of psychological dependence can develop. That is, once physical dependence exists and the person becomes familiar with the symptoms of abstinence, the person may develop a craving for the drug that is based on the person's fear or anxiety of experiencing the abstinence syndrome. Therefore, the person seeks out and administers the drug to alleviate the fear or anxiety. This type of psychological dependence is sometimes referred to as **secondary psychological dependence,** in order to distinguish it from the primary psychological dependence described earlier, which can occur whether or not the person is physically dependent on the drug.

Although tolerance and physical dependence often accompany each other, they are not necessarily related. At least some degree of drug tolerance inevitably precedes physical dependence, but physical dependence does not always follow when tolerance to a drug develops. In other words, if someone is physically dependent on a drug, that person will have developed tolerance to many of its effects. However, if a person has developed tolerance to a drug's effects, it does not mean that the person is physically dependent on the drug. This is most likely due to the fact there are many mechanisms for inducing tolerance, and only some of them may also result in physical dependence (Wuster et al., 1985).

We might note at this point that before the terms *psychological dependence* and *physical dependence* were in vogue, the term **drug addiction** was used. Over 30 years ago the World Health Organization (WHO) defined drug addiction as a state of periodic or chronic intoxication detrimental to the individual or society, produced by the repeated consumption of a drug. Its characteristics were described as an overpowering desire or need (compulsion) to continue taking the drug, because of either psychological or physical dependence on the effects of the drug, and a tendency to increase the dose or frequency of use.

Prior to the twentieth century, the term *addiction* meant simply a strong inclination toward certain kinds of conduct, with little or no stigma associated with it. Often it referred to a habit—good or bad, but more often good, such as an addiction to reading. However, as the term came to be more and more associated with drugs, the term became stigmatic. Furthermore, it often became synonymous with physiological dependence, in spite of the WHO definition indicating that either psychological dependence or physical dependence (or both) may be involved. For these reasons, many experts today try to avoid using the term addiction with respect to drugs. However, because the term has become so ingrained in our language, it will continue to be used. When, on occasion, it is used in the remainder of this book, it will be used in the sense of the WHO definition. In this context, whenever the term addict is used in this text, it will refer to someone who has a strong compulsion to use a particular substance.

Some psychotropic drugs have a relatively strong potential for producing both physical and psychological dependence; others appear capable of inducing one without the other;

and still others do not appear to induce either to any significant degree. I would hesitate to say that any psychotropic drug is incapable of inducing either or only one kind of dependence; it is just that there is no clear evidence one way or another in some cases. However, the argument has been made that just about any psychotropic drug, if the organism is exposed to it in large enough doses and for a long enough period of time, will provoke abstinence symptoms when the drug is rapidly eliminated from the body (Hollister, 1987).

Classes of drugs for which there is clear evidence of a moderate to strong potential for both physical and psychological dependence would include all drugs with sedative–hypnotic properties. Among them are alcohol, barbiturates, nonbarbiturate sedative–hypnotics, antianxiety drugs (sometimes called "minor tranquilizers"), and the narcotics, such as heroin, morphine, codeine, and methadone. Drugs that have a high potential for inducing psychological dependence, but for which physical dependence is either questionable or relatively mild, would include the psychostimulants, such as cocaine, amphetamines, and related compounds, and psychosis-mimicking drugs, such as LSD, mescaline, psilocybin, and marijuana.

Some drugs have minimal potential for inducing psychological dependence, but if taken for a period of time, will induce physical dependence and provoke withdrawal symptoms if the person ceases taking them. (Nasal spray, although not a psychotropic drug, is capable of having this effect.) Certain narcotics with mixed agonist–antagonist properties are in this category.

Finally, drugs used in the treatment of major mental and emotional disturbances, such as lithium, antidepressants, and antipsychotics, have minimal potential for inducing psychological dependence or signs of abstinence. In fact, many patients would prefer to stop taking these types of drugs because of the unpleasant side effects associated with them.

As stated earlier, even drugs that traditionally have not been recognized as being capable of inducing physical dependence (cocaine, for instance) may, if given in large enough quantities and for a long enough period of time, upon cessation of drug administration induce physiological and psychological disturbances opposite to the drug-induced effects. Perhaps we have not recognized these symptoms as withdrawal because they do not resemble, quantitatively or qualitatively, the symptoms associated with the sedative–hypnotics and the narcotics. This issue will be dealt with more fully when these drugs are discussed in later chapters. (Several years ago, when I pointed out the possibility of physical dependence with all psychotropic drugs, a student suggested that if this were true, giving LSD chronically in large amounts to schizophrenics might result in their becoming rational and nondelusional upon withdrawal. I quickly pointed out that although it was an intriguing hypothesis, there are exceptions to every generalization.)

Factors in Dependence

A multitude of sociological, psychological, and genetic factors have been suggested to be involved in the abuse of drugs (see Shadel et al., 2000, and National Institute on Drug Abuse monographs edited by Harris, 1980, 1981, and Thompson & Johanson, 1981, for extensive reviews of this topic). Genetic influences appear to be nearly universally important in determining sensitivity to drugs, and several hundred reports have appeared documenting genetic differences in sensitivity or toxic responses to almost all drugs subject to abuse

(Crabbe et al., 1994). Family, twin, and adoption studies have provided overwhelming evidence that variation in the liability to substance abuse is influenced by differences in individual genetic makeup (Vanyukov & Tarter, 2000). Twin studies suggest that genetic factors may account for up to 79 percent of the variation in the liability to any illicit drug abuse or dependence in both males and females, and may account for 73 percent (males) and 61 percent (females) in liability for alcoholism. Heritability estimates for tobacco initiation have ranged from 32 percent to 70 percent in females and from 31 percent to 40 percent in males. Genetic factors have consistently accounted for 60 percent to 71 percent in variation smoking persistence. Liability for use and abuse of various categories of drugs, alcohol, and tobacco has been shown to share a considerable proportion of genes, which suggests that some common genetic background predisposes individuals to exhibiting a variety of pathological characterisics involving drug use—the particular type or types being generated by environmental factors that are not yet clearly delineated.

Variations in genes controlling both pharmacodynamic (e.g., differences in dopamine D_2 receptors) and pharmacokinetic (e.g., differences in enzymes that metabolize ethanol, opiates, and nicotine) processes have been implicated in the predisposition to develop substance abuse disorders. Unfortunately, many recent findings in this area are difficult to replicate. For example, there is controversy over the potential role in alcoholism and other drug addictions of a particular form (allele) of the gene for the D_2 dopamine receptor (one of the five major receptors for dopamine), called the DRD_2 Al allele. Some studies have indicated that there is a strong association between the frequency and prevalence of this allele and the incidence of abuse for a variety of drugs, suggesting that this gene is a reinforcement or reward gene involved in the reactions to a variety of abused substances (Nobel, 1998a, 1998b), whereas others have not found this association (Edenberg et al., 1998; Bierut et al., 2000). Thus, it appears we will have to wait for further evidence before we can make any firm conclusions regarding this gene and the propensity for developing addiction to drugs.

Sociological factors in drug involvement have been discussed at length by a multitude of authors (Harris, 1980, 1981). With respect to extensive illicit drug use, the strongest and most direct factor is the user's selling of drugs, which in turn is strongly related to factors such as drug availability, significant others' labeling of the person as deviant, peer influence, early childhood deviance, poor school adjustment, and weak family influence (Clayton & Voss, 1981). For example, when one's family influence (defined in terms of family control, closeness of mother, and communication with parents) is weak, there is a higher likelihood during the early teens that the person will (1) exhibit signs of early deviance (i.e., be involved in unconventional or deviant activities); (2) be strongly influenced by peers who are delinquent, steal, engage in gang fights, drink alcohol, smoke marijuana, or use other drugs; and (3) exhibit poor school adjustment (i.e., dislike school and get low grades). Early deviance will also tend to increase the degree of peer influence and decrease the person's school adjustment. These factors then increase the person's likelihood of becoming labeled as a troublemaker and increasing the person's drug availability. These then make the person more likely to sell and use illicit drugs.

Generally ignored as a factor in drug abuse, but one of the most consistently replicated correlates of nonabuse, is religion (Gorsuch, 1988). With respect to alcohol use, for example, people in all religious denominations use less alcohol than do nonreligious people, with those denominations traditionally opposed to alcohol using it less. Of those who do drink, people who are religious abuse alcohol less than do people who are nonreligious.

Although race or ethnic group might be expected to be a factor in the incidence of drug abuse, the findings are not consistent with the impressions that many people in the United States have about drug-use rates. One of the more interesting findings from population-based epidemiologic studies conducted in the mid-1990s is that Whites, in comparison with African Americans and Hispanics, reported having the highest prevalence of lifetime use of most types of drugs (with the exception of heroin and crack cocaine). Perhaps not coincidentally, Whites were least likely to perceive risks for substance abuse (Ma & Shive, 2000). Whites also reported higher prevalence rates of recent alcohol and smokeless tobacco use. (African Americans, however, may have greater secondary problems arising out of substance abuse than Whites—for example, liver damage, cancer, pulmonary disease, malnutrition, hypertension, and birth defects.) Hispanics reported a higher prevalence of heavy alcohol use, and African Americans were more likely to use crack cocaine and heroin in their lifetime. In the Monitoring the Future surveys (O'Malley et al., 1995), compared with Whites and African Americans, Hispanic students report the highest use for all illicit drug categories and alcohol at eighth grade, but by the twelfth grade, Hispanics are highest only for cocaine, heroin, and steroids. Compared with adolescents of other American ethnic and racial groups, Native American adolescents are likely to use tobacco products, alcohol, and other drugs more frequently, and earlier, and with more serious health, social, and economic consequences (Schinke et al., 2000).

Exposure to licit substances, such as alcohol and tobacco, is also a major factor in abuse of both licit and illicit substances. In fact, numerous studies have demonstrated that there has been a reasonably consistent sequence of stages of drug involvement in North American and similar cultures over the last 30 years or so (Blaze-Temple & Lo, 1992; Fleming et al., 1989; Kandel, 1975). Generally the sequence begins with the use of more socially accepted substances like tobacco and beer, and is followed by an increased likelihood of using hard liquor and marijuana; for example, in one study less than 2 percent of middle school students reported trying marijuana without trying cigarettes first (Fleming et al., 1989). This stage then leads to an increased likelihood of using other illicit drugs such as cocaine, heroin, and LSD. (Note the use of the words "increased likelihood of using." These words should not be construed as meaning "a likelihood of using.") In other words, it is very rare in American culture for a person to start using hard liquor or marijuana without first using tobacco or beer, or other illicit drugs without first using marijuana or hard liquor.

The developmental processes of substance use are complex. Some abstainers progress to drug use, others remain abstinent, and still others shift from a pattern of use to nonuse (Coombs et al., 1986). Thus, escalation into more extensive patterns of drug use is not inevitable, nor is it always a gradual, progressive occurrence.

A number of hypotheses for predisposing factors in chronic drug use have emphasized personality characteristics, such as sensation- or novelty-seeking traits, extroversion and introversion, antisocial personality characteristics, anxiety, and other social motives. The most consistent finding is that many substance abusers exhibit a history of antisocial behavior (e.g., nonconformity, acting out, and impulsivity) and a high level of depression or low self-esteem (Marlatt et al., 1988). Another consistent observation is that high sensation seekers are much more likely to abuse all types of psychotropic drugs than low sensation seekers (Zuckerman, 1979).

There is considerable epidemiological and clinical evidence of high comorbidity (i.e., two or more disorders are observed in the same person) between drug dependence and psychiatric disorders, particularly depression. These findings have led to the hypothesis that for many abusers their drug use is a form of self-medication (Khantzian & Treece, 1985; Markou et al., 1998), although in many cases it is not clear whether these individuals' painful affective (mood or feeling) states existed prior to their drug abuse or came about as a consequence of their abuse. In support of this hypothesis, many (but not all) studies have shown that antidepressant drug treatment can significantly enhance the patients' mood as well as reduce their use of opiates, psychostimulants, alcohol, and nicotine (Cornelius et al., 2000; Markou et al., 1998). Further support for this hypothesis comes from family and twin studies (e.g., see page 159) that indicate that there are genetic links between depression and a variety of substance abuse disorders.

In addition to preexisting motivational variables associated with drug dependence, once drug taking begins, a number of physiological and conditioning factors enter into the process (Marlatt et al., 1988). If drug taking is shortly followed by the reinforcing effects of the drug, instrumental conditioning is involved and leads to drug seeking and further drug taking. Since drugs serve as unconditioned stimuli, the person's negative mood state or the environmental context in which one takes drugs can come to serve as conditioned stimuli for *conditioned drive states,* that is, drug craving (Childress et al., 1994; O'Brien et al., 1993). As discussed earlier in this chapter, conditioned responses that are compensatory to the drug-induced effects (that is, are opposite to the drug effects) may also occur. Thus, exposure to these environmental cues will potentially lead to drive states and withdrawal-like effects, which will further increase the desire to engage in drug-taking behavior (Stewart & Eikelboom, 1987). Furthermore, if the drug is capable of inducing pharmacodynamic physical dependence, it can create a physiological drive state most conducive to continuing drug-taking behavior. Once this condition has been created, secondary psychological dependence may be an additional motive for drug taking.

Perhaps a few examples will enhance your appreciation of the potency of these conditioning factors in drug dependence. It has long been recognized that individuals who self-administer drugs are more likely to abuse them than are passive recipients of drugs. For example, doctors who administer narcotics to themselves show a much higher incidence of narcotic abuse than do their patients, to whom narcotics are administered (Leavitt, 1982). Because there are many reasons why this result might occur (for example, doctors have easy access to pharmaceutical-grade narcotics), we cannot say for sure that it is the act of self-administering the drug that is the primary factor in this differential abuse rate.

Studies with rats have shown that they are more likely to exhibit signs of withdrawal following a few days of alcohol exposure if they have previously been administered alcohol chronically and have undergone withdrawal. That is, rats that have not previously experienced withdrawal will not exhibit withdrawal signs following only a few days exposure to alcohol (Leavitt, 1982). In humans undergoing narcotic detoxification, the severity of withdrawal symptoms has often been shown to be more closely related to the patient's anxiety and degree of expected distress than to the amount of narcotic used or the length of narcotic use (Phillips et al., 1986).

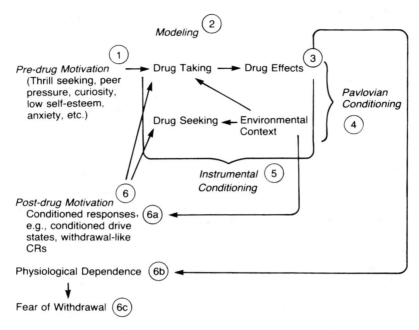

FIGURE 6–3 Summary of the basic steps and factors involved in the drug-dependence process.

In clinical studies with drug abusers, stimuli that are predictive of drug availability increase self-reports of craving and the motivation to consume drugs and have been shown to increase drug-seeking and self-administration of drugs (O'Brien et al., 1992). A *conditioned withdrawal* phenomenon has been established in the laboratory with patient volunteers maintained on a methadone regimen by pairing naloxone, a drug (UCS) that induces withdrawal (UCR) in opiate addicts, with a novel stimulus (CS). Upon injecting a placebo instead of naloxone (the injection procedure is the CS), the resulting CRs resembled the withdrawal UCRs. Similar behavioral withdrawal and subjective craving responses (a CR similar to, but not identical to, the withdrawal-type CR) have been shown to occur in abstinent narcotic users watching videotapes of themselves or others administering drugs or seeing other drug-related stimuli (Childress et al., 1986a, 1986b). Furthermore, this cue reactivity in opiate-addicted subjects has been shown to persist as long as 12 months after intensive inpatient treatment (Franken et al., 1999).

These are just a few examples indicating the power of conditioning processes, both instrumental and Pavlovian, in the development of drug dependence. Figure 6–3 summarizes the involvement of these processes in drug-taking behavior in terms of the following steps:

1. Predisposing factors motivate the individual to try a drug.
2. With drug availability, drug-taking behavior is initially modeled after drug-taking behavior in parents, peers, and so forth.

3. The individual experiences primary reinforcing and physiological effects of the drug.

4. Pairing of the environmental context with drug effects constitutes a Pavlovian conditioning trial.

5. Drug-taking behavior is followed by primary (or secondary) reinforcing effects of the drug in the environmental context, which constitutes instrumental conditioning.

6. Postdrug motivational states induced through Pavlovian processes (6a), or because continued exposure to drug effects results in physiological dependence (6b) and fear of undergoing withdrawal (6c), leads to further drug-seeking and drug-taking.

Note that genetic predispositions may interact or be involved in most, if not all, of the steps.

A number of lessons can be gained from all of this. First of all, there are many predisposing factors leading to initial drug use. Second, once drug-taking begins, there are many additional factors that can lead to the maintenance of drug-taking behavior. Third, conditioned withdrawal-type effects can often be confused with pharmacodynamic withdrawal effects. Fourth, although there has long been a concern that physical dependence is a factor in the maintenance of drug-taking behavior, it may be a relatively minor aspect in the maintenance of an addict's habit. Therefore, methods that simply focus on the control of physiological withdrawal are not going to work in the long run (Schuster & Johanson, 1981).

General Factors in Treatment for Drug Dependency

The first step in the treatment for drug dependency involves recognizing that a person's drug use is a problem. This recognition is not always easy to make. Once dependence processes begin with drug use, they almost always lead to numerous detrimental consequences for the user, the user's significant others, and, potentially, society in general. (Some specific consequences of drug dependency will be discussed more fully in subsequent chapters.) One would think that these consequences would be recognized by the users, or their friends and family, and would be sufficient reason to get the users to stop or at least seek help. However, two psychological processes generally prevent these things from happening: *denial* and *enabling.*

One of the symptoms of alcoholism and other chemical dependencies is *denial,* a defense mechanism that prevents users from consciously recognizing that they have a problem. Others may see the problem, but the users cannot. Perhaps at some level the users know their drug use is a problem, but they make excuses, minimize the magnitude of the problem, and blame others for their unpleasant feelings instead of blaming their relationship with mood-altering chemicals.

On the other hand, many of us do well-meaning things for our drug-dependent friends that actually encourage their drug use. Doing such things is called *enabling,* since it enables drug use to continue. We allow them to keep denying their problem whenever we do anything to help them escape the harmful consequences of their drug use. We do it out of love or concern, but it only makes things worse. We enable when we lie or make excuses for them to friends or employers, lend them money after they have spent their own on drugs, deny that they have a compulsive disorder, drink or take other drugs along with them, stop talking about their drug use because they become angry when we do so, or join them in blaming others for their own bad feelings. In short, any action we take to rescue them from the harmful consequences of their drug use is enabling. It sounds irrational, but when we take away their discomfort, we take away the only thing that might help them see that they are in trouble.

Therefore, the two essential keys to any effective treatment for drug abuse and dependence are these: (1) The person must recognize or be convinced that his or her drug use is a problem; and (2) he or she must have the incentive to change. These statements do not mean that these two conditions must be met before treatment can begin. In most cases, even voluntary patients submit themselves to treatment initially only because of strong social pressure or external coercion; their primary goal is to convince everyone (including themselves) that they do not have a problem (Cummings, 1979).

In fact, treatment outcome studies strongly suggest that coercion may be fundamental to addiction treatment and the achievement of favorable outcomes from therapeutic interventions (Miller & Flaherty, 2000). Often drug abusers must feel, face, or experience the "consequences" of their drug use before the denial of their problem can be penetrated and motivation for treatment can develop. Typically, coercion involves giving the drug abuser the choice between an opportunity to comply with treatment or an opportunity to receive the "alternative consequences," which could include such things as loss or receipt of employment or benefits, incarceration or probation (if he or she has engaged in drug-related criminal activity), if compliance with treatment is not met. Several lines of evidence suggest that coercion can be a therapeutic step in initiating treatment interventions and facilitating long-term recovery from abuse and dependence. If applied therapeutically, it can result in improved psychosocial status for patients; can reduce costs from criminal, health, and employment consequences; and can reduce illegal drug use or the criminal activity engendered by their drug use. Research indicates that coercion may be effective in the majority of individuals with drug abuse disorders.

Any treatment program for addiction will probably have to deal with the predisposing psychological and sociological factors that originally led to drug taking. (This can be a very difficult task when dealing with a person who has a poor self-image, has labeled himself or herself as a drug user, has a history of deviance, comes from a broken home, or has few education-related skills.) Strategies that empirical research has suggested may be helpful are discussed in Chapter 8 with respect to the treatment of alcoholism (the area in which the bulk of research on treatment effectiveness has been conducted). Most of these strategies are applicable to the treatment of other types of drug abuse and dependence.

To deal with cue-dependent cravings that may lead to relapse, a treatment program might include permanently removing the addict from drug-associated environmental stimuli. However, because this approach would rarely be feasible for most people, a more practical approach would be to expose the addict to the original drug-taking environment without allowing him or her to experience the rewarding effects of the drug so that the conditioned craving can be extinguished (O'Brien et al., 1993). Such a program could involve therapy sessions in which patients listen to audiotapes and watch videos of drug deals, handle drug paraphernalia, and look at or handle anything else that triggers their craving for the drug. It has been suggested that the extinction procedure should resemble actual drug-taking conditions as closely as possible, even to the extent of providing the real possibility of consuming the drug one is dependent on, in order to elicit conditioned reactions that can then be adequately extinguished (Corty et al., 1988). (Unfortunately, Pavlov demonstrated many years ago that even with extensive extinction training, the spontaneous recovery of CRs can occur with the simple passage of time.) Since cue reactivity (i.e., the intensity of the CR) has been suggested to be greater in drug-dependent persons when they are in a negative mood, and such individuals commonly report negative mood states as the most frequent initiator of relapse, exposure to negative emotional cues has sometimes been added to cue exposure therapy (Bradizza et al., 1999). However, there is no clear evidence that negative mood (using procedures that can temporarily induce such moods) alters cue reactivity in drug-dependent persons (Jansma et al., 2000; Robbins et al., 2000).

As will be discussed in subsequent chapters, a number of drugs have been or are being used as adjuncts to the treatment of drug abuse/dependence. Some drugs may be helpful because they reduce the negative affective states that may be a motivational factor underlying the person's drug-taking (for example, antidepressants). Drug substitutes—drugs with similar pharmacological properties as the drug(s) of abuse but with less toxic effects—may also be employed, either for detoxification during withdrawal (for example, benzodiazepines for alcohol withdrawal) or for maintenance purposes. In the latter instance, the drug may simultaneously reduce the craving for the original drug(s) as well as reduce their rewarding properties because of cross-tolerance (for instance, methadone for heroin addiction). Other drugs may serve as pure drug antagonists, which simply block the rewarding effects of the abused drug (for example, naltrexone for heroin addiction). Alternatively, drugs may be used that result in aversive bodily reactions whenever the addict takes the drug of abuse (for example, disulfiram in the treatment of alcoholism).

The ideal drug for this type of treatment would have the following characteristics (in order of importance): (1) possess significantly less toxicity and/or side effects than the drug of abuse; (2) inhibit craving for the abused drug; (3) provide an unsurmountable blockade of the effects of the abused drug; (4) block the effects of all drugs of abuse; (5) be long lasting; and (6) be orally effective. Obviously, the first characteristic is extremely important; a treatment that is more toxic than the drug you're trying to get the person to stop abusing is counterproductive. A drug with the second characteristic would be very valuable because it would eliminate much of the motivation to use the drug of abuse in the first place. Characteristic 3 is important because you want to prevent the rewarding effects of the abused drug as well as prevent the person from attempting to override the blockade with very high doses of the drug that may be toxic. Characteristic 4 is important because in many cases abusers of one drug also abuse other drugs or if prevented from using one drug will substitute another type of abused drug. Finally, drugs that are long lasting and are orally effective are preferable for the sake of convenience and cost of treatment and for keeping the drug abuser in the treatment program.

It has been suggested that drugs with NMDA antagonist properties may fit many of these characteristics. Since several lines of evidence suggest that NMDA receptors mediate the common adaptive processes that are involved in the development, maintenance, and expression of addiction to a wide variety of drugs, it has been proposed that NMDA antagonists may have multiple functions in treating addictions. These include the attenuation of withdrawal, the normalization of the mood changes following initiation of abstinence, and an attenuation of conditioned responses arising from drug-related stimuli (Bisaga & Popik, 2000). A variety of compounds with NMDA antagonistic actions (e.g., dextromethorphan, amantadine, memantine, ibogaine, acamprosate, and lamotragine) have been or are being tested in drug-dependent persons, but none has yet produced more than modest benefits, and some of these may exert potentially adverse reactions that would severely limit their use.

Numerous therapeutic interventions have been attempted in order to deal with drug addiction. All of them appear to work some of the time with some individuals. Often the efficacy of a technique depends on what stage of change the drug abuser is in: "precontemplation" (the person does not perceive that he or she has a problem or needs help and is not considering a change); "contemplation" (the person perceives that he or she may have a problem and partially wants to change and partially does not); "preparation" (the person finally recognizes a change is needed); "action" (the person chooses a strategy for change and pursues it); and "maintenance" (the person attempts to maintain the gains he or she has made and keep from relapsing) (Prochaska et al., 1992; Velicer et al., 1995).

No single technique works for the majority of individuals, perhaps because their efficacy is contingent upon the patient's voluntary participation in the treatment. Furthermore, even when treatment appears successful, relapse is common. However, the likelihood of relapse is reduced when the drug user (1) is under compulsory supervision or experiences a consistent aversive reaction related to drinking or other drug use (e.g., use of disulfiram or suffering from a painful ulcer); (2) finds a substitute dependency to compete with drug use (e.g., meditation, compulsive gambling, overeating, running); (3) obtains new social supports (e.g., a grateful employer or new significant other); or (4) becomes a member of an inspirational group (e.g., a religious group, Alcoholics Anonymous, Narcotics Anonymous) (Vaillant, 1988).

Relapse prevention may be enhanced by teaching addicts how to (1) anticipate, identify, and manage high-risk situations that may lead to relapse; (2) cope effectively if (or, more likely, when) relapse occurs to minimize its negative consequences and maximize learning from the experience; and (3) reduce global health risks and replace lifestyle imbalance with balance and moderation (Brownell et al., 1986; Dimeff & Marlatt, 1995).

The bottom line is—based on the criteria of reduction in substance use, improvement in personal health and social function, and reduction in public health and safety risks—treatment for drug abuse has been shown to be effective, especially when compared to alternatives such as no treatment or incarceration (Miller & Flaherty, 2000). For example, in one extensive study conducted in California, in which treatment effectiveness was assessed in randomly selected drug abusers who participated in four types of treatment programs (residential, residential "social model," outpatient, and outpatient methadone), it was determined that, on the average, for every one dollar of treatment costs, the state saved at least seven dollars in other medical and social costs (Gerstein et al., 1994).

State-Dependent Learning

The phenomenon to be described in this section is normally discussed in the context of how drugs may influence learning and memory. However, because it can have a profound influence on the maintenance of drug-taking behavior, it seems appropriate to discuss it here in the context of drug dependence. Approximately 30 years ago, some studies were performed in which animals learned tasks under one set of drug conditions and then were tested for their retention of the behavior under another set of drug conditions. The results indicated that the animals did not perform the tasks during the test as well as they would have if the retention test had been conducted under the same drug conditions as those present during the learning phase. This was found to be the case whether a drug was present during the acquisition phase and a nondrug condition was present during the retention phase, or vice versa. In other words, if learning was accomplished under nondrug conditions, retention was best under nondrug conditions; and if learning was accomplished under a drug, retention was best when the drug was present. The phenomenon was noted to occur with a wide variety of drugs and tasks, and it was found to occur in humans (Horton & Mills, 1984). It became known as **state-dependent learning** (also known as **drug-dissociative learning** or **drug-state learning**). In essence, it can be defined as learning under one set of drug (or nondrug) conditions that does not completely transfer to another set of drug conditions.

The usual explanation for the phenomenon is that certain cues—in this case, drug-related cues (perhaps internally produced)—present during the acquisition of information or behaviors become associated with the information or behaviors. Therefore, in order to successfully retrieve that information or perform that behavior during retention, those cues must be present. The more the context cues change between learning and retention, the greater the difficulty in exhibiting the information or behavior.

It should not be difficult now to see how state-dependent learning can become a factor in the continuation of drug-taking behavior. That is, if a person is exposed to a drug on a number of occasions, he (or she) is bound to acquire some new strategies or skills for dealing with the world. If the person then tries to perform those skills at a later time without the drug, he may experience difficulty in doing so and feel that he must be under the influence of the drug in order to perform appropriately. This experience starts a vicious cycle in which the more the person engages in the behavior under the drug's influence, the more likely he will be to feel the need to administer the drug in order to perform the behavior. For example, there are many anecdotal reports of alcoholic writers who have discovered that they are no longer able to write while sober, in spite of the fact that we generally expect people to think and write better without alcohol (particularly large doses). Thus, in order to maintain their success as writers, they continue to expose themselves to a chemical that will eventually lead to a great deal of psychological, neurological, and physiological damage.

State-dependent learning may also play a role in the potential benefits of psychotherapy in a patient who is also taking psychotropic medications. That is, patients may develop new coping strategies during therapy that may be lost or diminished when the patients' drug state changes or they go off their medication. A patient may feel that the therapy was a failure or may become dependent on the medication. Therapists should be aware of this possibility.

Websites for Further Information

Information on the concept of homeostasis as it relates to drug tolerance and dependence:

> http://www.augsburg.edu/psych/psy355/homeostasis.html

The National Institute for Drug Abuse criteria for substance-dependence diagnosis:

> http://www.nida.nih.gov/DSR.html

Site providing news on substance abuse issues:

> http://www.jointogether.org/

Web of Addictions (information on a multitude of aspects of drugs, their use and abuse):

> http://www.well.com/user/woa/

Bibliography

Baker, T. B., & Tiffany, S. T. (1985). Morphine tolerance as habituation. *Psychological Review, 92,* 78–108.

Bierut, L. J., Rice, J. P., Edenberg, H. J., et al. (2000). Family-based study of the association of the dopamine D2 receptor gene (DRD2) with habitual smoking. *American Journal of Medical Genetics, 90,* 299–302.

Bisaga, A., & Popik, P. (2000). In search of a new pharmacological treatment for drug and alcohol addiction: N-methyl-D-aspartate (NMDA) antagonists. *Drug and Alcohol Dependence, 59,* 1–15.

Blaze-Temple, D., & Lo, S. K. (1992). Stages of drug use: A community survey of Perth teenagers. *British Journal of Addiction, 87,* 215–225.

Bradizza, C. M., Gulliver, S. B., Stasiewicz, P. R., et al. (1999). Alcohol cue reactivity and private self-consciousness among male alcoholics. *Addictive Behaviors, 24,* 543–549.

Brecher, E. M. (Ed.). (1972). *Licit and illicit drugs.* Boston: Little, Brown.

Brownell, K. D., Marlatt, G. A., Lichtenstein, E., & Wilson, G. T. (1986). Understanding and preventing relapse. *American Psychologist, 41,* 765–781.

Carrera, M. R., Ashley, J. A., Parsons, L. H., et al. (1995). Suppression of psychoactive effects of cocaine by active immunization. *Nature, 378,* 727–730.

Childress, A. R., Ehrman, R., McLellan, A. T., et al. (1994). Can induced moods trigger drug-related responses in opiate abuse patients? *Journal of Substance Abuse Treatment, 11,* 17–23.

Childress, A. R., McLellan, T., & O'Brien, C. P. (1986a). Abstinent opiate abusers exhibit conditioned craving, conditioned withdrawal and reductions in both through extinction. *British Journal of Addiction, 81,* 655–660.

Childress, A. R., McLellan, T., & O'Brien, C. P. (1986b). Conditioned responses in a methadone population. *Journal of Substance Abuse Treatment, 3,* 173–179.

Chin, J. H., & Goldstein, D. B. (1977). Drug tolerance in biomembranes: A spin label study of the effects of ethanol. *Science, 196,* 684–685.

Clayton, R. R., & Voss, H. L. (1981). *Young men and drugs in Manhattan: A causal analysis* (NIDA Research Monograph No. 39). Rockville, MD: National Institute on Drug Abuse, Department of Health and Human Services.

Cochin, J. (1970). Possible mechanisms in development of tolerance. *Federation Proceedings, 29,* 19–27.

Coombs, R. H., Fawzy, F. I., & Gerber, B. I. (1986). Patterns of cigarette, alcohol, and other drug use among children and adolescents: A longitudinal study. *International Journal of the Addictions, 21,* 897–913.

Cooper, M. L. (1994). Motivations for alcohol use among adolescents: Development and validation of a four-factor model. *Psychological Assessment, 6,* 117–128.

Cornelius, J. R., Salloum, I. M., Haskett, R. F., et al. (2000). Fluoxetine versus placebo in depressed alcoholics: A 1-year follow-up study. *Addictive Behaviors, 25,* 307–310.

Cornish, J. L., Duffy, P., & Kalivas, P. W. (1999). A role for nucleus accumbens glutamate transmission in the relapse to cocaine-seeking behavior. *Neuroscience, 93,* 1359–1367.

Corty, E., O'Brien, C. P., & Mann, S. (1988). Reactivity to alcohol stimuli in alcoholics: Is there a role for temptation? *Drug and Alcohol Dependence, 21,* 29–36.

Crabbe, J. C., Belknap, J. K., & Buck, K. J. (1994). Genetic animal models of alcohol and drug abuse. *Science, 264,* 1715–1723.

Cummings, N. (1979). Turning bread into stones. *American Psychologist, 34,* 1119–1129.

Dahchour, A., & De Witte, P. (2000). Ethanol and amino acids in the central nervous system: Assessment of the pharmacological actions of acamprosate. *Progress in Neurobiology, 60,* 343–362.

Dimeff, L. A., & Marlatt, G. A. (1995). Relapse prevention. In R. K. Hester & W. R. Miller (Eds.), *Handbook of alcoholism treatment approaches* (pp. 176–194). Boston: Allyn and Bacon.

Edenberg, H. J., Foroud, T. Koller, D. L., et al. (1998). A family-based analysis of the association of the dopamine D2 receptor (DRD2) with alcoholism. *Alcoholism, Clinical and Experimental Research, 22,* 505–512.

Feingold, A., & Rounsaville, B. (1995). Construct validity of the abuse-dependence distinction as measured by DSM-IV criteria for different psychoactive substances. *Drug & Alcohol Dependence, 39,* 99–109.

Ferraro, D. P. (1976). A behavioral model of marihuana tolerance. In M. C. Braude & S. Szara (Eds.), *The phar-*

macology of marihuana tolerance (pp. 475–486). New York: Raven Press.

Fleming, R., Leventhal, H., Glynn, K., & Ershler, J. (1989). The role of cigarettes in the initiation and progression of early substance use. *Addictive Behaviors, 14,* 261–272.

Franken, I. H., De Haan, H. A., Haffmans, P. M., et al. (1999). Cue reactivity and effects of cue exposure in abstinent posttreatment drug users. *Journal of Substance Abuse Treatment, 16,* 81–85.

Gardner, E. L., & Lowinson, J. H. (1991). Marijuana's interaction with brain reward systems: Update 1991. *Pharmacology Biochemistry & Behavior, 40,* 571–580.

Gerstein, D. R., Johnson, R. A., Harwood, H., et al. (1994). *Evaluating recovery services, the California Drug and Alcohol Treatment Assessment (CALDATA).* Sacramento: State of California Department of Drug and Alcohol Programs.

Gold, M. S., & Dackis, C. A. (1984). New insights and treatments: Opiate withdrawal and cocaine addiction. *Clinical Therapeutics, 7,* 6–21.

Gorsuch, R. L. (1988). Psychology of religion. *Annual Review of Psychology, 39,* 201–221.

Grant, S., London, E. D., Newlin, D. B., et al. (1996). Activation of memory circuits during cue-elicited cocaine craving. *Proceedings of the National Academy of Sciences of the United States, 93,* 12040–12045.

Gray, J. A., Young, A. M. J., & Joseph, M. H. (1997). Dopamine's role. *Science, 278,* 1548–1549.

Grilly, D. M., & Gowans, G. C. (1986). Acute morphine dependence: Effects observed in shock and light discrimination tasks. *Psychopharmacology, 88,* 500–504.

Harris, L. S. (Ed.). (1980). *Problems of drug dependence, 1980.* Rockville, MD: National Institute on Drug Abuse.

Harris, L. S. (Ed.). (1981). *Problems of drug dependence, 1981.* Rockville, MD: National Institute on Drug Abuse.

Hinson, R. E., & Siegel, S. (1982). Nonpharmacological bases of drug tolerance and dependence. *Journal of Psychosomatic Research, 26,* 495–503.

Holland, P. C. (1984). Origins of behavior in Pavlovian conditioning. *The Psychology of Learning and Motivation, 18,* 129–173.

Hollis, K. L. (1984). The biological function of Pavlovian conditioning: The best defense is a good offense. *Journal of Experimental Psychology: Animal Behavior Processes, 10,* 413–425.

Hollister, L. E. (1987). Postmarketing surveillance of psychotherapeutic drugs: Concluding comments. *Psychopharmacology Bulletin, 23,* 405–406.

Horton, D. L., & Mills, C. B. (1984). Human learning and memory. *Annual Review of Psychology, 35,* 361–394.

Jansma, A. Breteler. M. H. M., Schippers, G. M., et al. (2000). No effect of negative mood on the alcohol cue reactivity on in-patient alcoholics. *Addictive Behaviors, 25,* 619–624.

Kandel, D. (1975). Stages in adolescent involvement in drug use. *Science, 190,* 912–914.

Kesner, R. P., & Cook, D. G. (1983). Role of habituation and classical conditioning in the development of morphine tolerance. *Behavioral Neuroscience, 97,* 4–12.

Khantzian, E. J., & Treece, C. (1985). DSM-III psychiatric diagnosis of narcotic addicts. *Archives of General Psychiatry, 42,* 1067–1071.

Koob, G. F. (1996). Drug addiction: The yin and yang of hedonic homeostasis. *Neuron, 16,* 893–896.

Leavitt, F. (1982). *Drugs and behavior.* New York: John Wiley & Sons.

Lefkowitz, R. J., Kobilka, B. K., & Caron, M. G. (1989). The new biology of drug receptors. *Biochemical Pharmacology, 38,* 2941–2951.

Lennartz, R. C., & Weinberger, N. M. (1992). Analysis of response systems in Pavlovian conditioning reveals rapidly versus slowly acquired conditioned responses: Support for two factors, implications for behavior and neurobiology. *Psychobiology, 20,* 93–119.

Ma, G. X., & Shive, S. (2000). A comparative analysis of perceived risks and substance abuse among ethnic groups. *Addictive Behaviors, 25,* 361–371.

Macenski, M. J., & Meisch, R. A. (1994). Oral drug reinforcement studies with laboratory animals: Applications and implications for understanding drug-reinforced behavior. *Current Directions in Psychological Science, 1,* 22–27.

Mahan, L. C., McKernan, R. M., & Insel, P. A. (1987). Metabolism of alpha- and beta-adrenergic receptors in vitro and in vivo. *Annual Review of Pharmacology and Toxicology, 27,* 215–235.

Markou, A., Kosten, T. R., & Koob, G. F. (1998). Neurobiological similarities in depression and drug dependence: A self-medication hypothesis. *Neuropsychopharmacology, 18,* 135–174.

Marlatt, G. A., Baer, J. S., Donovan, D. M., & Kivlahan, D. R. (1988). Addictive behaviors: Etiology and treatment. *Annual Review of Psychology, 39,* 223–252.

Miller, N. S., & Flaherty, J. A. (2000). Effectiveness of coerced addiction treatment (alternative consequences). A review of the clinical research. *Journal of Substance Abuse Treatment, 18,* 9–16.

Motzo, C., Porceddu, M. L., Dazzi, L., et al. (1997). Enhancement by flumazenil of dopamine release in the nucleus accumbens of rats repeatedly exposed to diazepam or imidazenil. *Psychopharmacology, 131,* 34–39.

Nathanson, N. M. (1987). Molecular properties of the muscarinic acetylcholine receptor. *Annual Review of Neuroscience, 10,* 195–236.

Nestler, E. J. (1996). Under siege: The brain on opiates. *Neuron, 16,* 897–900.

Newcomb, M. D., & Bentler, P. M. (1989). Substance use and abuse among children and teenagers. *American Psychologist, 44,* 242–248.

Noble, E. P. (1998a). DRD2 gene and alcoholism. *Science, 281,* 1287–1288.

Noble, E. P. (1998b). The D2 dopamine receptor gene: A review of association studies in alcoholism and phenotypes. *Alcohol, 16,* 33–45.

O'Brien, C. P. (1996). Drug addiction on drug abuse. In A. G. Gilman, L. S. Goodman, J. G. Hardman, L. E. Limbard, P. B. Molinoff, & R. W. Ruddon (Eds.), *The pharmacological basis of therapeutics* (pp. 557–577). New York: McGraw-Hill.

O'Brien, C. P., Childress, A. R., McLellan, A. T., & Ehrman, R. (1993). Developing treatments that address classical conditioning. *NIDA Research Monograph, 135,* 71–91.

O'Brien, C. P., Childress, A. R., McLellan, A. T., et al. (1992). Classical conditioning in drug-dependent humans. *Annals of the New York Academy of Sciences, 654,* 401–414.

Okamoto, M., Rao, S., & Walewske, J. L. (1986). Effect of dosing frequency on the development of physical dependence and tolerance to pentobarbital. *Journal of Pharmacology and Experimental Therapeutics, 238,* 1004–1008.

Olds, J., & Milner, P. (1954). Positive reinforcement produced by electrical stimulation of septal area and other regions of rat brain. *Journal of Comparative and Physiological Psychology, 47,* 419–427.

O'Malley, P. M., Johnston, L. D., & Bachman, J. G. (1995). Adolescent substance abuse: Epidemiology and implications for public policy. *Substance Abuse, 42,* 241–260.

Phillips, G. T., Gossop, M., & Bradley, B. (1986). The influence of psychological factors on the opiate withdrawal syndrome. *British Journal of Psychiatry, 149,* 235–238.

Prochaska, J. O., DiClemente, C. C., & Norcross, J. C. (1992). In search of how people change. Applications to addictive behaviors. *American Psychologist, 47,* 1102–1114.

Robbins, S. J., Ehrman, R. N., Childress, A. R., et al. (2000). Mood state and recent cocaine use are not associated with levels of cocaine cue reactivity. *Drug and Alcohol Dependence, 59,* 33–42.

Rosen, O. M. (1987). After insulin binds. *Science, 237,* 1452–1458.

Ross, E. M. (1996). Pharmacodynamics: Mechanisms of drug action and the relationship between drug concentration and effect. In A. G. Gilman, L. S. Goodman, J. G. Hardman, L. E. Limbird, P. B. Molinoff, & R. W. Ruddon (Eds.), *The pharmacological basis of therapeutics* (pp. 29–41). New York: McGraw-Hill.

Rothman, R. B. (1992). A review of the role of anti-opioid peptides in morphine tolerance and dependence. *Synapse, 12,* 129–138.

Schinke, S. P., Tepavac, L., & Cole, K. C. (2000). Preventing substance use among Native American youth: Three-year results. *Addictive Behaviors, 25,* 387–397.

Schuster, C. R., & Johanson, C. E. (1981). An analysis of drug-seeking behavior in animals. *Neuroscience and Biobehavioral Reviews, 5,* 315–324.

Sdao-Jarvie, K., & Vogel-Sprott, M. (1986). Mental rehearsal of a task before or after ethanol: Tolerance facilitating effects. *Drug and Alcohol Dependence, 18,* 23–30.

Self, D. W., & Nestler, E. J. (1995). Molecular mechanisms of drug reinforcement and addiction. *Annual Review of Neuroscience, 18,* 463–495.

Simons, J., Correia, C. J., & Carey, K. B. (2000). A comparison of motives for marijuana and alcohol use among experienced users. *Addictive Behaviors, 25,* 153–160.

Shadel, W. G., Shiffman, S., Niaura, R., et al. (2000). Current models of nicotine dependence: What is known and what is needed to advance understanding of tobacco etiology among youth. *Drug and Alcohol Dependence, 59,* S9–S21.

Sobrero, A. P., & Bouton, M. E. (1989). Effects of stimuli present during oral morphine administration on withdrawal and subsequent consumption. *Psychobiology, 17,* 179–190.

Sokolowski, J. D., Conlan, A. N., & Salamone, J. D. (1998). A microdialysis study of nucleus accumbens core and shell dopamine during operant responding in the rat. *Neuroscience, 86,* 1001–1009.

Stewart, J., & Eikelboom, R. (1987). Conditioned drug effects. In L. L. Iversen, S. D. Iversen, & S. H. Snyder (Eds.), *Handbook of psychopharmacology* (Vol. 19, pp. 1–57). New York: Plenum Press.

Thompson, T., & Johanson, C. E. (Eds.). (1981). *Behavioral pharmacology of human drug dependence.* Rockville, MD: National Institute on Drug Abuse.

Tiffany, S. T., Petrie, E. C., Baker, T. B., & Dahl, J. L. (1983). Conditioned morphine tolerance in the rat: Absence of a compensatory response and cross-tolerance with stress. *Behavioral Neuroscience, 97,* 335–353.

Vaillant, G. E. (1988). What can long-term follow-up teach us about relapse and prevention of relapse in addiction? *British Journal of Addiction, 83,* 1147–1157.

Vanyukov, M. M., & Tarter, R. E. (2000). Genetic studies of substance abuse. *Drug and Alcohol Dependence, 59,* 101–123.

Velicer, W. F., Hughes, S. L., Fava, J. L., et al. (1995). An empirical typology of subjects within stage of change. *Addictive Behaviors, 20,* 299–320.

Wickelgren, I. (1998). Teaching the brain to take drugs. *Science, 280,* 2045–2047.

Wise, R. A. (1998). Drug-activation of brain reward pathways. *Drug and Alcohol Dependence, 51,* 13–22.

Woods, J. H. (1978). Behavioral pharmacology of drug self-administration. In M. A. Lipton, A. DiMascio, & K. F. Killam (Eds.), *Psychopharmacology* (pp. 595–607). New York: Raven Press.

Wuster, M., Schulz, R., & Herz, A. (1985). Opioid tolerance and dependence: Re-evaluating the unitary hypothesis. *Trends in the Pharmacological Sciences, 6,* 64–67.

Zuckerman, M. (1979). *Sensation seeking: Beyond the optimal level of arousal.* Hillsdale, NJ: Erlbaum.

Chapter *7*

Psychotropic Drug Classification

Classifying drugs is no easy task, since in most cases no sharp distinctions can be made among them. Drugs with almost identical molecular structures may induce entirely different effects, while other drugs whose molecular structures are quite different may induce almost identical effects (Barden & Mason, 1977; Weissman & Milne, 1979). Some drugs may have one effect at one dose and an entirely different effect at another. A drug may have multiple psychological effects in a certain dose range, and depending on the population taking them (or the persons prescribing them), some of these effects may be viewed as desirable in one person and undesirable in another. For example, certain marijuana-like substances may effectively reduce nausea in cancer patients undergoing chemotherapy but may lead to an undesirable clouding of consciousness. In other groups of individuals, these "side effects" are the effects desired. Therefore, it is not surprising that different textbooks may classify drugs in a number of different ways.

Molecular Structure–Activity Relationships

One classification scheme that appears to be intuitively reasonable involves grouping drugs according to their chemical structure (Biel et al., 1978; Petracek, 1978). Although this scheme may often group together drugs that have very similar behavioral effects, in many cases what appear to be relatively minor changes in the molecular structure of a drug can considerably change its basic activity in the body.

Figure 7–1 displays the molecular structures of six different compounds. The first is simply the structure of one of the basic neurotransmitters, dopamine. The second structure is that of amphetamine. As will be described in Chapter 9, the actions of certain doses of amphetamine are very similar to the actions of dopamine. This similarity is not surprising, because amphetamine has several biochemical actions that essentially amplify dopamine's actions. One of amphetamine's biochemical actions is to temporarily inhibit the enzyme

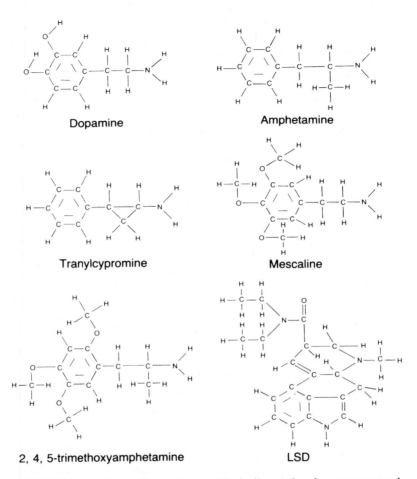

FIGURE 7–1   Examples of drugs with similar molecular structure and similar effects; similar structures and qualitatively different effects; and different structures but qualitatively similar effects.

monoamine oxidase (MAO). The third structure in Figure 7–1 is that of tranylcypromine, a drug with antidepressant properties. While its structure is quite similar to that of amphetamine, it is several thousand times more potent in its ability to inhibit MAO. The fourth structure is that of mescaline. Both mescaline and amphetamine have structural similarities, elevate mood in low doses, and are capable of inducing psychosis-mimicking effects, such as distortions in perceptions and, in some cases, hallucinations. However, the "psychosis" associated with mescaline is readily distinguishable from naturally occurring psychoses, whereas the "psychosis" induced by amphetamine is not. The fifth structure in Figure 7–1 is that of a drug with mescaline-like effects, but it is 10 to 100 times more potent than mescaline. The sixth structure is that of lysergic acid diethylamide (LSD). Although LSD is considerably more potent than mescaline, it is capable of inducing effects that are practically indistinguishable from those of mescaline. To summarize, in the first five relatively similar structures, we see actions that in some ways are quite similar and in other ways are quite dissimilar. We also see very similar actions in two drugs with very dissimilar structures.

There are many cases in which molecules that are identical except for their being mirror images of each other often have very different effects on the body. Such molecules are called *optical isomers* (or, more technically, *enantiomers*), which are commonly differentiated by the prefixes *levo* (or simply *l*, as in *l*-dopa) and *dextro* (or simply *d*, as in *d*-amphetamine) because the two forms in solution rotate plane-polarized light in different directions—to the left with the *levo* isomer and to the right with the *dextro* isomer. When the two isomers display differential receptor-binding properties (for instance, when one isomer binds and the other does not) and therefore induce different effects, they are said to be **stereospecific.**

Parts (a) and (b) of Figure 7–2 show skeleton molecular structures for the levo (active) and dextro (inactive) isomers of morphine. They are mirror images (isomers) of the morphine molecule; one produces analgesia, and the other does not. A slight modification of the active molecule produces the molecular structure shown in part (c), nalorphine, an antagonist of morphine. However, nalorphine still has some weak, narcotic-like effects. It has mixed agonist–antagonist properties. It is thought that when the chain attached to the nitrogen atom is in the "down" position, it acts as an antagonist, whereas when it swings around and "up"— indicated by the dashed lines—it acts as an agonist (note the similarity of the active morphine molecule in this position). Another modification of the active morphine molecule produces naloxone, shown in part (d), a narcotic antagonist without any narcotic action at all. It has only antagonist properties. In this case, the added OH group may prevent the chain attached to the nitrogen atom from swinging into an agonist conformation.

Thus, we see that slight modifications in a molecule can change it from an active molecule at its receptor into an inactive molecule, a mixed agonist–antagonist, or a "pure" antagonist. On the other hand, the structure shown in part (f) of the figure—that of the peptide leu-enkephalin—has actions very similar to those of morphine (e). Despite the dissimilarity of their molecular structures, studies have indicated that they do possess analogous regions that probably allow them to both bind to and activate opioid receptors (Barden & Mason, 1977). The peptide can be "twisted" so that critical components of the molecule necessary for receptor occupation correspond to analogous regions on the morphine molecule.

Despite the apparent inconsistencies between drug molecule structures and their activities in the nervous system, a great deal of progress has been made toward understanding structure–activity relationships (Pool, 1992). Biologists, using sophisticated molecular computer modeling programs and visualization software, can now easily create proteins on a computer screen and experiment with them—bringing other molecules up close to them and determining which drugs will fit best into their active sites. This capability is particularly valuable for pharmaceutical companies, whose drug designers can test thousands of potential drugs on a computer to find the most promising candidate for producing a specified effect.

Depressant versus Stimulant Classifications

Another way that many authors attempt to classify drugs is according to the activation dimension (Leavitt, 1982; Wallace & Fisher, 1999). In this context, drugs are often described

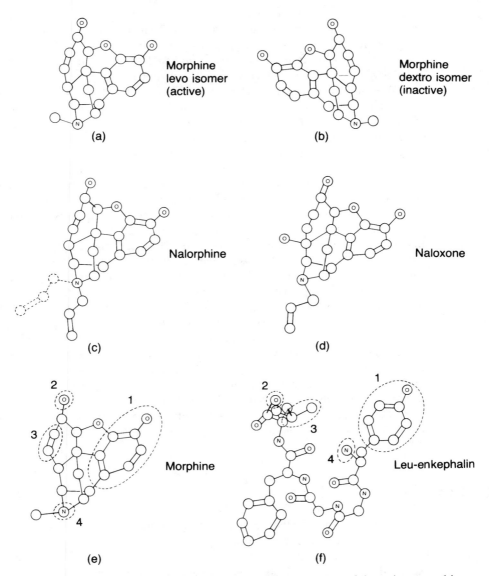

FIGURE 7–2   Skeleton molecular structures of the isomers of the opiate morphine, two opiate antagonists (one with opiate properties), and one of the enkephalins. (O = oxygen, N = nitrogen, unlabeled atoms are carbon, and hydrogen atoms are not shown.)

as (CNS) depressants or stimulants. Unfortunately, classifying drugs as stimulants or depressants can often be misleading. One might expect a depressant to decrease mood, motor activity, and the body's metabolic and physiological activities; reduce alertness and induce sleep; decrease brain activity and neurotransmitter turnover; and shift the EEG toward lower frequencies and higher amplitude waves (a physiological correlate of becoming less aroused). One might expect stimulants to do just the reverse. However, it is not that simple. As you will see in the upcoming chapters, drugs rarely do any of these things simultaneously. Thus, the terms *depressant* and *stimulant* do not mean much unless one specifies at which biological level the depression or stimulation is occurring, or the dose of the drug.

For example, a drug may stimulate the receptors of a particular set of neurons, but if these receptors allow the influx of negative ions and hyperpolarize the cells, the excitability of the neurons will decrease. Alternatively, the drug may increase the firing rate of one set of neurons or stimulate the release of a particular type of neurotransmitter. However, if the neurotransmitter released happens to be at inhibitory synapses, the drug, in effect, would decrease the excitability of the receiving cells, decrease their firing rate, and decrease the neurotransmitter they release. Conversely, a drug may depress a particular set of neurons in terms of their excitability and their rate of firing. However, if these neurons play an inhibitory role with respect to other neurons, the latter neurons' excitability may increase.

One may talk about a drug's depressant or stimulant role with respect to behavior or emotion, but, again, if one does not specify a particular set of behaviors or emotions and the dose of the drug, the terms *depressant* and *stimulant* impart little information. Although a drug may decrease the relative frequency of one set of behaviors, it may increase the relative frequency of other sets of behaviors. A drug at one dose may elevate mood, but at another dose it may depress mood. For example, alcohol and barbiturates (drugs commonly referred to as depressants) act as depressants biochemically, in that they decrease neurotransmitter turnover rate, and neuropharmacologically, in that they decrease the excitability of individual neurons. However, in low doses, these drugs increase the general activity and mood of many individuals. In high doses, a general suppression of activity and mood will probably occur. Amphetamine (a drug commonly referred to as a stimulant) increases the rate of firing of some neurons while simultaneously decreasing the rate of firing of others. It increases the production of some behaviors and reduces the frequency of others. Furthermore, behaviors that are increased at low doses of amphetamine may be depressed with much higher doses (see, for example, Figure 2–1).

Drug Use Classification

For these reasons, most authors (including this one) in this field prefer to classify drugs according to what they are predominantly used for (Leavitt, 1982; Usdin, 1978; Wallace & Fisher, 1999). Unfortunately, though, this system is far from perfect, because drugs may be used for different purposes in different doses and in different individuals. Nevertheless, in this textbook, drugs will be classified in this context. Before we begin, note that a single drug has several official names (Nies & Spielberg, 1996). Initially, when a pharmaceutical company discovers or synthesizes a promising new drug, it is given a **code name,** generally consisting of two or more letters and a series of numbers. Its **chemical name** provides a complete description of a particular molecule according to specific rules of organic chemistry. The **generic name** of the compound indicates its legal, official, or nonproprietary name, which is typically the official name cited in research reports on the drug. Once it has been approved for marketing, the drug will have a **brand** or **proprietary name,** given to it by its manufacturer.

So, for example, Prozac is the well-recognized brand name for the generic fluoxetine, which originally was given the code name Lilly 110140, which appeared in the early research publications describing its characteristics. It's pretty obvious why its chemical name, 3-(p-trifluoromethylphenoxy)-N-methyl-3-phenylpropyline, isn't used very often. After 17 years, when the patent on a compound runs out, anybody can market it, so it may then have several other brand names. Finally, if the drug is marketed illicitly or used recreationally, it may have a variety of "street" names. (For example, see the websites for street-drug slang terms at the end of this chapter.)

Because there may be a number of proprietary (brand) names for a single drug and because these may differ from country to country, the nonproprietary (generic) name for drugs will be used throughout this text. However, because most students reading this text are more likely to recognize various drugs by their brand names, along with their generic names, they will be referred to by their most common or initially used brand names the first time they are mentioned. Use of street names for drugs has generally been avoided because there are so many—as soon as one becomes popular, another is generated to take its place. For example, there are well over 100 different street names for heroin.

One of the most frequently used reference books that describes psychotropic drugs according to their medical uses is the *Physicians' Desk Reference* (PDR). Product descriptions in the PDR include lengthy explanations of the drugs' chemical structure, how they work, conditions for which they have been approved for use (but not necessarily those they may actually be used for), dosage, and administration. There are also warnings about possible adverse reactions or drug interactions, and indications as to whether a drug can be used in children, pregnant women, or nursing mothers. What it doesn't provide are drug prices and comparison information on which of several drugs in the same category may be most appropriate for a particular type of condition or set of symptoms.

Sedative–hypnotics (sometimes referred to as depressants) sedate, calm, or relax most individuals at low doses and, at somewhat higher doses, induce sleep in most individuals. It should be pointed out that the hypnotic effect of these drugs—sleep—is very different from the phenomena associated with hypnosis. The confusion comes about because it was once believed that hypnosis induced a sleeplike trance. However, we now know that hypnotized people are very much awake. Drugs included in the sedative–hypnotic category are ethyl alcohol (ethanol); barbiturates, such as secobarbital, phenobarbital, and pentobarbital; chloral hydrate; and numerous drugs with barbiturate-like effects, such as glutethimide (Doriden) and methaqualone (Quaalude). Many drugs in this class (for example, phenobarbital) are effective in reducing seizure activity and may be termed **anticonvulsants.** They may also be used as muscle relaxants, although muscle relaxation is secondary to their effects on the CNS.

Anxiolytics, or **antianxiety drugs,** are used in treating disorders where the prevailing symptom is anxiety—for instance, neuroses. The term *minor tranquilizers* is sometimes used to describe the drugs in this category. However, because these drugs are sometimes confused with the major tranquilizers (see the subsequent discussion of antipsychotics), and the word *minor* is often misinterpreted as meaning mild (it actually refers to the fact that these drugs are used to reduce less severe symptoms of psychological dysfunction), it is deemed an inappropriate term by many authors. Prior to the 1900s, several sedative–hypnotics were used to calm anxious and disturbed patients (for example, bromide, chloral hydrate, paraldehyde, urethan, and sulfonal). For the most part, these were replaced by the barbiturates in the early 1900s. Fewer than a dozen other sedatives were successfully marketed before 1960. The nonbarbiturate meprobamate (Miltown) was introduced as an antianxiety agent with great fanfare in 1955. However, over the past 35 years a class of drugs referred to as **benzodiaz-epines** has pretty much replaced all of these. Common examples of this class of drug would be chlordiazepoxide (Librium) and diazepam (Valium). Many of the drugs in this class may also be effective anticonvulsants. The properties of these drugs are quite similar to those of the sedative–hypnotics, except that the benzodiazepines don't have anesthetic properties and have a much higher therapeutic index.

The newest member of the anxiolytic category is buspirone (BuSpar). Its molecular structure is uniquely different from the rest of the anxiolytics. It also lacks their hypnotic, anticonvulsant, and muscle-relaxant properties. It does not appear to act synergistically with alcohol, and it is likely to possess a much lower potential for abuse and dependence than the sedative–hypnotics and other anxiolytics.

Psychostimulants (sometimes referred to as stimulants), in low to moderate doses, in-crease alertness, reduce fatigue, and elevate mood in most individuals. Drugs in this cate-gory include the amphetamines, cocaine, caffeine, and nicotine. Note that for drugs in this category, the use context is a recreational one, because these drugs are not presently medi-cally prescribed for these uses. In a medical context, some of these drugs may be used as appetite suppressants (**anoretics** or **anorectics**); others may be used in the treatment of *nar-colepsy* (a disorder in which the person has sudden, uncontrollable tendencies to sleep at irregular intervals, such as during the day) or the *attention deficit (hyperactivity) disorder.* In some very special cases, psychostimulants may be prescribed for mild depression.

Antipsychotics are drugs used in the treatment of major mental and emotional distur-bances (psychoses). Other authors often refer to these as major tranquilizers, because these drugs calm highly excited patients with schizophrenia or mania. However, the term may be inappropriate in certain cases; for instance, they may also enhance the social interactions and increase the activity of catatonic patients. The term may also lead to their being confused with the so-called minor tranquilizers, a class of drugs that differs greatly from antipsychotics. Therefore, most practitioners prefer not to refer to these drugs as major tranquilizers. Another term often used for these drugs is **neuroleptic.** However, since this term literally means a drug capable of inducing severe neurological symptoms (*lepsis* is Greek for seizing or taking), it is obviously inappropriate in the present classification context. Commonly used antipsychotics include chlorpromazine (Thorazine), thioridazine (Mellaril), clozapine (Clozaril), risperi-done (Risperdal), and haloperidol (Haldol). Reserpine (Serpasil), a drug that will be men-tioned in several contexts in this text, was one of the first of this category of drugs to be introduced, but it is no longer used in the treatment of psychotic disorders.

Humans normally exhibit wide variations in mood states, or *affective states,* as they are technically called. In some individuals, however, these are so chronic or become so extreme that the individuals become dysfunctional, and in some cases suicidal. In most of these in-dividuals, their exaggerated mood is predominantly one of depression, and such individuals are diagnosed as having a *unipolar disorder.* Others may exhibit depressed episodes at times; at other times, they may exhibit episodes of mania, characterized by frenzied psy-chomotor activity, excitement, a rapid passing or flight of ideas, exaltation, exaggerated confidence, and unstable attention. Such individuals are commonly diagnosed as having *manic depression* or a *bipolar disorder.* Drugs used to treat these affective disorders are commonly referred to as **antidepressants** and **mood stabilizers.**

Antidepressants are used in severe, unremitting cases of depression, generally for those depressions for which there appear to be no outstanding causal events. Classic examples of these drugs are fluoxetine (Prozac), imipramine (Tofranil), amitriptyline (Elavil), tranylcypromine (Parnate), and phenelzine (Nardil). Although, as mentioned, the psychostimulants generally raise mood in normal individuals, psychostimulants have not proved to be useful in the treatment of depression (except for some very unusual cases) for several reasons to be discussed later.

Mood stabilizers are most useful in the treatment of manic symptoms, but they may also be useful in the treatment of other symptoms that appear to be only tangentially related to mood. The drug of choice is generally a lithium salt, such as lithium carbonate. An alternative to lithium is carbamazepine (Tegretol), which is more commonly prescribed for seizure disorders (epilepsy). These drugs are referred to as mood stabilizers because they are generally successful in decreasing rapid mood swings—from mania to depression. Although the antipsychotics are quite effective in reducing manic symptoms and are often used for the initial treatment of mania, they are generally not used for chronic treatment in affective disorders because of their potentially severe side effects.

Drugs taken specifically to severely distort one's perception of reality, disturb cognitive processes, or induce hallucinations are referred to by many names. They are most commonly called **hallucinogens** (for hallucination-generating), **psychotomimetics** (for psychosis-mimicking), or **psychedelics** (for mind-manifesting). However, as discussed in Chapter 11, none of these terms is entirely appropriate, in that most substances in this category do not produce the types of psychoses naturally found in humans, nor do they always produce true hallucinations. The third term has even less functional meaning than the other two; nobody really understands what the mind is, or what is meant by the term *manifested* when applied to the mind.

Although these types of drugs are presently used predominantly in a recreational context, some of them, such as LSD, have been used in medical contexts or are presently being used experimentally in medical contexts (for example, compounds related to those found in marijuana). Examples of these types of drugs are LSD, mescaline, psilocybin, phencyclidine (PCP), and cannabinoids (those compounds found in *Cannabis sativa,* more popularly known as marijuana). Anticholinergic compounds, including scopolamine and atropine, may also be included in this category, although several unpleasant characteristics of these latter drugs probably account for their infrequent recreational use.

A wide variety of psychotropic compounds used in the treatment of pain are called either **anesthetics** (without feeling) or **analgesics** (without pain). These include the narcotics (morphine, heroin, codeine, meperidine [Demerol], and methadone [Dolophine]); inhalants like ether and nitrous oxide; many of the sedative–hypnotics (generally given in large doses); cocaine (as a local anesthetic); and ketamine (Ketalar), a phencyclidine-like drug. Many of these drugs are also used recreationally, usually for purposes quite unrelated to medical treatment.

The fact that a drug may have many uses is of particular concern to those in the area of drug therapeutics. When a drug has been shown to be reasonably safe and effective for some specific symptoms, it is approved for medical use by the Food and Drug Administration

(FDA) and officially labeled (Kessler & Feiden, 1995). This labeling includes the information that appears both on the container the drug comes in and on the package insert. The FDA is legally responsible for ensuring that all statements made by the drug manufacturer in labeling the drug are backed by substantial evidence. The FDA has final approval over what the manufacturer may recommend the drug for and what it may say in its advertisements and marketing publications. The FDA also determines whether the drug must be obtained by prescription—generally the case with any new drug—or can be obtained over-the-counter without a prescription—which generally occurs after the drug has been used long enough and by enough people to determine that it has an acceptably low incidence of adverse reactions or significant side effects.

However, the FDA does not have any authority over the practice of medicine. There is no federal law prohibiting physicians from prescribing an approved drug for anything they choose, although some states place restrictions on what certain drugs can be prescribed for. As a result, many drugs that have been approved for specific symptoms or disorders are commonly prescribed for entirely different purposes (or unlabeled uses) than those stated by the manufacturer (Pugh & Pugh, 1987). For example, drugs approved for use in the treatment of cardiovascular disease (propranolol), high blood pressure (clonidine), nausea associated with cancer chemotherapy (metaclopramide), and depression and bed-wetting (imipramine) can also be found being prescribed for stage fright, morphine withdrawal, tardive dyskinesia (see Chapter 12), and chronic pain, respectively. However, because a new approved use of a drug by the FDA can enhance its marketability, pharmaceutical companies will sometimes undergo the clinical trials to obtain approval for that use—oftentimes with a new proprietary name. So, for example, fluoxetine, which originally was approved for use as an antidepressant (as Prozac), has been approved for the use in Premenstrual Dysphoric Disorder (as Serafem); buproprion, which originally was approved for use as an antidepressant (as Wellbutrin), has been approved for use in the treatment of tobacco addiction (as Zyban); and naltrexone, which was originally approved for use in the treatment of opiate addiction (as Trexan), has been approved for use in the treatment of alcoholism (as ReVia).

The primary problems with the use classification scheme are readily apparent.

1. A drug may be used for several widely disparate symptoms. For example, phenobarbital may be used as an anticonvulsant, a sedative, or a hypnotic. Certain antidepressants have been used in the treatment of a wide variety of conditions without a clear connection to depression—for example, obsessive–compulsive disorder, panic disorders, phobias, premenstrual tension, eating disorders, substance abuse, chronic pain, dementia, and a number of personality disorders (Boyer, 1992). Some anxiolytics appear to be as effective in the treatment of certain types of depression as antidepressants, and some antidepressants successfully alleviate a number of anxiety symptoms. Cannabis may be used recreationally to alter "consciousness," or medically to reduce nausea in cancer patients undergoing chemotherapy (in which case, the altered consciousness may be deemed an undesirable side effect).

2. Some drugs that would seem to have the ideal properties for alleviating certain symptoms do not work in the long run. For example, amphetamine, which enhances mood in normal individuals, does not usually do so in depressed individuals. Even if it did, it would likely worsen their depression shortly after the person stopped taking it, and it should not be used to treat depression.

3. In many cases, the qualitative effects of a drug are dependent upon dosage or on how long the drug has been taken. For these reasons, even authors who categorize drugs using the same basic rationale as that used in this text tend to have somewhat different classification schemes.

Schedule-Controlled Drugs

One final classification system is provided by the United States government. Ever since the Harrison Narcotic Act of 1914, the federal government has classified psychoactive drugs for legal purposes. The most recent of such drug classification schemes came out of the Controlled Substances Act of 1970, which was designed by the government to improve the administration and regulation of manufacturing, distributing, and dispensing of potentially dangerous drugs. The present branch of the government responsible for this task is the Drug Enforcement Administration (DEA).

The drugs that come under the jurisdiction of the Controlled Substances Act are divided into five schedules and are referred to as **controlled substances.** Schedule I drugs are those that have no currently accepted medical use in treatment in the United States, are presumed to have a high potential for abuse, and lack accepted safety for use under medical supervision; such drugs can only be used for experimental research purposes. Schedule II drugs are those that have some currently accepted medical uses in the United States but have a high abuse potential. Schedule III, IV, and V drugs are those with current medical uses and successively lower abuse potentials than those of Schedules I and II. As one might expect, the penalties for nonprescription possession or sale of schedule-controlled drugs increase dramatically as one goes from Schedule V to Schedule I.

Table 7–1 provides some examples of different controlled substances according to schedule. Note that, in several cases, drugs are placed under different schedules, not so much because of differences in their mechanisms of action, but because of differences in pharmacokinetics. For example, the narcotic drugs heroin and morphine have the same action in the brain; they differ only in terms of their ability to penetrate the blood–brain barrier. The barbiturates secobarbital and phenobarbital both exert basically the same action in the brain, but again differ in how rapidly they penetrate the blood–brain barrier. Dronabinol (also known as delta-9-tetrahydrocannabinol) is the major psychoactive compound in marijuana; in its oral form, it is a Schedule III drug, but in its smokeable form (i.e., marijuana), it is a Schedule I drug. Placement in these schedules may also be dependent on what a drug is combined with (e.g., codeine with aspirin as opposed to codeine with Actifed) or the concentration of the drug (mg/ml); for example, opium-containing compounds can be placed in Schedules II–V depending on the concentration of opium in them.

The fact that small alterations in a drug molecule can produce minimal changes in its effects at one time led to considerable problems for the DEA, which is responsible for controlling illegal drugs. By slightly altering the structure of an already illegal drug, "underground chemists" attempted to produce new compounds—often referred to as **designer**

TABLE 7–1 Examples of Controlled Substances According to Schedule

Schedule I
  Bufotenine
  Dimethyltryptamine
  Heroin
  Lysergic acid diethylamide—LSD
  Marijuana
  Mescaline
  Psilocybin

Schedule II
  Cocaine
  Dextroamphetamine (Dexedrine)
  Meperidine (Demerol)
  Methadone (Dolophine)
  Methylphenidate (Ritalin)
  Morphine
  Secobarbital (Seconal)

Schedule III
  Dronabinol (Marinol)
  Glutethimide

  Nalorphine
  Phendimetrazine (Adipost)
  Some codeine-containing compounds

Schedule IV
  Alprazolam (Xanax)
  Chloral hydrate
  Chlordiazepoxide (Librium)
  Diazepam (Valium)
  Phenobarbital
  Propoxyphene (Darvon)
  Sibutramine (Meridia)

Schedule V
  Buprenorphine (Buprenex)
  Some codeine-containing compounds
  Some opium-containing compounds

Note: Common brand name is in parentheses.

drugs—with the same properties as the illegal drug. Until the new chemical structure was specifically designated by the DEA as illegal, its manufacture, sale, and use were legal. Most designer drugs have been analogues (that is, drugs with similar structures) of amphetamine, fentanyl (a very potent synthetic narcotic), meperidine (a synthetic narcotic), or phencyclidine. Although these designer drugs gained the attention of the mass media, it appears that their production and use has declined significantly over the past several years. This decline has been attributed to reports of lethal and toxic reactions to some of these compounds (see the discussion of MPTP in Chapter 10), prosecution of the few individuals with the biochemical expertise and equipment necessary to develop them, and the passing of the Controlled Substance Analogues Enforcement Act in 1986, which essentially treats any analogue of a controlled substance intended for human consumption as a Schedule I controlled substance (Frank Sapienza, DEA agent, 1988, personal communication).

Laypersons and the mass media often refer to drugs as "hard" or "soft," although it is never clear what characteristics of drugs are being referred to when these terms are used. One might expect that the hard-drug category would correspond to Schedule I and II drugs, and soft drugs would correspond to legal drugs or Schedule IV and V drugs. However, if hard drugs are those with high abuse potential, or those that are relatively toxic to the body, or those that are likely to produce notable behavioral or emotional disturbances, as discussed in later chapters, alcohol and nicotine certainly fit this description. On the other hand, marijuana, a Schedule I drug, is often viewed as one of the soft drugs. Thus, describing drugs as hard or soft really does not provide one with any useful information about them. It should be made clear that all psychotropic drugs can be safe or harmful, depending on the circumstances in which they are used, how frequently they are used, or how much is used.

Websites for Further Information

The DEA's homepage (focuses on controlled substances and federal drug enforcement):

http://www.usdoj.gov/dea/

The National Institute for Drug Abuse classification of abused drugs:

http://www.nida.nih.gov/DrugsofAbuse.html

List of FDA-approved drugs:

http://www.fda.gov/cder/ob/default.htm

Information on drugs from the FDA:

http://www.fda.gov/

Dictionaries of street-drug slang terms:

http://www.drugs.indiana.edu/slang/home.html
http://www.addictions.org/slang.htm

Information on organic chemical drugs and their synonyms:

http://chemweb.com/databases/negwer

Bibliography

Barden, J. A., & Mason, P. (1977). Conformation of (leu^5)enkephalin from x-ray diffraction: Features important for recognition at opiate receptor. *Science, 199,* 1214–1215.

Biel, J. H., Bopp, B., & Mitchell, B. D. (1978). Chemistry and structure-activity relationships of psychotropic drugs: Part 2. In W. G. Clark & J. del Guidice (Eds.), *Principles of psychopharmacology* (pp. 140–168). New York: Academic Press.

Boyer, W. F. (1992). Potential indications for the selective serotonin reuptake inhibitors. *International Clinical Psychopharmacology, 6 suppl. 5,* 5–12.

Kessler, D. A., & Feiden, K. L. (1995). Faster evaluation of vital drugs. *Scientific American, 272*(3), 48–54.

Leavitt, F. (1982). *Drugs and behavior,* 2nd ed. New York: John Wiley & Sons.

Nies, A. S., & Spielberg, S. P. (1996). Principles of therapeutics. In A. G. Gilman, L. S. Goodman, J. G. Hardman, L. E. Limbird, P. B. Molinoff, & R. W. Ruddon, 9th ed. *The pharmacological basis of therapeutics* (pp. 43–62). New York: McGraw-Hill.

Petracek, F. J. (1978). Chemistry and structure-activity relationships of psychotropic drugs: Part 1. In W. G. Clark & J. del Guidice (Eds.), *Principles of psychopharmacology* (pp. 134–139). New York: Academic Press.

Pool, R. (1992). The third branch of science debuts. *Science, 256,* 44–47.

Pugh, M. C., & Pugh, C. B. (1987). Unlabeled uses for approved drugs. *American Druggist, 195,* 127–138.

Usdin, E. (1978). Classification of psychotropic drugs. In W. G. Clark & J. del Guidice (Eds.), *Principles of psychopharmacology* (pp. 193–246). New York: Academic Press.

Wallace, B., & Fisher, L. E. (1999). *Consciousness & behavior,* 4th ed. Boston: Allyn & Bacon.

Weissman, A., & Milne, G. (1979). Cannabinoids: Definitional ambiguities and a proposal. *Neuroscience and Biobehavioral Reviews, 3,* 171–174.

Chapter 8

Sedative–Hypnotics and Anxiolytics

Drugs with sedative–hypnotic properties are perhaps the most commonly used and abused drugs in U.S. society, with alcohol topping the list. Despite the fact that they possess all the qualities that society deems unacceptable with respect to drugs (namely, toxicity, lethality, social disruptiveness, and psychological and physical dependence), and despite the fact that they are more destructive to individuals and society than all other drugs combined, they are readily accepted in both recreational and medicinal contexts. It has been estimated that alcoholics alone represent approximately 20 percent of the patients seen in psychiatric facilities (Guze et al., 1986). Therefore, it is imperative that everyone in U.S. society be fully aware of what these substances can do to cognitive functioning, behavior, and the body.

The term **sedative–hypnotic** is used because, in most individuals, the lower doses of these drugs have a psychological calming effect, and somewhat higher doses have a hypnotic, or sleep-inducing, effect. As mentioned in Chapter 7, the term *hypnotic* in this context should not be confused with the state induced by hypnosis, which is a state in which the individual is actually very much awake. These drugs are also commonly called **CNS depressants,** because their predominant tendency is to inhibit the excitability of neurons. However, as indicated on several earlier occasions, the term *CNS depression* may not be appropriate when one is describing the net effect of a drug on all the neurons of the CNS, since not all neurons decrease their rate of firing, particularly at the lower doses. In fact, while many neurons decrease their rate of firing with these drugs, others may increase their rate of firing because of the removal of the inhibitory influence of other neurons—an inhibition of inhibition.

Alcohol (technically ethanol) is the most used and abused recreational sedative–hypnotic drug in U.S. society, and barbiturates and benzodiazepines are among the most frequently abused prescription sedative–hypnotics. In addition, there are many drugs with very similar properties, including chloral hydrate, ethchlorvynol (Placidyl), glutethimide (Doriden), and methaqualone (Quaalude), most of which are no longer marketed (legitimately) because of their abuse potential. For the most part, all of these drugs differ primarily in their quantitative aspects—that is, the latency of onset, the intensity of effect, and the duration of action—without having any distinct qualitative differences. Their qualitative effects are directly dose related. Lower doses induce sedation; moderate doses induce sleep somewhat similar to natural sleep, in which the person is still responsive to pain; high doses induce sleep to the point of anesthesia; and successively higher doses can cause coma, respiratory arrest, and death. In the lower dose range, excitement, increased activity, gregariousness, and aggression may occur in some individuals. This phenomenon has commonly been attributed to the disruption of neural pathways of higher cortical origin that play an inhibitory function on subcortical centers of the brain (a phenomenon commonly referred to as *disinhibition*).

To some extent the anxiolytics (minor tranquilizers or antianxiety drugs) share a similar spectrum of effects, although their effects tend to be somewhat more selective in their ability to reduce anxiety without significantly altering other cognitive or perceptual processes or bodily activities, like respiration. For example, whereas Seconal (a barbiturate) significantly depresses respiration at hypnotic doses and can induce anesthesia with 10 times the hypnotic dose, the benzodiazepines have minimal effects on respiration in hypnotic doses, and true anesthesia, sufficient to allow surgery, is very difficult to achieve with them. Furthermore, benzodiazepine anxiolytics have considerably higher therapeutic indices than other compounds with sedative–hypnotic qualities.

Alcohol (Ethanol)

Pick 20 American adults at random and the odds are that 14 of them drink moderately or occasionally, two drink to the point at which their drinking may be considered by others to be a problem, and one drinks excessively and chronically to the point at which we can consider him or her an **alcoholic** (a compulsive alcohol user). Because of alcohol's prevalent use and potential abuse in U.S. society, I will discuss the properties and characteristics of this drug at some length.

Alcohol has a number of characteristics that make it somewhat unique in comparison to most other drugs (Ritchie, 1985). First, it is a rather bulky drug, requiring several grams to exert noticeable effects, rather than the milligram amounts needed with other drugs. It takes somewhere between 25 and 50 mg of ethanol per 100 milliliters of blood (a blood alcohol content, or BAC, of 0.025 percent to 0.05 percent) to exert measurable effects in most individuals. A limit of 0.08 BAC for determination of legal intoxication in terms of driving was established by federal legislation in 2000, which requires states to impose this standard or lose federal funds for highway improvement. (*Illegal* means that a BAC level above the set limit is a violation in and of itself—impairment need not be demonstrated.) A person can achieve this level by consuming one drink (0.6 ounce ethanol) for every 50 pounds of body weight in one hour. (In this context, a drink equals 1.5 ounces of 80-proof liquor, 6 ounces of wine, or 12 ounces of beer.)

Alcohol also has somewhat different pharmacokinetic properties than most other drugs. Unlike many drug molecules, the ethanol molecule is a relatively small, neutrally charged particle. These characteristics make it readily absorbed from all compartments of the G.I. tract. In contrast to many psychoactive drugs, it is highly water-soluble. Its oil/water partition coefficient is just high enough for it to readily pass the blood–brain barrier, but low enough so that it is not fat-soluble. Therefore, its onset of action is rather quick and its duration of action rather short. Its low fat solubility also generally results in females achieving somewhat higher plasma concentrations than males, even when the same amount of alcohol is ingested and they weigh the same, because females have more body fat proportionally than males. Unlike most other drugs, whose rate of metabolism is proportional to their concentration, alcohol is metabolized (by the P450 enzyme alcohol dehydrogenase [ADH]) at a fairly constant rate (i.e., it exhibits zero-order kinetics). Furthermore, with most drugs where there is considerable first-pass metabolism, the liver is responsible. With alcohol, it also occurs at an upper G.I. tract site (DiPadova et al., 1987). Women have only about half the ADH in their stomachs as men, which (in addition to possessing a higher body fat to water ratio) explains their relatively higher levels of intoxication when consuming similar amounts of alcohol as men.

Finally, alcohol is a high-calorie liquid that is almost always ingested orally as a beverage. Thus, it provides the body with a ready source of calories. The alcohol in wine is derived through the interaction of yeast and sugar (fermentation) in fruits, whereas beer and distilled spirits are derived through the interaction of yeast and sugar in grains (after the starch in the grain is converted enzymatically to sugar). The alcohol content of these beverages is generally specified in terms of **proof,** which is exactly double the actual percentage of ethyl alcohol (ethanol) they contain. For example, 90-proof whiskey is 45 percent ethanol.

To some extent, these characteristics contribute to some of the unique problems associated with alcohol. For example, chronic users of alcohol often suffer from liver damage, partially because the liver spends a lot of time and energy trying to metabolize alcohol, and brain damage, partially because the individuals are consuming a large portion of their calories in alcohol and neglecting to eat proper amounts of other foods containing proteins, vitamins, and minerals essential for neuron maintenance (Rao et al., 1986; Ritchie, 1985).

Psychological Effects of Ethanol

Alcohol has been used for centuries, and by many cultures, for a variety of effects. Some of these effects are due to pharmacology, but a great many of the effects of alcohol are due to set and expectancy (Critchlow, 1986; Cutter et al., 1986; Hull & Bond, 1986). The most notable and global expectancy about alcohol is that it serves as a positive transforming agent that enhances social and physical pleasure; enhances sexual performance and responsiveness; increases power, social assertiveness, and aggression; and reduces tension (Marlatt et al., 1988). Individuals may acquire these beliefs even before beginning to drink, and they appear to be powerful predictors of both adolescent drinking status and adult alcoholism. Heavy drinkers generally expect more positive and fewer negative consequences than do light drinkers.

Because some individuals become more active, excited, and aggressive under low to moderate doses of alcohol (Pihl & Zacchia, 1986), the common view among laypersons is that alcohol is a stimulant. However, as mentioned earlier, the apparent stimulation is due to the loss of inhibitory control by those parts of the brain (such as the reticular activating system and the cortex) involved in the most highly integrated mental functions, which are dependent on social conditioning and experience, and which generally lead to sobriety and self-control (Hobbs et al., 1996).

These effects, in turn, are reflected in more of the undesirable consequences of alcohol, such as engaging in criminal activity (for example, homicide, robbery, rape, and arson) and family violence (like spouse beating and child abuse). Statistically, alcohol consumption is the single most common denominator to all of these activities; in approximately half of all these examples, either the perpetrators or the victims were determined to be under the influence of alcohol (Cychosz, 1996; Guze et al., 1986). About 40 percent of all fatal traffic accidents in North America and Europe are alcohol-related, and the risk of a fatal car accident increases exponentially with a driver's BAC, which has prompted recommendations to lower the legal BAC limit for driving and piloting aircraft (Naranjo & Bremner, 1993). Over 20 percent of work-related accidents are likely to involve alcohol use. (It should be noted that numerous surveys indicate that undesirable effects of alcohol are believed to be much more likely to occur in others—that is, people are much less likely to report that they occur in themselves.)

Alcohol tends to disrupt ongoing psychological processes in a dose-dependent manner. In general the types of faculties affected by increasingly larger doses of alcohol are depressed in the reverse order in which they were originally developed: first, complex cognitive skills (for example, planning and problem solving); then fine learned motor skills (golfing); then gross learned motor skills (walking); and finally, visual accommodation and unconditioned reflexes (hand jerk upon touching a hot surface, breathing).

Various processes involved with learning and memory are also disrupted by alcohol (Mello, 1978; Nelson et al., 1986) (see Figure 9–2 for a summary of the various stages involved in learning and memory). Attention to relevant stimuli, ability to encode new information, and short-term memory (ability to maintain new information in storage for several seconds) all decrease. In the most extreme case, these processes may be so affected that the person may experience *blackouts*—that is, complete amnesia regarding events that took place over much of the period of intoxication. These dose-related blackouts occur in approximately a quarter of social drinkers and may occur in up to 90 percent of problem drinkers and alcoholics (Anthenelli et al., 1994; Campbell & Hodgins, 1993). More often, long-term memory is affected, primarily with respect to our ability to retrieve information from storage, possibly because of state-dependency. Interestingly, based on findings from recent studies of the effects of low doses of ethanol on the EEG patterns of normal individuals, it has been suggested that ethanol may induce some of its intoxicating effects by introducing a level of randomness or "noise" on brain electrical activity and neuronal processing (Ehlers et al., 1998). (Could this be why individuals say they have a "buzz" when they are mildly intoxicated with alcohol?) Although alcohol induces sleep, it is not exactly a natural sleep, since REM (the sleep stage in which rapid eye movements and vivid dreams are most pronounced) is considerably reduced (Ritchie, 1985).

Alcohol has numerous effects on tissues other than the brain. It increases blood circulation to the skin, causing a warm, flushing sensation. However, this change increases the rate of loss of body heat when exposed to the cold. The galvanic skin response, or GSR (actually a measure of sweat gland activity), is suppressed, and heart rate decreases, although in some individuals the initial effect of alcohol is to increase blood pressure, heart rate, and blood sugar level. These increases are probably related to an elevation in catecholamine blood levels stemming from a decrease in their clearance from the blood, possibly due to alcohol's disruption of norepinephrine neuronal reuptake (Ritchie, 1985). After an hour or so, these activities often decline below normal. Alcohol stimulates production of acid and pepsin in the stomach (potentially contributing to ulcers), and this effect could explain why some people's appetites are enhanced by alcohol. Alcohol inhibits the release of antidiuretic hormone from the hypothalamus, causing water to be eliminated at a high rate. Thus drinking alcoholic beverages to relieve thirst is counterproductive.

Ethanol Pharmacokinetics

It takes approximately one hour for 90 percent of the alcohol in a drink to get into the bloodstream. However, because alcohol is rapidly and readily absorbed from the stomach, its accumulation in the brain is rapid enough to exert noticeable effects within minutes. Carbonated alcoholic beverages tend to enhance the absorption of alcohol because the carbonation forces the alcohol into the small intestine, where there is greater surface area for the absorption to take place and, thus, more rapid accumulation of alcohol in the brain.

Alcohol is metabolized at a rate of approximately 12 to 18 ml/hour, or 1.0 to 1.5 ounces of 80-proof vodka per hour (Ritchie, 1985). The liver accounts for approximately 90 percent of the alcohol metabolized. The first metabolite is acetaldehyde, a highly toxic substance capable of inducing nausea, headache, and high blood pressure, as well as causing cellular damage. Acetaldehyde is then rapidly metabolized into acetic acid, which is further metabolized into carbon dioxide and water, which are then excreted. Approximately 5 percent of alcohol is excreted by way of the lungs, and a minimal amount of alcohol is directly eliminated in the urine.

Alcohol also interferes with the normal metabolic activities of the liver because of its own metabolism. Alcohol reduces the rate at which the liver forms glucose, oxidizes fats, and releases complex fats. As a result, when there is extensive exposure to alcohol, the liver accumulates fat, and blood sugar levels are depressed. Free fatty acids are not broken down and are deposited in the liver cells themselves. Thus, early stages of chronic alcohol consumption are characterized by fatty livers. Eventually, the cells may rupture or become isolated and die. Cell death is followed by the formation of fibrous connective tissue (fibrosis), which is nonfunctional, at least with respect to what the liver is supposed to do. Some individuals eventually develop *cirrhosis* (severe hardening and contraction of the liver).

Chronic exposure to ethanol can significantly change its rate of metabolism (as well as other drugs) and alter its BAC levels. Initially, ethanol induces greater synthesis of the P450 enzymes responsible for its metabolization, thus enhancing the rate at which ethanol is metabolized. However, in those individuals who use large doses of alcohol chronically and develop liver damage, the rate at which alcohol is metabolized can be dramatically reduced, which increases ethanol levels and prolongs its stay in the body—the ramifications of which should be apparent.

Although there is some relationship between plasma level of alcohol and its behavioral effects, there is a considerable lack of correspondence between the peak plasma levels of alcohol in the blood and the peak behavioral and subjective effects induced (Figure 8–1). That is, it has long been recognized that the behavioral effects of alcohol are far greater when plasma levels are on the rise than when they are falling (Ritchie, 1985). At one time, it was

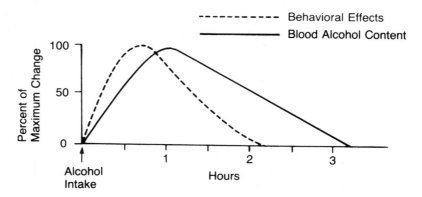

FIGURE 8–1   Percentage change in BAC levels and behavioral variables as a function of time since alcohol is administered. Note that the peak behavioral effects of alcohol occur prior to attaining peak BAC levels and that the behavioral effects dissipate considerably before all the alcohol has left the body.

believed that this effect was due to the fact that it takes considerably longer for alcohol levels in the forearm veins (where blood for alcohol analysis was drawn) to equal concentrations in intracranial arteries. However, subsequent studies assessing the time course for actual brain levels of alcohol found this belief to be unfounded. The fact that the same brain concentrations of ethanol during the rising and falling portions of the time-concentration function (a matter of an hour or two) induce substantially different effects suggests the development of acute tolerance (tachyphylaxis). This is probably due to some homeostatic adjustments in the neuronal membranes in the presence of alcohol.

Considering its widespread use, one would hope that the relative margin of safety of alcohol would be high. Unfortunately, it is not. The BAC of persons who have died of acute alcohol exposure is typically around 0.5 percent (a level achieved in a 165-pound male drinking 23 drinks in four hours). Since responsible social drinking generally results in BACs of around 0.05 percent (achieved in the same man drinking four drinks in four hours), the therapeutic index of alcohol is around 10—not very high. Fortunately, there are two built-in mechanisms that generally prevent lethal levels from being reached. If one approaches a BAC of around 0.12 percent rapidly enough, vomiting may occur, because of local irritation of the G.I. tract, disturbances in vestibular functioning, or the accumulation of acetaldehyde in the brain. Past this point, most persons become stuporous or pass out when a BAC of around 0.35 percent is reached. Therefore, the lethal limit would only be achieved in those who consume alcohol rapidly enough to achieve higher concentrations before they pass out.

Ethanol Pharmacodynamics

Whereas most psychoactive drugs directly alter functions at the synapse, alcohol alters practically every aspect of conduction and synaptic neurotransmission. At the neuropharmacological level, alcohol is believed to act directly on neuronal membranes by altering their basic semisolid structure and making them more "fluid" (Goldstein, 1989). At high doses this fluidizing action may inhibit the movements of the Na^+ and K^+ ions across the membranes and interfere with the ability of the neuron to generate and conduct action potentials. At lower doses that lead to intoxication, alcohol has been shown to enhance the activity of GABA at $GABA_A$ receptors, which, in turn, hyperpolarizes neurons by allowing more Cl^- to enter (Zorumski & Isenberg, 1991). This action, which may be related to the just-mentioned fluidizing action on the membrane, can be completely blocked by a benzodiazepine derivative (Ro15–4513), which may be acting as an inverse agonist (Britton et al., 1988). Although Ro15–4513 blocks alcohol's intoxicating properties, it does not reduce the lethal effects of high doses of alcohol. Therefore, the drug is unlikely to come into clinical use, because if people drink to get drunk and they take the drug beforehand, they could end up drinking so much alcohol in order to override the drug's effect that they could die. Recent research suggests that ethanol's enhancement of Cl^- conductance via $GABA_A$ receptors may be due to its ability to elevate levels of a neuroactive steroid (allopregnanolone) that is a potent modulator of this receptor subtype (VanDoren et al., 2000).

Another action of alcohol, which also occurs with intoxicating doses, is to inhibit the excitatory effects of glutamate and aspartate at the NMDA receptor-ion complex (Weight et al., 1993). This action results in less Ca^{++} and Na^+ ion flow into neurons and a decreased ability for the cell to depolarize. The mechanism through which alcohol inhibits NMDA receptors is not known, but it does not appear to be related to its well-known neuronal membrane disordering properties (Peoples & Weight, 1995).

In summary, alcohol's ability to potentiate the action of GABA at $GABA_A$ receptors appears to mediate its anxiolytic and sedative–hypnotic effects, an action shared by other sedative–hypnotic drugs. Its ability to inhibit the action of glutamate at NMDA receptors appears to mediate some other primary reinforcing properties. By reducing these receptors' tonic control over dopaminergic neurons in the ventral tegmental area, there is an increase in the release of dopamine in the nucleus accumbens (Tabakoff & Hoffman, 1996), which are actions shared by nonsedative drugs of abuse (for example, cocaine, nicotine, amphetamine). Thus, the effect of ethanol is not always that of depressing neuronal function. Furthermore, low concentrations of certain depressant drugs, such as alcohol, can induce excitatory effects (neuronal as well as behavioral) either due to a transient increase in the release of excitatory transmitters or to depression of inhibitory systems (Pohorecky, 1977).

Although alcohol has the ability to disrupt all neuronal membranes, some neurons may be more sensitive to its effects than others, so lower doses of alcohol may decrease the excitability of some neurons while leaving others unaffected, except at higher concentrations. Thus, if the neurons whose excitability is decreased normally play an inhibitory role in the activity of those neurons that are not affected by low doses of alcohol, the latter's rate of firing may increase due to the loss of inhibitory control. However, once concentrations of alcohol reach higher levels, these neurons may also become less excitable, and their rate of firing will decrease.

Chronic Effects of Alcohol Use

It should be apparent from the preceding discussion that the liver is one of the organs most likely to be affected by chronic alcohol consumption. Alcohol-induced liver disease is primarily restricted to the fatty liver and is a benign and asymptotic condition. However, after years of alcohol abuse, a minority of alcoholics (heavy alcohol users) suddenly develop the potentially lethal condition called *alcoholic hepatitis,* characterized by cellular death and organ inflammation (Schanne et al., 1981). Although liver damage associated with alcohol consumption was once believed to be primarily due to malnutrition, research has shown that excellent nutrition does not prevent the development of alcoholic hepatitis or its progression to cirrhosis (Hobbs et al., 1996).

It is not clear what mediates the transformation of fatty liver into cirrhosis, but there is evidence that some general physical effects of alcohol on cellular membranes render cells susceptible to otherwise nonlethal injuries. In other words, normally random exposure of the liver to membrane-active toxins (such as viruses and products of intestinal bacteria), which are normally well tolerated, overwhelm the homeostatic mechanisms of the cells in the presence of chronic alcohol exposure (Lieber, 1994). This mechanism may also account for alcohol-induced disease in other organs, including the heart, the pancreas, and the nervous system. Another mechanism for cellular damage involves the reduced ability of liver mitochondria to metabolize acetaldehyde, which in turn promotes the perpetuation of liver damage (Lieber, 1994). Whatever the mechanism, once the liver cells lose their ability to metabolize alcohol, the individual's reaction to alcohol and other drugs actively metabolized by the liver is considerably exaggerated with respect to both duration and accumulation (Mazoit et al., 1987).

A wide variety of studies have indicated that, as a group, chronic alcoholics develop a relatively enduring pattern of cognitive and motor deficits (McEntee & Mair, 1978; Oscar-Berman, 1980; Svanum & Schladenhauffen, 1986). These deficits are generally not large, nor are they consistent across studies. Some of the lack of consistency is likely due to differences in how alcoholism is defined (to be discussed shortly), the ages of the subjects, the number of years of drinking, and how soon the tests were administered after abstinence. In general, global I.Q. scores of alcoholics are in the normal range. Although most studies have indicated that nonverbal I.Q. is somewhat lower than verbal I.Q. among alcoholics, other studies have not found such differences. Impairments are often displayed in abstract reasoning ability, new learning, problem solving, and perceptual motor functions. Inability to shift cognitive and attentional sets may also occur (for example, a person who has developed one strategy for a task or who attends to one type of stimulus may continue using that strategy when it is no longer appropriate or may not perceive a new type of stimulus if one is suddenly presented).

Unfortunately, all of the studies attempting to assess physiological or neurological dysfunction in alcoholics are retrospective; that is, they are done only after the diagnosis of alcoholism. Thus, it is not clear to what extent the deficits noted may have existed prior to the alcoholism phase and may, in fact, have contributed to the person's becoming alcoholic in the first place. As yet, research has not demonstrated a clear and consistent relationship between levels of alcohol consumption and neuropsychological deficits.

A considerable body of evidence suggests that right-hemisphere functions (e.g., visual-spatial skills and visual-perceptual analysis) are more impaired in alcoholics than left-hemisphere functions (e.g., verbal-linguistic abilities). Because this pattern of cognitive decline in chronic heavy drinkers is similar to that observed in aged individuals, some have suggested that alcoholism is associated with "premature aging" of cognitive capabilities

(Ryan, 1982). However, a review of empirical research findings on cerebral asymmetries in alcoholics indicates that, although general information-processing mechanisms may decline in alcoholics, particularly for tasks that stress the person's acquired skills and abilities, there is probably no change in the balance of hemispheric specialization that accounts for the cognitive deficits observed (Ellis & Oscar-Berman, 1989).

It has generally been assumed that the disturbance to cognitive functions in alcoholics is the result of what alcohol does to the brain. However, a study of alcoholics who received liver transplants has challenged this assumption (Arria et al., 1991). A year after receiving new livers, all but two of the 13 alcoholics assessed returned to basically normal functioning in tests assessing psychomotor, visual, and perceptual abilities. The main exception, a lack of improvement in memory capacity, could be related to the results of other studies suggesting that chronic alcohol intake irreversibly damages the hippocampus—a brain structure heavily involved in memory formation (Wilson et al., 1987).

Chronic alcohol consumption has also been associated with brain shrinkage and a number of functional deficits in cerebral and cerebellar function (Carlen et al., 1978; Golden et al., 1981). Alcoholics suffering from these conditions can show some recovery when abstinence is maintained over periods of weeks to many months (Carlen et al., 1978), with similar improvements occurring regardless of gender or family history of alcoholism (Drake et al., 1995; Mann et al., 1992). Rapid recovery may be attributed to the resolution of the alcohol withdrawal syndrome—a biochemical process—whereas gradual functional improvement may have a structural basis—a reversible atrophy indicative of the plasticity in the CNS (Mann et al., 1993).

The mechanisms for cellular death with respect to the CNS are also not well understood, although there is clear evidence that a great deal of damage is indirectly due to alcohol consumption. Much of the alcohol-associated brain damage (Wernicke's disease) and the resulting impairment in learning and memory (Korsakoff's syndrome) have traditionally been attributed to malnutrition, especially thiamine deficiency, rather than to the direct neurotoxic effect of ethanol (Rao et al., 1986; Hobbs et al., 1996). These problems come about because a large portion of the alcoholic's diet is derived from alcohol, which happens to be very high in calories but contains no other essential nutrients, and the consumption of proper amounts of proteins, vitamins, and essential nutrients is low. Poor diet associated with chronic alcohol intake can also depress appetite and prevent proper absorption of nutrients from the G.I. tract (Pezzarossa et al., 1986). Therefore, treatment of these neurological disorders with thiamine and glucose is generally helpful (Gold, 1995; Zubaran et al., 1997), although it will not reverse symptoms that are the result of neuronal losses, because neurons in the brain typically do not regenerate.

Although the relationship between diet and neuropathy is clear, it is nevertheless the case that both neuropathological and neuropsychological deficits have been observed in some alcoholic patients who have no history of malnutrition. In some cases, these deficits can be traced to head injuries stemming from falls, fights, or car accidents (Svanum & Schladenhauffen, 1986). A genetic predisposition may be involved in other cases. Finally, studies with animals maintained on nutritional diets and given large quantities of alcohol chronically have reported significant loss of specific CNS neurons, such as those in the hippocampus (Riley & Walker, 1978; Walker et al., 1980). The functional significance of these findings for human alcoholics is not clear, because the concentrations of alcohol used in these studies is much higher than those sustained in humans. It is likely that the pathophysiology of alcoholic brain damage is due to a variety of factors—for example, synergistic effects of alcohol, acetaldehyde, thiamine deficiency, liver disease, and excessive NMDA receptor activity during ethanol withdrawal (Butterworth, 1995; Hunt, 1993; Kril, 1995; Lancaster, 1995).

Chronic alcohol consumption can also severely affect numerous sexual functions. Male alcoholics, with or without overt liver disease, exhibit certain underactive gonadal functions, including testicular atrophy, impaired sperm production, impotence, and decreased libido, as well as abnormalities in the metabolism of sex hormones. Much of the evidence suggests that these deficits are due to increased activities of the drug-metabolizing enzymes in the liver resulting from chronic alcohol exposure, which, in turn, severely reduces testosterone levels (Van Thiel et al., 1974).

Beneficial Effects of Alcohol

As discussed earlier, alcohol (or expectations about it) induces a variety of effects that users find pleasurable or beneficial to them. Furthermore, despite all that I have said about alcohol up to this point, there is no evidence that chronic exposure to less than 2 ounces of ethanol per day (approximately three drinks) is associated with any untoward health consequences for the user. (As discussed a little later on, this statement probably does not apply to a developing fetus.) In fact, drinking of these amounts—often described as moderate drinking—may have some health benefits.

A number of studies examining the association between alcoholic drinks and mortality have reached essentially the same conclusion; statistically there is a U- or J-shaped function between mortality and the average amount of alcohol reportedly drunk, regardless of the type of alcoholic beverage used, or the person's gender, education, or income (Dawson, 2000; Gaziano et al., 2000; Liao et al., 2000). In other words, relative to abstainers, moderate drinkers (that is, those who drink one to three drinks per day) have the lowest mortality rate, and heavy drinkers (that is, those who drink over three drinks per day) have the highest mortality rate, with the mortality rate increasing monotonically with higher alcohol intake. The higher mortality rate associated with heavy alcohol consumption is due to increased incidence of liver disease, cancer, and drunken driving, along with other factors. The lower mortality rate among moderate drinkers has been attributed to a decreased risk of cardiovascular and cerebrovascular disease, possibly due to alcohol's ability to stimulate production of an enzyme, t-PA, that helps break down blood clots (Ridker et al., 1994) or to raise the body's levels of HDL cholesterol—the type of cholesterol that keeps the arteries free of dangerous buildups (Gaziano & Hennekens, 1995). Enhanced quality of life and decreased arousal from stress may also be a factor in this phenomenon.

However, the case for moderate drinking leading to longer life may be overstated, because many of the studies investigating this link ignored factors such as the participants' socioeconomic status and overall health, or lumped together two kinds of individuals—life-long teetotalers and former drinkers—to form their nondrinker reference group. Evidence suggests that former drinkers exhibit risk characteristics that could enhance their mortality, and that, compared with light or occasional drinkers or lifelong teetotalers, these individuals may have the highest risk of mortality from all causes (Fillmore et al., 1998; Shaper & Wannamethee, 2000).

Tolerance, Dependence, and Alcoholism

As is the case with most drugs, tolerance to ethanol develops at different rates, depending on the measures one employs to evaluate it, and there is no uniform underlying mechanism responsible (Cicero, 1978; Pohorecky et al., 1986). In addition to the tachyphylaxis phenomenon described earlier, a low to moderate degree of tolerance develops to most of the behavioral and mood-altering effects of alcohol, such that the chronic user must take larger and larger amounts in order to obtain the desired effects. Minimal tolerance develops to the lethal effects of alcohol, so that, in effect, the therapeutic index for the drug gets smaller and smaller (O'Brien, 1996). There is cross-tolerance among alcohol and all the sedative–hypnotic drugs.

Just about all of the mechanisms described in Chapter 6 for the development of tolerance seem to operate with alcohol. There is some pharmacokinetic tolerance in that the drug-metabolizing enzymes of the liver may be increased by approximately 15 percent to 30 percent with chronic use (Ritchie, 1985). There is evidence that pharmacodynamic tolerance occurs with respect to ethanol's actions at $GABA_A$ and NMDA receptors (recall that acutely ethanol facilitates activity at the former and inhibits activity at the latter). Several lines of evidence suggest that chronic ethanol exposure in animals induces down-regulation of certain subunits of the $GABA_A$ receptor and up-regulation of brain NMDA receptors (Davidson et al., 1995; Mhatre & Ticku, 1993; Tabakoff & Hoffman, 1996). The adaptive changes in the $GABA_A$ receptor system may have a more significant relationship to the development of ethanol tolerance than to withdrawal, whereas the change in NMDA receptors appears to play a significant role in both tolerance development as well as many of the symptoms associated with ethanol withdrawal (for example, seizures, dysphoric mood) (Tabakoff & Hoffman, 1996). Some of alcohol's acute biological effects appear to be the result of an increase in fluidity and chemical composition of cell membranes, whereas enhanced membrane rigidity with chronic alcohol exposure is believed to result in cellular tolerance to alcohol (Goldstein, 1989). This enhanced rigidity occurs as a consequence of a compensatory shift in the composition of the cell membrane whereby polyunsaturated fats are replaced by saturated fats and cholesterol, rendering the membrane less susceptible to fluidization.

Much of the tolerance to alcohol is believed to be due to behavioral compensation; that is, the individual learns to compensate for the detrimental effects of the drug on behavior (O'Brien, 1996). Finally, studies with nonhumans indicate that some tolerance may be due to the development of Pavlovian conditioned compensatory responses, which may counter the direct actions of alcohol (Crowell et al., 1981). Both of these mechanisms imply that the degree of intoxication with alcohol is very situationally dependent; that is, the effects of alcohol are most pronounced in novel situations or tasks.

Alcohol, like other sedative–hypnotics, has a strong potential for inducing both psychological and physiological dependence. When either or both of these occur with alcohol, the term **alcoholism** is used, and the individual is referred to as an **alcoholic.** It is not clear exactly what is so positively reinforcing about alcohol. Its taste is obnoxious to practically everybody at first, and nonhumans are somewhat equivocal in their tendency to self-administer it. Most strains of rats and monkeys avoid drinking alcohol unless they are positively reinforced for doing so, or unless the catheter infusion method is used (Woods, 1978). Ethanol has numerous effects (for example, temporary relief from stress or anxiety) that could account for its positive reinforcing effects in humans. Most of the evidence from animal studies suggests that ethanol's ability, via its actions on either GABA or NMDA receptors, to directly or indirectly amplify dopaminergic input into the nucleus accumbens (an action shared by most drugs of abuse) plays a prominent role in its primary reinforcing effects (Henriksen, 1993; Tabakoff & Hoffman, 1996).

Although physical dependence on alcohol generally requires several months or years of exposure to alcohol to develop, many experts believe that a single day's exposure to a large quantity of alcohol can induce an abstinence syndrome, which is commonly experienced as a hangover (Gauvin et al., 1993). The fact that reexposure to alcohol can "cure" a hangover ("the hair of the dog that bit you") supports this belief. Some of the symptoms of a hangover may be related to a buildup of acetaldehyde in the brain, depletion of norepinephrine, lack of sleep, dehydration, and low blood sugar. In addition, alcohols other than ethanol (referred to as congeners) may enhance a hangover, which is probably why some alcoholic beverages induce greater hangovers than others.

The previously mentioned up-regulation of NMDA receptors, and possibly the down-regulation of $GABA_A$ receptor subunits, which occur with chronic ethanol exposure, most likely contributes to the CNS hyperexcitability during withdrawal. Abstinence symptoms following chronic use of greater than moderate doses of alcohol (say, a pint of whiskey per day for several weeks) may be limited to prolonged disturbances in the EEG during sleep. After cessation of larger doses, the symptoms may be evidenced as a high degree of arousal associated with weakness, tremor, anxiety, and elevated blood pressure, pulse rate, and respiratory rate. In severe reactions, 12 to 48 hours after the person stops drinking, convulsions may occur, and a toxic psychosis may appear with symptoms such as irritability, headaches, fever, nausea, agitation, confusion, and visual hallucinations. This latter syndrome is referred to as **delirium tremens** or the D.T.s, which typically appear 2 to 4 days after drinking stops (Romach & Sellers, 1991). Withdrawal-related symptoms have been noted in numerous clinical studies to become increasingly more severe after repeated episodes of alcohol intoxication and withdrawal, perhaps through a "kindling" process (e.g., see page 211), in which each episode of withdrawal "sensitizes" the brain toward progressively more intense withdrawal responses (Booth & Blow, 1993). A recent study using a positron emission tomography (PET) scan technique has suggested that reduced blood flow to certain areas of the brain following withdrawal periods may be a factor in this phenomenon (George et al., 1999). Because of the convulsions and the associated respiratory arrest, withdrawal from alcohol and other short-duration sedative–hypnotics can be lethal. Therefore, medical treatment is strongly advised.

What Is Alcoholism?

There has been a considerable amount of discussion as to exactly what constitutes alcohol dependence, or alcoholism, and definitions of this disorder vary. The idea that alcoholism is a disease dominates U.S. treatment programs, with advocates of such a model hypothesizing an underlying process based on physical dependency, genetic disposition, and the assumption that it is progressive (Marlatt et al., 1988). Other experts are critical of such a view because it depends on how one defines a disease. This model also fails to account for commonalities among addictions that do not involve substance use (e.g., compulsive gambling), and it does not explain how and why many people appear to overcome their addictions without any treatment or why they seem to benefit from a variety of treatment approaches (Marlatt et al., 1988).

Some authorities prefer to view alcoholism as a compulsive drug-use disorder, arguing that until the chronic exposure to alcohol induces physiological damage there is nothing distinctive about alcoholics except for their inability to regulate their use of alcohol in spite of experiencing adverse consequences. In 1988 the U.S. Supreme Court ruled that the government may continue viewing alcoholism as "willful misconduct" rather than an uncontrollable disease when awarding veterans' education benefits. However, the disease designation—adopted by the American Medical Association in 1957—is commonly accepted, if only to counteract the disorder's social stigma and to establish that it is treatable and arrestable (Guze et al., 1986). Some experts describe alcoholism in terms of the amount of alcohol consumed, whereas others feel the consequences of alcohol and the attendant behaviors associated with it, whatever the amount ingested, should be emphasized. With so many different criteria, determining the incidence of alcoholism is difficult, but according to the National Household Survey on Drug Abuse, there were an estimated 12.4 million heavy drinkers out of 105 million Americans age 12 and older who reported current use of alcohol in 1999. Thus, around one out of 10 drinkers could be considered an alcoholic. However, alcoholism rates are highly dependent on age, with these rates reaching a peak at age 21 and generally declining for successively older age groups.

Alcoholism is characterized by continuous or periodic impaired control over drinking, preoccupation with alcohol, use of alcohol despite numerous adverse consequences, and distortions in thinking, most notably denial. For example, there may be one or more unsuccessful efforts to cut down on or control alcohol use, or the person may continue to use alcohol despite knowledge of having persistent or recurrent social, psychological, or physical problems that are caused by their alcohol use. The person may have numerous driving accidents under the influence of alcohol, physically abuse the spouse or children, spend a great deal of money on alcohol, miss work because of drinking alcohol or recovering from its effects, or experience ulcers or high blood pressure. Alcoholics may also display a marked tolerance to alcohol and a characteristic withdrawal syndrome when alcohol use ceases. It should be emphasized that physical dependence is not a necessity in order for a person to be deemed an alcoholic; many individuals who are not physically dependent on alcohol are still considered alcoholic if the other characteristics are evidenced. However, if one is physically dependent on alcohol, then the person is definitely an alcoholic. The prevailing view is that even after such persons stop drinking for some length of time, they are still considered to be alcoholic because, should they return to drinking alcohol, the likelihood of the noted characteristics being evidenced is quite high.

Loss of control over one's consumption of alcohol is one factor that is highly debated (Fingarette, 1988). Some experts in the area of alcoholism view alcoholics as being qualitatively different from nonalcoholics in this dimension, as if alcohol acts like an "on-off" switch for them. Others view loss of control along a continuum of degrees of control. This is not a subtle distinction, as it has important bearing on the type of treatment prescribed for alcoholism. For those who believe that alcohol acts like an "on" switch, the primary treatment goal is complete abstinence from alcohol (Mello, 1978). For those who believe that there is a continuum of control, drinking in moderation is not only feasible but is perhaps a more appropriate goal in many individuals with an alcohol problem (Robertson et al., 1986). The reasoning here is that some individuals will avoid all treatment modalities, such as Alcoholics Anonymous, that emphasize complete abstinence, because they cannot see themselves going through life without ever taking another drink.

Etiology of Alcoholism

Alcoholism is found in all classes of society and in all walks of life. The ratio of male to female alcoholics is approximately 6:1 (Guze et al., 1986). There is no consistent evidence to indicate that a particular personality type develops the disorder; however, individuals high in antisocial characteristics, as measured by a variety of personality tests, have been consistently shown to be prone to alcoholism (Cadoret et al., 1987; Cloninger, 1987; Schuckit et al., 1995). Such individuals are generally males whose pattern of drinking is fairly continuous. They often engage in thrill-seeking behavior, fights, and criminal activities; rarely binge drink; display little guilt or anxiety over their drinking; and are low in the need for social rewards. Individuals with these characteristics are sometimes designated at Type II alcoholics (Cloninger, 1987). Conversely, Type I alcoholics are much more likely to abstain from drinking for periods of time and then binge once they start drinking. They tend not to engage in thrill-seeking and antisocial activities, they have high social reward dependence, and they often feel guilty or fearful about their alcohol dependence. Female alcoholics are more likely to display Type I characteristics, but many male alcoholics also share these characteristics.

Many studies have indicated that there are specific genetic bases for many forms of this disorder (Cadoret et al., 1987; Cloninger, 1987; Plomin et al., 1994; Vanyukov & Tarter, 2000). First of all, numerous studies assessing the acute responses of normal humans to alcohol have shown some degree of genetic control in a wide variety of responses (Reed & Hanna, 1986). For example, many Asians possess a type of gene that results in an inactive form of an enzyme that normally metabolizes acetaldehyde (a metabolite of alcohol), which allows for acetaldehyde levels to build up. As a result, these individuals experience a more intense reaction to alcohol, with some reactions being pleasant (that is, "high") and others being aversive (that is, facial flushing, nausea), which may contribute to their lower tendency to drink excessively (Wall et al., 1992). Within-race, genetically controlled differences have been shown to occur with respect to rates of absorption, metabolism, EEG alterations, heart rate, and blood pressure.

Second, with respect to alcoholism per se, several studies have noted that the *concordance rate** for alcoholism in identical twins is double that obtained in fraternal twins (approximately 55 percent versus 28 percent) (Kendler et al., 1992). People whose biological parents (one or both) display alcoholism and who were adopted as children by nonalcoholic parents have an almost four times higher incidence of alcoholism than adoptees whose biological parents were not alcoholics (Cloninger, 1987; Vaillant & Milofsky, 1982). This finding appears to be particularly true for the pattern of alcoholism discussed earlier involving antisocial characteristics (von Knorring et al., 1987). In general, most of the more recent evidence suggests that genetic factors account for about half of the variance in liability to alcoholism and that they are of similar etiologic importance for alcoholism in women and men (Kendler et al., 1992; Pickens et al., 1991). However, recent analyses suggest that Type II alcoholism (more common in men) has a very high genetic influence (estimated heritability of 90 percent), whereas Type I alcoholism (more common in women) is only moderately influenced by genetic factors (estimated heritability of less than 40 percent) (McGue, 1999). Also, there appear to be differences in the development of alcoholism in men and women (e.g., a history of child abuse is predictive of women but not men and age of onset of alcoholism is typically later in women than in men) (McGue, 1999). Interestingly, there is evidence that genetics may have a stronger influence in the amount of alcohol consumed than alcoholism (Plomin et al., 1994).

For the past two decades, researchers have been trying to identify biological characteristics or even actual genes that are associated with a predisposition to alcoholism—so far without much success. Although there is general agreement that many genes are involved in the disorder and that they are different for different groups of individuals, many scientists suspect that there are no specific genes for alcoholism per se. More likely there are a variety of genes that lead to a susceptibility to a number of compulsive behaviors—for example, alcohol or other drug addictions, gambling, or eating disorders—in which the type of disorder is shaped by environmental and temperamental factors. This suggestion is supported by the fact that there is a tremendous variability among alcoholics. Though close to a third of alcoholics also exhibit symptoms of other mental disorders—such as anxiety, depression, manic depression, childhood conduct disorder, and antisocial personality—most alcoholics do not (Schuckit et al., 1995). Also, alcoholism can set in early and fast or gradually develop over decades; some are binge drinkers while others are chronic maintenance drinkers. Thus, it is likely to be some time before we can fit all the disparate pieces of the puzzle together so that the predisposing factors behind this disorder are established with some certainty.

Over the years several studies have suggested that there are a number of biological and behavioral characteristics or markers of alcoholics. For example, studies have suggested that alcoholics metabolize alcohol into acetaldehyde at a faster rate and convert acetaldehyde into acetic acid at a slower rate than do nonalcoholics. A genetic basis for these metabolic differences was indicated by studies showing that similar differences occur between relatives of al-

---

*Concordance rate refers to the percentage of pairs of individuals who share some trait or characteristic. Say, for example, you locate 70 pairs of twins and you observe that in 5 pairs both members share the trait, but only one member in each of 5 other pairs displays the trait. In this case the concordance rate for that trait is 50 percent ([5/10]×100 = 50%). (Note that in 60 pairs, neither individual displays the trait, but these pairs do not figure into the determination of concordance rate.) If the concordance rate for alcoholism was 1 percent in pairs of genetically unrelated people raised apart, and was 100 percent in pairs of identical twins raised apart (that is, in every case either both members of a pair were alcoholic or neither member was alcoholic), then there would be overwhelming evidence that genetics was the sole determinant of alcoholism. Conversely, if the concordance rates were 1 percent in both unrelated and genetically identical sets, the evidence would be overwhelmingly in favor of environmental factors.

coholics (relatives who drank little or no alcohol) and relatives of nonalcoholics (Schuckit & Rayses, 1979; Watterlond, 1983).

Most studies looking for biological differences between alcoholics and nonalcoholics have been retrospective; that is, these characteristics were noted after alcoholism was evidenced. Thus, it is not clear whether these characteristics preceded heavy alcohol use or were caused by it. To circumvent the problem, researchers have attempted to determine whether non-alcohol-abusing young adults with a family history of alcoholism (FH+) differ, in terms of their reactions to alcohol, from those without a family history of alcoholism (FH–). The general findings in these studies are that young adult FH+ males, when given alcohol, are more sensitive to alcohol's effects during the rising arm of the BAC curve (see Figure 8–1) and exhibit reduced effects (that is, they exhibit acute tolerance) as the BAC level falls, compared with FH– males, despite the fact that the groups do not differ in their BAC curves (Newlin & Thomson, 1990; Schuckit, 1994a). This suggests that males at risk for alcoholism find alcohol more rewarding because the pleasurable, excitatory aspects at the early stage of intoxication are accentuated and the dysphoric feelings—that is, anxiety and depression—that predominate as BAC levels drop are attenuated. In fact, the differential reactions to alcohol in these males have been found to be a potent predictor of their becoming alcoholic 8 to 12 years later (Schuckit, 1994b). (Note that very few studies of this nature from which one can draw general conclusions have been conducted with females, due primarily to the much lower incidence of alcoholism in females; thus, there are fewer subjects of this type for researchers to study—a considerable problem for this particular methodological approach. Also, until recently, there was a common belief that there was much less of a genetic basis for alcoholism in females.) On the other hand, there is evidence that individuals at risk for alcoholism experience more frequent and intense hangover effects than do low-risk individuals, which may be a factor in their initiating further drinking to relieve these aversive symptoms (Earleywine, 1993; Newlin & Pretorius, 1990).

Other studies have noted that brain wave deficits that are often seen in alcoholics also appear in the sons of alcoholics before the individuals have ever used alcohol (Porjesz & Begleiter, 1991). These results, in addition to supporting the view that some of the variation in the propensity for alcoholism is biologically based, suggest that it may be possible to determine which individuals are prone to alcoholism prior to their becoming heavy users of alcohol and to warn such individuals about their predisposition to developing the disorder.

Environmental factors also are implicated in the vulnerability to alcoholism (Zucker & Gomberg, 1986). As noted above, even in identical twins the concordance rates are nowhere close to 100 percent. Furthermore, one-third of alcoholics have no family history of alcoholism, and only 17 percent to 25 percent of sons of alcoholics become alcoholics (Vanyukov & Tarter, 2000). For years environmental factors have been assumed to explain the findings of studies showing that different cultures have different alcoholism rates that are not easily tied in with per capita consumption of alcohol. For example, in France, where per capita consumption of alcohol is high, there is a high rate of alcoholism. However, in Italy and Greece, where per capita alcohol consumption is high, the rate of alcoholism is low. In the United States and Sweden, which have relatively low per capita consumption of alcohol, alcoholism is relatively high. In viewing the drinking habits and attitudes of these cultures, it appears that the lowest incidence of alcoholism occurs when (1) the children are exposed to alcohol early in life in a family or religious setting, with parents presenting an example of moderate drinking; (2) alcohol is served in small or diluted quantities, usually with meals; (3) abstinence is socially acceptable and excessive drinking is not; (4) drinking is not viewed as proof of adulthood or virility; and (5) there are well-established ground rules for drinking behavior (Aronow, 1980).

Despite the apparent cultural differences in alcoholism rates, no specific environmental factors have been shown to correlate with alcoholism. Some studies have shown that adoptees of adoptive parents who display alcohol-related problems are no more likely to become alcoholics than the general population. Others have shown that alcohol-related problems in the adoptive family do predict increased adoptee alcohol abuse. Still others have shown that alcohol-related problems in the adoptive family only predict adoptee alcohol abuse if there was a concomitant genetic disposition—that is, the adoptee had a biological parent who was alcoholic (Cadoret et al., 1987; Cloninger, 1987). Although considerably speculative, there is some evidence that environments that contribute to alcoholic vulnerability (1) do not promote impulse control; (2) view drunkenness as acceptable behavior; (3) reduce a person's cognitive ability to appraise information that might limit alcohol consumption; or (4) do not provide nondrug alternative sources of gratification (Heilbrun et al., 1986; Mello, 1978).

Obviously, there are numerous factors, many of which have probably not even been considered, that contribute to the induction of alcoholism. Perhaps the only thing that is certain is that impurities in alcoholic beverages, vitamin deficiencies, and hormonal changes are not factors (when hormonal changes occur, they are probably an effect of the disorder rather than a cause) (Ritchie, 1985).

Treatment of Alcoholism

The first step in any treatment for alcoholism is getting the alcoholic into treatment. Unfortunately, as indicated in Chapter 6, persons with alcohol or other drug problems typically are in denial over the difficulties their drug use is causing and do not recognize their need for help. When their difficulties do become obvious to them (e.g., they need a liver transplant to survive), their problems may be too extreme to do much about them. However, there are strategies to get individuals into treatment before this happens. For example, coercion techniques, in which the alcoholic is given a choice between complying with treatment or receiving "alternative consequences" (e.g., jail time or probation, loss of child or custody, loss of employment or benefits), have been shown to be highly effective for engaging and retaining alcoholics in treatment (Miller & Flaherty, 2000). Clients who have been coerced by their employer or the judicial system to enter alcoholism treatment may be just as successfully treated as those who have entered treatment voluntarily.

One of the more popular coercion techniques is the Johnson Intervention (Johnson, 1986). It is a specialized therapeutic technique in which members from the person's social network (e.g., family members, friends, employer), following a period of formal training and rehearsal, confront the alcoholic about the damage their drinking has caused and the action they will take if treatment is refused. It has been shown to be highly effective in engaging and retaining clients in both inpatient and outpatient treatment programs, although a variety of coercive methods appear to be comparable in getting clients to complete a treatment program (Loneck et al., 1996).

There are a multitude of ways of treating alcoholism, none of which has had universal success with all individuals (Miller et al., 1995). One thing is clear: for any of them to work, the alcoholic must not be physically dependent, because the motivational forces for continuing to drink are just too great in the physically dependent alcoholic. Since withdrawal from alcohol can be lethal, medical intervention is advisable. This generally entails substituting a long-acting anxiolytic—for example, diazepam (Valium)—and then gradually reducing the dose over several days (Romach & Sellers, 1991). However, anxiolytics that remain in the body for a shorter period of time, such as oxazepam (Serax), may be preferable because they allow physicians to more easily adjust dosages as needed. Carbamazepine (Tegretol), an anticonvulsant and mood stabilizer with no abuse potential, has been shown to be effective in the treatment of acute alcohol withdrawal and may also have efficacy in the long-term treatment of alcohol dependence (Mueller et al., 1997).

Once the physical dependence phase is over with, other interventions can be applied (chemical, psychological, or both). Chemical treatments for maintaining abstinence have ranged from drugs that induce nausea when accompanied by alcohol to drugs that attempt to promote insight into the causes of one's drinking. One of the most common chemical interventions involving disulfiram (Antabuse) has been used for over 45 years (Fuller, 1995). This drug competes for the same enzyme that normally metabolizes the alcohol metabolite acetaldehyde into acetic acid. Thus, with the intake of alcohol, there is a build-up of acetaldehyde in the body, and a toxic reaction occurs, consisting of nausea and a headache. The patient is either told of these unpleasant reactions or is given small test amounts of alcohol to precipitate the reaction, so that he or she will know what to expect.

Theoretically, this approach should keep the alcoholic abstinent. Unfortunately, however, most well-controlled studies on the efficacy of disulfiram treatment have indicated that the drug is no more effective than a placebo (Fuller, 1995). One of the basic problems with disulfiram is that its effectiveness as a drinking deterrent depends entirely on the person's willingness to comply with the treatment regimen or even accept it in the first place—both of which are rare (Brubaker et al., 1987). Another problem is that disulfiram may not even work (that is, produce a disulfiram-alcohol reaction) in patients with significant liver disease, because of insufficient build-up of acetaldehyde levels (Wicht et al., 1995). Furthermore, since the craving for alcohol is still present, the person needs only to stop taking the disulfiram for a few days in order to start drinking again. There are other problems associated with disulfiram treatment. One is that the person must be very careful to avoid all substances that might contain alcohol, such as cough medicine. Another is that several side effects—for example, psychotic-like reactions—can occur with chronic disulfiram exposure.

Antabuse was introduced as a treatment for alcoholism in 1948. It took almost 50 years for the FDA to approve for use (in 1995) the next drug for this purpose. It is naltrexone (ReVia), which was originally approved for the treatment of opiate addiction in 1984 (and marketed as Trexan). Several studies have now demonstrated that naltrexone is effective in the rehabilitation of alcoholics, presumably because of its ability to reduce alcohol-induced euphoria and to dampen the craving for another drink (O'Malley et al., 1996a; O'Malley et al., 1996b; Volpicelli et al., 1995a; Volpicelli et al., 1995b). For example, in one study the relapse rate in naltrexone-treated alcoholics was half that of placebo-treated alcoholics (23 percent versus 54 percent) over a 3-month period, and among patients who did revert to drinking, those given naltrexone were much less likely to drink heavily. Naltrexone works, it is theorized, because it blocks the receptors for endorphins, which in alcoholics may be unusually elevated when they drink. Endorphin receptor blockade prevents the sensation of pleasure that entices the drinker to further indulge.

Nalmefene (Revex), a newer opioid antagonist that is structurally similar to naltrexone, has also been found to be effective in preventing relapse to heavy drinking relative to placebo in alcohol-dependent outpatients (Mason et al., 1999). It has a number of potential pharmacological advantages over naltrexone for the treatment of alcohol dependence, including no dose-dependent association with toxic effects to the liver, greater oral bioavailability, longer duration of antagonist action, and more competitive binding with opioid receptor subtypes that are thought to reinforce drinking.

It is too early to determine whether opiate antagonists will actually be of much practical value in the treatment of alcoholism—or even accepted by practitioners, who may be reluctant to use a drug that may give their patients the false impression that they can now drink safely if they use it. It is clear, as all researchers of these drugs have emphasized, that opiate antagonist treatment should always be combined with psychosocial therapies in order to help alcoholics avoid relapse and achieve sobriety.

In between Antabuse and Revex, a number of other drug therapies for alcoholism have been tried—most of which have failed or remain unproved. For example, anthropological reports have suggested that Native Americans belonging to the Native American Church, which uses the mescaline-containing peyote plant in their religious ceremonies, have a lower incidence of alcohol problems than other Indian groups. In the early 1960s, a few pilot studies with LSD were conducted with alcoholics to see if the supposedly insight-promoting properties of this drug would be useful in reducing their alcohol problem (Brecher, 1972). These generally involved one or two exposures to LSD under medical supervision. Although there was some indication of an initial reduction in alcohol consumption, 6-month follow-ups showed no greater improvement with LSD than with a placebo. However, before more extensive research could be conducted with LSD, governmental restrictions became so difficult for researchers that no further studies were attempted.

Lithium, commonly used in the treatment of manic depression, has been periodically touted as an effective treatment for alcoholism since the 1970s, but a recent exhaustive study of this treatment failed to support its efficacy in this regard (Dorus et al., 1989). However, because manic depression has been found to be one of the most likely of major mental disorders to co-occur with alcohol or other drug abuse (Brady & Sonne, 1995), there may be a specific subgroup of alcoholics that may profit from treatment with lithium or some other type of mood stabilizer (see Chapter 13).

Acamprosate, a drug with putative GABA-enhancing and glutamate-inhibiting properties, has been tested in numerous clinical trials in Europe for several years and has been found to reduce relapse and drinking frequency in alcoholics, although its effects on enhancing abstinence or reducing time to first drink are unclear (Dahchour & De Witte, 2000; Garbutt et al., 1999). At this point, the efficacy of acamprosate appears to be comparable to that of the opiate antagonists in the treatment of alcoholism. As is the case with the opiate antagonists, the practical value of acamprosate treatment in alcoholism is questionable, particularly if not used in combination with other psychosocial therapies. For example, in a recent 6-month randomized controlled study of acamprosate versus placebo in preventing relapse in detoxified alcoholic patients, only 57 percent of the patients were judged to be taking at least 90 percent of their tablets after 2 weeks, and only 35 percent of the patients completed the study (Chick et al., 2000). Not surprisingly, there was no significant difference between the two groups in the total days of abstinence and the percentage of complete abstainers at the end of the study. In contrast, in a similarly designed study, but in which the patients also participated in an outpatient program that included medical counseling, psychotherapy, and self-help groups, only 25 percent of the patients dropped out after 6 months, and the abstinence rate and cumulative days of abstinence was significantly better in the acamprosate-treated group (Tempesta et al., 2000).

Because several lines of evidence suggest that serotonergic dysfunction may be a factor in alcoholism, the efficacy of serotonergic agents, including SSRIs (discussed later in this chapter and in Chapter 13), has been assessed in numerous clinical trials. The evidence from these trials is not very promising, although most studies of this nature have been confounded by high rates of comorbid mood disorders in the patients (Garbutt et al., 1999). In patients with comorbid major depressive disorder and alcohol dependence, long-term treatment with the SSRI fluoxetine has been shown to produce substantial reductions in depressive symptoms and drinking behaviors relative to placebo treatment, although none of the subjects in either treatment group was completely abstinent from alcohol throughout the entire period (Cornelius et al., 2000).

Recently, on the basis of evidence that early-onset alcoholism differs from late-onset alcoholism by its association with greater serotonergic abnormality and antisocial behaviors, treatment with ondansetron, a selective 5-HT$_3$ receptor antagonist, was assessed in early- and late-onset alcoholics. (Evidence suggests that 5-HT$_3$ receptors may be heteroreceptors that promote dopamine release in mesocorticolimbic neuronal terminals. Blocking 5-HT$_3$ receptors, which attenuates dopamine release, has been shown to reduce alcohol consumption in several animal species.) As predicted, low doses of ondansetron were found to be superior to placebo in increasing percentage of days abstinent and total days abstinent per study week in the patients with early-onset alcoholism (Johnson et al., 2000). These results indicate that ondansetron (at a specific dosage) may be an effective treatment for patients with early-onset alcoholism; they also suggest that the efficacy of pharmacological treatments may depend on the specific type of alcoholism.

Among the psychologically based treatments, a number of traditional psychodynamic approaches, behavior modification techniques, and group therapies have been applied in the treatment of alcoholism. Strategies that empirical research has suggested may be helpful in the treatment of alcoholism include self-help groups (for instance, Alcoholics Anonymous, Narcotics Anonymous, Cocaine Anonymous) (McCrady & Delaney, 1995), marital and family therapy (O'Farrell, 1995), coping and social skills training (Monti et al., 1995), anxiety and stress management (Stockwell, 1995), and behavior modification utilizing social, recreational, familial, and vocational reinforcers (Smith & Meyers, 1995). Cue exposure therapy, in which patients are exposed to potential conditioned stimuli (e.g., the sight and smell of alcohol) associated with alcohol's reinforcing effects in order to extinguish alcoholics' conditioned craving for alcohol, has produced some promising results in terms of reducing alcoholics' responsivity to alcohol cues (Staiger et al., 1999). However, its long-term efficacy for achieving and maintaining abstinence (the only viable goal with such an approach) remains to be established. Strategies that empirical research has uniformly found to be ineffective include relaxation training, confrontational counseling, videotape self-confrontation, individual psychotherapy, general alcoholism counseling, and educational lectures/films (Miller et al., 1995).

Perhaps one of the most accepted approaches to dealing with alcoholism is the one taken by Alcoholics Anonymous (AA). This organization, founded by a group of alcoholics in 1935, believes that alcoholism is a disease, that abstinence is required to deal with the disease, and that faith in a higher spiritual being is important in the recovery process. From a psychological perspective, this group provides peer education about alcoholism and its consequences for the individual, and provides support through the testimonials of many individuals who share the problems of alcoholism (McCrady & Delaney, 1995). These individuals also serve the vital function of being able to respond to the denials and rationalizations that inevitably occur in the alcoholic and that prevent the alcoholic from accepting that he or she has a problem. Unfortunately, there is considerable difficulty in determining the actual effectiveness of AA, since the group is reluctant to give researchers access to their records or members. Furthermore, participation in AA is almost always voluntary, raising questions of how self-selection might be a factor in the efficacy of AA. In one study, fewer than half of those treated for alcoholism in formal settings (discussed next) chose to attend AA meetings (Elal-Lawrence et al., 1987). In another study, it was found that those who chose to participate in AA were less pathological in their personality profile than those who did not voluntarily participate (Thurstin et al., 1986). Research suggests that problem drinkers who choose to participate actively in AA experience more favorable outcomes than those who just attend meetings—that is, those who are mandated or coerced to attend meetings by the courts or by employers—for whom controlled studies have found no unique efficacy of AA (Montgomery et al., 1995).

Over the past 30 years, a number of treatment centers for chemical dependency have sprung up around the United States. These centers use a relatively predictable combination of elements that characterize what is commonly referred to as the "Minnesota model" program, which continues to dominate treatment of addictions in the United States—a milieu advocating a spiritual 12-step (AA) philosophy, typically augmented with group psychotherapy, educational lectures and films, and relatively unspecified general alcohol counseling, often of a confrontational nature (W. R. Miller, 1995). The environment is highly structured, activities are regimented, and there is a heavy emphasis on peer-group therapy. It is difficult to determine the overall impact of these treatment centers in dealing with the age-old problem of alcoholism, particularly because these centers are selective in terms of the clients they accept and the treatment is expensive, which further restricts the types of clients who undergo this type of treatment.

The ability to select one's clients greatly influences the outcome of any treatment, because there is strong evidence that there are a number of characteristics of alcoholics that predict successful treatment (Holden, 1987). Alcoholics who respond well, regardless of treatment, are those with jobs, stable family relationships, minimal psychopathology, no history of past treatment failures, and minimal involvement with other drugs. Unfortunately, however, most alcoholics do not fall into this favored category. Furthermore, alcohol abusers whose history suggests a primary diagnosis of depression have been found to respond to treatment better than substance abusers with a diagnosis of antisocial personality.

In short, it is important to take with a grain of salt any claim of effective alcoholism treatment unless the characteristics of the clients are indicated. The fact is, on the basis of reviews of controlled comparisons among treatment settings (where different types of patients have been clumped together), there is little evidence that there is an overall advantage for residential over nonresidential settings, for longer over shorter inpatient programs, for more cost-intensive over less cost-intensive programs, or for inpatient over outpatient programs (Agosti, 1994; Holden, 1987; Miller & Hester, 1986, 1989).

However, a study comparing minimal versus intensive controlled-drinking treatment interventions for low to moderate dependence problem drinkers indicated that the intensive group reduced consumption and increased abstinent days significantly more than the minimal group (Robertson et al., 1986). Similar benefits were noted in a more recent study of employed problem drinkers randomly assigned to one of three rehabilitation regimens: compulsory inpatient treatment, compulsory attendance at AA meetings, or a choice of options. Though the estimated costs for the hospital group were about 10 percent higher than for the other two groups, the other two groups required more subsequent treatment (inpatient) and evidenced lower rates of abstinence and continuous sobriety 2 years after initial treatment (Walsh et al., 1991).

Virtually all strategies involved in the treatment of alcoholism in the United States focus on abstinence as the goal—primarily due to the belief that once an individual becomes an alcoholic, it is not possible for that individual to return to moderate drinking. However, there are a number of authorities who have suggested that controlled drinking training may still be a viable alternative for those individuals exhibiting less severe forms of alcoholism—that is, problem drinkers who have not developed a heavy physical dependence on alcohol (although I'm sure many experts cringe at such a suggestion) (Elal-Lawrence et al., 1987; Marlatt et al., 1993; Robertson et al., 1986). As mentioned earlier, there is a concern that many problem drinkers will simply not seek treatment if abstinence is the only option. The fact is, many individuals who receive extensive treatment for their alcoholism return to what can be considered controlled drinking (defined as less than 2.5 and 2.0 ounces of ethanol per day for men and women, respectively) following the period of abstinence required while they are in treatment. For example, in long-term follow-up studies of alcoholic patients treated in abstinence-oriented programs, controlled drinkers constitute 10 percent to 30 percent of the treated sample and abstainers constitute an additional 10 percent to 30 percent, with relapsers often comprising the largest outcome group (Booth et al., 1992; Miller et al., 1992). Those who return to moderate drinking are more likely to have received some type of training in controlled drinking, such as self-recording of drinking and blood alcohol levels; setting daily and weekly consumption limits; pacing drinking by sipping, diluting, and alternating alcoholic and non-alcoholic beverages; learning about the antecedents of drinking; learning how to refuse drinks; changing drinking environments and companions; and learning alternatives to drinking (Alden, 1988; Booth et al., 1992).

Whereas there is considerable resistance to the implementation of controlled drinking strategies into U.S. and Canadian treatment programs, where it is commonly believed that abstinence is the only acceptable outcome for patients, controlled drinking training is widely accepted in the United Kingdom as a viable treatment for alcoholism (Rosenberg et al., 1992; Rosenberg & Davis, 1994). The success of controlled drinking programs is still unclear, with some studies finding uncontrolled drinking frequently following a period of moderate drinking (Finney & Moos, 1991), and others finding that moderate drinking was sustained for follow-up periods of a year or longer (Booth et al., 1992; Miller et al., 1992).

No single personal characteristic has been consistently predictive of long-term success of controlled drinking treatments, but there is convincing evidence that a lower severity of dependence and a persuasion that controlled drinking is possible are associated with controlled drinking after treatment (Rosenberg, 1993). Although it may be argued that the majority of alcoholics who undergo behavioral self-control training will drink problematically or in excess of the controlled drinking limit at some time after follow-up, it is important to note that the distribution of approximately equal abstinent and nonabstinent successful outcomes is similar to that found following treatment programs that promote a single goal of abstinence (Booth et al., 1992; Miller et al., 1992).

Only about 15 percent of alcoholics ever receive formal treatment; many end up in jail, die of traffic or other accidents, or die of medical complications of their alcoholism. Depending on the criteria used for assessing treatment outcomes, somewhere between one-third and two-thirds of the alcoholics who are treated can be viewed as successes; that is, the person becomes abstinent or engages in nonproblem drinking (Marlatt et al., 1988). Interestingly, numerous studies have indicated that many alcohol abusers are able to positively change their use patterns without the assistance of formal treatment. Factors associated with successful self-change include a high level of motivation and commitment to change, public announcements, social support, alterations in one's social and leisure-time activities, general lifestyle changes that decrease exposure to conditioned craving cues, development of stress-coping strategies, and the generation of negative expectations over continued use and positive expectations concerning continued abstinence (Marlatt et al., 1988). A recent epidemiologic-based sample of individuals who remitted from alcohol abuse or alcohol dependence suggests that there may be two primary categories of drinkers with distinct pathways to remission: (1) those who experience significant problems for an extended period of time but then resolve to abstinence through the use of treatment services; and (2) those who drink heavily at some point in their lives, experience some problems, and then "mature out" of this stage in their life as they age and take on other life roles (Cunningham et al., 2000).

Fetal Alcohol Syndrome

Fetal alcohol syndrome (FAS) is the leading cause of mental retardation in the United States and is completely preventable, because it is caused by prenatal exposure to alcohol (Williams et al., 1994). First described in 1968, FAS is commonly characterized by mild to moderate mental retardation, small head circumference, absence of the groove between the nose and upper lip, inordinate profusion of hair on the face at birth, folds on eyelids, underdeveloped jaw area, cleft palate, joint anomalies, and cardiac irregularities. FAS children show smaller head circumference, smaller brain size, and proportionally smaller basal ganglia, diencephalon, and corpus callosum areas than do normal children (Mattson et al., 1994; Riley et al., 1995). Behavioral characteristics are reported in more than 50 percent of the cases. Compared with normal children, FAS children generally have poor attention spans; exhibit a lack of guilt after misbehaving; are impulsive, poorly coordinated, hyperactive, and irritable; and exhibit strange behavior and speech problems (Janzen et al., 1995; Wekselman et al., 1995). Many of their behavioral symptoms are very similar to those of children with Attention Deficit Hyperactivity Disorder (discussed in Chapter 14). It is generally accepted that alcohol-related birth defects exist along a continuum, with complete FAS at one end of the spectrum and incomplete features of FAS, termed **fetal alcohol effects** (FAE), which include more subtle cognitive-behavioral deficits, at the other.

Many of the symptoms of FAS decline as the children get older, but in most cases, these children remain at a considerable disadvantage in comparison to normal children (Steinhausen & Spohr, 1986). For example, one study found that I.Q. in FAS patients remained stable from a mean age of 8 years, 4 months (mean I.Q. of 66) to a mean age of 16 years, 7 months (mean I.Q. of 67) (Streissguth et al., 1991). Follow-up studies of FAS children have found that short stature persists into adolescence and adulthood, although weight may catch up to normal or above-normal levels (Wekselman et al., 1995).

For the most part, the cognitive impairment in these individuals (e.g., impaired academic performance) remains stable into their adult years (Phelps, 1995). Behaviorally, their hyperactivity is replaced by inattentiveness, distractibility, restlessness, and agitation. Adults with FAS tend to use poor judgment, make poor decisions, lack self-direction, and demonstrate difficulty in recognizing social cues. In adulthood, prenatal alcohol exposure has been found to be associated with high rates of trouble with the law, inappropriate sexual behavior, depression, suicide, and failure to care for children (Kelly et al., 2000).

The incidence of FAS and the severity of the symptoms are directly related to the amount of alcohol consumed by the mother during the first trimester. Numerous mechanisms have been proposed for the production of FAS (Keir, 1991). Some studies have pointed to ethanol's ability to disrupt the synthesis of retinoic acid, a metabolite of vitamin A, as a mechanism for inducing FAS, since an optimal level of retinoic acid is needed for normal development of the limbs and CNS (Shean & Duester, 1993). Others have suggested that the teratogenic effects of alcohol are due to altered umbilical–placental blood flow (Randall & Saulnier, 1995) or to the formation of free radicals (Guerri et al., 1994). Recently, alcohol's well-established ability to antagonize NMDA receptor activity has been proposed as a potential causal factor in FAS/FAE (Ikonomidou et al., 2000). This study found that a variety of agents that produced transient blockade of NMDA receptors caused sensitive neurons in the rat brain to die by a process that resembles the programmed cell death that occurs naturally in the developing brain. The window of vulnerability for humans would include the entire third trimester of pregnancy, because expression of NMDA receptors peaks during this period.

To account for why most women who drink during pregnancy do not give birth to FAS/FAE children, it has been argued that specific sociobehavioral risk factors—for example, those associated with low socioeconomic status, such as excessive pollutant exposure and poor nutrition—provide the context for biological factors—for example, maternal/fetal hypoxia and free radical formation—to provoke FAS/FAE in vulnerable fetuses (Abel & Hannigan, 1995). The risk of FAS has been reported to be sevenfold higher in Blacks than in Whites, even after adjustment for the frequency of maternal alcohol intake, occurrence of chronic alcohol problems, and number of children borne (Sokol et al., 1986), raising the question of some kind of genetic susceptibility to FAS.

The minimal amount of alcohol necessary for inducing FAS has not been determined, but most of the evidence suggests that it can occur when more than 1 ounce of ethanol is consumed per day. One cannot assume, however, that smaller amounts do not have any adverse effect on fetal brain growth and differentiation. Nor can one assume that such effects will not occur during the last trimester of pregnancy, when the fetus is generally considered to be least susceptible to environmental influence. In fact, one study indicated that pregnant women who drank heavily during the first two trimesters but were able to abstain or significantly reduce their alcohol consumption prior to the third trimester, produced offspring with no significant growth retardation (Rosett & Weiner, 1985). In contrast, more than a third of the neonates of mothers who drank heavily throughout pregnancy exhibited growth retardation. These findings suggest not only that damage can occur in the last trimester, but also that much of the damage that may occur during the first two trimesters may be reduced if drinking stops prior to the third trimester. Very little research has been done on pregnant women to determine the effects of binge drinking on fetuses. However, drinking seven drinks once a week is more likely to induce fetal abnormalities than having one or two drinks on a daily basis.

Barbiturates and Other Sedative–Hypnotics

Barbiturates have become the dinosaurs of drugs; they enjoyed a long period of use as sedative and hypnotic agents, but aside from a few specialized uses today, they have been displaced by the benzodiazepines. Furthermore, these and other drugs in the sedative–hypnotic class have effects so similar to alcohol's effects (Harvey, 1985) that little further discussion of them is needed, except to note that long-term alcohol exposure probably has more toxic physiological consequences (see earlier discussion on alcohol's unique characteristics and chronic effects of alcoholism). Since the mid-1800s, when the first barbiturate was derived (it is believed that the name came about either because the urine of a girl named Barbara was used to derive the compound or because the compound was synthesized on Saint Barbara's Day), more than 2,000 compounds with the same basic structure have been developed. Sedative–hypnotic compounds without the barbiturate structure, such as methaqualone and glutethimide, have been synthesized, but their actions are essentially indistinguishable from those of the barbiturates (Harvey, 1985).

In 1903, barbitone became the first of these compounds to be used clinically. Since that time, these substances have been used as general anesthetics for surgery, as treatments for anxiety-related symptoms, as sleep aids, and as anticonvulsants. Barbiturates differ from each other primarily in terms of pharmacokinetics, which determines how quickly the drugs act, their intensity of action, and their duration of action. All three of these properties are tied together. The differences in these properties are a major factor in determining what these drugs are used for. Representative barbiturates are thiopental, a fast-acting, ultrashort-duration (approximately 15 minutes) drug used primarily as an anesthetic; secobarbital, a short-duration (approximately 1.5 hours) drug used as a sleep inducer; pentobarbital and amobarbital, short- to intermediate-duration (approximately 4 hours) drugs used for either their sedative or sleep-inducing qualities; and phenobarbital, a relatively long-acting (approximately 6 hours) drug used as a sedative or an anticonvulsant.

The medical uses for these drugs have declined considerably over the past 30 years, primarily because of the development of newer compounds with less toxicity or dependence liability (such as the benzodiazepines, which will be discussed shortly) (Harvey, 1985). The primary advantage of the barbiturates at present is their cost. They are no longer under patent, and thus they are very inexpensive.

Despite lacking the barbiturate molecular structure, the substitute sedative–hypnotics mentioned earlier in this chapter have no properties, desirable or undesirable, that distinguish them from the barbiturates. In fact, at least one of these compounds—Quaalude (methaqualone)—was eventually withdrawn from the market because of its almost purely recreational use and abuse potential.

A consistent feature of barbiturates (and the nonbarbiturate alternatives) in humans is to increase EEG slow wave activity (theta and delta waves) and reduce alpha wave and fast beta wave activity (Patat, 2000). (Alpha activity predominates when a person is in a relaxed awake state with their eyes closed; beta activity is more frequent when a person concentrates on a task with their eyes open, and is associated with alertness; theta activity often occurs when a person has the eyes closed under resting conditions, and is linked to sleepiness; and delta waves, when they predominate, correspond to sleep.) The general tendency of these drugs is to decrease the excitability of neurons throughout the nervous system (Harvey, 1985). Although barbiturates depolarize some neurons, their predominant action throughout the nervous system is to hyperpolarize neurons. The inhibitory influence of barbiturates has been postulated to be due to their ability to enhance GABA's activity at the $GABA_A$-type receptor, which results in the opening of Cl^- channels, allowing Cl^- to flow into neurons and hyperpolarizing them. The primary action of barbiturates appears to be one of prolonging the duration that these channels remain open. The inhibitory effects of barbiturates may also be due to increases in potassium (K^+) conductance (that is, the flow of K^+ inside neurons to the outside) (O'Beirne et al., 1986). Accompanying these activities is an increase in the levels of most neurotransmitters, in all likelihood because of their decreased utilization. The rate of oxygen consumption and cerebral glucose metabolism in all areas of the brain is reduced with these drugs (Hibbard et al., 1987).

A wide variety of behaviors, perceptual processes, and mental activities are affected by even the low doses of these drugs that are used for their calming and sedating effects. As mentioned previously, these actions are almost indistinguishable from those of alcohol. Although they are all used for enhancing or inducing sleep, the pattern of sleep induced is not really what one would consider normal. In general, during an 8-hour night of sleep, we go through several stages of sleep. These stages differ with respect to how easy it is to wake the person, how physiologically aroused the body is, the mental content, the types of brain waves (EEG) produced, and the person's eye movements. All stages have been presumed to have some functional significance, but there is no consensus as to what specific functions they have. Most nonbenzodiazepine sedative–hypnotics tend to prolong the deeper stages of sleep and reduce the stage known as REM (rapid eye movement) (Harvey, 1985). REM is the stage in which vivid dreams are most common. However, the ability to suppress REM sleep is not restricted to the sedative–hypnotics. This characteristic has been noted to occur with many other types of drugs as well, including psychostimulants and marijuana.

The mechanisms for inducing tolerance to alcohol apply to the barbiturates, although the latter appear to have a greater effect than alcohol on the drug-metabolizing enzymes of the liver (increasing their levels up to five times their normal level) (Harvey, 1985). As indicated earlier, cross-tolerance occurs with all of these substances, and the psychological and physical dependence associated with them is quite similar. The faster-acting compounds, which also have more intense effects and shorter durations, are more likely to be abused, and the abstinence syndrome associated with them is likely to be more intense, but less protracted, than that associated with the longer-acting compounds.

Inhalants: Anesthetic Gases and Solvents

Inhalants consist of a wide variety of gases (ether, halothane, nitrous oxide, chloroform) and industrial solvents (for example, toluene, a component of some glues) that have sedative–hypnotic properties. Some of these are used as general anesthetics to put patients to sleep before surgery. Others are used for their intoxicating and euphoric properties. Inhalants, although not necessarily illicit drugs, are often used illicitly to get "high," particularly by very young individuals, for whom the prevalence rate of use is perhaps the highest of all abused drugs. Inhalants comprise one of the "gateway" drugs to further illicit drug use, but unlike almost all other substances that are used to get high, use of inhalants actually declines from the eighth grade to the end of high school (O'Malley et al., 1995).

Although these substances comprise a rather heterogeneous group of drugs, most of them are believed to work indiscriminatively by dissolving in neuronal membranes to somehow modify neuronal ion channel activity, because their potency is highly correlated with their lipid-solubility. However, some anesthetic gases, such as isoflurane, appear to act by binding directly to specific proteins in the CNS, because different isomers exert stereospecific effects on neuronal ion channels (Franks & Lieb, 1991). Whatever the mechanism of action, high doses of most of these substances decrease neuronal activities; at low doses they may increase some types of neuronal activity, most likely as a result of disinhibition (Jaffe, 1990).

Typically, after several minutes of inhalation, dizziness and intoxication occur. The characteristics of this high commonly include euphoria, visual and auditory hallucinations, a sense of empowerment, loss of motor coordination, nausea, and decreased heart and respiratory rates. Following the high, a period of drowsiness and stupor may persist for several hours (Miller & Gold, 1991).

Because of the heterogeneity of actions and because few of the many compounds of this nature have been systematically studied, little is known about their intoxicating properties. Some of them have been shown to have addictive qualities; for example, animals will self-administer nitrous oxide, chloroform, and toluene (Jaffe, 1990). Tolerance occurs with those substances that have been tested, but cross-tolerance may occur between some of these but not others.

Clinical problems associated with chronic use of many of the inhalants—for example, hexane and toluene—include cardiac arrhythmias, bone marrow depression, cerebral degeneration, and damage to the liver, kidney, and peripheral nerves (Jaffe, 1990; O'Brien, 1996). Deaths have occasionally been attributed to inhalant abuse; most of these are associated with heart failure, suffocation, or accidents (Johns, 1991).

Anxiolytics

At their core, anxiety disorders involve unrealistic, irrational fears or anxiety of disabling intensity. There are several primary types of anxiety disorders. Collectively, these disorders are the most frequently observed type of mental disorders in adults. For centuries, alcohol and to some extent opiate-type drugs were commonly used to reduce the symptoms of anxiety disorders; more recently the barbiturates (and drugs with similar properties) were used in their treatment. However, because of the high abuse potential and toxicity of these drugs, along with the development of drugs with more selective actions, the use of the former drugs (alcohol, barbiturates, and so forth) in treating anxiety disorders has virtually ceased, with perhaps the exception involving those individuals who use them for "self-medication" purposes. Anxiety disorders are now treated with drugs that are collectively referred to as **anxiolytics,** because they induce a "dissolution" or "loosening" of anxiety. A number of these drugs have pharmacological and behavioral properties similar to alcohol and barbiturates—differing only in a matter of degree. Others in this class, most developed in the past decade or so, have very different pharmacological and behavioral properties. In many cases the latter drugs have a higher efficacy rate, are less prone to abuse, and generally have minimal potential for inducing death through overdose.

Anxiety Disorders Treated with Anxiolytics

Phobias are characterized by persistent and disproportionate fear of some specific object or situation that presents little or no actual danger to the person. When persons with a phobia encounter a feared object or situation, they often experience the flight-or-fight response, which prepares them for escaping from the situation. *Specific phobias* generally involve fears of other species (for example, snakes, spiders) or fears of specific features of the environment (for example, large bodies of water, heights). *Social phobias* involve fears of social situations in which the individual feels exposed to the scrutiny of other people (such as during public speaking) and is afraid of acting in a humiliating or embarrassing way.

Panic disorder is related to phobias but is much less common. It is characterized by recurrent panic attacks, which are accompanied by heart palpitations or chest pain, a choking or smothering feeling, dizziness, numbness and tingling in the hands or feet, sweating, and trembling. The symptoms come on quite suddenly and unpredictably. The individual is persistently worried over experiencing a panic attack and "going crazy" or losing control. Long-term sufferers may begin to feel anxious in anticipation of an attack.

Agoraphobia is a common complication of panic disorder (although it can occur without experiencing prior panic attacks), in which the individual fears being in places or situations from which escape would be difficult or embarrassing should they experience a panic attack or something bad happen to them. In extreme cases, agoraphobics don't even venture outside their homes.

Generalized anxiety disorder (GAD) is characterized by chronic excessive worry over just about everything (that is, family, finances, work, or personal illness). Not only do individuals with this disorder exhibit much higher levels of worry over these than normal, but they also can't control or prevent their worrying. Other symptoms of this disorder include muscle tension, insomnia, attention and concentration problems, and social withdrawal.

Obsessive–compulsive disorder (OCD) is characterized by the occurrence of unwanted and intrusive obsessive thoughts or distressing images; these are usually accompanied by compulsive behaviors that may temporarily neutralize the obsessive thoughts or images or prevent some anticipated dreaded event or situation. Both obsessions and compulsions may occur in the disorder, or they may occur separately.

Posttraumatic stress disorder (PTSD) is characterized by a pathological reexperiencing of prior traumatic events in the form of intrusive thoughts, flashbacks, and dreams; avoidance of situations reminiscent of the trauma; and numbed responsiveness to the environment, manifested as diminished interest in significant activities, detachment from others, and restricted affect as well as symptoms of hyperarousal, including hypervigilance, exaggerated startle response, sleep disturbances, and impairment of concentration.

Benzodiazepines

Over the years, a number of drugs have come into clinical use with claims of being highly selective in their ability to reduce anxiety symptoms without inducing other undesirable effects. In the 1950s meprobamate (Miltown) was highly touted as one of these. However, it did not quite live up to its reputation in subsequent clinical tests and was not found to be significantly different from earlier sedative–hypnotic compounds. The introduction of chlordiazepoxide (Librium) into clinical use in 1961 ushered in the era of a new class of drugs called the benzodiazepines, and they have essentially taken over as the prototypic anxiolytic (Hobbs et al., 1996). These drugs are also sometimes referred to as "minor tranquilizers," because they are used predominantly in minor or less severe cases of pathology. Of the over 3,000 benzodiazepines synthesized, about three dozen are in clinical use in various parts of the world. In the United States the most commonly prescribed benzodiazepines for anxiety are chlordiazepoxide, diazepam (Valium), oxazepam (Serax), clorazepate (Tranxene), lorazepam (Ativan), prazepam (Centrax), alprazolam (Xanax), and halazepam (Paxipam). For many years the Valium brand of diazepam was the most popular drug of this group, but Xanax has replaced it as the most commonly prescribed anxiolytic, probably because of growing fears of addiction with Valium, competition from generic forms of diazepam, and limited evidence that Xanax may possess somewhat better antidepressant, antipanic, and antiphobic effects (DeVane et al., 1991).

The properties of benzodiazepines are very similar to those just described for the sedative–hypnotics. For example, they are effective anticonvulsants and muscle relaxants, they reduce a variety of aggressive tendencies, and they decrease anxiety. However, the actions of these drugs are hypothesized to be more specific than barbiturates and similar compounds in affecting the limbic system (which modulates emotionality, fear, aggression, sexuality, motivation, and pleasure) at doses that do not affect the reticular activating system (involved in maintaining a high level of consciousness and awareness) or the cerebral cortex (involved in higher mental processes like thinking and problem solving). In contrast to barbiturates, the benzodiazepines are not effective as general anesthetics.

There are a number of differences between the benzodiazepine anxiolytics and earlier compounds (including meprobamate) used in the treatment of anxiety-related disorders. The most striking difference is their high therapeutic index (Hobbs et al., 1996). Very few deaths are attributable to overdoses of benzodiazepines by themselves, although they have been involved in a number of deaths when combined with other sedative-like drugs, because of their additive effects. Their high therapeutic index is probably due to their specific ability to enhance the activity of a normally endogenous inhibitory neurotransmitter (GABA), as opposed to the more generalized neuronal suppressive effects of other sedative–hypnotic drugs. This may also account for why benzodiazepines have minimal general anesthetic effects except at very high doses. Another advantage is that they have minimal effects on the drug-metabolizing enzymes of the liver, and therefore do not enhance the hepatic metabolism of themselves or other drugs.

Part of the more selective action of the benzodiazepines is due to the fact that there are specific receptors for them, located in neuronal cell membranes, that mediate their action in the CNS. These benzodiazepine receptors seem to be highly specific for benzodiazepine agonists and antagonists (the latter appear to induce the symptoms of anxiety) and some nonbenzodiazepine compounds with similar psychoactive properties. The highest concentrations of these receptors are found in the cerebral cortex, limbic structures, and the cerebellum. Although the function of these receptors is unclear, the action of benzodiazepines at these receptors has been suggested to be one of facilitating the activity of GABA, which is predominately one of enhancing the flow of Cl^- ions into neurons and hyperpolarizing them.

Benzodiazepines are indirect GABA agonists, as they do not bind directly to GABA receptors, but appear to occupy receptor sites that enhance the ability of GABA to bind to and activate $GABA_A$ receptors (Costa & Guidotti, 1996; Zorumski & Isenberg, 1991). Thus, the benzodiazepines may be referred to as *allosteric modulators* of GABA (the term *allosteric* refers to the fact that the benzodiazepine recognition site is physically distinct from the GABA recognition site). As a result, the degree of effect of benzodiazepines depends on the concentration of GABA; that is, they produce marked effects at low GABA concentrations and minimal effects when high GABA concentrations are present. The lack of effect on maximal GABA responses may, in part, account for the lower toxicity of benzodiazepines compared with barbiturates in cases of overdose, because at high doses a number of barbiturates increase Cl^- flow into neurons in the absence of GABA—that is, they act more like direct GABA agonists (Hobbs et al., 1996).

Some of the endogenous ligands for these "benzodiazepine" receptors, termed *DBIs* for diazepam-binding inhibitors, have been identified (Barbaccia et al., 1988). Some of these may function to exert a natural anxiolytic action, whereas others have been shown to induce anxiety reactions (which presumably may have been adaptive in certain situations at some point in evolution). Some drugs (such as, Ro15–4513, beta-carbolines) have been found to induce the latter effects; because these drugs produce actions opposite of the benzodiazepines and their actions can be blocked with benzodiazepine antagonists (for example, flumazenil), they have been termed *inverse agonists.*

The action and thus the effects of benzodiazepines can be blocked completely with flumazenil (Romazicon). Flumazenil acts by competitively displacing benzodiazepines from their specific binding sites. In addition to its valuable use in locating and identifying specific benzodiazepine receptor sites, flumazenil has been used to rapidly reverse the effects of benzodiazepines used in surgical procedures, as an antidote in cases of benzodiazepine poisoning, and to reverse benzodiazepine comas (Hoffman & Warren, 1993).

The benzodiazepines are effective in reducing anxiety-related symptoms in approximately 70 percent to 80 percent of the persons with these symptoms. Their clinical efficacy must be evaluated against the fact that these symptoms vary considerably across time, and remission of symptoms with a placebo occurs in approximately 25 percent to 30 percent of patients. Perhaps for this reason, physicians who believe in the efficacy of these drugs seem to have greater success with their patients than do physicians who do not believe in their efficacy (Leavitt, 1982). The drug's effectiveness may also depend upon its effects on the patients' other defenses for combatting anxiety or behaviors they typically find useful to them. For instance, a professional golfer who takes a benzodiazepine to deal with tournament anxiety may actually play worse, and subsequently feel worse, because the drug disrupts motor abilities. Persons who are least likely to benefit from anxiolytic therapy are those with chronic dissatisfaction or insecurity, and those with character disorders, such as an antisocial personality. Such individuals are more likely to escalate their dosage, engage in impulsive overdosing, and succumb to physical dependence.

Many of the benzodiazepines are good anxiolytics because they are absorbed relatively slowly when given orally, with peak plasma levels occurring after several hours. This allows them to be taken only once or twice a day and induces a smooth, long-lasting effect. Diazepam is rapidly absorbed and reaches peak plasma levels in about an hour, which may account for its popularity both in clinical practice and on the streets. Most of the benzodiazepines are converted into active metabolites, which may partially account for the long duration of their action (Harvey, 1985). Their duration of action may be up to three or four times longer in premature neonates and the elderly than in young adults and children (Kerns, 1986).

Benzodiazepines that are highly lipid-soluble and do not form active metabolites may be useful in treating sleep disorders, because they have a fast onset of action but do not interfere with the next day's activities. However, aside from pharmacokinetic differences, in general there is no evidence that one benzodiazepine is more effective than another or that benzodiazepines labeled as hypnotics are more effective for sleep or less effective for daytime anxiety (Dubovsky, 1990). Benzodiazepines may also be used as anticonvulsants and as muscle relaxants.

One benzodiazepine that has gained considerable notoriety for its uses recently is Rohypnol (flunitrazepam). Although not marketed in the United States, there has been an increase in the illicit use and abuse of this drug, which is used clinically primarily as a sleeping aid (Rickert et al., 1999). The fact that it is quite potent—five to 10 times more potent than Valium—thus requiring very small amounts to be effective, coupled with its propensity to impair judgment and motor skills and to induce amnesia—particularly when combined with alcohol—has led to its use as a "date rape" drug. Several reports have appeared around the country in which women have awakened in unfamiliar surroundings with no clothes on or have been sexually assaulted after unknowingly (or knowingly) consuming Rohypnol. Its amnesia-inducing effects may prevent users from remembering how or why they took the drug or even having taken it, making investigation of sexually related offenses associated with its use very difficult. Because of its reputation for abuse, the DEA has recently classified flunitrazepam as a Schedule I drug—the first benzodiazepine to be so classified. Severe felony penalties have also been enacted for possession of Rohypnol and other similar drugs with the intent to commit a violent crime, including sexual assault.

As is the case with other drugs with sedative–hypnotic properties, tolerance develops to some of the pharmacological actions of benzodiazepines (File, 1985), and cross-tolerance may occur. However, the rate of tolerance may be slow (for example, to the anxiolytic effects), fast (for example, to sedative and anticonvulsant actions), or nonexistent (as in stimulant-type actions). The tolerance to benzodiazepines does not appear to be critically dependent upon altered metabolism or Pavlovian conditioning processes (Griffiths & Goudie, 1987). As discussed shortly, alterations in the GABA receptor complex may be responsible for some degree of tolerance.

Benzodiazepines have moderate psychological dependence liability. For instance, monkeys may self-administer them but not to the degree to which they self-administer cocaine (Johanson, 1987). Their abuse liability can be lessened considerably by formulating them in extended-release preparations, which slow their absorption rate without reducing their overall anxiolytic efficacy (Mumford et al., 1995). Physical dependence may also occur when doses considerably above therapeutic levels are administered. The severity of withdrawal is inversely related to the plasma half-life of the benzodiazepine (DeVane et al., 1991). However, since many benzodiazepines, and their active metabolites, accumulate and persist in the body for several days, withdrawal symptoms after chronic use may not appear for a week or so after abrupt discontinuation of these drugs, and the withdrawal symptoms are generally less intense than those occurring with other sedative–hypnotics. Furthermore, high doses must be given for a considerable length of time before marked withdrawal symptoms develop.

Following chronic usage of moderate dosages of benzodiazepines, abrupt discontinuation of use induces withdrawal symptoms consisting of anxiety and agitation (which could be confused with the symptoms for which the drugs were initially prescribed), increased sensitivity to light and sound, strange sensations, muscle cramps and twitches, sleep disturbance, and dizziness (Hobbs et al., 1996). Following high-dose usage, panic, depression, seizures, and delirium can develop. Withdrawal following chronic benzodiazepine exposure can also be triggered by the administration of the benzodiazepine antagonist flumazenil. As might be expected, chronic exposure to benzodiazepines is associated with progressive development of GABA receptor sensitization, which is concomitant with the development of tolerance as well as withdrawal symptoms upon discontinuation of these drugs (Lader, 1994).

The toxic reactions and side effects of benzodiazepines are similar to those of the barbiturates. In some cases, a paradoxical increase in hostility and irritability, and even anxiety, as well as vivid or disturbing dreams, may accompany benzodiazepine use (Hobbs et al., 1996). Confusional states in the elderly are commonly induced with these and other sedative compounds, and these states may be incorrectly attributed to senility. Other potential side effects of these drugs include amnesia, hallucinations, skin rashes, nausea, headaches, vertigo, light-headedness, sexual impotence, lowered white cell counts, and menstrual irregularities.

Several drugs (such as imidazenil, divaplon) have been developed that have a high affinity for benzodiazepine receptors but which elicit less amplification of GABA action at most $GABA_A$ receptor subtypes than benzodiazepines (Costa & Guidotti, 1996). These "partial allosteric modulators" (in contrast to benzodiazepines, which are "full allosteric modulators") have a pharmacological profile that may allow them to exert anxiolytic and anticonvulsant effects without most of the side effects of benzodiazepines. For example, tests with nonhumans indicate that they don't induce the cognitive impairments or motor disturbances induced by benzodiazepines (and, in fact, block these benzodiazepine-induced effects), don't potentiate the sedative effects of alcohol and barbiturates, and appear to have negligible potential for inducing tolerance and dependence. However, their therapeutic potential for treating anxiety and epileptic disorders in humans has not yet been tested.

Few reasonable clinicians would take the position that anxiety-related symptoms should be treated solely with drugs or solely with psychotherapy. It is difficult to compare efficacy rates between pharmacotherapy and psychotherapy, since there are so many factors determining the efficacy of drugs by themselves and so many different types of psychotherapy. Both seem to be in the same efficacy range in comparison to a placebo; that is, the average treated person is better off than 75 percent of placebo-treated patients (Smith & Glass, 1977). There is no consensus about combining anxiolytics with psychotherapy. Many clinicians feel that it is impossible to do successful psychotherapy (that is, behavioral, cognitive, or interpersonal therapy) in the presence of drug therapy. They believe the presence of discomfort is a motivating force for psychotherapy and that if the drug lessens the discomfort, patients will avoid dealing with the forces that are making them uncomfortable in the first place. Other clinicians feel that anxiolytics may be useful adjuncts to psychotherapy—if for no other reason than that if one treatment does not work, the other might.

Buspirone

After 20 years and umpteen different variations on the basic benzodiazepine molecule (resulting in numerous patented drugs with the same properties), pharmacologists finally synthesized a novel anxiolytic agent unrelated to the benzodiazepines and other sedative–hypnotics in structure and pharmacological profile. The drug is buspirone (BuSpar). As is typical in this field, the drug was originally developed for something other than what it may actually be most useful for. Initially, it looked like it might have antipsychotic properties. However, extensive clinical studies have shown buspirone to be comparable to the benzodiazepines diazepam and clorazepate in the treatment of anxiety (Sussman, 1994). It is also effective in patients with mixed anxiety and depression (Gammans et al., 1992). However, buspirone may be more effective in reducing the psychic problems of anxiety (that is, anger, hostility, worry, concentration difficulty) than the somatic symptoms (that is, muscle tension, insomnia). This may account for its lack of efficacy in treating panic disorder (Sheehan et al., 1993)—a more physical/somatic manifestation of anxiety—although it may enhance the effects of cognitive behavior therapy in the treatment of patients with panic disorder with agoraphobia (Cottraux et al., 1995).

Unlike the benzodiazepines, buspirone (1) lacks hypnotic, anticonvulsant, and muscle-relaxant properties; (2) takes 1 or 2 weeks of daily treatment before the onset of its anxiolytic effects is noted; (3) is much less likely to induce drowsiness and fatigue; (4) does not impair psychomotor or cognitive function; (5) has no potential for abuse and dependence (in fact, it may have dysphoric properties in moderate doses); (6) has no synergistic effect with alcohol; and (7) is not cross-tolerant with benzodiazepines and does not help reduce benzodiazepine withdrawal (Lader & Olajide, 1987). Pharmacokinetic interactions of buspirone with other coadministered drugs seem to be minimal (Chouinard et al., 1999). The most frequently reported adverse events with buspirone treatment are dizziness, headache, and nausea, although adverse events are typically mild and do not generally lead to treatment discontinuation (Sramek et al., 1999).

Buspirone lacks affinity for the benzodiazepine receptor and does not appear to act via GABA mechanisms. The mechanism of action of the drug is not well characterized, but it may exert its effect by acting on the dopaminergic system in the CNS or by binding to serotonin (5-HT) receptors (Mahmood & Sahajwalla, 1999). Its primary pharmacodynamic property is that of a 5-HT_{1A} partial agonist. Because 5-HT_{1A} receptors serve as somatodendritic serotonin autorecepters, buspirone suppresses serotonergic activity with acute exposure, but its proposed mechanism of action regarding its anxiolytic properties is one of down-regulating 5-HT_{1A} and 5-HT_2 receptors, which may explain why chronic exposure is needed before its benefits are evidenced (Charney et al., 1990).

Buspirone's unique properties have led to its being labeled as "anxioselective." It appears that it will be most useful in anxious patients, for whom daytime alertness is particularly important, and in the elderly, in whom the benzodiazepines may exacerbate cognitive impairment and cause adverse psychomotor effects (Steinberg, 1994). However, for patients who would benefit from a fast onset of action, or sedative and muscle-relaxant effects, the benzodiazepines would be preferred. Also, because there is no cross-tolerance with benzodiazepines, patients who are switched immediately from a benzodiazepine to buspirone may perceive the drug as ineffective. In fact, in patients who have been on a benzodiazepine for a long time and are then switched to buspirone, withdrawal symptoms may occur. These may be misinterpreted by the patients as an indication of the drug's ineffectiveness or as side effects. For patients with generalized anxiety disorder, the more recent their prior exposure to benzodiazepines, the less effective buspirone appears to be (DeMartinis et al., 2000). However, if anxious patients are first stabilized on benzodiazepines and then shifted to buspirone while the benzodiazepine is gradually tapered off, the anxiolytic efficacy can be retained without the patient experiencing rebound anxiety or benzodiazepine-withdrawal (Delle Chiaie et al., 1995).

Since its approval for use for GAD by the FDA in 1986, numerous studies have examined the efficacy and safety of buspirone for patients with other symptoms and disorders. Although relatively few placebo-controlled trials have been conducted on patients with problems other than GAD, an ever-growing body of research suggests that buspirone may be beneficial in the treatment of a variety of disorders. These include panic disorder, major depressive disorder, obsessive–compulsive disorder, body dysmorphic disorder, social phobia, posttraumatic stress disorder, selective serotonin reuptake inhibitor–induced adverse events, dementia, behavioral disturbances, attention deficit–hyperactivity disorder, and tobacco dependency (Apter & Allen, 1999).

Antidepressants as Anxiolytics

Anxiety disorders share a common affective state characterized by high psychological arousal, ranging from excessive worry to anxiety to extreme fear. Thus, it would seem that these disorders would be most amenable to treatment with anxiolytics. Curiously, however, while most research indicates that benzodiazepines, now the most commonly used anxiolytics, can reduce the symptoms of these disorders, other drugs not commonly viewed as anxiolytics have been shown to be equally or more effective in the treatment of these disorders (Davis & Gelder, 1991).

In clinical settings, anxiety and depression symptoms frequently coexist. Thus, a variety of antidepressants have been used in the treatment of patients with anxiety with some degree of success. While all of the classes of antidepressants described in Chapter 13 appear to be effective in many patients with these disorders, not all are effective in all patients with what appear to be very similar symptoms. Tricyclic antidepressants, such as imipramine (Tofranil), have been shown to be effective treatments for panic and phobic disorders, with an efficacy rate comparable to benzodiazepines such as alprazolam (Xanax) (Mattick et al., 1990). The monoamine oxidase inhibitors (MAOIs) have also been recommended for treatment of these disorders (Den Boer et al., 1995), but their use may be limited by potential interactions with other drugs or by dietary precautions that are necessary for preventing a hypertensive crisis. Curiously, the efficacy of antidepressants in the treatment of anxiety-related symptoms does not appear to be related to whether or not the patient is depressed.

If panic attacks or phobic reactions are controlled by an MAOI or tricyclic, but residual anxiety over experiencing symptoms is present, a benzodiazepine may be added to the drug regimen and then gradually removed as the patient becomes less fearful of suffering from another attack. As an adjunctive therapy to reduce the peripheral manifestations of these disorders (heart pounding and increased blood pressure), beta-adrenergic-blocking drugs, such as propranolol, may be tried. Unless the symptoms of these disorders are accompanied by clear signs of psychosis, antipsychotics are not appropriate in their treatment.

Over the past decade, a group of drugs, collectively called "selective serotonin reuptake inhibitors," or SSRIs, have come into clinical use. Originally developed for the treatment of depression (see Chapter 13 for a more complete description of these drugs), their clinical use has broadened dramatically, and they are being used in the treatment of a wide variety of disorders, including several in the anxiety category. SSRIs presently in clinical use include fluoxetine (Prozac), sertraline (Zoloft), paroxetine (Paxil), fluvoxamine (Luvox), and clomipramine (Anafranil). Reviews of drug treatment of patients with obsessive–compulsive disorder (OCD) concluded that clomipramine, fluoxetine, fluvoxamine, and sertraline are superior to placebo (Greist et al., 1995; Piccinelli et al., 1995), with approximately 60 percent to 70 percent of patients exhibiting at least moderate relief from their OCD symptoms. The SSRIs have been shown to be more effective in the treatment of OCD than antidepressant drugs that do not have selective serotonergic properties. While some studies have suggested that clomipramine induces greater overall improvement in OCD patients than the other SSRIs, other studies have concluded that the therapeutic efficacy among these drugs is comparable, although clomipramine is more prone to inducing anticholinergic and antiadrenergic side effects. In good responders, maintenance therapy with SSRIs for up to 2.5 years has been shown to provide substantial protection against OCD symptom worsening, compared to patients not receiving active medication, even when the maintenance SSRI dose is half that of the acute treatment dose (Ravizza et al., 1996).

The SSRIs also have demonstrated clinical efficacy in the treatment of panic disorder (with or without agoraphobia) (Bakish et al., 1996), generalized anxiety disorder and social phobia (Jefferson, 1995; Roy-Byrne et al., 1993), and posttraumatic stress disorder (van der Kolk et al., 1994). In most of these disorders, the efficacy of SSRIs is comparable to, or in some cases better than, the efficacy of more established drug treatments. For example, a recent meta-analysis revealed that the SSRIs are superior to imipramine and alprazolam in alleviating panic attacks (Boyer, 1995). Furthermore, the SSRIs are effective even in patients without symptoms of depression. Compared to TCAs and MAOIs, the SSRIs exhibit a better side-effect profile and possess greater safety in overdose. In addition, SSRIs do not pose the risk of addiction and withdrawal that may occur with the benzodiazepines. Thus, it is not surprising that this class of drugs is becoming more popular in the treatment of a variety of anxiety-related disorders.

Because many of the anxiety disorders present very specific behavioral symptoms, behavior therapy techniques such as biofeedback, systematic desensitization, and progressive relaxation may be useful in their treatment. Considerable research suggests this to be the case. Therefore, behavior therapy programs should definitely be involved in the treatment of these disorders, either in lieu of or in conjunction with drug therapy (Davis & Gelder, 1991).

Kava: An Herbal Anxiolytic?

The use of herbal preparations as alternative medical treatments has increased dramatically over the past several years in the United States and other parts of the world. Kava, a beverage prepared from the oceanic kava plant (*Piper methysticum*) and used extensively throughout the South Pacific for recreational and medicinal purposes, is one plant-based therapeutic option for treating anxiety. In 1998 it was among the top-selling herbs in the United States (Brevoort, 1998). Based on anecdotal reports of its calming influence, several double-blind, randomized, placebo-controlled trials of its efficacy have been conducted. Virtually all of these trials suggest that, relative to placebo, kava extract can significantly reduce anxiety (Pittler & Ernst, 2000). Although some of these trials reported adverse effects in a very small percentage of patients—such as stomach complaints, restlessness, drowsiness, tremor, headache, and tiredness—two of the trials, comprising approximately a third of the studied patients reported no adverse effects. Based on *in vitro* studies of kavapyrones, the pharmacologically active components of kava extracts, the effects are probably due to actions in the CNS, with the possibility of actions mediated through $GABA_A$ receptors (Davies et al., 1992; Jussofie et al., 1994). CNS effects of kava derivative have also been demonstrated by using EEG measurements in humans (Saletu et al., 1989). Although more research on the risk–benefit of kava needs to be done, it appears that kava extracts may be a relatively safe and effective alternative treatment for anxiety.

Sedative–Hypnotics and Insomnia

Insomnia is a sleep disorder that involves (1) the real or perceived inability to get to sleep or to stay asleep at night, resulting in subjective feelings of fatigue; (2) the chronic inability to maintain the amount and quality of sleep necessary for efficient daytime functioning; and (3) complaints of poor sleep, unrefreshing sleep, and sleep punctuated by abnormal restlessness. Chronic insomniacs not only report higher rates of difficulty with concentration, memory, and ability to cope with minor irritations, but also have two and a half times more fatigue-related automobile accidents than do good sleepers (Mendelson & Jain, 1995).

In doses somewhat higher than those needed to sedate, the sedative–hypnotics induce sleep, and for many years barbiturates were the most common treatment for insomnia. However, the use of barbiturates for this purpose has virtually ceased, primarily because they have been supplanted by somewhat safer drugs. It has long been recognized that the barbiturate sedative–hypnotics have numerous liabilities. Among these are their relatively low therapeutic index, their strong tendency to suppress REM sleep, their high psychological dependence potential, and their potentially lethal withdrawal effects when physical dependence develops. Furthermore, there is a relatively fast tolerance development to their sleep-inducing effects. While the functions of REM sleep and the consequences of suppressing it are still being debated, it is clear that, once the suppressing factors have been removed, REM activity increases dramatically for a few days and the dream content tends to be very bizarre and emotionally upsetting (Wallace & Fisher, 1999).

Because of these properties, drugs in the benzodiazepine class, such as flurazepam (Dalmane), became a popular treatment for insomnia. These drugs have considerably higher therapeutic indexes, have minimal effects on REM sleep, have less psychological dependence potential, and are less likely to induce severe physical dependence and withdrawal effects. However, benzodiazepines do have characteristics that make them less than ideal treatments for insomnia. They can raise the arousal threshold to such an extent that outside noises that should awaken the person, such as a smoke alarm, do not do so (Johnson et al., 1987). Also, there is evidence that benzodiazepines disrupt the deeper stages of sleep (stages 3 and 4) (Harvey, 1985), an effect that may prove to be just as significant as REM inhibition. On the other hand, this may be a factor in the efficacy of benzodiazepines in the treatment of sleepwalking and night terrors (the latter involving a sudden and intense arousal from slow-wave, deep sleep, accompanied by sharp body movements, a rise in heart rate and respiration, mental confusion, and extreme fright), which are most commonly observed to occur during the deeper stages of sleep (Rall, 1990).

Flurazepam and its several active metabolites tend to accumulate in the body over several days of use. This accumulation can produce daytime aftereffects such as lethargy and decreased coordination (also possible with the sedative–hypnotics). A more recently developed drug in this class, temazepam (Restoril), does not appear to have detrimental effects on next-day performance in psychomotor activities. This advantage is primarily due to its having no active metabolites. On the other hand, shorter-acting drugs, like temazepam and triazolam (Halcion), are more likely to induce early-morning insomnia (an increase in wakefulness during the final hours of drug nights), similar to rebound insomnia that occurs after withdrawal from the drug (Kales et al., 1983). In fact, reports on Halcion's side effects—rebound insomnia, daytime nervousness, panic attacks, and amnesia—led some experts to suggest that it be removed from the market. Although it is still available for clinical use, prescriptions for it declined considerably from 1988 to 1990. However, contrary to previous suggestions that such adverse effects as rebound insomnia and anterograde amnesia are unique to Halcion, hypnotically equivalent doses of Halcion have not been shown to produce these effects more frequently than other short-acting hypnotics (Mendelson & Jain, 1995).

All of the benzodiazepines used in the treatment of insomnia have a number of problems in common. They are all synergistic with alcohol and other CNS depressants; their combination with alcohol or other CNS depressants is one of the major causes of "overdose" deaths. In the elderly, who traditionally complain and suffer from insomnia, the diminished alertness that can come about with the use of these drugs can be confused with senility or dementia. The fact that these drugs do effectively induce sleep may prevent a patient from dealing with the problems causing insomnia. Finally, one must question the use of a potentially hazardous drug for the treatment of a disorder that may not necessarily be hazardous to one's health. In many cases, complaints of insomnia are exaggerated, and without knowing the purpose of sleep, it is difficult to determine how much sleep one should get and what represents normality or insomnia.

Zolpidem (Ambien) is a nonbenzodiazepine that was approved for treatment of insomnia in the United States in 1992 and is now the most commonly prescribed hypnotic (Rush, 1998). It has demonstrated efficacy equal to that of benzodiazepines, in terms of shortening sleep latency and prolonging total sleep time in insomniacs, and has actions resembling the latter class of drugs, but its advantages are that it appears to have low potential for inducing rebound insomnia or tolerance and withdrawal effects with chronic use (Hoehns & Perry, 1993). Furthermore, unlike the benzodiazepines, zolpidem has little effect on the stages of sleep in normal human subjects. At therapeutic doses, zolpidem infrequently produces residual daytime sedation or amnesia, and the incidence of other adverse effects (such as gastrointestinal complaints, dizziness) is also low. As is the case with benzodiazepines, zolpidem does not produce severe respiratory depression with large doses, unless other sedative–hypnotic type agents are also ingested. While the available data indicate that under most these circumstances the risk of abuse or dependence with zolpidem is minimal, there are several case reports of zolpidem abuse and dependence (Courtet et al., 1999). Furthermore, studies conducted with humans suggest that, on the basis of its reinforcing and pharmacokinetic properties, zolpidem's abuse potential is comparable to that of the hypnotic benzodiazepines (e.g., triazolam) (Rush, 1998).

Like the benzodiazepines, zolpidem appears to potentiate GABA-ergic transmission by increasing the frequency of Cl^- ion channels opening and inhibiting neuronal excitability. However, it has been proposed that zolpidem has more selective actions than the benzodiazepines because it has a relatively high affinity for one subtype of $GABA_A$ receptor, containing what is called the BZ1 (omega 1) receptor, and very low affinity for a second subtype of $GABA_A$ receptor, containing what is called the BZ2 (omega 2) receptor. In contrast, the benzodiazepines have approximately equivalent affinity for both receptor subtypes. BZ1 (omega 1) receptors have been suggested to be associated with sleep-inducing activity but not motor incoordination, and agonists at these receptors appear to produce little or no tolerance and dependence (Sanger et al., 1994).

Although this newer nonbenzodiazepine hypnotic seems to be equally efficacious as the short-acting benzodiazepines in the treatment of insomnia and has a better adverse-effect profile, neither it nor any other drug treatment for insomnia should be used as the sole treatment, but should be used in conjunction with nonpharmacological techniques, such as adherence to good sleep hygiene, sleep restriction, stimulus control, and biofeedback (Mendelson & Jain, 1995).

Websites for Further Information

The National Institute on Alcohol Abuse and Alcoholism home page:

http://www.niaaa.nih.gov/

Rutgers University's Center of Alcohol Studies home page (see "Facts on Alcohol"):

http://www.rci.rutgers.edu/~cas2/

Sites related to Fetal Alcohol Syndrome (FAS):

http://www.nofas.org/ (Home page for the National Organization on Fetal Alcohol Syndrome)
http://www.shadeslanding.com/clean-water/ (Home page of Clean Water International—
dedicated to purifying the fetal environment and preventing FAS)
http://w3.ouhsc.edu/fas/ (information on FAS and photographs of common FAS facial abnormalities)

Home pages for several alcoholism-related support groups:

http://www.alcoholics-anonymous.org/ (Alcoholics Anonymous)
http://www.adultchildren.org/ (Adult Children of Alcoholics)
http://www.health.org/nacoa/ (National Association for Children of Alcoholics)
http://www.al-anon-alateen.org/ (Al-Anon and Alateen)

Sites related to the temperance movement and prohibition:

http://www.history.ohio-state.edu/projects/prohibition/contents.htm
http://www.druglibrary.org/schaffer/alcohol/alcohol.htm

Information on barbiturates and benzodiazepines:

http://faculty.washington.edu/chudler/sleep.html
http://www.benzodiazepines.net/

Information on the latest research on GABA receptors and structures of GABA drugs:

http://gaba.ust.hk/Agent.html

Bibliography

Abel, E. L., & Hannigan, J. H. (1995). Maternal risk factors in fetal alcohol syndrome: Provocative and permissive influences. *Neurotoxicology & Teratology, 17,* 445–462.

Agosti, V. (1994). The efficacy of controlled trials of alcohol misuse treatments in maintaining abstinence: A meta-analysis. *The International Journal of the Addictions, 29,* 759–769.

Alden, L. E. (1988). Behavioral self-management controlled-drinking strategies in a context of secondary prevention. *Journal of Consulting and Clinical Psychology, 56,* 280–286.

Anthenelli, R. M., Klein, J. L., Tsuang, J. W., et al. (1994). The prognostic importance of blackouts in young men. *Journal of Studies on Alcohol, 55,* 290–295.

Apter, J. T., & Allen, L. A. (1999). Buspirone: Future directions. *Journal of Clinical Psychopharmacology, 19,* 86–93.

Aronow, L. (1980). *Alcoholism, alcohol abuse, and related problems: Opportunities for research.* Washington, DC: National Academy Press.

Arria, A. M., Tarter, R. E., Starzl, T. F., & Van Thiel, D. H. (1991). Improvement in cognitive functioning of alcoholics following orthotopic liver transplantation. *Alcoholism: Clinical and Experimental Research, 15,* 956–962.

Bakish, D., Hooper, C. L., Filteau, M. J., et al. (1996). A double-blind placebo-controlled trial comparing fluvoxamine and imipramine in the treatment of panic disorder with or without agoraphobia. *Psychopharmacology Bulletin, 32,* 135–142.

Barbaccia, M. L., Costa, E., & Guidotti, A. (1988). Endogenous ligands for high-affinity recognition sites of psychotropic drugs. *Annual Review of Pharmacology and Toxicology, 28,* 451–476.

Booth, B. M., & Blow, F. C. (1993). The kindling hypothesis: Further evidence from a U. S. national study of alcoholic men. *Alcohol and Alcoholism, 28,* 593–598.

Booth, P. G., Dale, B., Slade, P. D., & Dewey, M. E. (1992). A follow-up study of problem drinkers offered a goal choice option. *Journal of Studies of Alcohol, 53,* 594–600.

Boyer, W. (1995). Serotonin uptake inhibitors are superior to imipramine and alprazolam in alleviating panic attacks: A meta-analysis. *International Clinical Psychopharmacology, 10,* 45–49.

Brady, K. T., & Sonne, S. C. (1995). The relationship between substance abuse and bipolar disorder. *Journal of Clinical Psychiatry, 56* (Suppl), 19–24.

Brecher, E. M. (Ed.). (1972). *Licit and illicit drugs.* Boston: Little, Brown.

Brevoort, P. (1998). The booming US botanical market: A new overview. *Herbalgram, 44,* 36–46.

Britton, K. T., Ehlers, C. L., & Koob, G. F. (1988). Is ethanol antagonist Ro15–4513 selective for ethanol? *Science, 239,* 648–649.

Brubaker, R. G., Prue, D. M., & Rychtarik, R. G. (1987). Determinants of disulfiram acceptance among alcohol patients: A test of the theory of reasoned action. *Addictive Behaviors, 12,* 43–51.

Butterworth, R. F. (1995). Pathophysiology of alcoholic brain damage: Synergistic effects of ethanol, thiamine deficiency and alcoholic liver disease. *Metabolic Brain Disease, 10,* 1–8.

Cadoret, R. J., Troughton, E., & O'Gorman, T. W. (1987). Genetic and environmental factors in alcohol abuse and antisocial personality. *Journal of Studies on Alcohol, 48,* 1–8.

Campbell, W. G., & Hodgins, D. C. (1993). Alcohol-related blackouts in a medical practice. *American Journal of Drug and Alcohol Abuse, 19,* 369–376.

Carlen, P. L., Holgate, R. C., Wortzman, G., & Wilkinson, D. A. (1978). Reversible cerebral atrophy in recently abstinent chronic alcoholics measured by computed tomography scans. *Science, 200,* 1076–1078.

Charney, D. S., Krystal, J. H., Delgado, P. L., & Heninger, G. R. (1990). Serotonin-specific drugs for anxiety and depressive disorders. *Annual Review of Medicine, 41,* 437–446.

Chick, J., Howlett, H., Morgan, M. Y., et al. (2000). United Kingdom multicentre acamprostate study (UKMAS): A 6-month prospective study of acamprostate versus placebo in preventing relapse after withdrawal from alcohol. *Alcohol and Alcoholism, 35,* 176–187.

Chouinard, G., Lefko-Singh, K., & Teboul, E. (1999). Metabolism of anxiolytics and hypnotics: Benzodiazepines, buspirone, zoplicone, and zolpidem. *Cellular and Molecular Neurobiology, 19,* 533–552.

Cicero, T. J. (1978). Tolerance to and physical dependence on alcohol: Behavioral and neurobiological mechanisms. In M. A. Lipton, A. DiMascio, & K. F. Killman (Eds.), *Psychopharmacology* (pp. 1603–1618). New York: Raven Press.

Cloninger, C. R. (1987). Neurogenetic adaptive mechanisms in alcoholism. *Science, 236,* 410–416.

Cornelius, J. R., Salloum, I. M., Haskett, R. F., et al. (2000). Fluoxetine versus placebo in depressed alcoholics: A 1-year follow-up study. *Addictive Behaviors, 25,* 307–310.

Costa, E., & Guidotti, A. (1996). Benzodiazepines on trial: A research strategy for their rehabilitation. *Trends in the Pharmacological Sciences, 17,* 192–200.

Cottraux, J., Note, I. D., Cungi, C., et al. (1995). A controlled study of cognitive behaviour therapy with buspirone or placebo in panic disorder with agoraphobia. *British Journal of Psychiatry, 167,* 635–641.

Courtet, P., Pignay, V., Castelnau, D., et al. (1999). Abuse of and dependence on zolpidem: A report of seven cases. *Encephale, 25,* 652–657.

Critchlow, B. (1986). The powers of John Barleycorn: Beliefs about the effects of alcohol on social behavior. *American Psychologist, 41,* 751–763.

Crowell, C. R., Hinson, R. E., & Siegel, S. (1981). The role of conditional drug responses in tolerance to hypothermic effects of ethanol. *Psychopharmacology, 73,* 51–54.

Cunningham, J. A., Lin, E., Ross, H. E., & Walsh, G. W. (2000). Factors associated with untreated remissions from alcohol abuse or dependence. *Addictive Behaviors, 25,* 317–321.

Cutter, H. S. G., O'Faffell, T. J., Whitehouse, J., & Dentch, G. M. (1986). Pain changes among men from before to after drinking: Effects of expectancy set and dose manipulations with alcohol and tonic as mediated by prior experience with alcohol. *International Journal of the Addictions, 21,* 937–945.

Cychosz, C. M. (1996). Alcohol and interpersonal violence: Implications for educators. *Journal of Health Education, 27,* 73–77.

Dahchour, A., & De Witte, P. (2000). Ethanol and amino acids in the central nervous system: Assessment of the pharmacological actions of acamprosate. *Progress in Neurobiology, 60,* 343–362.

Davidson, M., Shanley, B., & Wilce, P. (1995). Increased NMDA-induced excitability during ethanol withdrawal: A behavioural and histological study. *Brain Research, 674,* 91–96.

Davies, L. P., Drew, C. A., Duffield, P., et al. (1992). Kava pyrones and resin: Studies on GABAA,

GABAB, and benzodiazepine binding sites in rodent brain. *Pharmacology and Toxicology, 71,* 120–126.

Davis, J. D., & Gelder, M. (1991). Long-term management of anxiety states. *International Review of Psychiatry, 3,* 5–17.

Dawson, D. A. (2000). Alcohol consumption, alcohol dependence, and all-cause mortality. *Alcoholism, Clinical and Experimental Research, 24,* 72–81.

Delle Chiaie, R., Pancheri, P., Casacchia, M., et al. (1995). Assessment of the efficacy of buspirone in patients affected by generalized anxiety disorder, shifting to buspirone from prior treatment with lorazepam: A placebo-controlled, double-blind study. *Journal of Clinical Psychopharmacology, 15,* 12–19.

DeMartinis, N., Rynn, M., Rickels, K., et al. (2000). Prior benzodiazepine use and buspirone response in the treatment of generalized anxiety disorder. *Journal of Clinical Psychiatry, 61,* 91–94.

Den Boer, J. A., Van Vliet, I. M., & Westenberg, H. G. (1995). Recent developments in the psychopharmacology of social phobia. *European Archives of Psychiatry & Clinical Neuroscience, 244,* 309–316.

DeVane L., Ware, M. R., & Lydiard, R. B., (1991). Pharmacokinetics, pharmacodynamics, and treatment issues of benzodiazepines: Alprazolam, adinazolam, and clonazepam. *Psychopharmacology Bulletin, 27,* 463–473.

DiPadova, C., Worner, T. M., Julkunen, R. J. K., & Lieber, C. S. (1987). Effects of fasting and chronic alcohol consumption on the first-pass metabolism of ethanol. *Gastroenterology, 92,* 1169–1173.

Dorus, W., Ostrow, D. G., Anton, R., et al. (1989). Lithium treatment of depressed and nondepressed alcoholics. *Journal of the American Medical Association, 262,* 1646–1652.

Drake, A. I., Butters, N., Shear, P. K., et al. (1995). Cognitive recovery with abstinence and its relationship to family history for alcoholism. *Journal of Studies on Alcohol, 56,* 104–109.

Dubovsky, S. L. (1990). Generalized anxiety disorder: New concepts and psychopharmacologic therapies. *Journal to Clinical Psychiatry, 51* (Suppl), 3–10.

Earleywine, M. (1993). Personality risk for alcoholism covaries with hangover symptoms. *Addictive Behavior, 18,* 415–420.

Ehlers, C. L., Havstad, J., Prichard, D., et al. (1998). Low doses of ethanol reduce evidence for nonlin-ear structure in brain activity. *Journal of Neuroscience, 18,* 7474–7486.

Elal-Lawrence, G., Slade, P. D., & Dewey, M. E. (1987) Treatment and follow-up variables discriminating abstainers, controlled drinkers and relapsers. *Journal of Studies on Alcohol, 48,* 39–46.

Ellis, R. J., & Oscar-Berman, M. (1989). Alcoholism, aging, and functional cerebral asymmetries. *Psychological Bulletin, 106,* 128–147.

File, S. E. (1985). Tolerance to the behavioural actions of benzodiazepines. *Neuroscience and Biobehavioral Reviews, 9,* 113–121.

Fillmore, K. M., Golding, J. M., Graves, K. L., et al. (1998). Alcohol consumption and mortality. *Addiction, 93,* 183–203.

Fingarette, H. (1988). *Heavy drinking: The myth of alcoholism as a disease.* Berkeley: University of California Press.

Finney, J. W., & Moos, R. H. (1991). The long-term course of treated alcoholism: I. Mortality, relapse and remission rates and comparisons with community controls. *Journal of Studies on Alcohol, 52,* 44–54.

Franks N. P., & Lieb, W. R. (1991). Stereospecific effects of inhalational general anesthetic optical isomers on nerve ion channels. *Science, 254,* 427–430.

Fuller, R. K. (1995). Antidipsotropic medications. In R. K. Hester & W. R. Miller (Eds.), *Handbook of alcoholism treatment approaches* (pp. 123–133). Boston: Allyn & Bacon.

Gammans, R. E., Stringfellow, J. C., Hvizdos, A. J. Seidhamel, R. J., Cohn, J. B., Wilcox, C. S., et al. (1992). Use of buspirone in patients with generalized anxiety disorder and coexisting depressive symptoms: A meta-analysis of eight randomized, controlled studies. *Neuropsychobiology, 25,* 193–201.

Garbutt, J. C., West, S. L., Carey, T. S., et al. (1999). Pharmacological treatment of alcohol dependence: A review of the evidence. *JAMA, 281,* 1318–1325.

Gauvin, D. V., Cheng, E. Y., & Holloway, F. A. (1993). Recent developments in alcoholism: Biobehavioral correlates. *Recent Developments in Alcoholism, 11,* 281–304.

Gaziano, J. M., & Hennekens, C. (1995). Royal colleges' advice on alcohol consumption. *British Medical Journal, 311,* 3–4.

Gaziano, J. M., Gaziano, T. A., Glynn, R. J., et al. (2000). Light-to-moderate alcohol consumption and mortality in the Physicians' Health Study enrollment cohort. *Journal of the American College of Cardiology, 35,* 96–105.

George, M. S., Teneback, C. C., Malcolm, R. J., et al. (1999). Multiple previous alcohol detoxifications are associated with decreased medial temporal and paralimbic function in the postwithdrawal period. *Alcoholism: Clinical and Experimental Research, 23,* 1077–1084.

Gold, P. E. (1995). Role of glucose in regulating the brain and cognition. *American Journal of Clinical Nutrition, 61* (Suppl), 987S–995S.

Golden, C. J., Graber, B., Blose, I., Berg, R., Coffman, J., & Bloch, S. (1981). Difference in brain densities between chronic alcoholic and normal control patients. *Science, 211,* 508–510.

Goldstein, D. B. (1989). Alcohol and biological membranes. In H. W. Goedde & D. P. Agarwal (Eds.), *Alcoholism* (pp. 87–98). New York: Pergamon Press.

Greist, J. H., Jefferson, J. W., Kobak, K. A., & Katzelnick, D. J. (1995). Efficacy and tolerability of serotonin transport inhibitors in obsessive-compulsive disorder. A meta-analysis. *Archives of General Psychiatry, 52,* 53–60.

Griffiths, J. W., & Goudie, A. J. (1987). Analysis of the role of behavioural factors in the development of tolerance to the benzodiazepine midazolam. *Neuropharmacology, 26,* 201–209.

Guerri, C., Montoliu, C., & Renau-Piqueras, J. (1994). Involvement of free radical mechanism in the toxic effects of alcohol: Implications for fetal alcohol syndrome. *Advances in Experimental Medicine & Biology, 366,* 291–305.

Guze, S. B., Cloninger, C. R., Martin, R., & Clayton, P. J. (1986). Alcoholism as a medical disorder. *Comprehensive Psychiatry, 27,* 501–510.

Harvey, S. C. (1985). Hypnotics and sedatives. In A. G. Gilman, L. S. Goodman, T. W. Rall, & F. Murad (Eds.). *The pharmacological basis of therapeutics* (pp. 339–371). New York: Macmillan.

Heilbrun, A. B., Cassidy, J. C., Diehl, M., et al. (1986). Psychological vulnerability to alcoholism: Studies in internal scanning deficit. *British Journal of Medical Psychology, 59,* 237–244.

Henriksen, S. J. (1993). Neuropharmacology of ethanol. In S. G. Korenman & J. D. Barchas (Eds.), *Biological basis of substance abuse* (pp. 309–326). New York: Oxford University Press.

Hibbard, L. S., McGlone, J. S., Davis, D. W., & Hawkins, R. A. (1987). Three-dimensional representation and analysis of brain energy metabolism. *Science, 236,* 1641–1646.

Hobbs, W. R., Rall, T. W., & Verdoorn, T. A. (1996). Hypnotics and sedatives: Ethanol. In A. G. Gilman, L. S. Goodman, J. G. Hardman, L. E. Limbard, P. B. Molinoff, & R. W. Ruddon (Eds.), *The pharmacological basis of therapeutics* (pp. 361–396). New York: McGraw-Hill.

Hoehns, J. D., & Perry, P. J. (1993). Zolpidem: A nonbenzodiazepine hypnotic for treatment of insomnia. *Clinical Pharmacy, 12,* 814–828.

Hoffman, E. J., & Warren, E. W. (1993). Flumazenil: A benzodiazepine antagonist. *Clinical Pharmacy, 12,* 641–656.

Holden, C. (1987). Is alcoholism treatment effective? *Science, 236,* 20–22.

Hull, J. G., & Bond, C. F. (1986). Social and behavioral consequences of alcohol consumption and expectancy: A meta-analysis. *Psychological Bulletin, 99,* 347–359.

Hunt, W. A. (1993). Are binge drinkers more at risk of developing brain damage? *Alcohol, 10,* 559–561.

Ikonomidou, C., Bittigau, P., Ishimaru M. J., et al. (2000). Ethanol-induced apoptotic neurodegeneration and fetal alcohol syndrome. *Science, 287,* 1056–1059.

Jaffe, J. (1990). Drug addiction and drug abuse. In A. G. Gilman, T. W. Rall, A. S. Nies, & P. Taylor (Eds.), *The pharmacological basis of therapeutics* (pp. 522–573). New York: Pergamon Press.

Janzen, L. A., Nanson, J. L., & Block, G. W. (1995). Neuropsychological evaluation of preschoolers with fetal alcohol syndrome. *Neurotoxicology & Teratology, 17,* 273–279.

Jefferson, J. W. (1995). Social Phobia: A pharmacologic treatment overview. *Journal of Clinical Psychiatry, 56* (Suppl.), 18–24.

Johanson, C. E. (1987). Benzodiazepine self-administration in rhesus monkeys: Estazolam, flurazepam and lorazepam. *Pharmacology, Biochemistry, and Behavior, 26,* 521–526.

Johns, A. (1991). Volatile solvent abuse and 963 deaths. *British Journal of Addiction, 86,* 1053–1056.

Johnson, B. A., Roache, J. D., Javors, M. A., et al. (2000). Ondansetron for reduction of drinking among biologically predisposed alcoholic patients: A randomized controlled trial. *JAMA, 284,* 963–971.

Johnson, L. C., Spinweber, C. L., Webb, S. C., & Muzet, A. G. (1987). Dose level effects of triazolam on sleep and response to a smoke detector alarm. *Psychopharmacology, 91,* 397–402.

Johnson, V. (1986). *Intervention: How to help someone who doesn't want help.* Minneapolis, MN: Johnson Institute Books.

Jussofie, A., Schmiz, A., & Hiemke, C. (1994). Kavapyrone enriched extract from Piper methysticum as modulator of the GABA binding site in different regions of rat brain. *Psychopharmacology, 116,* 469–474.

Kales, A., Soldatos, C. R., Bixler, E. O., & Kales, J. D. (1983). Early morning insomnia with rapidly eliminated benzodiazepines. *Science, 220,* 95–97.

Keir, W. J. (1991). Inhibition of retinoic acid synthesis and its implications in fetal alcohol syndrome. *Alcoholism Clinical and Experimental Research, 15,* 560–564.

Kelly, S. J., Day, N., & Streissguth, A. P. (2000). Effects of prenatal alcohol exposure on social behavior in humans and other species. *Neurotoxicology and Teratology, 22,* 143–149.

Kendler, K. S., Heath, A. C., Neale, M. C., et al. (1992). A population-based twin study of alcoholism in women. *Journal of the American Medical Association, 268,* 1877–1882.

Kerns, L. L. (1986). Treatment of mental disorders in pregnancy. *The Journal of Nervous and Mental Disease, 174,* 652–659.

Kril, J. J. (1995). The contribution of alcohol, thiamine deficiency and cirrhosis of the liver to cerebral cortical damage in alcoholics. *Metabolic Brain Disease, 10,* 9–16.

Lader, M. (1994). Biological processes in benzodiazepine dependence. *Addiction, 89,* 1413–1418.

Lader, M., & Olajide, D. (1987). A comparison of buspirone and placebo in relieving benzodiazepine withdrawal symptoms. *Journal of Clinical Psychopharmacology, 7,* 11–15.

Lancaster, F. E. (1995). Alcohol and the brain: What's NO got to do with it? *Metabolic Brain Disease, 10,* 125–133.

Leavitt, F. (1982). *Drugs and behavior.* New York: John Wiley & Sons.

Liao, Y., McGee, D. L., Cao, G., et al. (2000). Alcohol intake and mortality: Findings from the National Health Interview Surveys (1998 and 1990). *American Journal of Epidemiology, 151,* 651–659.

Lieber, C. S. (1994). Alcohol and the liver: 1994 update. *Gastroenterology, 106,* 1085–1105.

Loneck, B., Garrett, J. A., & Banks, S. M. (1996). A comparison of the Johnson intervention with four other methods of referral to outpatient treatment. *American Journal of Alcohol Abuse, 22,* 233–246.

Mahmood, I., & Sahajwalla, C. (1999). Clinical pharmacokinetics and pharmacodynamics of buspirone, an anxiolytic drug. *Clinical Pharma-cokinetics, 36,* 277–287.

Mann, K., Batra, A., Gunthner, A., Schroth, G. (1992). Do women develop alcoholic brain damage more readily than men? *Alcoholism, Clinical & Experimental Research, 16,* 1052–1056.

Mann, K., Mundle, G., Langle, G., & Peterson, D. (1993). The reversibility of alcoholic brain damage is not due to rehydration: A CT study. *Addiction, 88,* 649–653.

Marlatt, G. A., Baer, J. S., Donovan, D. M., & Kivlahan, D. R. (1988). Addictive behaviors: Etiology and treatment. *Annual Review of Psychology, 39,* 223–252.

Marlatt, G. A., Larimer, M. E., Baer, J. S., & Quigley, L. A. (1993). Harm reduction for alcohol problems: Moving beyond the controlled drinking controversy. *Behavior Therapy, 24,* 461–503.

Mason, B. J., Salvator, F. R., Williams, L. D., et al. (1999). A double-blind, placebo-controlled study of oral nalmefene for alcohol dependence. *Archives of General Psychiatry, 56,* 719–724.

Mattick, R. P., Andrews, G., Hadzi-Pavlovic, D., Christensen, H. (1990). Treatment of panic and agoraphobia. An integrative review. *Journal of Nervous & Mental Disease, 178,* 567–576.

Mattson, S. N., Jernigan, T. L., & Riley, E. P. (1994). MRI and prenatal alcohol exposure: Images provide insight into FAS. *Alcohol Health & Research World, 18,* 49–52.

Mazoit, J. -X., Sandouk, P., Zetlaoui, P., & Scherrmann, J. -M. (1987). Pharmacokinetics of unchanged morphine in normal and cirrhotic subjects. *Anesthetic Analgesics, 66,* 293–298.

McCrady, B. S., & Delaney, S. I. (1995). Self-help groups. In R. K. Hester & W. R. Miller (Eds.), *Handbook of alcoholism treatment approaches* (pp. 160–175). Boston: Allyn & Bacon.

McEntee, W. M., & Mair, R. G. (1978). Memory impairment in Korsakoff's psychosis: A correlation with brain noradrenergic activity. *Science, 202,* 905–907.

McGue, M. (1999). The behavioral genetics of alcoholism. *Current Directions in Psychological Science, 8,* 109–115.

Mello, R. E. (1978). Alcoholism and the behavioral pharmacology of alcohol, 1967–1977. In M. A. Lipton, A. DiMascio, & K. F. Killman (Eds.), *Psychopharmacology* (pp. 1619–1638). New York: Raven Press.

Mendelson, W. B., & Jain, B. (1995). An assessment of short-acting hypnotics. *Drug Safety, 13,* 257–270.

Mhatre, M. C., & Ticku, M. K. (1993). Alcohol: Effects on GABA$_A$ receptor function and gene expression. *Alcohol and Alcoholism, 2* (Suppl), 331–335.

Miller, N. S., & Flaherty, J. A. (2000). Effectiveness of coerced addiction treatment (alternative consequences): A review of the clinical research. *Journal of Substance Abuse Treatment, 18,* 9–16.

Miller, N. S., & Gold, M. S. (1991). Organic solvent and aerosol abuse. *American Family Physician, 44,* 183–189.

Miller, W. R. (1995). Increasing motivation for change. In R. K. Hester & W. R. Miller (Eds.), *Handbook of alcoholism treatment approaches* (pp. 89–104). Boston: Allyn & Bacon.

Miller, W. R., Brown, J. M., Simpson, T. L., et al. (1995). What works? A methodological analysis of the alcohol treatment outcome literature. In R. K. Hester & W. R. Miller (Eds.), *Handbook of alcoholism treatment approaches* (pp. 12–60). Boston: Allyn & Bacon.

Miller, W. R., & Hester, R. K. (1986). Inpatient alcoholism treatment. *American Psychologist, 41,* 794–805.

Miller, W. R., & Hester, R. K. (1989). Inpatient alcoholism treatment: Rules of evidence and burden of proof. *American Psychologist, 44,* 1245–1246.

Miller, W. R., Leckman, A. L., Delaney, H. D., & Tinkcom, M. (1992). Long-term follow-up of behavioral self-control training. *Journal of Studies of Alcohol, 53,* 249–261.

Montgomery, H. A., Miller, W. R., & Tonigan, J. S. (1995). Does Alcoholics Anonymous involvement predict treatment outcome? *Journal of Substance Abuse Treatment, 12,* 241–246.

Monti, P. M., Rohsenow, D. J., Colby, S. M., & Abrams, D. B. (1995). Coping and social skills training. In R. K. Hester & W. R. Miller (Eds.), *Handbook of alcoholism treatment approaches* (pp. 221–239). Boston: Allyn & Bacon.

Mueller, T. I., Stout, R. L., Rudden, S., et al. (1997). A double-blind, placebo-controlled pilot study of carbamazepine for the treatment of alcohol dependence. *Alcoholism, Clinical and Experimental Research, 21,* 86–92.

Mumford, G. K., Evans, S. M., Fleishaker, J. C., Griffiths, R. R. (1995). Alprazolam absorption kinetics affects abuse liability. *Clinical Pharmacology and Therapeutics, 57,* 356–365.

Naranjo, C. A., & Bremner, K. E. (1993). Behavioural correlates of alcohol intoxication. *Addiction, 88,* 25–35.

National Household Survey on Drug Abuse. (1999). National estimates of drug abuse. <http://www.health.org.govstudy/bkd376/Chapter2.htm#> (2000, October 23)

Nelson, T. O., McSpadden, M., Fromme, K., & Marlatt, G. A. (1986). Effects of alcohol intoxication on metamemory and on retrieval from long-term memory. *Journal of Experimental Psychology: General, 115,* 247–254.

Newlin, D. B., & Pretorius, M. B. (1990). Sons of alcoholics report greater hangover symptoms than sons of nonalcoholics: A pilot study. *Alcoholism, Clinical & Experimental Research, 14,* 713–716.

Newlin, D. B., & Thomson, J. B. (1990). Alcohol challenge with sons of alcoholics: A critical review and analysis. *Psychological Bulletin, 108,* 383–402.

O'Beirne, M., Gurevich, N., & Carlen, P. L. (1986). Pentobarbital inhibits hippocampal neurons by increasing potassium conductance. *Canadian Journal of Physiological Pharmacology, 65,* 36–41.

O'Brien, C. P. (1996). Drug addiction and drug abuse. In A. G. Gilman, L. S. Goodman, J. G. Hardman, L. E. Limbard, P. B. Molinoff, & R. W. Ruddon (Eds.), *The pharmacological basis of therapeutics* (pp. 557–577). New York: McGraw-Hill.

O'Farrell, T. J. (1995). Marital and family therapy. In R. K. Hester & W. R. Miller (Eds.), *Handbook of alcoholism treatment approaches* (pp. 195–220). Boston: Allyn & Bacon.

O'Malley, P. M., Johnston, L. D., & Bachman, J. G. (1995). Adolescent substance abuse: Epidemiology and implications for public policy. *Substance Abuse, 42,* 241–260.

O'Malley, S. S., Jaffe, A. J., Chang, G., et al. (1996a). Six-month follow-up of naltrexone and psychotherapy for alcohol dependence. *Archives of General Psychiatry, 53,* 217–224.

O'Malley, S. S., Jaffe, A. J., Rode, S., & Rounsaville, B. J. (1996b). Experience of a "slip" among alcoholics treated with naltrexone or placebo. *American Journal of Psychiatry, 153,* 281–283.

Oscar-Berman, M. (1980). Neuropsychological consequences of long-term chronic alcoholism. *American Scientist, 68,* 410–419.

Patat, A. (2000). Clinical pharmacology of psychotropic drugs. *Human Psychopharmacology: Clinical and Experimental, 15,* 361–387.

Peoples, R. W., & Weight, F. F. (1995). Cutoff in potency implicates alcohol inhibition of N-methyl-D-aspartate receptors in alcohol intoxication. *Proceedings of the National Academy of Sciences of the United States of America, 92,* 2825–2829.

Pezzarossa, A., Cervigni, C., Ghinelli, F., et al. (1986). Glucose tolerance in chronic alcoholics after alcohol withdrawal: Effect of accompanying diet. *Metabolism, 35,* 984–988.

Phelps, L. (1995). Psychoeducational outcomes of fetal alcohol syndrome. *School Psychology Review, 24,* 200–212.

Piccinelli, M., Pini, S., Bellantuono, C., & Wilkinson, G. (1995). Efficacy of drug treatment in obsessive-compulsive disorder. A meta-analytic review. *British Journal of Psychiatry, 166,* 424–443.

Pickens, R. W., Svikis, D. S., McGue, M., et al. (1991). Heterogeneity in the inheritance of alcoholism. *Archives of General Psychiatry, 48,* 19–29.

Pihl, R. O., & Zacchia, C. (1986). Alcohol and aggression: A test of the affect-arousal hypothesis. *Aggressive Behavior, 12,* 367–375.

Pittler, M. H., & Ernst, E. (2000). Efficacy of kava extract for treaty anxiety: Systematic review and meta-analysis. *Journal of Clinical Psychopharmacology, 20,* 84–89.

Plomin, R., Owen, M. J., & McGuffin, P. (1994). The genetic basis of complex human behaviors. *Science, 264,* 1733–1739.

Pohorecky, L. K. (1977). Biphasic action of ethanol. *Neuroscience and Biobehavioral Reviews, 1,* 231–240.

Pohorecky, L. K., Brick, J., & Carpenter, J. A. (1986). Assessment of the development of tolerance to ethanol using multiple measures. *Alcoholism: Clinical and Experimental Research, 10,* 616–622.

Porjesz, B., & Begleiter, H. (1991). Neurophysiological factors in individuals at risk for alcoholism. *Recent Developments in Alcoholism, 9,* 53–67.

Rall, T. W. (1990). Hypnotics and sedatives: Ethanol. In A. G. Gilman, T. W. Rall, A. S. Nies, & P. Taylor (Eds.), *The pharmacological basis of therapeutics* (pp. 345–382). New York: Pergamon Press.

Randall, C. L., & Saulnier, J. L. (1995). Effect of ethanol on prostacyclin, thromboxane, and prostaglandin E production in human umbilical veins. *Alcoholism, Clinical & Experimental Research, 19,* 741–746.

Rao, G. A., Larkin, E. C., & Derr, R. F. (1986). Biologic effects of chronic ethanol consumption related to a deficient intake of carbohydrates. *Alcohol and Alcoholism, 21,* 369–373.

Ravizza, L., Barzega, G., Bellino, S., et al. (1996). Drug treatment of obsessive-compulsive disorder (OCD): Long-term trial with clomipramine and selective serotonin reuptake inhibitors (SSRIs). *Psychopharmacology Bulletin, 32,* 167–173.

Reed, T. E., & Hanna, J. M. (1986). Between- and within-race variation in acute cardiovascular responses to alcohol: Evidence for genetic determination in normal males in three races. *Behavior Genetics, 16,* 585–598.

Rickert, V. I., Wiemann, C. M., & Berenson, A. B. (1999). Prevalence, patterns, and correlates of voluntary flunitrazepam use. *Pediatrics, 103,* E6.

Ridker, P. M., Vaughan, D. E., Stampfer, M. J., et al. (1994). Association of moderate alcohol consumption and plasma concentration of endogenous tissue-type plasminogen activator, *JAMA, 272,* 929–933.

Riley, E. P., Mattson, S. N., Sowell, E. R., et al. (1995). Abnormalities of the corpus callosum in children prenatally exposed to alcohol. *Alcoholism, Clinical & Experimental Research, 19,* 1198–1202.

Riley, J. N., & Walker, D. W. (1978). Morphological alterations in hippocampus after long-term alcohol consumption in mice. *Science, 201,* 646–648.

Ritchie, J. M. (1985). The aliphatic alcohols. In A. G. Gilman, L. S. Goodman, T. W. Rall, & F. Murad (Eds.), *The pharmacological basis of therapeutics* (pp. 372–386). New York: Macmillan.

Robertson, I., Heather, N., Dzialdowski, A., et al. (1986). A comparison of minimal versus intensive controlled drinking treatment interventions for problem drinkers. *British Journal of Clinical Psychology, 25,* 185–194.

Romach, M. K., & Sellers, E. M. (1991). Management of the alcohol withdrawal syndrome. *Annual Review of Medicine, 42,* 323–340.

Rosenberg, H. (1993). Prediction of controlled drinking by alcoholics and problem drinkers. *Psychological Bulletin, 113,* 129–139.

Rosenberg, H., & Davis, L. (1994). Acceptance of moderate drinking by alcohol treatment services in the

United States. *Journal of Studies on Alcohol, 55,* 167–172.

Rosenberg, H., Melville, J., Levell, D., & Hodge, J. E. (1992). A 10-yr follow-up survey of acceptability of controlled drinking in Britain. *Journal of Studies on Alcohol, 53,* 441–446.

Rosett, H. L., & Weiner, L. (1985). Alcohol and pregnancy: A clinical perspective. *Annual Review of Medicine, 36,* 3–80.

Roy-Byrne, P., Wingerson, D., Cowley, D., & Dager, S. (1993). Psychopharmacologic treatment of panic, generalized anxiety disorder, and social phobia. *Psychiatric Clinics of North America, 16,* 719–735.

Rush, C. R. (1998). Behavioral pharmacology of zolpidem relative to benzodiazepines: A review. *Pharmacology Biochemistry and Behavior, 61,* 253–269.

Ryan, C. (1982). Alcoholism and premature aging: A neuropsychological perspective. *Alcoholism: Clinical and Experimental Research, 6,* 79–96.

Saletu, B., Gruenberger, J., Linzmayer, L., et al. (1989). EEG-brain mapping, psychometric and psychophysiological studies on central effects of kavain: A kava plant derivative. *Human Psychopharmacology Clinical and Experimental, 4,* 169–190.

Sanger, D. J., Benavides, J., Perrault, G., et al. (1994). Recent developments in the behavioral pharmacology of benzodiazepine (omega) receptors: Evidence for the functional significance of receptor subtypes. *Neuroscience & Biobehavioral Reviews, 18,* 355–372.

Schanne, F. A. X., Zucker, A. H., & Farber, J. L. (1981). Alcohol-dependent liver cell necrosis in vitro: A new model. *Science, 212,* 338–340.

Schuckit, M. A. (1994a). A clinical model of genetic influences in alcohol dependence. *Journal of Studies on Alcohol, 55,* 5–17.

Schuckit, M. A. (1994b). Low level of response to alcohol as a predictor of future alcoholism. *American Journal of Psychiatry, 151,* 184–189.

Schuckit, M. A., & Rayses, V. (1979). Ethanol ingestion: Differences in blood acetaldehyde concentrations in relatives of alcoholics and controls. *Science, 202,* 54–56.

Schuckit, M. A., Tipp, J. E., Smith, T. L., et al. (1995). An evaluation of Type A and B alcoholics. *Addiction, 90,* 1189–1203.

Shaper, A. G., & Wannamethee, S. G. (2000). Alcohol intake and mortality in middle aged men with diagnosed coronary heart disease. *Heart, 83,* 394–399.

Shean, M. L., & Duester, G. (1993). The role of alcohol dehydrogenase in retinoic acid homeostasis and fetal alcohol syndrome. *Alcohol and Alcoholism, 2* (Suppl), 51–56.

Sheehan, D. V., Raj, A. B., Harnett-Sheehan, K., Soto, S., & Knapp, E. (1993). The relative efficacy of high-dose buspirone and alprazolam in the treatment of panic disorder: A double-blind placebo-controlled study. *Acta Psychiatrica Scandinavica, 18,* 1–11.

Smith, J. E., & Meyers, R. J. (1995). The community reinforcement approach. In R. K. Hester & W. R. Miller (Eds.), *Handbook of alcoholism treatment approaches* (pp. 263–266). Boston: Allyn & Bacon.

Smith, M. L., & Glass, G. V. (1977). Meta-analysis of psychotherapy outcome studies. *American Psychologist, 32,* 752–760.

Sokol, R. J., Ager, J., Martier, S., et al. (1986). Significant determinants of susceptibility to alcohol teratogenicity. *Annals of the New York Academy of Sciences, 477,* 87–102.

Sramek, J. J., Hong, W. W., Hamid, S., et al. (1999). Meta-analysis of the safety and tolerability of two dose regimens of buspirone in patients with persistent anxiety. *Depression and Anxiety, 9,* 131–134.

Staiger, P. K., Greeley, J. D., & Wallace, S. D. (1999). Alcohol exposure therapy: generalization and changes in responsivity. *Drug and Alcohol Dependence, 57,* 29–40.

Steinberg, J. R. (1994). Anxiety in elderly patients. A comparison of azapirones and benzodiazepines. *Drugs and Aging, 5,* 335–345.

Steinhausen, H. C., & Spohr, H. -L. (1986). Fetal alcohol syndrome. In B. B. Lahey, & A. E. Kazdin (Eds.), *Advances in clinical child psychology* (Vol. 9, pp. 217–243). New York: Plenum Press.

Stockwell, T. (1995). Anxiety and stress management. In R. K. Hester & W. R. Miller (Eds.), *Handbook of alcoholism treatment approaches* (pp. 242–250). Boston: Allyn & Bacon.

Streissguth, A. P., Randels, S. P., & Smith, D. F. (1991). A test-retest study of intelligence in patients with fetal alcohol syndrome: Implications for care. *Journal of the American Academy of Child and Adolescent Psychiatry, 30,* 584–587.

Sussman, N. (1994). The uses of buspirone in psychiatry. Symposium: Buspirone: Seven year update. *Journal of Clinical Psychiatry Monograph Series, 12,* 3–21.

Svanum, S., & Schladenhauffen, J. (1986). Lifetime and recent alcohol consumption among male alcoholics. *The Journal of Nervous and Mental Disease, 174,* 214–220.

Tabakoff, B., & Hoffman., P. L. (1996). Alcohol addiction: An enigma among us. *Neuron, 16,* 909–912.

Tempesta, E., Janiri, L., Bignamini, A., et al. (2000). Acamprosate and relapse prevention in the treatment of alcohol dependence: A placebo-controlled study. *Alcohol and Alcoholism, 35,* 202–209.

Thurstin, A. H., Alfano, A. M., & Sherer, M. (1986). Pretreatment MMPI profiles of A. A. members and nonmembers. *Journal of Studies on Alcohol, 47,* 468–471.

Vaillant, G. E., & Milofsky, E. S. (1982). The etiology of alcoholism. *American Psychologist, 37,* 494–503.

van der Kolk, B. A., Dreyfuss, D., Michaels, M., Shera, D., Berkowitz, R., Fisler, R., et al. (1994). Fluoxetine in posttraumatic stress disorder. *Journal of Clinical Psychiatry, 55,* 517–522.

VanDoren, M. J., Matthews, D. B., Janis, G. C., et al. (2000). Neuroactive steroid 3α-hydroxy-5α-pregnan-20-one modulates electrophysiological and behavioral actions of ethanol. *Journal of Neuroscience, 20,* 1982–1989.

Van Thiel, D. H., Gavaler, J., & Lester, R. (1974). Ethanol inhibition of vitamin A metabolism in the testes: Possible mechanism for sterility in alcoholics. *Science, 186,* 941–942.

Vanyukov, M. M., & Tarter, R. E. (2000). Genetic studies of substance abuse. *Drug and Alcohol Dependence, 59,* 101–123.

Volpicelli, J. R., Clay, K. L., Watson, N. T., O'Brien, C. P. (1995a). Naltrexone in the treatment of alcoholism: Predicting response to naltrexone. *Journal of Clinical Psychiatry, 57* (Suppl 7), 39–44.

Volpicelli, J. R., Watson, N. T., King, A. C., et al. (1995b). Effect of naltrexone on alcohol "high" in alcoholics. *American Journal of Psychiatry, 152,* 613–615.

von Knorring, L., Oreland, L., & von Knorring, A.-L. (1987). Personality traits and platelet MAO activity in alchohol and drug abusing teenage boys. *Acta Psychiatrica Scandanavica, 75,* 301–314.

Walker, D. W., Barnes, D. E., Zornetzer, S. F., et al. (1980). Neuronal loss in hippocampus induced by prolonged ethanol consumption in rats. *Science. 209,* 711–713.

Wall, T. L., Thomasson, H. R., Schuckit, M. A., & Ehlers, C. L. (1992). Subjective feelings of alcohol intoxication in Asians with genetic variations of ALDH2 alleles. *Alcoholism, Clinical and Experimental Research, 16,* 991–995.

Wallace, B., & Fisher, L. E. (1999). *Consciousness and behavior,* (4th ed.). Boston: Allyn & Bacon.

Walsh, D. D., Hingson, R. W., Merrigan, D. M., et al. (1991). A randomized trial of treatment options for alcohol-abusing workers. *New England Journal of Medicine, 325,* 775–782.

Watterlond, M. (1983, June). The telltale metabolism of alcoholics: A new interpretation of standard blood tests may lead to early diagnosis. *Science, 83,* 72–76.

Weight, F. F., Peoples, R. W., Wright, J. M., et al. (1993). Ethanol action on excitatory amino acid activated ion channels. *Alcohol and Alcoholism, 2* (Suppl), 353–358.

Wekselman, K., Spiering, K., Hetteberg, C., et al. (1995). Fetal alcohol syndrome from infancy through childhood: A review of the literature. *Journal of Pediatric Nursing, 10,* 296–303.

Wicht, F., Fisch, H. U., Nelles, J., Raisin, J., et al. (1995). Divergence of ethanol and acetaldehyde kinetics and of the disulfiram-alcohol reaction between subjects with and without alcoholic liver disease. *Alcoholism, Clinical and Experimental Research, 19,* 356–361.

Williams, B. F., Howard, V. F., & McLaughlin, T. F. (1994). Fetal alcohol syndrome: Developmental characteristics and directions for further research. *Education and Treatment of Children, 17,* 86–97.

Wilson, B., Kolb, B., Odland, L., & Wishaw, I. Q. (1987). Alcohol, sex, age, and the hippocampus. *Psychobiology, 15,* 300–307.

Woods, J. H. (1978). Behavioral pharmacology of drug administration. In M. A. Lipton, A. DiMascio, & K. F. Killman (Eds.), *Psychopharmacology* (pp. 595–607). New York: Raven Press.

Zorumski, C. F., & Isenberg, K. E. (1991). Insights into the structure and function of GABA-benzodiazepine receptors: Ion channels and psychiatry. *American Journal of Psychiatry, 148,* 162–173.

Zubaran, C., Fernandes, J. G., & Rodnight, R. (1997). Wernicke-Korsakoff syndrome. *Postgraduate Medical Journal, 73,* 27–31.

Zucker, R. A., & Gomberg, E. S. L. (1986). Etiology of alcoholism reconsidered: The case for a biopsychosocial process. *American Psychologist, 41,* 783–792.

C h a p t e r **9**

Psychostimulants

Another category of drugs that, for the most part, were originally derived for their clinical use but are now being used more extensively for recreational purposes, consists of the **psychostimulants.** This term is used because, in low to moderate doses, these drugs produce heightened mood (at its extreme, it is described as euphoria), increase vigilance and alertness, and reduce fatigue and the tendency to sleep. Generally, signs of increased sympathetic nervous system activity, such as increased heart rate and blood pressure, are evidenced. As one might expect with such actions, the EEG frequency shifts to higher frequencies.

Other frequently used terms for these drugs are *behavioral stimulants* and *CNS stimulants*; however, these terms do not do justice to the actual common properties of these drugs. Although some behaviors may increase in some individuals with these drugs, others may dramatically decrease, depending on the dose, the frequency of the behavior typically observed without the drug, and the individual (Grilly, 1977; Tecce & Cole, 1974; Wender et al., 1981). Likewise, while some neurons become more excitable and increase their rate of firing, others dramatically reduce their rate of firing. Actually, none of the terms mentioned adequately describes the effects of these drugs if the drugs are used in large amounts acutely or moderate amounts chronically. Some of these effects will be dealt with shortly.

Within this category are several structurally different types of drugs (see Figure 9–1 for their basic molecular structures). By far, the most commonly used psychostimulant is caffeine. Nicotine is another popular drug with psychostimulant properties. The amphetamines, together with other structurally related drugs, comprise another popular class. In a class by itself (no pun intended) is perhaps the most notorious of the group—cocaine. Other classes of drugs that might fit in this category are the antidepressants, some convulsants, and pemoline.

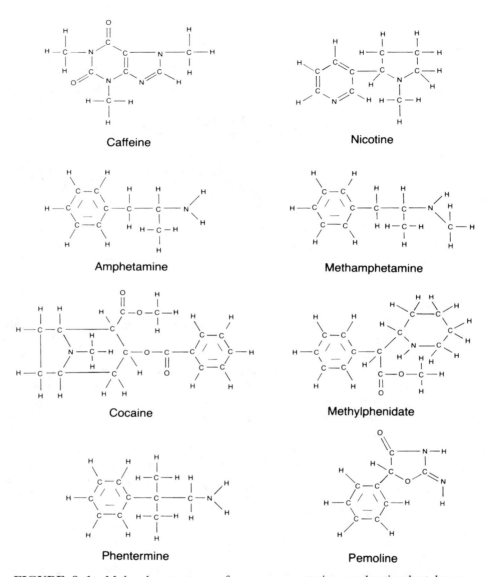

FIGURE 9–1   Molecular structures of some representative psychostimulant drugs.

Caffeine

Caffeine is the most widely used behaviorally active drug in the world (Barone & Roberts, 1996). Your morning cup of coffee, your soda pop at lunch, your afternoon cup of tea, and your chocolate sundae all contain this relatively mild psychostimulant (Table 9–1). It is one of several substances referred to as methylxanthines. The typical adult in the United States

TABLE 9–1   **Caffeine in Beverages and Foods**

	Caffeine (milligrams)
Coffee (5-ounce cup)	
Brewed, drip method	60–180
Brewed, percolator	40–170
Instant	30–120
Decaffeinated	2–5
Tea (5-ounce cup)	
Brewed	20–110
Instant	25–50
Cocoa (5-ounce cup)	2–20
Chocolate milk (8 ounces)	2–7
Chocolate (one ounce)	1–35
Soft drinks (12 ounces) (in which caffeine is listed as an ingredient)	30–60

Source: "The Latest Caffeine Scorecard" by C. Lecos, 1984, *Consumer's Research, 67,* 35–36.

consumes about 200 to 300 mg of caffeine a day, with coffee and tea consumption accounting for the majority of total caffeine intake (Barone & Roberts, 1996). Based on typical patterns of use throughout the day and a plasma half-life of approximately 5 hours, peak caffeine plasma levels typically occur in the early evening (Benowitz, 1990). However, owing to variability in absorption, metabolization, and excretion, as well as the fact that numerous metabolites of caffeine are formed that are also psychoactive (e.g., theophylline, theobromine, and paraxanthine), it is difficult to determine the overall time course and impact of caffeine on an individual.

What makes caffeine or coffee so popular is still unclear. In intravenous drug self-administration experiments with animals, caffeine has been shown to have reinforcing effects in some cases but not in others. Likewise, with humans, the reinforcing effects of caffeine have been variable, and in some individuals caffeine has been found to induce dysphoric effects. Most evidence suggests that caffeine is rated as having the most desirable and pleasant reactions in heavy coffee drinkers, particularly after they have not had any coffee for several hours. Coffee abstainers are more likely to report unpleasant and undesirable reactions to caffeine. This finding suggests that many of the reinforcing effects of caffeine stem from its ability to terminate caffeine withdrawal (Griffiths et al., 1986). However, research indicates that the average caffeine intake of coffee consumers does not predict the occurrence of withdrawal (Hughes et al., 1993). On the other hand, when coffee consumers are tested over a series of days without knowing whether they are consuming caffeinated or decaffeinated coffee, they are more likely to self-administer caffeinated than decaffeinated coffee (Hughes et al., 1993).

The effects of caffeine vary considerably among individuals in terms of wakefulness, psychomotor coordination, mood alterations, and autonomic nervous system response (Lombardo, 1986). Two cups of coffee, which contains approximately 150 mg of caffeine (unless it is decaffeinated), has the mood-elevating and fatigue-relieving properties of threshold doses of amphetamine (approximately 2 to 5 mg). However, larger doses generally do not have more of a mood-elevating effect, and 7 to 10 cups of coffee may cause insomnia, restlessness, mild sensory disturbances, or muscle tenseness (collectively called "caffeinism"), or may precipitate anxiety or panic attacks in susceptible individuals (Charney et al., 1985). Caffeine can raise blood pressure slightly, or it may have no effect. Similarly, heart rate changes are variable and, with some caffeine doses, may actually decrease. Increases in galvanic skin conductance level and reactivity are generally noted (Davidson & Smith, 1991). Thus, the evidence suggests that caffeine may not increase all indexes of arousal or change them in the same way in all persons (Zahn & Rapoport, 1987).

Persons who consume low to moderate doses of caffeine (30 to 450 mg) typically display dose-dependent improvements in indices of arousal, daytime alertness, vigilance, and some aspects of psychomotor performance and cognitive functions, such as reaction time, sustained attention, and information processing, and they experience predominantly positive subjective effects on mood, characterized by increased well-being, energy, and concentration (Graham et al., 1994; Patat et al., 2000; Zwyghuizen-Doorenbos et al., 1990). These beneficial effects are particularly evidenced when the individuals are tested under conditions of caffeine deprivation or total abstinence in regular caffeine users or following partial or total sleep deprivation. As little as 32 mg of caffeine has been shown to significantly improve auditory vigilance and visual reaction time (Lieberman et al., 1987). Caffeine can produce an increased capacity for both muscular work and sustained intellectual effort (Sawyer et al., 1982), but it can also disrupt arithmetic skills and task performance when delicate muscular coordination and accurate timing are required (Rall, 1985). The effects of caffeine on endurance (and probably other aspects of performance) are biphasic; that is, lower doses (3–6 mg/kg) enhance performance and higher doses have no significant effects (Graham & Spriet, 1995).

Several studies on efficiency of information processing in humans have shown that the effects of caffeine are dependent upon dose, task demands, the subject's sex, and the subject's typical level of arousal (Anderson & Revelle, 1983; Erikson et al., 1985). Some studies have concluded that extroverts (or high impulsives) tend to show dose-dependent improvements in performance, whereas introverts (or low impulsives) show improvements with lower doses and decrements with higher doses (Eysenck, 1967; Gupta & Gupta, 1990). Others have shown either no change or decrements in information processing, depending on the sex of the subject and the task demands (Erikson et al., 1985). (The dose ranges of caffeine used in these studies were equivalent to zero to four cups of regular coffee.) Thus, other than the conclusion that the behavioral effects of caffeine are quite subtle, there does not appear to be a consensus as to whether caffeine improves information-processing efficiency in general (Battig, 1991). It may all depend on whether the individual is a heavy consumer of coffee in the first place.

It is a common belief that caffeine can counteract the effects of sedative–hypnotic type drugs, but the empirical evidence for this belief is equivocal. The equivalent of two or three cups of coffee (250 mg caffeine) has been shown to significantly reduce next-day benzodiazepine-induced drowsiness (Johnson et al., 1990). Caffeine has also been shown to reduce the detrimental effects of alcohol on various types of complex reaction time. However, in terms of the subjective feelings of drunkenness and for most tasks—such as manual dexterity, balance, numerical reasoning, and verbal fluency—the deleterious effects of alcohol intoxication are not reduced by caffeine (Azcona et al., 1995; Fudin & Nicastro, 1988). Thus, an intoxicated driver, after consuming a few cups of coffee, might feel more alert, but he or she will still be impaired in terms of the motor coordination and decision making required for properly driving a motor vehicle.

The pharmacodynamics of caffeine are complex. The most important mechanism of caffeine's stimulant effects is antagonism of central adenosine receptors (Benowitz, 1990). Since adenosine is a potent inhibitor of synaptic transmission at central and peripheral synapses, its antagonism by caffeine results in an increase in the firing of cortical neurons and the locus coeruleus (a major regulator of arousal and vigilance), and an increase in behavioral activity; at high doses it elicits convulsions (Benowitz, 1990). Some of caffeine's actions also seem to be mediated by the catecholamines epinephrine and norepinephrine, since caffeine has discriminable properties in common with more potent psychostimulants, particularly cocaine and methylphenidate (Holtzman, 1986, 1987). Also, caffeine-induced stimulation of locomotor activity in animals can be prevented with alpha-adrenergic-blocking drugs, or when catecholamine synthesis is inhibited prior to caffeine treatment.

Tolerance develops to many of the effects of caffeine, most likely due to up-regulation of adenosine receptors in the brain (Graham et al., 1994). Withdrawal symptoms are uncommon, except following heavy use (around 500 mg per day) (Sawyer et al., 1982). Headaches are the most common symptom. They may be due to a rebound effect from caffeine's normal vasoconstrictive properties. (Perhaps this effect explains why so many over-the-counter analgesic preparations combine caffeine with aspirin.) Caffeine withdrawal symptoms may also include increased fatigue, sleepiness, and laziness, and decreased vigor and alertness. A neonatal withdrawal syndrome, consisting of irritability, jitteriness, and vomiting, has been reported in infants born to mothers who consumed large amounts of caffeine during pregnancy (Benowitz, 1990). However, clinical indicators of dependence, such as difficulty in stopping the use of caffeine and use despite harm, have not been documented (Hughes et al., 1992). The very low dependence liability of caffeine is consistent with findings with rats which indicate that low doses of caffeine typical of the human level of consumption do not activate the reward circuits in the brain (i.e., the mesolimbic–dopaminergic system) as most other drugs of abuse do (Nehlig & Boyet, 2000).

It is important to note that cigarette smokers, who generally consume more coffee than nonsmokers, metabolize caffeine at an accelerated rate. Upon smoking cessation, caffeine plasma levels increase on average more than 200 percent and may remain elevated for as long as 6 months, which could increase the person's "jitteriness" and be a contributing factor in tobacco withdrawal symptoms (Benowitz, 1990; Swanson et al., 1994).

Amphetamines and Related Drugs

In contrast to caffeine, amphetamines and structurally related drugs exert more intense and distinct emotional and cognitive effects, which may account for their popular recreational use and abuse potential. From the 1940s through the 1970s, these drugs were major drugs of abuse. Their use has declined somewhat since the 1970s because of governmental changes in their classification (at present they are Schedule II drugs), pressures on manufacturers to reduce the quantities produced, and pressures on physicians to reduce the types of clinical uses for them.

Amphetamine was initially synthesized in the late 1800s, but medical uses for it were not developed until the late 1920s. Although it is quite effective when administered orally, it was initially marketed in the form of inhalers for use in asthma treatment. It quickly gained popularity because of its potent CNS effects (Brecher, 1972). Shortly thereafter, amphetamine (marketed as Benzedrine in the United States) was discovered to be made up of two isomers, *l*- and *d*-amphetamine. The latter was found to be considerably more potent and was marketed as Dexedrine. A minor modification in the amphetamine molecule yielded the slightly more potent methamphetamine (Desoxyn, Methedrine). With the recognition of the potential psychopathological toxicity and dependence associated with the amphetamines, other compounds with very similar molecular structures were synthesized, including methylphenidate (Ritalin), pipradol (Meratran), phenmetrazine (Preludin), and phentermine (Ionamin). These amphetamine-related substances exert basically the same qualitative effects as the amphetamines do. (Some of these drugs are no longer on the market or the brand names they are marketed under have changed.)

Minor changes in the chemical structure of the basic amphetamine molecule can significantly alter the particular spectrum of its pharmacological and biochemical activities (Biel, 1970). Some changes may abolish both psychostimulant and appetite suppressant (anorexic) effects. Others may decrease only the anorexic effects, and others may decrease only the psychostimulant effects. Other changes profoundly enhance the MAO-inhibiting properties of the compound; for example, the amphetamine-like antidepressant tranylcypromine (Parnate) is some 5,000 times more potent than amphetamine in terms of MAO inhibition. Other modifications result in some psychotomimetic compounds, such as DOM (dimethoxymethylamphetamine), that produce effects similar to those of mescaline, but possess considerably higher potency. Many of these compounds will be dealt with in later chapters.

Psychological Effects of Amphetamines

The specific behavioral effects of amphetamine and related compounds depend to a great extent on the task requirements, the normal frequency of the behavior, the dose, and individual characteristics. Although psychostimulants are commonly believed to have effects in hyperactive children that are different from those observed in normal children or adults, empirical evidence indicates that, other than the magnitude of observed effects, amphetamines produce qualitatively similar effects in all three groups (Rapoport et al., 1980). (For further discussion of this issue see Chapter 14.)

In terms of quality of performance on various tasks, the most striking beneficial effects are noted when the person is fatigued (Lombardo, 1986). However, even in nonfatigued individuals, low to moderate doses tend to facilitate performance of tasks dependent on sustained attention (for instance, detecting infrequently occurring objects on radar screens) or those requiring quickness and strength (such as blocking and tackling in football, swimming, and track events) (Grilly & Loveland, 2001). High doses generally interfere with performance of these types of tasks. In tasks requiring smooth, accurate motions, low doses induce variable effects in individuals, in some cases enhancing, but in most cases interfering with, performance. In moderate to high doses, performance is hindered. Perhaps these task–drug interactions are the reason football players (at least linemen and linebackers) may be more prone to use these substances, whereas golfers and tennis players invariably avoid them.

Although amphetamine-related drugs often increase many kinds of activity, some kinds of behaviors, particularly those that occur frequently to begin with, are actually reduced by these drugs. Part of the reason for these differential effects is that not all behaviors can be increased simultaneously because one type of activity may compete with another (Grilly, 1977). Thus, for example, undifferentiated motor activity (hyperactivity) observed in many children with attention deficit disorder may be reduced with psychostimulants because on-task activity is enhanced.

In humans, mood and alertness tend to be enhanced with acute doses of *d*-amphetamine up to about 0.5 mg/kg (Jaffe, 1990). Paradoxically, a sizable minority of humans show the opposite effects, at least for the first hour or so, after taking amphetamine (Tecce & Cole, 1974). Somewhere in the 0.7 mg/kg dose range, humans experience dysphoria, social withdrawal, and depression (Griffith et al., 1970). Exposure to higher doses can precipitate a psychosis with symptoms very similar to paranoid schizophrenia (Jonsson & Gunne, 1970; Lyon et al., 1986). Behavior often becomes very stereotyped and repetitive. Simple movements such as continuous chewing, rubbing of the tongue on the inside of the lips, and teeth grinding occur. The individual may engage in a repetitious thought or meaningless acts for hours. Often users seem fascinated or preoccupied with their own thought processes and with philosophical concerns on a grand scale. The person may get very suspicious of others and become antisocial, and in some cases may become very prone to violence. Similar actions have been described with the other amphetamine-like substances—for example, methylphenidate.

Very similar behavioral effects have been noted to occur in all mammals, although in each case the specific type of stereotypic reaction is dependent on the species. Rats typically bob their heads back and forth and display gnawing behaviors. Monkeys have been observed to exhibit continuous grooming-like movements of body and limbs without actually grooming, and chimpanzees have been observed to rock and sway back and forth. Because of the similarities between the behavioral effects of high doses of amphetamines in humans and nonhumans, and because the human reactions are so similar to paranoid schizophrenia, the effects in nonhumans induced by higher doses of amphetamine are commonly viewed as a way of producing a model animal "psychosis" (Ellison, 1993).

With chronic use, tolerance to the reinforcing effects of amphetamine may be marked, leading to administration of very high drug doses (Hyman, 1996). In contrast, one of the curious aspects of amphetamine-induced motor and psychosis-mimicking effects in animals is that repeated exposure to amphetamine appears to sensitize, rather than reduce, the organism's susceptibility to them. This phenomenon can occur even if the exposures are several days apart (Kilbey & Ellinwood, 1977). Exposure to similar-acting drugs, such as cocaine, and severe stress also appear to sensitize the organism to the psychosis-mimicking effects (Antelman et al., 1980; Fitzgerald et al., 1996; MacLennan & Maier, 1983). These findings have led to the speculation that humans who have been exposed to stress or drugs of this nature may also be predisposed to developing the psychotic reactions to amphetamine or cocaine. Several explanations for these sensitization effects with these drugs have been proposed. One possibility is that the prolonged depletion of catecholamines following heavy use (see "Dependence on Amphetamines") induces increased receptor sensitivity or receptor up-regulation. Sensitization may also be the result of neuronal damage. Some studies indicate that stress-induced sensitization appears to be mediated by stress-induced secretion of stress-related hormones, called glucocorticoids, that promote increases in extracellular dopamine concentrations in the nucleus accumbens when psychostimulants like amphetamine and cocaine are administered (Rougé-Pont et al., 1995). Furthermore, excessive exposure to both glucocorticoids and amphetamine has been shown to exert neurotoxic effects in the brains of several species (Ellison, 1993; Sapolsky, 1996), which, at least with amphetamine, have been linked to its ability to sensitize the animal-type psychosis (Ellison, 1993).

Limited evidence also suggests that amphetamine-induced sensitization can occur in humans. Two studies, in which 0.25 mg/kg dextroamphetamine was administered orally to amphetamine-naïve human volunteers on two or three separate occasions 48 hours apart, found greater subjective effects during the second or third drug exposure than the first, suggestive of sensitization (Strakowski et al., 1996; Strakowski & Sax, 1998). Because the drug exposures were conducted with the same contextual cues present, this effect could have been due to Pavlovian conditioning; that is, a conditioned response added to the unconditioned response to the drug could have increased the net effect observed. In another study, in which 0.3 mg/kg amphetamine was administered intravenously to amphetamine-naïve humans on two separate occasions 7 to 35 days apart, neither tolerance nor sensitization in the second drug-exposure test was observed on either dopamine release in the brain or on the subjective effects of the drug (Kegeles et al., 1999). One study observed acute exacerbation of a paranoid psychotic state by methamphetamine in 16 of 21 patients who had been treated for chronic methamphetamine psychosis (Sato et al., 1983). Four of these patients relapsed following a single methamphetamine exposure to an amount less than initially used, and one relapsed without evidence of methamphetamine use. A positive prophylactic effect of small doses of the antipsychotic haloperidol on the acute exacerbation in eight of the patients suggested that dopaminergic supersensitivity may have been a mechanism for the paranoid psychotic state.

In addition to their central effects, amphetamines and related compounds have a number of sympathomimetic effects. They increase blood pressure and heart rate, constrict the blood vessels to the viscera, increase body temperature and muscle tension, and induce intestinal relaxation and bronchial dilation.

Clinical Uses for Amphetamines

The acute effects of low to moderate doses of amphetamine in humans include increased energy, concentration, alertness, and self-confidence, and mood elevation. In some individuals these effects can occur almost to the point of elation and euphoria (Jaffe, 1990). Social interactions, such as increased talkativeness, friendliness, and activity, may be enhanced. Amphetamine also suppresses appetite (anorexia).

The clinical uses of amphetamine and related drugs reflect these effects. Following its use in the treatment of asthma, one of amphetamine's first clinical uses for its CNS effects was in the treatment of *narcolepsy,* a rare but serious disorder in which the person falls asleep repeatedly during the day, often without warning. Shortly thereafter, amphetamine was found to significantly reduce many of the symptoms of children whose cognitive functioning was impaired by the inability to concentrate and who were overly active (a disorder now called *attention deficit hyperactivity disorder*). Currently, these are the only two disorders for which most experts agree amphetamines may be legitimately prescribed, although there are a number of other uses for them—most notably in the treatment of obesity (Holmes, 1995). (See Chapter 14 for further description of some of amphetamine's clinical uses.)

Over the past 65 years, amphetamines have been used for a variety of purposes. During World War II, most of the armed forces on both sides of the war issued amphetamines to their men to counteract fatigue, elevate mood, and heighten endurance (Brecher, 1972). Whether this practice hurt or helped their cause in the long run is debatable, for as we shall see, escalating the dose of amphetamine is a tempting probability in such times of stress. It can lead to a psychotic state involving a severe case of perceptual and cognitive disorganization. Some historians have suggested that at the end of the war, Adolf Hitler's increasingly bizarre behavior may have been due to his use of amphetamines, along with a variety of other stimulants. As stated by one historian:

> No one who has read about his behavior during this time or about his pronouncements at the situation conferences on 23, 25 and 27 April 1945, then still being recorded, can fail to recognize what it was that made him conjure up in all good faith such patently harebrained schemes. The rapid alternation of depression and euphoria, exhaustion and artificially induced buoyancy clearly reflect Hitler's dependence on the stimulants prescribed by Morell. (Maser, 1971, pp. 228–229)

After the war, amphetamines were routinely prescribed for weight control and mood depression, now recognized as inappropriate because amphetamine can lead to a person becoming even more depressed and suicidal. To blunt the nervousness and sleep-disrupting properties of amphetamine, individuals often combined it with a sedative–hypnotic, or tranquilizer, which in some cases produced other deleterious side effects.

Pharmacokinetics and Pharmacodynamics of Amphetamines

Amphetamines are relatively high in lipid-solubility and are very well absorbed when taken orally or inhaled as a vapor. Intravenous administration results in brain penetration within seconds. Although most amphetamines are not sufficiently volatile to vaporize when smoked, a new form of methamphetamine hydrochloride (called "ice" because of its transparent, sheetlike crystals) has been developed so that it can be inhaled through smoking. Inhalation allows it to produce a rapid onset of effect, similar to smoking cocaine, but as with other amphetamines, its effects last much longer—on the order of several hours (Cho, 1993).

Although the amphetamines and related compounds bear a strong molecular resemblance to the catecholamines (norepinephrine and dopamine), little of their activity appears to be due to a direct agonist action at catecholamine receptors. Instead, they have neuropharmacological properties that enhance the level of catecholamines in the synaptic cleft, which then increases catecholamine receptor activation. Amphetamine also increases extracellular levels of serotonin, but this action appears to play a minimal role in most of its behavioral effects.

Amphetamine has multiple actions on catecholamine systems. First, it increases release of catecholamines by increasing both their spontaneous leakage from neurons and their stimulated (action potential–induced) release. Second, it inhibits the reuptake of catecholamines back into the terminals. Third, it has a mild, temporary, inhibitory action on the enzyme MAO (which, you may recall, normally metabolizes the monoamines intraneuronally into inactive molecules) (Cole, 1978; Sulzer et al., 1995). Most of the catecholamines released appear to be from newly synthesized stores in the axon terminal—that is, outside the vesicles. Some studies further suggest that amphetamine redistributes dopamine from the synaptic vesicles to the cytoplasm and promotes reverse transport of dopamine—that is, release from neurons through the transporter protein that normally serves as the mechanism for the reuptake of dopamine from the extracellular fluid back into the neuron (Giros et al., 1996; Sulzer et al., 1995). Presumably, the other amphetamine-like substances have similar biochemical actions, although there appear to be minor differences in degree and type of action. Methylphenidate, for example, has much the same activity as amphetamine except that it seems to release primarily catecholamines that are stored in vesicles (Moore et al., 1977).

Although amphetamine and related psychostimulants (and cocaine) enhance catecholamine activity throughout the nervous system, which then results in a variety of effects on mood and behavior, most studies have indicated that the primary reward properties of these drugs are due to their ability to enhance dopaminergic activity in a part of the limbic system called the nucleus accumbens. Amphetamine and many of its congeners nonselectively elevate synaptic levels of dopamine, norepinephrine, and also serotonin, but their reinforcing properties and abuse potential are best correlated with their ability to increase extracellular levels of dopamine, because the rewarding effects of these agents are attenuated by selective dopamine antagonists and not by selective noradrenergic or serotonergic antagonists (Wise, 1998).

While amphetamine and related drugs are commonly referred to as CNS stimulants, this terminology is misleading. For example, one study has shown that regional cerebral metabolic rate for glucose, an index of local functional activity in the brain, may actually be reduced in many areas of the human brain by euphorigenic doses of amphetamine (Wolkin et al., 1987)—emphasizing a point I have made previously that increases in behavioral variables, such as mood, do not necessarily coincide with increases in neuronal activity in the CNS in general. In fact, amphetamine can dampen the activity of some of the brain's electrical and chemical circuits while enhancing others. This was demonstrated in a study in which people were given either placebo or dextroamphetamine and their regional cerebral blood flow was assessed with PET scans while they performed two different cognitive tasks—one heavily dependent on the hippocampus and the other heavily dependent on the prefrontal cortex (Mattay et al., 1996). When engaging in the hippocampus-dependent task, amphetamine increased activity in the hippocampus (relative to the control subjects) and decreased activity in the prefrontal cortex. When engaging in the prefrontal cortex–dependent task, amphetamine increased activity in the prefrontal cortex (relative to the controls) and decreased activity in the hippocampus. These findings illustrate that amphetamine-related drugs tend to "focus" neural activity and highlight the specific neural network that is specific to a particular cognitive task.

The actions just described occur with acute drug exposure. However, with chronic drug exposure, a multitude of changes have been documented to take place in the brain. With sufficiently high dosages of amphetamine, catecholamines can be depleted as a result of neurotoxic processes (discussed shortly), increased metabolization by extraneuronal COMT, or decreased synthesis resulting from excessive catecholamine autoreceptor activation (Paulson et al., 1991; Robinson & Becker, 1986). These changes could account for some tolerance phenomena and mood depression following amphetamine exposure and withdrawal. Alterations in catecholamine receptors (e.g., down-regulation of catecholamine autoreceptors and postsynaptic receptors) can occur with chronic amphetamine exposure, with the former accounting for some sensitization to amphetamine (due to loss of the inhibitory control over catecholaminergic neuron activity) and the latter accounting for some tolerance phenomena.

Interestingly, some of these neuroadaptations may depend on whether amphetamine is self-administered by the organism or is passively administered to the organism. For example, rats that had been allowed to self-administer methamphetamine for 5 weeks and were then withdrawn from methamphetamine for 24 hours showed marked decreases in somatodendritic dopamine D_2 autoreceptor levels in midbrain regions, with a corresponding downregulation of dopamine D_1 receptors in the nucleus accumbens. These changes were not observed in rats that passively received the same amounts of methamphetamine with the same temporal pattern of exposure (Stefanski et al., 1999).

Although most of the evidence for these changes has come from research with nonhumans exposed to much higher dosages than humans would likely administer, reduced levels of dopamine, tyrosine hydroxylase (the primary enzyme necessary for catecholamine synthesis), and fewer dopamine reuptake sites have been found in the striatum (nucleus accumbens, caudate, putamen) of deceased chronic methamphetamine users (Wilson et al., 1996). Lower concentrations of G proteins (major components of catecholamine receptor activation) have also been found in the nucleus accumbens of deceased methamphetamine users (McLeman et al., 2000).

Dependence on Amphetamines

In the early 1970s, more than 30 amphetamine-containing preparations were on the market. Some government sources estimated that there were enough doses of amphetamine and related compounds being marketed in the United States to supply every man, woman, and child several times daily. Furthermore, there were plenty of unscrupulous and ignorant physicians around willing to prescribe them. In addition to amphetamine's medically prescribed uses, it was being used by truck drivers who were doing long hauls without adequate rest, students who were cramming for exams, and "speed freaks" who were injecting it just to get high. With all of its use and potential misuse, something had to give. Beginning in the mid-1970s, the use of amphetamines gradually decreased, for many reasons. First, the government began to exert legal pressures on pharmaceutical companies to decrease their production. Second, the number of legitimate medical uses was drastically reduced. Third, the general population and physicians became more educated about the potential hazards and misuse. Fourth, compounds with less abuse potential and more specific actions with respect to major mood depression were developed—for example, antidepressants. Finally, cocaine, which users were led to believe was much less harmful than amphetamine, came on the scene to replace it as a drug for recreational use.

Unfortunately, in the 1990s there was a resurgence in the illicit use of amphetamine, in this case methamphetamine, with the expected consequences of earlier amphetamine epidemics—an increase in violence, criminal behavior, deaths, psychotic behavior, and extreme addiction (Kleiman & Satel, 1996). Making the situation worse is the fact that the quality (i.e., purity) of methamphetamine has improved drastically over the past several years, due to refinements in the manufacturing process and marketing factors—apparently so much is available that dealers aren't cutting (diluting) the drug as much as they used to.

Despite the dysphoric effects of high doses or chronic use, the dependence liability of amphetamine and similar-acting drugs is considered to be among the highest of all drugs (Jaffe, 1990). Although physical dependence may be a factor, unequivocal evidence for abstinence symptoms associated with these drugs is lacking. There is no question that when individuals stop taking amphetamines after a few days of moderate to heavy amphetamine exposure, they generally "crash"; that is, they experience exhaustion, depression, lethargy, and hunger. These are all symptoms opposite to the direct effects of the drug. However, rather than being signs of an abstinence syndrome, these symptoms may be due to lack of decent sleep, low blood sugar, or depletion of dopamine or norepinephrine, among other things. One can speculate that because of the enhanced activity at catecholamine receptors, there may also be a short-lived decrease in the sensitivity of postsynaptic catecholamine receptors, an effect that would be consistent with a true abstinence syndrome. (However, note that this speculation contrasts with the possibility for up-regulation of receptors following catecholamine depletion.) Even if the postdrug symptoms associated with chronic psychostimulant use are due to a true abstinence syndrome, they clearly are qualitatively and quantitatively very different from those symptoms associated with the sedative–hypnotics and the narcotics. Furthermore, it is questionable whether these symptoms are a major factor in the maintenance of drug-taking behavior with this class of drugs.

On the other hand, the psychological dependence associated with amphetamines and related drugs can be overwhelming. The euphoria, feelings of well-being, and enhanced self-confidence in both physical and mental ability serve as powerful primary reinforcers—even more powerful than food in a hungry animal (Aigner & Balster, 1978). Even animals find their effects very reinforcing. Self-administration studies with nonhumans have indicated that, if given free access to amphetamines or cocaine, they are highly likely to administer larger and larger amounts—in many cases to the point of administering lethal doses (which induce convulsions) (Aigner & Balster, 1978; Brady & Griffiths, 1977). This phenomenon rarely occurs with narcotics like heroin, where animals typically stabilize at a fairly constant daily dosage somewhat below lethal levels. Thus, it appears that these drugs have very strong primary reinforcing properties, and it is these properties that potentially lead to the heavy psychological dependence on them.

As with all psychotropic drugs, there is considerable individual variability in vulnerability to dependence on amphetamines. Some users go for months or years before becoming daily users, whereas others report such an intense positive response with the first dose that addiction occurs almost immediately. Some of the factors leading to this variability are likely to be genetic (e.g., differential reactivity to novel stimulation), whereas others may be environmental (e.g., the result of differential exposure to stressful events during some critical period of life) (Piazza et al., 1989).

Effects of Chronic Amphetamine Exposure

Even in animals that do not administer lethal amounts, continued exposure to amphetamines and related drugs eventually leads to problems associated with malnutrition, nonhealing ulcers, high blood pressure, and brain damage resulting from restricted blood flow to the brain. These effects can also occur in humans. Repeated administration of high doses of amphetamines has also been found to induce irreversible neuronal damage in animals (Wagner et al., 1985). This includes long-lasting depletion of central monoamine concentrations, a decrease in the number of monoamine uptake sites, a decrease in monoamine synthesis, and nerve terminal degeneration. It has been speculated that these effects are due to amphetamine's ability to enhance the release of both dopamine and serotonin from synaptic vesicles into the cytoplasm as well as inhibit MAO activity, which leads to the nonenzymatic oxidation of these monoamines into neurotoxins that trigger terminal degeneration (Cubells et al., 1994; Sonsalla et al., 1989). Consistent with this view are studies that have demonstrated that the neurotoxic actions of methamphetamine can be attenuated by pretreatment with vitamin C (an antioxidant) and alpha-methyl-p-tyrosine (a catecholamine synthesis inhibitor), and can be exacerbated by pretreatment with reserpine (a drug that enhances cytoplasmic pools of monoamines). PET scan studies indicating that humans with a history of abusing methamphetamine or methcathinone (a similar-acting drug discussed later) have reduced dopamine transporter density in the basal ganglia suggest that these neurotoxic effects may also occur with doses used by humans (McCann et al., 1998), although these results may be a cause or effect of their drug use, among other factors. Many of these neurotoxic effects may be reversible, as evidenced by the finding of considerable recovery of dopamine function in monkeys several weeks after acute, high-dosage amphetamine- and methamphetamine-induced neurotoxicity (Melega et al., 1997).

Cocaine

South American Indians have been using cocaine for centuries to increase their endurance and reduce fatigue and hunger. The early European explorers of South America, who essentially enslaved the natives, soon found the natives' fondness of the coca leaf to be useful as an incentive for performing hard labor. Eventually, the coca leaf was introduced in Europe with little fanfare. In the mid-1800s cocaine was isolated from coca extracts, but its general use did not begin until the late 1800s. Sir Arthur Conan Doyle's famous fictional detective, Sherlock Holmes, was reported to have injected cocaine (circa 1888) occasionally between cases. He said he found it "transcendentally stimulating and clarifying to the mind" (Grilly, 1980). (A recent novel revolving around Holmes's cocaine use—*The Seven-Per-Cent Solution* by Nicholas Meyer—is obviously not authentic, because it often confuses the effects of cocaine with those of opiates, and cocaine is clearly not an opiate.)

Perhaps the earliest leading proponent of cocaine's clinical use, for its antidepressant and antifatigue properties, was a young physician by the name of Sigmund Freud (Brecher, 1972). Between 1884 and 1887 Freud performed the functions of a psychopharmacologist by testing the various mood- and behavior-altering properties of cocaine, primarily on himself and a few friends. Freud initially concluded that cocaine had many beneficial characteristics. He found that it could be used to enhance mood, alleviate depression, reduce the effects of fatigue, and enhance sexual potency. He felt it could be a potential treatment for morphine and alcohol addiction, numerous psychological disorders (such as hysteria and hypochondria), and a variety of physical debilities (for example, diseases involving tissue degeneration, asthma, and digestive problems). Finally, he suggested that its local anesthetic properties might be of value.

Although Freud initially believed that cocaine was a wonder drug through which he could establish his medical reputation (as well as provide himself with recreation), he eventually became disillusioned with the drug (Jones, 1953). One reason may have been that his own work indicated that there was tremendous individual variability in the reaction to cocaine. He also attempted to wean a good friend off of his dependence on morphine, using cocaine as a substitute. Although the friend was successfully weaned from his morphine habit, he quickly developed a very strong cocaine dependence. After observing the effects of both kinds of dependence, Freud was perhaps the first to recognize that dependence on cocaine can have far more deleterious effects than morphine dependence. As will be discussed in Chapter 10, chronic morphine use has relatively benign effects on the person, whereas chronic cocaine use induces a psychotic state, extreme loss of appetite leading to nutritional deficiencies, impaired interpersonal relations, and a variety of other pathological effects.

Freud has long been recognized as a high achiever who wanted to become famous—something that was unattainable as long as he was associated with a drug with such a poor reputation. In recognizing his error in judgment regarding cocaine's therapeutic promise, Freud turned away from pursuing physical, organic approaches to the treatment of mental illness—perhaps leading him toward an approach emphasizing unconscious forces in its cause. However, his work with cocaine may have led to its use by an eye surgeon, Karl Koller, as a local anesthetic in the eye. It was the first drug physicians had for this purpose. Cocaine was later used as therapy for asthma and colic. Although Freud's work with cocaine ceased, he continued to use cocaine regularly until at least 1895, and probably quite a bit longer (but encouraged the widely held view that he stopped using the drug in 1887). Many have speculated that his cocaine use not only was a factor in his prodigious writings, but also may have played a causal role in the early development of his psychoanalytic theories by facilitating his capacity for introspection and self-analysis (Fuller, 1992).

Psychological Effects of Cocaine

Because of the similarities of the neurochemical effects of cocaine and those induced by amphetamine, it is not surprising that their mood-altering and behavioral effects are also quite similar. With few exceptions, the effects noted earlier for amphetamine apply to cocaine. These effects include euphoria, enhanced arousal and vigilance, reversal of fatigue-induced deficits in performance, and increases in blood pressure and heart rate. Furthermore, like amphetamine, euphorigenic doses of cocaine have been shown to decrease cerebral metabolism of glucose in most regions of the human and monkey brain (London et al., 1990; Lyons et al., 1996).

Although users of cocaine and amphetamine will often assert that the effects of the two drugs are different, there is little scientific research to support this belief. In fact, most studies have found that, when users of cocaine and amphetamine are administered these drugs intravenously, they are unable to distinguish between them, except for the duration of the drug effect (Van Dyke & Byck, 1982). The time course for amphetamine is approximately 2 to 3 hours, whereas cocaine's effects dissipate in about 30 minutes. In studies with animals, the behavioral effects of cocaine and amphetamine are quite similar in a variety of procedures. Also, after chronic exposure to either substance, those effects exhibiting tolerance to one will sometimes confer tolerance to the other (Fischman et al., 1985; Wood & Emmett-Oglesby, 1986). Similarly, when enhanced sensitivity is observed with one, sometimes it will also be evidenced with the other (Kilbey & Ellinwood, 1977; Short & Shuster, 1976). On the other hand, neither is cross-tolerant with opiates like morphine (Short & Shuster, 1976; Jaffe, 1990).

High doses of cocaine induce the same psychopathological effects noted earlier with respect to amphetamine: suicidal thoughts, irritability, anxiety, rebound depression, and paranoid ideation. (Robert Louis Stevenson gives us a glimpse of this behavior in his story "The Strange Case of Dr. Jekyll and Mr. Hyde," which he wrote in six days and nights under the influence of cocaine [Siegel, 1989]. Presumably, the drug that Dr. Jekyll took that turned him into the demonic murderer Mr. Hyde was modeled after cocaine.) The most common of the perceptual changes and pseudohallucinations induced by cocaine are tactile disturbances, in which there is a sensation of bugs running over the skin (referred to as *formication*), and visual disturbances (termed *snow lights*) (Jaffe, 1990).

There are some differences between cocaine and amphetamine in addition to those mentioned earlier. Although the potency of cocaine is about 60 percent that of amphetamine when the two drugs are administered intravenously, it is considerably less potent when they are administered orally (Jaffe, 1990). Oral cocaine, because of its alkaloid nature and the effects of G.I. secretions, is not well absorbed, whereas amphetamine is readily absorbed from the G.I. tract. There is also a difference between them when taken intranasally; cocaine has local anesthetic properties, whereas amphetamine does not. This local anesthetic action also appears to make it difficult for cocaine users to distinguish cocaine from other local anesthetics with minimal CNS actions, such as procaine (Novocain) (Van Dyke & Byck, 1982). Perhaps some of the subjective differences between amphetamine and cocaine are due to reputation, expectation, and setting, all of which are potent factors in many so-called drug-induced effects.

Pharmacokinetics of Cocaine

Despite the South American Indians' long-term use of cocaine, there are no reports of them suffering from any unpleasant side effects or toxicity. On the other hand, in the 1980s in the United States, we began to experience an epidemic of use and abuse of, and extreme dependence on, cocaine. Why is there such a difference in these two cultures' reactions to cocaine? Basically the difference lies in the way in which the drug is administered. The South

American Indians generally chew the coca leaf, which contains very small amounts of cocaine. Since cocaine in the coca plant is an alkaloid that is slowly absorbed from the G.I. tract, very little cocaine accumulates in the brain. North American users administer a highly concentrated form of cocaine intranasally, intravenously, or, most recently, through inhalation—all of which result in a rapid and high concentration of the drug in the brain (American Society for Pharmacology, 1987).

South American Indians have traditionally administered cocaine in its untransformed alkaloid form by chewing the leaves with an alkaloid substance so that absorption through the oral mucous membranes is enhanced. Apparently, there are very few cases in which this practice results in acute overdosage, psychosis, neglect of one's responsibility, or extensive focus on cocaine use. More recently, though, some young South Americans in urban areas have begun to mix the cocaine paste, which is extracted from the leaves for subsequent synthesis into cocaine hydrochloride, with tobacco and smoke it. In these individuals, the same patterns of pathological states, neglect of work, and preoccupation with cocaine use seen in North American users are evidenced (Jaffe, 1990).

In North America and other developed countries, cocaine hydrochloride is commonly self-administered by sniffing it (referred to as "snorting") so that it is absorbed through the nasal membranes. This leads to a somewhat faster onset of action and higher brain concentrations than when it is ingested orally (Van Dyke & Byck, 1982). The local vasoconstrictive properties of cocaine result in slower absorption and longer effects when the drug is snorted as opposed to smoked. Cocaine's vasoconstrictive properties in the nose also lead to tissue degeneration (for example, a perforated septum) because of ischemia (localized tissue anemia). Although much higher brain concentrations of cocaine can be achieved when administered intravenously (I.V.), this mode of administration is uncommon in the vast majority of users, perhaps because users recognize the hazards associated with this route of administration. On the other hand, the smoking of cocaine became popular in the 1980s because it allows high concentrations of cocaine to accumulate in the brain in a fashion very similar to intravenous administration, but avoids the hazards of injections—particularly the development of the inevitably lethal disease AIDS. Also, since users generally have had experience with smoking marijuana, they do not have to learn a new drug administration procedure.

Because cocaine hydrochloride is volatilized at temperatures that degrade it, in order for it to be effective when smoked, it must be reconverted chemically to its alkaloid (base) state. This practice is generally called **free-basing,** and in its crystalline form the compound is commonly referred to as **crack.** In this mode it is easily volatilized in active form at relatively low temperatures. Crack is relatively inexpensive—a moderate day's use can be financed for $10 to $20—and produces a rapid-onset, intense high, which makes it extremely addictive. Unfortunately, the toxic and lethal effects of cocaine, as well as the profound dependency, are just as readily induced by smoking the drug as with I.V. administration (American Society for Pharmacology, 1987). Because of incomplete absorption, the potency of smoked cocaine is somewhat lower than I.V. cocaine, but several of the positive subjective effects of cocaine (e.g., "stimulated," "high," "liking") may actually be greater when it is smoked than when it is administered intravenously, even when the cocaine plasma levels are similar (Foltin & Fischmann, 1991).

The dependence liability of cocaine with either of these modes of administration may actually be greater than that of amphetamine, because the subjective "crash" following smoking or I.V. administration of cocaine is much more noticeable than with amphetamine (American Society for Pharmacology, 1987). This outcome is probably related to cocaine's very short duration of action.

Once in the body, cocaine is widely distributed throughout the body and is rapidly metabolized. Minimal amounts of cocaine are excreted in an unmetabolized form. Although cocaine's plasma half-life is around 30 to 90 minutes, several metabolites can be detected by way of urinalysis for up to 2 to 5 days after a cocaine binge, with the major metabolite (benzoylecgonine) being detectable in the urine of heavy users for up to 10 days following a binge (O'Brien, 1996).

Use of alcohol along with cocaine, a common occurrence in users, results in increased plasma concentrations of cocaine and the formation of a psychoactive metabolite, cocaethylene, both of which enhance and prolong the subjective euphoria and cardiovascular effects of cocaine (McCance et al., 1995). These phenomena potentially play a role in the toxicity and abuse associated with this drug combination. Cocaethylene and cocaine both dramatically increase the extracellular levels of dopamine in the primate brain (Iyer et al., 1995), although in humans cocaethylene appears to have a somewhat longer elimination half-life and somewhat lower potency than cocaine in its subjective and cardiovascular effects (Perez-Reyes et al., 1994).

Pharmacodynamics of Cocaine

Although, as indicated in Chapter 4, cocaine has local anesthetic properties because of its ability to block neural conduction, its CNS effects are mediated primarily by its potent ability to inhibit the reuptake of the monoamines, that is, serotonin, norepinephrine, and dopamine from the synaptic cleft (Moore et al., 1977). It has now been fairly well established that the reinforcing properties of cocaine are predominantly due to its dopamine-reuptake–inhibiting properties (Giros et al., 1996; Ritz et al., 1987), which with acute exposure to cocaine results in large increases in extracellular levels of dopamine. There is, however, debate over the primary region of the brain that is responsible for the rewarding actions of cocaine—with some evidence favoring the nucleus accumbens and other evidence favoring the medial prefrontal cortex (Wise, 1998). Both of these areas are primary terminal areas for dopaminergic input originating in the ventral tegmental area of the midbrain. Cocaine also appears to weakly facilitate the release of catecholamines from axon terminals.

The neurochemical effects of cocaine are similar to those of methylphenidate, amphetamine, and some antidepressants, although in many cases there are subtle, but potentially important, differences. Methylphenidate, for example, binds to the same uptake sites in the brain as cocaine, but cocaine's clearance from the brain is significantly faster, which promotes its more frequent self-administration (Volkow et al., 1995). Amphetamine has weaker catecholamine-reuptake–blocking properties than cocaine but more potent catecholamine-releasing actions (Moore et al., 1977). Furthermore, cocaine appears to have considerably more dopaminergic activity, whereas amphetamine has considerably more noradrenergic activity.

Finally, although some antidepressants, such as imipramine (to be discussed in Chapter 13), share cocaine's monoamine-reuptake–inhibiting properties, they do not elevate mood until after several days of exposure, nor do they elevate mood in nondepressed individuals. Some of these differences may be due to these drugs having considerably weaker effects at the dopamine-uptake–binding site than cocaine; for instance, it would account for their lacking reinforcing effects in humans and animals. In order to achieve blood levels of imipramine that would induce dopamine-reuptake blockade comparable to that of cocaine, the imipramine blood levels would be in the range of human lethality (Ritz et al., 1987).

Cocaine Dependence

Although most reports prior to 1980 indicated that cocaine had relatively benign effects on most individuals, the majority of reports in the 1980s and 1990s indicated considerable concern over cocaine's dependence liability and toxicity. These reports indicated that, particularly when administered intravenously or through smoking, cocaine can induce a very strong psychological dependence (Gawin, 1993). For example, cocaine addicts report that virtually all thoughts are focused on cocaine during binges (which can last up to several days); nourishment, sleep, money, loved ones, responsibility, and survival lose all significance. It is estimated that one out of 10 recreational users of intranasal cocaine becomes heavily dependent or experiences numerous severe consequences. However, cocaine abusers in treatment report that 2 to 4 years intervene between initial exposure to cocaine and the development of addiction—a delay that may have contributed to the lack of recognition of its addictive and toxic properties.

Until recently there was some question whether tolerance occured with cocaine use. There is now considerable evidence that tolerance does develop to many of the physiological and subjective rewarding effects of cocaine, and in some cases it develops very rapidly (Fischman et al., 1985; Mendelson et al., 1998; Wood & Emmett-Oglesby, 1986). Some acute tolerance to cocaine's effects may be due to the activation of negative-feedback systems, that is, autoreceptor activation, which reduces monoamine neurotransmitter release, whereas long-term tolerance with chronic cocaine exposure may be related to the depletion of monoamines and/or down-regulation of monoamine receptors (with implications for dependence, which will be discussed shortly) (Volkow et al., 1990). Recent evidence suggests that cocaine exposure modifies subsequent responsiveness to the drug through a complicated intracellular cascade—culminating in gene expression—via what is called the transcription factor CREB (adenosine 3', 5'-monophosphate response element binding protein) in the nucleus accumbens. It has been suggested that overexpression of CREB in this region decreases the rewarding effects of cocaine and makes low doses of the drug aversive (Carlezone et al., 1999), which may be the result of a diminished release of dopamine in the nucleus accumbens. In cases in which cocaine disrupts task performance, lowers reinforcement availability, or increases exposure to aversive stimuli (punishment), the learning of compensatory behaviors (e.g., instrumental conditioning) has long been viewed as a mechanism for tolerance development.

It has also been recognized that, as is the case with amphetamine, exposure to cocaine can induce sensitization to many of cocaine's effects in animals, most notably its locomotor and stereotypy-inducing effects (Stripling & Ellinwood, 1977). A similar phenomenon has been observed in humans, in which sensitization to the psychosis-mimicking properties of cocaine appears to occur in a substantial percentage of heavy cocaine users (Bartlett et al., 1997; Brady et al., 1991; Satel et al., 1991b). Thus, with repeated use of cocaine in humans, the rewarding effects often diminish and are overshadowed by unpleasant side effects such as anxiety, irritability, and delusional paranoia. Interestingly, despite these effects, the individuals continue to use cocaine.

Whether tolerance or sensitization occurs with chronic cocaine use appears to depend on complex interactions among dose, the behavior involved, the pattern of use, and the species, as well as other as yet unknown factors (Grabowski & Dworkin, 1985). For example, in animals exposed continuously to cocaine for several days (for instance, by way of a small pump implanted under the skin), tolerance to the behavioral effects may occur. In contrast, in animals exposed intermittently to the same total daily amount of cocaine for the same number of days (for instance, one subcutaneous injection per day), sensitization to the behavioral effects may occur (King et al., 1994; Martin-Iverson & Burger, 1995). Along with these behavior phenomena, a puzzling array of alterations in dopamine receptors, as well as other receptors (for example, opioidergic, glutamatergic) that regulate dopaminergic functions, have been reported to occur with different cocaine administration regimens (Fitzgerald et al., 1996; Maisonneuve & Kreek, 1994; Unterwald et al., 1994a, 1994b). Perhaps this should not be surprising, since the neurons affected by cocaine, which has potent but short-duration actions, are literally getting mixed messages—at certain points during the day there is dopaminergic overactivity, and at other points there is dopamineragic underactivity.

The relevance of these findings to humans is unclear, as human cocaine abusers commonly combine these patterns by binging (administering cocaine every 10 to 30 minutes for several hours or even days) and then abstaining for one or more days before binging again. It is this pattern of use that often leads to the development of symptoms of paranoid psychosis in the user (Gawin, 1993). In human laboratory research, in which the doses of cocaine are much lower and the length of exposure is much shorter than those typically reported by street abusers, acute tolerance to the subjective and cardiovascular effects is commonly observed (Ambre, 1993; Foltin & Fischman, 1991; Foltin et al., 1995). Similarly, when low doses of cocaine are used to maintain self-administration in rats, tolerance to its reinforcing effects has been shown to develop with chronic exposure to cocaine, whether cocaine was given contingently (that is, self-administered by the rats) or noncontingently (that is, infused by the experimenter) (Emmett-Oglesby et al., 1993). It has been proposed that repeated use of cocaine sensitizes the person to the "wanting" or "desire" for cocaine, but induces tolerance to the "liking" or "pleasure" induced by cocaine (Berridge & Robinson, 1995). In other words, addicts come to want cocaine more and more, even if they like it less and less.

It has been demonstrated in nonhumans that some sensitization phenomena associated with cocaine exposure can be attributable to the environmental context and Pavlovian conditioning (Post et al., 1987). However, with sufficiently high doses of cocaine, an environment context-independent sensitization effect can also appear. In humans, panic attacks and seizures may develop with chronic cocaine use. It has been speculated that these are due to the biochemical properties of cocaine that produce its local anesthetic actions. Local anesthetics, when administered repetitively in high doses, produce an alteration in the threshold for seizures such that previously subconvulsive doses become capable of eliciting major motor seizures. (This phenomenon appears to be similar to that of electrophysiological "kindling," in which repeated electrical stimulation below the convulsive threshold eventually provokes full-blown seizures.) However, studies with animals have shown that, in contrast to seizures kindled by lidocaine (a local anesthetic with minimal euphoric properties), which are generally well tolerated for weeks or months of repetitions, cocaine-induced seizures are extremely lethal. The hypothesis that links electrical kindling in the limbic system (leading to seizures) to sensitivity to cocaine's effects was a factor in the use of anticonvulsant drugs in the treatment of cocaine dependence (discussed shortly).

Studies have also strongly suggested that withdrawal-like effects do occur after extensive cocaine use. Furthermore, anecdotal reports from cocaine-dependent persons suggest that withdrawal involves several phases, with mixtures of different dependence-inducing processes being implicated (Gawin, 1993). During the first few hours after a binge (which generally ceases only when all the cocaine is gone), the user feels depressed and agitated, lacks appetite, and experiences high cocaine craving. In the next several hours or days, the user experiences extreme hunger, although cocaine craving is absent. In some individuals there is also a strong abhorrence for cocaine during this time period, and the need for sleep is overwhelming. During the next several days, the user's sleep patterns and mood return to normal, and there is little cocaine craving. However, subsequently the user experiences anxiety, a lack of energy, an inability to enjoy normal activities, and high cocaine craving that is exacerbated by environmental cues previously associated with cocaine use. After several weeks, the user's mood and pleasure response return to normal, and he or she experiences only episodic cocaine craving, which again is most common in the presence of specific environments. If the person begins taking cocaine again at any point, he or she generally returns to the first phase.

In contrast to this phasic model of cocaine withdrawal, other studies conducted with cocaine-dependent persons undergoing abstinence in both outpatient and inpatient settings over 3- or 4-week periods have reported mild symptoms of cocaine craving, anxiety, depression, physical discomfort, and drug withdrawal, which decreased in a linear fashion over the course of the studies (Coffey et al., 2000; Satel et al., 1991a; Weddington et al., 1990). Thus, it is unclear under what conditions, if any, the phasic model of cocaine withdrawal is applicable to the majority of cocaine-dependent persons.

Differential time-related changes in brain glucose metabolism in frontal cortex regions and other regions have been observed in cocaine abusers undergoing cocaine withdrawal: increases in activity occurring within 1 week, normal levels occurring at 2 to 4 weeks, and subsequent decreases persisting for 3 to 4 months after detoxification (Volkow et al., 1991; Volkow et al., 1993). Furthermore, the greatest cocaine craving occurred during the period in which the glucose metabolism activity was highest (Volkow et al., 1991).

The intensity and persistence of cocaine craving following cocaine exposure is a major factor behind its abuse, with higher levels of cocaine craving being reported by cocaine-dependent persons when they are experiencing negative mood states (Robbins et al., 2000). Cocaine craving and other types of Pavlovian conditioned responses have been shown to be triggered by environmental stimuli or by internal mood states associated with the drug experience (Ehrman et al., 1992; Jaffe et al., 1989). Cue-induced craving in humans has been found to be associated with increases in activity (based on cerebral blood flow) in areas of the limbic system (amygdala and anterior cingulate cortex) and decreases in the basal ganglia (Childress et al., 1999). Interestingly, both pleasant (e.g., "high," "aroused") and unpleasant (e.g., "craving," "withdrawal," "negative mood") conditioned responses can be elicited in cocaine-dependent persons (Robbins et al., 2000). Cocaine craving can also be initiated in cocaine abusers by the administration of small doses of cocaine or similar-acting drugs, a phenomenon called *priming* (Spealman et al., 1999). Research with animals indicates that these priming effects can be mimicked by activation of the ventral tegmental area dopaminergic system (Stewart, 1984). Although both D_1-like and D_2-like dopamine receptors appear to mediate the reinforcing effects of cocaine, research has suggested that stimulation of D_2-like receptors is responsible for the priming effect, whereas stimulation of D_1-like receptors actually has the opposite effect (Self et al., 1996). The implication is that agonists that are highly specific to D_1-like receptors may be useful in the treatment of cocaine abuse, as well as other drugs of abuse that act through this dopaminergic system.

In addition, there is abundant evidence that pharmacologically induced biochemical disruptions, particularly central dopamine neuronal systems, play a role in the craving for cocaine. One model proposes that chronic cocaine exposure leads to a depletion of intraneuronal dopamine (Dackis & Gold, 1985; Maisonneuve et al., 1995). That is, it is assumed that acute exposure to cocaine inhibits dopamine reuptake and abruptly elevates extraneuronal dopamine levels. This increase is followed by a rapid return to normal dopamine levels, due presumably to the activation of a negative-feedback system, such as dopamine autoreceptor activation, which in turn leads the user to administer more cocaine. With continued cocaine exposure there is a depletion of intraneuronal dopamine stores, either because of reduced synthesis via autoreceptor activity or enhanced catabolization via COMT (extraneuronally) or MAO (intraneuronally). On the other hand, studies utilizing PET scan techniques suggest that chronic cocaine exposure decreases postsynaptic dopamine receptor availability (i.e., down-regulation), presumably due to the excessive and chronic dopamine exposure (Volkow et al., 1991; Volkow et al., 1993). In either case, decreased dopaminergic function is suggested to underlie cocaine addiction.

Any aspect of a drug that may increase its likelihood of being used on subsequent occasions may be a factor in its being a positive reinforcer and being abused (Stolerman & Jarvis, 1995). Cocaine has a reputation of enhancing a person's subjective self-worth, competence, and performance, and we would expect this to be a factor in the maintenance of cocaine drug use. Cocaine has been shown to enhance the performance of sleep-deprived individuals, but evidence that cocaine can enhance the learning or performance of nonfatigued individuals is weak (Johnson et al., 1998). Animal studies have shown that low doses of cocaine can enhance certain aspects of performance, such as accuracy and reaction time, in some tasks—even when the animals are not fatigued (Grilly et al., 1989; Grilly & Grogan, 1990).

In terms of patterns of use, cocaine is one of the few controlled substances in which the chances of initiating its use persist or increase well into adulthood (Kozel & Adams, 1986). As noted in Chapter 6, its use generally follows exposure to more licit drugs, such as tobacco and alcohol, and marijuana. Epidemiological studies are needed to answer more specific questions about predictors for initiation and maintenance of cocaine use, what interventions might mitigate these, and how frequently cocaine use impacts other aspects of the user's life, such as use of other drugs, socioeconomic status, health, and driving.

Direct Adverse Consequences of Cocaine

Many of the problems attributed to cocaine, such as lower productivity, financial losses, family disruptions, legal difficulties, and so on, are indirectly related to its use. These problems come about because of the user's preoccupation with the drug or the U. S. legal system's views on its possession and use. However, unlike opiates, where most of the problems with their use are due to these factors rather than to direct effects on the body, cocaine also has several potential direct adverse consequences. As noted previously, the adverse effects of heavy amphetamine use—for example, psychosis, profound irritability, misperception, paranoid thought, impaired interpersonal relations, and eating and sleeping disturbances—have also been well-documented to occur with heavy cocaine use (Post & Contel, 1983). Cocaine has also been shown to precipitate panic attacks, which may subsequently recur without further cocaine use (Aronson & Craig, 1986).

Cocaine can produce a variety of neurological problems, including seizures, headache, and transient symptoms such as sensory loss on one side of the body, visual impairment, and tremor (Rowbotham & Lowenstein, 1990). Other than seizure activity, which is dose related, there does not appear to be a correlation between these neurological problems and the dose, route of administration, or prior cocaine use patterns. Although neurocognitive impairments may precede cocaine use (and may be a factor in its initial use), there is considerable support for the conclusion that subgroups of cocaine-abusing patients may demonstrate sustained and persistent neurocognitive deficits that are consequences of their cocaine use (Strickland & Stein, 1995).

While news reports in the 1980s, such as those discussing the deaths of well-known athletes like Maryland basketball player Len Bias and Cleveland Browns football player Don Rogers, tended to emphasize cocaine's potential lethality, it is not clear how many deaths are directly due to cocaine overdoses. Statistics regarding fatalities attributable to cocaine use are not particularly reliable, but it does appear that only about one-quarter of the deaths are actually due directly to the recreational use of cocaine. The majority of cocaine-associated deaths can be attributed to suicide induced by or facilitated by cocaine; accidental overdoses (for example, the person swallowed cocaine for smuggling purposes or to elude detection when arrested); homicides; death from natural causes; or the combining of cocaine with other drugs (primarily opiates) (Finkle & McCloskey, 1977; Lichtenfeld et al., 1984). For most individuals, the lethal dose of cocaine—approximately 1 to 2 grams in an hour—would be quite expensive. Cocaine use may cause sudden death because of cerebral hemorrhaging (bleeding within the brain) (Lichtenfeld et al., 1984), convulsion induction (Ellinwood et al., 1977), lethal cardiac arrhythmias (Chakko & Myerberg, 1995), or acute myocardial infarction (sudden insufficiency of blood to the heart muscles)—even in individuals with no preexisting arterial dysfunctions (Isner & Chokshi, 1991). The mechanism behind sudden deaths is still obscure, but evidence suggests that even low doses of cocaine can lead to inflammation of the muscular walls of the heart in certain individuals. Also, contrary to what is commonly believed, intranasal cocaine can lead to sudden death (Finkle & McCloskey, 1977).

As noted in Chapter 3, most psychoactive substances are likely to be teratogenic. Considering cocaine's lipid solubility, there is no reason to believe that cocaine is an exception. Although only a small fraction of babies exposed to cocaine in the womb develop medical problems, since 1985 a number of studies, with both humans and nonhumans, have documented the potential teratogenic effects of cocaine (Slutsker, 1992). In humans, cocaine abuse has been associated with an increased stillbirth rate and premature delivery. Physically, cocaine-exposed neonates exhibit lower average birth weights, body lengths, and head circumferences. There is also evidence that such infants exhibit retarded brain growth and skull defects. Behaviorally, these infants exhibit more jitteriness and irritability and appear less attentive than non–cocaine-exposed infants. After birth, there is evidence that cocaine-exposed neonates are more prone to sudden unexplained infant death syndrome. Many of these effects are likely to be the result of impaired fetal oxygenation caused by cocaine's tendency to constrict blood vessels. Cocaine also produces a number of biochemical disruptions that may be responsible for many of its observed neurobehavioral effects. For example, recent studies with animals suggest that in utero exposure to cocaine can produce dysfunction of dopamine D_1 receptor signaling and induce abnormal dendritic growth patterns of some cerebral cortical neurons (Jones et al., 2000).

Unfortunately, the true extent of the severity and incidence of the harmful effects of prenatal cocaine exposure in humans is simply not known, because of a number of methodological problems in the studies addressing this issue. Among many problems, for example, the women in these studies (1) are more likely to be poor and undereducated (factors that, for a variety of reasons, can be detrimental to pre- and postnatal development); (2) may differ considerably in the amount, frequency, and time of cocaine use; (3) commonly use other drugs, such as alcohol (by itself a potent teratogen), nicotine, marijuana, and heroin, that may also compromise prenatal development; (4) may under- or overreport their drug use; and (5) may practice other poor health behaviors, such as inadequate nutrition and pre- and postnatal care (Griffith et al., 1994; Gonzalez & Campbell, 1994).

Recent analyses of a large number of studies suggest that the effects of prenatal cocaine exposure on language and cognitive functioning of children are more subtle than previously assumed (e.g., an average decrease of 3.26 I.Q. points) (Lester et al., 1998). However, these effects can have profound consequences for the success of these children in school and for the cost of special education services. For example, a downward shift in the I.Q. distribution of 3.26 I.Q. points would result in 1.5-fold increase in the number of children typically requiring early intervention and special education services (often defined by a child exhibiting I.Q. scores less than 70, or in some cases less than 78). If the estimates of 375,000 cocaine-exposed children being born each year are correct, the additional number of children necessitating special education services would range from around 1,700 to 38,000, and the additional monetary costs would range from $4 million to $80 million per year. Finally, since the mothers' cocaine use often occurs in the context of poverty and other known risks to children, including tobacco, alcohol, and other drug use, these children's prenatal exposure to cocaine compounds their problems.

Methcathinone

Methcathinone is the newest of the potent psychostimulants to be introduced into the United States, and it appears to be as addictive as crack cocaine and methamphetamine (Emerson & Cisek, 1993). It is a derivative of a naturally occurring stimulant drug, cathinone, which is found in the "Khat" plant native to Africa and the southern Arabian peninsula. Methcathinone was originally synthesized in Germany in 1928 and used in the Soviet Union as an antidepressant drug in the 1930s and 1940s. In the mid-1950s, an American pharmaceutical company conducted preliminary studies on its potential medical uses. After determining that it had substantial side effects, with effects essentially identical to those of amphetamine, the company abandoned its research with methcathinone. In the 1980s, it reappeared on the illicit market after a student working at the company stole samples and documentation on the manufacturing process. In 1990, associates of the student began manufacturing the drug (a relatively simple process) in clandestine laboratories and selling it—a practice that rapidly spread to several states.

It appears that methcathinone has psychopharmacological properties that are indistinguishable from those just described for cocaine and amphetamine (Emerson & Cisek, 1993; Glennon et al., 1995). The most common means of taking methcathinone is intranasally, but it is also administered orally, intravenously, or by smoking. Often there is a binge pattern of use similar to that of other illicit psychostimulants. The effects of short-term intoxication are similar to those produced by crack cocaine or methamphetamine: stimulation of heart rate and respiration; feeling of euphoria; loss of appetite; and increased alertness. The pupils may be dilated and body temperature may be slightly elevated. Acute intoxication at higher doses may also result in insomnia, tremors and muscle twitching, fever, headaches, convulsions, irregular heart rate and respiration, anxiety, restlessness, paranoia, and hallucinations and delusions. Following a binge, users report a crash that often includes severe psychological depression and suicidal thoughts. In short, methcathinone is a new drug with the same old problems.

Treatment of Cocaine and Amphetamine Abuse

The important factor in drug dependence is the dynamics among the individual's environment, genetic predispositions, behavior, and drug exposure—not the drug. The key to treatment is getting compulsive drug users to acknowledge that they are out of control and should do whatever they need to to get well; thus, social, behavioral, and cognitive treatments for psychostimulant abuse are often the same as those described earlier for alcohol abuse. Furthermore, a large number of psychostimulant abusers also meet the diagnostic criteria for alcohol dependence (Gossop et al., 2000; Higgins et al., 1994a). Because most of the recent research on treatment for psychostimulant dependence has focused on cocaine, I will focus my comments on this drug, but with few exceptions they can be applied equally to the amphetamines as well.

Getting the cocaine addict to quit taking cocaine is not the major problem in treatment; it is preventing relapse—often triggered by intense cravings for cocaine—that appears most difficult. Rehabilitation by way of self-help groups, behavioral modification procedures (for example, vouchers given for cocaine-free urine samples), involvement of significant others in the treatment, helping the patient learn to cope with everyday problems and stress, and extinction of cue-triggered cravings result in significant improvement in the majority of cocaine abusers (Gossop et al., 2000; Higgins et al., 1994b, 1994c; O'Brien et al., 1993; Simpson et al., 1999; Withers et al., 1995).

These improvements consist of not only reductions in the use of cocaine and other psychostimulants (on the order of 70% to 80% reductions in amounts used), but also sizeable reductions in other drug use (alcohol, opiates, benzodiazepines), acquisitive crimes and selling drugs, drug injecting and sharing of needles, and physical and psychological health problems. However, drugs that can serve as adjunctive treatments have been actively sought to facilitate the therapeutic process.

There are some differences in the chemical interventions potentially used in the treatment of psychostimulant dependence, as opposed to sedative–hypnotic or narcotic dependence. In the case of the psychostimulants, physical withdrawal is neither life-threatening nor exceedingly uncomfortable (Satel et al., 1991a; Weddington et al., 1990). Thus, there is no need to substitute a long-acting psychostimulant (if there were such a compound) and then gradually reduce the dosage because of concern over precipitating a convulsive episode or cardiovascular collapse.

Because symptoms of depression commonly precede cocaine use and may be a factor in its initial use—and almost always follow chronic heavy use—the efficacy of antidepressants in the treatment of cocaine abuse has been investigated in numerous studies. Desipramine, a tricyclic antidepressant with primarily norepinephrine reuptake–inhibiting properties, has been found to have effectiveness in reducing cocaine use and craving in some individuals who have less severe forms of dependence along with symptoms of depression. However, the majority of studies have not found desipramine, or any other tricyclic antidepressant, to be of much benefit in the majority of addicts (Mendelson & Mello, 1996). The newer selective serotonin reuptake inhibitor antidepressants have been reported to be of benefit in reducing craving and the use of cocaine in addicts in several uncontrolled studies, but the most recent, large-scale, double-blind, placebo-controlled study found neither of these benefits (Grabowski et al., 1995). Mood stabilizers (drugs used in the treatment of bipolar affective disorders), such as lithium and carbamazepine, have been shown to be no more effective than placebos in providing benefits to cocaine addicts (Mendelson & Mello, 1996). Phenytoin, an anticonvulsant commonly used in the treatment of epilepsy, has been shown in a double-blind study to significantly lower cocaine use in cocaine-using subjects, as well as to reduce craving intensity (Crosby et al., 1996).

Based on the hypothesis that a dopamine deficiency contributes to discomfort of cocaine addicts upon abstinence, a number of drugs that enhance dopaminergic function have been tested for efficacy in treatment. Bromocriptine (Parlodel), a direct dopamine receptor agonist, and amantadine (Symmetrel), a drug that releases dopamine and norepinephrine from neuronal storage sites, have been found to be beneficial in reducing cocaine craving and other withdrawal symptoms (Schuckit, 1994). However, the benefits appeared to be minimal or absent in several controlled studies, and both drugs produce problematical side effects. Placebo-controlled studies have also failed to find benefits of treatment with the dopamine precursors tyrosine or L-dopa (Chadwick et al., 1990; Wolfsohn et al., 1993). Methylphenidate, with actions similar to cocaine but with a longer duration of action, has been found to increase rather than decrease the craving for cocaine. Finally, neither mazindol, which inhibits the binding of cocaine to dopamine transporters, nor bupropion, an antidepressant that weakly facilitates dopaminergic function, has been found to be more effective than placebos in treating cocaine dependence (Mendelson & Mello, 1996). A number of dopamine agonists that are highly selective for each of the major subtypes of dopamine receptors have been developed and show promise in animal models of dependence, but further testing is necessary before we will know whether they provide any more specific benefits than those of other drugs that enhance dopaminergic functioning.

Because many of the reinforcing effects of psychostimulants depend critically on their ability to elevate extracellular dopamine levels in the mesolimbic dopamine system, blockade of dopamine receptors (e.g., with drugs typically used in the treatment of schizophrenia) has been proposed as a potential treatment for cocaine dependence (Wise, 1995). While these types of drugs do block the rewarding effects of cocaine, they don't reduce the craving for cocaine. Furthermore, the risk of side effects (e.g., tardive dyskinesia) and the dysphoric effects of these types of drugs make compliance a problem in their use.

As discussed elsewhere (see Chapter 11), ibogaine (Endabuse) has been proposed to possess broad-spectrum antiaddiction properties that may be useful in the treatment of psychostimulant dependence (Mash et al., 1998). In animal studies, ibogaine has been shown to reduce a number of cocaine- and amphetamine-induced effects, including self-administration and locomotion effects—in some cases for several days following ibogaine exposure—although these effects and their persistence may depend upon the dose, dose pattern, and species and sex of the animals (Popik et al., 1995). Multiple mechanisms of action are responsible for ibogaine's effects, but two prominent actions that are likely to be relevant are its ability to block NMDA receptor-activated ion channels and its ability to block 5-HT reuptake sites and elevate extracellular 5-HT levels. Numerous lines of evidence suggest that these types of actions can interrupt drug-seeking behavior in animals. Clinical trials are presently being conducted in a number of centers around the world to test the safety and efficacy of ibogaine as a treatment for addiction.

For cocaine addicts concurrently dependent on opiates, treatment with the mixed opioid agonist/antagonist buprenorphine (discussed in Chapter 10) has been examined in several studies (Compton et al., 1995). However, clinical evidence of buprenorphine's effectiveness in treating cocaine abuse has not been clearly demonstrated. The dose of buprenorphine used may be a critical factor in the attenuation of cocaine effects, with higher doses being more effective than lower doses (Stine & Kosten, 1994).

Thus far, all studies of medications used to help prevent relapse to cocaine dependence have revealed modest benefits at best (O'Brien, 1996). One of the basic problems with drugs used in the treatment for dependence on cocaine, or any other drug, is their lack of long-term effects. That is, even with the longest acting drugs, the effects last only a few days. Thus, if the addict stops taking them, perhaps with the desire to reexperience the effects of cocaine, their efficacy is lost. This may have been a factor in a study finding that fluoxetine (a selective serotonin reuptake inhibitor antidepressant) was not effective in reducing cocaine use in cocaine-dependent subjects (Grabowski et al., 1995). The main outcome in the study was that fluoxetine treatment dose-dependently increased the dropout rate of the subjects over the 12-week study phase. One interpretation of this result is that the subjects (most of whom apparently continued to use cocaine) found the effects of cocaine unfulfilling and dropped out of the study so that they could reexperience the pleasurable effects of the drug.

One strategy that has been explored to induce long-lasting suppression of the psychoactive effects of cocaine has employed the immunization approach, which has been used in medicine for many years as a prophylactic treatment for a variety of pathogen-induced diseases (Slusher & Jackson, 1996). Studies have shown that animals given active immunization with a new, stable cocaine conjugate, which theoretically should reduce the actions of the drug by preventing it from entering the CNS, does in fact decrease many of its effects (Carrera et al., 1995). However, whether the process can be applied to humans and how long the immunization lasts remains to be determined. It is also important to determine whether addicts can use higher doses of cocaine to override the immunization, which addicts may very well do since the process does nothing to reduce cocaine craving. In this case, the toxic effects of cocaine on other parts of the body—for example, the heart—may still be evident.

Nicotine

Every year thousands of young people take up smoking tobacco. Over time their use changes from sporadic, occasional use to more continuous, daily use. On the other hand, thousands of people who have smoked for years try to stop; in most cases these attempts fail because the process is so aversive. In fact, several years ago the Surgeon General of the United States issued a report that stated that the pharmacologic and behavioral processes that determine tobacco addiction are similar to those that determine addiction to drugs such as heroin and cocaine. Most people—smokers and nonsmokers—recognize that there are costs for smoking. Although cheap in comparison to most other drug habits, smoking is not inexpensive. "Pack-a-day" smokers currently pay around $1,000 a year for their habit. However, this expense is a drop in the bucket compared to the potential health costs of lung cancer, emphysema, cardiovascular dysfunction, and other diseases associated with cigarette smoking. The problems are compounded by the fact that cigarette smoking is prominent among most abusers of other drugs; for example, more than 90 percent of alcoholic inpatients are smokers (Bien & Burge, 1990). Smoking exacerbates their health risks and complicates their treatment. (For example, it is not clear whether treatment for alcohol, cocaine, or heroin dependence would be facilitated or worsened by concomitant cessation of smoking.)

Questions as to why people start smoking in the first place and what makes stopping smoking so difficult for the majority of heavy smokers have been addressed by researchers for years. So far, only pieces of the puzzle exist. A large majority of adult smokers in the United States report that they began smoking when they were adolescents (Eissenberg & Balster, 2000). A wide variety of studies have indicated that there are numerous predictors of adolescent tobacco use. These include being male and White, holding positive attitudes toward smoking, having concerns over body weight, having parents who smoke or have permissive attitudes toward smoking, perceiving that smoking has positive benefits, having low expectations for school achievement, having easy access to tobacco, and having a number of smoking friends (Mayhew et al., 2000). Adolescents who take up smoking tend to exhibit lower self-esteem, perceive themselves as having less internal control over their lives, and have higher levels of trait anxiety than those who do not take up smoking (Penny & Robinson, 1986). About one-third to one-half of those who experiment with cigarettes become regular users. Although there has been a reduction in the prevalence of smoking among many segments of the U. S. population—particularly among adults and Black adolescents—and a decline in per capita consumption, there has been minimal progress in reducing smoking by adolescents, especially Whites and males (Giovino et al., 1995).

Once smoking begins, genetic factors probably play a role in developing nicotine dependency. It has long been recognized that nicotine dependency is strongly associated with alcohol dependency, which, as we have noted earlier, has an established linkage to genes. Studies have also noted that nicotine-dependent persons, at some point in their lives, are more than twice as likely as nondependent nicotine users (or nonusers) to have suffered from major depression, which has also been viewed as involving a genetic predisposition

(Glassman et al., 1990). In one study, teenagers with a depressive disorder had odds of nicotine dependence that were 2.3 times those of teenagers without a depressive disorder (Fergusson et al., 1996). In addition, persons with histories of major depression or any anxiety disorder tend to report more severe nicotine withdrawal symptoms than persons with neither of these disorders (Breslau et al., 1992). However, a recent study suggests that the causal link between cigarette use and the development of depressive symptoms may be opposite of what has been previously presumed. In that study, depression was not found to be an antecedent to heavy cigarette use among teens (Goodman & Capitman, 2000). On the other hand, teen smokers who were not depressed at baseline were about four times as likely to develop highly depressed symptoms during a year's time.

Despite a multitude of studies on tobacco use, it is still not clear what is so reinforcing about the practice. For the majority of individuals, the initial smoking experiences are more likely to be unpleasant than pleasant (Eissenberg & Balster, 2000). Apparently, the psychosocial rewards, such as peer acceptance and role-model identification, are sufficiently strong to maintain smoking behavior until the individuals learn to monitor the amount of smoke and the unpleasant side effects subside. Nicotine has been long presumed to be the most important, but not the only, reinforcing factor behind smoking tobacco (Henningfield & Goldberg, 1988). If it were the only factor, then chewing nicotine gum would induce effects similar to smoking tobacco, which it does not do, and the treatment for smoking using nicotine gum would be much more effective than it is (Pickworth et al., 1986). In fact, most tobacco smokers cannot describe any attractive effect except what they might describe as the "taste" of tobacco smoke in their mouth, lungs, and nasal passages (Schelling, 1992). One important factor in maintaining the use of tobacco is its ability to reduce negative affective states—transient aversive emotional states such as sadness, boredom, anxiety, which may occur as a function of endogenous characteristics of the individual (for example, depression), environmental stressors, and, of course, nicotine withdrawal (Brandon, 1994). Finally, smoking may be reinforcing because it gives one something to do with one's hands, it may affect one's public image (although lately the image of a smoker has become considerably more negative), or it may be associated with other social reinforcers, such as acceptance by one's peers.

On the other hand, there are several lines of evidence that indicate that nicotine is the principal reinforcer for smoking behavior. First, human tobacco users who were administered low doses of nicotine (0.01 mg/kg) intravenously reported enhancement of mood and drug liking, although higher doses (0.04 mg/kg) produced aversive effects (Lundahl et al., 2000). Both effects can be blocked with nicotinic receptor blockade. Second, nicotine administered to animals increases extracellular and synaptic concentrations of dopamine in the nucleus accumbens (Mihailescu & Drucker-Colin, 2000), which, as discussed previously, is a phenomenon observed with many drugs of abuse and is associated with primary reward. Third, animals have been shown to self-administer nicotine via both oral and intravenous routes of administration (Donny et al., 1999; Maehler et al., 2000). However, self-administration of nicotine in animals is often not as robust as it is with most other drugs of abuse, and its efficacy as a reinforcer may depend on administration under certain environmental conditions. For example, in one study, monkeys self-administered nicotine at a relatively high rate if a discrete signal came on just as the nicotine infusions were delivered, but their rate of administering nicotine dropped sharply when the signal did not occur (Goldberg et al., 1981). Perhaps this relationship explains why nicotine by way of smoking is the most popular route of administration; that is, with this route, discrete stimuli (smoke upon exhalation) always accompany the nicotine just before it reaches the brain (Schelling, 1992).

Working on the hypothesis that chronic smokers maximize the reinforcing effects of nicotine by titrating their intake, several studies have attempted to determine whether or not cigarette smokers can effectively regulate the amount of nicotine in their blood when given high- and low-nicotine cigarettes to smoke (Henningfield & Goldberg, 1988). Most agree that while some regulation of nicotine plasma levels is often achieved—by increasing the number of low-nicotine cigarettes or reducing the number of high-nicotine cigarettes consumed—it is nowhere near perfect. In two of the studies that varied nicotine and tar content independently, the number of cigarettes smoked was inversely related to nicotine content, not tar content. Finally, studies in which the subjects were preloaded with nicotine (in gum or in capsules) found a decrease in cigarettes consumed, whereas when a nicotine antagonist was administered, cigarette smoking increased.

In some individuals, nicotine has a mild psychostimulant effect, particularly with respect to enhanced vigilance (Jaffe, 1990). In fact, socially relevant doses of nicotine may be comparable to socially relevant doses of caffeine in facilitating choice reaction time, motor tracking, and short-term memory retrieval, as well as antagonizing some of the debilitating effects of alcohol (Kerr et al., 1991). In most cases nicotine shifts EEG patterns toward those often associated with increased psychological arousal—that is, higher-frequency, lower-amplitude waves—and are most pronounced when the individual is relaxed with eyes closed (Pickworth et al., 1986). On the other hand, smokers often report that a cigarette calms them down and reduces tension (Schelling, 1992)—perhaps because it relieves their craving for a cigarette or stops withdrawal.

The effects of nicotine on performance are typically subtle and variable. Various lines of evidence suggest that nicotine can enhance task performance, memory, cognition and learning in some individuals, in some situations, some of the time (Gentry et al., 2000; Heishman, 1998; Heishman et al., 1994; Sherwood, 1993; Waters & Sutton, 2000). The problem in determining the who, where, and when is that there are so many potential factors involved: (1) whether the person being tested is a tobacco user or not (most studies are done with users); (2) the degree of nicotine dependence and deprivation level at the time of testing; (3) the route of administration (smoking, injection, nasal spray, nicotine gum, nicotine patch), which influences the onset and duration of effects; (4) the dose (dose–response functions of performance-enhancing drugs are typically inverted U-shaped); (5) the predrug psychological state of the person; (6) the type of task used; and so forth. Furthermore, nicotine can affect mood, cognition, or arousal, all of which can interact in complicated ways; for example, cognition could be enhanced directly by nicotine or it could be enhanced because nicotine improves the person's mood.

It is clear that nicotine and smoking can reverse deprivation-induced deficits in certain abilities in abstinent smokers. Studies conducted with nondeprived smokers and nonsmokers have shown that nicotine may enhance finger-tapping rate and motor responding in tests of focused attention. Additionally, nicotine has been shown to enhance sustained attention and recognition memory in both nondeprived smokers and nonsmokers. In simulated driving tests, nondeprived smokers have been shown to exhibit decreased braking time and improved tracking after smoking. Enhanced performance most typically occurs in relatively simple tasks requiring sustained attention or fast reaction times. In more complex tasks, such as understanding articles or solving problems, nicotine may actually be detrimental to performance. At the present time, no studies have reported true enhancement of sensory abilities, selective attention, learning, and other cognitive (e.g., problem solving, reasoning) abilities.

Presumably these psychological effects occur because of nicotine's ability to stimulate nicotinic receptor sites normally activated by acetylcholine. Which of the particular receptors are most important is not clear, since nicotine acts on receptors found throughout the nervous system. Furthermore, nicotinic receptors outside the brain may be involved. In the peripheral nervous system, activation of nicotinic receptors produces sympathomimetic effects, primarily because the nicotinic receptors found in the adrenal gland trigger the release of adrenaline (epinephrine) from the adrenal gland into the bloodstream. Adrenaline, in turn, is transported to adrenergic receptors in the heart and blood vessels, leading to increases in heart rate and elevated blood pressure (through constriction of blood vessels). Although adrenaline may potentially affect CNS function, it is unlikely to have much effect because it does not cross the blood–brain barrier very well. (Since there are nicotinic receptors on postganglionic parasympathetic neurons, activation of nicotinic receptors would also be expected to enhance parasympathetic activity, but the sympathetic effects predominate over the parasympathetic effects.) Despite these multiple PNS effects, they are probably not of major importance in reinforcing smoking because they can be blocked without appreciably altering the psychological effects of nicotine in humans.

There are also numerous nicotinic receptors in the CNS, which could account for nicotine's ability to alter cortical neuron function. Recent research indicates that nicotine enhances both inhibitory and excitatory transmission in the CNS by acting on receptors located on presynaptic nerve endings, which increase intracellular Ca^{++} levels and enhance release of a variety of transmitters—for example, glutamate, acetylcholine, norepinephrine, GABA, and dopamine (Mihailescu & Drucker-Colin, 2000). Which (if any) of these actions is relevant to the effects of nicotine in humans is unknown. The importance of cholinergic systems on working memory (discussed in Chapters 11 and 14) suggests that nicotine may facilitate some aspects of this type of memory (Levin & Simon, 1998).

In addition to the nicotine in tobacco, research suggests that an unidentified ingredient in tobacco smoke reduces levels of monoamine oxidase B (the enzyme that breaks down dopamine) in smokers (Fowler et al., 1996). Thus, these two factors may synergistically lead to higher dopamine levels, enhancing the reward and the high associated with smoking tobacco. These actions may also explain the prevalence of, and increase in smoking in, patients treated with antipsychotics, which are dopamine receptor blockers (McEvoy et al., 1995). It is also possible that the light-headed feeling that one gets by depriving the brain of oxygen—because of the carbon monoxide in smoke—is perceived as pleasurable.

Following chronic tobacco exposure, nicotine may also be reinforcing because it immediately stops withdrawal symptoms, indicative of the physical dependence on nicotine that many believe exists. The onset of withdrawal symptoms may occur within hours of the last cigarette. In addition to a craving for tobacco, these symptoms may consist of decreased heart rate, EEG slowing, irritability, increased hunger, sleep disturbances, gastrointestinal disturbances, drowsiness, headache, and impairment of concentration, judgment, and psychomotor performance (Hughes et al., 1987; Sommese & Patterson, 1995).

Some of these withdrawal symptoms may be mediated by changes in nicotinic-acetylcholine receptors (nAchRs) that may occur with chronic nicotine exposure (Mihailescu &

Drucker-Colin, 2000). In general, long-term nicotine exposure increases the actual number of nAchRs—opposite to what one might normally expect from agonist-receptor interactions (that is, receptor down-regulation). However, the nAchR is a bit unusual in that after an agonist binds to it and activates it, the nAchR quickly desensitizes. Low levels of nicotine may cause significant nAchR desensitization, and over the long term, the nAchRs may enter a long-lasting inactive state, which then triggers a homeostatic up-regulation of the nAchRs. Thus, aspects of nicotine tolerance could be explained by nAchRs undergoing desensitization and inactivation, and withdrawal could be explained by their slowly recovering to functional states from various levels of desensitization and inactivation. Also, the increased number of nAchRs could account for why the first smoke of the day in chronic smokers is particularly enjoyable.

However, observations that none of these abstinence symptoms may occur, that they may be delayed for several days, or that they may wax and wane over a period of months suggest that many of these symptoms may be more psychological than pharmacodynamic in origin (Henningfield & Goldberg, 1988). In other words, if the symptoms were purely physiological in origin, they would be strongly and inversely related to how much the person had been smoking recently and how long it had been since the person's last cigarette. If this were the case, all heavy smokers (those smoking at least 20 cigarettes a day) would undergo withdrawal every morning, because nicotine plasma levels are essentially zero at this time; yet some do not start smoking until the afternoon. Others may forgo smoking altogether for proscribed periods of time without undue discomfort—for example, Orthodox Jews on the Sabbath.

Conversely, if abstinence symptoms were psychological in origin, they would be directly related to the type of environment, social setting, and mood states that regularly have accompanied cigarette smoking, as well as the person's expectations and attitudes about cigarette withdrawal. The fact that these vary considerably within and among individuals more easily accounts for the variability in the degree of discomfort and the times when it occurs. For example, one study found that smokers in a treatment program who believed they were getting nicotine gum, but actually were receiving a placebo, reported fewer withdrawal symptoms and smoked fewer cigarettes during the first week of quitting smoking than those smokers who thought they were getting a placebo (Gottlieb et al., 1987). Also, there was no relationship between the actual nicotine content of the gum and reported withdrawal symptoms or eventual relapse rates. Unfortunately, as stressed in Chapter 6, once the underlying conditioning factors take place and the expectations develop, their presence may be felt for the rest of the person's life.

In summary, despite the inconsistencies in the evidence, there is a very strong case that nicotine is addictive (Stolerman & Jarvis, 1995). Patterns of use by most smokers are consistent with compulsive use. Although a majority of chronic smokers report the desire to quit, the likelihood of success in a cessation attempt is low, relapse is a common occurrence, and nicotine replacement enhances outcomes in smoking cessation. There is evidence of both tolerance development to nicotine's effects and abstinence symptoms upon cessation. Nicotine has both positive (enhancement of mood or performance) and negative (relief of abstinence symptoms) reinforcing properties. Nonhumans will self-administer nicotine, albeit under more limited conditions than with a number of other addictive drugs. Finally, nicotine shares some discriminative properties with cocaine and amphetamine, and many of its biochemical actions are shared by a variety of other addictive drugs.

Although concerns over cigarette smoking have probably been a factor in the decline of smoking in young men and women over the past two decades, use of smokeless tobacco—namely, snuff and chewing tobacco—has increased at an alarming rate in young males (National Institutes of Health, 1986). This increase has been attributed to the perception that smokeless tobacco is safer and more socially acceptable than cigarette smoking, and that smokeless tobacco enhances athletic performance. While the health risks of smokeless tobacco use are indeed much lower than those associated with tobacco smoking (Vigneswaran et al., 1995), smokeless tobacco is not harmless. Its use has been associated with oral and pharyngeal cancer, numerous dental and gum problems, and cardiovascular abnormalities related to elevated blood pressure and heart rate. Also, smokeless tobacco does not appear to facilitate performance, since differences between users and nonusers of smokeless tobacco have not been observed with respect to neuromuscular reactivity or perceptual-motor task performance (Edwards & Glover, 1986; Edwards et al., 1987).

Many people "mature out" of their drug habits because their drug use ceases to match a change in their lifestyle—for example, marriage, job, or parenthood. Hardly anybody matures out of cigarettes. Smokers quit, but not through loss of interest—quitting requires determination (Schelling, 1992). The most promising aids to quitting are medicines that contain nicotine, such as chewing gum (Nicorette) or nicotine-containing skin patches (ProStep, Habitrol, Nicoderm), which release a constant, small amount of nicotine into the bloodstream and presumably lessen the craving for cigarettes. After a few weeks patients can chew less gum or receive smaller patches that release less nicotine until they are weaned off the substance. When used in conjunction with appropriate nonpharmacologic interventions, these nicotine-replacement therapies roughly double the rate of quitting smoking, in comparison to placebo treatments (Fiore et al., 1992; Haxby, 1995). For example, in over a dozen studies, nicotine patches produced 6-month abstinence rates of 22 percent to 42 percent, compared to 5 percent to 28 percent rates with placebo patches. These nicotine-replacement systems reduce most, but not all, nicotine withdrawal symptoms, including craving for cigarettes, negative moods, hypoarousal, and increased appetite. In addition, the satisfaction and good taste of cigarettes appear to be decreased in subjects using nicotine-replacement therapies (Levin et al., 1994), although it should be emphasized that while using these aids, smoking tobacco should be avoided, because of nicotine's potential cardiovascular toxicity at high doses. The evidence for their efficacy and safety has been deemed sufficient for both types of nicotine-replacement systems to be approved as nonprescription drugs. The nicotine patch may be the more effective treatment because it is easier to use and comply with than gum.

Convulsants

Mention the word *strychnine* to most people, and their immediate impression is that it is a poison used to kill rodents. Its lethality is due to the induction of convulsions, which are followed by impaired respiration and hypoxia. However, strychnine is a *convulsant* (something that induces brain seizures) and in low doses, convulsants do have some properties of other psychostimulants (Franz, 1985). Their ability to increase arousal at low doses is primarily the result of their antagonistic action at postsynaptic receptors for glycine, which serve an inhibitory function in numerous interneurons in the brain stem (Cooper et al., 1996). In other words, these neurons are released from inhibition by these drugs. However, their therapeutic indexes are very low, and they are thus highly toxic and lethal in relatively small amounts. I am not aware of any self-administration studies with nonhumans that could assess whether these drugs have any primary reinforcing effects, but humans do not use these drugs, perhaps because they are so aware of their toxic qualities. Convulsants, like other types of drugs, seem to facilitate retention in the passive avoidance task (discussed later in this chapter), but studies with humans are obviously limited because of the toxicity of these drugs.

Antidepressants

Because of their mood-elevating properties, antidepressants, which will be discussed in Chapter 13, would seem to be the type of drugs that would be appropriately classified as psychostimulants. However, most of the drugs used for the treatment of depression do not increase attention and vigilance or relieve fatigue; nor do they enhance mood in nondepressed individuals. In fact, several major types of antidepressants may cause drowsiness and induce mental confusion. Although a number of antidepressants (such as imipramine, desipramine) have an affinity for the dopamine uptake transporter and inhibit catecholamine reuptake into neurons in a fashion similar to cocaine and amphetamines (Ritz et al., 1987), their potency in this respect is very weak, and these drugs are not self-administered by nonhumans. Other antidepressants (such as tranylcypromine, phenelzine) have monoamine oxidase–inhibiting properties, a characteristic shared by amphetamine; but again, these drugs have little ability to enhance attention or mood in nondepressed individuals. Thus, despite a similarity in pharmacological profile, the antidepressants have none of the behavioral properties of typical psychostimulants and are typically not classified as such.

Pemoline

Pemoline (Cylert) increases attention, reduces reaction time in cognitive tasks, and relieves fatigue in a fashion similar to methylphenidate, which is consistent with its pharmacological profile of releasing catecholamines and blocking the dopamine transporter protein and blocking dopamine reuptake at clinically relevant concentrations (Sallee et al., 1992). It appears to have an affinity for the dopamine transporter on the same order as methylphenidate. Curiously, unlike other psychostimulants with these pharmacological properties, pemoline has not been shown to be self-administered by nonhumans, and there are few reports of pemoline abuse in humans, which may be due to its somewhat slower onset of action (Langer et al., 1986). As a result, it is classified as a Schedule IV controlled substance, in contrast to methylphenidate and the amphetamines, which are Schedule II controlled substances. Its primary use is in the treatment of attention deficit disorders (see Chapter 14 for further discussion of this).

Modafinil

Narcolepsy is a disabling neurological disorder characterized by excessive daytime sleepiness, which is similar to the feeling experienced by normal people when they are sleep deprived. Individuals with this disorder often experience uncontrollable "sleep attacks" in which there is a sudden episode of muscle weakness. In severe episodes the person may become temporarily paralyzed and fall down. Attacks generally last a few seconds, but they may last for several minutes. The individual is usually awake at the start of the attack and may remain conscious and alert throughout the episode. However, in longer attacks, the individual may fall into REM sleep and experience vivid hallucinations (auditory, visual, tactile). After the episode, the individual typically regains full muscle strength, although in some cases the paralysis may continue for a short time after awakening.

As a lifelong disorder, narcolepsy requires long-term management of symptoms, which may involve nonpharmacological interventions such as lifestyle changes, and often requires drug treatment (Fry, 1998). For years, the psychostimulants such as the amphetamines, pemoline, and methylphenidate have been used in the treatment of narcolepsy to increase wakefulness, vigilance, and performance. However, these stimulants are associated with dependence liability, sympathomimetic side effects, limitations in efficacy, and negative effects on nighttime sleep. Recently, modafinil (Provigil), a new wake-promoting agent, has been approved by the FDA for the treatment of narcolepsy. Several double-blind, placebo-controlled trials have shown modafinil to be effective in reducing daytime sleepiness in patients with narcolepsy (US Modafinil, 2000). Patients receiving modafinil report significant improvement in all subjective and objective measures of sleepiness. Modafinil appears to be well tolerated, with headache being the only adverse event typically reported, although the incidence may not be significantly greater than with placebo. Nighttime sleep does not appear to be adversely affected with modafinil treatment compared with placebo treatment. Its efficacy has been maintained for many weeks, with no evidence of tolerance development. During treatment discontinuation, patients who had been receiving modafinil experienced a return of their symptoms to baseline levels, but they did not experience symptoms associated with amphetamine withdrawal syndrome.

In a recent double-blind evaluation of the abuse potential of modafinil, the effects of modafinil were compared with methylphenidate in male volunteers with a history of polysubstance abuse that included the stimulant cocaine (Jasinski, 2000). The subjects discriminated both modafinil and methylphenidate from placebo and liked the effects of both drugs. However, modafinil differed from methylphenidate in its lack of a significant response on a scale commonly used to assess amphetamine-like effects of drugs. The profile of physiological effects for modafinil also differed from methylphenidate in that modafinil showed greater inhibition of observed and reported sleep, less facilitation of orthostatic tachycardia, and less reduction of caloric intake. These findings were consistent with previous data suggesting that modafinil is not an amphetamine-like agent. The data indicate that modafinil has an excellent safety profile.

Psychostimulants, Learning, and Memory

Because of the enhanced mood and alertness associated with low doses of amphetamines and similar drugs, one might expect this type of drug to enhance learning. Indeed, this has been a common assumption of many a college student for years. But do these drugs really enhance learning? The evidence on the issue is equivocal, primarily because learning is never observed directly and involves a variety of complex processes for it to take place. Therefore, before beginning a discussion of this issue, one must be familiar with the basic

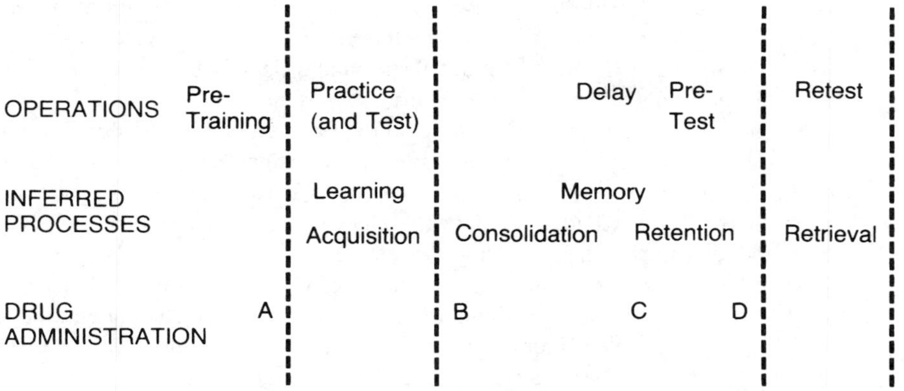

OPERATIONS	Pre-Training	Practice (and Test)		Delay Pre-Test	Retest

INFERRED PROCESSES — Learning Acquisition — Memory Consolidation Retention — Retrieval

DRUG ADMINISTRATION — A — B — C   D

FIGURE 9–2   Schematic representation of operations over time and phases of inferred processes in the study of effects of drugs on learning and memory (modified from Heise, 1981).

phases of learning and memory. These consist of an acquisition phase, a consolidation phase, a retention phase, and a retrieval phase (Heise, 1981).

Acquisition is the phase in which the behavior or information is initially practiced and encoded. *Retention* is the preservation of this behavior or information between the end of the training period and the period during which it is utilized. *Retrieval* is the phase during which the organism attempts to utilize the behavior or information acquired earlier. Note that the acquisition phase corresponds to what we commonly refer to as learning, and the retention and retrieval phases correspond to what we refer to as memory. Memory is commonly viewed as consisting of two different storage systems. The first is short-term memory, lasting a few seconds or minutes; in humans this is commonly referred to as *working memory,* which is a larger, more elaborate system that not only maintains limited amounts of information temporarily, but also involves conscious processes that regulate attention, retrieval, and symbolic encoding of information. The second is long-term memory, which is relatively permanent. During the time that it takes to create the long-term changes (perhaps resulting from the creation of new proteins that modify the permanent responsiveness of neurons), the information is maintained in short-term memory. There is a time period during which only temporary (short-term) memory exists and the permanent memory has not yet been established. The establishment of permanent traces from temporary ones is called *consolidation,* and the time it takes to form the permanent traces is called the consolidation phase.

A schematic representation of these four phases is shown in Figure 9–2. In the figure, times A, B, C, and D indicate where a drug would be administered in order to assess its effects on different components of learning and memory. Differences in performance between drug-treated and non–drug-treated animals are assessed during retest procedures. Any differences would be due to the drug's effects on acquisition processes (for example, attention, motivation, and general arousal) if the drug were administered at time A, consolidation if administered at time B (or if the duration of action of the drug given at A was such that it was also present during time B), retention if administered at time C, and retrieval if administered at time D (modified from Heise, 1981). From this discussion, we can see that when we ask the question of whether a particular drug affects learning or memory, we must first clarify during which phase(s) the drug is present.

Under conditions in which the person is fatigued or has an attention deficit disorder (see Chapter 14), there do seem to be some beneficial effects of low doses of amphetamine in the acquisition of new information, presumably because of increased attention to the material (Jaffe, 1990; Wender et al., 1981). Under conditions in which the person is already alert and rested, or with higher doses of amphetamine, the evidence is not as clear. In some cases it facilitates and in some cases it interferes with acquisition. Perhaps these contradictory results occur because, although amphetamine may enhance attentional processes, it may also increase one's attention to irrelevant details or tangential material. Thus, relevant information may not be acquired. Regardless of whether there are benefits to the acquisition process or not, there are questions as to whether the information will be efficiently retrieved at appropriate times later on. This issue will be dealt with shortly.

If exposure to adrenaline-stimulating drugs, like amphetamine, occurs immediately following a novel experience (that is, during consolidation), there is some evidence that this can affect the experience's subsequent retention—with retention being enhanced by low doses and impaired by high doses (McGaugh, 1990). These influences appear to be mediated by activation of noradrenergic receptors, particularly beta-adrenergic receptors, within the part of the limbic system called the amygdala (McGaugh et al., 1993). Most of the evidence for these phenomena comes from studies with nonhumans learning a very particular type of behavior referred to as passive avoidance. Briefly, the task involves placing a rat or a mouse in an area that it generally will move away from, such as on a platform raised an inch or so off the ground. Normally, the animal will step down off the platform after a few seconds. It is then subjected to a brief aversive shock, and then transferred back to its home cage. Later, after about 24 hours, the animal is placed on the platform again, to see how long it takes to step down. Animals that were not shocked earlier will generally step down very quickly, whereas animals that had been shocked will generally stay on the platform for a considerably longer period of time, presumably because they remember what happened the last time they stepped down. If the animal is administered an appropriate dose of amphetamine just after the initial shock, it generally will stay on the platform the next time even longer than saline-treated (undrugged) animals, presumably because it remembers even better what had happened to it the first time it stepped down.

Similar enhancements of retention in nonhumans with adrenaline-stimulating drugs have been obtained using positively motivated discrimination tasks (McGaugh, 1990). However, the tasks used to assess the effects of drugs on the consolidation phase of learning involve very special situations that may have no counterpart in the everyday learning experiences of humans. Thus we cannot really say that information acquired by humans will be similarly enhanced if it is immediately followed by amphetamine exposure, although there is evidence that enhanced memory associated with emotional events in humans does involve activation of the beta-adrenergic system (Cahill et al., 1994).

Once information has been acquired and consolidated, there is little likelihood that amphetamine and similar-acting drugs will facilitate retrieval at a later time, unless the person is particularly fatigued to begin with. In fact, there is evidence of state-dependent learning with amphetamine. This means that if learning occurred without the drug, its presence during retention may actually interfere with the retrieval of the previously learned material. For example, in one study, hyperactive and normal children engaged in a paired-associate learning task (one in which the subjects are required to learn a set of stimulus–response pairs, such that when a stimulus item is presented, the subjects are supposed to produce the appropriate response) after being administered a placebo or Ritalin. They were then tested at a later time for their retention of the material, again after being given Ritalin or a placebo. Both groups showed greater retention when the drug state during retesting was the same as that during learning, as opposed to when the drug state was changed between the learning and testing phases (Swanson & Kinsbourne, 1976).

Websites for Further Information

Cocaine Anonymous website:

http://www.ca.org/

A site covering many aspects of cocaine, along with a number of links:

http://www.erowid.org/entheogens/coca/coca.shtml

Site providing information on the influence of interdiction efforts on price for cocaine:

http://books.nap.edu/books/0309064775/html/29.html

Bibliography

Aigner, T. G., & Balster, R. L. (1978). Choice behavior in rhesus monkeys: Cocaine versus food. *Science, 201*, 534–535.

Ambre, J. J. (1993). Acute tolerance to pressor effects of cocaine in humans. *Therapeutic Drug Monitoring, 15*, 537–540.

American Society for Pharmacology and Experimental Therapeutics and Committee on Problems of Drug Dependence. (1987). Scientific perspectives on cocaine abuse. *The Pharmacologist, 29*, 20–27.

Anderson, K. J., & Revelle, W. (1983). The interactive effects of caffeine, impulsivity and task demands on a visual search task. *Personality and Individual Differences, 4*, 127–134.

Antelman, S. M., Eichler, A. J., Black, C. A., & Kocan, D. (1980). Interchangeability of stress and amphetamine in sensitization. *Science, 207*, 329–331.

Aronson, T. A., & Craig, T. J. (1986). Cocaine precipitation of panic disorder. *American Journal of Psychiatry, 143*, 643–645.

Azcona, O., Barbanoj, M. J., Torrent, J., & Jane, F. (1995). Evaluation of the central effects of alcohol and caffeine interaction. *British Journal of Clinical Pharmacology, 40*, 393–400.

Bartlett, E., Hallin, A., Chapman, B., & Angrist, B. (1997). Selective sensitization to the psychosis-inducing effects of cocaine: A possible marker for addiction relapse vulnerability. *Neuropsychopharmacology, 16*, 77-82.

Barone, J. J., & Roberts, H. R. (1996). Caffeine consumption. *Food and Chemical Toxicology, 34*, 119–129.

Battig, K. (1991). Coffee, cardiovascular and behavioral effects: Current research trends. *Reviews on Environmental Health, 9*, 53–84.

Benowitz, N. L. (1990). Clinical pharmacology of caffeine. *Annual Review of Medicine, 41*, 277–288.

Berridge, K. C., & Robinson, T. E. (1995). The mind of an addicted brain: Neural sensitization of wanting versus liking. *Journal of the American Psychological Society, 4*, 71–76.

Biel, J. H. (1970). Structure-activity relationships of amphetamine and derivatives. In E. Costa & S. Garattini (Eds.), *International symposium on amphetamines and related compounds* (pp. 3–19). New York: Raven Press.

Bien, T. H., & Burge, R. (1990). Smoking and drinking: A review of the literature. *International Journal of the Addictions, 25*, 1429–1454.

Brady, K. T., Lydiard, R. B., Malcolm, R., & Ballenger, J. C. (1991). Cocaine-induced psychosis. *Journal of Clinical Psychiatry, 52,* 509–512.

Brady, J. V., & Griffiths, R. R. (1977). Drug-maintained performance and the analysis of stimulant reinforcement effects. In E. E. Ellinwood & M. M. Kilbey (Eds.), *Cocaine and other stimulants* (pp. 599–614). New York: Plenum Press.

Brandon, T. H. (1994). Negative affect as motivation to smoke. *Journal of the American Psychological Society, 3,* 33–37.

Brecher, E. M. (Ed.). (1972). *Licit and illicit drugs.* Boston: Little, Brown and Company.

Breslau, N., Kilbey, M. M., & Andreski, P. (1992). Nicotine withdrawal symptoms and psychiatric disorders: Findings from an epidemiologic study of young adults. *American Journal of Psychiatry, 149,* 464–469.

Cahill, L., Prins, B., Weber, M., & McGaugh, J. L. (1994). Beta-adrenergic activation and memory for emotional events. *Nature, 371,* 702–704.

Carlezon, W. A., Thome, J., Olson, V. G., et al. (1998). Regulation of cocaine reward by CREB. *Science, 282,* 2272–2275.

Carrera, M. R., Ashley, J. A., Parsons, L. H., et al. (1995). Suppression of psychoactive effects of cocaine by active immunization. *Nature, 378,* 727–730.

Chadwick, M. J., Gregory, D. L., & Wendling, G. (1990). A double-blind amino acids, L-tryptophan and L-tyrosine, and placebo study with cocaine-dependent subjects in an inpatient chemical dependence treatment center. *American Journal of Drug Alcohol Abuse, 16,* 275–286.

Chakko, S., & Myerberg, R. J. (1995). Cardiac complications of cocaine abuse. *Clinical Cardiology, 18,* 67–72.

Charney, D. S., Heninger, G. R., & Jatlow, P. I. (1985). Increased anxiogenic effects of caffeine in panic disorders. *Archives of General Psychiatry, 42,* 233–243.

Childress, A. R., Mozley, D., McElgin, W., et al. (1999). Limbic activation during cue-induced cocaine craving. *American Journal of Psychiatry, 156,* 11–18.

Cho, A. K. (1993). Ice: D-methamphetamine Hydrochloride. In S. G. Korenman & J. D. Barchas (Eds.), *Biological basis of substance abuse* (pp. 119–142). New York: Oxford University Press.

Coffey, S. F., Dansky, B. S., Carrigan, M. H., & Brady, K. T. (2000). Acute and protracted cocaine abstinence in an outpatient population: A prospective study of mood, sleep and withdrawal symptoms. *Drug and Alcohol Dependence, 59,* 277–286.

Cole, S. O. (1978). Brain mechanisms of amphetamine-induced anorexia, locomotion, and stereotypy: A review. *Neuroscience and Biobehavioral Reviews, 2,* 89–100.

Compton, P. A., Ling, W., Charuvastra, V. C., & Wesson, D. R. (1995). Buprenorphine as a pharmacotherapy for cocaine abuse: A review of the evidence. *Journal of Addictive Diseases, 14,* 97–114.

Cooper, J. R., Bloom, F. E., & Roth, R. H. (1996). *The biochemical basis of neuropharmacology,* 7th ed. New York: Oxford University Press.

Crosby, R. D., Pearson, V. L., Eller, C., et al. (1996). Phenytoin in the treatment of cocaine abuse: A double-blind study. *Clinical Pharmacology & Therapeutics, 59,* 458–468.

Cubells, J. F., Rayport, S., Rajendran, G., & Sulzer, D. (1994). Methamphetamine neurotoxicity involves vacuolation of endocytic organelles and dopamine-dependent intracellular oxidative stress. *Journal of Neuroscience, 14,* 2260–2271.

Dackis, C. A., & Gold, M. S. (1985). New concepts in cocaine addiction: The dopamine depletion hypothesis. *Neuroscience and Biobehavioral Reviews, 9,* 469–477.

Davidson, R. A., & Smith, B. D. (1991). Caffeine and novelty: Effects on electrodermal activity and performance. *Physiology Biochemistry and Behavior, 49,* 1169–1175.

Donny, E. C., Caggiula, A. R., Mielke, M. M., et al. (1999). Nicotine self-administration in rats on a progressive ratio schedule of reinforcement. *Psychopharmacology, 147,* 135–142.

Edwards, S., & Glover, E. (1986). Snuff and neuromuscular performance. *American Journal of Public Health, 76,* 45.

Edwards, S., Glover, E., & Schroeder, K. (1987). The effects of smokeless tobacco on heart rate and neuromuscular reactivity in athletes and nonathletes. *The Physician and Sportsmedicine, 15,* 141–147.

Ehrman, R. N., Robbins, S. J., Childress, A. R., & O'Brien, C. P. (1992). Conditioned responses to cocaine-related stimuli in cocaine abuse patients. *Psychopharmacology, 107,* 523–529.

Eissenberg, T., & Balster, R. L. (2000). Initial tobacco use episodes in children and adolescents: Current knowledge, future directions. *Drug and Alcohol Dependence, 59,* S41–S60.

Ellinwood, E. H., Kilbey, M. M., Castellani, S., & Khoury, C. (1977). Amygdala hyperspindling and seizures induced by cocaine. In E. H. Ellinwood & M. M. Kilbey (Eds.), *Cocaine and other stimulants* (pp. 303–326). New York: Plenum Press.

Ellison, G. D. (1993). Paranoid psychosis following continuous amphetamine or cocaine: Relationship to selective neurotoxicity. In S. G. Korenman & J. D. Barchas (Eds.), *Biological basis of substance abuse* (pp. 355–372). New York: Oxford University Press.

Emerson, T. S., & Cisek, J. E. (1993). Methcathinone: A Russian designer amphetamine infiltrates the rural midwest. *Annals of Emergency Medicine, 22,* 1897–1903.

Emmett-Oglesby, M. W., Peltier, R. L., Depoortere, R. Y., et al. (1993). Tolerance to self-administration of cocaine in rats: Time course and dose-response determination using a multi-dose method. *Drug and Alcohol Dependence, 32,* 247–256.

Erikson G. C., Hager, L. B., Houseworth, C., et al. (1985). The effects of caffeine on memory for word lists. *Physiology and Behavior, 35,* 47–51.

Eysenck, H. J. (1967). *Biological basis of personality.* Springfield, IL: Thomas Charles.

Fergusson, D. M., Lynskey, M. T., & Horwood, L. J. (1996). Comorbidity between depressive disorders and nicotine dependence in a cohort of 16-year-olds. *Archives of General Psychiatry, 53,* 1043–1047.

Finkle, B. S., & McCloskey, K. L. (1977). The forensic toxicology of cocaine. In R. C. Peterson & R. C. Stillman (Eds.), *Cocaine: 1977.* National Institute of Drug Abuse-Research Monograph Series, *13,* pp. 153–179.

Fiore, M. C., Jorenby, D. E., Baker, T. B., & Kenford, S. L. (1992). Tobacco dependence and the nicotine patch. Clinical guidelines for effective use. *Journal of the American Medical Association, 268,* 2687–2694.

Fischman, M. W., Schuster, C. R., Javaid, J., et al. (1985). Acute tolerance development to the cardiovascular and subjective effects of cocaine. *Journal of Pharmacology and Experimental Therapeutics, 235,* 677–682.

Fitzgerald, L. W., Ortiz, J., Hamedani, A. G., & Nestler, E. J. (1996). Drugs of abuse and stress increase the expression of GluR1 and NMDAR1 glumate receptor subunits in the rat ventral tegmental area: Common adaptations among cross-sensitizing agents. *Journal of Neuroscience, 16,* 274–282.

Foltin, R. W., & Fischman, M. W. (1991). Smoked and intravenous cocaine in humans: Acute tolerance, cardiovascular and subjective effects. *Journal of Pharmacology and Experimental Therapeutics, 157,* 247–261.

Foltin, R. W., Fischman, M. W., & Levin, F. R. (1995). Cardiovascular effects of cocaine in humans: Laboratory studies. *Drug and Alcohol Dependence, 37,* 193–210.

Fowler, J. S., Volkow, N. D., Wang, G. J., et al. (1996). Inhibition of monoamine oxidase B in the brains of smokers. *Nature, 379,* 733–736.

Franz, D. N. (1985). Central nervous system stimulants. In A. G. Gilman, L. S. Goodman, T. W. Rall, & F. Murad (Eds.), *The pharmacological basis of therapeutics* (pp. 582–588). New York: Macmillan.

Fry, J. M. (1998). Treatment for narcolepsy. *Neurology, 50,* S43–S48.

Fudin, R., & Nicastro, R. (1988). Can caffeine antagonize alcohol-induced performance decrements in humans? *Perceptual and Motor Skills, 67,* 375–391.

Fuller, R. C. (1992). Biographical origins of psychological ideas: Freud's cocaine studies. *Journal of Humanistic Psychology, 32,* 67–86.

Gawin, F. H. (1993). Cocaine addiction: Psychology, neurophysiology, and treatment. In S. G. Korenman & J. D. Barchas (Eds.), *Biological basis of substance abuse* (pp. 425–442). New York: Oxford University Press.

Gentry, M. V., Hammersley, J. J., Hale, C. R., et al. (2000). Nicotine patches improve mood and response speed in a lexical decision task. *Addictive Behaviors, 25,* 549–557.

Giovino, G. A., Henningfield, J. E., Tomar, S. L., & Escobedo, L. G. (1995). Epidemiology of tobacco use and dependence. *Epidemiologic Reviews, 17,* 48–65.

Giros, B., Jaber, M., Jones, S. R., et al. (1996). Hyperlocomotion and indifference to cocaine and amphetamine in mice lacking the dopamine transporter. *Nature, 379,* 606–612.

Glassman, A. H., Helzer, J. E., Covey, L. S., et al. (1990). Smoking, smoking cessation, and major depression. *Journal of the American Medical Association, 264,* 1546–1549.

Glennon, R. A., Young, R., Martin, B. R., & Dal Cason, T. A. (1995). Methcathione ("cat"): An enantiomeric potency comparison. *Pharmacology Biochemistry & Behavior, 50,* 601–606.

Goldberg, S. R., Spealman, R. D., & Goldberg, D. M. (1981). Persistent behavior at high rates maintained by intravenous self-administration of nicotine. *Science, 214,* 573–575.

Goodman, E., & Capitman, J. (2000). Depressive symptoms and cigarette smoking among teens. *Pediatrics, 106,* 748–755.

Gonzalez, N. M., & Campbell, M. (1994). Cocaine babies: Does prenatal exposure to cocaine affect development? *Journal of the American Academy of Child and Adolescent Psychiatry, 33,* 16–19.

Gossop, M., Marsden, J., & Stewart, D. (2000). Treatment outcomes of stimulant misusers: One-year follow-up results from the National Treatment Outcome Research Study (NTORS). *Addictive Behaviors, 25,* 509–522.

Gottlieb, A. M., Killen, J. D., Marlatt, G. A., & Taylor, C. B. (1987). Psychological and pharmacological influences in cigarette smoking withdrawal: Effects of nicotine gum and expectancy on smoking withdrawal symptoms and relapse. *Journal of Counseling and Clinical Psychology, 55,* 606–608.

Grabowski, J., & Dworkin, S. E. (1985). Cocaine: An overview of current issues. *International Journal of the Addictions, 20,* 1065–1088.

Grabowski, J., Rhoades, H., Elk, R., et al. (1995). Fluoxetine is ineffective for treatment of cocaine dependence or concurrent opiate and cocaine dependence: Two placebo-controlled, double-blind trials. *Journal of Clinical Psychopharmacology, 15,* 163–174.

Graham, T. E., Rush, J. W., & Van Soeren, M. H. (1994). Caffeine and exercise: Metabolism and performance. *Canadian Journal of Applied Physiology, 19,* 111–138.

Graham, T. E. & Spriet, L. L. (1995). Metabolic, catecholamine, and exercise performance responses to various doses of caffeine. *Journal of Applied Physiology, 78,* 867–874.

Griffith, D. R., Azuma, S. D., & Chasnoff, I. J. (1994). Three-year outcome of children exposed prenatally to drugs. *Journal of the American Academy of Child and Adolescent Psychiatry, 33,* 20–27.

Griffith, J. D., Cavanaugh, J. H., Held, J., & Oates, J. A. (1970). Experimental psychosis induced by the administration of d-amphetamine. In E. Costa & S. Garattini (Eds.), *International symposium on amphetamines and related compounds* (pp. 897–904). New York: Raven Press.

Griffiths, R. R., Bigelow, G. E., & Liebson, I. A. (1986). Human coffee drinking: Reinforcing and physical dependence producing effects of caffeine. *Journal of Pharmacology and Experimental Therapeutics, 239,* 416–425.

Grilly, D. M. (1977). Rate dependent effects of amphetamine resulting from behavioral competition. *Biobehavioral Reviews, 1,* 87–93.

Grilly, D. M. (1980). Sherlock Holmes and cocaine: Fact and fiction. *Sherlock Holmes Journal, 15,* 11–13.

Grilly, D. M., & Grogan, T. W. (1990). Cocaine and level of arousal: Effects on vigilance task performance in rats. *Pharmacology Biochemistry & Behavior, 35,* 269–271.

Grilly, D. M., Gowans, G. C., McCann, D. S., & Grogan, T. W. (1989). Effects of cocaine and d-amphetamine on sustained and selective attention in rats. *Pharmacology Biochemistry Behavior, 33,* 733–739.

Gupta, U., & Gupta, B. S. (1990). Caffeine differentially affects kinesthetic aftereffect in high and low impulsives. *Psychopharmacology, 102,* 102–105.

Haxby, D. G. (1995). Treatment of nicotine dependence. *American Journal of Health-System Pharmacy, 52,* 265–281.

Heise, G. A. (1981, June). Learning and memory facilitators: Experimental definition and current status. *Trends in the Pharmacological Sciences,* pp. 158–160.

Heishman, S. J. (1998). What aspects of human performance are truly enhanced by nicotine? *Addiction, 93,* 317–320.

Heishman, S. J., Taylor, R. C., & Henningfield, J. E. (1994). Nicotine and smoking: Review of effects on human performance. *Experimental and Clinical Psychopharmacology, 2,* 345–395.

Henningfield, J. E., & Goldberg, S. R. (1988). Pharmacologic determinants of tobacco self-administration by humans. *Pharmacology, Biochemistry, and Behavior, 30,* 221–226.

Higgins, S. T., Budney, A. J., Bickel, W. K., et al. (1994a). Alcohol dependence and simultaneous cocaine and alcohol use in cocaine-dependent patients. *Journal of Addictive Diseases, 13,* 177–189.

Higgins, S. T., Budney, A. J., Bickel, W. K., & Badger, G. J. (1994b). Participation of significant others in outpatient behavioral treatment predicts greater cocaine abstinence. *American Journal of Drug and Alcohol Abuse, 20,* 47–56.

Higgins, S. T., Budney, A. J., & Bickel, W. K. (1994c). Applying behavioral concepts and principles to the treatment of cocaine dependence. *Drug and Alcohol Dependence, 34,* 87–97.

Holmes, V. F. (1995). Medical use of psychostimulants: An overview. *International Journal of Psychiatry in Medicine, 25,* 1–19.

Holtzman, S. G. (1986). Discriminative stimulus properties of caffeine in the rat: Noradrenergic mediation. *Journal of Pharmacology and Experimental Therapeutics, 233,* 706–714.

Holtzman, S. G. (1987). Discriminative stimulus effects of caffeine: Tolerance and cross-tolerance with methylphenidate. *Life Sciences, 40,* 381–389.

Hughes, J. R., Gust, S. W., & Pechacek, T. F. (1987). Prevalence of tobacco dependence and withdrawal. *American Journal of Psychiatry, 144,* 205–208.

Hughes, J. R., Oliveto, A. H., Bickel, W. K., et al. (1993). Caffeine self-administration and withdrawal: Incidence, individual differences and interrelationships. *Drug and Alcohol Dependence, 32,* 239–246.

Hughes, J. R., Oliveto, A. H., Helzer, J. E., et al. (1992). Should caffeine abuse, dependence, or withdrawal be added to DSM-IV and ICD-10? *American Journal of Psychiatry, 149,* 33–40.

Hyman, S. E. (1996). Addiction to cocaine and amphetamine. *Neuron, 16,* 901–904.

Isner, J. M., & Chokshi, S. K. (1991). Cardiac complications of cocaine abuse. *Annual Review of Medicine, 42,* 133–138.

Iyer, R. N., Nobiletti, J. B., Jatlow, P. I., & Bradberry, C. W. (1995). Cocaine and cocaethylene: Effects on extracellular dopamine in the primate. *Psychopharmacology, 120,* 150–155.

Jaffe, J. H. (1990). Drug addiction and drug abuse. In A. G. Gilman, T. W. Rall, A. S. Nies, & P. Taylor (Eds.), *The pharmacological basis of therapeutics* (pp. 522–573). New York: Pergamon Press.

Jaffe, J. H., Cascella, N. G., Kumor, K. M., & Sherer, M. A. (1989). Cocaine-induced cocaine craving. *Psychopharmacology, 97,* 59–64.

Jasinski, D. R. (2000). An evaluation of the abuse potential of modafinil using methylphenidate as a reference. *Journal of Psychopharmacology, 14,* 53–60.

Johnson, B., Overton, D., Wells, L., et al. (1998). Effects of acute intravenous cocaine on cardiovascular function, human learning, and performance in cocaine addicts. *Psychiatry Research, 77,* 35–42.

Johnson, L. D., Spinweber, C. L., & Gomez, S. A. (1990). Benzodiazepines and caffeine: Effect on daytime sleepiness, performance, and mood. *Psychopharmacology, 101,* 160–167.

Jones, E. (1953). *Life and work of Sigmund Freud, Volume I (1856–1900).* New York: Basic Books.

Jones, L. B., Stanwood, G. D., Reinoso, B. S., et al. (2000). In utero cocaine-induced dysfunction of dopamine D1 receptor signaling and abnormal differentiation of cerebral cortical neurons. *Journal of Neuroscience, 20,* 4606–4614.

Jonsson, L. E., & Gunne, L. M. (1970). Clinical studies of amphetamine psychosis. In E. Costa & S. Garattini (Eds.), *International symposium on amphetamines and related compounds* (pp. 929–936). New York: Raven Press.

Kegeles, L. S., Zea-Ponce, Y., Abi-Dargham, A., et al. (1999). Stability of [123I] IBZM SPECT measurement of amphetamine-induced striatal dopamine release in humans. *Synapse, 31,* 302–308.

Kerr, J. S., Sherwood, N., & Hindmarch, I. (1991). Separate and combined effects of the social drugs on psychomotor performance. *Psychopharmacology, 104,* 113–119.

Kilbey, M. M., & Ellinwood, E. H. (1977). Reverse tolerance to stimulant-induced abnormal behavior. *Life Sciences, 20,* 1063–1076.

King, G. R., Joyner, C., Lee, T., et al. (1994). Intermittent and continuous cocaine administration: Residual behavioral states during withdrawal. *Pharmacology Biochemistry & Behavior, 43,* 243–248.

Kleiman, M. A. R., & Satel, S. (1996, May 7). Speed is rushing back. *The Plain Dealer,* p. B8.

Kozel, N. J., & Adams, E. H. (1986). Epidemiology of drug abuse: An overview. *Science, 234,* 970–974.

Langer, D. H., Sweeney, K. P., Bartenbach, P. M., & Meander, D. K. B. (1986). Evidence of lack of abuse or dependence following pemoline treatment: Results of a retrospective survey. *Drug and Alcohol Dependence, 17,* 213–227.

Lecos, C. (1984). The latest caffeine scorecard. *Consumer's Research, 67,* 35–36.

Lester, B. M., LaGasse, L. L., & Seifer, R. (1998). Cocaine exposure and children: The meaning of subtle effects. *Science, 282,* 633–634.

Levin, E. D., & Simon, B. (1998). Nicotinic acetylcholine involvement in cognitive function in animals. *Psychopharmacology, 138,* 217–230.

Levin, E. D., Westman, E. C., Stein, R. M., et al. (1994). Nicotine skin patch treatment increases abstinence, decreases withdrawal symptoms, and attenuates rewarding effects of smoking. *Journal of Clinical Psychopharmacology, 14,* 41–49.

Lichtenfeld, P. J., Rubin, D. B., & Feldman, R. S. (1984). Subarachnoid hemorrhage precipitated by cocaine snorting. *Archives of Neurology, 41,* 223–224.

Lieberman, H. R., Wurtman, R. J., Emde, G. G., et al. (1987). The effects of low doses of caffeine on human performance and mood. *Psychopharmacology, 92,* 308–312.

Lombardo, J. A. (1986). Stimulants and athletic performance (part 1 of 2): Amphetamines and caffeine. *The Physician and Sportsmedicine, 14,* 128–139.

London, E. D., Cascella, N. G., Wong, D. F., et al. (1990). Cocaine-induced reduction of glucose utilization in human brain. *Archives of General Psychiatry, 47,* 567–574.

Lundahl, L. H., Henningfield, J. E., & Lukas, S. E. (2000). Mecamylamine blockade of both positive and negative effects of IV nicotine in human volunteers. *Pharmacology Biochemistry and Behavior, 66,* 637–643.

Lyon, N., Mejsholm, B., & Lyon, M. (1986). Stereotyped responding by schizophrenic outpatients: Cross-cultural confirmation of perseverative switching on a two-choice task. *Journal of Psychiatric Research, 20,* 137–150.

Lyons, D., Friedman, D. P., Nader, M. A., & Porrino, L. J. (1996). Cocaine alters cerebral metabolism within the ventral striatum and limbic cortex of monkeys. *Journal of Neuroscience, 16,* 1230–1238.

MacLennan, A. J., & Maier, S. F. (1983). Coping and the stress-induced potentiation of stimulant stereotypy in the rat. *Science, 219,* 1091–1092.

Maehler, R., Dadmarz, M., & Vogel, W. H. (2000). Determinants of the voluntary consumption of nicotine in rats. *Neuropsychobiology, 41,* 200–204.

Maisonneuve, I. M., Ho, A., & Kreek, M. J. (1995). Chronic administration of a cocaine "binge" alters basal extracellular levels in male rats: An in vivo microdialysis study. *Journal of Pharmacology and Experimental Therapeutics, 272,* 652–657.

Maisonneuve, I. M., & Kreek, M. J. (1994). Acute tolerance to the dopamine response induced by a binge pattern of cocaine administration in male rats: An in vivo microdialysis study. *Journal of Pharmacology and Experimental Therapeutics, 268,* 916–921.

Martin-Iverson, M. T., & Burger, L. Y. (1995). Behavioral sensitization and tolerance to cocaine and the occupation of dopamine receptors by dopamine. *Molecular Neurobiology, 11,* 31–46.

Maser, W. (1971). *Adolf Hitler: Legend, myth, and reality.* New York: Harper & Row.

Mash, D. C., Kovera, C. A., Buck, B. E., et al. (1998). Medication development of ibogaine as a pharmacotherapy for drug dependence. *Annals of the New York Academy of Sciences, 844,* 274–292.

Mattay, V. S., Berman, K. F., Ostrem, J. L., et al. (1996). Dextroamphetamine enhances "neural network-specific" physiological signals: A positron-emission tomography rCBF study. *Journal of Neuroscience, 16,* 4816–4822.

Mayhew, K. P., Flay, B. R., & Mott, J. A. (2000). Stages in the development of adolescent smoking. *Drug and Alcohol Dependence, 59,* S61–S81.

McCance, E. F., Price, L. H., Kosten, T. R., & Jatlow, P. I. (1995). Cocaethylene: Pharmacology, physiology and behavioral effects in humans. *Journal of Pharmacology and Experimental Therapeutics, 274,* 215–223.

McCann, U. D., Wong, D. F., Yokoi, F., et al. (1998). Reduced striatal dopamine transporter density in abstinent methamphetamine and methcathinone users: Evidence from positron emission tomography studies with [11C] WIN-35,428. *Journal of Neuroscience, 18,* 8417–8422.

McEvoy, J. P., Freudenreich, O., Levin, E. D., & Rose, J. E. (1995). Haloperidol increases smoking in patients with schizophrenia. *Psychopharmacology, 119,* 124–126.

McGaugh, J. L. (1990). Significance and remembrance: The role of neuromodulatory systems. *Psychological Science, 1,* 15–25.

McGaugh, J. L., Introini-Collison, I. B., Cahill, et al. (1993). Neuromodulatory systems and memory storage: Role of the amygdala. *Behavioral Brain Research, 58,* 81–90.

McLeman, E. R., Warsh, J. J., Ang, L., et al. (2000). The human nucleus accumbens is highly susceptible to G protein down-regulation by methamphetamine and heroin. *Journal of Neurochemistry, 74,* 2120–2126.

Melega, W. P., Raleigh, M. J., Stout, D. B., et al. (1997). Recovery of striatal dopamine function after acute amphatamine- and methamphetamine-induced neurotoxicity in the vervet monkey. *Brain Research, 766,* 113–120.

Mendelson, J. H., & Mello, N. K. (1996). Management of cocaine abuse and dependence. *The New England Journal of Medicine, 334,* 965–972.

Mendelson, J. H., Sholar, M., Mello, N. K., et al. (1998). Cocaine tolerance: Behavioral, cardiovascular, and neuroendocrine function in men. *Neuropsychopharmacology, 18,* 264–271.

Mihailescu, S., & Drucker-Colin, R. (2000). Nicotine, brain nicotinic receptors, and neuropsychiatric disorders. *Archives of Medical Research, 31,* 131–144.

Moore, K. E., Chiueh, C. C., & Zeldes, G. (1977). Release of neurotransmitters from the brain in vivo by amphetamine, methylphenidate and cocaine. In E. H. Ellinwood & M. M. Kilbey (Eds.), *Cocaine and other stimulants* (pp. 143–160). New York: Plenum Press.

National Institutes of Health Consensus Development Conference Statement. (1986). Health implications of smokeless tobacco use. *Cancer Journal for Clinicians, 36,* 310–317.

Nehlig, A., & Boyet. S. (2000). Dose-response study of caffeine effects on cerebral functional activity with a specific focus on dependence. *Brain Research, 858,* 71–77.

O'Brien, C. P. (1996). Drug addiction and drug abuse. In A. G. Gilman, L. S. Goodman, J. G. Hardman, L. E. Limbard, P. B. Molinoff, & R. W. Ruddon (Eds.), *The pharmacological basis of therapeutics* (pp. 557–577). New York: McGraw-Hill.

O'Brien, C. P., McLellan, A. T., & Alterman, A. (1993). Effectiveness of treatment for substance abuse. In S. G. Korenman & J. D. Barchas (Eds.), *Biological basis of substance abuse* (pp. 487–510). New York: Oxford University Press.

Patat, A., Rosenzweig, P., Enslen, M., et al. (2000). Effects of a new slow release formulation of caffeine on EEG, psychomotor and cognitive functions in sleep-deprived subjects. *Human Psychopharmacology: Clinical and Experimental, 15,* 153–170.

Paulson, P. E., Camp, D. M., & Robinson, T. E. (1991). Time course of transient behavioral depression and persistent behavioral sensitization in relation to regional brain monoamine concentrations during amphetamine withdrawal in rats. *Psychopharmacology, 103,* 480–492.

Penny, G. N., & Robinson, J. O. (1986). Psychological resources and cigarette smoking in adolescents. *British Journal of Psychology, 77,* 351–357.

Perez-Reyes, R. M., Jeffcoat, A. R., Myers, M., et al. (1994). Comparison in humans of the potency and pharmacokinetics of intravenously injected cocaethylene and cocaine. *Psychopharmacology, 116,* 428–432.

Piazza, P. V., Deminiere, J.-M., Le Moal, M., & Simon, H. (1989). Factors that predict individual vulnerability to amphetamine self-administration. *Science, 245,* 1511–1513.

Pickworth, W. B., Herning, R. I., & Henningfield, J. E. (1986). Electroencephalographic effects of nicotine chewing gum in humans. *Pharmacology, Biochemistry, and Behavior, 25,* 879–882.

Popik, P., Layer, R. T., & Skolnick, P. (1995). 100 years of ibogaine: Neurochemical and pharmacological actions of a putative anti-addictive drug. *Pharmacological Reviews, 47,* 235–253.

Post, R. M., & Contel, 4N. R. (1983). Human and animal studies of cocaine: Implications for development of behavioral pathology. In I. Creese (Ed.), *Stimulants: Neurochemical, behavioral, and clinical perspectives* (pp. 169–202). New York: Raven Press.

Post, R. M., Weiss, S. R. B., & Pert, A. (1987). The role of context and conditioning in behavioral sensitization to cocaine. *Psychopharmacology Bulletin, 23,* 425–429.

Rall, T. W. (1985). Central nervous stimulants (continued). In A. G. Gilman, L. S. Goodman, T. W. Rall, & F. Murad (Eds.), *The pharmacological basis of therapeutics* (pp. 589–603). New York: Macmillan.

Rapoport, J. L., Buchsbaum, M. S., Weingartner, H., et al. (1980). Dextroamphetamine: Its cognitive and behavioral effects in normal and hyperactive boys and normal men. *Archives of General Psychiatry, 37,* 933–943.

Ritz, M. C., Lamb, R. J., Goldberg, S. R., & Kuhar, M. J. (1987). Cocaine receptors on dopamine transporters are related to self-administration of cocaine. *Science, 237,* 1219–1223.

Robbins, S. J., Ehrman, R. N., Childress, A. R., et al. (2000). Mood state and recent cocaine use are not associated with levels of cocaine cue reactivity. *Drug and Alcohol Dependence, 59,* 33–42.

Robinson, T. E., & Becker, J. B. (1986). Enduring changes in brain and behavior produced by chronic amphetamine administration: A review and evaluation of animal models of amphetamine psychosis. *Brain Research, 396,* 157–198.

Rougé-Pont, F., Marinelli, M., Le Moal, M. L., et al. (1995). Stress-induced sensitization and glucocorticoids. II. Sensitization of the increase in extracellular dopamine induced by cocaine depends on stress-induced corticosterone secretion. *The Journal of Neuroscience, 15,* 7189–7195.

Rowbotham, M. C., & Lowenstein, D. H. (1990). Neurologic consequences of cocaine use. *Annual Review of Medicine, 41,* 417–422.

Sallee, F. R., Stiller, R. L., & Perel, J. M. (1992). Pharmacodynamics of pemoline in attention deficit disorder with hyperactivity. *Journal of the American Academy of Child and Adolescent Psychiatry, 31,* 244–251.

Sapolsky, R. M. (1996). Why stress is bad for your brain. *Science, 273,* 749–750.

Satel, S. L., Price, L. H., Palumbo, J. M., et al. (1991a). Clinical phenomenology and neurobiology of cocaine abstinence: A prospective inpatient study. *American Journal of Psychiatry, 148,* 1712–1716.

Satel, S. L., Southwick, S. M., & Gawin, F. H. (1991b). Clinical features of cocaine-induced paranoia. *American Journal of Psychiatry, 148,* 495–498.

Sato, M., Chen, C. C., Akiyama, K., et al. (1983). Acute exacerbation of paranoid psychotic state after long-term abstinence in patients with previous methamphetamine psychosis. *Biological Psychiatry, 18,* 429–440.

Sawyer, D. A., Julia, H. L., & Turin, A. C. (1982). Caffeine and human behavior: Arousal, anxiety, and performance effects. *Journal of Behavioral Medicine, 5,* 415–439.

Schelling, T. C. (1992). Addictive drugs: The cigarette experience. *Science, 255,* 430–433.

Schuckit, M. A. (1994). The treatment of stimulant dependence. *Addiction, 89,* 1559–1563.

Self, D. W., Barnhart, W. J., Lehman, D. A., & Nestler, E. J. (1996). Opposite modulation of cocaine-seeking behavior by D1 and D2-like dopamine receptor agonists. *Science, 271,* 1586–1589.

Sherwood, N. (1993). Effects of nicotine on human psychomotor performance. *Human Psychopharmacology: Clinical and Experimental, 8,* 155–184.

Short, P. H., & Shuster, L. (1976). Changes in brain norepinephrine associated with sensitization to *d*-amphetamine. *Psychopharmacology, 48,* 59–67.

Siegel, R. K. (1989). *Intoxication.* New York: Pocket Books.

Simpson, D. D., Joe, G. W., Fletcher, B. W. et al. (1999). A national evaluation of treatment outcomes for cocaine dependence. *Archives of General Psychiatry, 56,* 507–514.

Slusher, B. S., & Jackson, P. F. (1996). A shot in the arm for cocaine addiction. *Nature Medicine, 2,* 26–27.

Slutsker, L., (1992). Risks associated with cocaine use during pregnancy. *Obstetrics and Gynecology, 79,* 778–789.

Sommese, T., & Patterson, J. C. (1995). Acute effects of cigarette smoking withdrawal: A review of the literature. *Aviation Space and Environmental Medicine, 66,* 164–167.

Sonsalla, P. K., Nicklas, W. J., & Heikkila, R. E. (1989). Role for excitatory amino acids in methamphetamine-induced nigrostriatal dopaminergic toxicity. *Science, 243,* 398–400.

Spealman, R. D., Barrett-Larimore, R. L., Rowlett, J. K., et al., (1999). Pharmacological and environmental determinants of relapse to cocaine-seeking behavior. *Pharmacology Biochemistry and Behavior, 64,* 327–336.

Stefanski, R., Ladenheim, B., Lee, S. H., et al. (1999). Neuroadaptations in the dopaminergic system after active self-administration but not after passive administration of methamphetamine. *European Journal of Pharmacology, 371,* 123–135.

Stewart, J. (1984). Reinstatement of heroin and cocaine self-administration behavior in the rat by intracerebral application of morphine in the ventral tegmental area. *Pharmacology Biochemistry & Behavior, 20,* 917–923.

Stine, S. M., & Kosten, T. R. (1994). Reduction of opiate withdrawal-like symptoms by cocaine abuse during methadone and buprenorphine maintenance. *American Journal of Drug & Alcohol Abuse, 20,* 445–458.

Stolerman, I. P., & Jarvis, M. J., (1995). The scientific case that nicotine is addictive. *Psychopharmacology Bulletin, 117,* 2–10.

Strakowski, S. M., & Sax, K. W. (1998). Progressive behavioral response to repeated d-amphetamine challenge: Further evidence for sensitization in humans. *Biological Psychiatry, 44,* 1171–1177.

Strakowski, S. M., Sax, K. W., Setters, M.J., et al. (1996). Enhanced response to repeated *d*-amphetamine challenge: Evidence for behavioral sensitization in humans. *Biological Psychiatry, 40,* 872–880.

Strickland, T. L., & Stein, R. (1995). Cocaine-induced cerebrovascular impairment: Challenges to neuropsychological assessment. *Neuropsychology Review, 5,* 69–79.

Stripling, J. S., & Ellinwood, E. H. (1977). Sensitization to cocaine following chronic administration in the rat. In E. H. Ellinwood & M. M. Kilbey (Eds.), *Cocaine and other stimulants* (pp. 327–352). New York: Plenum Press.

Sulzer, D., Chen, T. K., Lau, Y. Y., et al. (1995). Amphetamine redistributes dopamine from synaptic vesicles to the cytosol and promotes reverse transport. *Journal of Neuroscience, 15,* 4102–4108.

Swanson, J. M., & Kinsbourne, M. (1976). Stimulant-related state-dependent learning in hyperactive children. *Science, 192,* 1354–1356.

Swanson, J. A., Lee, J. W., & Hopp, J. W. (1994). Caffeine and nicotine: A review of their joint use and possible interactive effects in tobacco withdrawal. *Addictive Behaviors, 19,* 229–256.

Tecce, J. J., & Cole, J. O. (1974). Amphetamine effects in man: Paradoxical drowsiness and lowered electrical brain activity (CNV). *Science, 185,* 451–453.

Unterwald, E. M., Ho, A., Rubenfeld, J. M., & Kreek, M. J. (1994a). Time course of the development of behavioral sensitization and dopamine receptor up-regulation during binge cocaine administration. *Journal of Pharmacology and Experimental Therapeutics, 270,* 1387–1396.

Unterwald, E. M., Rubenfeld, J. M., & Kreek, M. J. (1994b). Repeated cocaine administration upregulates kappa and mu, but not delta, opioid receptors. *Neuroreport, 5,* 1613–1616.

U.S. Modafinil in Narcolepsy Multicenter Study Group. (2000). Randomized trial of modafinil as a treatment for the excessive daytime somnolence of narcolepsy. *Neurology, 54,* 1166–1175.

Van Dyke, C., & Byck, R. (1982). Cocaine. *Scientific American, 246,* 128–141.

Vigneswaran, N., Tilashalski, K., Rodu, B., & Cole, P. (1995). Tobacco use and cancer. A reappraisal. *Oral Surgery, Oral Medicine, Oral Pathology, Oral Radiology, and Endodontics, 80,* 178–182.

Volkow, N. D., Ding, Y. S., Fowler, J. S., et al. (1995). Is methylphenidate like cocaine? Studies on their pharmacokinetics and distribution in the human brain. *Archives of General Psychiatry, 52,* 456–463.

Volkow, N. D., Fowler, J. S., Wang, G. J., et al. (1993). Decreased dopamine D2 receptor availability is associated with reduced frontal metabolism in cocaine abusers. *Synapse, 14,* 169–177.

Volkow, N. D., Fowler, J. S., Wolf, A. P., et al. (1991). Changes in brain glucose metabolism in cocaine dependence and withdrawal. *American Journal of Psychiatry, 148,* 621–626.

Volkow, N. D., Fowler, J. S., Wolf, A. P., et al. (1990). Effects of chronic cocaine abuse on postsynaptic dopamine receptors. *American Journal of Psychiatry, 147,* 719–724.

Wagner, G. C., Carelli, R. M., & Jarvis, M. F. (1985). Pretreatment with ascorbic acid attenuates the neurotoxic effects of methamphetamine in rats. *Research Communications in Chemical Pathology and Pharmacology, 47,* 221–228.

Waters, A. J., & Sutton, S. R. (2000). Direct and indirect effects of nicotine/smoking on cognition in humans. *Addictive Behaviors, 25,* 29–43.

Weddington, W. W., Brown, B. S., Haertzen, C. A., et al. (1990). Changes in mood, craving, and sleep during short-term abstinence reported by male cocaine addicts. A controlled, residential study. *Archives of General Psychiatry, 47,* 861–868.

Wender, P. H., Reimherr, F. W., & Wood, D. R. (1981). Attention deficit disorder ("minimal brain dysfunction") in adults. *Archives of General Psychiatry, 38,* 449–456.

Wilson, J. M., Kalasinsky, K. S., Levey, A.I., et al. (1996). Striatal dopamine nerve terminal markers in human, chronic, methamphetamine users. *Nature Medicine, 2,* 699–703.

Wise, R. A. (1995). D_1 and D_2-type contributions to psychomotor sensitization and reward: Implications for pharmacological treatment strategies. *Clinical Neuropharmacology, 18,* S74-S83.

Wise, R.A. (1998). Drug activation of brain reward pathways. *Drug and Alcohol Dependence, 51,* 13–22.

Wolfsohn, R., Sanfilipo, M., & Angrist, B. (1993). A placebo-controlled trial of L-dopa/carbidopa in early cocaine abstinence. *Neuropsychopharmacology, 9,* 49–53.

Wolkin, A., Angrist, B., Wolf, A., et al. (1987). Effects of amphetamine on local cerebral metabolism in normal and schizophrenic subjects as determined by positron emission tomography. *Psychopharmacology, 92,* 241–246.

Wood, D. M., & Emmett-Oglesby, M. W. (1986). Characteristics of tolerance, recovery from tolerance and cross-tolerance for cocaine used as a discriminative stimulus. *Journal of Pharmacology and Experimental Therapeutics, 237,* 120–125.

Zahn, T. P., & Rapoport, J. L. (1987). Acute autonomic nervous system effects of caffeine in prepubertal boys. *Psychopharmacology, 91,* 40–44.

Zwyghuizen-Doorenbos, A., Roehrs, T. A., Lipschutz, L., et al. (1990). Effects of caffeine on alertness. *Psychopharmacology, 100,* 36–39.

Chapter 10

Opioids (Narcotics) and Their Antagonists

Some of the oldest psychotropic drugs used by humans are morphine and codeine; their use may go back 7,000 years. Originally these drugs were used in the form of extracts from the poppy plant, which contains opium, and in purified form they are still used extensively. They belong to a class of drugs that includes the most potent pain relievers available, so they are the most commonly used analgesic treatments for moderate to severe pain. Since users often experience euphoria, drowsiness, and mental clouding—perhaps resulting in the feeling that all their problems are trivial—these drugs are also used recreationally and are highly subject to abuse.

The most common term for morphine and similar-acting drugs is **narcotic,** which is a derivation of the Greek word for stupor (narkē). Unfortunately, the term *narcotic* has taken on many unwarranted connotations. It has been used primarily to refer to a class of drugs that promote sleep and induce analgesia, but many laypersons often think of narcotics as any highly abusable or addicting drug. From this perspective, drugs that bear little similarity to morphine in terms of their neurochemical actions or their psychological effects (like cocaine and marijuana) have been designated as narcotics for legal purposes. However, pharmacologically, only a drug with the following qualities can be appropriately classified as a narcotic: (1) It generally has sedative–hypnotic and analgesic properties; (2) it acts stereospecifically on endorphin/enkephalin receptors; and (3) its actions are antagonized by naloxone (Narcan). In essence, narcotics are restricted to extracts of opium (**opiates**), opiate derivatives, and synthetic drugs with opiate properties. Perhaps because of the confusion surrounding the term *narcotic,* many authorities now refer to these substances as **opioids.** Routinely throughout this chapter, I will refer to these substances as *narcotics, opiates,* and *opioids* interchangeably. In this way, you will become familiar with all three terms.

Endogenous Opioid Peptides and Their Receptors

The definition of a narcotic has become more confusing and complex since the discovery of a multitude of substances, endogenous to the brain and body, with opiate properties (researchers often refer to these as *endogenous opioid peptides*). Three distinct families have been identified thus far: the *enkephalins,* the *endorphins,* and the *dynorphins* (Akil et al., 1984). However, as mentioned previously, these are often categorized in a general sense as endorphins. Each family is derived from different precursor polypeptides, more than 200 amino acids long, with different anatomical distributions. Each precursor contains a number of biologically active opioid and nonopioid peptides, which are cleaved (split) at specific sites by specific enzymes (called *proteases*) to produce the active agents (Marx, 1987). For example, the precursor pro-opiomelanocortin contains three separate hormones, one of which contains the opioid peptide beta-endorphin, which in turn contains the opioid peptide met-enkephalin (a peptide of five amino acids with methionine at one end). The precursor proenkephalin contains several met-enkephalin segments and a leu-enkephalin segment (the same amino acid sequence as met-enkephalin except that leucine is substituted for methionine). The precursor prodynorphin contains two endorphin segments, three leu-enkephalin segments, and two types of the opioid peptide dynorphin.

Pro-opiomelanocortin peptides are found in the pituitary gland (indicating that they play a role in a variety of neuroendocrine functions) and in relatively limited areas of the CNS. Peptides from the other two precursors are distributed widely throughout the CNS, particularly on those regions related to the modulation of pain perception (such as the spinal cord and midbrain), affective states (for example, amygdala, hippocampus, locus coeruleus, and cerebral cortex), and the autonomic nervous system (for example, medulla). They are also found in other parts of the body, such as the stomach and intestines.

Though the endogenous opioid peptides are believed to function as neurotransmitters, neurohormones, or neuromodulators, their physiological role is not well understood. Furthermore, they frequently coexist with other hormones or neurotransmitters within a given neuron. However, it is clear that specific types of stimulation (e.g., acute stressors and expectation cues and/or conditioning) are capable of activating endogenous opioid systems. For example, some placebo analgesic responses have been shown to be mediated by endogenous opioids, and these responses do not necessarily affect the whole body but can be very specific to the part of the body where the placebo-induced expectancy is directed (Benedetti et al., 1999).

At least three distinct opioid receptors have been identified, and there are subtypes of each of these (Reisine & Pasternak, 1996). The actions and selectivities of representative ligands and drugs for these various opioid receptors are shown in Table 10–1 (based on Ferrante, 1996; Reisine & Pasternak, 1996). Those designated as *mu* receptors are morphine- and naloxone-selective (that is, morphine and naloxone bind to them more readily than enkephalins do) and probably mediate the euphorigenic properties of typical opiates (such as morphine, methadone). Other prominent effects of mu receptor agonists include supraspinal and spinal analgesia, respiratory depression, cardiovascular effects, slowing of G.I. motility, and sedation. *Delta* receptors are more enkephalin-selective and induce spinal analgesia. *Kappa* receptors have a high affinity for dynorphin and may mediate spinal analgesia as well as sedation. Kappa receptors also probably mediate aversive, psychosis-mimicking opiate effects, and this fact may explain why some narcotics that are primarily kappa agonists (for

TABLE 10–1   Opioid Receptors and Their Ligands

Opioid/Ligand	mu (μ)	delta (δ)	kappa (κ)
Endogenous agonists			
Met-enkephalin	++	+++	
Leu-enkephalin	++	+++	
β-endorphin	+++	+++	
Dynorphin A	++		+++
Dynorphin B	+	+	+++
α-neoendorphin	+	+	+++
Exogenous agonists			
Morphine	+++		+
Methadone	+++		
Fentanyl	+++		
Meperidine	+++		
Hydromorphone	+++		
Etorphine	+++	+++	+++
Mixed agonist–antagonists			
Buprenorphine	Partial agonist		−−
Nalorphine	−−−		++
Pentazocine	−		++
Cyclazocine	−−−		++
Antagonists			
Naloxone	−−−	−	−−
Naltrexone	−−−	−	−−
Nalmefene	−−−		
Diprenorphine	−−−	−−	−−−

Note: Activities of drugs are given at the receptors for which the agent has documented affinity in nonhumans. Agonists are indicated by + and antagonists are indicated by –, with the degree of potency indicated by the number of symbols.

example, cyclazocine) do not produce drug-seeking behavior (Slifer & Dykstra, 1987). These three types of receptors may represent independent and structurally different entities, but they do not always act independently of one another; that is, stimulation of one type of opioid receptor can affect another opioid receptor. As opioid research progresses, it is likely that other putative opioid receptors will be discovered and their functions determined.

Typical Opiates

Considering the various types and subtypes of opioid receptors, it should not come as any surprise that not all drugs classified as narcotics have identical effects. In some cases, drugs with narcotic-like effects by themselves may actually block the effects of other narcotics.

In addition to the natural opiates (morphine and codeine), derivatives or semisynthetic opiates, like heroin, nalorphine, and hydromorphone (Dilaudid), have resulted from minor modifications in structure. A number of other drugs with very similar properties, but very dissimilar molecular structures, have been synthesized, including meperidine (Demerol), fentanyl (Sublimaze), propoxyphene (Darvon), and methadone (Dolophine).

In addition to having somewhat different pharmacological effects, these drugs differ with respect to potency, intensity, duration of action, and oral effectiveness, in many cases because of differences in pharmacokinetics (Oldendorf et al., 1972). For example, heroin is considered to be one of the most potent of the nonendogenous types of opiates. It is approximately two to four times more potent than morphine when injected (that is, one-third as much is needed to achieve the same degree of analgesia as morphine). Because of this difference in potency, many individuals have campaigned to make heroin, which is presently a Schedule I drug, a legally available medication in the United States for the treatment of severe pain for use in terminally ill patients (Holden, 1977). However, what most people do not realize is that the differential potency is due to pharmacokinetics and not to intrinsic activity at receptors. First, the potency of heroin and morphine is equivalent when taken orally. Second, the heroin molecule is simply a slight modification of morphine. This modification allows heroin to penetrate the blood–brain barrier much more rapidly than morphine does. This characteristic allows it to accumulate in the brain much more quickly. Once in the brain, heroin is metabolized into morphine, but because it gets there so much more quickly, it exerts effects that are much more rapid and intense.

Administered subcutaneously for analgesia in humans, methadone has approximately the same potency as morphine and approximately half the potency of heroin (Reisine & Pasternak, 1996). With respect to suppression of opiate withdrawal symptoms, methadone is about twice as potent as heroin and four times as potent as morphine. It is much more effective than either heroin or morphine when administered orally and has an action approximately three to four times longer than that of morphine. Codeine is approximately 12 times less potent than morphine when injected; however, it is more readily absorbed through oral administration than morphine. Neither heroin nor morphine, being weak alkaloids, are readily absorbed orally; heroin administered orally is about 100 times less potent than when it is administered intravenously. The endogenous opioid peptides are far more potent than heroin (Smith & Griffin, 1978), but they are rapidly inactivated by enzymes throughout the body (Schulties et al., 1989). Fentanyl is one of the most potent of the nonendogenous opiates (approximately 50 times more potent than heroin when injected I.M.). Its short duration of action makes it useful as an adjunctive treatment during surgical procedures, but its potency can lead to lethal overdoses in individuals who believe they are injecting heroin. Fentanyl has recently been formulated into a flavored lozenge on a handle (Actiq) for oral transmucosal administration, which allows it to be rapidly absorbed and provide better pain control for cancer patients. The handle allows the lozenge to be removed from the mouth if excessive opioid effects appear during administration.

Behavioral and Physiological Effects of Opiates

Although the predominant effect of narcotics is a sedative–hypnotic one, there may be a brief stimulant-like effect immediately after administration, particularly if administered intravenously. Some species, such as cats, and some people show only the stimulant type of effect (Jaffe & Martin, 1985). The most prominent clinically useful effect of opiates is to reduce pain—a complex perceptual and emotional phenomenon dependent on several neurotransmitter systems located in the spinal cord and supraspinal structures (i.e., areas above the spinal cord such as the locus coeruleus and medulla). Opiates have relatively little influence on the sharp pain initially induced by a noxious stimulus; their major effectiveness is in reducing the dull ache that persists after a noxious stimulus. This is why opiates are typically used in chronic pain conditions and in treatment of postoperative pain but are not by themselves effective during surgery.

The discovery of multiple pathways involved in pain perception should allow us to control chronic pain more effectively while reducing the tolerance and dependence that now limit the usefulness of most opiates. For example, when a patient shows signs of tolerance to morphine, which has a high affinity for mu receptors in supraspinal structures, he or she could be switched to a compound with a high affinity for delta receptors, which are more prominent in the spinal cord, in order to maintain analgesic activity (Pasternak, 1988).

Better methods of administering opiates have been developed to improve their efficacy, reduce their side effects, or lower the cost of treatment—for example, transdermally administered opioid analgesics and patient-controlled opiate analgesia, in which the patient is allowed to self-administer opiates (with some constraints to protect against inadvertent overdose), either orally or by pushing a button on an electronically controlled pump that delivers small doses of morphine through an I.V. tube (Bloor et al., 1994; Reisine & Pasternak, 1996).

Some of the most notable effects of narcotics are shown in Table 10–2. In addition to their analgesic properties, opiates, presumably because of activity in the limbic system, also relieve what some call psychological pain—that is, anxieties, feelings of inadequacy, and hostile or aggressive drives—as well as inducing extremely pleasant mood states or euphoria in the majority of users. Intravenous administration, or so-called mainlining, results in

TABLE 10–2   Effects of Opiate Administration and Opiate Withdrawal

Opiate Administration	Opiate Withdrawal
Hypothermia	Hyperthermia
Decrease in blood pressure	Increase in blood pressure
Peripheral vasodilation, skin flushed and warm	Piloerection (gooseflesh), chilliness
Miosis (pupillary constriction)	Mydriasis (pupillary dilation)
Drying of secretions	Lacrimation, rhinorrhea
Constipation	Diarrhea
Respiratory depression	Yawning, panting
Decreased urinary 17-ketosteroid levels	Increased urinary 17-ketosteroid levels
Antitussive	Sneezing
Decreased sex drive	Spontaneous ejaculations and orgasms
Relaxation	Restlessness, insomnia
Analgesia	Pain and irritability
Euphoria	Depression

Source. From Jaffe (1985) and Jaffe and Martin (1985).

what is subjectively referred to as a "whole-body orgasm" or "rush," an experience for which there is presently no explanation. However, in general, chronic narcotic use severely reduces the user's sex drive and leads to impotence.

Actions in the medulla decrease the rate and depth of breathing (respiratory depression—a primary cause of death associated with narcotic use), suppress the cough reflex, and induce vomiting (emesis) and nausea. This last effect generally occurs with the first administration, unless the person is in pain or is lying down, but shows relatively rapid tolerance.

Narcotics have a number of peripheral actions. Most notably, they induce a marked constriction of the pupil, called "pinpoint pupil" or miosis (primarily found with morphine, heroin, and hydromorphone, but not with meperidine), and they slow the movement of the contents of the G.I. tract, resulting in constipation.

Some drugs that are classified as narcotics have unusual properties that distinguish them from the prototype narcotics like morphine and heroin. Some, like nalorphine and cyclazocine, have an analgesic effect, but they may induce a dysphoric reaction, cause anxiety, or have psychotomimetic effects. These are also capable of blocking the effects of the prototype narcotics. Because these drugs have agonist as well as antagonist properties—depending on the type of opioid receptor—they are often referred to as **mixed agonist–antagonists.** Although these drugs have no psychological dependence liability (for example, there is an absence of craving for them), if taken chronically, discontinuing their use can precipitate an abstinence syndrome similar to that of other narcotics, indicating that they can induce physical dependence. However, as indicated in Chapter 6, because physical dependence plays a minimal role in motivating drug-seeking behavior, these drugs are viewed as having little or no potential for abuse. Other mixed agonist–antagonist drugs that have the more typical narcotic effects that make them prone to induce drug-seeking have been synthesized. Pentazocine (Talwin) is such a drug. Nevertheless, they are capable of blocking the effects of prototypic (mu-type) narcotics, and in fact, may provoke withdrawal if taken by someone physically dependent on morphine or heroin.

Although the chronic use of narcotics might be expected to lead to significant deterioration in the body, many studies have found no major damage to any organ of the body that is solely due to the presence of a narcotic—even heroin (Brecher, 1972). Most of the damage that is found is due to the poor nutritional practices of addicts, the use of adulterated drugs under nonsterile conditions, concomitant use of other drugs, and the general lifestyle of the addicts. Also their narcotic use decreases their ability to recognize pain that normally is present when something is pathologically wrong with them, and thus they fail to seek treatment. Their recognition that medical treatment may also reveal their addiction and lead to termination of their drug use may also be a factor in failing to seek treatment. If pure narcotics are taken under sterile conditions and proper nutritional practices are followed, there is little damage to the body. It is possible for chronic exposure to narcotics to permanently alter the body's synthesis or regulation of endorphins and their receptors, so that normal psychological processes that are believed to be associated with them, like pain perception, mood, and pleasure, may be affected for the remainder of the person's lifetime.

It has long been observed that opiate addicts have increased susceptibility to infections. Whether this is a result of the addict's lifestyle or a direct result of opioid exposure is not clear, since opiates have been shown to exert detrimental effects on immune functions of the body (Carballo-Dieguez et al., 1994; Weber & Pert, 1989). For example, opiate agonists tend to suppress antibody production, alter the ability of white blood cells to respond to substances that stimulate white blood cell transformation, and decrease the toxicity of other types of natural killer cells. Many of these effects are mediated through opiate receptors in the midbrain. Research with animals has indicated that chronic opiate exposure may also disrupt immune responsiveness indirectly through the increased production of adrenal corticosteroids (by opiate activation of what is called the "hypothalamic–pituitary–adrenal axis") (Freier & Fuchs, 1994). It has been well established that chronic exposure to corticosteroids can have a variety of toxic consequences, one of which is an increase in a person's susceptibility to infection from a variety of bacterial and fungal pathogens (Schimmer & Parker, 1996).

There may be significant damage to a fetus and neonate if a woman is chronically exposed to narcotics during pregnancy (Bauman & Levine, 1986). Newborns of narcotic-dependent women tend to have lower birth weights and be more excitable and irritable than normal babies. Some of these symptoms are probably due to their experiencing narcotic withdrawal at birth. Symptoms that persist for several weeks or months, or longer, may be due to any number of factors. Prior to birth, the developing nervous system of the fetus may be particularly sensitive to the periodic withdrawal that the mother (and the fetus) probably undergoes (Kuwahara & Sparber, 1981). Or there may be alterations in the endorphin systems of the fetus during development. After birth, the mother–infant bonding may be disrupted, inadequate maternal care or nutrition may be provided, and dependent mothers may perform less adaptively in areas of intelligence, personality, and parenting behaviors. For example, a recent study assessing 2-year-old children born to methadone-using women determined that mother–infant interactions following birth were a factor in their children's developmental outcome, but that methadone exposure alone did not have a negative impact on the developmental measures studied (Bernstein & Hans, 1994).

Opioid Pharmacodynamics

Opiates depress the rate of neuronal firing in most areas of the brain, but some groups of neurons increase their rate of firing, possibly because they are released from the inhibitory control by other neurons whose rate of firing has been directly depressed by opiates (Cooper et al., 1996). Opioid receptors act through G-protein secondary messenger systems to inhibit adenylate cyclase and cyclic AMP. Activation of opiate receptors on presynaptic axon terminals inhibits the Ca^{++} influx that underlies release of neurotransmitters. At the postsynaptic membrane, their activation hyperpolarizes the membrane by enhancing K^+ flow out of neurons. In some cases these two processes appear to operate independently, and in others they appear to work synergistically to reduce transmission in neuronal pathways, for instance, those underlying pain transmission (Taddese et al., 1995). The euphoria, tranquility, and other mood changes induced by mu and delta opioid agonists have been linked to their ability to indirectly activate dopaminergic neurons projecting to the nucleus accumbens—quite likely due to their inhibition of inhibitory interneurons. However, the finding that dopamine antagonists do not consistently prevent the reinforcing effects of opiates in animals suggests that some nondopaminergic mechanism may also play a role in these effects (Reisine & Pasternak, 1996). Kappa receptor agonists exert aversive qualities in animal tests, possibly due to their ability to decrease mesolimbic release of dopamine in the nucleus accumbens (Mansour et al., 1995).

Tolerance and Dependence on Opiates

After continued use of an opiate, especially if it is taken often and in fairly high doses, the user becomes very tolerant to many of its effects, and cross-tolerance occurs to all of the narcotics, including the endorphins. After several months of heavy use, some users can administer 40 to 50 times the dose that would kill the nontolerant individual. In a recent study in which rats were trained to self-administer heroin via intravenous infusions and allowed to administer it 24 hours a day, they increased their heroin intake from under 2 mg/kg/day to up to 336 mg/kg/day (a dose that was lethal in drug-naïve rats) within a 29- to 39-day period (Sim-Selley et al., 2000). Tolerance occurs to some but not all effects of narcotics. The rush and euphoria probably show the fastest tolerance, whereas there is little or no tolerance developed to the constipation and pupil constriction. In addition to these chronic opioid tolerance phenomena, which may develop with an incubation period of 8 to 10 days and last for a long period, acute opioid tolerance (tachyphylaxis) may also develop within a few hours after a single exposure to opiates (Wang & Ho, 1994). The two forms of opioid tolerance may differ in terms of their characteristics and the mechanisms behind them.

Many of the mechanisms for inducing tolerance discussed in Chapter 6 have been suggested to be involved in tolerance development to narcotics with chronic exposure (Collin & Cesselin, 1991; Reisine & Pasternak, 1996). A slight elevation in the drug-metabolizing enzymes of the liver has been shown. This could lead to faster metabolic inactivation of opiates. Despite extensive investigations, the neuronal bases for opiate tolerance and dependence remains unclear. While *in vitro* studies have been fairly consistent in demonstrating opiate receptor down-regulation with chronic opiate exposure, this phenomenon has been more difficult to demonstrate in animals, with up-regulation, down-regulation, or no change in receptor number being observed (Harrison et al., 1998). Furthermore, when down-regulation does occur, the time course does not correspond to the time course of tolerance development.

Opioid receptors belong to the family of inhibitory G-protein–coupled receptors. Both *in vitro* and *in vivo* studies have suggested that many of the cellular adaptations underlying tolerance and physical dependence to opiates occur at the level of the signal-transducing G-protein—that is, a desensitization of opiate receptors and a corresponding up-regulation or loss of inhibition of the adenylate cyclase cyclic AMP system (Sim-Selley et al., 2000; Wang & Gintzler, 1995). These phenomena appear to occur at least in part at the level of gene expression (Maldonado et al., 1996). This mechanism may also explain why nonopioid agonists—for example, the alpha-2-adrenergic agonist clonidine—that also inhibit this secondary messenger system may be effective in reducing the symptoms of opiate withdrawal.

Since opiates inhibit the release of several types of neurotransmitters, the receptors for these neurotransmitters may exhibit adaptation in terms of up-regulation or sensitization, which could also account for some of the physical withdrawal symptoms that occur with opiate use. Research has suggested that continual stimulation of opiate receptors may gradually increase the activity of anti-opioid peptide systems that counteract opiate effects. These systems could also account for some tolerance and dependence phenomena associated with opiate use (Stinus et al., 1995). Several studies have also demonstrated that a variety of treatments that suppress the immune system significantly reduce the severity of withdrawal signs in morphine-dependent animals (Dougherty et al., 1990). Thus, at least with opiates, it appears that the immune system may play a role in abstinence symptoms.

NMDA receptors may also be a factor in the development of opiate tolerance and dependence, since antagonists (for example, MK-801, phencyclidine) at this type of receptor have been shown to reduce morphine analgesia tolerance and withdrawal symptoms but do not affect morphine-induced analgesia (Trujillo & Akil, 1994). Although NMDA receptors are a subtype of glutamate receptor important in mediating several forms of neural and behavioral modifiability—for instance, learning—it appears that pharmacodynamic rather than learning mechanisms are involved in these phenomena.

In addition to these pharmacodynamic processes, learning processes (Pavlovian and instrumental conditioning, habituation) can account for some tolerance and dependence phenomena associated with chronic opiate use (see the discussion in Chapter 6). The Pavlovian model, which hypothesizes that environmental cues associated with the drug elicit compensatory CRs (i.e., CRs that oppose the drug-induced UCRs), is particularly controversial. Although some studies indicate that environmental cues associated with the drug effects can be a factor in tolerance to some of morphine's effects, others suggest that environmental cues can have an additive effect (Eikelboom & Stewart, 1982). Other researchers suggest that the context-specific tolerance is not due to a Pavlovian CR, because most attempts to demonstrate specifically the presence of a compensatory response with opiates have generally failed (Tiffany et al., 1983), but that the context-specific tolerance to opiates is actually due to simple stimulus habituation.

The symptoms of withdrawal from opiates are essentially opposite of the direct effects of these drugs (see Table 10–1 for examples of some of the direct and withdrawal effects associated with opiates). The intensity and duration of the abstinence syndrome are directly correlated with the intensity and duration of the particular drug's effects (Figure 10–1). For example, the withdrawal from heroin, which induces rapid and intense effects of short duration, is relatively intense but dissipates within a few days. On the other hand, withdrawal from methadone, which induces gradual and mild effects of long duration, is relatively mild, but the syndrome takes several days to weeks to subside (O'Brien, 1996). For this reason, many opiate addicts find methadone withdrawal to be more disruptive and disturbing than heroin withdrawal.

The opioid withdrawal syndrome can be very unpleasant, consisting of symptoms much like those experienced during a bad case of the flu. It begins 6 to 12 hours after the last dose of a short-acting opiate like heroin and may be delayed up to 72 to 84 hours after a very long-lasting opiate (O'Brien, 1996). Several investigators have suggested that many of the physical complaints are really of psychological rather than physical origin, in which case they would be very context-specific (Childress et al., 1986a, 1986b). In fact, in one study the psychological factors of neuroticism and the expected degree of distress were more related to the severity of withdrawal symptoms during methadone detoxification than either the methadone dose

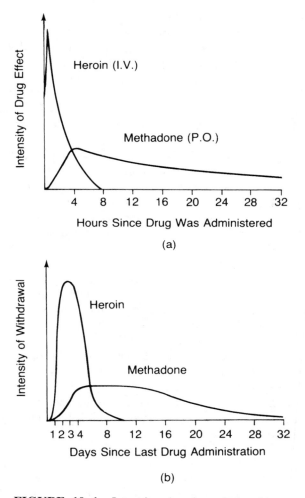

FIGURE 10–1   Intensity–duration relationships for the direct effects (a) and abstinence symptoms (b) of the narcotics heroin and methadone.

or the length of opiate use prior to methadone treatment (Phillips et al., 1986). Unlike the withdrawal associated with the sedative–hypnotics and alcohol, opiate withdrawal is rarely life-threatening, unless there are preexisting cardiovascular problems that could result in stroke or heart failure during the heightened sympathetic nervous system activity.

For a number of years, many experts believed that the physical dependence on opiates was the primary motivating factor in continued drug taking. However, study after study has noted that even after the abstinence syndrome has long since dissipated, the vast majority of addicts, if left without further treatment, eventually start taking opiates again. Addicts often report that the craving for opiates may be present even after several months of abstinence. This craving has been attributed to the development of a Pavlovian conditioned drive state, which is triggered any time the person is in a context previously associated with the drug experience. This type of CR is different from the compensatory CR discussed earlier, but functionally it does the same thing; that is, it creates an unpleasant state that can be effectively eliminated by administering a narcotic. Studies demonstrating how the context can trigger conditioned reactions that could subserve the craving subsequently supported these reports (Childress et al., 1986a, 1986b). Also, as noted in Chapter 6, conditioned abstinence symptoms have been shown to develop when organisms undergo physical withdrawal when opiate actions are terminated rapidly in specific contexts (which would occur with a short-acting opiate such as heroin, or if an opiate antagonist were administered). Thus, the prevailing view now is that the psychological dependence on opiates is the far more powerful factor, in the long run, in maintaining opiate drug-taking behavior.

All forms of dependence—primary and secondary psychological, as well as physiological—have been documented to occur with narcotics. Other than these effects, heroin and other narcotics are not particularly damaging as far as the body is concerned. However, they have such primary reinforcing value that people will engage in some very maladaptive behaviors (such as using dirty syringes and dirty water, exposing themselves to unknown adulterants, or engaging in criminal activities) to obtain them and experience their effects (O'Brien, 1996). (As will be discussed shortly, many of these maladaptive behaviors are due to American culture's legal system regarding access to narcotics.) The high incentive value of narcotics may also decrease the person's desire for engaging in more socially acceptable activities.

Contrary to popular belief, patients taking opiates solely to control pain generally do not become addicted, that is, develop an uncontrollable compulsion to use opiates. The common misconception, however, has resulted in their being undertreated and having to experience unnecessary agony (Grossman, 1993). The traditional approach has been to administer morphine or other opiates at fixed intervals, with the expectation that the analgesia will last 4 to 6 hours. Unfortunately, the pain may then become so severe that a larger dose is needed, which then increases the likelihood of side effects, such as mental clouding and nausea. A more enlightened approach that has come into use involves the patient-controlled approach described earlier. Numerous studies have shown that patients generally maintain their doses at a reasonable level, often using lower amounts of morphine than when it is administered in the traditional fashion, experience more effective pain relief, and decrease their dosage when pain diminishes. Rarely do such patients develop rapid and marked tolerance to, and dependence on, the narcotic; those that do usually are patients who have a history of psychological disturbance or substance abuse (Ferrante, 1996; Melzack, 1990).

Treatment for Opiate Dependence

Although some chronic compulsive opiate users eventually stop of their own accord, for the most part dependence on opiates is so strong that some type of intervention is required in order to overcome it. A variety of treatments have been tried, all with limited success. Some addicts go into therapeutic communities, like Synanon and Daytop, that have been established by addicts to support narcotic users through the most difficult periods of their dependence. One study of a Synanon group in West Berlin found that over a 10-year period approximately 15 percent of the individuals who stayed in the community were still abstaining from narcotic use and that only about 4 percent of those who left the community were still abstinent (Cohen, 1981).

The finding that abstinent opiate abusers (who completed a 30-day treatment program in a therapeutic community setting) experienced intense drug craving and withdrawal symptoms when exposed to drug-related stimuli has led to attempts to eliminate these responses through the process of extinction. This process basically involves exposing the person to the conditioned stimuli that provoke the craving without allowing the person to experience the drug (that is, the unconditioned stimulus). This has been found to virtually eliminate the conditioned craving and withdrawal symptoms within 20 hour-long treatment sessions (Childress et al., 1986a). How long these reductions last and how well they generalize to other drug-related stimuli after the patients' discharge remains to be determined.

Some of the more common treatments for narcotic addicts involve the use of drugs that either block narcotic effects or are substitute narcotics with less disruptive effects than those on which the person is dependent (O'Brien, 1996). One of the first drug treatments for narcotic dependence involved the administration of narcotic antagonists, thereby theoretically breaking up the relationship between the drug-taking behavior and the reinforcing effects of these drugs. Initially, nalorphine and cyclozocine were used. While these drugs did block the effects of heroin and morphine, they had a number of properties that prevented them from being practical tools in the treatment of narcotic dependence. These drugs sometimes induced dysphoric side effects, and taken chronically, they were capable of inducing a mild physical dependence. The introduction of the pure narcotic antagonist naloxone (Narcan) eliminated these problems because it induced neither dysphoria nor physical dependence. The disadvantages of naloxone were its short duration and its ineffectiveness when taken orally. These problems were surmounted with the subsequent development of naltrexone (Trexan, now marketed as ReVia), which is not only more effective when taken orally but also has opiate-blocking actions for up to 3 days, thus eliminating the need for several daily administrations.

While the use of pure opiate antagonists like naltrexone in the treatment of opiate abuse and dependence sounds great in theory, it is not an approach that is likely to be very effective in the treatment of most compulsive opiate users because these drugs do not deal with the major motivating factor behind the narcotic use; that is, they do not eliminate the psychological craving for narcotics. Therefore, without any further intervention, these individuals will probably stop taking the antagonist and go back to taking narcotics. In addition, unlike the opiate agonist methadone, which can be adminsitered at any stage of addiction, treatment with opiate antagonists such as naltrexone typically would not begin until after all signs of abstinence have dissipated (i.e., the addict has been detoxified) because these drugs would induce a rapid onset of abstinence symptoms that could be quite severe. (However, see the discussion of ultrarapid opiate detoxification on p. 258.) It is argued that these drugs would only be useful in highly motivated individuals. These concerns have been supported by a study indicating that only 27 percent of naltrexone-maintained narcotic addicts remained in treatment for the 12-week observation period, whereas 87 percent of methadone-maintained addicts remained in treatment (Osborn et al., 1986). However, opiate-addicted professionals who routinely have ready access to opiates (for example, doctors, nurses, pharmacists) make excellent candidates for this treatment approach (O'Brien, 1996).

Perhaps one of the most successful drug treatments for narcotic dependence is not really a treatment at all, in that it involves substituting one narcotic for another. However, the substitute narcotic has more socially acceptable qualities and fewer disruptive effects on the individual. The narcotic is methadone (Dolophine), a synthetic narcotic developed in Nazi Germany during World War II. Although it is a very effective analgesic, it did not come into use in the United States until the late 1960s.

The way in which methadone came into use for the treatment of narcotic dependence is an interesting story (Dole & Nyswander, 1976). It came about somewhat by accident through the combined efforts of Dr. Vincent Dole, a specialist in metabolic disorders, and Dr. Marie Nyswander, a psychiatrist who specialized in the treatment of narcotic addicts. Dole was interested in establishing whether narcotic addicts had a metabolic disorder that resulted in their craving for narcotics, and Nyswander was interested in pursuing alternatives to the multiple approaches to the treatment of addiction that were being used in the 1960s, and that almost always failed.

To pursue the metabolism research, a few heroin addicts were first maintained on morphine. This required several injections per day and kept the patients in a generally lethargic and inactive state. For detoxification purposes, the patients were given methadone, which was known to produce a more protracted, but less intense, withdrawal. However, rather than immediately beginning to decrease the dose of methadone, the patients were maintained on rather high doses so that the metabolic studies could be repeated with methadone. Although the metabolic research did not turn up anything notable, the researchers noticed a number of other developments in their patients. First, the patients' craving for narcotics was eliminated, and second, they began to engage in socially relevant activities. Follow-ups with more patients revealed other developments. There was a dramatic decrease in their heroin use and drug-related crimes, and an increase in their ability to function in the community. Patients began attending school, receiving passing grades, maintaining a family, and working at a job.

In summary, Dole and Nyswander concluded that, despite most of their patients' preexisting disadvantages of low socioeconomic levels, poor education, prison records, and years of addiction, the majority of those individuals maintained on methadone became self-supporting, law-abiding citizens. Furthermore, the longer they were maintained on methadone, the more probable this scenario became. Since that report, a large number of studies has led to essentially the same conclusion—that is, of all treatments for heroin dependence, methadone maintenance treatment has the most evidence of benefit in terms of reducing heroin use, as well as other illicit drug use, mortality, criminal activity, and risk of HIV infection, and of improving social rehabilitation (Bertschy, 1995; Fairbank et al., 1993; Taj et al., 1995; Wodak, 1994).

The primary advantages of methadone over other narcotics are that it is readily and reliably absorbed orally and has a relatively long duration of action—approximately 24 hours. These characteristics eliminate the hazards of the injection method and, although it has some mood-elevating effects, methadone induces a more gradual and stable effect on the individual than heroin or morphine does. Tolerance develops to methadone, and through cross-tolerance, methadone blocks the effects of other narcotics unless they are taken in very high (and expensive) amounts. Because it is active at opiate receptors, it greatly reduces the craving for narcotics generally experienced by addicts and reduces their motivation for returning to their original drug-taking behavior. The side effects of methadone— namely, constipation and impotence—are qualitatively the same as those of other narcotics (Reisine & Pasternak, 1996).

Using sufficiently high daily doses of methadone (optimally using plasma methadone concentrations as a guide) is a critical factor in its efficacy (Banys et al., 1994; Caplehorn et al., 1993; Hartel et al., 1995; Kell, 1995). Higher methadone dosages may be necessary in individuals with higher degrees of psychopathological symptoms, regardless of their heroin-use history (Maremmani et al., 1993). Also, exposure to high-quality medical and psychosocial services, clear orientation toward social rehabilitation and treatment retention (to allow a sufficient duration of treatment), and a slow detoxification regimen of well-stabilized patients are all factors contributing to better efficacy with methadone treatment (Bertschy, 1995; Wodac, 1994).

Methadone is used either as a maintenance drug, much as insulin is used by diabetics, or as a drug that can be administered in smaller and smaller doses to gradually reduce the addict's physical dependence on narcotics. Most studies indicate that the former approach is more satisfactory in decreasing illicit narcotic use. Further decreases in illicit drug use can be obtained if the dose of methadone is made contingent on drug-free urinalysis; for example, when the urine is drug-free, the client receives a higher dose of methadone (Stitzer et al., 1986; Taj et al., 1995).

While methadone does decrease the use of illicit narcotics, it does not eliminate their use in a large portion of addicts. They often get into methadone treatment, gradually reducing the dose until their tolerance to narcotics decreases, and then return to their original drug-taking activities. Addicts under methadone are also more likely to have higher employment rates than nontreated addicts and are less likely to engage in criminal activities. However, access to methadone does not eliminate criminal behavior entirely, since most addicts in the United States have developed over the years a number of skills, such as selling drugs and stealing, that may still be useful to them, even though they may not be needed for obtaining narcotics any more.

The scientific data are substantial in showing that methadone therapy helps control illicit drug use and prevent associated diseases such as AIDS. Unfortunately, methadone has been available only under strict federal and state laws and licensing procedures that control dosage. In 1997, an expert panel organized by the National Institutes of Health recommended that officials relax these controls and encourage more physicians to become more involved in treating the nation's estimated 600,000 opiate addicts (NIH, 1999). It is not clear at this time whether public officials have paid much attention to this recommendation.

Other opiate drugs used in the treatment of narcotic dependence are LAAM (levo-alpha-acetyl-methadol, Orlamm) and buprenorphine (Buprenex). LAAM is a narcotic agonist similar to methadone, and buprenorphine is a mixed opiate agonist–antagonist (Reisine & Pasternak, 1996). Both of these have even longer durations of action than methadone. Thus, they induce a much more stable effect on mood and psychological processes and induce a very mild withdrawal when drug administration is terminated. The efficacy of both of these drugs has been shown to be comparable to that of methadone in terms of suppressing addicts' use of heroin, effectiveness in withdrawal detoxification, blocking the effects of other opiates, and satisfying their craving for opiates (Fischer et al., 1999; Prendergast et al., 1995; Schottenfeld et al., 1997). They have advantages over methadone specifically with regard to only requiring one to three doses weekly, possible cost savings, and possible improved clinic–community relations.

LAAM has been approved as a maintenance treatment for opiate addiction. Buprenorphine is presently approved for use in pain management. On the basis of the controlled trials comparing buprenorphine and methadone maintenance in the treatment of opiate dependence, which have generally found very favorable results regarding buprenorphine's efficacy and safety, it is likely that buprenorphine will be approved for maintenance treatment of opiate addiction quite soon (or will be by the time you read this). The manufacturer is expected to seek approval for a buprenorphine–naloxone combination tablet to reduce further its potential for illicit use. One of the advantages of buprenorphine over other opiates is the absence of dangerous respiratory depression—even at doses 100 times those necessary for inducing analgesia. Preliminary studies have found buprenorphine to be acceptable to heroin addicts who will not accept methadone maintenance treatment, either because they view methadone as "just another addicting drug" with less desirable effects than heroin or have experienced methadone effects as aversive (Resnick et al., 1992). Buprenorphine maintenance treatment in opiate-dependent pregnant women has also shown to be well accepted by them, and is associated with a low incidence of neonatal abstinence syndrome (Fischer et al., 2000). Because of preclinical studies finding that buprenorphine reduced cocaine self-administration in non–opiate-dependent animals, researchers have suggested that buprenorphine might have some specific additional value in reducing cocaine use in opiate addicts. However, studies with humans have not shown buprenorphine to be particularly effective—that is, compared with methadone—in this regard (Compton et al., 1995; Schottenfeld et al., 1997).

One potential problem with the use of very long acting narcotics is that, after a history of taking other narcotics daily or several times daily, addicts may not feel subjectively that the longer-acting substance is actually working. Therefore, they may feel some psychological discomfort with a compound that only needs to be taken once or twice a week. On the other hand, research with LAAM has indicated that many opiate addicts prefer LAAM over methadone because they need to attend a clinic less frequently, experience fewer side effects, and feel that LAAM has a better maintenance effect (Tennant et al., 1986).

With the discovery of the endogenous opioid peptides, there was hope that one or more of these might be usefully employed as a nonaddicting substitute for opiates. Unfortunately, the duration of effect of these peptides proved to be short because they are rapidly inactivated in the body by enzymes. Furthermore, tolerance occurs with chronic endorphin or enkephalin exposure, and withdrawal may occur when administration ceases (Cooper et al., 1991).

Clonidine, a nonopiate alpha-2-adrenoceptor agonist, has been found to significantly alleviate opiate withdrawal without inducing euphoria (Gold, 1993). Detoxification with clonidine is generally faster, and may be more effective, than with methadone. Its efficacy appears to be due to its ability to reduce noradrenergic activity within the locus coeruleus, a part of the reticular activating system. It projects extensively to limbic regions and autonomic centers. Firing rates and norepinephrine release from locus coeruleus neurons tend to be inhibited by opiates initially, but these effects show tolerance with repeated opiate use.

When opiate use ceases, locus coeruleus cells become hyperactive. Clonidine significantly reduces this hyperactivity via its actions at these cells' autoreceptors; that is, it activates the inhibitory feedback system regulating norepinephrine synthesis and release. While facilitating opiate detoxification, clonidine is not a drug likely to be beneficial in reducing the psychological cravings for opiates, perhaps because these feelings are more directly tied to opiate receptor activity. Furthermore, clonidine is only effective in suppressing withdrawal symptoms specifically associated with heightened activity in the locus coeruleus of the CNS and the sympathetic nervous system (both are heavily noradrenergic) (Jaffe, 1985). Anxiety, restlessness, insomnia, and muscular aching are suppressed only minimally.

As discussed in previous chapters, the hallucinogenic alkaloid ibogaine has been claimed to possess broad-spectrum antiaddictive properties. In some, but not all, studies with nonhumans it has been shown to reduce self-administration of morphine, to inhibit morphine-induced locomotor activity, and to inhibit at least some components of the morphine withdrawal syndrome (Popik et al., 1995). Anecdotal and case reports with humans have also suggested that ibogaine can decrease the intensity and duration of withdrawal in opiate addicts and reduce opiate craving (Sheppard, 1994). In several instances, the effects appeared to last several days or even weeks. However, the putative antiaddictive properties of ibogaine require more rigorous validation in humans, after careful assessment of its neurotoxic potential. (See Chapter 11 for a more complete description of ibogaine's properties.)

Many users of narcotics never seek treatment. Those who do not are less likely to have severe non–drug-related problems (for example, employment, legal, or psychiatric problems) than those who do (Corty & Ball, 1986). Many of those who do not seek treatment may eventually become abstinent on their own—a process called "maturing out." While maturing out tends to be a time-related phenomenon, it is less likely to occur in addicts who are deeply involved in crime and drug dealing (Brecht et al., 1987).

The "Overdose" Phenomenon

Perhaps one of the more notable properties of narcotics in the eyes of the general public is their lethality. Reports occur periodically in the mass media describing what appears to be a death induced by an overdose of a narcotic. However, there is little scientific evidence that the vast majority of these deaths are actually due to narcotic overdose. An excellent discussion of this phenomenon was presented in 1972 (Brecher, 1972), but remarkably little has been done to advance our knowledge of it since then. First of all, although respiratory depression and death do occur at high doses of narcotics, such doses are much higher than those that addicts are likely to use. We don't know what the minimum lethal dose of pure heroin is in humans, but in normal, pain-free adults there is no serious toxicity with less than 30 mg of morphine given parenterally (O'Brien, 1996), and it takes approximately 7 mg/kg of morphine to kill nontolerant baboons (Brecher, 1972). Assuming that humans are physiologically similar to baboons and that heroin is three times more potent than morphine, it would take somewhere between 10 and 160 mg of heroin administered intravenously to kill the average nontolerant human. To the vast majority of addicts, that is a lot of heroin to be administered at one time. A gram (1,000 mg) of illicitly obtained heroin, which may cost around $100, may actually contain 5 percent to 30 percent heroin (50 to 300 mg), and injecting that amount all at once is highly unlikely. Furthermore, addicts generally have developed tolerance to narcotics. Second, there is little evidence from autopsies of addicts who supposedly have died from narcotics that an excessive amount of narcotic was in the body. Nor is there clear evidence that the concentration of heroin found in the syringe or supplies used by the person was particularly high. Third, addicts often share a supply of heroin, but only one may die from the injection. Finally, in some cases, death is so rapid that the needle is still in the arm of the deceased, whereas sufficient respiratory depression to cause death with narcotics generally occurs after several minutes or hours.

If the majority of deaths associated with illicit narcotics are not due to excessive amounts of narcotics, then to what can these deaths be attributed? One possibility is that they are due to an interaction between an opiate and another drug (a phenomenon common to a wide variety of drug-related deaths). The fact is, it is a rare narcotic user who uses only narcotics. Alcohol use is quite abundant. Mixing a narcotic with cocaine (commonly called a speedball) or with a drug that has sedative–hypnotic properties (like Valium) is also common. Such drug mixtures can have synergistic effects or interact in ways still not understood. The deaths of Janis Joplin, Jimi Hendrix, and Elvis Presley, as well as many other well-known celebrity narcotic-related deaths, probably occurred in this fashion. Although Elvis's autopsy did not reveal large concentrations of any particular drug, traces of a dozen or so psychoactive substances, including opiates, were found in his body. John Belushi died following an injection of heroin and cocaine, administered after a heavy night's drinking.

The adulterants mixed with illicit narcotics may also be a factor. There is an interesting direct correlation between death rates associated with heroin use and the percentage of quinine mixed with heroin. Adding quinine to heroin was first done in the 1930s as a way of preventing malaria, but it was soon discovered to be an effective way of disguising the actual purity of heroin because of its taste and because it acted synergistically with heroin. Since the 1930s, as adding quinine to heroin became more common, the death rates associated with heroin use increased dramatically. It is also possible that many narcotic-related deaths are due to *anaphylactic shock*—an immediate, transient kind of extreme allergic reaction characterized by contraction of smooth muscle and dilation of capillaries resulting from the release of histamine and other pharmacologically active substances (Reisine & Pasternak, 1996). Such a reaction could result in rapid pulmonary edema (a filling of the lungs with fluid) and asphyxiation, which are not uncommon among narcotic-related deaths. The Pavlovian conditioning model of tolerance has even been proposed as a factor (Hinson & Siegel, 1982). That is, an addict may inject a narcotic—perhaps one that is more pure than usual—in a novel environment. In such an environment, compensatory CRs normally elicited by the environment associated with the drug would not be present to counteract the drug UCRs. In effect, much of the tolerance to the drug would be lost, and the person could die.

Whatever the case, there are a multitude of factors, other than simply an overdose of narcotics, that may contribute to deaths associated with their use. For example, of the almost 2,000 narcotic-related deaths in New York City in 1986, approximately 12 percent were regarded as general overdose deaths. The remainder were attributed to AIDS (45 percent) and other diseases resulting from the addicts' lifestyles (e.g., pneumonia, liver damage, cardiovascular complications, tuberculosis) (Stoneburner et al., 1988).

In cases of true pure opiate overdoses, which would be evidenced by the triad of coma, pinpoint pupils, and depressed respiration, an injection of naloxone rapidly reverses these symptoms—although too high a dose of naloxone can precipitate severe withdrawal and induce cardiac arrhythmias and pulmonary edema (Reisine & Pasternak, 1996). Based on evidence that patients with severe pain may tolerate larger doses of morphine, it is likely that exposure to a painful stimulus may have a stimulatory effect and temporarily reverse the respiratory depression induced by opiate overdose.

Legal Factors in the Narcotics Problem

It seems appropriate at this point to discuss briefly the legal system's contribution to the present problem with narcotics in the United States (Brecher, 1972; Stephens, 1987). Up until the early 1900s, it was possible to obtain any drug available over the counter for a relatively small price. A wide variety of tonics and medicines contained unknown mixtures of alcohol, opium, cocaine, and other psychoactive substances. We can assume that, with such easy access to these mixtures, dependence was widespread. But we can also assume that the dependence was rather mild, because the common route of administration was oral. With the recognition of increasing dependence associated with these drugs, a number of governments around the world became concerned about the ramifications of this problem. In 1914 the United States legislated the Harrison Act to deal with it. In essence, it classified a number of drugs as narcotics (curiously, cocaine was among these) and made it illegal for them to be sold except by prescription obtained from a physician, who could only prescribe them during the course of professional practice. Initially, this restriction presented no problem to those dependent on opium or heroin, because they simply went to their local doctor for a prescription. However, before long, some law officials began prosecuting physicians for prescribing narcotics to dependent persons, because addiction was not viewed as a disease and, therefore, prescribing narcotics solely to alleviate the symptoms of withdrawal was not an acceptable medical practice. Physicians soon stopped prescribing narcotics to their addicted patients.

Immediately, some enterprising individuals, recognizing the ready market for narcotics, set up shop and started dispensing narcotic drugs—at somewhat inflated prices. The law's attempts to prosecute these individuals, as well as to legislate more severe penalties for the sale and possession of narcotics, started a vicious cycle that escalated for more than a half century.

With higher and higher prices for narcotics, individuals turned to crime to support their habits. Little money went for proper nutrients, and the physical health of the average addict began to decline. More and more misrepresentation of drugs, in terms of quantity, quality, and type of drug, and the addition of adulterants led to increased toxicity and lethality in the addicted population.

The danger of adulteration was well illustrated in the 1980s by the discovery that the sloppy laboratory practices of a man attempting to synthesize analogues of the narcotic meperidine for street sale in northern California resulted in the chemical 1-methyl-4-phenyl-1,2,5,6-tetrahydro-pyridine (MPTP) (Lewin, 1984). The substance has been found to metabolize in the brain into a compound that kills midbrain dopaminergic cells whose axons project to neurons in the basal ganglia. This effect produces clinical symptoms essentially identical to those of Parkinson's disease. This phenomenon was first described in 1979 in the case of a 23-year-old graduate student who had developed a parkinsonian-like condition after injecting a meperidine-like drug that he had synthesized in his own laboratory. In taking shortcuts in his manufacturing process, the student contaminated his chosen product with MPTP. Unfortunately, the student was not the only one who used the adulterated substance, and several dozen young users of this synthetic opiate succumbed to a similar fate—a lifetime (which could be quite short) of tremors, partial or complete paralysis, and abnormal posture. Unfortunately, these symptoms can only be temporarily reversed with the drug most commonly used in the treatment of Parkinson's disease (L-dopa), and they get worse with time.

Low availability of narcotics also eventually led to the more dangerous intravenous method of administration. Problems with the injection procedure were compounded by the failure to protect against infectious diseases, in part because of lack of education. Finally, vigorous enforcement of narcotics laws in the United States allowed organized crime to strengthen itself with the immense profits associated with narcotic sales. That is, the greater the penalties for sale, the higher the price and the greater the profit from selling. This phenomenon persists to this day. The basic problem is that the majority of the money spent to buy illicit drugs like heroin or cocaine goes to the bottom level of the market—to the street and near-street sellers. Only a small portion of the final price goes to the production and smuggling sector. As a result, seizures of big drug shipments, which may cost the government on the order of $1 million per drug seizure, have almost no impact on buyers and thus no impact on demand or on the huge profits to be made (Marshall, 1988).

In essence, what started out as an effort to protect consumers from becoming mildly dependent on relatively nontoxic substances resulted in their becoming strongly dependent on very toxic and lethal substances. The question many of us ask is: Would we have been better off to have left well enough alone? Although there is no way of knowing the answer to this question as far as the United States is concerned, another "experiment," conducted in Great Britain at about the same time, leads many to answer yes to the question, or at least suggests that an alternative route might have been more productive.

Around the time the United States legislated the Harrison Act, Great Britain was instituting its own similar legislation. However, it viewed dependence from a less moralistic perspective, as something to be treated. Thus, narcotic addicts in Great Britain were able to obtain heroin and other narcotics by prescription from their family physicians, while the law attempted to keep illicit narcotics out of the hands of nonaddicts. Thus, illicit trade in narcotics was minimized and the population of addicts was maintained at a fairly constant level until the 1960s. Unfortunately, some physicians were rather lackadaisical in their prescription practices, and more narcotics were being prescribed than was necessary to maintain just the addicted population (Spear, 1994). This excessive prescribing led to a change in policy in 1968, whereby only specifically licensed physicians are allowed to prescribe heroin, some other abused opiates, and cocaine to addicts on a maintenance basis (Power, 1994). In addition, until 1996 addicts treated by these physicians had to be reported to what is called the Home Office (Hall et al., 2000). Most of these physicians are affiliated with special drug treatment centers (called Drug Dependence Units), although any physician can apply for a license to write prescriptions for these drugs for their addicted patients (Connell & Strang, 1994). Over the past 30 years, there has been a trend in Great Britain to emphasize (push?) oral methadone as the most appropriate drug treatment for heroin addiction, and any medical physician in the United Kingdom is permitted to prescribe methadone for the purpose of treating opiate dependence. Due to a variety of reasons (e.g., hassles with bureaucracy, not wanting to be identified by the government, insufficient amounts of opiates prescribed), the true addict population is approximately two to 10 times the number reported.

Great Britain's policy with respect to narcotic addiction is not a panacea. Addicts still die of narcotic-related causes and suffer infectious diseases because of nonsterile injection procedures (Hall et al., 2000). There is still a black market trade in narcotics, and the rate of addiction in Great Britain is still growing (Fountain et al., 2000). In any event, the problems with narcotics in Great Britain appear to be of a lower magnitude than those in the United States, and the lower incidence of criminal activities by addicts who do not need much money to obtain clean supplies of narcotics definitely benefits the general population.

Opiate Antagonists: Potential Uses

For over two decades, the relatively pure opioid receptor antagonists naloxone and naltrexone have been the mainstays of research and treatments associated with the opioids and their receptors. Naloxone is fast acting, with a short duration of action (less than 4 hours), and is poorly absorbed when taken orally. Naltrexone is more potent than naloxone and is quite effective when taken orally, and its duration of opiate-blocking action is between 24 and 48 hours. Nalmefene (Revex) is a relatively new, pure opiate antagonist that is structurally similar to naloxone and naltrexone. Compared with naloxone, nalmefene is more potent in blocking opiate receptors, more readily absorbed when taken orally, acts as quickly, and lasts somewhat longer. However, it is not clear whether it has any other particular properties that distinguish it from naloxone and naltrexone.

These opioid antagonists have a variety of clinical uses, and numerous other uses have been suggested for them. Naloxone and nalmefene are currently being used primarily for their ability to reverse the effects of narcotics in acute overdose cases and as a diagnostic tool for assessing the degree of opiate physical dependence. Interestingly, a recent survey conducted in Great Britain found that while the majority of injecting drug abusers had experienced or witnessed at least one drug overdose (mostly involving opiates), with perhaps a third witnessing a fatal overdose, only 35 percent were aware of the existence and effects of naloxone (Strang et al., 1999). The results suggested that at least two-thirds of witnessed overdose fatalities could be prevented by administration of home-based supplies of naloxone. Naltrexone and nalmefene are being used as a prophylactic measure in opiate addicts who have terminated their opiate use but who are concerned that they may relapse. Should they do so and administer a narcotic such as heroin, they are aware that they would not experience any of the effects and that it would be a waste of money.

Naloxone may also be used to reduce the illicit use of prescription opiates. Some opiates that are normally taken orally for their analgesic effects often are converted for illicit use into injectable form for intravenous administration. This enhances the opiate's euphoric properties as well as its dependence liability. However, if naloxone is added to the tablet, injecting the combination is ineffective. That is, naloxone, which in small amounts is ineffective orally, does not reduce an opiate's effectiveness if taken orally. But when the combination is injected, sufficient amounts of naloxone get into the brain to effectively block the opiate's action. This significantly reduces its likelihood of being channeled into illicit use. Such an approach has been taken with the opiate analgesic pentazocine (Talwin Nx). Unfortunately, if the combination is injected, it can cause severe, potentially lethal, reactions. Again, it appears that our attempts to reduce illicit opiate use can sometimes lead to worse consequences for the user than the opiate itself.

Naltrexone is a key ingredient in a new technique that is gaining popularity—called ultrarapid opioid detoxification—in which opiate-dependent patients are anaesthetized or heavily sedated and exposed to high, repetitive doses of nalmefene, naloxone, or naltrexone for 24 to 48 hours (Spanagel, 1999). The patients undergo physiological withdrawal but are not consciously aware of it. Maintenance treatment with naltrexone is provided following this rapid detoxification. Proponents claim that a significant proportion of these patients remain abstinent after completion of the treatment. However, the efficacy and safety of this treatment are still questionable. The treatment is more expensive than conventional procedures because of the additional procedures involved, carries more risks, such as pulmonary and renal failure and cardiovascular complications, and increases the risk of overdose should the patient return to opiate use (Pfab et al., 1999; Spanagel, 1999). Finally, several deaths have been attributed to this procedure. Whether relapse rates are significantly different with this technique than with more traditional approaches remains to be determined, for while the physical withdrawal from opiates is a factor in maintaining opiate dependence, it is the psychological components to dependence that are the key factors in relapse.

Because opiates have some neuropharmacological actions that are shared with several other drugs of abuse (for example, cocaine, amphetamine, alcohol, nicotine), a number of studies have attempted to determine whether opiate antagonists may be useful in the treatment of other drug addictions. As discussed in Chapter 8, the most promising results have been in the area of alcoholism treatment.

Opioid antagonists may have a variety of other potential uses outside the scope of drug dependence. With the discovery of a variety of endogenous opioid peptides in the body, there has been much speculation as to their function. Obviously, one of these is in the area of pain regulation, but there are many other areas. It has been speculated that endogenous opioids are involved in a variety of psychopathological conditions, including autism, self-injurious behavior, schizophrenia, obsessive–compulsive disorders, eating disorders such as bulimia, sleep apnea syndrome (disruptions in breathing possibly associated with sudden infant death syndrome), and attention deficit disorders.

As discussed in later chapters, numerous studies have explored the potential involvement of opioids in these disorders and the use of opioid antagonists in reducing the symptoms of these disorders, unfortunately with very limited success. While positive reports have been frequently been made, failures to replicate are quite common. In many cases, this may be due to initial investigations being done without appropriate controls (for example, use of the double-blind procedure in which neither the person receiving the drug nor the person measuring the effects is aware of the actual drug given), or small sample sizes. In some studies noting positive effects, the test procedures themselves may have been stressful. It has now been established that acute stressors may activate endorphin systems. If the test procedures were sufficiently stressful to activate endorphin activity and exacerbate the pathological symptoms being measured, then it would appear that the symptoms would be reduced if an opiate antagonist were administered. In other cases, the heterogeneity of the factors causing similar symptoms may lead to discrepant findings. Finally, the degree to which opioid antagonists have therapeutic effects may depend on whether endogenous opioids are active all the time in a particular disorder or only under specific conditions, if indeed they are involved at all. Clearly, much work remains to be done in this area before we will have any definitive answers regarding the efficacy of opiate antagonists in these disorders.

Websites for Further Information

Site providing information on the opium war of the nineteenth century (an interesting historical twist on the "war on drugs"):

http://ourworld.compuserve.com/homepages/OLDNEWS/opium.htm

Site covering many aspects of heroin, along with a number of links (images, chemistry, law):

http://erowid.org/entheogens/heroin/heroin.shtml

Information on methadone and the treatment of opiate dependence, along with a number of links:

http://erowid.org/pharms/methadone/methadone.shtml

Bibliography

Akil, H., Watson, S. J., Young, E., et al. (1984). Endogenous opioids: Biology and function. *Annual Review of Neuroscience, 7,* 223–225.

Banys, P., Tusel, D. J., Sees, K. L., & Reilly, P. M. (1994). Low (40 mg) versus high (80 mg) dose methadone in a 180-day heroin detoxification program. *Journal of Substance Abuse Treatment, 11,* 225–232.

Bauman, P. S., & Levine, S. A. (1986). The development of children of drug addicts. *International Journal of the Addictions, 21,* 849–863.

Benedetti, F., Arduino, C., & Amanzio, M. (1999). Somatotopic activation of opioid systems by target-directed expectations of analgesia. *Journal of Neuroscience, 19,* 3639–3648.

Bernstein, V. J., & Hans, S. L. (1994). Predicting the developmental outcome of two-year-old children born exposed to methadone: Impact of social-environmental risk factors. Special issue: Impact of poverty of children, youth, and families. *Journal of Clinical Child Psychology, 23,* 349–359.

Bertschy, G. (1995). Methadone maintenance treatment: An update. *European Archives of Psychiatry and Clinical Neuroscience, 245,* 114–124.

Bloor, L. B., Leese, B., & Maynard, A. (1994). The cost of managing severe cancer pain and potential savings from transdermal administration. *European Journal of Cancer, 30A,* 463–468.

Brecher, E. M. (Ed.). (1972). *Licit and illicit drugs.* Boston: Little, Brown.

Brecht, M. L., Anglin, M. D., Woodward, J. A., & Bonett, D. G. (1987). Conditional factors of maturing out: Personal resources and preaddiction sociopathy. *International Journal of the Addictions, 22,* 55–69.

Caplehorn, J. R., Bell, J., Kleinbaum, D. G., & Gebski, V. J. (1993). Methadone dose and heroin use during maintenance treatment. *Addiction, 88,* 119–124.

Carballo-Dieguez, A., Sahs, J., Goetz, R., & El Sadr, W. (1994). The effect of methadone on immunological parameters among HIV-positive and HIV-negative drug users. *American Journal of Drug & Alcohol Abuse, 20,* 317–329.

Childress, A. R., McLellan, A. T., & O'Brien, C. P. (1986a). Abstinent opiate abusers exhibit conditioned craving, conditioned withdrawal and reductions in both through extinction. *British Journal of Addiction, 81,* 655–660.

Childress, A. R., McLellan, A. T., & O'Brien, C. P. (1986b). Conditioned responses in a methadone population. *Journal of Substance Abuse Treatment, 3,* 173–179.

Cohen, S. (1981). *The substance abuse problems.* New York: Haworth Press.

Collin, E., & Cesselin, F. (1991). Neurobiological mechanisms of opioid tolerance and dependence. *Clinical Neuropharmacology, 14,* 465–488.

Compton, P. A., Ling, W., Charuvastra, V. C., & Wesson, D. R. (1995). Buprenorphine as a pharmacotherapy for cocaine abuse: A review of the evidence. *Journal of Addictive Diseases, 14,* 97–114.

Connell, P., & Strang, J. (1994). The creation of the clinics: Clinical demand and the formation of policy. In J. Strang & M. Gossop (Eds.), *Heroin addiction and drug policy: The British system* (pp. 167–177). Oxford: Oxford University Press.

Cooper, J. R., Bloom, F. E., & Roth, R. H. (1991). *The biochemical basis of neuropharmacology,* 6th ed. New York: Oxford University Press.

Cooper, J. R., Bloom, F. E., & Roth, R. H. (1996). *The biochemical basis of neuropharmacology,* 7th ed. New York: Oxford University Press.

Corty, E., & Ball, J. C. (1986). What can we know about addiction from the addicts we treat? *International Journal of the Addictions, 21,* 1139–1144.

Dole, V. P., & Nyswander, M. E. (1976). Methadone maintenance treatment. *Journal of the American Medical Association, 235,* 2117–2119.

Dougherty, P. M. Pellis, N. R., & Dafny, N. (1990). The brain and the immune system: An intact immune system is essential for the manifestation of withdrawal in opiate addicted rats. *Neuroscience, 36,* 285–289.

Eikelboom, R., & Stewart, J. (1982). Conditioning of drug-induced physiological responses. *Psychological Review, 89,* 507–528.

Fairbank, J. A., Dunteman, G. H., & Condelli, W. S. (1993). Do methadone patients substitute other drugs for heroin? Predicting substance use at 1-year follow-up. *American Journal of Drug and Alcohol Abuse, 19,* 465–474.

Ferrante, F. M. (1996). Principles of opioid pharmacotherapy: Practical implications of basic mechanisms. *Journal of Pain and Symptom Management, 11,* 265–273.

Fischer, G., Gombas, W., Eder, H., et al. (1999). Buprenorphine versus methadone maintenance for the treatment of opioid dependence. *Addiction, 94,* 1337–1347.

Fischer, G., Johnson, R. E., Eder, H., et al. (2000). Treatment of opioid-dependent pregant women with buprenorphine. *Addiction, 95,* 239–244.

Fountain, J., Strang, J., Gossop, M., et al. (2000). Diversion of prescribed drugs by drug users in treatment: Analysis of the UK market and new data from London. *Addiction, 95,* 393–406.

Freier, D. O., & Fuchs, B. A. (1994). A mechanism of action for morphine-induced immunosuppression: Corticosterone mediates morphine-induced suppression of natural killer cell activity. *Journal of Pharmacology and Experimental Therapeutics, 270,* 1127–1133.

Gold, M. S. (1993). Opiate addiction and the locus coeruleus. The clinical utility of clonidine, naltrexone, methadone, and buprenorphine. *Psychiatric Clinics of North America, 16,* 61–73.

Grossman, S. A. (1993). Undertreatment of cancer pain: Barriers and remedies. *Supportive Care in Cancer, 1,* 74–78.

Hall, W., Lynskey, M., & Degenhardt, L. (2000). Trends in opiate-related deaths in the United Kingdom and Australia, 1985-1995. *Drug and Alcohol Dependence, 57,* 247–254.

Harrison, L. M., Kastine, A. J., & Zadina, J. E. (1998). Opiate tolerance and dependence: Receptors, G-proteins, and antiopiates. *Peptides, 19,* 1603–1630.

Hartel, D. M., Schoenbaum, E. E., Selwyn, P. A., & Kline, J. (1995). Heroin use during methadone maintenance treatment: The importance of methadone dose and cocaine use. *American Journal of Public Health, 85,* 83–88.

Hinson, R. E., & Siegel, S. (1982). Nonpharmacological bases of drug tolerance and dependence. *Journal of Psychosomatic Research, 26,* 495–503.

Holden, C. (1977). New look at heroin could spur better medical use of narcotics. *Science, 198,* 807–809.

Jaffe, J. H. (1985). Drug addiction and drug abuse. In A. G. Gilman, L. S. Goodman, T. W. Rall, & F. Murad (Eds.), *The pharmacological basis of therapeutics* (pp. 532–581). New York: Macmillan.

Jaffe, J. H., & Martin, W. R. (1985). Opioid analgesics and antagonists. In A. G. Gilman, L. S. Goodman, T. W. Rall, & F. Murad (Eds.), *The pharmacological basis of therapeutics* (pp. 491–531). New York: Macmillan.

Kell, M. J. (1995). Utilization of plasma and urine methadone concentration measurements to limit narcotics use in methadone maintenance patients: II. Generation of plasma concentration response curves. *Journal of Addictive Diseases, 14,* 85–108.

Kuwahara, M. D., & Sparber, S. B. (1981). Opiate withdrawal in utero increases neonatal morbidity in the rat. *Science, 212,* 943–947.

Lewin, R. (1984). Trail of ironies to Parkinson's disease. *Science, 224,* 1083–1085.

Maldonado, R., Blendy, J. A., Tzavara, E., et al. (1996). Reduction of morphine abstinence in mice with mutation in the gene encoding CREB. *Science, 273,* 657–659.

Mansour, A., Fox, C. A., Akil, H., & Watson, S. J. (1995). Opioid-receptor mRNA expression in the rat CNS: Anatomical and functional implications. *Trends in Neuroscience, 18,* 22–29.

Maremmani, I., Zolesi, O., Agueci, T., & Castrogiovanni, P. (1993). Methadone doses and psychopathological symptoms during methadone maintenance. *Journal of Psychoactive Drugs, 25,* 253–256.

Marshall, E. (1988). A war on drugs with real troops? *Science, 241,* 13–15.

Marx, J. L. (1987). A new wave of enzymes for cleaving prohormones. *Science, 235,* 285–286.

Melzack, R. (1990). The tragedy of needless pain. *Scientific American, 262,* 27–33.

NIH consensus panel recommends expanding access to and improving methadone treatment programs for heroin addiction. (1999). *European Addiction Research, 5,* 50–51.

O'Brien, C. P. (1996). Drug addiction and drug abuse. In A. G. Gilman, L. S. Goodman, J. G. Hardman, L. E. Limbard, P. B. Molinoff, & R. W. Ruddon (Eds.), *The pharmacological basis of therapeutics* (pp. 557–577). New York: McGraw-Hill.

Oldendorf, W. H., Hyman, S., Braun, L., & Oldendorf, S. Z. (1972). Blood-brain barrier: Penetration of morphine, codeine, heroin and methadone after carotid injection. *Science, 178,* 984–986.

Osborn, E., Grey, C., & Reznikoff, M. (1986). Psychosocial adjustment, modality choice, and outcome in naltrexone versus methadone treatment. *American Journal of Drug and Alcohol Abuse, 12,* 383–388.

Pasternak, G. W. (1988). Multiple morphine and enkephalin receptors and the relief of pain. *Journal of the American Medical Association, 259,* 1362–1367.

Pfab, R., Hirtl, C., & Zilker, T. (1999). Opiate detoxification under anesthesia: No apparent benefit but suppression of thyroid hormones and risk of pulmonary and renal failure. *Journal of Toxicology. Clinical Toxicology, 37,* 43–50.

Phillips, G. T., Gossop, M., & Bradley, B. (1986). The influence of psychological factors on the opiate withdrawal syndrome. *British Journal of Psychiatry, 149,* 235–238.

Popik, P., Layer, R. T., & Skolnick, P. (1995). 100 years of ibogaine: Neurochemical and pharmacological actions of putative anti-addictive drug. *Pharmacological Reviews, 47,* 235–250.

Power, R. (1994). Drug trends since 1968. In J. Strang & M. Gossop (Eds.), *Heroin addiction and drug policy: The British system* (pp. 29–41). Oxford: Oxford University Press.

Prendergast, M. L., Grella, C., Perry, S. M., & Anglin, M. D. (1995). Levo-alpha-acetylmethadol (LAAM): Clinical, research, and policy issues of a new pharmacotherapy for opioid addiction. *Journal of Psychoactive Drugs, 27,* 239–247.

Reisine, T., & Pasternak, G. (1996). Opioid analgesics and antagonists. In A. G. Gilman, L. S. Goodman, J. G. Hardman, L. E. Limbard, P. B. Molinoff, & R. W. Ruddon (Eds.), *The pharmacological basis of therapeutics* (pp. 521–555). New York: McGraw-Hill.

Resnick, R. B., Galanter, M., Pycha, C., et al. (1992). Buprenorphine: An alternative to methadone for heroin dependence treatment. *Psychopharmacology Bulletin, 28,* 109–113.

Schimmer, B. P., & Parker, K. L. (1996). Adrenocorticotropic hormone; adrenocortical steroids and their synthetic analogs; inhibitors of the synthesis and actions of adrenocortical hormones. In A. G. Gilman, L. S. Goodman, J. G. Hardman, L. E. Limbard, P. B. Molinoff, & R. W. Ruddon (Eds.), *The pharmacological basis of therapeutics* (pp. 1459–1485). New York: McGraw-Hill.

Schottenfeld, R. S., Pakes, J. R., Oliveto, A., et al. (1997). Buprenorphine vs methadone maintenance treatment for concurrent opioid dependence and cocaine abuse. *Archives of General Psychiatry, 54,* 713–720.

Schulties, G., Weinberger, S. B., & Martinez, J. L., Jr. (1989). Plasma uptake and in vivo metabolism of (leu)enkephalin following its intraperitoneal administration to rats. *Peptides, 10,* 913–919.

Sheppard, S. G. (1994). A preliminary investigation of ibogaine: Case reports and recommendations for further study. *Journal of Substance Abuse Treatment, 11,* 379–385.

Sim-Selley, L. J., Selley, D. E., Vogt, L. J., et al. (2000). Chronic heroin self-administration desensitizes μ opioid receptor-activated G-proteins in specific regions of rat brain. *Journal of Neuroscience, 20,* 4555–4562.

Slifer, B. L., & Dykstra, L. A. (1987). Discriminative stimulus effects of N-Allylnormetazocine in rats trained to discriminate a kappa from a sigma agonist. *Life Sciences, 40,* 343–349.

Smith, G. D., & Griffin J. F. (1978). Conformation of (leu5) enkephalin from x-ray diffraction: Features important for recognition at opiate receptor. *Science, 199,* 1214–1216.

Spanagel, R. (1999). Is there a pharmacological basis for therapy with rapid opioid detoxification? *The Lancet, 354,* 2017.

Spear, B. (1994). The early years of the 'British System' in practice. In J. Strang & M. Gossop (Eds.), *Heroin addiction and drug policy: The British system* (pp. 3–28). Oxford: Oxford University Press.

Stephens, R. C. (1987). *Mind-altering drugs.* Newbury Park, CA: Sage.

Stinus, L., Allard, M., Gold, L., & Simonnet, G. (1995). Changes in CNS neuropeptide FF-like material, pain sensitivity, and opiate dependence following chronic morphine treatment. *Peptides, 16,* 1235–1241.

Stitzer, M. L., Bickel, W. K., Bigelow, G. E., & Liebson, I. A. (1986). Effect of methadone dose contingencies on urinalysis test results of polydrug-abusing methadone-maintenance patients. *Drug and Alcohol Dependence, 18,* 341–348.

Stoneburner, R. L., Des Jarlais, D. C., Benezra, D., et al. (1988). A larger spectrum of severe HIV-1-related disease in intravenous drug users in New York City. *Science, 242,* 916–919.

Strang, J., Powis, B., Best, D., et al. (1999). Preventing opiate overdose fatalities with take-home naloxone: Pre-launch study of possible impact and acceptability. *Addiction, 94,* 199–204.

Taddese, A., Seung-Yeol, N., & McCleskey, E. W. (1995). Selective opioid inhibition of small nociceptive neurons. *Science, 270,* 1366–1369.

Taj, R., Keenan, E., & O'Connor, J. J. (1995). A review of patients on methadone maintenance. *Irish Medical Journal, 88,* 218–219.

Tennant, F. S., Rawson, R. A., Pumphrey, E., & Seecof, R. (1986). Clinical experiences with 959 opioid-dependent patients treated with levo-alpha-acetylmethadol (LAAM). *Journal of Substance Abuse Treatment, 3,* 195–202.

Tiffany, S. T., Petrie, E. C., Baker, T. B., & Dahl, J. L. (1983). Conditioned morphine tolerance in the rat: Absence of a compensatory response and cross-tolerance with stress. *Behavioral Neuroscience, 97,* 335–353.

Trujillo, K. A., & Akil, H. (1994). Inhibition of opiate tolerance by non-competitive N-methyl-D-aspartate receptor antagonists. *Brain Research, 633,* 178–188.

Wang, J. J., & Ho, S. T. (1994). Acute and chronic opioid tolerance: A pharmacological review. *Acta Anaesthesiologica Sinica, 32,* 261–267.

Wang, L., & Gintzler, A. R. (1995). Morphine tolerance and physical dependence: Reversal of opioid inhibition to enhancement of cyclic AMP formation. *Journal of Neurochemistry, 64,* 1102–1106.

Weber, R. J., & Pert, A. (1989). The periaqueductal gray matter mediates opiate-induced immunosuppression. *Science, 245,* 188–190.

Wodak, A. (1994). Managing illicit drug use. A practical guide. *Drugs, 47,* 446–457.

Chapter *11*

Psychotomimetics, Psychedelics, and Hallucinogens

What does one call a class of drugs taken primarily because of their ability to elicit in normal individuals such alterations as visual or auditory hallucinations, depersonalization, perceptual disturbances, and disturbances of thought processes at doses that exert minimal changes in other bodily functions? Before we answer this question, note that both the quantitative and the qualitative effects of these drugs are heavily dependent on the dose. Lower doses may alter mood and thought content with minimal sensory disturbances; somewhat higher doses may induce clear perceptual distortions without inducing true hallucinations (strongly experienced false perceptions that have a compulsive sense of the reality of the object but that have no relevant or adequate stimuli for their induction); and higher doses may actually induce true hallucinations. Common examples of such drugs with which you may be familiar are LSD, mescaline, and marijuana.

Since hallucinations are one of the more striking symptoms associated with such drugs, many authors commonly refer to this class of drugs as **hallucinogens.** Others prefer to use the term **psychotomimetic** (literally psychosis-mimicking) or **psychotogenic** (for psychosis-generating) because these drugs induce actual hallucinations only at the higher doses, whereas with the lower doses some of the fundamental characteristics of psychosis are still evidenced (such as gross distortion or disorganization of a person's mental capacity, affective response, and capacity to recognize reality, communicate, and relate to others). However, these two terms are also somewhat inappropriate. First, numerous drugs referred to in this fashion rarely induce a condition that mimics the types of psychoses naturally found in humans—namely, schizophrenia and mania. Second, doses of some drugs that do mimic natural psychotic states, such as large doses of cocaine and amphetamine, are not voluntarily taken for this expressed purpose. The term **psychedelic** (for mind-expanding, -manifesting,

-clarifying, or -revealing) has also been applied to these drugs, but the functional meaning of this term is also unclear. Philosophers and psychologists have grappled for years with the question of what the mind is or what it means. So what do we mean when we say it is expanded? Perhaps a new term should be coined for these drugs, but I will not be coining a new one here. For the purposes of this chapter, I will refer to them as psychotomimetic/ psychedelic/hallucinogenic substances, or simply P/P/Hs. (See Jaffe, 1985, for further discussion of this issue.)

Many have been intrigued by the P/P/Hs for a variety of reasons. For centuries, a variety of aboriginal groups have used P/P/H-containing plants in their rituals and ceremonies for healing and sacramental purposes and to promote group cohesiveness, spirituality, and mystical experiences—for example, the peyote (mescaline) sessions of the Native American Church, yage or hoasca (harmine) ceremonies of South American Amazon Indians, ingestion of sacred mushrooms (psilocybin) by a number of Indian tribes in Mexico, or the iboga (ibogaine) rites of some tribes in Central-West Africa (Dobkin de Rios, 1996; Grof, 1980). In many cases, these practices are still conducted today, with evidence that they may contribute to reduction in psychopathological characteristics of the participants (Grob et al., 1996). Over the past 45 years, a number of conventional psychotherapists have proposed the use of P/P/Hs as adjuncts in the treatment of a variety of mental disorders. Many scientists have utilized a variety of P/P/Hs as potential tools for understanding the biochemical bases of psychoses. And, of course, our society in general is so deeply concerned over their recreational use, abuse, and potential toxicity that we have raised most of them to our highest official status of controlled substance—Schedule I.

Some General Characteristics of P/P/Hs

Although P/P/Hs are used occasionally in a clinical context, the preponderant use of these substances is recreational. There are four major classes of P/P/Hs:

1. The **monoamine-related substances,** whose molecular structures and biochemical activity suggest that their effects are mediated by alterations in the activity of serotonin, dopamine, and norepinephrine in the CNS.
2. The **cannabinoids,** derivatives of the *Cannabis sativa* (marijuana) plant or synthetic analogues.
3. **Anticholinergics,** which block acetylcholine activity in the brain.
4. **Dissociative anesthetics,** which are analgesic–anesthetic drugs with P/P/H effects.

Another P/P/H drug that will be discussed in this chapter is **ibogaine**—a drug with pharmacological properties so unique that it doesn't fit into any of the four classes but shares some properties with at least two of them.

Most of these drugs gain their reinforcing value for humans because of their ability to alter consciousness and perceptual processes, rather than because they exert their effects on the primary reward centers of the brain, as do some of the drugs described earlier. I say this for several reasons. First, the subjective reports of humans consistently contain references to the perceptual and cognitive aspects of the drug-induced experience, while comments on the mood and emotions evoked appear secondary to these (Feeney, 1976; Wallace & Fisher, 1999). Second, although euphoria is commonly expressed as an effect of these drugs, it is highly context-specific. In some cases, an extreme dysphoric reaction, described as a panic or paranoid feeling, may occur without warning and may persist for several minutes to hours (Jaffe, 1985).

A third line of evidence that the reward value of most P/P/Hs is not directly related to their effects on the primary reward centers of the brain comes from research with nonhumans. Nonhumans will not self-administer many of the P/P/Hs in their pure form (Jaffe, 1985), whereas they will do so with psychostimulants, sedative–hypnotics, and narcotics. There are reports of animals ingesting plants that contain P/P/H substances, but because they have nutritional value, it is not clear whether they are eating them for their P/P/H properties or for the nutrients (Siegel, 1979).

When pure LSD or mescaline is used with the catheter infusion method, animals avoid administering them. There are exceptions to this general rule, though. For example, in one report of monkeys self-administering a P/P/H substance under experimental conditions, the monkeys were completely isolated from all visual and auditory stimulation (Siegel & Jarvik, 1980). They were then allowed to self-administer the very short-acting P/P/H dimethyltryptamine (DMT) by way of a smoking response. Under these conditions, two of the three monkeys did so. Unfortunately, the interpretation of these observations is unclear because of the well-documented stress that occurs with isolation. Under such conditions, any perceptual experience, drug-induced or not, can have reinforcing properties. Furthermore, when the monkeys were returned to their normal test environment with visual and auditory stimulation, they refused to administer the DMT, even when the monkeys were water-deprived and water reward was made contingent on DMT smoking. Three types of P/P/Hs that are readily administered by nonhumans are delta-9-tetrahydrocannabinol (the major psychoactive ingredient in marijuana), phencyclidine (PCP), and derivatives of amphetamine with P/P/H properties (such as MDMA). However, this finding is still not unambiguous evidence that nonhumans will administer P/P/Hs for their consciousness-altering or perceptual effects, because these drugs have a variety of properties that could account for their reinforcing effects.

Before beginning a discussion on P/P/Hs, it should be pointed out that research on most P/P/Hs over the last 25 years, particularly with humans, has been very limited, primarily because of governmental restraints and a lack of funding for this type of research (Neill, 1987). Furthermore, since many of these substances are classified as Schedule I drugs, researchers have to apply for a special DEA license to conduct research with them. Some of the restraints have come about because of public wariness over the potent consciousness-altering properties of these drugs (Holden, 1980). In some cases the early research was conducted without proper controls, with subjects who were not sufficiently informed of the type of research being conducted (or were not informed at all that they were involved in a drug experiment). Some subjects experienced very dysphoric, and occasionally long-lasting, reactions. During the 1960s, literally thousands of people experienced the effects of P/P/Hs, either in clinical settings as a potential therapeutic tool or in recreational settings. Unfortunately, information from these individuals consists mostly of self-reports of a highly variable nature.

Because present ethical concerns limit the type of research conducted with P/P/Hs in humans, much of the research with these substances is done with animals. Many of the questions we would like to address concerning P/P/Hs are somewhat limited by the nature of the primary properties of P/P/Hs. That is, animals cannot communicate about the highly subjective drug-induced experience, so their role is primarily one of determining what the neuropharmacological and biochemical actions of these drugs are. Unfortunately, trying to relate these actions to the cognitive and perceptual effects of P/P/Hs in humans is exceedingly difficult.

One very powerful tool for assessing subjective effects of P/P/H drugs (or any other psychoactive drugs) in animals is a technique known as the **drug discrimination paradigm** (Appel et al., 1982). Essentially, animals are trained to tell the difference (discriminate) between the effects of a placebo injection (saline) and those produced by a particular drug. For example, a hungry rat may be rewarded with food occasionally for pressing a left lever if it was injected with saline a few minutes earlier and rewarded for pressing a right lever if injected with a small dose of LSD. Rats can learn to make the appropriate choice fairly quickly. After the rat learns to respond on the appropriate lever more than 90 percent of the time, it is injected with a test compound. If the test compound induces subjective effects similar to LSD, the rat will press the lever previously associated with the LSD cue; if the effects are not LSD-like, the lever previously associated with saline will be pressed. This procedure can also be used to see which neurotransmitter systems are involved in a particular drug's subjective effects. After an animal has learned to discriminate between the presence and absence of a particular drug, the animal can be injected with a drug whose properties at specific receptors are known, prior to being injected with the placebo or the particular drug being tested. If, for example, we want to know if a particular drug works by activating 5-HT receptors, we could inject the drug after injecting a known 5-HT antagonist and test the animal to see whether it will press the lever that has been associated with the placebo. Thus, the drug discrimination paradigm is a useful way in which to use animals to compare and contrast drugs with unknown CNS effects with those whose CNS effects have been established with humans, as well as to determine the specific sites at which a drug acts.

Monoamine-Related P/P/Hs

Monoamine-related drugs are so named because they share a basic similarity with the molecular structures of the monoamine neurotransmitters serotonin, dopamine, and norepinephrine (see Figure 11–1 for representative P/P/Hs of this type) (Glennon & Rosecrans, 1982). Examples of the serotonin-type (indoleamine) P/P/H are lysergic acid diethylamide (LSD), psilocybin and psilocin (found in the *Psilocybe* genus of mushroom), bufotenine (found in glands of certain toads, e.g., *Bufo alvarius*), dimethyltryptamine (DMT), and diethyltryptamine (DET). Examples of the catecholamine-type P/P/H are mescaline (found in the peyote cactus); dimethoxymethylamphetamine (DMMA, the main ingredient in the street drug known as STP); 3,4-methylenedioxyamphetamine (MDA); and methoxymethylenedioxyamphetamine (MMDA). Most of the discussion of this group of drugs will center on LSD, because the majority of work has been done with this compound.

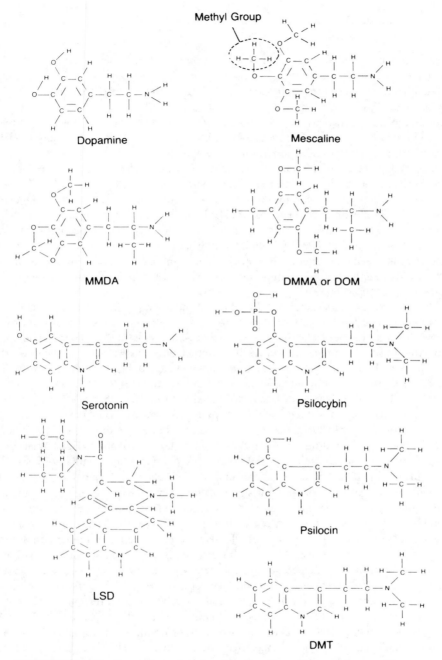

FIGURE 11-1 Examples of molecular structures of some drugs with psychotomimetic properties and two of the monoamine neurotransmitters in the brain. Note that all the psychotomimetic molecules have a number of methyl (CH_3) groups attached to them.

The subjective effects of the monoamine-related P/P/Hs in the dose ranges that are effective are quite similar and often indistinguishable in both humans and animals. For example, in animal drug discrimination procedures, the indoleamine- and catecholamine-type P/P/Hs generalize to each other (Appel et al., 1982). However, their potency may vary tremendously; for example, LSD is approximately 100 times more potent than psilocybin and approximately 4,000 times more potent than mescaline in humans (Jaffe, 1985). They may also differ in terms of their durations of action; for instance, the effects of LSD may last for several hours, whereas the effects of DMT may dissipate within 1 hour. The durations of action of mescaline, psilocin, and psilocybin are in between these two.

The effects of monoamine P/P/Hs range from those very similar to amphetamine (strongly psychostimulant-like and weakly hallucinogenic, such as MDA) to those very similar to LSD (weakly psychostimulant-like and strongly hallucinogenic, such as mescaline and psilocybin) (Jaffe, 1985; Nichols, 1986). In some cases, the type of effect is largely dependent on which isomer of the compound is administered. For example, the dextro isomer of MDA induces amphetamine-like effects, whereas the levo isomer induces LSD-like effects (Nichols, 1986).

Most drugs in this category induce fairly rapid tolerance to both their mental and sympathomimetic effects; tolerance appears to be complete after three or four daily exposures (Freedman & Halaris, 1978). They are also cross-tolerant with each other, but do not appear to exhibit cross-tolerance with drugs in the other three P/P/H classes. The one exception seems to be DMT, in which tolerance (in humans) has not been shown to develop (Strassman, 1996); nor does tolerance development to LSD transfer to DMT (Jaffe, 1985). However, the lack of tolerance to DMT may be due to the fact that DMT has a very short duration of action of less than 30 minutes (perhaps tolerance would develop if an organism were exposed to DMT on an hourly basis for several days). In most cases, tolerance is lost after a few days of no drug exposure. As far as we know, there are no signs of an abstinence syndrome following chronic exposure to any of the monoamine-related P/P/Hs.

In addition to the similarity of the subjective effects of the monoamine-related P/P/Hs, as one might expect of drugs with some of the properties of the psychostimulants, they share the tendency to produce bodily effects largely sympathomimetic in nature. These may consist of pupillary dilation, increases in blood pressure and heart rate, exaggeration of deep tendon reflexes, tremor, nausea, piloerection (hair erection), and increased body temperature. As will be discussed later in this chapter, the other classes of P/P/Hs share these characteristics in some respects but differ greatly in other respects. For example, anticholinergics may increase heart rate and blood pressure and produce pupillary dilation, but unlike the monoamine-related P/P/Hs, the pupillary dilation is not responsive to light. While the monoamine-related P/P/Hs induce signs of heightened arousal, anticholinergics and cannabinoids tend to induce sedative-like effects, drowsiness, and fatigue. You should note other fundamental differences in the effects of the other P/P/Hs discussed in this chapter as we go along.

LSD's Historical Significance

Although the effects of LSD have only been experienced over the past 50 years or so, it has been speculated that its naturally occurring cousin ergot, which is present in bread blighted by ergot-producing fungi and produces a wide variety of neuropsychiatric and vascular symptoms, may have contributed to historical accounts of the emergence of Jewish mystical movements in Europe and the bizarre behaviors of the young adolescent girls who accused the townsfolk of witchcraft during the Salem witchcraft trials in 1692 (Packer, 1998; Woolf, 2000). However, there is little empirical evidence to support these speculations. We do know that in 1938 a pharmacologist, Albert Hofmann, synthesized LSD while working with several derivatives of ergot. Five years later, Hofmann was the first to describe its profound effects on consciousness, after he accidently ingested the compound while working on it in the laboratory. As Hofmann also found out rather quickly (after purposely taking what he considered to be a trivial amount—one-quarter of a milligram—and experiencing a psychotic reaction), it is one of the most potent pharmacological agents known. It can exert subjectively detectable effects in most people with doses as low as 50 micrograms (about the weight of a grain of table salt). It is up to 10 times more potent than our own hormones at its sites of action.

Following Hofmann's discovery of LSD, interest in it went through three distinct phases (Neill, 1987). The first was an interest in LSD's potential use for revealing the biochemical basis of psychosis, a phase that began to wane in the mid-1950s—primarily because it was determined that its effects did not mimic the symptoms of any natural psychosis. The second phase began in 1953 when it was proposed to be a potentially useful adjunct to various psychotherapeutic techniques, principally Freudian and Jungian psychoanalysis. Therapists, who often took LSD themselves so that they could better understand the therapeutic process in their clients, felt the drug could facilitate regression to obtain early childhood memories, shorten therapy, and, in particular, open up heretofore difficult patients, such as obsessive–compulsives (who curiously turned out to be very resistant to LSD's effects [Grof, 1980]). LSD was also used to treat other disorders, such as alcoholism, drug addiction, and the emotional distress and physical pain of terminally ill patients. For example, in the 1960s one study of over 100 alcoholics found that half of the high-dose LSD treatment participants reported abstinence 6 months after treatment, in comparison to one-third of those in a low-dose LSD group and only 12 percent in a conventionally treated group. Other research in the 1960s indicated that a majority of cancer patients suffering from anxiety, depression, and uncontrollable pain showed improvement in their physical and emotional status after LSD treatment. The researchers also observed that many of these LSD-treated patients reported that their desire for addictive pain medicines, such as morphine, diminished or vanished, along with the pain. In fact, at that time the National Institute of Mental Health recognized that the use of LSD in these types of patients was legitimate.

This LSD therapy phase began to wane in the mid-1960s for two primary reasons. First, the psychiatric community was unable to decide how LSD should be used in the therapeutic process or to document its efficacy scientifically. Second, by the mid-1960s, nonmedical use of LSD, especially by young people comprising a counterculture that was opposed to traditional values ("hippies"), led to the belief that LSD had become a public health problem. As a result the U.S. government passed a law that banned the use and sale of LSD, as well as peyote, mescaline, and several similar drugs, by the public. At that point, legitimate research on its effects on humans and on its potential therapeutic uses declined precipitously—not only because of the legal difficulties and maze of bureaucratic procedures required, but also because psychedelic research with humans was not viewed as reputable by the vast majority of those in the scientific community.

In this third phase, LSD and similar drugs became just another class of abusable drugs that mainstream culture attempted to suppress. Psychedelic drug therapy still goes on unofficially—practitioners would not continue using it under difficult conditions unless they believed that they were accomplishing something. Whether it will ever return to mainstream use remains to be seen. However, in the 1990s the FDA has sought ways to allow human studies to test LSD and other Schedule I psychedelic drugs to assess their potential medical usefulness and has granted IND status to several psychedelic drugs (Kurtzweil, 1995). (The IND status means that the drugs have been studied in the laboratory for their major physical and chemical properties and tested in laboratory animals for their pharmacological and toxic effects.) The National Institute on Drug Abuse funds some of these studies. It is still difficult for researchers to conduct human research with psychedelic drugs, but at least this type of research has returned to some degree of respectability.

Pharmacodynamics of LSD and Related Compounds

LSD is absorbed within 30 to 60 minutes after oral administration, and its high lipid–solubility allows it to rapidly penetrate the blood–brain barrier and stay in the body for up to 15 hours. The potency of LSD is even more emphasized by the fact that there is general distribution of the drug throughout the body, with relatively low levels found in the brain, where there is widespread regional distribution of LSD binding sites (Freedman & Halaris, 1978). Thus, its mechanism and precise sites of action are difficult to determine because of the very small doses needed to induce its effects. Despite its potency with respect to perceptual, emotional, and cognitive alterations, there is only a single documented case of fatal poisoning by LSD in the literature (Fysh et al., 1985).

The mechanism through which LSD and other monoamine P/P/Hs induce their subjective effects is unknown but is most likely linked to serotonergic systems in the brain. Because of structural similarities between the LSD and 5-HT molecule and because LSD causes a cessation of spontaneous firing of serotonergic neurons of the reticular activating system, it was initially proposed that LSD acted as a presynaptic agonist on these neurons (Rech & Rosecrans, 1982). This hypothesis fit nicely with the observation that during normal REM sleep, when dreams are most vivid, these neurons also cease firing. Thus, LSD could be viewed as inducing the intense emotions and vivid imagery of the dream state while the person was awake (Jacobs, 1976).

However, several subsequent lines of evidence were incompatible with this theory—the most important being that tolerance to its psychotomimetic effects occurred with chronic LSD exposure, but tolerance to its inhibitory actions on serotonergic neuron firing did not. These phenomena led to the theory that LSD and other P/P/Hs with its subjective effects acted as agonists postsynaptically—specifically via postsynaptic 5-HT_2 receptors (Jacobs, 1987). This theory was supported by two major observations. First, the affinity of LSD-like P/P/Hs for 5-HT_2 receptors correlated highly with their potencies for causing hallucinations in humans. Second, 5-HT_2 antagonists were found to block the discriminative cue properties of LSD-like P/P/Hs in animals (Cunningham & Appel, 1987). But, again, subsequent research failed to support the theory—the most notable observation being that some highly specific 5-HT_2 antagonists did not block the discriminative cue properties of LSD (Pierce & Peroutka, 1990).

The most recent research on this issue still points to alterations in serotonergic functions, but the picture is much more complicated than previous theories assumed. By 1990, it was apparent that (1) LSD-like P/P/Hs bind to a variety of 5-HT receptors; (2) the hallucinogenic potencies of LSD-like P/P/Hs correlate well with their binding affinity at many of these receptors; (3) some of these 5-HT receptors are autoreceptors and some are postsynaptic receptors; and (4) depending on the type of receptor, LSD-like P/P/Hs may act as agonists, partial agonists, or antagonists (Frazer et al., 1990; Pierce & Peroutka, 1990; Sanders-Bush & Breeding, 1991).

By the mid-1990s, with further refinement in subcategorizing 5-HT receptors, research findings suggested that the 5-HT_{1A}, 5-HT_{2A}, and 5-HT_{2C} receptor subtypes, for which LSD is an agonist, were the major receptors responsible for the stimulus effects of monoamine-related hallucinogens—at least in nonhumans (Fiorella et al., 1995; Krebs & Geyer, 1994; Penington & Fox, 1994). Unfortunately, we have not narrowed down their location and function to the point at which we can conclusively determine the primary mechanisms through which these drugs act to induce the complete hallucinogenic experience.

As the foregoing discussion should indicate, LSD-like drugs would be expected to exert a mixture of excitatory and inhibitory actions on serotonergic functioning. For example, inhibition of 5-HT release by somatodendritic 5-HT_{1A} receptor activation could reduce competition between 5-HT and LSD-like drugs for agonistic activity at postsynaptic 5-HT_{2A} and 5-HT_{2C} receptors—thus altering the mixture of intrinsic activity at these receptors. However, even if alterations in serotonergic systems were solely responsible for the psychological effects these drugs produce, it is not at all clear how the combination of actions is related to the effects.

In addition to altering serotonergic function directly, monoamine-related P/P/Hs also affect noradrenergic and dopaminergic function, blocking reuptake (Nichols, 1986) in several areas of the brain. One area of the reticular activating system that has been shown to be affected similarly by many monoamine-related P/P/Hs is the *locus coeruleus,* a noradrenergic system that distributes axon terminals directly to wide regions and most layers of the cerebral cortex, as well as to the cerebellar cortex (Rasmussen & Aghajanian, 1986). This nucleus has been implicated in modulating global brain functions such as emotion and vigilance. Both LSD and mescaline have been shown to depress the spontaneous activity of locus coeruleus neurons while simultaneously facilitating the activation of the locus coeruleus by external stimuli. These actions are most likely mediated by 5-HT_2 receptors located outside the locus coeruleus itself (Rasmussen & Aghajanian, 1986). Although it is tempting to speculate that these actions of monoamine-related P/P/Hs on the locus coeruleus may be important for their perceptual and emotional effects (such as enhancing the organism's responsiveness to both externally and internally produced stimuli), their general behavioral relevance remains to be established. From the preceding discussion, it is clear that much work remains to be done before we can gain an understanding of the mechanisms involved in P/P/H drug effects.

Psychological Effects of Monoamine P/P/Hs

The psychological effects of LSD and other P/P/Hs are very difficult to describe because they are almost entirely subjective and depend on self-reports (Strassman et al., 1994). Furthermore, the effects are very dependent on the context and on the expectations of the person. The person may express deep religious feelings one moment, sexual feelings another, and extreme sadness, anxiety, and paranoia at another. Bizarre thoughts and feelings may represent a major break with reality and may lead the person to believe that he or she can fly, stop automobiles by stepping in front of them, or perform some other amazing feat. Occasionally, these feelings can lead to self-destructive behavior, such as attempting suicide or jumping out of windows.

In many instances, users report that they develop insights that never occurred to them before or that they see things regarding themselves or others that they have never seen before—much like looking into a mirror that strips away all preconceived notions about how they look, who they are, and the meaning of their existence. In some cases, this transcendental experience can leave them feeling quite at peace with themselves and their world; in others, it can be very disturbing.

Perceptual alterations are usually visual, auditory, or tactile and may involve extreme distortions of the physical environment or, with higher doses, actual hallucinations. With the eyes closed, the person experiences a virtual kaleidoscope of changing patterns and intense colors. Synesthesia, the transposition of sensations such as sounds into visual images, may occur. In a recent study with humans administered DMT, many subjects remarked on the strong degree of similarity between their dreams and their subjective experiences following the higher doses of DMT (Strassman et al., 1994). As one of the participants commented, "This was a dream, not a hallucination. Dreams have story lines as I experienced today; hallucinations do not."

Dysphoric reactions, often referred to as bad trips, generally occur if users take a larger than usual dose of these substances and suddenly get the feeling that they are completely losing control over the experience and that they may never return to normal. People and objects in the environment, as well as the person's own body image, may become so distorted that they are grotesque and threatening. Anxiety, panic, and paranoia (the belief that people are out to get you) are very common. Although these feelings may lead to assaultive behavior, the person is generally so paralyzed with fear that this is unlikely.

Although these acute effects dissipate rapidly (within 6 to 12 hours after ingesting LSD), a very small minority of individuals continue to experience psychotic-like effects, such as mental confusion, perceptual distortions, and poor concentration beyond this time—in some cases for days or weeks (Abraham & Aldridge, 1993). In very rare cases, individuals have complained about mental and emotional disturbances several years after being exposed to LSD. The incidence of prolonged psychosis (that is, lasting more than 48 hours) following LSD in research or clinical settings falls in the range of 0.08 percent to 4.6 percent, with the lower estimates derived from experimental subjects and the higher estimates derived from clinical populations (Abraham & Aldridge, 1993).

Incidentally, several individuals have tried to sue the U.S. government because of mental or emotional problems they allegedly suffered from involuntarily being administered LSD in experimental projects funded by or carried out by governmental agencies between 1953 and 1973. Although governmental officials have generally conceded that these projects were unethical, because of complicated circumstances these suits have not been successful. In one case—*U.S. v. Stanley*, 107 S. Ct. 3054 [1987]—the Supreme Court held that a former Army serviceman who was secretly administered LSD four times as part of an Army experiment could not seek redress through a suit for violations of his constitutional rights on the ground that the suit was barred by a doctrine that precludes governmental liability for injuries to servicemen resulting from activity incident to service. In another suit—*Orlikow v. U.S.,* 682 F. Supp. 77 [D.D.C. 1988]—nine individuals claimed that they suffered mental or emotional problems resulting from their psychiatric treatment in a CIA-subsidized experimental program that included being administered LSD without their knowledge. The case dragged through the courts for a number of years until an out of court settlement was reached in October 1988.

One of the key questions is whether the occasional prolonged psychotic-like reaction to LSD-like P/P/Hs constitutes a distinct syndrome or is a nonspecific reaction in personalities vulnerable to stress. Although this issue has not been resolved, most of the findings support the position that it is a drug-induced schizophrenia-like reaction in persons vulnerable to both substance abuse and psychosis (Vardy & Kay, 1983).

Antipsychotic drugs like chlorpromazine and haloperidol are effective in blocking most of the effects of LSD-like P/P/Hs, but these treatments are generally not needed in cases of dysphoric reactions. Furthermore, antipsychotics may intensify the experience if the LSD-like drug has been adulterated with another type of P/P/H (for example, PCP, scopolamine). In most cases, placing the person in a quiet environment and talking him or her "down"—that is, talking to the person and offering continual reassurances that the effects will dissipate soon—are sufficient to calm the person (Jaffe, 1985). However, in cases in which this process is difficult to accomplish—for instance, in the emergency room—administering a benzodiazepine has been shown to induce rapid and effective relief from LSD toxicity (Abraham & Aldridge, 1993).

In a recent review of studies in which neuropsychological tests were administered to users of LSD or other hallucinogens to assess whether there was evidence of residual toxicity, it was concluded that there are few, if any, long-term neuropsychological deficits attributable to hallucinogen use (Halpern & Pope, 1999). Unfortunately, all of the studies had methodological problems that limit interpretation of the findings; for example, most studies failed to control for premorbid attributes of the hallucinogen users versus controls, and virtually all failed to control for the subjects' use of other illicit drugs and alcohol. However, there is considerable evidence for neurotoxicity associated with the chronic use of the mildly hallucinogenic MDMA, which will be discussed shortly.

Some users of LSD (and other P/P/Hs) may experience what they report as brief episodes similar to the LSD-induced state—commonly termed **flashbacks**—several weeks or months after they have ingested LSD. These are often, but not always, in the form of altered visual perceptions: geometric pseudohallucinations (patterns or figures that are clearly recognized by the observer as not being real), illusionary movements in the peripheral visual field, images that trail moving objects, flashes of color, intensified color for brief periods of time, and prolonged afterimages. Emergence into a dark environment is one of the most common precipitants of the disturbances (Abraham, 1983). Flashbacks may be very upsetting to some individuals, or they may be viewed as novel, curious phenomena by others. In cases in which the flashback experience is disturbing and long lasting, the diagnosis of *posthallucinogen perceptual disorder* may be made.

Explanations for these phenomena are hard to come by because of confounding factors in the individuals who experience them (for example, multiple drug use or the presence of eccentric personality characteristics). Also, there is no way of determining when they might occur or of experimentally validating them. A pharmacological mechanism is an exceedingly remote possibility; these drugs simply do not stay in the body long enough (Cohen, 1981). Furthermore, the tendency to experience LSD flashbacks does not appear to be related to the time since the drug was last used, nor is there a clear relationship between the percentage of users who experience flashbacks and the number of times they have used LSD (Abraham, 1983). As noted previously, since the incidence of psychotic episodes (schizophrenia type) in the general population is not uncommon (approximately 1 percent to 2 percent), it is possible that the prolonged reactions to LSD occur in those individuals predisposed to psychosis and that the intense psychological disturbances of the LSD state then trigger the endogenous psychosis-like symptoms.

It has been suggested that flashbacks represent some type of learning phenomenon that occurs in predisposed individuals during acute stress (Cohen, 1981). Studies of individuals who have experienced flashbacks suggest that these individuals had strong tendencies to fantasize and were highly suggestible prior to their LSD use (Silling, 1980). Therefore, it is possible that after an LSD experience they may encounter a situation that reminds them of the experience (for example, a stressful situation that induces sympathetic arousal) and elicits a small conditioned response that they are able to elaborate on and interpret as a druglike experience. Others have hypothesized that some flashbacks represent episodes of visual seizures (Abraham, 1983). This theory would be consistent with reports that anti-psychotics, which may reduce the seizure threshold (see Chapter 12), may actually enhance flashback episodes in some individuals.

Ever since the effects of LSD were first expressed, there has been much speculation about the similarity between these effects and those that occur during endogenous psychoses like schizophrenia. A number of authors have noted that there is a considerable difference between the two conditions (Jacobsen, 1968). With LSD, the hallucinations are mostly visual, generally consist of extreme distortions of the existing environment, and are viewed predominantly as pleasant or neutral in content. The LSD-induced psychotic state is highly responsive to suggestions from others. Finally, persons under the influence of LSD tend to be greatly concerned about their interpersonal relations. With schizophrenia, the hallucinations are almost entirely auditory, are generally superimposed on the environment, and are almost universally viewed as threatening and unpleasant. Schizophrenics are exceedingly resistant to suggestion (which makes psychotherapy difficult), and there is an almost total lack of concern over interpersonal relations. Finally, reports from schizophrenics in remission who have taken LSD indicate that they can distinguish between the two kinds of psychotic states.

Although the preceding accounts of both LSD and schizophrenia are highly simplified, they do suggest that different mechanisms are involved in the two conditions. However, it is important to point out that to some extent we may be comparing apples with oranges; with LSD, the psychosis is generally known by the person to be drug-induced and is short-lived, whereas, with schizophrenia, the psychotic episodes have no explainable cause and may be chronic or recurrent. These factors may contribute to some of the differences between the two kinds of psychoses. For example, if one's ability to communicate effectively with others is severely disrupted for a length of time, one might very well withdraw from contact with others and avoid any attempt to have normal interpersonal relations.

MDMA ("Ecstasy")

The latest controversy over monoamine-related P/P/Hs is centered on a chemical relative of methamphetamine known as "ecstasy" or MDMA (3,4-methylenedioxymethamphet-amine). It is commonly referred to as a designer drug, but it was synthesized by a legitimate pharmaceutical company long before the concept of designer drugs came into being. It has been suggested that MDMA possesses both amphetamine-like and LSD-like effects, although it is relatively free of the hallucinations produced by the LSD-related compounds (Greer & Tolbert, 1986; Nichols, 1986). Users claim that it leaves them feeling more empathetic, insightful, and aware. Some psychotherapists who have used MDMA in their practice claim that it is useful in facilitating more direct communication between people involved in a significant emotional relationship. Others claim that it induces a state of reduced anxiety and lowered defensiveness, which makes it attractive to therapists wishing to speed up the therapeutic process (Greer & Tolbert, 1986).

A more recently reported use pattern for MDMA has been in the context of large, organized social settings known as "raves," which are typically held in large warehouses or dance halls and involve all-night dancing to high-tech music, computer-generated video, and laser light shows (Steele et al., 1994). Party goers, who may number in the thousands, typically use MDMA and often drink beverages with amino acids (so-called smart drugs) added to them (perhaps they think this will prevent the neurotoxicity that has been associated with MDMA).

MDMA is a derivative of MDA (a P/P/H of the 1960s that had a reputation as a "love drug"), and the effects of the two are quite similar. MDMA was originally synthesized more than 70 years ago, but until recently it received very little attention. Neuroscientists are just beginning to explore its potential mechanisms of action and its behavioral effects. As is the case with other monoamine P/P/Hs, serotonin seems to be heavily involved in the effects of both MDMA and MDA. However, rather than reducing serotonin release, as is the case with LSD, both have been found to be potent serotonin-releasing agents (Steele et al., 1994). As is the case with amphetamine, MDMA and MDA have some dopamine-releasing action. Studies with MDMA and animals have shown that following the serotonin-releasing action there is an acute depletion of cortical serotonin between 3 and 6 hours after administration, with recovery of normal serotonin levels within 24 hours. However, a second phase of depletion may occur several days later, which is suggestive of a neurotoxic reaction (Schmidt, 1987). Apparently, both the *d* and *l* isomers are involved in the first phase, whereas only the *d* isomer (or one of its metabolites) is involved in the second phase.

Because low doses appear to produce experiences characterized by consciousness-altering effects unaccompanied by intense hallucinations, users have often argued that MDMA is a unique drug that is distinctively different from mescaline and LSD. Tests with animals, using the drug discrimination procedure, support these assertions. MDA, but not MDMA, has been found to induce LSD-like stimulus properties, whereas MDMA has been found to induce amphetamine-like stimulus properties (Steele et al., 1994).

With higher doses, the perceptual effects of MDMA intoxication are typical of those induced by the classic monoamine-type P/P/Hs (Siegel, 1986). Users commonly report an orderly progression of visual imagery from simple geometric forms to complex scenes, a characteristic of these and other P/P/Hs. Auditory and body-image changes are also reported frequently.

As with other P/P/H drugs, MDMA intoxication is neither uniformly predictable nor uniformly controllable. Most users view the MDMA experience as positive and pleasant. The most common subjective positive effects include, in declining order of incidence, changes in feelings and emotions; enhanced communication, empathy, and understanding; cognitive insight or mental association changes; euphoria; perceptual distortions or hallucinations; and transcendental or religious experiences. Common negative effects are mostly of physiological origin and include, in declining order of incidence, elevation of blood pressure and pulse; muscle tension and jaw clenching; fatigue; insomnia; sweating; blurred vision; loss of motor coordination; and anxiety (Siegel, 1986).

The pattern of MDMA use is also typical of other P/P/H use, in that it is primarily social and experimental. Adverse reactions depend on the set and setting of the user or occur when higher than usual doses are taken. Most users adopt patterns of use and take doses that generally do not lead to dependence or significant psychopathology, although use of high doses can lead to prolonged physical and psychological reactions, such as anxiety. It does not appear that MDMA is conducive to regular and frequent use because tolerance is commonly reported to develop to the positive effects of MDMA, while negative effects increase with use (Solowij et al., 1992). As is the case with other P/P/Hs, MDMA may predispose people to a recurrence of previous psychological disturbance (Steele et al., 1994).

Numerous studies with a variety of animal species have indicated that even short-term exposure to doses of MDMA that closely approximate those used by humans can cause long-lasting, possibly irreversible, neurotoxic effects on serotonergic systems of the brain, particularly with respect to 5-HT axons (Steele et al., 1994). In agreement with these findings, many adverse neuropsychiatric consequences suggestive of serotonergic dysfunction have been noted in human MDMA users. Shortly after MDMA exposure, users may feel more depressed, abnormal, unsociable, unpleasant, and ill-tempered than control subjects. Long-lasting (up to 12 months following abstinence) adverse effects of recreational MDMA exposure in humans consistent with serotonergic dysfunction have been found with respect to sleep, memory, neuroendocrine function, impulsivity, and other dimensions of personality (Allen et al., 1993; Bolla et al., 1998; Gerra et al., 2000; Gouzoulis-Mayfrank et al., 2000; McCann et al., 1994, 1998; Morgan, 1999; Parrott, 2000). However, these findings cannot rule out the possibility that these dysfunctional characteristics may have existed prior to the users' exposure to MDMA.

Also, MDMA's potential dependence liability was revealed by studies showing that animals will self-administer MDMA by way of the catheter method (not true with the LSD-type P/P/Hs) (Lamb & Griffiths, 1987). These findings led to the DEA's classification of MDMA as a Schedule I drug. Interestingly, several psychiatrists contested this classification in court, saying that they should be allowed to explore the use of mind-altering drugs in psychotherapy, and the DEA was forced to remove the Schedule I classification. Six months later, the DEA reclassified MDMA as a Schedule I compound on the basis that it had no proven medical value, although the FDA has given approval for limited human MDMA studies to go forward (Steele et al., 1994).

Cannabinoids

The leaves and buds of the *Cannabis sativa* plant have been used as an intoxicant and as a medicinal herb for centuries, perhaps as far back as 2737 B.C. Only for the last 100 years or so have the recreational uses of this plant been emphasized. Its medicinal use gradually declined, partially because other drugs for which it was used came into being, with more selective action, and partially because the shelf-life of the active ingredients was short.

About the same time, its recreational use began to increase gradually. Perhaps reflecting this shift in use, the term *marijuana* (also spelled "marihuana") was coined after the Mexican-Spanish word *mariguana,* which means "intoxicant."

Because its use changed from a medicinal one to a recreational one, certain public officials, particularly a zealous commissioner of the Federal Bureau of Narcotics by the name of Harry Anslinger, became concerned about its use (Carroll, 1991). In the 1930s, Anslinger and other officials began to circulate stories about marijuana causing permanent brain damage and insanity, enhancing criminal and aggressive tendencies, and inducing sexual perversion. (These effects were duly noted in a 1936 film called "Reefer Madness," a completely serious movie that became a cult movie in the 1970s, when it came to be viewed by the audience as outrageously humorous. Despite depicting all the hazards of marijuana that Anslinger attributed to it, he did not like the film because he believed that just seeing drugs being used could provoke people to use them.) In reaction to these allegations, Congress enacted the Marijuana Tax Act of 1937, which made possession of marijuana without having paid a special tax on it a federal crime. (The "catch-22" was that one had to be in possession of the marijuana before one could obtain the tax stamp for it, and possession of marijuana without the stamp was illegal. Needless to say, nobody ever applied for the tax stamp, nor did the federal government ever grant one.)

A number of people were still skeptical of the potential damaging effects of marijuana. One of these was New York City's Mayor Fiorello La Guardia. In the early 1940s, he set up a special commission of experts to determine the actual consequences of marijuana use on people. The final report of La Guardia's panel suggested that marijuana was a fairly mild intoxicant with few side effects, even when used to excess. The panel's findings essentially concurred with those noted in the 1890s by the Indian Hemp Commission. Despite the findings of these presumably objective and unbiased observers, the report had little impact on the opinions of the majority of people in the United States. In most cases the report was ridiculed and criticized for its lack of rigor and its methodology—particularly by Anslinger, who effectively undermined the results of the report well before its publication (Brecher, 1972; Carroll, 1991).

In the 1950s the beliefs about marijuana's effects changed somewhat. Its use supposedly resulted in a strong psychological dependence, led users to escalate their use to more potent and dangerous drugs (such as the dreaded heroin), induced a so-called *amotivational syndrome,* and was a cause of permanent brain damage. A plethora of empirical research on the effects of marijuana in the late 1960s and early 1970s dispelled some of these beliefs but led to speculation over some new, potentially detrimental effects (Harris, 1978; Hollister, 1986). There was a report that substantiated the view that irreversible brain damage was associated with its use—a report that was quickly and severely criticized for its methodological deficiencies. Other researchers suggested that heavy marijuana use was the cause of severe personality changes. The amotivational syndrome was still being discussed. However, contrary to the notions that marijuana caused one to become a sex maniac, studies suggested that marijuana might actually cause sexual impotence and sterility in males due to reductions in the male sex hormone testosterone. Chromosomal aberrations, decreases in certain kinds of white blood cells and immunity, and alterations in DNA potentially leading to cancer were suggested by studies to be associated with cannabis use. The reliability and potential ramifications of these findings are still being debated.

Marijuana is not a drug itself; the word actually refers to the plant material, which contains over 400 different chemicals, more than 60 of which are specific to cannabis. These chemicals are referred to as *cannabinoids*. Most of these are probably not psychoactive even in high doses (Dewey, 1986; Hollister, 1986). The molecular structures of cannabinoids, which have no nitrogen atom and are not alkaloids, are very different from those of other classes of P/P/Hs. It appears that cannabinoids possess complex and particularly unique properties, even though they induce effects similar to numerous other drugs.

The major psychoactive chemical in marijuana is delta-9-tetrahydrocannabinol, or THC for short. (Due to differences in numbering systems in describing chemical structures, the molecule may also be referred to as delta-1-THC.) Two other cannabinoids, cannabinol and cannabidiol, may be active at high doses. Although these two drugs may have minimal effects in the amounts found in street marijuana, research has indicated that they interact with THC to modify its effects (Karniol & Carlini, 1972). This finding is consistent with the common belief that varieties of marijuana grown in different localities have different effects not wholly related to their THC content.

While numerous "authorities" have claimed that the potency of marijuana (technically, the concentration of THC in the plant material) has increased dramatically since the early 1970s, with the implication that it presents greater hazards now than then, this claim is not only inaccurate but probably irrelevant (Mikuriya & Aldrich, 1988). First, there is much published evidence about the availability of highly potent varieties of cannabis from the nineteenth century through the present day. Second, the sampling techniques used for testing have been so inconsistent over these years that direct comparisons are virtually worthless (e.g., marijuana confiscated by the DEA may sit on the shelf for variable periods of time while the THC degrades, whereas street samples submitted to laboratories for analysis may be due to the voluntary samples being submitted precisely because of their extraordinary potency). Third, an important consideration in regard to the potency issue is *autotitration*, the adjustment of dose by the individual user to obtain optimal effects and avoid unpleasant ones. Smoking marijuana, the customary practice in present social use of the drug, gives the user rapid feedback with regard to levels of effect, because the drug goes directly to the brain from the lungs, unimpeded by the gut or the liver, and whatever the potency of the drug used, individuals tend to smoke only the amount necessary to achieve the desired effect.

Psychological Effects of Marijuana

Interpreting the effects of marijuana on behavioral variables is complicated by the fact that set and setting variables—for example, context, the user's personality, previous marijuana experiences, and expectations—have been shown to play a critical role in changes in mood and behavior that occur following marijuana use (Ferraro, 1980), and may even influence the rate of THC metabolism (Cami et al., 1991). Thus, all the effects noted in this discussion of marijuana are likely to be due to the interaction between these factors and the actions of the drug on the nervous system.

The acute effects of marijuana (that is, being "stoned") generally consist of an increasingly dose-dependent impairment of memory and cognitive functions, such as attending, speaking, problem solving, and concept formation (Azorlosa et al., 1992; Dewey, 1986; Ferraro, 1980). The person's speech is fragmented, suggestive of disjointed thought patterns, and the speaker often forgets what (s)he or others have recently said. Ideas extraneous to the focus of an individual's attention appear to enter consciousness, producing a loosening of associations. Phenomena that are not usually associated with each other in normal waking life tend to appear connected under the influence of marijuana, and phenomena or ideas that are commonly associated in normal waking life may seem irrelevant or unconnected. Sometimes the person under the influence of marijuana gains insights of great importance. Unfortunately, while under the influence, the person's ability to reflect on or analyze the quality of these insights is greatly impaired, and when the intoxication phase is over, the great insights often turn out to be mundane or unworkable ideas.

A multitude of studies using a wide variety of cognitive tasks strongly suggest that many of the cognitive deficits produced by marijuana can be attributed to alterations in memory functions (Hooker & Jones, 1987). There is a great deal of variability in the degree to which marijuana disrupts cognitive functions, some of which is dependent upon differences in the drug dose used and the specific task (Azorlosa et al., 1992). It is also well established that the level of motivation to perform well may affect the degree to which marijuana impairs performance (Cami et al., 1991). Cognitive and behavioral tolerance to marijuana's effects can also occur, such that cognitive deficits noted in infrequent users may not be observed in individuals who use it frequently.

One of the primary effects of marijuana is interference with short-term memory (the ability to maintain access to newly acquired information for several seconds or minutes). This is found to occur with both verbal and graphic material. Marijuana also disrupts long-term memory retrieval (the ability to gain access to information acquired several hours, or longer, prior to marijuana intoxication). This effect is more predominant with recall (the ability to reproduce the previously learned material) than with recognition (the ability to choose from a number of items which of those the person has previously learned). Much of the memory disruption appears to be due to increased imagery and thought flow coming out of the intrusion of irrelevant associations (Hooker & Jones, 1987). However, there is little evidence that, once the person returns from the intoxicated state, retrieval of information learned prior to the intoxicated state is affected.

There is also evidence for weak state-dependent retrieval effects with marijuana, in which information acquired under the influence of marijuana is retrieved better under marijuana than under nondrug conditions. But these effects are more likely to occur under recall conditions that provide minimal external cues to the person (Eich et al., 1975).

Although there are no studies directly assessing the effects of marijuana on classroom learning experiences, the similarity between the types of activities relevant to such settings and those observed in the laboratory is so close as to strongly suggest that marijuana interferes with classroom functioning and knowledge acquisition. This is an important factor considering the extent of marijuana use among high school students today.

The detrimental effects of marijuana on complex psychomotor skills in the laboratory have also been observed in real-life situations of driving and flying (Hollister, 1986). While marijuana may be less detrimental to driving performance than alcohol is, it nevertheless is a potential causal factor in accidents that occur while driving or engaging in similar activities. Some of the detrimental effects on performance may persist for some time, possibly up to 24 hours, beyond the period of subjective intoxication (Pope et al., 1995; Pope &

Yurgelun-Todd, 1996). One factor that contributes to alcohol's detrimental effects on driving is its tendency to provoke risk taking, whereas in simulated and actual driving tests, marijuana typically makes drivers more cautious, and drivers under the influence of marijuana consciously attempt to compensate for its detrimental effects (Zimmer & Morgan, 1997).

Psychoactive cannabinoids have a sedative-like action in most people, as opposed to the sympathomimetic-like effects of the monoamine-related compounds. There is no cross-tolerance between these two classes, and the monoamine-related compounds are more potent in their perceptual and hallucinatory actions (Jaffe, 1985). While many people find the marijuana experience pleasurable, others do not. Those who do experience pleasurable effects may find them to wax and wane during the period of intoxication, and in some cases they may develop a dysphoric reaction. This generally occurs if the person ingests an amount that is considerably higher than he or she is used to. Such cases are more common with oral administration, because the absorption of THC from the G.I. tract is considerably slower than absorption through smoking, and because the person has difficulty in regulating the amount of marijuana ingested.

Other effects of marijuana that may be viewed positively by the user are its effects on appetite (Foltin et al., 1986) and sexual experiences, although these appear to be heavily dependent on cultural expectations (Meyer, 1978). For example, North Americans commonly report and, in some cases, exhibit increases in appetite (particularly sweets) and weight gain (Foltin et al., 1986). They also report that they experience enhanced sexual stimulation under the influence of marijuana (Meyer, 1978). In other countries, cannabis is used as a sexual depressant (in India, for example) or to suppress feelings of hunger (in Jamaica). While acute use of marijuana in low doses may enhance the sexual experience, high doses or prolonged use may lead to a depression of sexual desire and even impotence (Hollister, 1986).

Numerous studies indicate that cannabinoid agonists exert a profound decrease in the reaction of animals to painful stimuli (Ameri, 1999). These findings suggest that cannabinoid systems are involved in pain perception and that cannabinoids may be therapeutically useful as analgesics. However, studies with humans administered THC and other cannabinoid agonists have not found them to be particularly effective analgesics, and doses that do induce analgesia also produce a number of side effects, such as blurred vision, drowsiness, and mental clouding (Greenwald & Stitzer, 2000; Holdcroft et al., 1997; Jain et al., 1981; Jochimsen et al., 1978; Martin & Lichtman, 1998; Noyes et al., 1975). Selective mu opiate antagonists typically do not block the analgesic effects of cannabinoid agonists in either animals or humans (Ameri, 1999; Greenwald & Stitzer, 2000; Hamann & DiVadi, 1999), which is consistent with evidence that while the analgesic effects of cannabinoids and opiates may involve similar brain-stem circuitry, they are mediated by different receptor mechanisms (Meng et al., 1998).

What makes the marijuana experience rewarding? We really do not know. The ability of THC to enhance the release of dopamine in reward-relevant areas of the brain (discussed shortly) may be one factor. The transient cognitive and memory disruptions associated with marijuana may account for its popularity in some, but by no means all, humans (Feeney, 1976). That is, the new and unrelated intrusions into thought, the loosening of traditional or learned associations among stimuli and responses, the encoding of new information subject to associative links that normally would be inhibited, the ambiguity and variability in the perceptual experience, and so forth, result in novel experiences, feelings of creativity, and insightfulness (Feeney, 1976; Hooker & Jones, 1987). Those individuals who are not particularly anxious about the unfamiliar or the unconventional or about loss of control and the unpredictability of their world may find such effects pleasurable, as long as they can retain control over the time and degree of these effects. Those who are anxious about these may find such effects unpleasurable. Other drugs described in this chapter may have similar qualities, but marijuana's effects are relatively short-lasting and are easier to control, tolerance to them develops relatively slowly, and the immediate side effects associated with marijuana are less troublesome.

Cannabinoid Pharmacokinetics

Marijuana is most commonly administered by smoking a "joint" (an average joint contains approximately 10 to 20 milligrams of THC). However, most cannabinoids are highly lipid-soluble and are also readily absorbed orally (Agurell et al., 1986). Because of stomach acid degradation, enzyme alterations, and slow absorption, oral THC is about one-third as potent as THC that is smoked. Since, at most, only half of the original THC in the smoked cannabis is actually delivered and absorbed, inhalation may be five to 10 times as effective a mode of administration. However, if one takes sufficient amounts of THC orally in order to achieve the same peak intensity effects of smoked THC, because of the slower accumulation of the drug in the blood the effects last considerably longer than when the THC is smoked.

Initial metabolism of cannabinoids in marijuana smoke occurs in the lungs, whereas orally administered cannabinoids are metabolized in the G.I. tract and by the liver. There are more than 30 metabolites of THC, and over 20 each of cannabinol and cannabidiol. Many of these metabolites are also psychoactive. One of the principal psychoactive metabolites of THC is 11-hydroxy-delta-9-THC, which crosses the blood–brain barrier more readily than THC, and therefore may be more active than THC. However, because of the multitude of biotransformation pathways and metabolites and the complex interaction of the cannabinoids, no practical method has been developed for determining levels of intoxication based on detectable cannabinoids and metabolites.

What is quite apparent about cannabinoids is that their extremely high lipid-solubility results in their persisting in the body for long periods of time. Studies have shown that after a single administration of THC, detectable levels of THC are found in the body for weeks or longer, depending on how much was administered and the sensitivity of the assessment method. A number of investigators have suggested that this is an important factor in marijuana's effects, perhaps because cannabinoids may accumulate in the body, particularly in the lipid membranes of neurons. However, it is most likely that the major site of accumulation is adipose tissue (comprising some 10 percent to 20 percent of the human body), which would mean that these drugs would have no significant psychological consequences (Hollister, 1986).

Pharmacodynamics of Delta-9-THC

Little is known about the mechanisms of action of THC at the neuronal level. Our lack of understanding of these mechanisms is certainly not due to lack of interest or too little research in the area; rather, it is due to some unique characteristics of THC (Martin, 1986). First, THC has such high lipid-solubility that it is absorbed in high concentrations in practically all tissues. Second, THC alters just about every biological system in which it is examined. Unfortunately, establishing the significance of these effects with respect to THC's psychoactive properties is difficult.

THC exerts nonspecific "fluidizing" effects on lipid membranes—similar to those of general anesthetics and alcohol, but not to the same degree (Martin, 1986). This fluidizing could partially explain why THC has sedative-like effects without having anesthetic properties, but evidence for this possibility is still weak. Until recently, evidence for specific receptors for THC was circumstantial. As would be expected for a specific receptor interaction, modest structural modifications of the THC molecule can result in profound changes in its behavioral effects. Also, there is a definite stereospecificity of the THC molecule, with the levo isomer being from six to 100 times more active than the dextro isomer, depending on the species and the behavioral tests used.

Although receptor binding studies, which are normally used to assess the presence of specific receptors for ligands, have been hampered by THC's extreme lipid-solubility and its large degree of nonspecific binding to membranes, researchers have now confirmed the existence of at least two types of cannabinoid receptors, CB1 and CB2, with the CB1 receptor found primarily in the brain as well as in some peripheral tissues, and the CB2 receptor found exclusively in peripheral tissues (Ameri, 1999). Cannabinoids appear to alter mood and cognition by binding to one of these receptors (a G–protein–coupled receptor) and inhibiting a secondary messenger system (adenylate cyclase) in a dose-dependent stereospecific manner. Several lines of evidence suggest that cannabinoid agonists act on presynaptic CB1 receptors to inhibit calcium flow into neurons, which then reduces the release of a variety of neurotransmitters (Ameri, 1999).

Cannabinoid receptors are widely distributed in the brain, but the pattern is uneven. The highest levels are found in the cerebral cortex, hippocampus, hypothalamus, and amygdala. These areas are critically important for higher mental processes, memory formation, primary drive regulation, and emotional expression—all of which are altered to some degree by cannabinoids. High cannabinoid receptor densities have also been observed in the basal ganglia and cerebellum of the rodent brain, consistent with the marked effects of cannabinoids on spontaneous locomotory activity in rodents. In contrast, there is a low abundance of cannabinoid receptors in the human cerebellum, which is in line with the absence of gross motor disturbances in humans who use marijuana (Ameri, 1999)

At least one type of endogenous ligand for cannabinoid receptors has been isolated from brain tissue (Howlett, 1995). Like THC, the ligand is fat-soluble, but it is a simpler molecule that is derived from arachidonic acid, a fatty acid common to cell membranes. The ligand, which appears to occur in slightly different forms, has been christened "anandamide," from a Sanskrit word meaning internal bliss. What functions the cannabinoid receptor and its ligand actually serve in the CNS have yet to be determined, but these discoveries are likely to infuse new energy into the search for drugs with the therapeutic effects of marijuana (discussed later) without causing intoxication. Furthermore, the recent development of a selective and orally active antagonist (SR141716A) of the brain cannabinoid receptor should prove to be a powerful tool for investigating the *in vivo* functions of the anandamide/cannabinoid system (Rinaldi-Carmona et al., 1994).

Depending on the concentration, THC has been shown to either enhance or inhibit release of various neurotransmitters (Campbell et al., 1986). Similarly, electrical recordings of CNS neuronal activity have suggested both excitatory and inhibitory effects of THC. Despite these inconsistencies, electrical recordings in the hippocampus of rats have been shown to change dramatically when behaviorally effective doses of THC are administered. Thus, it is probable that THC-mediated changes in hippocampal operations are partly responsible for the distortions in memory and cognitive performance that commonly occur during marijuana intoxication (Campbell et al., 1986).

These speculations are supported by findings that suggest that THC disrupts cholinergic functioning because the hippocampus contains high concentrations of cholinergic neurons (Miller & Branconnier, 1983). The effects of cannabinoids on memory processes are similar to those found following administration of anticholinergics (such as scopolamine) and those found in neurological patients suffering from deficits in hippocampal (limbic) cholinergic functioning. Physiologically, cannabinoids exhibit some similarities to anticholinergics, including dry mouth, increased heart rate, decreased sweating, and bronchodilation (one notable exception is that whereas cannabinoids decrease pressure within the eyeball, anticholinergics increase it). It does not appear that THC operates at postsynaptic cholinergic receptors, since drugs that normally reverse the effects of competitive acetylcholine antagonists (such as physostigmine, a drug that reduces the enzymatic breakdown of acetylcholine in the synapse) do not change the subjective effects of THC. However, because THC (but not the weakly psychoactive cannabidiol) decreases acetylcholine turnover in the hippocampus, one mode of action of THC may involve a selective reduction of acetylcholine synthesis or its release from axon terminals, perhaps by acting through presynaptic cholinergic mechanisms. It has been shown that both anandamide and cannabinoids enhance GABAergic transmission (Wickens & Pertwee, 1993), which could account for some of their sedative-like properties. Although opioid systems have been suggested to mediate or modulate some effects of THC in nonhumans, because they can be antagonized with opiate receptor antagonists, the opiate receptor antagonists naloxone and naltrexone have not been shown to block or attenuate the subjective, physiological, and behavioral effects of THC in humans (Greenwald & Stitzer, 2000; Hamann & DiVadi, 1999; Wachtel & de Wit, 2000).

There is now fairly good evidence that some of marijuana's rewarding effects may be mediated by the same brain reward system (discussed in Chapter 6) through which other recreational and abuse-prone drugs act (Gardner & Lowinson, 1991; Tanda et al., 1997). For example, THC has been found to enhance electrical brain stimulation reward and to enhance both basal and stimulated dopamine release in reward-relevant loci (e.g., the nucleus accumbens), in animals. However, in contrast to most drugs of abuse, until recently, attempts to get laboratory animals to self-administer THC were unsuccessful—except under unusual conditions. For example, two studies indicated that rats would self-administer THC, but only under conditions in which the rats were food-deprived and received noncontingent food delivery during the sessions (Takashi & Singer, 1979, 1980). The negative findings have led many to conclude that marijuana is somewhat unique among drugs that are commonly abused by humans. However, reliable self-administration of THC via the intravenous catheter method has now been demonstrated in squirrel monkeys (Tanda et al., 2000). That the effect was due to the THC was supported by the finding that self-administration ceased when the CB1 receptor antagonist SR141716A was administered prior to the test sessions. Previous attempts may have failed due to the use of too-high doses of THC (possibly in combination with an inappropriate vehicle—typically a fluid in which the drug is suspended or dissolved that doesn't have psychoactive properties itself). For humans, there is a range of doses of THC delivered by smoking that produces pleasurable effects; doses below this range are ineffective and doses above this range produce dysphoric effects. When the doses of THC delivered intravenously by the monkeys approximated the doses obtained by humans smoking a typical joint, they self-administered the THC. When they were higher than these doses, the animals did not. Thus, THC joins the list of drugs, such as cocaine, heroin, nicotine, and alcohol, that are self-administered by nonhumans and abused by humans.

Psychopathological Effects of Marijuana

The acute panic anxiety reaction, noted particularly when unexpectedly strong marijuana is used, is the most common adverse psychological effect. More serious cannabis-related psychoses and other intellectual deficiencies have been reported in countries in which cannabis use is extensive. (Some of the individuals diagnosed as having cannabis psychosis had used cannabis for 5 years or more in amounts up to several grams per day; Imade & Ebie, 1991.) However, such reactions do not appear common in North America (Hollister, 1986). Interestingly, in a study evaluating the effect of cannabis on positive and negative symptoms in schizophrenics (described in Chapter 12), it was observed that negative symptoms were lower in schizophrenic cannabis abusers than nonabusers, supporting a self-medication hypothesis of cannabis abuse (Peralta & Cuesta, 1992).

Most studies that have investigated the effects of prolonged and heavy use of cannabinoids have not shown any systematic long-lasting decrements in mental activities suggestive of impairments of brain or cerebral function and cognition (Pope et al., 1995). For example, in one study of long-term cannabis use in 10 subjects born, raised, and educated in the United States, no cognitive deficits could be determined in any of the subjects, most of whom had engaged in extremely heavy use for over 7 years (the subjects used a cannabis-tobacco mixture daily as a sacrament of communion in the context of their particular religion) (Schaeffer et al., 1981). In fact, the intellectual functioning among the adults tested was above average, and in two of the subjects where similar tests had been conducted 15 and 20 years previously, the I.Q. scores were virtually unchanged. It should be stressed that these adults were well educated prior to their cannabis use; did not use other psychoactive substances; observed a good diet, consisting of vegetables, fruit, and small amounts of meat; and adhered to a strict religious doctrine. Obviously, such individuals are not particularly representative of a very broad spectrum of people.

Several studies conducted in the 1970s in Jamaica, Greece, and Costa Rica did not find any notable cognitive or physical differences between heavy users of cannabis (who had smoked approximately 10 joints a day for several years) and suitably matched nonusers (Hollister, 1986). Follow-up studies conducted on similar samples in Costa Rica and India also found no significant differences between users and nonusers on most tests of a variety of intellectual functions (Page et al., 1988; Varma et al., 1988). These later studies did find that users evidenced small, but reliable, deficits in some perceptual-motor tasks and sustained-attention and short-term memory tests requiring considerable mental effort. More recent studies, which assessed brain wave patterns during a complex auditory selective-attention task, have indicated that some chronic marijuana users had more difficulty than nonusers in setting up an accurate focus of attention and in filtering out irrelevant information, even after cessation of their cannabis use for several months (Hall & Solowij, 1998). Unfortunately from a methodological standpoint, the users in some of these studies were only asked to abstain from cannabis use 12 to 24 hours prior to testing; considering the amount of cannabis normally consumed by many of the users in these studies, it is quite possible they were still somewhat "stoned" during these tests. And, of course, in none of these studies were there pre-cannabis use measures on these individuals to assure that these deficits were not present prior to their cannabis use—deficits that could potentially be related to their use of cannabis in the first place.

In summary, in assessing residual neuropsychological effects of marijuana use, one must first differentiate among those effects that are direct effects of the drug or those that are symptoms of actual psychiatric disorders that are caused or exacerbated by marijuana from those that are simply attributes of heavy marijuana users. Then one must determine whether the drug residue effects are short-lived, due to the persistence of cannabinoids in the body, or are long lasting, due to toxic effects on the CNS that persist even after all cannabinoids have been eliminated from the body following prolonged abstinence. The data support a residual effect of marijuana on attention, psychomotor tasks, and short-term memory during the 12- to 24-hour period immediately after use, but evidence for a more prolonged residual drug effect or a toxic effect on the CNS that persists even after cannabinoids have left the body is weak. Some electrophysiological and neuropsychological studies show that long-term cannabis use may produce subtle impairments in memory, attention, and the ability to organize and integrate complex information, with the degree of cognitive impairment becoming more pronounced the longer cannabis is used (Hall & Solowij, 1998). These impairments are so subtle that it remains unclear how important they are for everyday functioning and whether they are reversed after an extended period of abstinence. It is clear that the long-term heavy use of cannabis does not produce the severe or grossly debilitating impairment of memory, attention, and cognitive function that is found with chronic heavy alcohol use.

There are also data to suggest that the development or recurrence of acute psychosis in the context of marijuana use may be associated with a genetic predisposition to schizophrenia (McGuire et al., 1995), although in many cases, individuals diagnosed with cannabis-induced psychosis may actually be individuals with paranoid schizophrenia who have used marijuana (Mathers & Ghodse, 1992). Interestingly, out of the hundreds of studies investigating the effects of acute exposure to marijuana or THC in thousands of human subjects, not one has reported a single case of a long-lasting psychotic reaction in the subjects—perhaps because individuals with a history of psychological problems were excluded from participating in the research.

It should be pointed out that the quality of the studies in this area is variable, and their results often conflict. Some of the variability no doubt can be attributed to the variability in the users' personalities and emotional dispositions, so that marijuana use may have either positive, negative, or benign effects on mental health and adjustment depending on the user's disposition (Zablocki et al., 1991). Also, it is difficult to distinguish between drug-induced psychological problems and preexisting determinants. It is often the case that extensive drug users are those who have had emotional problems prior to use (Hollister, 1986). Furthermore, use in North America is a relatively recent phenomenon, and the studies done with American users have involved relatively small samples of highly motivated college populations using smaller amounts of marijuana with lower amounts of THC. Whatever the case, most clinicians caution against the use of marijuana by persons with a history of serious psychological problems. This caution also applies to adolescents, who are generally going through a lot of turmoil regarding the psychosocial development of their identity, their role in the adult world ahead, and their cognitive and interpersonal skills.

While violence and aggression have sometimes been suggested to be associated with marijuana use, there is little evidence to support such an association (Dewey, 1986; Hollister, 1986). In fact, the predominant finding is that low doses of marijuana have little effect on aggression, and moderate to high doses tend to inhibit aggression in humans. There may be some individuals with poor impulse control or a proneness to violence, or who are under stress, for whom marijuana use may trigger an aggressive episode.

Rarely, the flashback phenomenon may also occur with cannabis use (Fischer & Taschner, 1991). However, there does not appear to be a correlation between the amount of cannabis consumed and the occurrence of a flashback. On the other hand, the probability of the occurrence of a flashback in a cannabis user seems to increase with the amount of LSD-like P/P/Hs the person has used (Abraham, 1983). Therefore, these individuals' cannabis use may simply be coincidental with their experiencing flashbacks, or it may be a precipitating factor in inducing LSD flashbacks. Although a flashback may range from a mild to a quite vivid recreation of the drug-induced experience, most clinicians feel that it requires little or no treatment.

Although concerns over the possibility that cannabis use may induce brain damage have been expressed for over a century, there is little evidence that doses typically used by humans are neurotoxic (Zimmer & Morgan, 1997). Several studies using echoencephalography and computerized transaxial tomography with heavy cannabis users failed to find any evidence of cerebral atrophy. (However, one's interpretation of these findings must be tempered by the fact that many individuals diagnosed with endogenous psychosis have no gross brain abnormalities that can be detected with present neuroassessment techniques—for example, a PET scan, MRI, or CAT scan.) Several laboratories have reported that chronic exposure to THC or marijuana extracts persistently alter the structure and function of the rat hippocampus (Scallet, 1991). However, the relevance of these studies is questionable because the studies employed massive doses of THC, which humans would never self-administer. Studies of monkeys after up to 12 months of daily exposure have not consistently reported neurotoxicity, and the results of longer exposures have not yet been studied. Interestingly, while some *in vitro* studies with cultured cortical neurons have indicated that cannabinoid agonists may exert neurotoxic effects on cortical neurons (Chan et al., 1998), others (*in vitro* and *in vivo*) have indicated that cannabinoids may protect cortical neurons from excitotoxicity associated with various types of brain insult and slow the progression of neurodegenerative diseases (Hampson et al., 2000; Nagayama et al., 1999; Shen & Thayer, 1998). The differences in these studies may depend on such factors as the specific procedures used, the source of the cells, the dosage and type of cannabinoid agonist, and so on, but at this point we still have not resolved the debate.

Tolerance and Dependence on Cannabis

Many users of marijuana report that continued use of it results in their becoming more sensitive to its effects (a so-called reverse tolerance). As suggested in Chapter 6, this phenomenon may be due to the novice user—exposed to low doses of THC—learning to be more aware of marijuana's subjective effects, or to drug accumulation, since cannabinoids are stored in fat. However, the vast majority of studies indicate that tolerance can develop to most of the psychological effects (Dewey, 1986), but as is the case with most drugs, tolerance development to THC is dose dependent. Apparently, the usual patterns of marijuana smoking by North Americans—on the order of a joint or less a day (about 10 mg THC)—is such that tolerance to marijuana's effects does not develop (Perez-Reyes et al., 1991). However, with sufficiently high dosages, tolerance to most of THC's effects is likely to occur. Considerable evidence suggests that much of the tolerance phenomena observed in humans is due to learned adaptations to marijuana's disruptive effects on behavioral and perceptual processes (Ferraro, 1976). Pharmacodynamic processes could account for some tolerance phenomena, since chronic treatment with THC in rats has been shown to produce down-regulation of cannabinoid receptors in some areas of the brain (Oviedo et al., 1993; Rodriguez de Fonseca et al., 1994). However, increased density of cannabinoid receptors in some areas of the rat brain have also been observed with chronic THC exposure (Romero et al., 1995). Rats treated chronically with THC have been shown to develop differential tolerance to the neurophysiological effects of THC on different dopaminergic systems in the brain, which could account for differential degrees of tolerance to marijuana's behavioral, physiological, and subjective effects (Wu & French, 2000). The relevance of these findings to humans is unknown, because the doses of THC used in these animal studies were extremely high.

Dependence on marijuana is primarily psychological—that is, it is due to its mood- and cognitive-altering properties. Although in some ways it is like comparing apples with oranges, most experts would probably agree that psychological dependence associated with cannabinoids (that is, the compulsive need to experience the effects) is of a considerably lower degree than that associated with alcohol and other sedative–hypnotics, opiates, or the psychostimulants (Dewey, 1986; Hollister, 1986; Jaffe, 1985; Zimmer & Morgan, 1997). Physical dependence as a result of social use of marijuana is even more atypical; until the mid-1970s most experts even denied its existence. However, studies conducted in the late 1970s and early 1980s demonstrated that cessation of extremely high dosage (e.g., 210 mg THC per day—equivalent to 10 to 20 average joints) chronic marijuana use by humans can precipitate an abstinence syndrome that may include one or more of the following: irritability, restlessness, decreased appetite, sleep disturbance, sweating, tremor, nausea, vomiting, and diarrhea. More recently, signs of withdrawal were shown in humans following 4 days of smoking four marijuana cigarettes (with 3.1 percent THC content—an amount typically found in illegal joints) a day (Haney et al., 1999). Interestingly, none of the participants in this study requested to be terminated from the study during the abstinence periods, suggesting that the withdrawal symptoms were not particularly uncomfortable. This is consistent with reports by heavy marijuana users that when withdrawal symptoms do occur, they tend to be mild (compared with those associated with other drugs like alcohol or opiates) and transitory. Although there has been a recent increase in the number of people entering treatment programs with a primary diagnosis of marijuana dependence, most of these are polydrug abusers who also report problems with alcohol, cocaine, amphetamine, tranquilizers, or heroin (Zimmer & Morgan, 1997).

Non–CNS-Related Effects of Marijuana

Although they are outside the scope of the present text, there are a number of other potential consequences of marijuana use that the reader should be aware of, so these will briefly be discussed (see Dewey, 1986, and Hollister, 1986, for a more complete description). The peripheral manifestations of acute marijuana intoxication are minimal and consist predominantly of tachycardia (rapid heart rate) and conjunctival reddening of the eyes. There may be a slight increase in blood pressure with low doses and a slight decrease with high doses. Some individuals may experience blurred vision or headaches. Following acute intoxication, there are generally no residual physiological effects analogous to the alcohol hangover, unless particularly large quantities are used. As an illustration of how high the dosage of THC must be to induce such effects, some of the studies cited earlier in this chapter reported no discomfort in the marijuana users who had smoked 10 to 15 joints a day for years (on the order of 150 mg THC a day) when they were asked to abstain from smoking for 12 to 24 hours.

Numerous studies have indicated that marijuana smoking produces inflammation, edema, and cell injury in lung tissues of smokers and may be a risk factor for lung cancer, although there is no empirical evidence for lung cancer related solely to marijuana smoking (Zimmer & Morgan, 1997). Studies in humans who smoked cigarettes containing THC indicate that marijuana smoke may be a source of cellular oxidative stress that could contribute significantly to cell injury and dysfunction in the lungs of smokers (Sarafian et al., 1999). As one might expect, because human marijuana smokers generally autotitrate to a desired level of intoxication, smoking higher potency (i.e., higher THC content) marijuana relative to lower potency marijuana has been shown to reduce pulmonary exposure to noxious smoke components due to a reduced intake of smoke and/or a reduced tar yield from the stronger marijuana preparations (Matthias et al., 1997). Comparisons of heavy, habitual smokers of marijuana alone, smokers of marijuana plus tobacco, regular smokers of tobacco alone, and nonsmokers of either substance have indicated that regular tobacco, but not marijuana, smoking is associated with greater annual rates of decline in lung function than is nonsmoking (Tashkin et al., 1997).

Some studies have suggested that reproductive functioning may be impaired with marijuana, which may be reflected in lower testosterone levels (although generally within normal levels), reduced sex drive, and less vigorous sperm motility in males and interference with fertility in females. Most studies, however, have failed to show any significant effects of chronic marijuana use on the reproductive hormones of either men or women (Block et al., 1991). Given the potential alterations in hormonal functions, and the importance of these in the developing fetus, marijuana use (or any other drug use) during pregnancy is strongly discouraged. Although some studies have suggested that marijuana may interfere with the immune response and affect chromosomes, the clinical significance of those studies is questionable. Furthermore, many other studies have found no effects of marijuana in these areas (Zimmer & Morgan, 1997).

On the other side of the coin, cannabinoids have been suggested to have some therapeutic value, an issue that is the subject of growing debate in the medical community (Hollister,

2000). THC (Marinol) is available for medical use in oral form (it is presently a Schedule III controlled substance). Smoked marijuana does not share this legal position, although several states have passed initiatives that would allow, contrary to federal regulations, the sale and use of smoked marijuana for a variety of medical indications. The primary advantages of smoked marijuana come from the ability to achieve a rapid onset of effect and of users to autotitrate the THC concentrations needed to produce the maximal benefits, whereas oral THC produces a slower onset of effect, with greater variability in degree of effect. Advocates cite anecdotal and clinical evidence that cannabinoids can reduce nausea and vomiting associated with chemotherapy for cancer, reverse the wasting syndrome associated with AIDS, ease muscle spasms in the paralyzed, and significantly reduce the pressure in the eye associated with glaucoma. Although cannabinoids generally are not superior to other medications used in these problems, they may prove useful in certain patients for whom these drugs are ineffective. Other doctors and federal health officials, however, say there is insufficient evidence to prove that marijuana is beneficial; some suggest that smoking it could be harmful, particularly for AIDS patients vulnerable to lung ailments. Because of the development of synthetic cannabinoid compounds with fewer intoxicating qualities and concerns over the potential harmfulness of marijuana, in 1992 the U.S. government stopped accepting new participants in its medicinal marijuana program, which, for some 15 years, had been supplying government-grown marijuana to patients suffering from cancer, glaucoma, and AIDS (Bowersox, 1992).

Dissociative Anesthetics: Phencyclidine and Ketamine

One of the most predominant effects of phencyclidine (or PCP, which stands for its chemical name phencyclohexyl piperidine) and its analogue ketamine is profound anesthesia. Because patients anesthetized with these drugs are awake but appear disconnected from their environment, perhaps the simplest term to be used to describe these drugs is **dissociative anesthetic** (Jaffe, 1985). As is almost universally the case, PCP was discovered serendipitously. In the 1950s, while searching for new psychoactive drugs with therapeutic properties, chemists synthesized the drug, which psychopharmacologists immediately recognized as having some very unique effects in animals (Domino, 1980). In rats it had an amphetamine-like action, but, as with sedative–hypnotics, it disrupted muscular coordination. In dogs it induced convulsions, and in monkeys low doses had a calming effect (the monkeys appeared so serene that the drug was later marketed as Sernylyn), while higher doses eliminated sensitivity to touch or pain. It was this anesthetic action that was most promising for therapeutics, since most drugs with general anesthetic activity also have a strong lethal potential—due to the depression of the body's vital functions—at doses approximately double the anesthetic dose. With PCP the lethal dose was approximately 10 times the anesthetic dose. At appropriate doses, PCP induced insensitivity to pain while increasing blood pressure and heart rate. Also unlike any other general anesthetic, the organism remained awake with the eyes open.

When PCP was tested in human volunteers, it soon became apparent that it shared the properties of another class of drugs, the P/P/Hs. However, unlike LSD, with its definitive visual distorting properties, PCP prompted distortions in body image, feelings of depersonalization, and a sense of timelessness—a transient feeling of being in outer space or dead or not having any arms or legs. In approximately a third of the individuals, the drug also prompted symptoms that mimicked very closely those of schizophrenia (apathy, ambivalence, autism, and an inability to associate thoughts or ideas), which, in some cases, persisted for several days or weeks. For this reason, the pharmaceutical company that developed Sernylyn withdrew it from the market, except for veterinary purposes. Until it was totally withdrawn from the market, Sernylyn was used primarily as an anesthetic in primates and not, as it is commonly assumed, as an animal tranquilizer.

For some of the same reasons that clinical use of PCP with humans was discontinued, illicit drug manufacturers in the 1960s started synthesizing the drug (a relatively easy process) and selling it as a substitute for LSD, THC, mescaline, and amphetamine. Until the 1970s it was rarely purchased intentionally as PCP (in which case, it was most commonly referred to as "angel dust"). Although still used by a very small minority of illicit drug users, PCP presents a very severe drug abuse problem in that it has been reliably linked to suicides (as a result of severe depression) and drownings, self-inflicted wounds, and violence (as a result of the dissociation from reality, incoordination, and hallucinations).

Pharmacodynamics and Psychological Effects of PCP

The CNS actions of PCP are quite complex and probably involve a wide variety of neurotransmitter systems. Stereospecific binding sites for PCP have been noted. Almost all of these sites appear to be located deep within an ion channel regulated by the NMDA receptor for the excitatory amino acids glutamate and aspartate; by binding to this site, PCP prevents Ca^{++} and Na^+ flow through the channel and into the neuron (Johnson & Jones, 1990). PCP's ability to antagonize NMDA-type glutamate receptor activity also appears to be a major factor in its ability to increase extracellular dopamine concentrations in the nucleus accumbens, prefrontal cortex, and basal ganglia (Hanson et al., 1995; Hondo et al., 1994; Yonezawa et al., 1995). Although these dopamine-enhancing effects may be responsible for some of PCP's rewarding properties and its psychotomimetic effects, there is evidence that PCP's blockade of NMDA receptor function is sufficient to explain both (Carlezon & Wise, 1996; Halberstadt, 1995). As is the case with most drugs of abuse, PCP has been shown to potentiate the effects of electrical stimulation of the brain (Carlezon & Wise, 1993).

Studies have also suggested that some of the properties of PCP are similar to those of the mixed agonist–antagonist narcotics like cyclazocine, which are generally viewed as kappa opioid receptor agonists (Pfeiffer et al., 1986). Adenosine receptors may be involved, since agonists at these receptors block the CNS properties of PCP (Browne & Welch, 1982). Finally, behavioral and pharmacodynamic measures in rats indicate that high doses of PCP can enhance serotonergic activity by binding to 5-HT transporters and inhibiting 5-HT reuptake (Hori et al., 2000).

Although PCP is often misrepresented as LSD, mescaline, or THC, the CNS effects of PCP are distinct from those of most other drugs, including amphetamine, THC, LSD, methaqualone, scopolamine, and morphine (Jaffe, 1985). PCP's CNS effects are also clearly different from those of the monoamine-related P/P/Hs. In the drug discrimination procedure, animals show no generalization between PCP and any monoamine P/P/H (Appel et al., 1982) or, for that matter, between PCP and any cholinergic, dopaminergic, serotonergic,

GABAergic, or opioid drugs (Johnson & Jones, 1990). PCP is one of the P/P/Hs, that animals have been shown (using catheter/infusion method) to self-administer (Balster & Chait, 1976). Finally, whereas chlorpromazine (the antipsychotic) blocks the effects of LSD, it tends to potentiate PCP's depressant actions (Balster & Chait, 1976).

Electrophysiologically, sensory impulses to the cortex appear to be grossly distorted by PCP, particularly those involved in proprioception (the perceptual processing of stimuli originating in muscles, tendons, and other internal tissues) (Domino, 1980). Peripherally, PCP has the sympathomimetic effects of increasing heart rate and blood pressure. The persistence of the PCP-induced effects can be traced to the fact that PCP has a relatively long plasma half-life, in some cases as long as 3 days (Jaffe, 1985). In addition to the confusing array of effects possessed by PCP, there are dozens of its metabolites, with potential psychoactive properties, that also persist in the body for several days.

Behaviorally in humans, low doses of PCP (1 to 5 mg) produce a drunken state, or "floaty" euphoria, with numbness in the hands and feet. Persons often describe their experience as involving grotesquely distorted body shape, unreal size of body parts, a sensation of floating or hovering in a weightless condition in space, or a leaving of the body. Radiantly colorful visions that include images of moving from one room to another and moving, glowing geometrical patterns and figures are also reported, and the user may experience a complete absence of time sense (Domino, 1980).

Moderate doses (5 to 15 mg) induce analgesia and anesthesia, and an excited, confused intoxication can develop. Communication is definitely impaired. A body position may be rigidly maintained over extended periods of time (catalepsy). Larger doses of PCP induce a very definite psychosis and, in rare cases, convulsions (although low doses of PCP generally have anticonvulsant properties due to NMDA-mediated response blockade). Death is rarely directly caused by PCP because of its moderately high therapeutic index. There are distinct species differences in terms of reaction to PCP; some animals become very excited, and others become very sedated. The anesthetic dose is dependent on the complexity of the organism; as one progresses up the phylogenetic scale, lower doses are needed to induce anesthesia (Domino, 1980).

Tolerance develops to many of the effects of PCP, but much of it appears to be due to behavioral adaptations. For example, monkeys administered PCP (1.0 mg/kg) daily for 4 months were less affected by 1.0 mg/kg PCP than nondrug-treated monkeys in terms of their ability to stand on their hind limbs to reach for a food pellet, their ability to track a food pellet moved laterally across the field of vision, and their ability to reach out and take an offered pellet. However, in terms of nystagmus (rhythmical oscillation of the eyeballs), both groups of monkeys were affected to the same degree (Balster & Chait, 1976). Notice that the dependent variables to which tolerance developed were the ones in which you would expect behavioral adjustments to occur. Other studies with animals have confirmed these findings. For example, studies have demonstrated that tolerance occurs to some behavioral effects with both PCP and ketamine, while the anticonvulsant action (with low doses) of these drugs remains unaffected after chronic drug exposure (Leccese et al., 1986).

PCP may also produce mild physical dependence, because abrupt withdrawal from PCP after chronic use may be followed by fearfulness, tremors, and facial twitches (Jaffe, 1985). Alterations in PCP receptors with chronic PCP exposure do not appear to play a major role in the production of PCP dependence (Burke et al., 1995). Some craving after stopping PCP use may also be experienced by chronic users.

With such a confusing array of pharmacological actions, it is not clear what accounts for PCP's popularity. The majority of PCP users report that they enjoy the intoxication state, viewing it as a novel experience that provides an escape from anxieties, depression, and other external pressures (Domino, 1980). To this outside observer, these effects seem a little like the effects from a combination of a sedative–hypnotic, a monoamine-related P/P/H, and an opiate.

PCP-Induced Psychosis

Although it has euphoriant effects in the majority of users, PCP can induce a distinct psychotic reaction in a significant minority of people (Erard et al., 1980). These people can generally be placed in one of three categories: (1) normal individuals who experience a schizophrenic-like syndrome lasting for several hours; (2) individuals with no previous history of psychotic episodes or other psychiatric problems, whose PCP-induced psychosis lasts an average of 2 weeks; and (3) those previously diagnosed with schizophrenia, in whom PCP triggers or exacerbates their original psychosis, a condition that may last for several weeks. Whether these three types of reactions are qualitatively different or are simply variations along a continuum involving persons with varying degrees of predisposition toward the development of schizophrenic symptoms is unclear.

The symptoms of PCP psychosis are indistinguishable from the core symptoms of schizophrenia (Ellison, 1995). Most patients treated for it present global paranoia, persecutory and grandiose delusions, and auditory hallucinations, with periods of suspiciousness alternating with extreme anger or terror. As is common with schizophrenia, affect is blunted, and patients are ambivalent toward close friends and relatives. In some cases, they profess superhuman strength and invulnerability, and they may become violent without provocation (it should be mentioned that this is rarely the case with schizophrenia). Other clinical signs are negativism, hostility, disorientation, repetitive motor behavior, and rigidity. In very rare cases, the psychosis is more similar to mania, with symptoms including elation, grandiose and paranoid delusions, and widely fluctuating affect, but no thought disorder or disorientation. Generally, the patients are amnesic for the events occurring during the PCP-induced state.

Schizophrenics are particularly sensitive to PCP and show profound disorganization in reaction to it (Erard et al., 1980). This is considerably different from their reaction to other P/P/Hs, such as LSD or mescaline. Intelligent schizophrenics can distinguish the effects of these latter drugs from their psychosis, and, as with normal individuals, they experience the kaleidoscopic visual effects (Jacobsen, 1968).

Although acute exposure to PCP can produce many of the symptoms characteristic of schizophrenia, the most complete spectrum of schizophrenic symptoms occurs with repeated exposures to PCP. First, while both acute and long-term exposure to PCP produces intense psychosis, hallucinations, delusions, thought disorder, and impaired cognition, these effects are considerably longer lasting with long-term than with acute exposure (e.g., days to weeks rather than a few hours). Second, whereas acute PCP exposure produces visual illusions, euphoric to catatonic affect, and increased frontal lobe blood flow, long-term PCP exposure is more likely to produce anxious, labile, or paranoid affect, auditory and paranoid hallucinations, delusions that are frequently religious, and decreased frontal lobe blood flow (Jentsch & Roth, 1999). The latter symptoms more completely model the behavioral and metabolic dysfunctions of schizophrenia.

Treatment for PCP Psychosis

The treatment of PCP toxic reactions is somewhat different from treatments for other P/P/Hs (Aronow et al., 1980), which for the most part simply require time passage and reassurance. Some of the psychotomimetic effects of PCP can be antagonized by the nonsedating antipsychotics like haloperidol (Haldol), although some clinicians feel that these drugs may exacerbate the behavioral dyscontrol of PCP. Diazepam may be used to help control muscle spasms and restlessness, and the anticonvulsant Dilantin may be used prophylactically against convulsions. Nondrug treatment generally involves lavage (washing out the G.I. tract with large amounts of fluid) or gastric suctioning if the psychosis is treated shortly after the drug has been administered. Since PCP is a weak alkaloid administered as a salt (phencyclidine hydrochloride), a technique called *ion trapping*, in which the urine is acidified to ensure ionization of the PCP base, is used to facilitate PCP's removal from the body. Unlike the "talking down" strategy suggested for dealing with LSD-like or cannabinoid psychoses, it is suggested that the person experiencing a PCP psychosis be placed in as quiet and nonstimulating an environment as possible, because he or she may exhibit unexpected violence or aggression.

Ketamine

After noting the many side effects of PCP, chemists synthesized a number of analogues of PCP. Ketamine (Ketalar) was found to have the most therapeutic value as an anesthetic. While possessing the desirable characteristics of PCP (that is, high therapeutic index, minimal effect on respiration, and elevation of blood pressure and cardiac output), it did not induce convulsions and was shorter-acting than PCP (recovery occurs in less than 2 hours) (Domino, 1980).

Ketamine's pharmacodynamic actions are very similar to those of PCP; that is, it antagonizes NMDA receptor-sensitive glutamatergic neurotransmission in the brain. Essentially the same perceptual distortions in vision, audition, body image, sense of time, and the like, noted with PCP can occur during the recovery period following ketamine anesthesia, but to a lesser degree (Hansen et al., 1988). Furthermore, like PCP, ketamine has been shown to induce positive and negative symptoms of schizophrenia (see Chapter 12) in both healthy subjects and schizophrenic patients (Krystal et al., 1999; Lahti et al., 1995). The symptoms in these schizophrenic patients were strikingly similar to those exhibited by the patients during active episodes of their illness. However, in neither group were the psychotic symptoms reduced with the typical antipsychotic haloperidol, although some of the disruptive effects of ketamine on cognitive functions of the healthy subjects were lessened with haloperidol. Interestingly, the atypical antipsychotic clozapine was found to significantly blunt the increase in positive symptoms induced by ketamine in antipsychotic drug-free schizophrenics (Malhotra et al., 1997). As discussed in Chapter 12, clozapine is one of several atypical antipsychotics with a different spectrum of actions and effects than those displayed with typical antipsychotics (e.g., haloperidol).

Anticholinergics

One of the oldest known groups of P/P/Hs is called the **anticholinergics** because of their specific blockade at acetylcholine receptors. The early writings of Homer describe potent agents with properties similar to those of the anticholinergics. These drugs are often called belladonna alkaloids because at one time women used one of these compounds *(Atropa belladonna)* to dilate their pupils and enhance their beauty *(belladonna* means "beautiful lady"). Throughout the Middle Ages, many witchcraft potions contained mushrooms and herbs with anticholinergic properties. The four deadly nightshades—*Atropa belladonna* (death's herb), *Datura stramonium* (Jamestown weed, jimson weed, thornapple, stinkweed), *Hyoscyamus niger* (henbane), and *Mandragora officinarum* (mandrake)—were also well known to oracles, assassins, seducers, and physicians. Jamestown weed was commonly used as an intoxicant by the early settlers of Jamestown, Virginia (circa 1676).

In addition to their CNS effects, anticholinergic drugs exert a number of peripheral effects, which led to their being included in a variety of over-the-counter (OTC) medications. In the 1970s more than 100 OTC medications contained anticholinergics. These included a variety of sleep aids (Sominex, Compoz, Serene), cold remedies (Contac), antacids (Trangest), cough syrups (Endotussin), antidiarrhea compounds (Donnagel), analgesics (Femicin), anti–motion sickness compounds (Travel-eze), and antiasthmatics (Asthmador). However, in the late 1970s and early 1980s, concerns over the effectiveness of OTC medications led the federal government to require that OTC medications be proven not only safe (a requirement established in the 1960s), but also effective in order for them to be marketed. These requirements led to the reformulation of most OTC medications containing anticholinergic drugs and, for the most part, the replacement of anticholinergics with more effective compounds (most of which are antihistamines).

At the present time, anticholinergics are not schedule-controlled substances, even though they can only be purchased through prescription, nor is there any law preventing the cultivation of plants containing these alkaloids, primarily because the recreational use and the abuse potential for these drugs is currently very minimal. They have a number of side effects that reduce their reward value, and there are other drugs available with similar euphoriant properties that do not have these side effects.

Effects of Anticholinergics

The three most common anticholinergics are atropine, scopolamine, and *l*-hyoscyamine. These drugs are discussed in this chapter because of their ability to induce hallucinatory experiences at sufficiently high doses, but they have myriad effects that are heavily dose-dependent (Weiner, 1985). In small doses, scopolamine induces quiet sedation, with euphoria, amnesia, and dreamless sleep (probably associated with reduced REM activity). Sometimes, however, especially when the person is in pain, scopolamine causes excitement, hallucinations, or delirium in small doses. In general, the effects of anticholinergics resulting from their CNS activity include the following: (1) confusion, slurred speech, disorientation similar to alcohol intoxication; (2) psychotic behavior similar to hebephrenia (a state in which the person acts very childish and silly); (3) hallucinations, primarily consisting of brightly colored objects and pleasant sounds; (4) drowsiness and fatigue; and (5) amnesia, whereby the person may forget the entire episode of intoxication. (At one time anticholinergics, in combination with morphine, were given to women in labor to induce a "twilight sleep" so that they would forget the pain of childbirth.) At extremely high doses, coma can result. Although these drugs can be lethal and have been used as poisons in the past, their margin of safety is actually rather large. Deaths attributed to them nowadays generally involve abusers who might wander off into heavy traffic or fall into swimming pools, and children who ingest berries or seeds containing belladonna alkaloids.

Anticholinergics generally shift the EEG rhythm to slower frequencies, an effect commonly found with sedative–hypnotic compounds (Weiner, 1985). As noted earlier, several cognitive and peripheral effects of marijuana resemble those of anticholinergics. In therapeutic doses they also reduce abnormal EEG waves in approximately half of those individuals with grand mal seizures and may be useful in some cases of petit mal seizure activity. These drugs also have antitremor activity and have been used for many years in the treatment of parkinsonism.

Peripherally, anticholinergics block activity of the parasympathetic nervous system (the system that regulates vegetative processes and that is most active when the organism is calm and relaxed). The reduction of parasympathetic input to the organs of the body results in effects that resemble those of drugs that amplify sympathetic nervous system activity (such as amphetamine), with respect to increased heart rate, blood pressure, and pupillary dilation. With anticholinergics, pupillary dilation is not responsive to light, and testing this response is a good way to diagnose poisoning with these substances. Many other peripheral effects generally result in fluid retention in all areas of the body; for example, the mouth and nose dry up, sweating is absent, urination becomes difficult, and there is intraocular (inside the eye) fluid build-up. The person becomes very thirsty, hot, and flushed. Other effects include poor eye accommodation (blurred vision), decreased G.I. activity (constipation), and bronchodilation. It was because of several of these properties that small amounts of anticholinergics were, until recently, often found in many OTC medications for the treatment of cold symptoms, excess stomach acid, cough, diarrhea, motion sickness, and asthma.

Tolerance to the belladonna alkaloids occurs in humans to a limited extent. Psychological dependence at the present time is extremely rare. Physical dependence is minimal, although vomiting, malaise, excessive sweating, and salivation have been recorded in parkinsonism patients treated with large doses (required for therapeutic benefit) of these compounds upon sudden withdrawal.

Pharmacodynamics of Anticholinergics

These drugs are pharmacological, competitive antagonists of acetylcholine (ACH) at muscarinic receptors (so named because the drug muscarine acts like acetylcholine at these receptors). Thus, they are often, and more appropriately, termed **antimuscarinics.** Their blocking action at ACH receptors activated by nicotine (nicotinic receptors) is very weak. The fact that they compete with ACH means that their effects can be overcome by increasing the amount of ACH released or by reducing its inactivation in the synaptic cleft. The latter technique is the most often used antidote to anticholinergic poisoning, carried out by administering physostigmine, a drug that inhibits the action of acetylcholinesterase (the enzyme that metabolizes ACH in the synaptic cleft). On the other hand, the use of antipsychotic drugs like chlorpromazine (Thorazine) in the treatment of anticholinergic-induced psychosis would only intensify the psychosis, because these drugs also have anticholinergic properties.

Since muscarinic receptors for ACH are found in both the peripheral and central nervous systems, antimuscarinics have profound effects on both bodily and psychological functions. Atropine has a greater effect on the G.I. tract, heart, and bronchi, while scopolamine has a greater effect on the eyes, glands, and brain.

Ibogaine

Ibogaine is one of several psychoactive indole alkaloids found in a shrub, *Tabernanthe iboga,* indigenous to Central-West Africa. Peoples of this region have used the shrub for many years for a variety of purposes—for instance, in initiation rite ceremonies (in which members ingesting the iboga root believe it allows them to make contact with ancestors in the spirit world), for the enhancement of endurance and strength of warriors, and as an aphrodisiac (Popik et al., 1995b). The plant was introduced to Western medicine over a century ago, and ibogaine was isolated from the plant in 1901. At that time, a number of potential medical uses were suggested for ibogaine, but interest in its therapeutic properties didn't gain momentum until the 1930s and 1940s, when it was promoted primarily as a tonic or stimulant in the treatment of fatigue, sleeping sickness (trypanosomiasis), and depression. In the 1960s, the use of ibogaine for its purported performance-enhancing effects in athletes and for its hallucinogenic effects among members of the counterculture ("hippies") led to its being prohibited in many countries, including the United States, which in 1970 classified ibogaine as a Schedule I controlled substance. Interest in ibogaine resurfaced again in the 1980s when Howard S. Lotsof acquired a series of patents for the use of ibogaine (called Endabuse) as a rapid and easy means of treating addiction to opiates, psychostimulants, alcohol, and nicotine. At the present time, a number of clinical trials are being conducted with ibogaine to evaluate its safety and efficacy in the treatment of a variety of drug addictions. For example, in one study of heroin addicts undergoing detoxification, the signs of opioid withdrawal were eliminated in 25 of 33 patients within 24 hours after ibogaine administration without further drug seeking behavior—an effect that was sustained throughout the 72-hour period of posttreatment observation (Alper et al., 2000).

Although stimulant-like effects predominate with lower doses of the crude extract of iboga, when taken in sufficiently high doses (which are sometimes fatal), iboga is reported by users to result in fantastic visions, feelings of excitement, drunkenness, mental confusion, and hallucinations. The verbal reports of users of ibogaine or the total iboga extract suggest that the subjective experience, which lasts about 6 hours, is very similar to that of the more potent monoamine-related P/P/Hs. This is consistent with the fact that ibogaine has a serotonin-like (indole amine) molecular structure and the finding that animals trained to discriminate between saline and the monoamine P/P/Hs LSD or DMMA in the two-choice drug discrimination paradigm respond to ibogaine as if it were the LSD or DMMA cue (Palumbo & Winter, 1992). On the other hand, in studies with humans, the drug has been reported to elicit a state of drowsiness in which the subjects did not want to move, open their eyes, or attend to the environment. Many subjects were light-sensitive and covered their eyes or asked that lights be turned off. Sounds or noises were disturbing. These are characteristics commonly observed with phencyclidine (PCP). As is the case with many P/P/Hs, severe anxiety and apprehension can accompany the hallucinations. Some reports indicate that the psychic state produced by ibogaine is similar to a dream state without the loss of consciousness, which some psychoanalytic therapists suggested might be useful as a psychological catalyst that could compress a long psychotherapeutic process into a shorter time period (Naranjo, 1969). Similar dreamlike experiences have been reported to occur with the indole amine–related P/P/H dimethyltryptamine (DMT) (Strassman et al., 1994).

Ibogaine is also reported to be a highly valued aphrodisiac in Africa. Whether this is due to a direct effect on sexual function or is due to an expectancy effect, an increase in self-confidence, or a decrease in fatigue is unknown.

What ibogaine's abuse potential is in humans is not clear at this point. There are no reports of animals' self-administering pure ibogaine (although in Africa wild animals have been observed by local inhabitants to dig up and eat the root of the iboga plant and then enter into a wild frenzy—which may have been how humans learned about the properties of the plant [Pope, 1969]). Furthermore, as noted in earlier chapters, ibogaine has been shown to inhibit the self-administration of drugs of abuse in animals.

Some effects of ibogaine have been observed up to 1 week after administration in both humans and animals. Because detectable levels of ibogaine are no longer present within about 12 hours after administration, it has been hypothesized that ibogaine may be metabolized into a long-lasting psychoactive compound. Although an active metabolite of ibogaine has been found (12-hydroxyibogamine), it is not clear that it accounts for ibogaine's long-term effects (Mash et al., 1995).

Ibogaine's pharmacodynamic properties are even more complex and varied, with potent actions on dopaminergic, opioid, and serotonergic systems, and NMDA and calcium channels, among others (Popik et al., 1995b), suggesting that multiple mechanisms of action are responsible for ibogaine's effects. One of its most prominent actions is to block NMDA receptor–activated ion channels by binding to a site within the channel (Popik et al., 1995a). This is also a property of phencyclidine, which, as described earlier, has psychotomimetic and subjective effects similar to ibogaine. Ibogaine and one of its metabolites also block 5-HT reuptake sites and elevate extracellular 5-HT levels. In addition to actions on several neurotransmitter systems, high doses of ibogaine in rats have been reported to cause the degeneration of a subset of neurons in the cerebellum (O'Hearn et al., 1995; O'Hearn & Molliver, 1993), which could account for some of ibogaine's long-lasting effects. Unfortunately, if neurotoxicity occurs with lower doses, or is the major factor in ibogaine's "antiaddiction" properties (should they be verified), justification of its therapeutic use will be difficult.

P/P/Hs: The Human Experience

We are built to process stimuli, and an important aspect of our living is our seeking out of stimuli to process. The popularity of P/P/Hs is a function of this general characteristic of stimulus seeking. The central property of any of the P/P/Hs is the enhancement of experience

(Aaronson & Osmond, 1970). They seem to increase the capacity of the human brain to respond to fine gradations of stimulus input, to enhance our responses to stimulation at both the upper and lower levels of perceptual processing, and to remove the constraints imposed by the different sensory pathways through which stimulation is received. They produce new perceptions, alter our ways of looking at the world, and in some cases induce hallucinations. The experience can be very exhilarating or very frightening. In contrast, the sedative–hypnotics and narcotics reduce our attention to sensory input, although these substances may induce hypnagogic and dreamlike states. Psychostimulants may enhance endurance, improve mood, and increase alertness, but they do not alter our attention to the fine nuances of sensory experience to the degree that P/P/Hs do.

However, in order for the enhanced capacity for experience to occur with P/P/Hs, an adequate range of stimuli must be available, because exposure to them under conditions of sensory deprivation seems to reduce their effects considerably (Aaronson & Osmond, 1970). On the other hand, as the complexity of the stimulus situation increases, the variability of the experiences and perceptual reactions increases. Furthermore, in addition to the setting, the person's attitudes, motivations, cognitive set, and expectations play such a large role in the experience that it is impossible to predict in advance the type of experience one may have with these substances. This unpredictability may, in fact, be another reason why humans use them.

Websites for Further Information

Site providing information on a wide variety of hallucinogens (e.g., psilocybin, cannabis, mescaline, LSD, PCP), along with a number of links:

http://erowid.org/general/big_chart.shtml

The Albert Hofmann Foundation website (the use of LSD to explore the unconscious):

http://www.hofmann.org/

Sites concerned with the history of legal restrictions on marijuana:

http://www.forces.org/articles/files/whiteb/white.htm (The History of the Non-Medical Use of Drugs in the U.S., by Charles Whitebread, USC Law School, 1995)

http://www.druglibrary.org/schaffer/hemp/taxact/taxact.htm_ (Testimony and documentation concerned with the Marijuana Tax Act of 1937)

http://www.druglibrary.org/schaffer/library/studies/nc/ncmenu.htm (The Report of the National Commission on Marihuana and Drug Abuse commissioned by Richard M. Nixon, 1972)

The National Organization for the Reform of Marijuana Laws' (NORML) home page:

http://www.norml.org/home.shtml

The nature and extent of marijuana use in the United States:

http://www.frw.uva.nl/cedro/library/Drugs16/usa3.html#nati

Site providing news about marijuana:

http://www.marijuananews.com/

Site providing information on proposed legislation to make marijuana legal for medical use:

http://dpf.guiworks.com/Archive/1999/3/2-1057.html

Bibliography

Aaronson, B., & Osmond, H. (1970). Introduction: Psychedelics, technology, psychedelics. In B. Aaronson & H. Osmond (Eds.), *Psychedelics* (pp. 3–18). Garden City: Anchor Books.

Abraham, H. D. (1983). Visual phenomenology of the LSD flashback. *Archives of General Psychiatry, 40,* 884–889.

Abraham, H. D., & Aldridge, A. M. (1993). Adverse consequences of lysergic acid diethylamide. *Addiction, 88,* 1327–1334.

Agurell, S., Halldin, M., Lindgren, J.-E., et al. (1986). Pharmacokinetics and metabolism of delta-1-tetrahydrocannabinol and other cannabinoids with emphasis on man. *Pharmacological Reviews, 38,* 21–43.

Allen, R. P., McCann, U. D., & Ricaurte, G. A. (1993). Persistent effects of (+/–)3,4-methylenedioxymethamphetamine (MDMA, "ecstasy") on human sleep. *Sleep, 16,* 560–564.

Alper, K. R., Lotsof, H. S., Frenken, G. M., et al. (2000). Ibogaine in acute opioid withdrawal. An open label case series. *Annals of the New York Academy of Sciences, 909,* 257–259.

Ameri, A. (1999). The effects of cannabinoids on the brain. *Progress in Neurobiology, 58,* 315–348.

Appel, J. B., White, F. J., & Holohean, A. M. (1982). Analyzing mechanisms of hallucinogenic drug action with drug discrimination procedures. *Neuroscience and Biobehavioral Reviews, 6,* 529–536.

Aronow, R., Miceli, J. N., & Done, A. K. (1980). A therapeutic approach to the acutely overdosed PCP patient. *Journal of Psychedelic Drugs, 12,* 259–266.

Azorlosa, J. L., Heishman, S. J., Stitzer, M. L., & Mahaffey, J. M. (1992). Marijuana smoking: Effect of varying delta-9-tetrahydrocannabinol content and number of puffs. *Journal of Pharmacology and Experimental Therapeutics, 261,* 114–122.

Balster, R. L., & Chait, L. D. (1976). The biobehavioral pharmacology of phencyclidine. *Clinical Toxicology, 9,* 513–529.

Block, R. I., Farinpour, R., & Schlechte, J. A. (1991). Effects of chronic marijuana use on testosterone, luteinizing hormone, follicle stimulating hormone, prolactin and cortisol in men and women. *Drug and Alcohol Dependence, 28,* 121–128.

Bolla, K. I., McCann, U. D., & Ricaurte, G. A. (1998). Memory impairment in abstinent MDMA ("ecstasy") users. *Neurology, 51,* 1532–1537.

Bowersox, J. (1992). PHS cancels availability of medicinal marijuana. *Journal of the National Cancer Institute, 84,* 475–476.

Brecher, E. M. (Ed.). (1972). *Licit and illicit drugs.* Boston: Little, Brown.

Browne, R. G., & Welch, W. M. (1982). Stereoselective antagonism of phencyclidine's discriminative properties by adenosine receptor agonists. *Science, 217,* 1157–1159.

Burke, T. F., Buzzard, S., & Wessinger, W. D. (1995). [3H]MK-801 binding to well-washed rat brain membranes following cessation of chronic phencyclidine treatment. *Pharmacology, Biochemistry, & Behavior, 51,* 435–438.

Cami, J., Guerra, D., Ugena, B., et al. (1991). Effect of subject expectancy on the THC intoxication and disposition from smoked hashish cigarettes. *Pharmacology, Biochemistry, and Behavior, 40,* 115–119.

Campbell, K. A., Foster, T. C., Hampson, R. E., & Deadwyler, S. A. (1986). Effects of delta-9-tetrahydrocannabinol on sensory-evoked discharges of granule cells in the dentate gyrus of behaving rats. *Journal of Pharmacology and Experimental Therapeutics, 239,* 941–945.

Carlezon, W. A., Jr., & Wise, R. A. (1993). Phencyclidine-induced potentiation of brain stimulation reward: Acute effects are not altered by repeated administration. *Psychopharmacology, 111,* 402–408.

Carlezon, W. A., Jr., & Wise, R. A. (1996). Rewarding reactions of phencyclidine and related drugs in nucleus accumbens shell and frontal cortex. *Journal of Neuroscience, 16,* 3112–3122.

Carroll, R. (1991). A rhetorical biography of Harry J. Anslinger, Commissioner of the Federal Bureau of Narcotics, 1930–1962 (Doctoral Dissertation, University of Pittsburgh, 1991). *Dissertation Abstracts International, 52,* 1569.

Chan, G. C., Hinds, T. R., Impey, S., et al. (1998). Hippocampal neurotoxicity of delta 9-tetrahydrocannabinol. *Journal of Neuroscience, 18,* 5322–5332.

Cohen, S. (1981). *The substance abuse problems.* New York: Haworth Press.

Cunningham, K. A., & Appel, J. B. (1987). Neuropharmacological reassessment of the discriminative stimulus properties of *d*-lysergic acid diethylamide (LSD). *Psychopharmacology, 91,* 67–73.

Dewey, W. L. (1986). Cannabinoid pharmacology. *Pharmacological Reviews, 38,* 151–178.

Dobkin de Rios, M. (1996). On "Human pharmacology of hoasca": A medical anthropology perspective. *The Journal of Nervous and Mental Disease, 184,* 95–98.

Domino, E. F. (1980). History and pharmacology of PCP and PCP-related analogs. *Journal of Psychedelic Drugs, 12,* 223–227.

Eich, J. E., Weingartner, H., Stillman, R. C., & Gillin, J. C. (1975). State-dependent accessibility of retrieval cues in the retention of a categorized list. *Journal of Verbal Learning and Verbal Behavior, 14,* 408–417.

Ellison, G. (1995). The N-methyl-D-aspartate antagonists phencyclidine, ketamine and dizocilpine as both behavioral and anatomical models of the dementias. *Brain Research-Brain Research Reviews, 20,* 250–267.

Erard, R., Luisada, P. V., & Peele, R. (1980). The PCP psychosis: Prolonged intoxication or drug-precipitated functional illness? *Journal of Psychedelic Drugs, 12,* 235–245.

Feeney, D. M. (1976). The marijuana window: A theory of cannabis use. *Biobehavioral Biology, 18,* 455–471.

Ferraro, D. P. (1976). A behavioral model of marihuana tolerance. In M. C. Braude & S. Szara (Eds.), *The pharmacology of marihuana* (pp. 475–486). New York: Raven Press.

Ferraro, D. P. (1980). Acute effects of marijuana on human memory and cognition. *NIDA Research Monograph Series 31* (pp. 98–119). National Institute on Drug Abuse, Department of Health and Human Services, Rockville, Md.

Fiorella, D., Rabin, R. A., & Winter, J. C. (1995). The role of the 5-HT2A and 5-HT2C receptors in the stimulus effects of hallucinogenic drugs. I. Antagonist correlation analysis. *Psychopharmacology, 121,* 347–356.

Fischer, J., & Taschner, K. L. (1991). Flashback following use of cannabis—A review. *Fortschritte der Neurologie, Psychiatrie, und Ihrer Grenzgebiete, 59,* 437–446.

Foltin, R. W., Brady, J. V., & Fischman, M. W. (1986). Behavioral analysis of marijuana effects on food intake in humans. *Pharmacology, Biochemistry, and Behavior, 25,* 577–582.

Frazer, A., Maayani, S., & Wolfe, B. B. (1990). Subtypes of receptors for serotonin. *Annual Review of Pharmacology and Toxicology, 30,* 307–348.

Freedman, D. X., & Halaris, A. E. (1978). Monoamines and the biochemical mode of action of LSD at synapses. In M. A. Lipton, A. DiMascio, & K. F. Killam (Eds.), *Psychopharmacology* (pp. 347–360). New York: Raven Press.

Fysh, R. R., Oon, M. C. H., Robinson, K. N., et al. (1985). A fatal poisoning with LSD. *Forensic Science International, 28,* 108–114.

Gardner, E. L., & Lowinson, J. H. (1991). Marijuana's interaction with brain reward systems: Update 1991. *Pharmacology, Biochemistry, and Behavior, 40,* 571–580.

Gerra, G., Zaimovic, A., Ferri, M., et al. (2000). Long-lasting effects of (±)3,4-methylenedioxymethamphetamine (ecstasy) on serotonin system function in humans. *Biological Psychiatry, 47,* 127–136.

Glennon, R. A., & Rosecrans, J. A. (1982). Indolealkylamine and phenalkylamine hallucinogens: A brief overview. *Neuroscience and Biobehavioral Reviews, 6,* 489–498.

Gouzoulis-Mayfrank, E., Daumann, J., Tuchtenhagen, F., et al. (2000). Impaired cognitive performance in drug free users of recreational ecstasy (MDMA). *Journal of Neurology, Neurosurgery, and Psychiatry, 68,* 719–725.

Greenwald, M. K., & Stitzer, M. L. (2000). Antinociceptive, subjective and behavioral effects of smoked marijuana in humans. *Drug and Alcohol Dependence, 59,* 261–275.

Greer, G., & Tolbert, R. (1986). Subjective reports of the effects of MDMA in a clinical setting. *Journal of Psychoactive Drugs, 18,* 319–327.

Grob, C. S., McKenna, D. J., Callaway, J. C., et al. (1996). Human psychopharmacology of hoasca, a plant hallucinogen used in ritual context in Brazil. *The Journal of Nervous and Mental Disease, 184,* 86–94.

Grof, S. (1980). *LSD Psychotherapy.* Ponoma, CA: Hunter House Inc.

Halberstadt, A. L. (1995). The phencyclidine-glutamate model of schizophrenia. *Clinical Neuropharmacology, 18,* 237–249.

Hall, W., & Solowij, N. (1998). Adverse effects of cannabis. *The Lancet, 352,* 1611–1616.

Halpern, J. H., & Pope, H. G., Jr. (1999). Do hallucinogens cause residual neuropsychological toxicity? *Drug and Alcohol Dependence, 53,* 247–256.

Hamann, W., & DiVadi, P. P. (1999). Analgesic effect of the cannabinoid analogue nabilone is not mediated by opioid receptors. *The Lancet, 353,* 560.

Hampson, A. J., Grimaldi, M., Lolic, M., et al. (2000). Neuroprotective antioxidants from marijuana. *Annals of the New York Academy of Sciences, 899,* 274–282.

Haney, M., Ward, A. S., Comer, S. D., et al. (1999). Abstinence symptoms following smoked marijuana in humans. *Psychopharmacology, 141,* 395–404.

Hansen, G., Jensen, S. B., Chandresh, L., & Hilden, T. (1988). The psychotropic effect of ketamine. *Canadian Journal of Psychology, 36,* 527–531.

Hanson, G. R., Midgley, L. P., Bush, L. G., & Gibb, J. W. (1995). Response of extrapyramidal and limbic neurotensin systems to phencyclidine treatment. *European Journal of Pharmacology, 278,* 167–173.

Harris, L. S. (1978). Cannabis: A review of progress. In M. A. Lipton, A. DiMascio, & K. F. Killam (Eds.), *Psychopharmacology* (pp. 1565–1574). New York: Raven Press.

Holdcroft, A., Smith, M., Jacklin, A., et al. (1997). Pain relief with oral cannabinoids in familial Mediterranean fever. *Anaesthesia, 52,* 483–486.

Holden, C. (1980). Arguments heard for psychedelics probe. *Science, 209,* 256–257.

Hollister, L. E. (1986). Health aspects of cannabis. *Pharmacological Reviews, 38,* 1–20.

Hollister, L. E. (2000). An approach to the medical marijuana controversy. *Drug and Alcohol Dependence, 58,* 3–7.

Hondo, H., Yonezawa Y., Nakahara, T., et al. (1994). Effect of phencyclidine on dopamine release in the rat prefrontal cortex: An in vivo microdialysis study. *Brain Research, 633,* 337–342.

Hori, T., Abe, S., Baba, A., et al. (2000). Effects of repeated phencyclidine treatment on serotonin transporter in rat brain. *Neuroscience Letters, 280,* 53–56.

Howlett, A. C. (1995). Pharmacology of cannabinoid receptors. *Annual Review of Pharmacology & Toxicology, 35,* 607–634.

Hooker, W. D., & Jones, R. T. (1987). Increased susceptibility to memory intrusions and the Stroop interference effect during acute marijuana intoxication. *Psychopharmacology, 91,* 20–24.

Imade, A. G. T., & Ebie, J. C. (1991). A retrospective study of symptom patterns of cannabis-induced psychosis. *Acta Psychiatrica Scandinavica, 83,* 134–136.

Jacobs, B. L. (1976, March). Serotonin: The crucial substance that turns dreams on and off. *Psychology Today,* pp. 70–73.

Jacobs, B. L. (1987). How hallucinogenic drugs work. *American Scientist, 75,* 386–392.

Jacobsen, E. (1968). The hallucinogens. In C. R. B. Joyce (Ed.), *Psychopharmacology: Dimensions and perspectives* (pp. 175–213). Philadelphia: J. B. Lippincott.

Jaffe, J. H. (1985). Drug addiction and drug abuse. In A. G. Gilman, L. S. Goodman, T. W. Rall, & F. Murad (Eds.), *The pharmacological basis of therapeutics* (pp. 532–581). New York: Macmillan.

Jain, A. K., Ryan, J. R., McMahon, F. G., et al. (1981). Evaluation of intramuscular levonantradol and placebo in acute postoperative pain. *Journal of Clinical Pharmacology, 21,* 320S–326S.

Jentsch, J. D., & Roth, R. H. (1999). The neuropsychopharmacology of phencyclidine: From NMDA receptor hypofunction to the dopamine hypothesis of schizophrenia. *Neuropsychopharmacology, 20,* 202–225.

Jochimsen, P. R., Lawton, R. L., VerSteeg, K. et al. (1978). Effect of benzopyranoperidine, a delta-9-THC congener, on pain. *Clinical Pharmacolgy and Therapeutics, 24,* 223–227.

Johnson, K. M., & Jones, S. M. (1990). Neuropharmacology of phencyclidine: Basic mechanisms and therapeutic potential. *Annual Review of Pharmacology and Toxicology, 30,* 707–750.

Karniol, J. G. & Carlini, E. A. (1972). The content of (–) delta-9-trans-tetrahydro-cannabinol (delta-9-THC) does not explain all biological activity of some Brazilian marihuana samples. *Journal of Pharmacy and Pharmacology, 24,* 833–835.

Krebs, K. M., & Geyer, M. A. (1994). Cross-tolerance studies of serotonin receptors involved in behavioral effects of LSD in rats. *Psychopharmacology, 113,* 429–437.

Krystal, J. H., D'Souza, D. C., Karper, L. P., et al. (1999). Interactive effects of subanesthetic ketamine and haloperidol in healthy humans. *Psychopharmacology, 145,* 193–204.

Kurtzweil, P. (1995). Medical possibilities for psychedelic drugs. *FDA Consumer, 29,* 1–5.

Lahti, A. C., Koffel, B., LaPorte, D., & Tamminga, C. A. (1995). Subanesthetic doses of ketamine stimulate psychosis in schizophrenia. *Neuropsychopharmacology, 13,* 9–19.

Lamb, R. J., & Griffiths, R. R. (1987). Self-injection of *d,*1-3,4-methylenedioxymethamphetamine (MDMA) in the baboon. *Psychopharmacology, 91,* 268–272.

Leccese, A. P., Marquis, K. L., Mattia, A., & Moreton, J. E. (1986). The anticonvulsant and behavioral effects of phencyclidine and ketamine following chronic treatment in rats. *Behavioural Brain Research, 22,* 257–264.

Malhotra, A. K., Adler, C. M., Kennison, S. D., et al. (1997). Clozapine blunts N-methyl-D-aspartate antagonist-induced psychosis: A study with ketamine. *Biological Psychiatry, 42,* 664–668.

Martin, B. (1986). Cellular effects of cannabinoids. *Pharmacological Reviews, 38,* 45–74.

Martin, B. R., & Lichtman, A. H. (1998). Cannabinoid transmission and pain perception. *Neurobiology of Disease, 5,* 447–461.

Mash, D. C., Staley, J. K., Baumann, M. H., et al. (1995). Identification of a primary metabolite of ibogaine that targets serotonin transporters and elevates serotonin. *Life Sciences, 57,* 45–50.

Mathers, D. C., & Ghodse, A. H. (1992). Cannabis and psychotic illness. *British Journal of Psychiatry, 161,* 648–653.

Matthias, P., Tashkin, D. P., Marques-Magallanes, J. A., et al. (1997). Effects of varying marijuana potency on deposition of tar and delta-9-THC in the lung during smoking. *Phamacology, Biochemistry and Behavior, 58,* 1145–1150.

McCann, U. D., Ridenour, A., Shaham, Y., & Ricaurte, G. A. (1994). Serotonin neurotoxicity after (+/-) 3,4-Methylenedioxymethamphetamine (MDMA; "Ecstasy"): A controlled study in humans. *Neuropsychopharmacology, 10,* 129–138.

McCann, U. D., Szabo, Z., Scheffel, U., et al. (1998). Positron emission tomographic evidence of toxic effect of MDMA ("ecstasy") on brain serotonin neurons in human beings. *The Lancet, 352,* 1433–1437.

McGuire, P. K., Jones, P., Harvey, I., et al. (1995). Morbid risk of schizophrenia for relatives of patients with cannabis-associated psychosis. *Schizophrenia Research, 15,* 277–281.

Meng, I. D., Manning, B. H., Martin, W. J., et al. (1998). An analgesia circuit activated by cannabinoids. *Nature, 395,* 381–383.

Meyer, R. E. (1978). Behavioral pharmacology of marijuana. In M. A. Lipton, A. DiMascio, & K. F. Killam (Eds.), *Psychopharmacology* (pp. 1639–1652). New York: Raven Press.

Mikuriya, T. H., & Aldrich, M. R. (1988). Cannabis 1988. Old drug, new dangers. The potency question. <http://www.druglibrary.org/schaffer/hemp/general/potency.htm> (2000, August 18).

Miller, L. L., & Branconnier, R. J. (1983). Cannabis: Effects on memory and the cholinergic limbic system. *Psychological Bulletin, 93,* 441–456.

Morgan, M. J. (1999). Memory deficits associated with recreational use of "ecstasy" (MDMA). *Psychopharmacology, 141,* 30–36.

Nagayama, T., Sinor, A. D., Simon, R. P., et al. (1999). Cannabinoids and neuroprotection in global and focal cerebral ischemia and in neuronal cultures. *Journal of Neuroscience, 19,* 2987–2995.

Naranjo, C. (1969). Psychotherapeutic possibilities of new fantasy-enhancing drugs. *Clinical Toxicology, 2,* 209–224.

Neill, J. R. (1987). "More than medical significance": LSD and American psychiatry. *Journal of Psychoactive Drugs, 19,* 39–45.

Nichols, D. E. (1986). Differences between the mechanism of action of MDMA, MBDB, and the classic hallucinogens. Identification of a new therapeutic class: Entactogens. *Journal of Psychoactive Drugs, 18,* 305–313.

Noyes, R., Jr., Brunk, S. F., Avery, D. A. H., et al. (1975). The analgesic properties of delta-9-tetrahydrocannabinol and codeine. *Clinical Pharmacology and Therapeutics, 18,* 84–89.

O'Hearn, E., & Molliver, M. E. (1993). Degeneration of the Purkinje cells in parasagittal zones of the cerebellar vermis after treatment with ibogaine or harmaline. *Neuroscience, 55,* 303–310.

O'Hearn, E., Zhang, P., & Molliver, M. E. (1995). Excitotoxic insult due to ibogaine leads to delayed induction of neuronal NOS in Purkinje cells. *Neuroreport, 6,* 1611–1616.

Oviedo, A., Glowa, J., & Herkenham, M. (1993). Chronic cannabinoid administration alters cannabinoid receptor binding in rat brain: A quantitative autoradiographic study. *Brain Research, 616,* 293–302.

Packer, S. (1998). Jewish mystical movements and the European ergot epidemics. *Israel Journal of Psychiatry and Related Sciences, 35,* 227–239.

Page, J. B., Fletcher, J., & True, W. R. (1988). Psychosociocultural perspectives on chronic cannabis use: The Costa Rican follow-up. *Journal of Psychoactive Drugs, 20,* 57–65.

Palumbo, P. A., & Winter, J. C. (1992). Stimulus effects of ibogaine in rats trained with yohimbine, DOM, or LSD. *Pharmacology, Biochemistry, & Behavior, 43,* 1221–1226.

Parrott, A. C. (2000). Human research on MDMA (3,4-methylene-dioxymethamphetamine) neurotoxicity:

Cognitive and behavioural indices of change. *Neuro-psychobiology, 42,* 17–24.

Penington, N. J., & Fox, A. P. (1994). Effects of LSD on CA++ currents in central 5-HT-containing neurons: 5-HT1A receptors may play a role in hallucinogenesis. *Journal of Pharmacology & Experimental Therapeutics, 269,* 1160–1165.

Peralta, V., & Cuesta, M. J. (1992). Influence of cannabis abuse on schizophrenic psychopathology. *Acta Psychiatrica Scandinavica, 85,* 127–130.

Perez-Reyes, M., White, W. R., McDonald, S. A., et al. (1991). The pharmacologic effects of daily marijuana smoking in humans. *Pharmacology, Biochemistry, and Behavior, 40,* 691–694.

Pfeiffer, A., Brantl, V., Herz, A., & Emrich, H. M. (1986). Psychotomimesis mediated by k opiate receptors. *Science, 233,* 774–775.

Pierce, P. A., & Peroutka, S. J. (1990). Antagonist properties of *d*-LSD at 5-hydroxytryptamine$_2$ receptors. *Neuropsychopharmacology, 3,* 503–508.

Pope, H. G. (1969). *Tabernantha iboga:* An African narcotic plant of social importance. *Economic Botany, 23,* 174–184.

Pope, H. G., Gruber, A. J., & Yurgelun-Todd, D. (1995). The residual neuropsychological effects of cannabis: The current status of research. *Drug and Alcohol Dependence, 38,* 25–34.

Pope, H. G., & Yurgelun-Todd, D. (1996). The residual cognitive effects of heavy marijuana use in college students. *JAMA, 275,* 521–527.

Popik, P., Layer, R. T., & Skolnick, P. (1995a). 100 years of ibogaine: Neurochemical and pharmacological actions of a putative anti-addictive drug. *Pharmacological Reviews, 47,* 235–250.

Popik, P., Layer, R. T., Fossom, L. H., et al. (1995b). NMDA antagonist properties of the putative anti-addictive drug, ibogaine. *Journal of Pharmacology and Experimental Therapeutics, 275,* 753–760.

Rasmussen, K., & Aghajanian, G. K. (1986). Effect of hallucinogens on spontaneous and sensory-evoked locus coeruleus unit activity in the rat: Reversal by selective 5-HT$_2$ antagonists. *Brain Research, 385,* 395–400.

Rech, R. H., & Rosecrans, J. A. (1982). Review of mechanisms of hallucinogenic drug action. *Neuroscience and Biobehavioral Reviews, 6,* 481–482.

Rinaldi-Carmona, M., Barth, F., Heaulme, M., et al., (1994). SR141716A, a potent and selective antagonist of the brain cannabinoid receptor. *FEBS Letters, 350,* 240–244.

Rodriguez De Fonseca, F., Gorriti, M. A., Fernandez-Ruiz, J. J., et al. (1994). Down-regulation of rat brain cannabinoid binding sites after chronic delta 9-tetrahydrocannabinol treatment. *Pharmacology Biochemistry and Behavior, 47,* 33–40.

Romero, J., Garcia, L., Fernandez-Ruiz, J. J., et al. (1995). Changes in rat brain cannabinoid binding sites after acute or chronic exposure to their endogenous agonist, anandamide, or to delta 9-tetrahydrocannabinol. *Pharmacology, Biochemistry & Behavior, 51,* 731–737.

Sanders-Bush, E., & Breeding, M. (1991). Choroid plexus epithelial cells in primary cultures: A model of 5HT$_{1C}$ receptor activation by hallucinogenic drugs. *Psychopharmacology, 105,* 340–346.

Sarafian, T. A., Magallanes, J. A., Shau, H., et al. (1999). Oxidative stress produced by marijuana smoke: An adverse effect enhanced by cannabinoids. *American Journal of Respiratory Cell and Molecular Biology, 20,* 1286–1293.

Scallet, A. C. (1991). Neurotoxicology of cannabis and THC: A review of chronic exposure studies in animals. *Pharmacology, Biochemistry and Behavior, 40,* 671–676.

Schaeffer, J., Andrysiak, T., & Ungerleider, J. T. (1981). Cognition and long-term use of ganja (cannabis). *Science, 213,* 465–466.

Schmidt, C. J. (1987). Neurotoxicity of the psychedelic amphetamine, methylenedioxymethamphetamine. *Journal of Pharmacology and Experimental Therapeutics, 240,* 1–7.

Shen, M., & Thayer, S. A. (1998). Cannabinoid receptor agonists protect cultured rat hippocampal neurons from excitoticity. *Molecular Pharmacology, 54,* 459–462.

Siegel, R. K. (1979). Natural animal addictions: An ethological perspective. In J. D. Keehn (Ed.), *Psychopathology in animals.* New York: Academic Press.

Siegel, R. K. (1986). MDMA: Nonmedical use and intoxication. *Journal of Psychoactive Drugs, 18,* 349–354.

Siegel, R. K., & Jarvik, M. E. (1980). DMT self-administration by monkeys in isolation. *Bulletin of the Psychonomic Society, 16,* 117–120.

Silling, S. M. (1980, January). LSD flashbacks: An overview of the literature for counselors. *American Mental Health Counselors Association Journal,* pp. 39–45.

Solowij, N., Hall, W., & Lee, N. (1992). Recreational MDMA use in Sydney: A profile of 'Ecstasy' users and their experiences with the drug. *British Journal of Addiction, 87,* 1161–1172.

Steele, T. D., McCann, U. D., & Ricaurte, G. A. (1994). 3,4-Methylenedioxymethamphetamine (MDMA, "Ecstasy"): Pharmacology and toxicology in animals and humans. *Addiction, 89,* 539–551.

Strassman, R. J. (1996). Human psychopharmacology of N, N-dimethyltryptamine. *Behavioral Brain Research, 73,* 121–124.

Strassman, R. J., Qualls, C. R., Uhlenhuth, E. H., & Kellner, R. (1994). Dose-response study of N,N-Dimethyltryptamine in humans. *Archives of General Psychiatry, 51,* 98–108.

Takahashi, R. N., & Singer, G. (1979). Self-administration of Δ9-tetrahydrocannabinol by rats. *Pharmacology Biochemistry and Behavior, 11,* 737–740.

Takahashi, R. N., & Singer, G. (1980). Effects of body weight levels on cannabis self-injection. *Pharmacology Biochemistry and Behavior, 13,* 877–881.

Tanda, G., Munzar, P., & Golderg, S. R. (2000). Self-administration behavior is maintained by the psychoactive ingredient of marijuana in squirrel monkeys. *Nature Neuroscience, 3,* 1073–1074.

Tanda, G., Pontieri, F., & Di Chiara, G. (1997). Cannabinoid and heroin activation of mesolimbic dopamine transmission by a common μ_1 opioid receptor mechanism. *Science, 276,* 2048–2050.

Tashkin, D. P., Simmons, M. S., Sherrill, D. L., et al. (1997). Heavy habitual marijuana smoking does not cause an accelerated decline in FEVI with age. *American Journal of Respiratory and Critical Care Medicine, 155,* 141–148.

Vardy, M. M., & Kay, S. R. (1983). LSD psychosis or LSD-induced schizophrenia? *Archives of General Psychiatry, 40,* 877–883.

Varma, V. K., Malhotra, A. K., Dang, R., et al. (1988). Cannabis and cognitive functions: A perspective study. *Drug and Alcohol Dependence, 21,* 147–153.

Wachtel, S. R., & de Wit, H. (2000). Naltrexone does not block the subjective effects of oral Δ9-tetrahydrocannabinol in humans. *Drug and Alcohol Dependence, 59,* 251–260.

Wallace, B., & Fisher, L. E. (1999). *Consciousness and Behavior,* 4th ed. Boston: Allyn & Bacon.

Weiner, N. (1985). Atropine, scopolamine, and related antimuscarinic drugs. In A. G. Gilman, L. S. Goodman, T. W. Rall, & F. Murad (Eds.), *The pharmacological basis of therapeutics* (pp. 130–144). New York: Macmillan.

Wickens, A. P., & Pertwee, R. G. (1993). Delta 9-tetrahydrocannabinol and anandamide enhance the ability of muscimol to induce catalepsy in the globus pallidus of rats. *European Journal of Pharmacology, 250,* 205–208.

Woolf, A. (2000). Witchcraft or mycotoxin? The Salem witch trials. *Journal of Toxicology. Clinical Toxicology, 38,* 457–460.

Wu, X., & French, E. D. (2000). Effects of chronic delta-9-tetrahydrocannabinol on rat midbrain dopamine neurons: An electrophysiological assessment. *Neuropharmacology, 39,* 391–398.

Yonezawa, Y., Kuroki, T., Tashiro, N., et al. (1995). Potentiation of phencyclidine-induced dopamine release in the rat striatum by the blockade of dopamine D2 receptor. *European Journal of Pharmacology, 285,* 305–308.

Zablocki, B., Aidala, A., Hansell, S., & White, H. R. (1991). Marijuana use, introspectiveness, and mental health. *Journal of Health and Social Behavior, 32,* 65–79.

Zimmer, L., & Morgan, J. P. (1997). *Marijuana myths, marijuana facts.* New York: The Lindesmith Center.

Chapter *12*

Antipsychotics

One of the most common major mental disorders for which drug treatment is almost inevitable is *schizophrenia*. This form of *psychosis* (a general term used to reflect a severe disorganization in personality, thought, emotion, and behavior) may afflict two out of 100 individuals at some point in their lives, and approximately one out of 200 individuals in the United States is currently being treated for this disorder with one or more drugs. It seems almost ironic that this chapter, which deals with drugs that we ask or coerce others to take to eliminate psychotic-like effects, would immediately follow a chapter dealing with drugs that some individuals take to purposely induce these kinds of effects. Perhaps, because the biochemical activities of the drugs discussed in Chapter 11 may have something in common with the endogenous condition, by understanding them we can somehow understand and treat schizophrenia and other psychotic disorders.

Schizophrenia is most commonly evidenced in young adulthood. The symptoms may occur suddenly, generally following severe environmental stress (often termed *reactive* schizophrenia), or they may develop gradually over a period of time (often termed *process* schizophrenia). Symptoms include distorted thinking (evidenced in delusions and in speech patterns wandering and failing to lead to their apparent goals), perceptual distortions and hallucinations (mostly auditory), flattened affect or inappropriate expression of emotion, withdrawal of the individual's interest from other people and the outside world, and altered motor behavior (ranging from complete immobilization to frantic, purposeless, or ritualistic activity), among many others. The symptoms of schizophrenia are often clustered into "positive" and "negative" categories. *Negative symptoms* represent a loss or diminution of functions that should be present, such as blunted affect, lack of energy, inability to experience pleasure, and poverty of speech and thought. *Positive symptoms* include phenomena that are distortions or exaggerations of normal functions, such as hallucinations, delusions, and thought disorder. Although these symptoms vary considerably from individual to individual, they almost always cause severe difficulties in everyday tasks and interpersonal relationships. Therefore, considerable intervention is generally required in order to reduce these difficulties.

People have been using drugs for thousands of years to counteract abnormal mental and emotional states. Unfortunately, though, until about 45 years ago, there was no drug (or any other treatment, for that matter) that specifically reduced the symptoms of schizophrenia without severely stupefying the individual and without inducing a strong physical dependence. This all changed with the discovery of the selective effects of chlorpromazine, a drug capable of both calming the excited schizophrenic and animating the totally withdrawn schizophrenic.

Prior to the 1950s, the major nondrug "therapies" for schizophrenia consisted of isolation, restraint, electroshock treatment, and surgery (prefrontal lobotomy). In 1954 there were approximately 600,000 hospitalized patients diagnosed as schizophrenics. Today, with the use of chlorpromazine and other antipsychotic drugs, there are fewer than one-third that number currently in hospitals. Unfortunately, these statistics do not mean that a cure for schizophrenia has been found, that fewer people are developing the disorder, that there are fewer people being admitted to hospitals for the disorder, or that these drugs are a panacea with few side effects or social consequences. The fact is that although these drugs reduce the core symptoms of schizophrenia in three out of four individuals, there is no known cure for the vast majority of them. Proportionally, there are the same number of individuals developing the disorder now as in the past, and the number of admissions to hospitals with the diagnosis of schizophrenia is far higher now than it was 45 years ago. Furthermore, regardless of the drugs used, the side effects associated with their use range from those that involve relatively minor discomfort to those with socially disabling qualities to those that may be lethal.

The basic rationale for the use of antipsychotic drugs is that they generally work better than nothing at all. In many cases they are used in conjunction with various kinds of behavior therapy and psychotherapy, which most clinicians believe would be totally useless without the drugs. Most experts believe that there are many causes of the symptoms of schizophrenia (perhaps the plural, schizophrenias, would be more appropriate in this context)—many of these having some common biochemical denominator. Although the evidence favors a strong hereditary component for the majority of these disorders, it is likely that the symptoms are the result of a complex interaction between environmental factors and genetic susceptibility (Tsuang, 2000). In addition to parental and societal factors, chemicals in the environment and nutritional factors, among other things, may be involved. For example, for many years alcohol abuse has been suggested to be an important etiological factor in some schizophrenia-like psychoses (Hays & Aidroos, 1986). Whatever the cause, by altering the biochemical functioning of the brain with drugs, we are able to reduce the symptoms.

Biochemical Hypotheses of Schizophrenia

Before describing some of the basic properties of the drugs used to treat schizophrenia, it may be instructive to discuss briefly some of the major hypotheses surrounding this disorder, to provide a context for its treatment with drugs. Perhaps the most prevalent biochemical hypothesis involves the neurotransmitter dopamine (DA) (Seeman, 1987).

The Dopamine Hypothesis of Schizophrenia

Basically, the *dopamine hypothesis* states that there is an overactive or hypersensitive DA system or systems (Figure 12–1) in many forms of schizophrenia. For example, there might

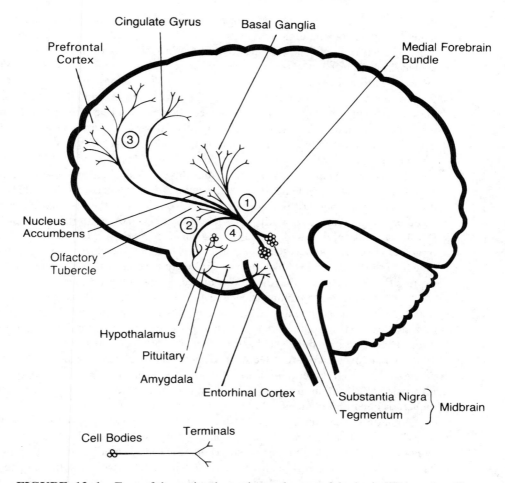

FIGURE 12–1   Four of the major dopamine pathways of the brain likely to be affected by antipsychotics and believed to be responsible for some of the beneficial effects of
these drugs with respect to schizophrenia as well as many of their side effects. (1) The
nigrostriatal tract connects the substantia nigra with the caudate-putamen complex of
the basal ganglia; (2) the mesolimbic tract connects the midbrain with various limbic
structures; (3) the mesocortical tract connects the midbrain with association areas of the
frontal cortex; and (4) the tuberoinfundibular tract connects the hypothalamus with the
pituitary gland. The presence versus absence of dopamine autoreceptors on the neurons
of these different tracts may account for the different time courses for psychosis symptom reduction and motor disturbance onset with antipsychotic drug treatment, as well as
the differences among antipsychotic drugs in inducing motor disturbances (see text for
further discussion).

be excessive DA levels or receptors or a deficiency in one or more transmitters that normally modulate dopaminergic activity, such as GABA, serotonin (5-HT), or norepinephrine (NE). There is little evidence for an excess of DA in schizophrenic patients, and most of the evidence points to DA receptors as the primary culprit in their symptoms. Unfortunately, there are a variety of DA receptors in the brain, often with opposing neurochemical actions. Until recently the DA receptors were designated as D_1 and D_2, with the major distinguishing feature being that D_1 receptors stimulated adenylate cyclase activity and D_2 receptors inhibited adenylate cyclase activity (although they differ in other respects, too). It has become clear that these receptors have subtypes, with important differences in their distribution in the brain as well as neurochemical actions (Cooper et al., 1996). Thus the D_1 receptors are now being called D_1-like, with subtypes designated as D_1 and D_5; the D_2 receptors are now being called D_2-like, with subtypes designated as D_2, D_3, and D_4. To complicate matters further, D_2-like receptors perform a role as both postsynaptic receptors and autoreceptors; for all we know, this may also apply to D_1-like receptors, but for the moment D_1-like receptors appear to be primarily postsynaptic receptors. Most of the focus has been on the D_2-like receptors as the type particularly relevant to schizophrenic symptoms, although both D_1-like and D_2-like receptors in concert probably play a complex role in their expression. We'll have further discussion on these later in this chapter.

The first clue that dopamine may be involved in schizophrenia came from the observation that drugs that specifically reduced many of the core symptoms of schizophrenia (antipsychotics) also induced motor disturbances, called extrapyramidal symptoms (EPS). These EPS were indistinguishable from those of Parkinson's disease, which, by the late 1960s, was known to be associated with DA deficiency and controllable with the dopamine precursor L-dopa. Furthermore, it was observed that when L-dopa was used to control the motor side effects of antipsychotics, it only made the psychosis worse. Within a few years, numerous other observations fell in line with the hypothesis.

First, substances that decrease DA levels tend to decrease the symptoms of schizophrenia (Carlsson, 1978). For example, reserpine (a drug used in the 1950s to control psychotic symptoms) prevents the binding of monoamines to the synaptic vesicles, allowing them to be metabolized by the enzyme MAO, and reduces the amount of DA that can be released from the axon. Synthesis of DA from its initial precursor tyrosine can be reduced with the drug alpha-methyl-p-tyrosine (AMPT). Both of these compounds are capable of reducing the symptoms of schizophrenia; however, since neither of these compounds exerts specific enough effects (for example, reserpine reduces the levels of all the monoamines, and AMPT reduces the levels of all catecholamines), they are not used clinically.

Second, substances that inhibit DA release or block its access to DA receptors are all effective in the treatment of schizophrenia. With respect to the traditionally used antipsychotic drugs, there is a high correlation between their clinical potency (determined on the basis of the average daily dose of the drug needed to reduce symptoms) and their potency in inhibiting the stimulated release of DA from brain slices (Seeman & Lee, 1975). There is also a high correlation between their clinical potency and their relative ability to bind to D_2 receptors (presumably while occupying the receptors they prevent DA from binding and activating the receptors) (Seeman, 1987).

However, once the DA-blocking properties of antipsychotics became known, the hypothesis required an explanation for the observation that these drugs generally needed to be given several weeks before the full treatment benefits were expressed. The explanation was that, because antipsychotics also block DA autoreceptors, DA neurons initially fired more frequently and released more DA into the synapse; that is, there was an increase in DA turnover. This in turn counteracted the drugs' blockade of postsynaptic DA receptors and prevented the therapeutic benefits. With chronic drug exposure, DA turnover was observed to return slowly to pretreatment levels, owing to inactivation of DA neuron firing (Lane & Blaha, 1987). Thus, as the DA hypothesis predicts, the time course for symptom remission appeared to correspond to the time it takes for inactivation of DA neurons to occur.

Third, substances that are agonists at DA postsynaptic receptors (such as apomorphine), or that increase DA levels (such as L-dopa, MAO inhibitors, and PCP), or that increase DA release (such as amphetamine and methylphenidate), or that block DA reuptake (such as cocaine) have been noted to worsen or produce schizophrenic symptoms (Lieberman et al., 1987; Moskovitz et al., 1978). Interestingly, while high doses of apomorphine may trigger psychotic symptoms, low doses of it may actually reduce schizophrenic symptoms (Tammiga et al., 1978). This contradictory effect has been attributed to its having a greater affinity for autoreceptors for DA than for postsynaptic DA receptors. Since autoreceptors play an inhibitory role in regulating DA synthesis and release, their activation would decrease the amount of DA normally released from the terminal. However, the reduced DA release is more than compensated for when higher doses of apomorphine are given, because the drug directly activates postsynaptic DA receptors. This phenomenon may also occur with L-dopa; that is, low doses may reduce and high doses may exacerbate schizophrenia symptoms (Seeman, 1987).

Fourth, a number of studies using radioactive ligands for dopamine receptors have reported elevated levels of D_2-like receptors, particularly the D_4 subtype, in the basal ganglia of deceased schizophrenics as well as living schizophrenic patients (utilizing positron emission tomography [PET] scan techniques) (Murray et al., 1995; Gjedde et al., 1995; Seeman et al., 1995). However, other studies have not found increased D_2-like receptors in schizophrenics (Nordstrom et al., 1995; Sedvall & Farde, 1995; Sedvall et al., 1995). Several methodological problems contribute to the confusion. For example, some studies utilized patients treated with dopamine blockers (antipsychotics), which tend to result in up-regulation of dopamine receptors. As mentioned earlier, the D_2-like receptors constitute a family of receptor subtypes (D_2, D_3, and D_4), and the degree of receptor selectivity of the radioactive ligands used to label these receptors differs from one study to another. Furthermore, for some dopamine receptors no selective ligands are yet available, so indirect methods—based on questionable assumptions—have been used to determine dopamine receptor binding. Finally, many studies of this nature utilize small numbers of patients; with a disorder that is so heterogeneous in its etiology, it's not surprising that the outcomes of these studies have been equally heterogeneous. Studies utilizing PET scan techniques have also reported intriguing results suggesting that an area of the brain of schizophrenic patients that is particularly sensitive to dopamine agonists—the cingulate gyrus—is also one of the areas in which there is heightened activity when schizophrenic patients are actively hallucinating (Dolan et al., 1995; Silbersweig et al., 1995).

As indicated earlier, other neurotransmitter systems may be indirectly involved in the DA hypothesis. For example, several NE tracts exist that may serve to dampen DA activity. Thus, if this modulatory role is decreased, DA activity may increase. This process is consistent with some studies suggesting that the brains of deceased schizophrenics may have lower than normal levels of the enzyme DA-beta-hydroxylase, which is necessary for the synthesis of NE from DA.[1] Also, drugs that inhibit DA-beta-hydroxylase, such as disulfiram (Antabuse) and fusaric acid, have been shown to induce schizophrenic-like symptoms in some individuals (Seeman, 1987). Note, however, that DA may be directly involved in these actions because NE is synthesized from DA. Without DA being metabolized into NE, DA levels would increase in neurons that normally release NE. One can only theorize as to what might happen if DA instead of NE were released from these neurons, and, if so, what would happen if DA activated NE receptors.

There is evidence that 5-HT released from axons of the reticular formation plays a modulatory role in dopaminergic activity. Ever since the discovery that LSD had psychosis-mimicking effects mediated by its actions on serotonergic neurons, disturbances in serotonergic systems have been implicated as a causal factor in schizophrenia. However, since the 1960s, with the recognition that LSD does not produce a model form of schizophrenia, along with the DA hypothesis becoming firmly established, the potential role of serotonin (5-HT) in this disorder received relatively little attention (Huttunen, 1995). With the discovery of the unique efficacy profile of some atypical antipsychotics and their potent antagonism of 5-HT_{2A} receptors, there has been a renewal of interest in the role of serotonin in schizophrenia. A considerable body of anatomical, biochemical, electrophysiological, and behavioral evidence supports the modulatory role of 5-HT_{2A} receptors on dopaminergic systems (Schmidt et al., 1995). However, the degree to which 5-HT_{2A} receptor blockade is involved in improving the negative symptoms of schizophrenia and/or reducing EPS effects—as well as the mechanism(s) involved—is still a matter of debate (Huttunen, 1995; Schmidt et al., 1995).

Several lines of evidence have suggested that schizophrenic symptoms may be due to reduced glutamatergic transmission at NMDA receptors (Halberstadt, 1995; Olney & Farber, 1995), causing an imbalance between glutamatergic and dopaminergic systems in structures of the basal ganglia and limbic system. For example, NMDA channel blockers, such as phencyclidine (PCP) and ketamine, induce both positive and negative symptoms of schizophrenia in nonschizophrenic persons with large doses and exacerbate the symptoms of chronic schizophrenics with smaller doses (Ellison, 1995). On the other hand, treatment with glycine, a potentiator of NMDA-mediated transmission, has been shown to significantly improve the negative symptoms of schizophrenic patients under medication with typical antipsychotics (Javitt et al., 1994). Other lines of research suggest that there is a selective loss of glutamatergic neurons in the brains of deceased schizophrenics (Squires et al., 1993), and increases in NMDA-associated binding sites have been reported in the brains of deceased schizophrenics, possibly due to postsynaptic compensation for impaired glutamatergic neurotransmission (Ishimaru et al., 1994).

Despite several lines of evidence supporting the DA hypothesis of schizophrenia, a number of unresolved questions remain to be answered. For example, why does it take sev-

---

[1]One should remember that DA is found in three types of neurons in the brain: (1) neurons in which DA is the primary neurotransmitter; (2) neurons in which DA is the precursor for NE, which is the primary neurotransmitter; and (3) neurons in which DA, and subsequently NE, is the precursor to epinephrine, which is the primary neurotransmitter.

eral days, or in some cases weeks or months, of continuous exposure to DA-receptor blockers (antipsychotics) before maximum relief from the core symptoms is evidenced? Why are most antipsychotic drugs more effective in reducing the positive symptoms of schizophrenia than the negative symptoms, and why do others appear to reduce both types of symptoms? And why are the latter drugs able to control the symptoms of schizophrenia while at the same time producing minimal disturbances of DA systems that commonly underlie many of the motor side effects associated with the former drugs? Possible answers to some of these questions will be provided later in this chapter, but in some cases answers are not yet available.

Over the past several years, the DA hypersensitivity model of schizophrenia has been modified into a DA dysregulation model, which basically proposes that the symptoms of schizophrenia are the result of DA hyperactivity in some areas of the brain, which may be responsible for the positive symptoms, and DA hypoactivity in other areas, which may be partly responsible for negative symptoms (Brunello et al., 1995). For example, Grace (1991) has provided a model that integrates a number of apparently conflicting observations regarding the role of DA in this disorder. Highly simplified, this model proposes that in schizophrenics a prolonged decrease in prefrontal cortical activity (e.g., due to cortical atrophy) reduces the tonic (i.e., sustained) release of DA in subcortical areas. Over time this reduction elicits homeostatic compensations in DA responsivity (e.g., DA receptor up-regulation) in these subcortical areas. These, in turn, increase overall DA responsivity in these subcortical areas and cause enhanced phasic (i.e., transient) DA release—presumably elicited by behaviorally relevant stimuli—to provoke abnormally large responses. It was further assumed that the tonic decrease in DA activity underlies the negative symptoms of the disorder, whereas the phasic increase in DA activity underlies the positive symptoms.

This model explains why traditional antipsychotics, which are potent D_2 receptor blockers, are more effective in reducing positive symptoms than negative symptoms and why the atypical antipsychotic clozapine, which decreases phasic DA release but increases tonic DA levels, reduces both types of symptoms. It also explains why amphetamine induces only positive symptoms, because it enhances both tonic and phasic DA release, whereas PCP induces both types of symptoms because it inhibits reuptake of phasically released DA while inhibiting DA released tonically via its action at NMDA ion channels. Although this model is intriguing and handles a lot of diverse phenomena associated with schizophrenia and its treatment, further verification of its various assumptions is needed. It must also be recognized that some cases or symptoms of schizophrenia may be totally unrelated to disturbances in dopaminergic functions.

Alternatives to the Dopamine Hypothesis

The DA hypothesis has been the most widely researched and accepted hypothesis over the past three decades, but several other biochemical hypotheses for schizophrenia have been proposed. One long-standing biochemical hypothesis about schizophrenia is that it is due to improper metabolizing of monoamine neurotransmitters. Note that the molecular structures of the psychotomimetic compounds in Figure 11–1 that bear a strong resemblance to the monoamine transmitters all have one or more CH_3 (methyl) groups. Thus, the so-called *transmethylation hypothesis* proposes that methylated transmitters, in conjunction with stress, produce the perceptual and thought distortions common to schizophrenia (Gillin et al., 1978).

Evidence for the transmethylation hypothesis of schizophrenia is very weak. Although numerous methylated neurotransmitter-like substances have been found in brain tissue, they occur in exceedingly small quantities, and there is no evidence that the brains of schizophrenics contain more of these than normal brains do. Some investigators have reported that substances that can act as methyl donors (such as the amino acid methionine) or cause methylation of DA (like the enzyme COMT) can exacerbate the symptoms of schizophrenia. Others have suggested that adding large amounts of substances that theoretically can act as methyl group acceptors (for example, the B_3 group consisting of niacin, niacinamide, nicotinamide, or nicotinic acid) can reduce the symptoms of schizophrenia, particularly those with an acute onset.

Unfortunately, large-scale studies done in the 1970s in Canada, specifically investigating the transmethylation hypothesis and the efficacy of *megavitamin therapy* (the use of large doses of the vitamins niacin, ascorbic acid, or pyridoxine in the treatment of mental disorders) in schizophrenia, were not supportive at all (Ban, 1975). These studies found that nicotinic acid, in doses of 3 grams per day, (1) was no more effective than a placebo in newly admitted schizophrenic patients; (2) was less effective than a placebo in newly admitted as well as chronic schizophrenic patients treated with antipsychotic drugs; (3) was less effective when combined with pyridoxine (75 mg/day) in antipsychotic-treated patients; (4) combined with ascorbic acid (vitamin C) was no more effective in antipsychotic-treated patients; and (5) could neither prevent nor counteract the psychopathology induced by the combined administration of an MAO inhibitor and methionine.

These findings also tend to negate the (rather old) hypothesis that schizophrenia is an incipient form of cerebral pellagra (a disease with symptoms of mental illness most commonly found in persons whose diet is low in tryptophan and niacin), based on idiosyncratic needs for exceptional amounts of vitamin B_3.

Anthropological observations indicate that cases of schizophrenia are rare in peoples consuming little or no cereal grain in their diet but that the incidence increases when these peoples shift to grain-containing diets (Dohan et al., 1984). Furthermore, people with celiac disease, predominantly a genetically based intestinal disturbance exacerbated by consumption of wheat gluten (an insoluble protein), often display symptoms similar to schizophrenia. These and other observations led to the hypothesis that some cases of schizophrenia are due to an intolerance to glutens in cereal grains—perhaps due to their enzymatic conversion into opioid peptides (called *exorphins*) that act on schizophrenia-specific abnormal opioid receptors, which in turn cause dopaminergic and cholinergic dysfunction and the symptoms of schizophrenia (Dohan, 1988). However, clinical tests to assess whether avoidance of wheat products by schizophrenic patients is beneficial have produced conflicting results, perhaps because only a small subset of patients (perhaps 4 percent to 10 percent) with schizophrenic symptoms may have wheat gluten sensitivity (King, 1985; Pfeiffer, 1984).

This diet-related hypothesis involving opioids was one of several hypotheses proposing a defect in endorphin activity as biochemical explanations for schizophrenia. One hypothesis was that there was too much endorphin activity, while another was that there was too little endorphin activity. However, numerous studies with schizophrenics administered opioid antagonists (e.g., naloxone, naltrexone) or opioid agonists (e.g., beta-endorphin, methadone) produced largely negative findings (Schmauss & Emrich, 1986; Welch & Thompson, 1994), which have pretty much dissipated the enthusiasm for both the overactive and underactive endorphin hypotheses regarding schizophrenia. However, endorphins have not been completely ruled out as a factor in this disorder, possibly through an altered opioid-DA interaction (Schmauss & Emrich, 1986). This possibility is consistent with several observations: (1) opioid receptors have been located on DA neurons; (2) lesions in nigrostriatal DA pathways (see Figure 12–1) have been associated with enhanced enkephalin levels; and (3) opiates generally reduce DA cell activity and alter behaviors mediated by DA.

Numerous other abnormalities, which have more to do with structural defects than biochemical defects, have been suggested to be involved with schizophrenia. New techniques for studying living brain structure and functions directly that will likely improve our understanding of this mental disorder include imaging techniques (such as computerized axial tomography and magnetic resonance imaging) and methods for measuring blood flow, metabolism, and receptor mapping (such as positron emission tomography). These techniques have revealed that schizophrenic patients as a group show excessive brain volume loss, exhibited as excessive ventricular enlargement and excessive expansion of the fluid space around the brain (Goodman & Pardee, 2000). Changes in the cellular architecture and circuitry in the prefrontal cortex and decreased density of interneurons in the hippocampus have also been observed in schizophrenic patients. There is evidence that the thalamus of schizophrenic patients is smaller and has significantly fewer neurons than normal (Andreasen et al., 1994; Young et al., 2000). This is a plausible site for a schizophrenic abnormality, because the thalamus serves as the major way station that receives input from the reticular activating system; limbic structures involved in emotion and memory, such as the amygdala and hippocampus; and cortical association areas. The thalamus seems to act as the filter or gate for reaching all cortical areas, so that if the filter is defective, the brain might be overloaded with information—or starved of it—and the result would be problems in understanding subtle social cues, monitoring one's own "inner speech," and interpreting information from the outside world. Other studies have found reduced blood flow in the frontal and prefrontal cortex of schizophrenics as well as decreases in metabolism in the basal ganglia that are reversed with antipsychotics (Buchsbaum et al., 1987).

Interpreting these findings is difficult because most biological abnormalities currently identified are not exhibited in all cases, and only present themselves as group differences. Furthermore, many of these abnormalities are found in unaffected individuals; for example, excessive brain volume loss can be found in the unaffected twin in monozygotic twin pairs discordant in exhibiting symptoms of schizophrenia (Goodman & Pardee, 2000). Some investigators question whether these effects precede—that is, cause—the disorder or are consequences of the different lifestyle or treatment often applied to the individuals.

There are many other problems with this area of research. Some of these are due to the nature of the illness itself. The diagnosis of schizophrenia is hardly cut-and-dried. Symptoms vary among and within individuals over time. Occasionally, the syndrome appears suddenly; more commonly the symptoms have a gradual onset. Often studies fail to employ the same diagnostic criteria to all patients included in them and fail to differentiate between long-hospitalized patients and recently admitted patients. For example, if one is trying to determine the efficacy of a particular therapeutic intervention and includes chronic, "burned-out" schizophrenics, failures may be due to the fact that some schizophrenics cannot improve because their illness is so chronic.

Related to this issue is the likelihood that schizophrenia is not a single disorder, but is actually a set of symptoms with varying etiology. Therefore, with a heterogeneous sample of individuals, particularly a small sample, it is highly unlikely that any therapeutic intervention, which may only benefit a few individuals in the sample, will result in significant differences between treated and untreated groups. It may be, for example, that there are individuals displaying the symptoms of schizophrenia who respond to megavitamin therapy, but in a large group of schizophrenics, they may not be detected.

Other problems in this line of research stem from not using a double-blind procedure (where neither the patient nor the treatment provider knows what treatment condition the patient is in) or from beginning the treatment assessment before a reasonable *washout period,* in which the patients stop taking all medication, has occurred. The fact is, the overall psychological functioning of many patients (such as nonresponsive chronic schizophrenics and patients whose symptoms remit regardless of whether antipsychotics are administered) actually improves when antipsychotic medications stop. Without a washout period, these patients' improvement would be attributed erroneously to the treatment.

Present-Day Antipsychotics

Antipsychotics (also termed *neuroleptics* and *major tranquilizers*) in clinical use today are unrelated chemically and pharmacologically to previously known sedative–hypnotics and anxiolytics (such as barbiturates and benzodiazepines). Although antipsychotics often have sedative-like qualities, and benzodiazepines may reduce schizophrenic symptoms in some patients (perhaps by reducing the impact of stressors that may mediate relapse), the bulk of evidence indicates that the antipsychotics are clearly superior in reducing the core symptoms of schizophrenia (Baldessarini, 1996; Stimmel, 1996). In addition, antipsychotics tend to increase muscle tone and tension, lower the convulsive threshold (which means the potential for seizure activity increases), and have a negligible potential for inducing psychological dependence. Sedative–hypnotics generally decrease muscle tension, increase the convulsive threshold, and have a considerable abuse potential. Antipsychotics have a wide assortment of potential side effects that are not found with sedative–hypnotics—most notably motor disturbances, anticholinergic effects, and allergic reactions. Unlike many sedative–hypnotics, antipsychotics do not produce anesthesia, although they may be used as preanesthetics to reduce patients' apprehension over pending surgery and to reduce the dose of anesthetic required. By themselves, their lethal toxicity is very low, but a lethal synergism may occur when they are combined with other sedative-type drugs. Although not particularly effective as antidepressants, these drugs may be beneficial in some cases of depression.

More than a dozen antipsychotics, comprising over half a dozen basic molecular groups, are currently approved for clinical use in the United States. Representative drugs in these groups are shown in Table 12–1, along with their clinically effective doses (for schizophrenia) and some of the more common side effects (to be discussed shortly). For years fol-

TABLE 12–1   **Relative Incidence of Common Side Effects to Typical and Atypical Antipsychotics**

Antipsychotic	Dose Range	Motor EPS	Sedative Activity	Anti-ACH Effects	Hypotension
Typical					
Chlorpromazine (Thorazine)	300–800	Mod	High	High	High
Fluphenazine (Prolixin)	2–20	High	Low	Low–Mod	Low
Mesoridazine (Serentil)	75–300	Low–Mod	Mod–High	Mod	Mod
Perphenazine (Trilafon)	8–32	Mod–High	Mod	Low–Mod	Low
Thioridazine (Mellaril)	200–600	Low	Mod–High	High	Mod–High
Trifluoperazine (Stelazine)	6–20	High	Low	Low–Mod	Low
Thiothixene (Navane)	6–30	Mod–High	Low	Low–Mod	Low–Mod
Haloperidol (Haldol)	6–20	High	Low	Very Low	Low
Molindone (Moban)	50–225	Low–Mod	Low–Mod	Low	Very Low
Loxapine (Loxitane)	60–100	Mod	Low–Mod	Low	Low
Atypical					
Clozapine (Clozaril)	200–650	Absent	Mod–High	Mod–High	Mod–High
Risperidone (Risperdal)	2–10	Very Low	Mod	Very Low	Mod
Olanzapine (Zyprexa)	7.5–20	Very Low	Mod	Low–Mod	Mod
Quetiapine (Seroquel)	150–800	Very Low	Mod	Mod	Mod
Ziprasidone (Zeldox)	40–160	Very Low	Low	Low	Mod

Source: Based on Baldessarini (1996), Baldessarini & Frankenburg (1991), Jibson & Tandon (1996), and Newton et al. (1978).

Notes: In parentheses under each generic name is its most common proprietary name. *Dose range* refers to the normal daily clinical oral dosage; *EPS* refers to extrapyramidal symptoms; *Anti-ACH effects* refers to anticholinergic effects. For the "typical" antipsychotics, there is a strong positive correlation between the midrange dose for each drug and the drug's tendency to induce sedation, anticholinergic effects, and orthostatic hypotension. On the other hand, there is a strong negative correlation between the midrange dose for each drug and the drug's tendency to induce EPS.

lowing the discovery of their efficacy in the treatment of schizophrenia, it was common to refer to antipsychotics according to the chemical class to which they belonged—for example, chlorpromazine and fluphenazine were classified as "phenothiazines," haloperidol was a "butyrophenone," thiothixene was a "thioxanthene," and so forth. However, it has become clear that this nomenclature is rather meaningless (a point I touched on in Chapter 7) because the efficacy of an antipsychotic drug appears to be unrelated to what drug class it belongs to—not all phenothiazines are effective antipsychotics and not all effective antipsychotics are phenothiazines. At the present time, it appears more fruitful to classify antipsychotics as *typical* and *atypical.* The primary distinguishing feature of atypical antipsychotics is the absence of extrapyramidal motor disturbances (EPS) and other motor disturbances (at least at doses that are effective in reducing the core symptoms of schizophrenia). Other features that some regard as atypical include (1) the ability to effectively reduce the symptoms of schizophrenia in patients that do not respond to typical antipsychotics; (2) a greater efficacy than the typical antipsychotics in reducing the negative symptoms of schizophrenia; and (3) absence of hyperprolactinemia (excessive prolactin blood levels) (Remington & Kapur, 2000).

Despite their very different molecular structures and potencies (in terms of the dosage needed to exert therapeutic effects), at the dosages noted the typical antipsychotics are remarkably similar in their effectiveness in reducing the positive symptoms of schizophrenia. In fact, because of the equivalence in efficacy of the typical antipsychotics, investigators exploring phenomena associated with antipsychotic treatment (such as relapse rates, drop-out rates, incidence of tardive dyskinesia as a function of years of treatment, and so forth) will often lump patients together within or across studies by converting the dosage of the different medications into **chlorpromazine equivalents.** For example, in terms of potency, 2 mg of haloperidol is equivalent to 100 mg chlorpromazine; thus, a patient receiving 7 mg/day of haloperidol would be calculated as receiving 350 chlorpromazine equivalents. On the other hand, although the typical antipsychotics generally share the same spectrum of side effects, their relative potential for inducing these at equivalent antipsychotic doses varies considerably.

Clozapine (Clozaril) was the first atypical antipsychotic to be developed—in fact, the first truly unique and clinically effective antipsychotic drug developed since chlorpromazine (Marsellis et al., 2000). Its pharmacological properties have been the inspiration for the development of virtually all of the recent antipsychotics approved for clinical use. It was unique for several reasons. First, it had minimal extrapyramidal effects, and there was no evidence that clozapine induces tardive dyskinesia (Safferman et al., 1991). (In fact, it was the absence of EPS that led the manufacturer of the drug to question its marketability in the 1960s, because the prevailing view at the time was that a drug's ability to reduce schizophrenic symptoms was closely tied to its ability to induce extrapyramidal motor disturbances.) Second, research indicated that it may be more effective in reducing the negative symptoms of schizophrenia than typical antipsychotics. Third, in addition to being an effective treatment in many schizophrenics who respond to typical antipsychotics, it was shown to reduce the symptoms of approximately one-third of schizophrenics who did not respond to typical antipsychotics. One major drawback to clozapine, however, was its greater potential to induce severe *agranulocytosis*—that is, to suppress white blood cell formation (1 percent to 2 percent incidence per year)—than typical antipsychotics. Because there is a considerable risk of mortality when agranulocytosis occurs, clinicians in most countries, particularly the United States, were reluctant to use the drug in their patients, and the drug's manufacturer was not encouraged to market it. However, once research indicated that this problem could be surmounted with appropriate patient monitoring, the FDA approved its use in the United States. Unfortunately, this monitoring system—the Clozaril Patient Management System—costs several thousand dollars a year to implement. This expense, of course, is still a major drawback for many patients, whose economic status makes the cost prohibitive. Until alternative systems are developed or allowed by the FDA, cost will continue to be a problem. As discussed shortly, the newer antipsychotics (also atypical in several ways) may eliminate some of these problems.

Efficacy of Antipsychotics

Numerous clinical trials with antipsychotic drugs have established their effectiveness in all subtypes of schizophrenia, at all stages of the illness, and at all ages (Baldessarini, 1996). Rarely does a patient treated with adequate doses of antipsychotics fail to show some degree of improvement, varying from complete remission of the psychosis to minimal symptomatic change. On the contrary, placebos and other sedatives (e.g., phenobarbital) produce little mean improvement in large groups of schizophrenics; some individuals improve with these treatments, but an equal number get worse.

Approximately 70 percent of the patients diagnosed with schizophrenia show great improvement in their symptomatology with antipsychotic treatment, and approximately 20 percent show minimal improvement. (These figures may change significantly as the atypical antipsychotics come into wider use.) As mentioned earlier, a few patients get worse with antipsychotic medications, perhaps because of toxic reactions at high doses. Neurochemical differences within the schizophrenic population are a likely factor in differential responsiveness to antipsychotics, but pharmacokinetic factors also may be involved (Verghese et al., 1991). This hypothesis is consistent with studies on institutionalized patients that have demonstrated that nonresponders may exhibit antipsychotic blood levels far lower (often two to seven times lower) than responders when given the same doses of antipsychotics. Another factor in nonresponse may relate to the difficulties in diagnosing schizophrenia; that is, some patients diagnosed with this disorder may actually be misdiagnosed unipolar or bipolar patients (discussed in Chapter 13) and may be more appropriately treated with lithium or antidepressants (Glazer et al., 1987).

As mentioned earlier, one of clozapine's unique characteristics is its efficacy in *treatment-refractory* schizophrenic patients (that is, patients who do not exhibit significant symptom reduction following treatment with at least two different typical antipsychotics for at least 6 weeks at dosages equivalent to 1000 mg/day of chlorpromazine). While the efficacy of clozapine is comparable to that of typical antipsychotics in reducing the positive symptoms of schizophrenia and may be more effective in reducing negative symptoms, because of the possibility of agranulocytosis and the accompanying overall cost of treatment with clozapine, its use is generally restricted to treatment-refractory patients or patients exhibiting disabling and persistent EPS, for example, tardive dyskinesia (Ames et al., 1996; Juarez-Reyes et al., 1995).

Once it became apparent that clozapine was indeed a unique antipsychotic—with one particularly fatal flaw—a variety of compounds with similar pharmacological profiles underwent clinical testing. The first of these to meet the FDA's criteria for efficacy and safety and to be approved for medical use was risperidone (Risperdal). It has rapidly become one of the most frequently prescribed first-line treatments for schizophrenia (meaning that it is a drug recommended immediately upon diagnosis). Risperidone is viewed as atypical because the incidence of EPS in patients receiving no more than 6 mg of risperidone daily—a dosage that is sufficiently effective in the majority of patients—has been shown to be no higher than those receiving placebo. At daily dosages of 10 mg or more, EPS may be observed. Controlled studies in several countries have also shown risperidone to be effective in the treatment of both positive and negative symptoms of schizophrenia (Borison et al., 1992; Chouinard et al., 1993; Claus et al., 1992). The odds are that over 40 percent more patients treated with risperidone will show significant reductions in negative symptoms than patients treated with typical antipsychotics (or 7 out of 10 risperidone-treated patients versus 5 out of 10 patients treated with typical antipsychotics) (Carman et al., 1995).

It is still unresolved whether atypical antipsychotics like clozapine and risperidone reduce negative symptoms directly or secondarily by exerting an antidepressant effect, by improving positive symptoms, or by not inducing extrapyramidal side effects that sometimes mimic negative symptoms. For example, in some instances typical antipsychotics may actually induce negative-type symptoms that may be reduced by a decrease in antipsychotic dosage (Volavka et al., 1996). One analysis has suggested that the benefits of risperidone may be almost evenly divided between a direct effect on negative symptoms and indirect effects through reduction in positive symptoms, EPS or depression (Moller et al., 1995).

Other atypical antipsychotics that have been approved by the FDA for clinical use include olanzapine (Zyprexa) and quetiapine (Seroquel), and ziprasidone (Zeldox), which could also be first-line therapies for schizophrenia (Ames et al., 1996; Borison, 1995). Each of these drugs is well tolerated and has a clinical profile very similar to risperidone, but they differ somewhat in side-effect profile and activity against negative symptoms (Jibson & Tandon, 1996). Agranulocytosis is rare with all of them. Their efficacy in treatment of refractory patients remains to be established.

As yet, there are no consistent pretreatment symptomatic predictors of antipsychotic response. Several studies have suggested that, in comparison with poor responders, good responders are more likely to have better social adjustment and less schizoid developmental history, are older at first hospitalization or onset of symptoms, and exhibit a rapid onset of symptoms (Bowers et al., 1987). There is also considerable evidence to support the view that the earlier schizophrenia is detected and treated with antipsychotics, the more favorable the clinical outcome (Tsuang et al., 2000).

Factors such as antipsychotic dose, major symptom characteristics, and chronicity are important in determining the efficacy of antipsychotics. In spite of the fact that some antipsychotics have been used for over 45 years, there is no general consensus as to the correct doses to be employed, but many clinicians are of the opinion that the doses of these drugs now in use are far in excess of what is required (Verghese et al., 1991; Pollack et al., 1995). In addition there may be a therapeutic window such that levels below or above the window are associated with poorer outcomes. There is widespread agreement that patients with positive symptoms are more likely to respond to typical antipsychotics, whereas those with negative symptoms respond poorly. It is also clear that a history of chronic hospitalization predicts poor response (Volavka & Cooper, 1987).

Analysis of the psychotic symptoms most affected by antipsychotics indicate a specificity in their activity. Agitated, belligerent, impulsive behavior in patients is markedly reduced, whereas withdrawn or autistic patients sometimes become more responsive and communicative. Generally over a period of days, psychotic symptoms of hallucinations, delusions, and disorganized or incoherent thinking tend to disappear (Baldessarini, 1996). Improvements in sleep, self-care, appetite, and sometimes seclusiveness occur. Improvement in insight, judgment, memory, and orientation are also likely in cases of acute psychosis, whereas in chronic schizophrenics, changes in these are variable and often unsatisfactory (Baldessarini, 1996). On the other hand, nonspecific schizophrenic symptoms such as anxiety, tension, and guilt may remain relatively unaffected by antipsychotics. Indeed, in mild cases of schizophrenia these symptoms may be aggravated. In chronic schizophrenic patients stabilized on an antipsychotic medication who experience moderate to severe symptoms of anxiety, use of a benzodiazepine anxiolytic, such as alprazolam (Xanax), has been shown to be useful as an adjunctive treatment (Morphy, 1986).

General improvement with antipsychotic treatment approximates a learning curve, in that there is a rapid change in the first few weeks of treatment, a slowing of improvement in the sixth to twelfth weeks, and a very slow change thereafter. However, symptom improvement in refractory patients treated with clozapine may continue for as much as a year after treatment begins (Ames et al., 1996). The rate of change for specific symptoms may vary; for example, hyperactive and manic symptoms may disappear after only a few doses of an antipsychotic, whereas delusions or hallucinations may persist with lessened affect after weeks of daily drug exposure. The abnormal thought and poor interpersonal relations of catatonic patients may improve weeks before the pathologic motor pattern is altered (Hollister, 1973).

There are some indications that the high-potency antipsychotics like haloperidol most rapidly control the manic patient. There were some early suggestions that these high-potency drugs given in large doses (for example, 100 mg or more of haloperidol) may be more effective when given at the beginning of treatment, with the dosage reduced considerably when schizophrenic symptoms subside. However, more recent studies have not found large-dose treatment to be any more effective than smaller doses of these drugs (Baldessarini, 1996).

There is uneven development of tolerance to the effects of antipsychotics (Baldessarini, 1996). Their ability to suppress psychotic symptoms is fairly stable, although symptoms can worsen or improve over time. In fact, once the symptoms subside, most authorities suggest that lower antipsychotic doses should be given unless the patient has a clear history of symptom worsening when the medication dose is decreased. Tolerance does tend to occur to a certain degree with respect to many of the side effects of these drugs, including sedative effects, hypotension, and anticholinergic effects.

Antipsychotic drugs do not generally possess any potential for inducing psychological dependence, primarily because of the numerous side effects associated with this class of drugs. However, they may induce mild abstinence symptoms after abrupt cessation of high doses; in some cases, there may be signs of malaise, gastrointestinal dysfunction, nausea and vomiting, and tremulousness. A transient worsening of psychotic symptoms may occur. Also, motor disturbances similar to those associated with tardive dyskinesia (discussed shortly) may occur, but then rapidly dissipate. Since most of these drugs have relatively long plasma half-lives or have active metabolites, plasma levels of active drug decline slowly, so that these symptoms are generally not very severe or noticeable.

After a patient has been stabilized with antipsychotic medication, the question of what to do next remains, particularly in light of the potential side effects (some of which may be irreversible) associated with chronic drug exposure. One possibility is to simply stop the medication. However, a review of 66 studies including over 4,000 patients indicated that, during a mean follow-up period of 10 months, slightly more than half of the patients relapsed (that is, exhibited symptom recurrence or worsening) when withdrawn from typical antipsychotic drug therapy, in contrast to only 16 percent who were maintained on typical antipsychotics (Gilbert et al., 1995). As one might expect, the rate of relapse was positively correlated with the length of the follow-up period. (At the present time, reliable estimates of relapse rates upon discontinuation of atypical antipsychotics are not available.) Thus, there was both good news and bad news. That is, some patients will relapse even if maintained on antipsychotics, whereas other patients do not require continued drug exposure and will not relapse even if taken off these drugs.

Fortunately, patients who relapse when taken off antipsychotics completely generally respond fairly quickly once drug treatment is reinstated (Gilbert et al., 1995). Some of these patients may benefit from a significant reduction in their medication dosage (for instance, a 50 percent decrease in dosage). Rather than stopping drug treatment completely, a slow tapering to the lowest effective antipsychotic dosage may be a preferred strategy in many patients. In some cases, these patients' overall psychological functioning may actually improve from the dose reduction (Faraone et al., 1986; Volavka et al., 1996).

Unfortunately, predicting which patients will relapse and which will not is very difficult. Some studies have indicated that patients of younger age or earlier age of onset of illness, patients with higher baseline antipsychotic dosage (that is, those whose symptoms may have been more difficult to control), and patients with recent psychiatric hospitalization appear to be more vulnerable to relapse following cessation of antipsychotic treatment. However, the specific predictors of relapse are not consistent across studies (Gilbert et al., 1995). Studies assessing psychosocial factors in the relapse of patients whose antipsychotic medications have been significantly reduced have suggested that interpersonal variables relating to stress and coping may mediate relapse. Patients may be at a greater risk of relapse if they live with highly critical and overinvolved relatives. Those with reduced risk of relapse either have been involved in behavioral treatments that improve social competence and family problem solving or have social network members with whom they can discuss problems in a helpful manner (Faraone et al., 1986).

Patients with good social adjustment who develop symptoms abruptly in response to stress and who usually respond rapidly to antipsychotics probably should not be maintained on them, since they may never develop the symptoms again. Furthermore, chronic hospitalized schizophrenics who respond only minimally to antipsychotics should also not be maintained on typical antipsychotics, since the risk of tardive dyskinesia outweighs the benefits of these drugs. The use of atypical antipsychotics may be useful in such patients.

Based on the evidence cited earlier in this chapter indicating that a glutamatergic transmission deficiency at NMDA receptors may play a role in the symptoms of schizophrenia, a number of preliminary studies have found that dietary supplements of glycine may augment the effectiveness of antipsychotic drug treatment (Heresco-Levy et al., 1996). Administration of glutamate itself cannot be done because it is too toxic. However, glycine, which is necessary for glutamate-induced NMDA receptor activation and can be viewed as a coagonist at these receptors, can be given in sufficient quantities to raise glycine in the brain and potentiate NMDA receptor–mediated neurotransmission without any apparent toxicity. Across these studies, a 15 percent to 30 percent improvement in negative symptoms was observed, with no corresponding worsening of positive symptoms. These studies suggest that supplementation with glycine or other glycinergic agents may be effective in the treatment of this disease.

Pharmacodynamics of Antipsychotics

As indicated earlier, most of the available evidence indicates that the primary biochemical effect of just about all antipsychotics is to competitively block DA's access to its receptors. As DA autoreceptors at the dopaminergic cell bodies and axon terminals are also blocked, the immediate consequences are an increase in dopaminergic cell activity (that is, firing) and an increase in DA synthesis and release. With chronic antipsychotic exposure, many of these effects are reversed; that is, dopaminergic cell activity decreases, and DA synthesis and release are reduced. The decreased release of DA with chronic antipsychotic exposure has generally been attributed to enhanced DA autoreceptor sensitivity at DA nerve terminals. Chronic exposure to antipsychotics may also produce cessation of firing activity in a majority of midbrain DA cells due to sustained depolarization of the cells' membrane potential as a consequence of prolonged excitation—a phenomenon called *depolarization block* (Grace et al., 1997). It has been proposed that depolarization block of mesolimbic and nigrostriatal DA neurons may contribute, respectively, to the therapeutic effect and extrapyramidal syndromes associated with typical antipsychotics (e.g., haloperidol), whereas the selective inactivation of mesolimbic DA neurons may reflect the reduced propensity for extrapyramidal syndromes associated with atypical antipsychotics (e.g., clozapine). This argument is supported by findings that repeated treatment with both typical and atypical antipsychotics produces depolarization block of midbrain DA neurons. However, although both typical and atypical antipsychotics inactivate mesolimbic DA neurons, only the typical inactivate nigrostriatal DA neurons. Recent behavioral evidence of differential depolarization block has also been demonstrated with haloperidol and clozapine, suggesting that the neural substrates mediating mesolimbic and nigrostriatal activities are functionally independent and differentially sensitive to typical and atypical antipsychotics (Boye & Rompre, 2000).

The ability of all presently used antipsychotics to reduce many of the core symptoms of schizophrenia—particularly the positive symptoms—appears to be due to their antagonism of D_2-like receptors, since they all block these receptors to some degree (Brunello et al., 1995; Meltzer, 1995). Furthermore, their clinical potency (determined by the daily dosage required to suppress schizophrenic symptoms) and relative affinity for D_2-like receptors are strongly positively correlated. In contrast their clinical potency and relative affinity for D_1-like receptors exhibit little correlation, and selective antagonists at D_1-like receptors have so far failed to exhibit antipsychotic actions (Karlsson et al., 1995). The primary difference between antipsychotic drugs—particularly between the typical antipsychotics (such as chlorpromazine and haloperidol) and the atypical antipsychotics (such as clozapine and risperidone)—appears to reside in their differential ability to block D_2-like (D_2, D_3, D_4) receptors and other neurotransmitter receptor subtypes.

Some notable pharmacological characteristics of clozapine that distinguish it from typical antipsychotics and may be contributing factors in the differences in their behavioral properties include the following: (1) clozapine has a relatively weak affinity for D_2 receptors in comparison to typical antipsychotics; (2) clozapine has approximately equal affinities for the D_1 and D_2 receptors in comparison to typical antipsychotics, which have higher affinities for D_2 than for D_1 receptors; (3) clozapine has a much higher affinity for D_4 than for D_2 receptors in contrast to typical antipsychotics that have equal or lower affinities for D_4 than D_2 receptors; and (4) clozapine has a much higher affinity for $5\text{-}HT_{2A}$ receptors than for D_2 receptors, in contrast to typical antipsychotics, which have lower affinities for $5\text{-}HT_{2A}$ receptors than for D_2 receptors (Marsellis et al., 2000).

The weak ability of clozapine to bind to D_2 receptors in the basal ganglia may contribute to the absence of EPS, since the degree of EPS produced by typical antipsychotics is directly related to D_2 receptor occupancy. Because D_1 and D_2 receptors have opposing actions on adenylate cyclase activity, it has been proposed that these receptors are linked to maintain levels of the second messenger cyclic AMP within narrow limits, despite large fluctuations in extracellular DA levels. Thus, a balanced blockade of these two types of receptors might allow antipsychotic effects to be achieved below the threshold for inducing EPS. The low affinity of clozapine for D_1 and D_2 receptors would allow for endogenous DA to compete for and activate these receptors sufficiently so that compensatory up-regulation of these receptors does not occur, thus preventing late-onset motor disturbances, such as tardive dyskinesia, from occurring. Clozapine's differential blockade of D_4 receptors over D_2 receptors may be responsible for its efficacy in the treatment of schizophrenic patients resistant to typical antipsychotics, since recent studies have suggested that it is the density (number) of the D_4 subtype of the D_2-like receptor family that seems to be particularly elevated in schizophrenics.

Most of the recent evidence for the beneficial effect of clozapine on negative symptoms of schizophrenia and its absence of EPS points to its potent $5\text{-}HT_{2A}$ receptor antagonism relative to its D_2 receptor antagonism. It was this particular pharmacological combination that lead to clinical tests with other compounds with these characteristics (Meltzer, 2000). One of these drugs was risperidone, which turned out to have an efficacy profile similar to clozapine and minimal production of EPS (at least at low doses). Virtually all of the atypical antipsychotics that have more recently been approved for clinical use (such as olanzapine and quetiapine) have this particular combination. A number of models attempt to explain why this combination may be particularly effective in the treatment of schizophrenia—all of which are too complicated to discuss here (see Brunello et al., 1995; Meltzer, 1995; Schmidt et al., 1995). Furthermore, with so many pharmacological combinations to consider, it is not clear which ones are most responsible for the differential behavioral effects of typical and atypical antipsychotics.

Another potential factor that may differentiate the typical from the atypical antipsychotics is their relative affinities for D_2 receptors. An agent's receptor affinity is determined by the rate at which it binds to receptors and the rate at which it dissociates from the receptors. In the case of antipsychotics, their D_2 binding rates are virtually identical, whereas their D_2 dissociation rates vary nearly a thousand-fold. Since atypical antipsychotics dissociate from D_2 receptors more rapidly than typical antipsychotics, they may allow the receptors to be more responsive to endogenous changes in dopamine levels, and thus be less likely to give rise to side effects such as EPS and prolactin elevation (Kapur & Seeman, 2000).

As already mentioned, an imbalance between glutamatergic (low) and dopaminergic (high) activity has been proposed as a causal factor in schizophrenic symptoms. At present, it is not clear whether the efficacy of clozapine and other atypical antipsychotics in reducing both the positive and negative symptoms of schizophrenia is related to their actions on glutamatergic systems. Some evidence suggests that they exert antiglutamatergic effects at NMDA receptors, while other evidence points to their acting as functional agonists at NMDA receptors (Brunello et al., 1995; Corbett et al., 1995).

The types of effects exerted by antipsychotics appear to depend on which of several dopaminergic systems in the brain is affected, since there are at least five specific dopaminergic pathways in the brain (Baldessarini, 1996). Four of these are shown in a cross section of the brain in Figure 12–1. The nigrostriatal pathway, often referred to as the extrapyramidal tract, can be thought of as regulating the responsiveness of the basal ganglia to the motor commands of the cortex (see Chapter 5). Thus, if there is insufficient DA input, motor commands are difficult to initiate and carry out. Parkinson's disease is a result of a degeneration of the substantia nigra neurons comprising this pathway. Essentially the same EPSs, sometimes referred to as *pseudoparkinsonism,* can occur as a result of dopaminergic blockade by antipsychotics.

Mesolimbic and mesocortical fibers terminate in many of the limbic areas known to affect emotions and emotional expressions. Electrical or chemical stimulation of these target areas has been reported to produce hallucinations and thought disturbances. Several behavioral and perceptual changes (for example, paranoid ideation, depersonalization, perceptual distortions, catatonia, and mood and emotional disturbances) accompany stimulation or ablation of various areas of the limbic system in humans (Paul, 1977). Therefore, it is the blockade of DA by antipsychotics in these areas that is most commonly believed to be relevant to their antipsychotic properties.

It appears that the typical antipsychotics exert essentially the same effects on the nigrostriatal, mesocortical, and mesolimbic tracts (namely, an increase in dopaminergic activity with initial drug exposure and subsequent decrease following chronic exposure), whereas the atypical antipsychotics like clozapine exert these effects on the mesolimbic and mesocortical tracts while exerting minimal effects on the nigrostriatal DA cells (Baldessarini & Frankenburg, 1991). These findings suggest that the inability of the atypical antipsychotic drugs to decrease the latter's activity may be related to their lower incidence of motor disturbances (namely, pseudoparkinsonism and tardive dyskinesia). They also indicate that the gradual inactivation of mesolimbic and mesocortical neurons may be involved in the delayed onset of therapeutic effects during antipsychotic treatment.

Antipsychotics also differ considerably in terms of their binding affinities for DA autoreceptors, which in turn differ markedly in their distribution of dopaminergic neurons (Meltzer, 1991). Dopamine neurons comprising some dopaminergic tracts possess somatodendritic autoreceptors, whereas others possess few if any of these. Conversely, some DA neurons have autoreceptors that modulate the synthesis and release of DA, whereas others do not. Thus, the differences in autoreceptor type and number among the prefrontal, mesocingulate, nigrostriatal, and mesolimbic DA neurons may be the basis for differences in their basal DA activity as well as differences in their response to DA agonists and antagonists.

Other dopaminergic pathways exist within the hypothalamus (the incertohypothalamic tract) and between the hypothalamus and the pituitary gland (the tuberoinfundibular tract) that are responsible for regulating neuroendocrine function and synthesis and secretion of several pituitary hormones—for example, prolactin. Dopamine receptor blockade in these areas is believed to be responsible for numerous endocrine changes and side effects, including abnormal lactation and menstruation, impotence, edema, and weight gain.

Antipsychotic Side Effects

As noted earlier, the primary differences among the drugs in this class are differential tendencies to induce the numerous side effects (see Table 12–1) associated with their use (Baldessarini, 1996). Perhaps the most noticeable and common of these side effects are the movement abnormalities referred to as *extrapyramidal symptoms* or EPS (so-called because they result from disturbances in the brain structures affecting bodily movement, excluding motor neurons, the motor cortex, and the pyramidal tract). Because many of these symptoms resemble those associated with Parkinson's disease, antipsychotics are said to induce pseudoparkinsonism. The symptoms consist primarily of tremor, *dystonia* (muscle rigidity), and *bradykinesia* (extreme slowness of movement). Other symptoms include *akathisia* (motor restlessness), *akinesia* (immobility), expressionless face, and subtle motor speech abnormalities.

Signs of motor disturbances usually begin within a few days of initiating typical antipsychotic medication and are almost always noticed within 3 months of treatment. As noted earlier, the absence of EPS is a key characteristic of the atypical antipsychotics. Clozapine has minimal EPS effects, even with high dosages, and risperidone only induces EPS at dosages somewhat higher than those necessary to control the core symptoms of schizophrenia. Extrapyramidal symptoms wax and wane. Acute dystonic reactions tend to dissipate quickly, pseudoparkinsonism symptoms may persist or decrease over several weeks, and tardive dyskinesia symptoms may begin to appear after several months (Baldessarini, 1996).

With the exception of the late-onset motor disturbances (tardive dyskinesia), most EPS can usually be controlled by lowering the dosage of antipsychotic or adding antiparkinsonism agents. These are generally drugs with antihistamine and anticholinergic properties (for example, Artane, Benadryl, and Cogentin). The fact that drugs with anticholinergic properties are effective in reducing both pseudoparkinsonism and parkinsonism has suggested to some researchers that these symptoms are due to a dopaminergic–cholinergic imbalance—that is, too little DA activity relative to acetylcholine activity.

Neuroendocrine side effects (weight gain, breast enlargement and tenderness, and decreased sex drive) may also occur. In females, hyperprolactinemia (abnormally high blood levels of prolactin) can result in irregular ovulation, milk accumulation in breasts, decreased vaginal secretions, and light, irregular, short, or no periods.

One rare, but potentially fatal, side effect of antipsychotics that has become widely recognized is the so-called *neuroleptic malignant syndrome* (Caroff & Mann, 1993). Core features of this syndrome, which lasts 7 to 10 days in uncomplicated cases, are severe muscle rigidity, instability of the autonomic nervous system (for example, elevated blood pressure, tachycardia), high fever, and mental status changes (for example, stupor). Early reports indicated that the syndrome was lethal in approximately 20 percent to 30 percent of patients developing this side effect, but more recent reports suggest that lethality has decreased to almost zero, perhaps because of earlier diagnosis, rapid drug discontinuation, and institution of intensive care, or use of dopamine-augmenting drugs (for example, amantadine, L-dopa, and bromocriptine) (Caroff & Mann, 1993). All antipsychotics, including clozapine (Tsai et al.,

1995), have been shown to induce this syndrome, and the potency of the drug is not a proven risk in this development. Upon recovery from the symptoms of this syndrome, the majority of patients can be safely returned to antipsychotic medication, although a significant risk of their recurrence does exist.

Although less disturbing than the EPS induced by antipsychotics, the side effects associated with acetylcholine blockade (such as blurred vision, dry mouth, nasal congestion, constipation, and difficulty in urinating) can be unpleasant. The lower potency compounds also have a higher incidence of orthostatic hypotension and allergic reactions than the high-potency compounds. Examples of such reactions are photosensitivity, dermatitis (skin rash), pigmentary changes (yellow skin and eyes), and agranulocytosis (decrease in white blood cells). The lower potency compounds may also be more prone to induce epileptic seizure activity (Baldessarini, 1996).

There is an absence of EPS with clozapine and a low incidence of EPS with other atypical antipsychotics at clinically effective dosages (Remington & Kapur, 2000). Atypical antipsychotics do have a number of other side effects, which they share with several other typical antipsychotics. The atypical antipsychotics can produce orthostatic hypotension (associated with alpha-adrenergic receptor blockade) and sedation or drowsiness (associated with alpha-adrenergic or histaminic blockade). All but risperidone may induce unwanted anticholinergic effects (associated with muscarinic receptor blockade), such as dry mouth, blurred vision, constipation, sedation, and confusion. (Oddly, one of clozapine's more common side effects is hypersalivation—a paradoxical reaction, since it generally has potent anticholinergic actions, which typically would produce a dry mouth.) These side effects can be particularly troublesome for the elderly. Orthostatic hypotension can result in patients' falling down and severely hurting themselves, and the anticholinergic side effects may increase confusion in cognitively impaired elderly patients.

The incidence of grand mal seizures and drug-induced EEG abnormalities is reportedly higher for clozapine than for any other antipsychotic, particularly at higher dosages (Baldessarini & Frankenburg, 1991). Curiously, however, evidence suggests that treatment-refractory patients who develop gross EEG abnormalities when treated with clozapine may actually have a more favorable outcome for clinical improvement than patients who do not develop such abnormalities (Risby et al., 1995). Since most of these EEG abnormalities are not predictive of developing epileptic seizures, these results do not support the routine administration of prophylactic anticonvulsant medications to clozapine-treated patients who develop abnormal EEGs in the absence of seizure activity.

Tardive Dyskinesia

Just about all of the side effects noted in the preceding section go away if antipsychotic medications are reduced in dosage or are eliminated. However, one potential and considerably troublesome side effect that in some cases may not disappear is *tardive dyskinesia* (Tarsy & Baldessarini, 1984). It is a movement disorder consisting of frequent, repetitive, involuntary movements of the lips, tongue, jaw, face, and sometimes trunk or limbs. The symptoms usually occur after prolonged antipsychotic treatment, and once established, they may persist for months or years following antipsychotic treatment. The symptoms decrease or disappear altogether with sedation or sleep and increase under emotional stress or during activities requiring repetition of motor activities or attention to fine motor tasks. Attempts to consciously control the symptoms may increase the movements. Curiously, however, changes within individual patients suggest that it is not unusual for the symptoms of tardive dyskinesia to exhibit spontaneous remissions over time.

The onset of tardive dyskinesia symptoms is typically subtle, and because the drugs that cause most of the symptoms also mask their manifestation, the symptoms may not become apparent until drug treatment ceases or the drug dosage is reduced. Furthermore, the symptoms of tardive dyskinesia often resemble abnormal movements sometimes observed in unmedicated schizophrenic patients (Fenton, 2000). The incidence of symptoms increases most obviously with the duration of antipsychotic drug exposure and with increasing age (Jeste, 2000).

The estimated annual risks of tardive dyskinesia with typical antipsychotics generally range between 4 percent and 8 percent per year of treatment in young and middle-aged patients (Glazer, 2000a). Symptoms of tardive dyskinesia may be five to six times more prevalent in elderly patients than in younger patients (Jeste, 2000), although the true incidence of antipsychotic-induced symptoms is difficult to determine because the prevalence of spontaneous dyskinesias in unmedicated patients also tends to increase as a function of age (Fenton, 2000). All the typical antipsychotics have been shown to induce tardive dyskinesia to approximately the same degree (Glazer, 2000a). The evidence is fairly clear that the incidence of tardive dyskinesia is virtually absent with chronic clozapine treatment and considerably lower with the other atypical antipsychotics (at low, clinically effective doses), and patients with tardive dyskinesia that are switched from typical to atypical antipsychotic drugs often display dramatic decreases in their symptoms over time (Glazer, 2000b). These findings are consistent with evidence that the ability to induce early EPS is associated with the induction of tardive dyskinesia. Higher antipsychotic dosage, female gender, poor response to antipsychotic treatment at the first psychotic episode, and evidence of neurologic soft signs of basal ganglia dysfunction prior to drug exposure have also been linked to tardive dyskinesia induction (Chakos et al., 1996; Latimer, 1995; Schultz et al., 1995).

Age is a factor in recovery from tardive dyskinesia symptoms. With young patients, discontinuation of antipsychotic medication generally increases the symptoms, but there may be steady improvement over a period of months or years, provided the antipsychotics are withheld. Most research shows that mild cases in the young are most easily reversible, with current remission rates of 50 percent to 90 percent being reported. With older patients, there is poor prognosis for recovery.

A variety of biochemical pathologies are likely involved in tardive dyskinesia. This side effect is believed to be due predominantly to prolonged DA receptor blockade, leading to supersensitive DA receptors and causing a relative dominance of DA over acetylcholine activity (just the opposite of pseudoparkinsonism) (Glazer, 2000c). Decreased activity in certain GABAergic striatonigral neurons and noradrenergic hyperactivity have also been suggested to be factors in the pathophysiology of tardive dyskinesia (Nordic Dyskinesia Study Group, 1986). The ability of antipsychotics to induce excessive levels of iron in the basal ganglia (Gold & Lenox, 1995) or to induce free radical damage to the basal ganglia neurons (Cadet & Kahler, 1994) have also been proposed as mechanisms behind tardive dyskinesia.

Early drug treatments for the disorder consisted of either trying to reduce DA activity or enhancing cholinergic activity. Unfortunately, the former tactic (for example, increasing the dose of antipsychotic) leads only to temporary relief and potential worsening of the condition later on. The latter tactic has been shown to exert temporary or negligible benefits or to induce other side effects. A number of other miscellaneous drugs, including lithium, pyridoxine, niacinamide, manganese, estrogen, baclofen, fusaric acid, tryptophan, barbiturates, morphine, naloxone, enkephalins, hydergine, amantadine, and methylphenidate (in other words, just about everything), have been tried and found to be of limited, negligible, or questionable clinical value in the treatment of tardive dyskinesia (Volavka et al., 1986). More recent studies utilizing the antioxidant vitamin E, which is a safe and highly potent scavenger of free radicals, have reported significant attenuation of tardive dyskinesia symptoms, especially in patients who have had tardive dyskinesia for 5 years or less (Cadet & Kahler, 1994; Lohr & Caligiuri, 1996).

It is clear that until a satisfactory treatment for tardive dyskinesia is found, the prevention and early diagnosis of these potentially socially disruptive symptoms must be emphasized (Simpson, 2000). Although clinicians have advocated that drug-free periods be used routinely to reduce the possibility of tardive dyskinesia and to determine whether the symptoms are developing, several studies have provided evidence that drug-free periods are actually accompanied by an increased risk of subsequent tardive dyskinesia, for reasons as yet unclear (Nordic Dyskinesia Study Group, 1986; Yassa et al., 1986). Effective prevention lies in cautious use of antipsychotics. The smallest doses that sustain improvement should be used, and patients who can maintain gains without drugs should be afforded such an opportunity. Switching the patient to an atypical antipsychotic, such as risperidone, olazapine, or quetiapine would also be an appropriate strategy (Casey, 1999). Although clozapine has the most evidence in favor of its reducing the symptoms of tardive dyskinesia over time, all of the newer atypical antipsychotics should be assessed for efficacy before switching to clozapine, because of its risk for inducing agranulocytosis. It is indeed unfortunate that a person exhibiting, and being treated for, one set of socially disruptive behaviors may someday exhibit another set of socially disturbing behaviors—or in severe cases, even more incapacitating or life-threatening symptoms—for which there is no treatment.

Current Pharmacotherapy for Schizophrenia

The atypical antipsychotics are rapidly replacing the typical antipsychotics as first-line agents for treating schizophrenia (Pearsall et al., 1998; Worrel et al., 2000). They exhibit a clear advantage in their lower incidence of inducing EPS and tardive dyskinesia, and they may also be less likely to induce a neuroleptic malignant syndrome and hyperprolactinemia. In several clinical trials in patients with non–treatment-resistant schizophrenia, the atypical antipsychotics clozapine, risperidone, and olanzapine have been shown to be superior to placebo for reducing positive and negative symptoms, and superior to the typical antipsychotic haloperidol for reducing negative symptoms. They also have been found to be superior to haloperidol in improving some global measures of quality of life (Hamilton et al., 1998; Revicki et al., 1999). Head-to-head efficacy comparisons of atypical antipsychotics in non–treatment-resistant schizophrenia have been inconclusive. While some studies have indicated that risperidone and olanzapine may be more effective than typical antipsychotics in the treatment of treatment-resistant schizophrenia, clozapine remains the standard agent for these cases (Marder, 1999; Worrel et al., 2000). However, it carries a risk of agranulocytosis and requires that the patients' white blood cell counts be monitored. Some studies also indicate that atypical antipsychotics may exert better therapeutic effects on depression symptoms, hostility, and suicidality than typical antipsychotics (Keck et al., 2000).

Unfortunately, none of the atypical antipsychotics are presently formulated for depot injection. Thus, for some patients requiring maintenance therapy who do not take their medications reliably, only typical antipsychotics like fluphenazine decanoate or haloperidol decanoate can be injected in a depot form to provide a very long duration of action (perhaps as long as 6 weeks with a single injection).

The profiles of adverse effects of clozapine and the newer atypical antipsychotics differ, with all but risperidone producing anticholinergic effects; clozapine producing more fatigue, hypersalivation, nausea, and orthostatic dizziness; and the newer atypical drugs, with the exception of olanzapine, producing more EPS (Tuunainen et al., 2000).

Atypical agents are substantially more expensive than their typical counterparts, but when one factors in outpatient and inpatient medical costs with the medication costs, the total medical costs are generally equivalent or lower for the atypical antipsychotics (Hamilton et al., 1998; Revicki, 1999; Revicki et al., 1999). For example, higher medication and outpatient costs for clozapine are offset by lower hospital costs for patients, because they relapse less frequently and spend less time in the hospital.

One caveat to these conclusions is that while they are based on well-designed, multicenter studies that utilized state-of-the-art research methods, most are based on studies that were designed, executed, and interpreted by investigators financed by the pharmaceutical industry (Marder, 1999). Thus, these conclusions should be scrutinized for bias until verified by independent investigators.

Websites for Further Information

General information on psychiatric disorders and pharmacotherapy:

http://uhs.bsd.uchicago.edu/~bhsiung/tips/tips.html

Information on schizophrenia and antipsychotic drugs:

http://www.schizophrenia.com/

Bibliography

Ames, D., Wirshing, W. C., & Marder, S. R. (1996). Advances in antipsychotic pharmacotherapy: Clozapine, risperidone, and beyond. *Essential Psychopharmacology, 1,* 5–26.

Andreason, N. C., Arndt, S., Swayze, V., et al. (1994). Thalamic abnormalities in schizophrenia visualized through magnetic resonance image averaging. *Science, 266,* 294–298.

Baldessarini, R. J. (1985). *Chemotherapy and psychiatry.* Cambridge, MA: Harvard University Press.

Baldessarini, R. J. (1996). Drugs and the treatment of psychiatric disorders: Psychosis and anxiety. In A. G. Gilman, L. S. Goodman, J. G. Hardman, L. E. Limbard, P. B. Molinoff, & R. W. Ruddon (Eds.), *The pharmacological basis of therapeutics* (pp. 399–430). New York: McGraw-Hill.

Baldessarini, R. J., & Frankenburg, F. R. (1991). Clozapine: A novel antipsychotic agent. *New England Journal of Medicine, 324,* 746–754.

Ban, T. A. (1975). Nicotinic acid in the treatment of schizophrenias. *Neuropsychobiology, 1,* 133–145.

Barnes, D. M. (1987). Biological issues in schizophrenia. *Science, 235,* 430–434.

Borison, R. L. (1995). Clinical efficacy of serotonin-dopamine antagonists relative to classic neuroleptics. *Journal of Clinical Psychopharmacology, 15,* 24S–29S.

Borison, R. L., Pathiraja, A. P., Diamond, B. I., & Meibach, R. C. (1992). Risperidone: Clinical safety and efficacy in schizophrenia. *Psychopharmacology Bulletin, 28,* 213–218.

Bowers, M. B., Swigar, M. E., Jatlow, P. I., et al. (1987). Early neuroleptic response: Clinical profiles and plasma catecholamine metabolites. *Journal of Clinical Psychopharmacology, 7,* 83–86.

Boye, S. M., & Rompre, P. (2000). Behavioral evidence of depolarization block of dopamine neurons after chronic treatment with haloperidol and clozapine. *Journal of Neuroscience, 20,* 1229–1239.

Brunello, N., Masotto, C., Steardo, L., et al. (1995). New insights into the biology of schizophrenia through the mechanism of action of clozapine. *Neuropsychopharmacology, 13,* 177–213.

Buchsbaum, M. S., Wu, J. C., DeLisi, L. E., et al. (1987). Positron emission tomography studies of basal ganglia and somatosensory cortex neuroleptic drug effects: Differences between normal controls and schizophrenic patients. *Biological Psychiatry, 22,* 479–494.

Cadet, J. L., & Kahler, L. A. (1994). Free radical mechanisms in schizophrenia and tardive dyskinesia. *Neuroscience and Biobehavioral Reviews, 18,* 457–467.

Carlsson, A. (1978). Mechanism of action of neuroleptic drugs. In M. A. Lipton, A. DiMascio, & K. F. Killam (Eds.), *Psychopharmacology* (pp. 1057–1070). New York: Raven Press.

Carman, J., Peuskens, J., & Vangeneugden, A. (1995). Risperidone in the treatment of negative symptoms of schizophrenia: A meta-analysis. *International Clinical Psychopharmacology, 10,* 207–213.

Caroff, S. N., & Mann, S. C. (1993). Neuroleptic malignant syndrome. *Medical Clinics of North America, 77,* 185–202.

Casey, D. E. (1999). Tardive dyskinesia and atypical antipsychotic drugs. *Schizophrenia Research, 35,* S61–S66.

Chakos, M. H., Alvir, J. M., Woerner, M. G., et al. (1996). Incidence and correlates of tardive dyskinesia in first episode of schizophrenia. *Archives of General Psychiatry, 53,* 313–319.

Chouinard, G., Jones, B., Remington, G., et al. (1993). A Canadian multicenter placebo-controlled study of fixed doses of risperidone and haloperidol in the treatment of chronic schizophrenic patients. *Journal of Clinical Psychopharmacology, 13,* 25–40.

Claus, A., Bollen, J., De Cuyper, H., et al. (1992). Risperidone versus haloperidol in the treatment of chronic schizophrenic inpatients: A multicentre double-blind comparative study. *Acta Psychiatrica Scandinavica, 85,* 295–305.

Cooper, J. R., Bloom, F. E., & Roth, R. H. (1996). *The biochemical basis of neuropharmacology,* 7th ed. New York: Oxford University Press.

Corbett, R., Camoacho, F., Woods, A. T., et al. (1995). Antipsychotic agents antagonize non-competitive N-methyl-D-aspartate antagonist-induced behaviors. *Psychopharmacology, 120,* 67–74.

Dohan, F. C. (1988). Genetic hypothesis of idiopathic schizophrenia: Its exorphin connection. *Schizophrenia Bulletin, 14,* 489–494.

Dohan, F. C., Harper, E. H., Clark, M. H., et al. (1984). Is schizophrenia rare if grain is rare? *Biological Psychiatry, 19,* 385–399.

Dolan, R. J., Fletcher, P., Frith, C. D., et al. (1995). Dopaminergic modulation of impaired cognitive activation in the anterior cingulate cortex in schizophrenia. *Nature, 378,* 180–182.

Ellison, G. (1995). The N-methyl-D-aspartate antagonists phencyclidine, ketamine and dizocilpine as both behavioral and anatomical models of the dementias. *Brain Research–Brain Research Reviews, 20,* 250–267.

Faraone, S. V., Curran, J. P., Laughren, T., et al. (1986). Neuroleptic bioavailability, psychosocial factors, and clinical status: A 1-year study of schizophrenic outpatients after dose reduction. *Psychiatry Research, 19,* 311–322.

Fenton, W. S. (2000). Prevalence of spontaneous dyskinesia in schizophrenia. *Journal of Clinical Psychiatry, 61,* 10–14.

Gilbert, P. L., Harris, M. J., McAdams, L. A., & Jeste, D. V. (1995). Neuroleptic withdrawal in schizophrenic patients. *Archives of General Psychiatry, 52,* 173–188.

Gillin, J. C., Stoff, D. M., & Wyatt, R. J. (1978). Transmethylation hypothesis: A review of progress. In M. A. Lipton, A. DiMascio, & K. F. Killam (Eds.), *Psychopharmacology* (pp. 1097–1112). New York: Raven Press.

Gjedde, A., Reith, J., & Wong, D. (1995). Dopamine receptors in schizophrenia. *Lancet, 346,* 1302–1303.

Glazer, W. M. (2000a). Review of incidence studies of tardive dykinesia associated with typical antipsychotics. *Journal of Clinical Psychiatry, 61,* 15–20.

Glazer, W. M. (2000b). Expected incidence of tardive dykinesia associated with atypical antipsychotics. *Journal of Clinical Psychiatry, 61,* 21–26.

Glazer, W. M. (2000c). Extrapyramidal side effects, tardive dyskinesia, and the concept of atypicality. *Journal of Clinical Psychiatry, 61,* 16–21.

Glazer, W. M., Pino, C. D., & Quinlan, D. (1987). The reassessment of chronic patients previously diagnosed as schizophrenic. *Journal of Clinical Psychiatry, 48,* 430–433.

Gold, R., & Lenox, R. H. (1995). Is there a rationale for iron supplementation in the treatment of akathisia? A review of the evidence. *Journal of Clinical Psychiatry, 56,* 476–483.

Goodman, A. B., & Pardee, A. B. (2000). Meeting report; "Molecular neurobiological mechanisms in schizophrenia: Seeking a synthesis," April 11–14, 1999. *Biological Psychiatry, 48,* 173–183.

Grace, A. A. (1991). Phasic versus tonic dopamine release and the modulation of dopamine system responsivity: A hypothesis for the etiology of schizophrenia. *Neuroscience, 41,* 1–24.

Grace, A. A., Bunney, B. S., Moore, H., et al. (1997). Dopamine-cell depolarization block as a model for the therapeutic actions of antipsychotic drugs. *Trends in Neurosciences, 20,* 31–37.

Halberstadt, A. L. (1995). The phencyclidine-glutamate model of schizophrenia. *Clinical Neuropharmacology, 18,* 237–249.

Hamilton, S. H., Revicki, D. A., Genduso, L. A., et al. (1998). Olanzapine versus placebo and haloperidol: Quality of life and efficacy results of the North American double-blind trial. *Neuropsychopharmacology, 18,* 41–49.

Hays, P., & Aidroos, N. (1986). Alcoholism followed by schizophrenia. *Acta Psychiatrica Scandinavica, 74,* 187–189.

Heresco-Levy, U., Silipo, G., & Javitt, D. C. (1996). Glycinergic augmentation of NMDA receptor-mediated neurotransmission in the treatment of schizophrenia. *Psychopharmacology Bulletin, 32,* 731–740.

Hollister, L. E. (1973). *Clinical use of psychotherapeutic drugs.* Springfield, IL: Charles C. Thomas.

Huttunen, M. (1995). The evolution of the serotonin-dopamine antagonist concept. *Journal of Clinical Psychopharmacology, 15,* 4–10.

Ishimaru, M., Kurumaji, A., & Toru, M. (1994). Increases in strychnine-insensitive glycine binding sites in cerebral cortex of chronic schizophrenics: Evidence for glutamate hypothesis. *Biological Psychiatry, 35,* 84–95.

Javitt, D. C., Zylberman, I., Zukin, S. R., et al. (1994). Amelioration of negative symptoms in schizophrenia by glycine. *American Journal of Psychiatry, 151,* 1234–1236.

Jeste, D. V. (2000). Tardive dyskinesia in older patients. *Journal of Clinical Psychiatry, 61* (Suppl 4), 27–32.

Jibson, M. D., & Tandon, R. (1996). A summary of research findings on the new antipsychotic drugs. *Essential Psychopharmacology, 1,* 27–37.

Juarez-Reyes, M. G., Shumway, M., Battle, C., et al. (1995). Effects of stringent criteria on eligibility for clozapine among public mental health clients. *Psychiatric Services, 46,* 801–806.

Kapur, S., & Seeman, P. (2000). Antipsychotic agents differ in how fast they come off the dopamine D2 receptors: Implications for atypical antipsychotic action. *Journal of Psychiatry & Neuroscience, 25,* 161–166.

Karlsson, P., Smith, L., Farde, L., et al. (1995). Lack of apparent antipsychotic effect of the D1-dopamine receptor antagonist SCH39166 in acutely ill schizophrenic patients. *Psychopharmacology, 121,* 309–316.

Keck, P. E. Jr., Strakowski, S. M., & McElroy, S. L. (2000). The efficacy of atypical antipsychotics in the treatment of depressive symptoms, hostility, and suicidality in patients with schizophrenia. *Journal of Clinical Psychiatry, 61,* 4–9.

King, D. S. (1985). Statistical power of the controlled research on wheat gluten and schizophrenia. *Biological Psychiatry, 20,* 785–787.

Lane, R., & Blaha, C. D. (1987). Chronic haloperidol decreases dopamine release in striatum and nucleus accumbens in vivo: Depolarization block as a possible mechanism of action. *Brain Research Bulletin, 18,* 135–138.

Latimer, P. R. (1995). Tardive dyskinesia: A review. *Canadian Journal of Psychiatry, 40,* S49–S54.

Lieberman, J. A., Kane, J. M., & Alvir, J. (1987). Provocative tests with psychostimulant drugs in schizophrenia. *Psychopharmacology, 91,* 415–433.

Lohr, J. B., & Caligiuri, M. P. (1996). A double-blind placebo-controlled study of vitamin E treatment of tardive dyskinesia. *Journal of Clinical Psychiatry, 57,* 167–173.

Marder, S. R. (1999). Newer antipsychotics in treatment-resistant schizophrenia. *Biological Psychiatry, 45,* 383–384.

Marsellis, M., Basile, V. S., Ozdemir, V., et al. (2000). Pharmacogenetics of antipsychotic treatment: Lessons learned from clozapine. *Biological Psychiatry, 47,* 252–266.

Meltzer, H. Y. (1991). The mechanism of action of novel antipsychotic drugs. *Schizophrenia Bulletin, 17,* 263–277.

Meltzer, H. Y. (1995). Role of serotonin in the action of atypical antipsychotic drugs. *Clinical Neuroscience, 3,* 64–75.

Meltzer, H. Y. (2000). An atypical compound by any other name is still a…. *Psychopharmacology, 148,* 16–19.

Moller, H. J., Muller, H., Borison, R. L., et al. (1995). A path-analytical approach to differentiate between direct and indirect drug effects on negative symptoms in schizophrenic patients. A re-evaluation of the North American risperidone study. *European Archives of Psychiatry and Clinical Neuroscience, 245,* 45–49.

Morphy, M. A. (1986). A double-blind comparison of alprazolam and placebo in the treatment of anxious schizophrenic outpatients. *Current Therapeutic Research, 40,* 551–560.

Moskovitz, C., Moses, H., & Klawans, H. L. (1978). Levodopa-induced psychosis: A kindling phenomenon. *American Journal of Psychiatry, 135,* 669–675.

Murray, A. M., Hyde, T. M., Knable, M. B., et al. (1995). Distribution of putative D4 dopamine receptors in postmortem striatum from patients with schizophrenia. *Journal of Neuroscience, 15,* 2186–2191.

Newton, M., Godbey, K. L., Newton, D. W., & Godbey, A. L. (1978, July). How you can improve the effectiveness of psychotropic drug therapy. *Nursing 78,* pp. 45–55.

Nordic Dyskinesia Study Group (1986). Effect of different neuroleptics in tardive dyskinesia and parkinsonism. *Psychopharmacology, 90,* 423–429.

Nordstrom, A. L., Farde, L., Eriksson, L., & Halldin, C. (1995). No elevated D2 dopamine receptors in neuroleptic-naive schizophrenic patients revealed by positron emission tomography and [11C]N-methylspiperone. *Psychiatry Research, 61,* 67–83.

Olney, J. W., & Farber, N. B. (1995). Glutamate receptor dysfunction and schizophrenia. *Archives of General Psychiatry, 52,* 998–1007.

Paul, S. M. (1977). Movement and madness: Towards a biological model of schizophrenia. In J. D. Maser & M. E. P. Seligman (Eds.), *Psychopathology: Experimental models* (pp. 358–386). San Francisco: W. H. Freeman.

Pearsall, R., Glick, I. D., Pickar, D., et al. (1998). A new algorithm for treating schizophrenia. *Psychopharmacology Bulletin, 34,* 349–353.

Remington, G., & Kapur, S. (2000). Atypical antipsychotics: Are some more atypical than others? *Psychopharmacology, 148,* 3–15.

Pfeiffer, C. C. (1984). Schizophrenia and wheat gluten enteropathy. *Biological Psychiatry, 19,* 279–280.

Pollack, S., Lieberman, J. A., Fleishhacker, W. W., et al. (1995). A comparison of European and American dosing regimens of schizophrenic patients on clozapine: Efficacy and side effects. *Psychopharmacology Bulletin, 31,* 315–320.

Revicki, D. A., (1999). Pharmacoeconommic studies of atypical antipsychotic drugs for the treatment of schizophrenia. *Schizophrenia Research, 35,* S101–S109.

Revicki, D. A., Genduso, L. A., Hamilton, S. H., et al. (1999). Olanzapine versus haloperidol in the treatment of schizophrenia and other psychotic disorders: Quality of life and clinical outcomes of a randomized clinical trial. *Quality of Life Research, 8,* 417–426.

Risby, E. D., Epstein, C. M., Jewart, R. D., Nguyen B. V., Morgan, W. N., Risch, S. C., et al. (1995). Clozapine-induced EEG abnormalities and clinical response to clozapine. *Journal of Neuropsychiatry and Clinical Neurosciences, 7,* 466–470.

Safferman, A., Leiberman, J. A., Kane, J. M., et al. (1991). Update on the clinical efficacy and side effects of clozapine. *Schizophrenia Bulletin, 17,* 247–257.

Schmauss, C., & Emrich, H. M. (1986). Dopamine and the action of opiates: A reevaluation of the dopamine hypothesis of schizophrenia with special considerations of the endogenous opioids in the pathogenesis of schizophrenia. *Biological Psychiatry, 20,* 1211–1231.

Schmidt, C. J., Sorensen, S. M., Kehne, J. H., et al. (1995). The role of 5-HT2A receptors in antipsychotic activity. *Life Sciences, 56,* 2209–2222.

Schultz, S. K., Miller, D. D., Arndt, S., et al. (1995). Withdrawal-emergent dyskinesia in patients with schizophrenia during antipsychotic discontinuation. *Biological Psychiatry, 38,* 713–719.

Sedvall, G., & Farde, L. (1995). Chemical brain anatomy in schizophrenia. *Lancet, 346,* 743–749.

Sedvall, G., Farde, L., Hall, H., et al. (1995). Utilization of radioligands in schizophrenia research. *Clinical Neuroscience, 3,* 112–121.

Seeman, P. (1987). Dopamine receptors and the dopamine hypothesis of schizophrenia. *Synapse, 1,* 133–152.

Seeman, P., Guan, H. C., & Van Tol, H. H. (1995). Schizophrenia: Elevation of dopamine D4-like sites, using [3H]nemonapride and [125I]epidepride. *European Journal of Pharmacology, 286,* R3–R5.

Seeman, P., & Lee, T. (1975). Antipsychotic drugs: Direct correlation between clinical potency and presynaptic action on dopamine neurons. *Science, 188,* 1217–1219.

Silbersweig, D. A., Stern, E., Frith, C., et al. (1995). A functional neuroanatomy of hallucinations in schizophrenia. *Nature, 378,* 176–179.

Simpson, G. M. (2000). The treatment of tardive dyskinesia and tardive dystonia. *Journal of Clinical Psychiatry, 61* (Suppl 4), 39–44.

Squires, R. F., Lajtha, A., Saederup, E., & Palkovits, M. (1993). Reduced [3H]flunitrazepam binding in cingulate cortex and hippocampus of postmortem schizophrenic brains: Is selective loss of glutamatergic neurons associated with major psychoses? *Neurochemical Research, 18,* 219–223.

Stimmel, G. L. (1996). Benzodiazepines in schizophrenia. *Pharmacotherapy, 16,* 1485–1515.

Tammiga, C. A., Schaffer, M. H., & Davis, J. M. (1978). Schizophrenic symptoms improve with apomorphine. *Science, 200,* 567–568.

Tarsy, D., & Baldessarini, R. J. (1984). Tardive dyskinesia. *Annual Review of Medicine, 35,* 605–623.

Tsai, G., Crisostomo, G., Rosenblatt, M. L., & Stern, T. A. (1995). Neuroleptic malignant syndrome associated with clozapine treatment. *Annals of Clinical Psychiatry, 7,* 91–95.

Tsuang, M. (2000). Schizophrenia: Genes and environment. *Biological Psychiatry, 47,* 210–220.

Tsuang, M. T., Stone, W. S., & Faraone, S. V. (2000). Towards the prevention of schizophrenia. *Biological Psychiatry, 48,* 349–356.

Tuunainen, A., Wahlbeck, K., & Gilbody, S. M. (2000). Newer atypical antipsychotic medication versus clozapine for schizophrenia. *Cochrane Database System Review, 2,* CD000966.

Verghese, C., Kessel, J. B., & Simpson, G. M. (1991). Clinical pharmacokinetics of neuroleptics. *Psychopharmacology Bulletin, 27,* 541–564.

Volavka, J., & Cooper, T. B. (1987). Review of haloperidol blood level and clinical response: Looking through the window. *Journal of Clinical Psychopharmacology, 7,* 25–30.

Volavka, J., Cooper, T. B., Czobor, P., & Meisner, M. (1996). Effect of varying haloperidol plasma levels on negative symptoms in schizophrenia and schizoaffective disorder. *Psychopharmacology Bulletin, 32,* 75–79.

Volavka, J., O'Donnell, J., Muragali, R., et al. (1986). Lithium and lecithin in tardive dyskinesia: An update. *Psychiatry Research, 19,* 101–104.

Welch, E. B., & Thompson, D. F. (1994). Opiate antagonists for the treatment of schizophrenia. *Journal of Clinical Pharmacy and Therapeutics, 19,* 279–283.

Worrel, J. A., Marken, P. A., Beckman, S. E., et al. (2000). Atypical antipsychotic agents: A critical review. *American Journal of Health-System Pharmacy, 57,* 238–255.

Yassa, R., Nair, V., & Schwartz, G. (1986). Early versus late onset psychosis and tardive dyskinesia. *Society of Biological Psychiatry, 21,* 1291–1297.

Young, K. A., Manaye, K. F., Liang, C., et al. (2000). Reduced number of mediodorsal and anterior thalamic neurons in schizophrenia. *Biological Psychiatry, 47,* 944–953.

Chapter *13*

Antidepressants and Mood Stabilizers

The primary symptoms of schizophrenia are most notable in the cognitive and perceptual spheres; distortions in mood and emotions are secondary and variable. However, with the affective disorders—depression, mania, and manic depression—mood and emotional disturbances are the primary symptoms, and these may be accompanied by distortions in thought patterns. (Unfortunately, these distinctions may not be particularly clear and can lead to variability in clinical diagnoses.) Studies indicate that as many as 17 percent of the population experience at least one severe depressive episode at some point in their lives. Since depression is a primary factor in tens of thousands of suicides every year, it is a major public health concern requiring intervention. The lifetime suicide risks for men and women diagnosed with major depression have been estimated to be 7 percent and 1 percent, respectively (although approximately twice as many women as men are diagnosed with depression); there is an 80 percent greater suicide risk for untreated suffers than their treated counterparts (Blair-West et al., 1999). Although mania is much less common, the destructive behaviors accompanying it also require intervention. In many of these cases, drugs are a primary form of intervention, either alone or in combination with other forms of psychotherapy.

The treatment of depression is made difficult by the fact that it is both a normal mood state, which a person encounters during periods of loss and which is generally transitory, and an emotional disorder. Depression can also result from a pattern of drug abuse that the person may be reluctant to change. Symptoms of depression as a disorder may remit spontaneously or may come and go over time. Therefore, it is hard to determine whether intervention is necessary or would even be beneficial. However, depression is viewed as an emotional disorder requiring intervention when the person is profoundly sad for a period of time, loses the ability to experience normal pleasure (anhedonia), denies past accomplishments, feels unworthy of current achievements, or expresses suicidal ideas. Physical complaints of loss of appetite and weight, insomnia, early-morning awakenings, aches and pains, and so forth may also be present. Under extreme conditions, a depressed person may severely distort reality and exhibit unusual beliefs or behaviors. Because fear and anxiety may accompany depression, the person may be physically active but may not be able to concentrate on any one task for very long.

The clinical criteria for what is commonly referred to as "clinical depression," or more technically *major depressive disorder*, stipulate at least five symptoms from a list that includes depressed mood; diminished interest; disturbances in concentration; poor self-esteem or guilt; disturbances in sleep, energy, and appetite; jitteriness; psychomotor slowing; and thoughts of death or suicide. The symptoms must have been present most of the time for a 2-month period, and they must have a deleterious impact on the individual's life, such as an impaired capacity to work. The milder mood disorder, *dysthymic disorder*, requires the presence of only two symptoms from this list, but the duration of the condition must be at least 2 years and it must result in substantial impairment (Yonkers, 1998).

For most individuals with symptoms of depression, the contrast with normal mood is in one direction; thus, the diagnosis is typically referred to as *unipolar disorder*. In about one-fifth of persons with symptoms of depression there may be periods in which there is an extreme shift in mood toward mania; in these cases the condition is called *manic depression* or *bipolar disorder*. (Although manic episodes are not always accompanied by depressive episodes, such cases are extremely rare.) During these manic episodes, the person may exhibit extreme elation, display unusually high activity levels, and be irrationally optimistic and overconfident. However, this mood is brittle—that is, easily and dramatically changed by the specific circumstances—and the person can become irritable if frustrated. The thought patterns during mania are often disturbed, with one thought rapidly following another (referred to as "flight of ideas"). While mild forms of mania, termed *hypomania*, may be beneficial to the person in social and vocational contexts, extreme forms of mania can be very destructive to the person's career and interpersonal relationships.

Some persons with the bipolar disorder may shift back and forth between the two extremes of depression and mania, while others may exhibit long periods of relatively normal functioning between episodes. Because depressive episodes are generally more common in these individuals, it is often difficult to determine whether a unipolar disorder or bipolar disorder is present. However, the distinction is important because the types of drugs that are most effective in the two disorders are quite different. Giving a bipolar patient medication appropriate for the unipolar depressive disorder may precipitate a manic episode, whereas giving a unipolar depressed patient medication appropriate for the bipolar patient may not be beneficial and may prolong unnecessary discomfort.

Biochemical Hypotheses of Affective Disorders

As is the case with schizophrenia, there are many theories about the causes of affective disorders. However, because this text deals with chemicals that alter cognitions, emotions, and behavior, presumably through altering the biochemistry of the brain, we will deal only with biochemically oriented theories.

As you read this section, it should become clear that we really have little understanding of what causes dysfunctional mood states or how present-day antidepressants or antimanics produce their benefits at a biochemical level. We know a lot about these drugs with respect to their actions on various neurotransmitter systems, but how these actions relate to their beneficial effects is still a puzzle. Clearly, some actions contribute primarily to side effects; others contribute to side effects and possibly to their beneficial effects; and others are probably linked to their beneficial effects. In reality, we just aren't sure. I wish I could give the readers some simple answers to their questions about these issues, but at present simple answers just aren't available. One thing we do know is that the basic biochemistry of the brain is heavily influenced by genetics and that genetics plays a prominent role in many cases of affective disorder, with the strongest genetic influence being involved in bipolar disorders (Kolata, 1986; Plomin et al., 1994).

The hypothesis that has dominated neuroscientists' thought for many years is known as the *catecholamine hypothesis of affective disorders* (McNeal & Cimbolic, 1986). This hypothesis proposed that depression may be related to a deficiency of norepinephrine and/ or dopamine (primarily norepinephrine) at functionally important CNS receptors and that mania may be related to the opposite set of conditions. However, as will soon become evident, studies indicated that deficits in serotonergic functioning may also be involved in mood disturbances, so the hypothesis has been modified and is often referred to as the *monoamine* (or simply *amine*) *hypothesis of depression* (Hirschfeld, 2000).

The role of catecholamines in affect is consistent with a great deal of research indicating that the catecholamines are highly involved in primary motivation and reward. These neurotransmitters are found in high concentrations in the limbic system and are heavily involved in areas of the brain in which electrical stimulation has reinforcing properties (Fibiger & Phillips, 1981). As noted earlier, one of the primary features of depressed individuals is their lack of drive and their inability to experience normal life activities as rewarding.

One of the first pieces of evidence for the hypothesis came from the observation that the drug reserpine not only reduced mania in humans but also precipitated a severe depression in some individuals treated with this drug. These phenomena correlate with the finding that reserpine depletes the brain of catecholamines by preventing their binding to the synaptic vesicles. Outside of the protection of the vesicles, the catecholamines are accessible to the enzyme monoamine oxidase (MAO), which is present intraneuronally; MAO then metabolizes the catecholamines into inactive molecules. Conversely, it was discovered that some drugs that had mood-elevating properties also were capable of inhibiting the action of MAO (thus they are called MAO inhibitors). Theoretically, this inhibiting action should allow catecholamines to accumulate in neuronal tissues and make more neurotransmitters available for release in the process of neurotransmission. Furthermore, MAO inhibitors were found to block the effects of reserpine; that is, even though reserpine prevents the monoamines from binding to vesicles, without MAO activity there would still be a pool of monoamines in the terminal available for release during an action potential.

Oddly, a few studies done in the late 1960s and early 1970s investigating the properties of alpha-methyl-p-tyrosine (AMPT) and its effects on mood and catecholamines were contradictory to the catecholamine hypothesis and appear to have been largely ignored until recently. These studies found that AMPT treatment, which depletes the brain catecholamines by preventing the conversion of tyrosine into the catecholamines, did not induce depression in healthy adults. However, AMPT did induce agitation in some adults with a previous history of depression, worsened depression in some patients who were already depressed, and reduced manic symptoms in some bipolar patients who were in a mania phase (Delgado et al., 1993). Thus, it should have been recognized early on that catecholamine deficiency may not be a direct cause of depression, although it may be a predisposing factor in some individuals (more on this issue shortly).

In contrast to the effects of AMPT, the actions and effects of the potent psychostimulants amphetamine and cocaine do appear to fit in with the catecholamine hypothesis. As noted in Chapter 9, it has long been recognized that these drugs elevate mood and can induce mania and that these effects correlate with their ability to temporarily increase the levels of catecholamines in the synapse (by increasing the amounts released or blocking their reuptake after release). However, prolonged use of these drugs depletes catecholamines (probably because they are used faster than they are synthesized). This depletion correlates with the depression and lethargy that often occur when the person stops taking these drugs.

Further evidence for the catecholamine hypothesis came with the discovery of the tricyclic antidepressants (so called because of their three-ringed molecular structure). Many studies noted that the primary biochemical action of these drugs was inhibition of the reuptake of catecholamines back into the axon terminal, thus allowing them to stay in the synaptic cleft longer and to have greater access to their receptors. Similar actions occur with more recently developed nontricyclic antidepressants. However, it was with these observations that the catecholamine hypothesis began to fall apart, because the reuptake-blocking action of tricyclics was observed to occur within minutes of exposure, but their mood-elevating effects generally take several days or weeks of chronic exposure. Furthermore, nondepressed humans evidence no signs of mood elevation when these drugs are administered.

Lithium is another drug with actions that on the surface appear to be consistent with the catecholamine hypothesis but that upon close examination are paradoxical. Lithium is a very effective treatment for manic symptoms, and it may also antagonize some effects of amphetamine and cocaine. Furthermore, several studies on the biochemical effects of lithium suggest that it either reduces the amount of catecholamine released from nervous tissue or enhances catecholamine reuptake (Baldessarini, 1996). However, as is the case with the tricyclics, these physiological effects occur rapidly, whereas remission (the clinical term for lessening or abating) of manic symptoms takes several days or weeks to occur. These biochemical actions are also hard to reconcile with the fact that lithium can significantly reduce the likelihood of depressive cycles in the manic-depressive patient.

Direct evidence for noradrenergic dysfunction in depressed patients is weak. The results of studies attempting to correlate levels of MHPG, the major norepinephrine metabolite, in urine or blood with depressive symptoms have been inconsistent (Delgado, 2000). Few studies have been conducted on the potential association between depressive symptoms and MHPG levels in the cerebrospinal fluid (CSF), which is more likely to represent noradrenergic activity in the CNS. However, a recent study has shown a substantial correlation between CSF MHPG concentrations and self-rated depression in abstinent alcoholics (Heinz et al., 1999). Several studies have suggested that depressed patients have higher densities or greater sensitivities of presynaptic alpha-2-adrenoceptors (autoreceptors), which could result in lower norepinephrine availability, and antidepressant response has been shown to be associated with decreases in the density or activity of these receptors (Delgado, 2000; Gurguis et al., 1999). Finally, up-regulation of beta-adrenoceptors has been suggested to occur in depressed patients, and the down-regulation of beta-adrenoceptors with drug treatment is often regarded as a marker of antidepressant efficacy (Delgado, 2000).

It is unlikely that a single neurotransmitter is responsible for mood and mood disorders. Dysfunction in serotonergic systems was proposed as a factor in affective disorders in the 1960s, but until the mid-1980s most attention was focused on noradrenergic systems in these disorders. However, recently there has been refocus on serotonin (5-HT) with the recognition that some very effective tricyclic antidepressants potently block 5-HT reuptake—actually having a greater affinity for the 5-HT uptake transport pump than for the NE pump. Furthermore, several studies have found that people who commit suicide are likely to have low levels of a serotonin metabolite, 5-HIAA, in their cerebrospinal fluid as well as more 5-HT$_2$ receptors in their prefrontal cortex—both of which are consistent with diminished serotonergic transmission (Arango et al., 1990). Thus, the monoamine serotonin is also viewed as being important in certain cases of depression. In fact, it was the belief that serotonin plays a role in depression that led to the development of the "selective serotonin reuptake inhibitors" (SSRIs) as a potential treatment. That the symptoms of depression may be the result of either insufficient noradrenergic or serotonergic activity would not be surprising, considering the fact that in the CNS both systems greatly overlap in terms of distribution and physiological activity (see, for example, Figure 5–4).

It would seem that the most direct way of determining whether insufficient levels of catecholamines or 5-HT in the CNS are direct causes of depression would be to deplete the brain of one or the other of these monomines in normal, healthy humans and see if they develop the symptoms of depression. Acute depletion of catechoamines can easily be accomplished by treatment with the drug alpha-methyl-p-tyrosine (AMPT), which prevents the conversion of the amino acid tyrosine into the catecholamines, or with the administration of an amino acid mixture that is deficient in the catecholamine precursors phenylalanine and tyrosine. Similarly, acute depletion of 5-HT can easily be accomplished with the administration of an amino acid mixture that is deficient in tryptophan (the amino acid precusor for 5-HT). (See pages 88–89 for an explanation for why this procedure affects CNS monoamine levels.) Although numerous studies of this nature have been conducted since the 1960s, no clear picture has emerged from their findings. While both catecholamine and 5-HT depletion have been shown to lower mood in many individuals without a history of depression, the effects are inconsistent and the mood-lowering effect is not as great as that seen in depressed patients (Delgado et al., 2000; Leyton et al., 1999: Smith et al., 1987; Young et al., 1985). The effect of these treatments on mood may depend on whether the individual has a genetic susceptibility for major affective disorders (Benkelfat et al., 1994; Ellenbogen et al., 1996), or is exposed to aversive psychological conditions (Leyton et al., 2000).

Similar studies conducted with unmedicated, depressed patients have not found that depletion of either catecholamines or 5-HT reliably worsens their depression (although this may be due to the patients already being close to "basement" levels). On the other hand, a consistent pattern of results has been found with depressed patients who differentially respond to either noradrenergic- or serotonergic-specific antidepressants (discussed later in this chapter). That is, patients who responded well to serotonergic-specific antidepressants were much more likely show relapse with 5-HT depletion than with catecholamine depletion, and patients who responded well to noradrenergic-specific antidepressants were much more likely to show relapse with catecholamine depletion than with 5-HT depletion (Delgado & Moreno, 2000).

Thus, the most clear-cut conclusions from these studies is that the availability of NE appears to be essential for maintaining an antidepressant response to noradrenergic-enhancing drugs and that the availability of 5-HT appears to be essential for maintaining an antidepressant response to serotonergic-enhancing drugs (Delgado, 2000). It also appears that there is no single mechanism of antidepressant drug action; both the noradrenergic and serotonergic systems are important. Finally, it appears unlikely that a simple deficiency or dysfunction in serotonergic and/or noradrenergic systems is the cause of depression.

In summary, while it is generally accepted that, acutely administered, most antidepressant drugs enhance monoaminergic neurotransmission, it is not clear how their actions are related to depression symptom remission. The NE or 5-HT reuptake blockade by the tricyclics and the SSRIs and the inhibition of MAO by MAO inhibitors are rapid, but the lifting of symptoms is slow. This clearly indicates that these drugs' acute actions per se are not responsible for the antidepressant response to these drugs, but it is the neuroadaptive changes in the nervous system that occur with chronic exposure that underlie the therapeutic response to them. Several lines of research suggest that these neuroadaptive changes include desensitization of the 5-HT reuptake process; desensitization of 5-HT autoreceptors (5-HT_{1A} and 5-HT_{1D} receptors) regulating serotonergic neuron firing and release of 5-HT; and desensitization of alpha-2-adrenoceptors that normally inhibit NE and/or 5-HT release. Most effective antidepressant treatments, including ECT, have been shown to have one or more of these properties, with the net effect of enhancing 5-HT neurotransmission (Blier & de Montigny, 1994; Cryan & Leonard, 2000; Stahl, 1998). However, there is an unresolved discrepancy between the effects of ECT, a very effective antidepressant treatment that seems to up-regulate 5-HT_2 receptors, and virtually all known antidepressant drugs, which are capable of down-regulating 5-HT_2 receptors with chronic exposure, a phenomenon that correlates well with the reduction in the symptoms of depression in depressed patients. (Unfortunately, when these studies were done, we didn't know that there are at least three receptor subtypes belonging to the 5-HT_2 family, so we don't know if we're talking about the same types of 5-HT_2 receptors.)

Since the 1960s, the monoamine hypothesis of affective disorders has been a useful model for our understanding of mood disorders and for developing of pharmacological treatments for them. Unfortunately, as the previous discussion suggests, the hypothesis has sufficient holes in it that it may be invalid. More recent studies measuring postmortem brains and utilizing *in vivo* brain-imaging techniques have begun to reveal some consistent findings that point to the role of atrophy or loss of neurons, as well as glia, in the prefrontal cortex and the hippocampus of patients with mood disorders, which may be caused by stress or other brain insults (Duman et al., 1997; Rajkowska et al., 1999). Other studies have suggested that chronic treatment with lithium and antidepressants may exert their beneficial effects by activating neurotrophic or neuroprotective processes that may reverse or ameliorate these neuropathological conditions (Duman & Charney, 1999; Moore et al., 2000). We shall have to wait and see if further research utilizing more sophisticated new techniques will be able to determine whether these new views on the causes and treatments for mood disorders can successfully replace the old views.

Acetylcholine has also been implicated in affective disorders. It has been suggested that an overactive acetylcholine system or an imbalance between acetylcholine and norepinephrine is a causative factor in depression (Fritze, 1993). This hypothesis is supported by the clinical finding that physostigmine, an inhibitor of the enzyme that normally inactivates acetylcholine, may aggravate depression and reduce mania. This is consistent with the fact that many antidepressants, some of which have minimal effects on either norepinephrine or serotonin reuptake, have anticholinergic properties. However, because more recently developed antidepressants (e.g., the SSRIs) are essentially void of anticholinergic properties, it is unlikely that excessive cholinergic activity plays much of a role in depression.

Decreased GABAergic function may play a role in various forms of endogenous depressions, because GABA-mimetic drugs have been found to be effective antidepressants. Consistent with this hypothesis are studies noting that the cerebrospinal fluid of severely depressed patients contains significantly higher concentrations of endogenous inhibitors of benzodiazepine agonists than found in age- and sex-matched normal volunteers (Barbaccia et al., 1988).

Finally, endorphins have also been implicated in some cases of depression. They are found in relatively high concentrations in the limbic system and appear to modulate many of its activities. Also, narcotics have long been recognized for their euphoric and antidepressant properties. There has been speculation that many narcotic addicts comprise a subclass of depressed individuals who take narcotics to feel "normal" (Khantzian, 1985). Unfortunately, should this hypothesis prove to be valid, it would make drug treatment difficult because all known substitutes for endorphins—both exogenous and endogenous—have the strong potential for inducing tolerance and physical dependence with chronic use.

Pharmacotherapy for Depression

The three major classes of drugs currently used in the United States for the treatment of depression are the SSRIs, the tricyclics, and the MAO inhibitors. Members of the last two classes were introduced in the 1950s, and the first of the SSRIs—fluoxetine (Prozac)—was approved for use in the late 1980s. The research literature suggests that, as a group, antidepressants are effective in 50 percent to 60 percent of patients with unipolar depression and that placebo treatment is effective in 20 percent to 30 percent, with higher placebo rates for patients with mild depression (Quitkin et al., 2000; Thase, 1999). Skeptics have argued that the difference in efficacy rate between antidepressant therapy and placebo may be largely illusionary (Kirsch, 2000), perhaps resulting from clinician bias (e.g., because clues from side effects of the active drug may be distinguished from inactive placebo). Others who have reanalyzed many of the original sources that led to these claims have failed to provide support for these arguments (Quitkin et al., 2000). Unfortunately, until proper controls are employed (which can be very costly to the pharmaceutical industry that provides the funding for most clinical trials), the question of how much of the actual efficacy of antidepressant drugs can be attributed to their peculiar biochemical properties remains unresolved.

No single antidepressant drug has been shown to be effective in relieving the symptoms of unipolar depression in more than two out of every three patients (Davis et al., 1993; Frank et al., 1993; Mulrow et al., 2000). However, drugs with very different pharmacological properties, while appearing comparable in terms of inducing global changes in depression, may differ considerably in terms of their ability to reduce specific symptoms (for example, depersonalization; depressed mood; early, middle, and late insomnia) commonly assessed in global depression inventories (for instance, the Hamilton Rating Scale for Depression, or HAM-D) (Leon et al., 1993). Because there is tremendous variation in the pharmacodynamics of different antidepressants and because depression may be caused by a variety of mechanisms, with sufficient patience and trials with different types of antidepressants, alone or combined with other drug therapy or psychotherapy, the overall treatment efficacy rate may approach 90 percent (McGrath et al., 1993; Thase, 1999). Unfortunately, about one out of every four patients will relapse, even when maintained on an antidepressant medication; again, shifting to another type of antidepressant will produce symptom remission in many of these patients.

Placebo efficacy rates vary considerably depending on a variety of factors—for example, approximately 40 percent efficacy in married or mildly depressed patients versus approximately 20 percent in single or more severely depressed patients (Wilcox et al., 1992). About half of these responders will relapse with placebo maintenance. There is some evidence that the difference in efficacy between active medications and placebo may increase after 6 weeks of treatment, but because of ethical and economic reasons, many studies of this nature do not go much beyond a 3- or 4-week evaluation period (Prien, 1988). In any case, one must consider the possibility that some patients who improve with these medications do so because of a true drug effect, while others do so because of nonspecific (placebo) factors. Evidence suggests that a true drug response is more likely to be delayed and more persistent than a nonspecific response and that those patients who relapse with continued antidepressant therapy are more likely to display placebo-response patterns (early onset and/or fluctuating course) (Harrison et al., 1988).

Actually, the early and substantial placebo response in depressed patients has led to the mistaken belief that antidepressant drugs take several weeks (2 to 6) to produce their therapeutic effects. The fact is detectable changes in some mood scales do occur within 7 days of drug treatment; the problem is in differentiating these effects from placebo effects. For example, in a series of studies by Martin Katz and his colleagues (reviewed in Derivan, 1995), it was found that tricyclic antidepressants do act in responders within the first week of treatment, with responders distinguishable from nonresponders in terms of improving affect and cognitive functioning (such as thinking and concentration). However, in general, it is not until the second week of treatment that active treatment effects begin to separate reliably from placebo treatment effects (Montgomery, 1995).

Selective Serotonin Reuptake Inhibitors (SSRIs)

As discussed shortly, the tricyclic antidepressants were the first-line agents used in the treatment of depression for many years and have been the prototype drugs against which all newcomers have been compared. While the evidence is clear that they are effective in the treatment of depression, they have a wide variety of potential side effects and a low therapeutic index, which is due to the fact that these drugs act on a wide variety of neurotransmitter receptors and uptake transporters. Because of these problems, along with the growing consensus that 5-HT was a vital component to normal mood, researchers set out to develop drugs that would have a high affinity for the 5-HT uptake site and a low affinity for other neurotransmitter uptake sites and receptors, and thus potentially produce an effective antidepressant without the side effects of the tricyclics. As a result of trial and error research, the **selective serotonin reuptake inhibitors, or SSRIs,** were born (Stanford, 1996). The first of these to be approved for clinical use in the United States in 1987 was fluoxetine (Prozac), and it has rapidly become one of the most widely prescribed of all antidepressants (Barondes, 1994). Members of this class of drugs available for prescription now include sertraline (Zoloft), paroxetine (Paxil), citalopram (Celexa), and fluvoxamine (Luvox). Ironically, while Prozac has provoked considerable scientific interest in the SSRIs as therapeutic drugs in the mental health field and has acquired public awareness that is not yet evident with other SSRIs, it may actually be the least selective of the SSRIs. That is, it does exhibit considerable effects on catecholamine function in the brain (Stanford, 1996).

Since their introduction in the late 1980s, the SSRIs have become the first-line drugs in the treatment of depression. Their popularity derives not from their exhibiting greater efficacy in reducing the core symptoms of depression, which is comparable to that of the tricyclics and MAOIs and may actually be lower than the efficacy of tricyclics in severe cases of depression (Anderson, 2000). It derives instead from their less objectionable side effects. That is, they don't have anticholinergic side effects such as dry mouth and abnormal heart rhythms, and they don't increase the risk of heart attacks (myocardial infarctions) as do the tricyclics (Cohen et al., 2000). This makes them more effective in the treatment of some patients—for example, the elderly. Furthermore, they are much less toxic than tricyclics in large doses and therefore pose less danger as a potential instrument for suicide. Also, they do not produce the toxic interaction with a number of foods that many of the MAO inhibitors are capable of. The SSRIs are generally better tolerated in combination with most medicines (notable exceptions are lithium and MAO inhibitors) or alcohol (Goodnick, 1991a), although the SSRIs do inhibit the action of a wide variety of P450 enzymes that are responsible for metabolizing most drugs (Kent, 2000). Thus, the plasma concentrations and actions of drugs such as caffeine, beta-blockers, antipsychotics, nonsteroidal anti-inflammatory analgesics, benzodiazepines, opiates, other SSRIs, and tricyclics, among many others, may be increased when taken with these drugs.

Due to fewer side effects, there is greater patient acceptance of the SSRIs and compliance with treatment, which often determines treatment outcome. However, the SSRIs have a wide range of side effects—most notably nausea, headaches, nervousness, insomnia, or sexual dysfunction (for instance, impotence, inability to achieve orgasm)—which some patients are unable to tolerate. Overall, the safety factor is overwhelmingly in favor of the SSRIs over the older tricyclics and MAO inhibitors, which is why they have become the first choice in the treatment of depression in such a short time (Swinkles & de Jonghe, 1995). However, as with all antidepressants, they are not effective in all patients, even at maximal dosages and with sufficiently long exposure, and some patients may find the side effects intolerable. In these cases, another class of antidepressant may be effective.

One potentially life-threatening complication with the SSRIs is their ability to induce a *serotonin syndrome* (Lane & Baldwin, 1997). More often this syndrome occurs when an SSRI is used concurrently with another substance that also increases extracellular levels of 5-HT (e.g., other antidepressants, St. John's wort). The symptoms include disorientation and confusion, behavioral agitation and restlessness, fever, shivering, profuse perspiration, diarrhea, and coordination impairment and involuntary muscle contraction, and they may go undetected because they are sometimes similar to symptoms induced by the SSRI. The difference between this syndrome and the occurrence of adverse effects caused by SSRIs alone is the clustering of the signs and symptoms, their severity, and their duration.

The SSRIs belong to different chemical families, and the only common property they share is their capacity to inhibit the uptake of 5-HT; thus, it is indisputable that they exert their therapeutic effect primarily via 5-HT systems (Blier & de Montigny, 1994). However, with over a dozen receptors for 5-HT to act on—many with distinct distributions—the relationship between their pharmacodynamic properties and their therapeutic effects is not clear. It is clear that the immediate actions of these drugs is only the beginning of a series of molecular changes in the brain that eventually leads to symptom relief, since the action of 5-HT reuptake inhibition by these drugs is almost immediate, whereas it generally takes 1 to 2 weeks—in some cases up to a month—of drug exposure for symptom relief to be clearly distinguishable from that which is achieved with a placebo, regardless of the disorder (Barondes, 1994).

Most of the SSRIs have relatively long elimination half-lives, e.g., 14 to 26 hours for paroxetine, sertraline, and fluvoxamine, so that they may be administered as a single daily dose (DeVane, 1994). The extended half-life of fluoxetine of 4 to 6 days—and of its active metabolite, norfluoxetine, of 4 to 16 days—requires an extended period of time to establish steady-state plasma levels and a prolonged washout period when dosing is discontinued. These drugs are all cleared from the body mostly through hepatic metabolism, and all except paroxetine and fluvoxamine are metabolized into pharmacologically active metabolites. Like the tricyclics, the SSRIs display a broad variability in steady-state plasma levels, but due to their greater safety/toxicity profile, the variability in clearance is of lesser importance than with the tricyclics. Unfortunately, no usable relationship between SSRI plasma concentration levels and therapeutic effects has been found, and widely varying concentrations appear to have little relationship to adverse effects.

As discussed in Chapter 8, the SSRI antidepressants have been found to be beneficial in a wide variety of anxiety-related disorders with no clear connection with depression. For example, they have been found to be the most effective drug treatment for obsessive–compulsive disorder. They have been prescribed for a number of other symptoms, many of which aren't even considered indicative of a mental disorder (Barondes, 1994). These include excessive sensitivity to criticism, fear of rejection, lack of self-esteem, a deficiency in the ability to experience pleasure, premature ejaculation, premenstrual dysphoric disorder, eating disorders, obesity, borderline personality disorders, self-injurious behavior in the developmentally disabled, alcoholism, and cocaine abuse. However, it should be noted that adequate documentation of the efficacy of these drugs in these symptoms (disorders), in comparison to placebo, is lacking.

None of the SSRIs have been associated with abuse or dependence. Abstinence symptoms of physiological and psychological discomfort (e.g., dizziness, gastrointestinal symptoms, and anxiety/dysphoria), can occur following abrupt discontinuation of chronic SSRI treatment, with the symptoms being more prominent with SSRIs with shorter plasma half-lives (Michelson et al., 2000). Documented evidence for tolerance development to their antidepressant properties is also lacking, but tolerance often occurs to the early-onset side effects of these drugs. In general, to prevent or lessen the magnitude of these effects, initial dosages start low and are gradually increased.

Shortly after fluoxetine came on the market and was recognized to be a novel, atypical antidepressant, numerous anecdotal reports came out suggesting that it might induce suicidal thoughts or actions in a small portion of patients. However, because these patients typically exhibit characteristics, such as depression, for which suicidal ideation is not uncommon, it was difficult to assess the degree to which fluoxetine was responsible. Large-scale studies have determined, whether causal or not, that the incidence of violent suicidal preoccupation with fluoxetine treatment is rare—less than 5 percent of patients treated—and does not appear to be significantly different from that which occurs with other antidepressants (Beasley et al., 1991; Fava & Rosenbaum, 1991). In fact, as one might expect from an antidepressant, reduction in suicidal ideation is much more likely to occur. For example, a study investigating the relationship between fluoxetine use and suicidal behavior in patients with anxiety disorders and/or depression showed that patients using fluoxetine had a significantly lower probability of making suicide attempts or gestures during the follow-up period than patients not using fluoxetine, although patients with more suicide risk factors at intake were more likely to be prescribed fluoxetine than those without these risk factors (Warshaw & Keller, 1996).

Tricyclic Antidepressants

Tricyclics are so named because they consist of three-ringed molecules. The most common clinically used tricyclic compounds in the United States are imipramine (Tofranil) and a primary metabolite desipramine (Norpramin), amitriptyline (Elavil) and a primary metabolite nortriptyline (Pamelor), doxepin (Sinequan), amoxapine, trimipramine (Surmontil), maprotiline (Ludiomil), and protriptyline (Vivactil). These drugs all block reuptake of norepinephrine (NE) and serotonin (5-HT), but they differ considerably in terms of their potency and selectivity in these actions (Baldessarini, 1996). For example, amitriptyline, doxepin, imipramine, and trimipramine tend to inhibit both NE and 5-HT reuptake; desipramine, maprotiline, nortriptyline, and protriptyline exhibit the most selectivity in blocking NE reuptake; and amoxapine tends to block both NE and DA reuptake. These drugs also exhibit wide differences with respect to blocking histamine (H_1), muscarinic, serotonin ($5-HT_2$), and dopamine (D_2) receptors.

Regardless of these differences, they all are equally effective in relieving depression, and they all take several days or weeks to alter the symptoms of depression (Davis et al., 1993; Frank et al., 1993). In most cases the core symptoms of depression are relieved with tricyclics. Patients feel more confident, their mood is improved, their physical symptoms are reduced, and their suicidal thoughts are eliminated.

Tricyclics appear to be most effective in severe cases of unipolar unremitting depression. Although it has generally been believed that they are more effective in treating endogenous depression (where there is no evidence of obvious precipitating events) characterized by regression and inactivity than exogenous depression (where there are clearly precipitating events, such as loss of a loved one), research has not supported the endogenous versus exogenous dichotomy. The reason that studies have not found tricyclics to be of much benefit in exogenous depression and mild depression may be that there is a high placebo-response rate or a high spontaneous remission rate in these cases, coupled with the slow onset of action by the drugs (Brown, 1988). Tricyclics are not recommended for use in bipolar depression because they may trigger a transition from depression to manic excitement and because this disorder is quite responsive to lithium, which generally induces fewer side effects. As discussed in other chapters of this book, psychological disturbances that do not have a clear link to depression may also show favorable response to tricyclics. According to a multimillion-dollar research treatment program sponsored by the National Institute on Mental Health, the short-term efficacy of tricyclics in the treatment of unipolar depression appears to be comparable to at least two forms of brief psychotherapy—cognitive behavior therapy and interpersonal psychotherapy (Elkin et al., 1989).

Tricyclic antidepressants can be extremely toxic, and they have relatively low therapeutic indexes—unfortunate characteristics for drugs used in the treatment of a disorder that can lead to suicide. In fact, tricyclics account for a quarter of all fatal overdoses in the United States, with 70 percent of tricyclic deaths never reaching the hospital (Jarvis, 1991). Therefore, a prudent approach to the treatment of depressed patients would be to give them no more than a 2-week supply of these medications.

As is the case with many antidepressants, tricyclics have the potential to induce epilepsy-like seizures (Tollefson, 1991). Because of their potent anticholinergic (specifically antimuscarinic) action, tachycardia, blurred vision, dry mouth, constipation, and urinary retention are common—adverse effects that probably account for why the dropout rate in clinical trials is significantly higher with tricyclics than with newer antidepressants (Mulrow et al., 2000). Therapeutic doses of these drugs have significant effects on the cardiovascular system, such as orthostatic hypotension (a drop in blood pressure upon standing up). In addition, an increased tendency for arrhythmia (irregularity in the heartbeat) to develop with these drugs has resulted in a number of unexpected deaths. With long-term exposure, the risk of heart attacks has been found to be over two times higher in users of tricyclic antidepressants than in users of SSRIs (Cohen et al., 2000). Therefore, great caution must be observed in their use in patients with cardiac problems. Weakness and fatigue may also occur infrequently. Although significant motor disturbances are rare, a fine tremor may occur, particularly in elderly patients. The relatively infrequent side effects of jaundice, agranulocytosis, rashes, weight gain, and orgasmic impotence have also been reported to occur with tricyclics.

Since high doses of these drugs can induce CNS-toxic reactions, there is a biphasic relationship between drug plasma levels and efficacy. That is, there is a therapeutic window; below or above a particular plasma level, the drug is not effective in elevating mood (Tollefson, 1991). Unfortunately, when idealized dosages are administered to different individuals, resulting steady-state plasma concentrations may vary tenfold or more (DeVane et al., 1991). These characteristics contribute to difficulties in establishing optimal dosage regimens for individual patients.

Tolerance development to the antidepressant properties of tricyclics appears to be rare, but there is some indication that tolerance may develop to the sedative and anticholinergic side effects and orthostatic hypotension. There is minimal potential for tricyclics to induce psychological dependence, as they are void of primary reinforcing properties and have numerous side effects. As you might expect, nonhumans also will not self-administer these drugs. Unlike the psychostimulants, there is no evidence that abrupt cessation of tricyclics induces depression. However, reduction of tricyclic medication should be gradual because an abstinence syndrome (sleep disturbance, nightmares, nausea, headache, and hypercholinergic-type effects) may occur if medication is stopped abruptly (Baldessarini, 1996).

Monoamine Oxidase Inhibitors

Monoamine oxidase (MAO) is an enzyme found in cells throughout the body. It is localized predominantly on the outer membrane of subcellular particles called mitochondria. It comes in two forms, designated Type A and Type B, depending on the substances that they act on. MAO is responsible for the intraneuronal metabolic inactivation (through deamination) of serotonin, dopamine, and norepinephrine. The **monoamine oxidase inhibitor (MAOI)** antidepressants comprise a group of heterogeneous drugs that share the ability to block this action of MAO. The first MAOI (iproniazid) was originally used in the treatment of tuberculosis and was only accidentally found to have mood-elevating properties. However, its toxicity eventually led to its withdrawal from the market, a fate common to many of these types of drugs. The three MAOIs presently used clinically as antidepressants in the United States are tranylcypromine (Parnate), phenelzine (Nardil), and isocarboxazid (Marplan).

As one might expect, the efficacy of MAOIs in treating depression appears to be related to the normal level of MAO activity in the patient; that is, depressed patients with low MAO activity to begin with are less responsive to MAOIs than patients with higher MAO activity (Georgotas et al., 1987). Although enhancement of monoamine activity is presumed to be the primary pharmacodynamic factor in their antidepressant properties, MAOIs have numerous other biochemical actions that may be involved in their effects (e.g., increases in GABA levels) (Parent et al., 2000). Furthermore, as is the case with other antidepressants, the MAO-inhibiting actions occur rapidly and precede symptom remission by as much as 2 or more weeks.

Although the antidepressant properties of the first MAOI were noted at about the same time as those of the first tricyclic, the therapeutic use of MAOIs has been very limited. Generally they are used only in patients who remain depressed after an adequate trial of one or two different types of tricyclics, SSRIs, or newer alternative antidepressants, because most early controlled comparisons between MAOIs and tricyclics suggested that MAOIs were significantly less effective in most cases of depression.

In addition, MAOIs are less commonly used than tricyclics or SSRIs because MAOIs may induce more toxic reactions when combined with certain drugs or foods. MAOIs can interact unpredictably with many adrenergic-related chemicals to induce a so-called *hypertensive crisis*—a very serious toxic effect that can lead to headaches, fever, intracranial bleeding, and, in some cases, death. This can occur when MAOIs are combined with tricyclics, psychostimulants, and L-dopa. For these reasons, the combination of MAOIs and tricyclic antidepressants is generally contraindicated. On the other hand, for reasons as yet unclear, postural hypotension (which can cause dizziness) is commonly observed when MAOIs are used by themselves.

MAOIs also interact in a similar fashion with foods containing the amino acid tyramine and other monoamines. Examples of such foods are cheese, yeast products, chocolate, some wines, milk, beer, pickled herring, chicken liver, and large amounts of coffee, among many others. This problem comes about because the MAO inhibition allows these biologically active amines, which hepatic MAO would normally deaminate into inactive molecules, to release catecholamines from axon terminals and produce sympathomimetic effects, which include a marked rise in blood pressure and other cardiovascular changes. MAOIs also interfere with various enzymes to prolong and intensify the effects of nonadrenergic-related drugs (such as sedative–hypnotics, general anesthetics, narcotics, and anticholinergics), and they interfere with the metabolization of various naturally occurring substances.

Because of these interactions, individuals being treated with MAOIs (and their families) are normally given a list of drugs and foods to avoid. (Unfortunately, such information has been used in the past by patients to derive a list of agents through which they can commit suicide.) Typically, these drugs are cleared from the body rapidly, so plasma levels are not correlated with MAO inhibition (Mallinger & Smith, 1991). However, since phenelzine and isocarboxazid bind irreversibly to MAO, it may take up to 2 weeks after discontinuing their use for the body to resynthesize new enzyme molecules and restore monoamine metabolism to normal (Parent et al., 2000). The effects of tranylcypromine are reversed more rapidly because it is not bound irreversibly to MAO. In either case, a period of several days to 2 weeks is recommended before switching a patient from an MAO inhibitor to another class of antidepressant (Baldessarini, 1996).

In spite of the long delay in therapeutic response, a number of toxic reactions to overdoses of MAOIs can occur within hours (Baldessarini, 1996). These may consist of agitation, hallucinations, high fever, convulsions, and hypotension or hypertension. Treatment of these symptoms is difficult because of the numerous interactions between MAOIs and other drugs that normally might be useful in dealing with these symptoms. The long duration of MAO inhibition requires that the patient be monitored for several days after a toxic reaction. Several side effects have been noted with doses of MAOIs lower than those inducing acute toxicity—for example, cellular damage to liver cells, tremors, insomnia, agitation, hypomania, hallucinations, dizziness, and anticholinergic-like effects. It is obvious from the list of potential toxic effects of the MAOIs that they are greater and more serious than those of most other psychotherapeutic drugs. Thus, not surprisingly, their use is reserved for patients who are not responsive to other drugs and refuse electroconvulsive shock therapy.

For reasons just discussed, the MAOIs have generally been considered to be a second- or third-line defense against most cases of depression, generally being used only after unsuccessful treatment with an adequate dosage of one or two different monoamine reuptake inhibitors (e.g., SSRIs, tricyclics). However, research on MAOIs has indicated that they have much more versatility than previously assumed (Rudorfer, 1992). For example, with adequate dosage in nonpsychotic depressed patients, MAOIs may be as effective in the treatment of typical major depressions as tricyclics. They have also been shown to be effective in the treatment of bipolar patients, if combined with lithium to prevent treatment-emergent mania or hypomania. Clinical reports have documented the safety of switching patients who have not responded to tricyclics to an MAOI without a washout period, thus potentially shortening the misery a depressed patient must undergo before a successful treatment is found. In fact, if done carefully, MAOIs can be combined with tricyclics or lithium to enhance treatment efficacy (Feighner et al., 1985). Although the dangerous interactions between MAOIs and other substances remain a limiting factor in MAOI use, new understanding into the mechanisms, prevention, and treatment of these toxicities has led to streamlining of instruction to patients, which enhances compliance and acceptability of MAOI treatment.

Depressed patients who are most likely to respond preferentially to MAOIs are those diagnosed with what is sometimes referred to as *atypical depression* in the clinical literature (Quitkin et al., 1993). Such patients commonly have a reactive mood and exhibit one or more atypical features of overeating (often with a particular craving for sweets), oversleeping, leaden paralysis, and rejection sensitivity. Atypical depressed patients may also exhibit a reversal of the usual diurnal variation; that is, rather than feeling better in the morning, with mood declining somewhat as the day goes on, they are more likely to feel worse in the morning. Depending on the diagnostic criteria used, patients with atypical depression may account for 10 percent to 40 percent of outpatient cases of depression (Zisook et al., 1993).

Another form of atypical depression that appears to respond well to phenelzine is termed *hysteroid dysphoria* (Kayser et al., 1985). Patients with this disorder (usually women) are characterized by immaturity, self-centeredness, attention-getting behavior, manipulativeness, and, quite often, vague seductiveness. They experience depressions that are often precipitated by rejection, especially the loss of a romantic attachment. Their depressed episodes are characterized by a tendency to oversleep or spend more than normal amounts of time in bed, to overeat or crave sweets, and a labile mood that temporarily improves when attention or praise is given.

MAOIs have also been shown in many studies to be as effective as tricyclics in elderly depressed patients (Volz et al., 1994) and may be used as an alternative treatment in elderly patients who cannot tolerate some of the side effects of tricyclics. Like the tricyclics, the MAOIs may exert considerable improvement in the moods and eating behavior of bulimics, although their use in a condition whose primary symptoms involve uncontrollable eating behavior may not be advisable (because of the dietary constraints already mentioned) (Walsh et al., 1984).

MAOIs may also exert a favorable response in people with certain neurotic illnesses with depressive features and in people who suffer from acute anxiety, phobias, and panic attacks (in which the person may experience light-headedness, dizziness, "rubbery" legs, choking, difficulty in breathing, a racing or palpitating heart, tingling sensations, and extreme fright) (Buigues & Vallejo, 1987). Disabling obsessive thoughts that are characteristic of the obsessive–compulsive disorder may also respond to MAOIs, whether major symptoms of depression are present or not.

As is the case with the tricyclic and SSRI antidepressants, there is little potential for tolerance development or psychological dependence with the MAOIs. Abstinence symptoms associated with MAOI cessation have not been identified.

Reversible Inhibitors of Monoamine Oxidase A (RIMAs)

The first-generation MAOIs just described are all effective in the treatment of depression and a variety of other disorders, but they possess three pharmacological properties that minimize their usefulness. First, these MAOIs interact with exogenous amines (for example, tyramine in food and pressor amine drugs), producing a potentially toxic reaction. Second, they bind irreversibly to MAO enzymes, so that after their use, up to 2 weeks are needed for these enzymes to be resynthesized by the body, which may delay initiating treatment with other drugs for depression or other medical problems the patient might have. Third, in addition to allowing for a build-up of NE and 5-HT, which appears to be crucial for their antidepressant effects, they also allow DA levels to build up, a result that does not appear to be relevant for their antidepressant properties but which may exacerbate or produce schizophrenic or manic symptoms in predisposed individuals. To counter these problems, a number of reversible inhibitors of the MAO-A enzyme (RIMAs) have been developed (Lavian et al., 1993). These drugs only inhibit the MAO-A enzyme, which is selective in metabolizing NE and 5-HT but not DA, and being reversibly bound to MAO, their duration of MAO inhibition is short. Also, these drugs may be displaced from their binding site in the intestine by ingested, indirectly acting sympathomimetic amines such as tyramine, which allows the MAO to inactivate these amines, thus avoiding the initiation of an extreme hypertensive reaction (Mayersohn & Guentert, 1995; Norman & Burrows, 1995). By themselves, they appear to exert minimal hypotensive effects, including orthostatic hypotension. Two of the recently developed RIMAs showing considerable clinical potential for use are moclobemide and brofaromine.

In clinical comparisons with other antidepressants, including tricyclics, SSRIs and the first generation MAOIs, the efficacy of RIMAs has been comparable in the treatment of depression, although, as is the case with most of the antidepressants, some depressed patients that are refractory to one type of antidepressant may show dramatic improvements in mood with RIMAs (Volz et al., 1994; Reynaert et al., 1995). Their efficacy has been demonstrated in the treatment of psychotic (that is, very severe, with delusional thought disturbance) and nonpsychotic depression, exogenous and endogenous depression (both unipolar and bipolar), retarded and agitated depression, and in depression that accompanies dementia (for example, Alzheimer's type) (Priest et al., 1995). As with the first-generation MAOIs and other classes of antidepressants, RIMAs show promise in the treatment of a variety of other disorders that may or may not be associated with depression—for example, attention deficit hyperactivity disorder, agoraphobia, bulimia, borderline personality disorder, PTSD (post-traumatic stress disorder), compulsive hair pulling, phobic disorders, as well as a variety of anxiety symptoms (Priest et al., 1995). Moclobemide and brofaromine lack significant effects on psychomotor performance and cognitive function, and lack anticholinergic effects, which make them particularly useful in elderly patients.

Unfortunately, despite their use worldwide, it is not likely that the RIMAs will be available in the United States in the foreseeable future because there appears to be insufficient financial incentive to support the additional research required for FDA approval (Lotufo-Neto et al., 1999). There is simply too much competition from existing approved antidepressants, particularly the SSRIs, which have a more extensive track record of safety, especially in overdose. And while head-to-head comparisons indicate that RIMAs may have slightly better antidepressant efficacy than SSRIs and induce fewer complaints of sexual dysfunction, they may induce more insomnia. There is also little evidence that RIMAs share the older MAOIs' utility for the treatment of atypical depressions.

Alternative Antidepressants

Following one or more trials with adequate dosages and periods of time—6 weeks of SSRIs, tricyclics, and MAO inhibitors as described in the preceding sections (that is, after several different types of drugs have been tried)—85 percent to 90 percent of patients with major depression will show significant symptom reduction. However, if none of these drugs are sufficiently effective, or induce intolerable side effects, several alternative antidepressant drugs with slightly different pharmacological profiles than those in these three categories might be efficacious. For example, trazodone (Desyrel) selectively inhibits 5-HT reuptake, but unlike the typical SSRIs has fairly strong sedative properties and a tendency to induce hypotension. Nefazodone (Serzone), has some 5-HT and NE reuptake-inhibiting properties, but its ability to block and down-regulate 5-HT_{2A} receptors may be its most potent mechanism of action (Horst & Preskorn, 1998). In contrast to the SSRIs, nefazodone does not induce nervousness nor suppress appetite and has a lower tendency to induce tremors, insomnia, sweating, diarrhea, and sexual dysfunction. On the other hand, it is more likely to induce confusion, dizziness, visual disturbances, and dry mouth (Preskorn, 1995; Robinson et al., 1996). Nefazodone may be particularly useful in depressed patients with agitation, anxiety, and insomnia (Lader, 1996). As with the other newer antidepressants, these drugs display no anticholinergic effects, cardiac effects, seizure activity, or weight gain, and exhibit a wide margin of safety (Horst & Preskorn, 1998).

Venlafaxine (Effexor) has been shown to potently block neuronal reuptake of NE and 5-HT, and, to a lesser extent DA (Morton et al., 1995). Its pharmacological profile and side-effect profile are very similar to that of the SSRI fluoxetine. Speculation that venlafaxine may have an earlier onset of action than previously available antidepressants, due to its ability to rapidly down-regulate beta receptors in rat brains, has not been proved in humans (Ellingrod & Perry, 1994). Nor have some clinical trials comparing venlafaxine to other antidepressants, such as imipramine or trazodone, shown significant advantages for venlafaxine in terms of efficacy or onset of effect (Morton et al., 1995). However, two studies using very high doses of venlafaxine (375 mg/day, which can produce an abnormally high incidence of side effects such as nausea, dizziness, somnolence, sweating, and sexual dysfunction) found a significant difference from placebo in decreased depression symptoms in 4 to 7 days (Mendlewicz, 1995). Perhaps because of its dual mechanisms of action, with greater potency in inhibiting 5-HT reuptake than NE reuptake at lower doses, venlafaxine may have greater efficacy in the treatment of clinical depression than the SSRIs at the higher ends of the effective dosage ranges (Horst & Preskorn, 1998; Rudolph & Feiger, 1999).

Some benzodiazepines, such as alprazolam (Xanax), may be used as antidepressants. Alprazolam has a potent GABA-enhancing effect similar to other benzodiazepines, but unlike others in this class, it has antidepressant efficacy comparable to older tricyclics, with a faster onset of action, primarily in the domain of insomnia relief. However, tolerance may develop to its antidepressant properties after a few weeks. Like the benzodiazepines, it has a low incidence of anticholinergic side effects, low cardiotoxicity, and minimal potential for lethality with overdose. However, drowsiness and lethargy are common, but generally well tolerated, side effects. Because of alprazolam's relatively short plasma half-life and its tendency to induce physical dependence with chronic use, dosages should be gradually tapered over several weeks when treatment with alprazolam is discontinued (Rickels et al., 1990).

Bupropion (Wellbutrin) has antidepressant efficacy comparable to the tricyclics, but it differs from previous antidepressants because its most potent influence is on inhibiting DA reuptake, with a weaker influence on NE reuptake and no effect on 5-HT reuptake (Horst & Preskorn, 1998). These actions may account for its exerting mild amphetamine-like effects (Goodnick, 1991b). (Its structure resembles that of amphetamine.) In addition, double-blind, placebo-controlled studies have demonstrated that a majority of patients who were intolerant to or resistant to tricyclics responded favorably when treated with bupropion (Preskorn, 1991). It possesses no MAO-inhibition effects and minimal anticholinergic or antihistaminic actions, which result in its producing a low incidence of side effects, sedation, orthostatic hypotension, and adverse cardiac effects. Also, its tendency to induce hypomanic or manic episodes in unipolar depressives appears low, although it may trigger manic episodes in bipolar patients. In contrast to the SSRIs, for which sexual side effects are common, bupropion appears to induce an unusually low incidence of sexual side effects and may actually improve sexual desire in some individuals (Segraves, 1998). The major problem with bupropion is its tendency to induce seizures and other forms of CNS toxicity—for example, delirium, psychosis, and extrapyramidal side effects—at high dosages (Preskorn, 1991). It may also induce mild dryness of the mouth, headache, nausea, constipation, and tremor.

The nonbenzodiazepine anxiolytic buspirone (BuSpar) has been shown to be effective in relieving symptoms of depression (Charney et al., 1990). Although its efficacy is more moderate than other drugs discussed in this section, its low toxicity and side effects, lack of dependence liability, and minimal interactions with other drugs (e.g., alcohol) make it an attractive alternative to these other drugs.

Two relatively new drugs with unique pharmacodynamic properties that may provide benefits beyond those typically provided by earlier antidepressants are mirtazapine (Remeron) and reboxetine (Kent, 2000). Mirtazapine potently blocks central alpha-2-adrenergic autoreceptors and heteroreceptors and 5-HT_2 and 5-HT_3 receptors while exhibiting minimal affinity for other receptors or uptake transporters. Presumably, NE release is enhanced by the autoreceptor blockade, and 5-HT release is enhanced by the blockade of the heteroreceptors on serotonergic neurons, as well as 5-HT_3 receptors that presynaptically influence 5-HT release. The most common side effects of mirtazapine are sleepiness (more likely with low doses), dizziness, weight gain (due to enhanced appetite), dry mouth, and constipation. It has minimal effects on P450 enzymes, which results in very low frequency of the drug–drug interactions typically found with older antidepressants. Numerous studies have indicated that mirtazapine is comparable in efficacy to various tricyclic antidepressants (Kent, 2000). Comparative studies of mirtazapine versus SSRIs have all reported statistically significant and clinically relevant differences in favor of mirtazapine—for example, faster onset of efficacy and rapid anxiolytic effects (Thompson, 1999; Wheatley et al., 1998). In one study with depressed patients who discontinued SSRI treatment because they experienced sexual dysfunction, all patients displayed significant improvement in depressive symptoms without experiencing sexual dysfunction (Koutouvidis et al, 1999).

Reboxetine (Edronax) is the obvious counterpart to the SSRIs in that it was developed as a selective inhibitor of NE reuptake. Because of its low affinity for other uptake transporters and receptors, it induces fewer anticholinergic side effects than the tricyclics and less nausea and sexual dysfunction than the SSRIs (Montgomery, 1999). It also exerts minimal effects on P450 enzymes. Several clinical trials have indicated its efficacy to be comparable to tricyclics and SSRIs in the treatment of moderate depression and to be more effective than SSRIs in the treatment of hospitalized depressed patients and those with severe depression (Massana et al., 1999; Moller, 2000). Enhancement of social functioning of depressed patients also appears to be greater with reboxetine than with SSRIs (Dubini et al., 1997a, 1997b).

The use of herbal medicines as alternative treatments for a variety of disorders has grown tremendously over the last several years. One herbal medicine that is gaining in popularity for treatment of depression is St. John's wort (*Hypericum perforatum*). It has been used in Europe as a folk remedy for depression for some time, and a number of clinical trials using extracts of this plant have suggested that it is effective in the treatment of mild to moderate cases of depression. Recent comparisons between hypericum extracts and the SSRI fluoxetine have suggested that there is comparable efficacy in the treatment of mild to moderate depression, with hypericum being superior to fluoxetine in overall incidence of side effects (Schrader, 2000; Volz & Laux, 2000). The primary active constituent in hypericum is believed to be hypericin. Some studies have indicated that it has some properties of other antidepressants, but as yet its mechanisms of action are unclear. Although it is reasonably safe, it can induce some potentially severe adverse reactions when combined with other drugs (Fugh-Berman, 2000). It is also fairly inexpensive compared with pharmaceutical antidepressants. However, because the FDA does not regulate it as a drug in the United States, preparations of St. John's wort may be variable in terms of quantity and quality.

Psychostimulants

Drugs like amphetamine and cocaine have several properties, particularly their fast onset of action, that would appear to make them ideal antidepressants. Although some clinically depressed patients do experience feelings of calmness, well-being, or euphoria when given these drugs, the majority of such patients experience mixed mood effects, or experience dysphoric feelings of tension and increased sadness (Post et al., 1974). Thus, their effects cannot be described as simply antidepressant. Furthermore, as was noted in Chapter 9, their euphoric effects in normal individuals show tolerance, and their chronic use can worsen or induce depression when drug exposure ceases. In fact, the rebound following cocaine use involves such a severe depression that it can be life-threatening by causing, or at least precipitating, suicidal behavior. Thus, these types of drugs are an outmoded and contraindicated treatment for severe depression (however, see next paragraph).

Drug Combinations in the Treatment of Depression

There is a very good chance that a major depression can be effectively treated with one of the drugs that are currently available. However, there are still a small number of patients who are treatment-resistant. There may be a complete lack of response to medication, a tendency to relapse after an initial response, or an inability to tolerate the drug's side effects. If drugs from the major classes—tricyclics, MAOIs, and SSRIs—and the newer alternative antidepressants have been tried in adequate doses for at least 6 weeks each and the patient still has not responded, or if the side effects cannot be tolerated, it may be fruitful to try some combinations of drugs and/or psychotherapy.

For example, in a recent study, just under half of the patients with chronic forms of major depression displayed a clinically beneficial response to short-term treatment with either an antidepressant or a cognitive behavioral analysis system of psychotherapy, whereas the combination of the two treatments was effective in 73 percent of the patients (Keller et al., 2000). A number of drug combinations have also been tried with success (Fava, 2000).

Numerous studies have shown that augmentation of antidepressants with lithium can produce robust improvements in a number of depressed patients that have not previously responded to single-drug therapy with tricyclics, MAOIs, or SSRIs. However, this strategy seems to have lost favor recently among psychiatrists, perhaps due to the potential toxicity associated with lithium, particularly when combined with SSRIs, and the need to carefully monitor lithium plasma concentrations. Thyroid hormone (T_3) augmentation of tricyclic therapy has also been used successfully in patients who are refractory to tricyclics, but there is little information on the use of this approach with SSRIs. There are published studies showing that augmentation with psychostimulants (methylphenidate, pemoline, dextroamphetamine) may enhance the efficacy of a variety of antidepressants—often with a rapid onset of action—but concerns over the potential for abuse of these drugs, particularly in patients with a history of substance abuse, limit this approach. The practice of combining antidepressants with different pharmacological profiles—for example, bupropion or buspirone with SSRIs—appears to be growing in popularity, but there are insufficient quality studies for determining the efficacy of this approach.

Conclusions

Present-day antidepressants differ considerably in terms of their molecular structure, their metabolic activities, and their specificity of actions, both within and between neurotransmitter systems. When selecting a particular antidepressant for treatment, at least four factors should be considered: symptom-profile efficacy, onset of action or latency of response to treatment, potential side-effect profile, and toxicity. There is general agreement that most antidepressants differ little with regard to efficacy and the period of time for onset of action; significant differences do occur with regard to side-effect profiles and potential toxicity. Side effects are of considerable clinical importance, not only because they may represent a health risk to the patient, but also because they may deter patient compliance, which in turn may lead to suboptimal outcome and can limit the clinician's ability to adjust the dosages into an adequate therapeutic range.

The older antidepressants are comparable to the newer antidepressants in terms of the percentage of patients exhibiting significant symptom reduction as well as the magnitude of symptom reduction, but they may exert more troubling side effects. Especially if one considers the importance of nonmonetary costs and benefits of different pharmacological treatments—that is, the overall quality of life of the patients (a multidimensional construct derived by looking at such things as side effects of the drug, mortality rate, productivity, psychosocial functioning, and so forth)—they may not be as effective as the newer antidepressants (Pleil, 1995). One of the benefits of older tricyclics over newer antidepressants would appear to be cost, because as generic drugs they are cheaper than brand-name drugs. For example, the cost of a 30-day supply of imipramine at maximum dosage would be around $25 versus $205 for Prozac or $52 for Serzone (in 2000 U.S. dollars). However, when one looks at the total resource costs for treating depression, which include drug-related costs (physician visits, ancillary treatment, and changes in medical service related to the drug), drug-induced costs (those incurred due to the follow-up created by intolerance of the side effects of the drug or suboptimal therapeutic response), as well as the monetary cost of the drugs, one may actually find the newer drugs to have a lower lifetime cost (Anton & Revicki, 1995).

With respect to the issue of how long antidepressant treatment should be maintained, the available evidence suggests that drug treatment should be continued on a long-term basis after the acute response, since premature discontinuation soon after symptomatic relief is associated with a return of depression in many patients (Montgomery, 1996). The recommendation is that all treatments for depression should continue for a minimum of 4 to 6 months to prevent relapse. The evidence strongly indicates that antidepressant treatment should be continued in patients at risk for symptom recurrence, and depending on the number of recurrences, lifelong prophylactic therapy may be warranted.

Pharmacotherapy in Mania and Bipolar Illnesses

The effectiveness of a particular drug treatment for mania may depend on whether the patient experiences only manic symptoms, which occur intermittently between episodes of normal mood, or experiences cycles of mania and depression, that is, bipolar disorders. Treatment efficacy may also depend on whether episodes of mania and depression occur infrequently and separately (typical bipolar disorder), or involve rapid cycling (for instance, patients experience four or more episodes per year), or involve dysphoric (mixed) mania, in which manic and depressive symptoms occur together. Drugs that generally decrease the intensity or duration of both manic and depressive episodes, or prevent them from occurring, are commonly referred to as **mood stabilizers.** Of these, lithium (Eskalith) is generally the initial drug used in the treatment of all bipolar disorders, but its effectiveness is most apparent in cases of typical bipolar disorder (Calabrese & Woyshville, 1995). Tricyclic or other antidepressants are commonly used in combination with lithium if the patient does not respond to lithium after several weeks or is experiencing a severe depressive episode. Some anticonvulsant drugs, either alone or in combination with lithium, appear to be somewhat more effective than lithium in the treatment of rapid-cycling or mixed bipolar patients. A number of other drug treatments (for instance, calcium blockers, cholinergic agents, adrenergic blockers) and nondrug treatments (for example, electroconvulsive shock, phototherapy, psychosurgery) have been explored as alternatives to these, but research supporting their efficacy is very limited, and none have gained widespread acceptance (Prien & Potter, 1990). Studies with the atypical antipsychotic drugs suggest that they may be useful alternatives or adjunctive treatments for bipolar disorders.

Lithium

The properties of lithium are unique, such that it stands alone among all the psychotherapeutic drugs (Baldessarini, 1996). Although the first report of its antimanic effects by Australian psychiatrist John Cade in 1949 would seem to put it at the forefront of the psychopharmacological revolution begun in the 1950s, it had little impact in the United States until 20 years later. One reason was its high toxicity, particularly when combined with low sodium intake. Several months prior to Cade's report, a number of deaths were reported in patients with kidney and heart problems who were given lithium salt as a substitute for ordinary table salt (sodium chloride). Thus, despite its remarkable antimanic properties, physicians were reluctant to use such a toxic drug. Furthermore, a few years later, chlorpromazine was noted to possess antimanic effects as well as considerably lower toxicity. A rapid succession of similar compounds, as well as antidepressants, new stimulants, sedatives, and hypnotics, came into being, each requiring considerable study with respect to their safety and efficacy. Another factor in the lack of enthusiasm for lithium was its minimal marketability because, as an element of nature, it was unpatentable. Eventually, however, lithium's remarkable properties became well recognized, and its use has become commonplace.

Lithium is unique for several reasons (Baldessarini, 1996). First, it is a light metal ion (positively charged) that exists in nature as a salt (lithium carbonate, lithium chloride). Although the ion is found in trace amounts in animal tissues, it plays no known physiological role. Second, therapeutic levels of lithium have almost negligible psychotropic effects in normal individuals—that is, there are no sedative, depressant, stimulant, or euphoriant effects. Third, and most important, it is highly specific in relieving manic symptoms without oversedating the person (a common problem with antipsychotics) or inducing depression (as was the case with reserpine). Furthermore, continued treatment with lithium salt can prevent or decrease the severity of future episodes of mania and depression in most bipolar patients (this is what experts mean when they say lithium has prophylactic properties).

Efficacy of Lithium in Mood Disturbances

The efficacy of lithium in treating acute mania and preventing subsequent episodes of both mania and depression in bipolar disorder is unquestioned, with approximately 60 percent to 80 percent of such cases displaying partial to complete symptom remission (Prien & Potter, 1990). Studies have suggested that persons with a strong genetic link to manic depression—for example, patients in whose families the disorder has occurred—may show the most favorable response to lithium (Campbell et al., 1984). Although many bipolar patients relapse, even with lithium maintenance treatment, whether there is a loss of prophylactic efficacy of lithium is controversial. Some authors have questioned its long-term effectiveness in general, and others have argued that loss of efficacy may be due to factors such as underdosing and noncompliance, or due to the fact that the natural course of affective disorders is capricious and tends to become more severe over time (Kleindienst et al., 1999). The general conclusion at this time is that while affective recurrences do occur in some bipolar patients after apparently successful treatment with lithium, there is no clear evidence that these are the result of a loss of lithium efficacy.

In some individuals maintained on lithium, there is an unusual mood stability, which might be viewed unfavorably by these patients (Johnson, 1979). Most bipolar patients probably do not want to experience the uncontrolled onset of depressive or manic moods, but would like to experience normal emotions. However, lithium patients often report being emotionless in situations where mood shifts are expected, or at least appropriate.

Although lithium appears to have little antidepressant activity in persons experiencing a depressive episode, it can prevent depressive episodes in some patients with recurrent unipolar depression. Several studies have reported impressive results indicating that patients who are refractory to traditional antidepressants (including lithium) may respond favorably to lithium in combination with traditional antidepressants (Goodnick & Schorr-Cain, 1991).

Side effects are not generally a factor in lithium's efficacy. Although the majority of patients experience some adverse consequences—such as tremor, thirst, fluid retention, weight gain, and frequent need to urinate—these are relatively minor problems. Lithium's potential interactions with other drugs that patients may also likely be taking (antipsychotics, diuretics, and nonsteroidal antiinflammatory drugs) may limit its efficacy (Tollefson, 1991).

Lithium salts have also been used with varying degrees of success in other disorders with an affective component that have a cyclical nature to them, such as recurrent hyperactivity in children (however, not in the attention deficit disorder described in Chapter 14) (Campbell et al., 1984), the premenstrual syndrome, and episodic anger or aggression. There is considerable evidence that lithium is effective in reducing aggressiveness with an affective component (explosiveness) in children aged 5 to 12 years with conduct disorder (Campbell et al., 1995). The benefits of lithium in these cases have been attributed to lithium's ability to reduce impulsiveness or explosiveness—as if a delay mechanism or filter device were inserted between stimulus analysis and decision mechanisms in patients who previously went automatically from stimulus to response (Johnson, 1979).

Pharmacokinetics of Lithium

Since lithium's therapeutic index can be as low as 2 or 3, it is important to monitor its concentrations in the body on a regular basis, at least until stable levels can be assured (Baldessarini, 1996). Lithium is usually administered orally in a salt form, most commonly lithium carbonate (the particular salt used is not important in the therapeutic action since the anionic partner serves only as an inert vehicle for transport). It is readily absorbed from the G.I. tract, with almost complete absorption occurring within 8 hours. Passage through the blood–brain barrier is slow, but once plasma levels have stabilized, cerebrospinal fluid levels stabilize at approximately half that of plasma concentrations. Because of its very low therapeutic index, lithium dosages are based on plasma concentration of lithium ion, generally determined in milliequivalent units per liter of blood (mEq/L) (*milliequivalent* refers to the number of grams of solute dissolved in 1 milliliter of a normal solution). Therapeutic doses are achieved when plasma levels of lithium reach 0.6 to 1.5 mEq/L (generally achievable with two to three 300-mg tablets of lithium carbonate per day).

Above these levels, toxic signs of diarrhea, vomiting, drowsiness, confusion, and muscular weakness may occur (Annitto, 1979). At levels above 2.0 mEq/L, ataxia, tinnitus, and interference with kidney function can occur, and levels above 3.0 mEq/L may result in coma, respiratory depression, and death. Even at therapeutic levels, side effects of fine hand tremors, nausea, thirst, and excessive sweating may occur. In comparison to most other drugs requiring chronic exposure, the side effects of therapeutic levels of lithium are rather mild or uncommon. Nevertheless, idiosyncratic reactions can occur; for instance, its use has been associated with diabetes, seizure activity, and neurological disturbances, particularly when combined with other drugs.

The pharmacokinetics of lithium may vary considerably among individuals, but they are relatively stable over time within individuals. Although lithium has a relatively long plasma half-life (about 20 to 24 hours), it is generally given in divided doses because of its low therapeutic index. Slow-release preparations have been developed that produce smoother lithium plasma level curves, allow administration once a day or every other day, and may have fewer side effects (Goodnick & Schorr-Cain, 1991). Concentration levels of lithium are heavily dependent on sodium intake. Lithium is generally excreted more readily with high sodium intake, and high, toxic concentrations of lithium may occur with low sodium intake or drug-induced sodium depletion (as might occur with diuretics) as a result of enhanced retention. Also, lithium's urinary retention and elimination half-life may double during mania (Goodnick & Schorr-Cain, 1991).

Pharmacodynamics of Lithium

Our understanding of lithium's neuropharmacological properties with respect to its ability to stabilize mood is particularly weak. As an ion, lithium has the potential for altering the distribution and exchange of ions involved in the process of conduction (see Chapter 4). Therefore, there has been some speculation that such interactions may account for lithium's mood-stabilizing properties, although it is uncertain whether important interactions with these ions occur at therapeutic concentrations of lithium (Tosteson, 1981). In brain tissue at therapeutic concentrations, lithium reduces the stimulation-produced and calcium-dependent release of catecholamines (but not serotonin) from nerve endings (Baldessarini, 1996). It may also enhance the reuptake of catecholamines. These actions are consistent with the catecholamine hypothesis of mania but do not really fit the opposite side of the hypothesis regarding catecholamines and depression. Lithium appears to have no direct influence on postsynaptic catecholamine receptors, nor does it affect the binding of ligands to catecholamine receptors.

In studies attempting to determine whether lithium is able to reduce the effects of amphetamine (which, you should recall, initially amplifies catecholamine release and reduces their reuptake), there have been a variety of outcomes. Although studies have found that lithium attenuates several of amphetamine's behavioral effects, in other tests it has either produced no change or has intensified amphetamine's effects (Cox et al., 1971; Flemenbaum, 1974; Furukawa et al., 1975; Matussek & Linsmayer, 1968).

The problem with these studies, in terms of trying to understand the relationship between lithium's actions and its ability to lessen manic symptoms, is that they are all acute studies. It is well established that a minimum of 7 to 10 days of chronic lithium administration is usually required before therapeutic benefits are observed. This time period corresponds to the time it takes for lithium to "stabilize" the relationship between tryptophan uptake in the brain and its synthesis into 5-HT (mentioned earlier in the discussion of the biochemical basis of affective disorders). Once this new equilibrium state has been achieved, the actions and effects of drugs like amphetamine and cocaine are greatly reduced (Cooper et al., 1996). So it may be this action of lithium that is most critical for its therapeutic effects.

More recent evidence points to lithium's actions on at least two independent signaling systems in the CNS that could be involved in its mood stabilizing effects (Jope, 1999). In both cases, lithium is proposed to increase basal neuronal activity but attenuate stimulus-induced (e.g., neurotransmitter-activated) increases in neuronal activity. For example, receptor-mediated production of cyclic AMP (one of the most prevalent second messengers in the brain) is controlled by a stimulatory G-protein (Gs) and a counterbalancing inhibitory G-protein (Gi), with the Gi influence predominating under basal conditions. Lithium appears to inhibit both G-protein–mediated processes, which would allow increases in basal cyclic AMP levels but reduce the stimulus-induced increases in cyclic AMP production. Thus, the ability for lithium to stabilize fluctuations in neuronal responses—a property shared with other mood stabilizers—could be the foundation for its mood stabilizing effects.

Alternatives to Lithium in the Treatment of Bipolar Disorders

Despite the evidence of lithium efficacy in the treatment of bipolar disorders, a number of naturalistic studies have found that bipolar patients exhibit frequent relapses, even with maintenance drug treatment (Gitlin et al., 1995; Goldberg et al., 1996). These studies have observed that 68 percent to 89 percent of bipolar patients relapse within 4 to 5 years, with the majority of these exhibiting multiple relapses during this time. As one might expect, bipolar patients with more previous episodes of mood dysfunction tend to relapse earlier than patients with fewer previous episodes. Poor psychosocial functioning—particularly, poor job functioning—is also associated with a shorter time to relapse, with depressive episodes most strongly related to social and family dysfunction. Thus, not surprisingly, concomitant psychotherapy and social support have been suggested to greatly improve the outcome of prophylactic drug therapy (Miklowitz et al., 1996; Werder, 1995). Nevertheless, alternatives to lithium clearly are needed because a substantial number of bipolar patients fail lithium prophylaxis, including those with a high frequency of prior episodes, mixed (dysphoric) mania, comorbid personality disturbances, and rapid cycling (Solomon et al., 1995).

Antipsychotic drugs have been used for almost 45 years in the treatment of bipolar disorders, particularly for the acute emergency management of mania. In many cases attempting to manage a manic patient with lithium alone is not practical during the first week of the illness, so antipsychotics or benzodiazepines, which suppress manic symptoms more quickly than lithium, are often combined with lithium (Werder, 1995). Alternatively, electroconvulsive therapy (ECT) may be used. In fact, in a series of studies conducted over a period of several years, ECT with sparing use of antipsychotics followed by lithium was found to be the most effective short-term intervention for acute mania in bipolar patients (Small et al., 1996).

If antipsychotic drugs are used, once the manic symptoms have subsided, many experts recommend that these drugs be withdrawn. Although chronic treatment with antipsychotics may be just as effective as lithium in preventing subsequent manic episodes, their vast spectrum of potentially debilitating side effects makes them less desirable than lithium for this purpose. Unfortunately, despite the risks of neurological and behavioral side effects associated with the protracted use of typical antipsychotics and the availability of agents with less severe side effects, a substantial number of bipolar patients receive maintenance treatment with antipsychotic agents. Because the efficacy of atypical antipsychotics is comparable to that of typical antipsychotics in the treatment of psychotic mood disorders but exhibit less problematic side effects (described in Chapter 12), these should be the preferred treatment for patients with bipolar disorders (Keck et al., 2000).

If a bipolar patient suffering from moderate depression has not responded to lithium treatment alone for several weeks, many, but not all, authorities recommend that a tricyclic or other antidepressant be combined with lithium (Prien & Potter, 1990). The rationale for giving lithium alone before adding an antidepressant is based on the presumption that standard antidepressants may precipitate mania, hypomania, or rapid cycling. This is also the reason that typical antidepressants by themselves are not recommended for use in bipolar patients.

In manic-depressive patients for whom lithium, alone or in combination with an antidepressant, has not been effective, at the present time, the foremost pharmacologic alternatives for long-term bipolar treatment are the anticonvulsants carbamazepine (Tegretol) and valproate (various forms; for example, valproic acid, sodium valproate, divalproex, Depakote, Depakene) (Bowden, 1995; Solomon et al., 1995; Guay, 1995). These drugs have been used for many years in the treatment of epilepsy.

A number of clinical trials have verified both of these drugs to be efficacious in the short-term management of bipolar manic symptoms, and the response may be maintained for extended periods of time. As yet, there is little evidence from rigorous clinical trials to support the widespread use of anticonvulsants in maintenance therapy for bipolar disorders (Dardennes et al., 1995; Solomon et al., 1995). There seems to be a consensus that these anticonvulsants are more effective in bipolar patients that respond poorly to lithium—those exhibiting mixed mania, rapid cycling, comorbid substance abuse (Bowden, 1995; Calabrese & Woyshville, 1995; Guay, 1995). Unfortunately, these drugs are capable of inducing severe toxic side effects—for example, fatal hepatic failure with valproate, and agranulocytosis and aplastic anemia (white and red blood cell deficiency) with carbamazepine. While these side effects are rare, their seriousness may limit these drugs' usefulness.

The mechanism of action that is responsible for their mood-stabilizing effects is unclear, but both of these anticonvulsants have been shown to limit the sustained repetitive firing of action potentials evoked by a sustained depolarization of mouse cortical neurons at therapeutically relevant concentrations. This action is mediated by prolonging the inactivation of voltage-activated Na^+ channels that occurs after depolarization of the neuron (Baldessarini, 1996).

The newest drugs suggested by clinical trials to be efficacious in the treatment of bipolar symptoms are the atypical antipsychotics clozapine and risperidone. Clozapine appears to be effective and well tolerated in the short-term and maintenance treatment of severe or psychotic mood disorders, particularly in the manic-excited phases of bipolar disorders (about 75 percent response rate), even in patients who have not responded well to conventional pharmacotherapies (Ciapparelli et al., 2000; Zarate et al., 1995). Clozapine may also have sustained mood-stabilizing activity, or at least a prophylactic antimanic effect. Acutely manic patients who respond to clozapine appear to do so within 2 weeks. Like most mood-stabilizing agents, clozapine may be more effective for mania than for unipolar or bipolar depression. Finally, clozapine may usefully and safely be combined with lithium or valproate in the long-term maintenance treatment of bipolar disorders. As discussed earlier, clozapine's tendency to induce agranulocytosis is a limiting factor in its use.

Because risperidone has only fairly recently been approved for clinical use, it is still too early to evaluate its long-term efficacy in bipolar disorders. However, preliminary clinical trials have indicated that risperidone may be a useful adjunctive treatment for bipolar disorders when used in conjunction with the typical mood stabilizers (Keck et al., 1995; Madhusoo-danan et al., 1995), although by itself it is ineffective in treating pure manic psychosis (Sajatovic et al., 1996).

Nondrug Treatments for Depression

Clearly, not all grief, misery, and general disappointments associated with life in human society call for drug intervention. Most episodes of these types, even severe cases, evidence a very high rate of spontaneous remission with sufficient time passage. Psychological intervention that changes the person's interpersonal relationships or belief structures may be beneficial in these cases. Several studies that have compared the effectiveness of interpersonal psychotherapy or cognitive therapy with that of pharmacotherapy (mostly tricyclics) have not found any notable differences between these two forms of psychotherapy and antidepressant medication (Frank & Thase, 1999). Some severe depressions may not respond to drug therapy, or a patient may be so suicidal that waiting for a drug to take effect would be inadvisable (Feighner et al., 1985). In such cases, electroshock therapy may be considered, because it remains the most rapid and effective treatment for severe acute depression and is potentially lifesaving for the suicidal patient (Fink, 1994).

Although physicians play the most direct role in pharmacotherapy for depression, those of you who will work or are now working in the mental health field outside of medicine may also serve important functions. Because you are the ones most likely to deal initially with a depressed client, or to have the most contact with such an individual during his or her treatment, you may serve as information gatherers to determine whether drug therapy may be a useful adjunct to traditional psychotherapies. You may also oversee the progress of a client who is under drug treatment. Your interaction with the patient during the evaluation and your reassurances may in themselves prove therapeutic. You can determine whether there are precipitating events underlying the clients' symptoms, assess how chronic the problem is and whether there is a cyclical nature to it, determine whether the client is suicidal, gather family history, and so on. This is valuable information in establishing whether or not a person may be a good candidate for drug intervention. Mere inquiry into the nature of your clients' dysphoria can challenge them to confront their lives and their inability to respond appropriately to these events. If your clients are taking medication for their disorders, you can look for side effects of the drugs and signs of drug toxicity. Your optimism over the likely benefits of a prescribed medication may have tremendous value in alleviating distress, guilt, and hopelessness in the patients and may be the difference between their compliance or noncompliance in sticking with a drug regimen that may take 2 to 4 weeks before any benefits are realized. Those of you who practice psychotherapy may find that antidepressants make your clients more amenable to your particular therapeutic techniques.

Websites for Further Information

Sites providing general information on affective disorders and pharmacotherapy:

http://uhs.bsd.uchicago.edu/~bhsiung/tips/tips.html
http://www.depression.com/

Bibliography

Anderson, I. M. (2000). Selective serotonin reuptake inhibitors versus tricyclic antidepressants: A meta-analysis of efficacy and tolerability. *Journal of Affective Disorders, 58,* 19–36.

Annitto, W. J. (1979, March). Recognizing lithium-associated neurotoxicity. *Drug Therapy,* pp. 45–51.

Anton, S. F., & Revicki, D. A. (1995). The use of decision analysis in the pharmacoeconomic evaluation of an antidepressant: A cost-effectiveness study of nefazodone. *Psychopharmacology Bulletin, 31,* 249–258.

Arango, V., Ernsberger, P., Marzuk, P. M., et al. (1990). Autoradiographic demonstration of increased serotonin 5-HT$_2$ and beta-adrenergic receptor binding sites in the brain of suicide victims. *Archives of General Psychiatry, 47,* 1038–1047.

Baldessarini, R. J. (1996). Drugs and the treatment of psychiatric disorders: Depression and mania. In A. G. Gilman, L. S. Goodman, J. G. Hardman, L. E. Limbard, P. B. Molinoff, & R. W. Ruddon (Eds.), *The pharmacological basis of therapeutics* (pp. 431–460). New York: McGraw-Hill.

Barbaccia, M. L., Costa, E., & Guidotti, A. (1988). Endogenous ligands for high-affinity recognition sites of psychotropic drugs. *Annual Review of Pharmacology and Toxicology, 28,* 451–476.

Barondes, S. H. (1994). Thinking about prozac. *Science, 263,* 1102–1104.

Beasley, C. M., Dornseif, B. E., Bosomworth, J. C., et al. (1991). Fluoxetine and suicide: A meta-analysis of controlled trials of treatment for depression. *British Medical Journal, 303,* 685–692.

Benkelfat, C., Ellenbogen, M. A., Dean, P., et al. (1994). Mood-lowering effect of tryptophan depletion: Enhanced susceptibility in young men at genetic risk for major affective disorders. *Archives of General Psychiatry, 51,* 687–697.

Blair-West, G. W., Cantor, C. H., Mellsop, G. W., & Eyeson-Annan, M. L. (1999). Lifetime suicide risk in major depression: Sex and age determinants. *Journal of Affective Disorders, 55,* 171–178.

Blier, P., & de Montigny, C. (1994). Current advances and trends in the treatment of depression. *Trends in the Pharmacological Sciences, 15,* 220–226.

Bowden, C. L. (1995). Predictors of response to divalproex and lithium. *Journal of Clinical Psychiatry, 56,* 25–30.

Brown, W. A. (1988). Predictors of placebo response in depression. *Psychopharmacology Bulletin, 24,* 14–17.

Buigues, J., & Vallejo, J. (1987). Therapeutic response to phenelzine in patients with panic disorder and agoraphobia with panic attacks. *Journal of Clinical Psychiatry, 48,* 55–59.

Calabrese, J. R. & Woyshville, M. J. (1995). Lithium therapy: Limitations and alternatives in the treatment of bipolar disorders. *Annals of Clinical Psychiatry, 7,* 103–112.

Campbell, M., Kafantaris, V., & Cueva, J. E. (1995). An update on the use of lithium carbonate in aggressive children and adolescents with conduct disorder. *Psychopharmacology Bulletin, 31,* 93–102.

Campbell, M., Perry, R., & Green, W. H. (1984). Use of lithium in children and adolescents. *Psychosomatics, 25,* 95–106.

Charney, D. S., Krystal, J. H., Delgado, P. L., & Heninger, G. R. (1990). Serotonin-specific drugs for anxiety and depressive disorders. *Annual Review of Medicine, 41,* 437–446.

Ciapparelli, A., Dell'Osso, L., Pini, S., et al. (2000). Clozapine for treatment-refractory schizophrenia, schizoaffective disorder, and psychotic bipolar disorder: A 24-month naturalistic study. *Journal of Clinical Psychiatry, 61,* 329–334.

Cohen, H. Gibson, G., & Alderman, M. H. (2000). Excess risk of myocardial infarction in patients treated with antidepressant medication: Association with use of tricyclic agents. *American Journal of Medicine, 108,* 2–8.

Cooper, J. R., Bloom, F. E., & Roth, R. H. (1996). *The biochemical basis of neuropharmacology,* 7th ed. New York: Oxford University Press.

Cox, C., Harrison-Read, P. E., Steinberg, H., & Tomkiewicz, M. (1971). Lithium attenuates drug-induced hyperactivity in rats. *Nature, 232,* 336–338.

Cryan, J. F., & Leonard, B. E. (2000). 5-HT1A and beyond: The role of serotonin and its receptors in depression and the antidepressant response. *Human Psychopharmacology: Clinical and Experimental, 15,* 113–135.

Dardennes, R., Even, C., Bange, F., & Heim, A. (1995). Comparison of carbamazepine and lithium in the prophylaxis of bipolar disorders. A meta-analysis. *British Journal of Psychiatry, 166,* 378–381.

Davis, J. M., Wang, Z., & Janicak, P. G. (1993). A quantitative analysis of clinical drug trials for the treatment of affective disorders. *Psychopharmacology Bulletin, 29,* 175–182.

Delgado, P. L. (2000). Depression: The case for a monoamine deficiency. *Journal of Clinical Psychiatry, 61,* 7–11.

Delgado, P. L., Miller, H. L., Salomon, R. M., et al. (1993). Monoamines and the mechanism of antidepressant action: Effects of catecholamine depletion on mood of patients treated with antidepressants. *Psychopharmacology Bulletin, 29,* 389–396.

Delgado, P. L., & Moreno, F. A. (2000). Role of norepinephrine in depression. *Journal of Clinical Psychiatry, 61,* 5–12.

Derivan, A. T. (1995). Antidepressants: Can we determine how quickly they work? Issues from the literature. *Psychopharmacology Bulletin, 31,* 23–28.

DeVane, C. L. (1994). Pharmacokinetics of the newer antidepressants: Clinical relevance. *American Journal of Medicine, 97,* 13S–23S.

DeVane, C. L., Rudorfer, M. V., & Potter, W. Z. (1991). Dosage regimen for cyclic antidepressants: A review of pharmacokinetic methods. *Psychopharmacology Bulletin, 27,* 619–632.

Dubini, A., Bosc, M., & Polin, V. (1997a). Noradrenaline-selective versus serotonin-selective antidepressant therapy: Differential effects on social functioning. *Journal of Psychopharmacology, 11,* S17–S23.

Dubini, A., Bosc, M., & Polin, V. (1997b). Do noradrenaline and serotonin differentially affect social motivation and behaviour? *European Neuropsychopharmacology, 7,* S49–S55.

Duman, R. S., & Charney, D. S. (1999). Cell atrophy and loss in major depression. *Biological Psychiatry, 45,* 1083–1084.

Duman, R. S., Heninger, G. R., & Nestler, E. J. (1997). A molecular and cellular theory of depression. *Archives of General Psychiatry, 54,* 597–606.

Elkin, I., Shea, T., Watkins, J. T., et al (1989). National Institute of Mental Health treatment of depression collaborative research program. *Archives of General Psychiatry, 46,* 971–982.

Ellenbogen, M. A., Young, S. N., Dean, P., et al. (1996). Mood response to acute tryptophan depletion in healthy volunteers: Sex differences and temporal stability. *Neuropsychopharmacology, 15,* 465–474.

Ellingrod, V. L., & Perry, P. J. (1994). Venlafaxine: A heterocyclic antidepressant. *American Journal of Hospital Pharmacy, 51,* 3033–3046.

Fava, M. (2000). New approaches to the treatment of refractory depression. *Journal of Clinical Psychiatry, 61,* 26–32.

Fava, M., & Rosenbaum, J. F. (1991). Suicidality and fluoxetine: Is there a relationship? *Journal of Clinical Psychiatry, 52,* 108–111.

Feighner, J. P., Herbstein, J., & Damlouji, N. (1985). Combined MAOI, TCA, and direct stimulant therapy of treatment-resistant depression. *Journal of Clinical Psychiatry, 46,* 206–209.

Fibiger, H. C., & Phillips, A. G. (1981). Increased intracranial self-stimulation in rats after long-term administration of desipramine. *Science, 214,* 683–685.

Fink, M. (1994). Indications for the use of ECT. *Psychopharmacology Bulletin, 30,* 269–275.

Flemenbaum, A. (1974). Does lithium block the effects of amphetamine? *American Journal of Psychiatry, 131,* 820–821.

Frank, E., & Thase, M. E. (1999). Natural history and preventative treatment of recurrent mood disorders. *Annual Review of Medicine, 50,* 453–468.

Frank, E., Karp, J. F., & Rush, A. J. (1993). Efficacy of treatments for major depression. *Psychopharmacology Bulletin, 29,* 457–476.

Fritze, J. (1993). The adrenergic-cholinergic imbalance hypothesis of depression: A review and a perspective. *Reviews in the Neurosciences, 4,* 63–93.

Fugh-Berman, A. (2000). Herb-drug interactions. *The Lancet, 355,* 134–138.

Furukawa, T., Ushizima, I., & Ono, N. (1975). Modifications by lithium of behavioral responses to methamphetamine and tetrabenazine. *Psychopharmacologia, 42,* 243–248.

Georgotas, A., McCue, R. E., Friedman, E., & Cooper, T. (1987). Prediction of response to nortriptyline and phenelzine by platelet MAO activity. *American Journal of Psychiatry, 144,* 338–340.

Gitlin, M. J., Swendsen, J., Heller, T. L., & Hammen, C. (1995). Relapse and impairment in bipolar disorder. *American Journal of Psychiatry, 152,* 1635–1640.

Goldberg, J. F., Harrow, M., & Leon, A. C. (1996). Lithium treatment of bipolar affective disorders under naturalistic followup conditions. *Psychopharmacology Bulletin, 32,* 47–54.

Goodnick, P. J. (1991a). Pharmacokinetics of second generation antidepressants: Fluoxetine. *Psychopharmacology Bulletin, 27,* 503–512.

Goodnick, P. J. (1991b). Pharmacokinetics of second generation antidepressants: Bupropion. *Psychopharmacology Bulletin, 27,* 513–520.

Goodnick, P. J., & Schorr-Cain, C. B. (1991). Lithium pharmacokinetics. *Psychopharmacology Bulletin, 27,* 475–492.

Guay, D. R. (1995). The emerging role of valproate in bipolar disorder and other psychiatric disorders. *Pharmacotherapy, 15,* 631–647.

Gurguis, G. N. M., Vo, S. P., & Griffith, J. (1999). Platelet alpha2A-adrenoceptor function in major depression. *Psychiatry Research, 89,* 73–95.

Harrison, W., Stewart, J. W., McGrath, P. J., et al., (1988). Is loss of antidepressant effect during continuation therapy related to a placebo effect? *Psychopharmacology Bulletin, 24,* 9–17.

Heinz, A., Weingartner, H., George, D., et al. (1999). Severity of depression in abstinent alcoholics is associated with monoamine metabolites and dehydroepiandrosterone-sulfate concentrations. *Psychiatry Research, 89,* 97–106.

Hirschfeld, R. M. A. (2000). History and evolution of the monoamine hypothesis of depression. *Journal of Clinical Psychiatry, 61,* 4–6.

Horst, W. D., & Preskorn, S. H. (1998). Mechanisms of action and clinical characteristics of three atypical antidepressants: Venlafaxine, nefazodone, bupropion. *Journal of Affective Disorders, 51,* 237–254.

Jarvis, M. R. (1991). Clinical pharmacokinetics of tricyclic antidepressant overdose. *Psychopharmacology Bulletin, 27,* 541–550.

Johnson, F. N. (1979). The psychopharmacology of lithium. *Neuroscience and Biobehavioral Reviews, 3,* 15–30.

Jope, R. S. (1999). A bimodal model of the mechanism of action of lithium. *Molecular Psychiatry, 4,* 21–25.

Kayser, A., Robinson, D. S., Nies, A., & Howard, D. (1985). Response to phenelzine among depressed patients with features of hysteroid dysphoria. *American Journal of Psychiatry, 142,* 486–488.

Keck, P. E., McElroy, S. L., Strakowski, S. M., et al. (2000). Antipsychotics in the treatment of mood disorders and risk of tardive dyskinesia. *Journal of Clinical Psychiatry, 61,* 33–38.

Keck, P. E., Jr., Wilson, D. R., Strakowski, S. M., et al. (1995). Clinical predictors of acute risperidone response in schizophrenia, schizoaffective disorder, and psychotic mood disorders. *Journal of Clinical Psychiatry, 56,* 466–470.

Keller, M. B., McCullough, J. P., Klein, D. N., et al. (2000). A comparison of nefazodone, the cognitive behavioral-analysis system of psychotherapy, and their combination for the treatment of chronic depression. *New England Journal of Medicine, 342,* 1462–1470.

Kent, J. M. (2000). SNaRIs, NaSSAs, and NaRIs: New agents for the treatment of depression. *The Lancet, 355,* 911–918.

Khantzian, E. J. (1985). The self-medication hypothesis of addictive disorders: Focus on heroin and cocaine dependence. *American Journal of Psychiatry, 142,* 1259–1263.

Kirsch, I. (2000). Are drug and placebo effect in depression additive? *Biological Psychiatry, 47,* 733–735.

Kleindienst, N., Greil, W., Ruger, B., & Moller, H.-J. (1999). The prophylactic efficacy of lithium–transient or persistent? *European Archives of Psychiatry and Clinical Neuroscience, 249,* 144–149.

Kolata, G. (1986). Manic depression: Is it inherited? *Science, 232,* 575–576.

Koutouvidis, N., Pratikakis, M., & Fotiadou, A. (1999). The use of mirtazapine in a group of 11 patients following poor compliance to selective serotonin reuptake inhibitor treatment due to sexual dysfuntion. *International Clinical Psychopharmacology, 14,* 253–255.

Lader, M. H. (1996). Tolerability and safety: Essentials in antidepressant pharmacotherapy. *Journal of Clinical Psychiatry, 57,* 39–44.

Lane, R., & Baldwin, D. (1997). Selective serotonin reuptake inhibitor-induced serotonin syndrome: Review. *Journal of Clinical Psychopharmacology, 17,* 208–221.

Lavian, G., Finberg, J. P., & Youdim, M. B. (1993). The advent of a new generation of monoamine oxidase inhibitor antidepressants: Pharmacologic studies with moclobemide and brofaromine. *Clinical Neuropharmacology, 16,* S1–S6.

Leon, A. C., Shear, M. K., Portera, L., & Klerman, G. L. (1993). Effect size as a measure of symptom-specific drug change in clinical trials. *Psychopharmacology Bulletin, 29,* 163–168.

Leyton, M., Young, S. N., Pihl, R. O., et al. (1999). A comparison of the effects of acute tryptophan depletion and acute phenylalanine/tyrosine depletion in healthy women. *Advances in Experimental Medicine and Biology, 467,* 67–71.

Leyton, M., Young, S. N., Pihl, R. O., et al. (2000). Effects on mood of acute phenylalanine/tyrosine depletion in healthy women. *Neuropsychopharmacology, 22,* 52–63.

Lotufo-Neto, F., Trivedi, M., & Thase, M. E. (1999). Meta-analysis of the reversible inhibitors of monoamine oxidase type A moclobemide and brofaromine for the treatment of depression. *Neuropsychopharmacology, 20,* 226–247.

Madhusoodanan, S., Brenner, R., Araujo, L., & Abaza, A. (1995). Efficacy of risperidone treatment for psychoses associated with schizophrenia, schizoaffective disorder, bipolar disorder, or senile dementia in 11 geriatric patients: A case series. *Journal of Clinical Psychiatry, 56,* 514–518.

Mallinger, A. G., & Smith, E. (1991). Pharmacokinetics of monoamine oxidase inhibitors. *Psychopharmacology Bulletin, 27,* 493–502.

Massana, J., Moller, H. J., Burrows, G. D., et al. (1999). Reboxetine: A double-blind comparison with fluoxetine in major depressive disorder. *International Clinical Psychopharmacology, 14,* 73–80.

Matussek, N., & Linsmayer, M. (1968). The effect of lithium and amphetamine or desmethylimipramine-RO 4-1284 induced motor hyperactivity. *Life Sciences, 7,* 371–375.

Mayersohn, M., & Guentert, T. W. (1995). Clinical pharmacokinetics of the monoamine oxidase-A inhibitor moclobemide. *Clinical Pharmacokinetics, 29,* 292–332.

McGrath, P. J., Stewart, J. W., Nunes, E. V., et al. (1993). A double-blind crossover trial of imipramine and phenelzine for outpatients with treatment refractory depression. *American Journal of Psychiatry, 150,* 118–123.

McNeal, E. T., & Cimbolic, P. (1986). Antidepressants and biochemical theories of depression. *Psychological Bulletin, 99,* 361–374.

Mendlewicz, J. (1995). Pharmacologic profile and efficacy of venlafaxine. *International Clinical Psychopharmacology, 10,* 5–13.

Michelson, D., Fava, M., Amsterdam, J., et al. (2000). Interruption of selective serotonin reuptake inhibitor treatment. Double-blind, placebo-controlled trial. *British Journal of Psychiatry, 176,* 363–368.

Miklowitz, D. J., Frank, E., & George, E. L. (1996). New psychosocial treatments for the outpatient management of bipolar disorder. *Psychopharmacology Bulletin, 32,* 613–621.

Moller, H. J. (2000). Are all antidepressants the same? *Journal of Clinical Psychiatry, 61,* 24–28.

Montgomery, S. A. (1995). Are 2-week trials sufficient to indicate efficacy? *Psychopharmacology Bulletin, 31,* 41–44.

Montgomery, S. A. (1996). Efficacy of long-term treatment of depression. *Journal of Clinical Psychiatry, 57,* 24–30.

Montgomery, S. A. (1999). Predicting response: Noradrenaline reuptake inhibition. *International Clinical Psychopharmacology, 14,* S21–S26.

Moore, G. J., Bebchuk, J. M., Hasanat, K., et al. (2000). Lithium increases N-acetyl-aspartate in the human brain: In vivo evidence in support of bcl-2's neurotrophic effects. *Biological Psychiatry, 48,* 1–8.

Morton, W. A., Sonne, S. C., & Verga, M. A. (1995). Venlafaxine: A structurally unique and novel antidepressant. *Annals of Pharmacotherapy, 29,* 387–395.

Mulrow, C. D., Williams, J. W., Jr., Chiquette, E., et al. (2000). Efficacy of newer medications for treating depression in primary care patients. *American Journal of Medicine, 108,* 54–56.

Norman, T. R., & Burrows, G. D. (1995). A risk-benefit assessment of moclobemide in the treatment of depressive disorders. *Drug Safety, 12,* 46–54.

Parent, M. B., Habib, M. K., & Baker, G. B. (2000). Time-dependent changes in brain monoamine oxidase activity and in brain levels of monoamines and amino acids following acute administration of the antidepressant/antipanic drug phenelzine. *Biochemical Pharmacology, 59,* 1253–1263.

Pleil, A. M. (1995). The importance of considering non-monetary costs and benefits in selecting pharmacologic interventions in mental health. *Psychopharmacology Bulletin, 31,* 727–734.

Plomin, R., Owen, M. J., & McGuffin, P. (1994). The genetic basis of complex human behaviors. *Science, 264,* 1733–1739.

Post, R. M., Kotin, J., & Goodwin, F. K. (1974). The effects of cocaine on depressed patients. *American Journal of Psychiatry, 131,* 511–517.

Preskorn, S. H. (1991). Should bupropion dosage be adjusted based upon therapeutic drug monitoring? *Psychopharmacology Bulletin, 27,* 637–643.

Preskorn, S. H. (1995). Comparison of the tolerability of bupropion, fluoxetine, imipramine, nefazodone, paroxetine, sertraline, and venlafaxine. *Journal of Clinical Psychiatry, 56,* 12–21.

Prien, R. F. (1988). Methods and models for placebo use in pharmacotherapeutic trials. *Psychopharmacology Bulletin, 24,* 4–8.

Prien, R. F., & Potter, W. Z. (1990). NIMH workshop report on treatment of bipolar disorder. *Psychopharmacology Bulletin, 26,* 409–428.

Priest, R. G., Gimbrett, R., Roberts, M., & Steinert, J. (1995). Reversible and selective inhibitors of monamine oxidase A in mental and other disorders. *Acta Psychiatrica Scandinavica, 386,* 40–43.

Quitkin, F. M., Rabkin, J. G., Gerald, J., et al. (2000). Validity of clinical trials of antidepressants. *American Journal of Psychiatry, 157,* 327–337.

Quitkin, F. M., Stewart, J. W., McGrath, P. J., et al. (1993). Columbia atypical depression. A subgroup of depressives with better response to MAOI than to tricyclic antidepressants or placebo. *British Journal of Psychiatry Supplement, 21,* 30–34.

Rajkowska, G., Miguel-Hidalgo, J. J., Wei, J., et al. (1999). Morphometric evidence for neuronal and glial prefrontal cell pathology in major depression. *Biological Psychiatry, 45,* 1085–1098.

Reynaert, C., Parent, M., Mirel, J., et al. (1995). Moclobemide versus fluoxetine for a major depressive episode. *Psychopharmacology, 118,* 183–187.

Rickels, K., Amsterdam, J., Clary, C., et al. (1990). Buspirone in depressed outpatients: A controlled study. *Psychopharmacology Bulletin, 26,* 163–168.

Robinson, D. S., Marcus, R. N., Archibald, D. G., & Hardy, S. A. (1996). Therapeutic dose range of nefazodone in the treatment of major depression. *Journal of Clinical Psychiatry, 57,* 6–9.

Rudolph, R. L., & Feiger, A. D. (1999). A double-blind, randomized, placebo-controlled trial of once-daily venlafaxine extended release (XR) and fluoxetine for the treatment of depression. *Journal of Affective Disorders, 56,* 171–181.

Rudorfer, M. V. (1992). Monoamine oxidase inhibitors: Reversible and irreversible. *Psychopharmacology Bulletin, 28,* 45–57.

Sajatovic, M., DiGiovanni, S. K., Bastani, B., et al. (1996). Risperidone therapy in treatment refractory acute bipolar and schizoaffective mania. *Psychopharmacology Bulletin, 32,* 55–62.

Schrader, E. (2000). Equivalence of St. John's wort extract (Ze 117) and fluoxetine: A randomized, controlled study in mild-moderate depression. *International Clinical Psychopharmacology, 15,* 61–68.

Segraves, R. T. (1998). Antidepressant-induced sexual dysfunction. *Journal of Clinical Psychiatry, 59,* 48–54.

Small, J. G., Klapper, M. H., Milstein, V., et al. (1996). Comparison of therapeutic modalities for mania. *Psychopharmacology Bulletin, 32,* 623–627.

Smith, S. E., Pihl, R. O., Young, S. N., et al. (1987). A test of possible cognitive and environmental influences on the mood lowering effect of tryptophan depletion in normal males. *Psychopharmacology, 91,* 451–457.

Solomon, D. A., Keitner, G. I., Miller, I. W., et al. (1995). Course of illness and maintenance treatments for patients with bipolar disorder. *Journal of Clinical Psychiatry, 56,* 5–13,

Stahl, S. M. (1998). Mechanism of action of serotonin selective reuptake inhibitors: Serotonin receptors and pathways mediate therapeutic effects and side effects. *Journal of Affective Disorders, 51,* 215–235.

Stanford, S. C. (1996). Prozac: Panacea or puzzle? *Trends in the Pharmacological Sciences, 17,* 150–154.

Swinkels, J. A., & de Jonghe, F. (1995). Safety of antidepressants. *International Clinical Psychopharmacology, 9,* 19–25.

Thase, M. E. (1999). How should efficacy be evaluated in randomized clinical trials of treatments for depression? *Journal of Clinical Psychiatry, 60,* 23–31.

Thompson, C. (1999). Mirtazapine versus selective serotonin reuptake inhibitors. *Journal of Clinical Psychiatry, 60,* 18–22.

Tollefson, G. D. (1991). Antidepressant treatment and side effect consideration. *Journal of Clinical Psychiatry, 52* (Suppl), 4–13.

Tosteson, D. C. (1981). Lithium and mania. *Scientific American, 244,* 164–174.

Volz, H. P., Heimann, H., Bellaire, J., et al. (1994). Brofaromine in non-endogenous major depressed inpatients—results of a preliminary dose-finding trial versus tranylcypromine. *Pharmacopsychiatry, 27,* 152–158.

Volz, H. P., & Laux, P. (2000). Potential treatment for subthreshold and mild depression: A comparison of St. John's wort extracts and fluoxetine. *Comprehensive Psychiatry, 41,* 133–137.

Walsh, B. T., Stewart, J. W., Roose, S. P., et al. (1984). Treatment of bulimia with phenelzine. *Archives of General Psychiatry, 41,* 1105–1109.

Warshaw, M. G., & Keller, M. B. (1996). The relationship between fluoxetine use and suicidal behavior in 654 subjects with anxiety disorders. *Journal of Clinical Psychiatry, 57,* 158–166.

Werder, S. F. (1995). An update on the diagnosis and treatment of mania in bipolar disorder. *American Family Physician, 51,* 1126–1136.

Wheatley, D. P., VanMoffaert, M., Timmerman, L., et al. (1998). Mirtazapine: Efficacy and tolerability in comparison with fluoxetine in patients with moderate to severe major depressive disorder. *Journal of Clinical Psychiatry, 59,* 306–312.

Wilcox, C. S., Cohn, J. B., Linden, R. D., et al. (1992). Predictors of placebo response: A retrospective analysis. *Psychopharmacology Bulletin, 28,* 157–162.

Yonkers, K. A. (1998). Assessing unipolar mood disorders in women. *Psychopharmacology Bulletin, 34,* 261–266.

Young, S. N., Smith, S. E., Pihl, R. O., et al. (1985). Tryptophan depletion causes a rapid lowering of mood in normal males. *Psychopharmacology, 87,* 173–177.

Zarate, C. A., Jr, Tohen, M., Banov, M. D., et al. (1995). Is clozapine a mood stabilizer? *Journal of Clinical Psychiatry, 56,* 108–112.

Zisook, S., Shuchter, S. R., Gallagher, T., et al. (1993). Atypical depression in an outpatient psychiatric population. *Depression, 1,* 268–274.

14

Pharmacotherapy for Miscellaneous Mental Disorders

Schizophrenia, affective disorders, and problems associated with anxiety are the conditions in which chemical intervention is most likely, but there are a number of other mental or emotional conditions in which the use of psychotropic drugs may also be involved. This chapter will deal briefly with some of the more common ones, paying particular attention to those that occur predominantly in children and the aged.

Because this book is chiefly concerned with psychotropic drugs, the interventions discussed will necessarily deal with drugs. However, as a psychologist, I would strongly suggest that any interventions in these disorders also include a variety of psychotherapies, such as cognitive or behavior therapy, family therapy, or group therapy. In many cases, these should be tried before pharmacotherapy. When drugs and psychotherapy are combined, the two may complement each other. They may be synergistic; for example, a drug may be used to achieve a mood or mental state in patients that makes them more amenable to a particular form of psychotherapy. The combination of pharmacotherapy and psychotherapy may work better than either one alone simply because one is more effective in one subset of patients while the other is more effective in another subset of patients—despite the fact that both sets appear to share the same overt symptoms. Such is the vagary of diagnostics and etiology of most psychopathology.

Disorders in Children

There are a number of childhood mental or behavioral problems for which drugs are used, and the prevalence of psychotropic drug treatment in children of all ages has increased dramatically in the United States during the last few decades (Zito et al., 2000). The major categories include (1) attention deficit disorders; (2) organic brain damage and retardation; (3) childhood schizophrenia; (4) infantile autism; and (5) affective disorders (generally in postpubertal children). (See Gadow, [1992] and Campbell & Cueva [1995] for a more complete review of these areas.)

Unfortunately, there are a number of major problems in evaluating the effectiveness of drugs in these disorders (Arnold, 1993). Among these are the requirements of clinical trials that both the parent(s) and child or adolescent must consent to the treatment and the treatment must have some potential benefit for the patient (unlike with adults who may volunteer for altruistic reasons). Thus, it is difficult to find appropriate subjects for conducting double-blind, placebo-controlled clinical trials. Second, accurate diagnoses are difficult to make. Verbal behavior, which is often crucial in determining the type of problems evidenced in adults, may be absent or poorly developed in a child, so that communication with the child is difficult or impossible. Also, the behavior of even normal children is pretty "psychotic"—they talk to nonexistent people, think inanimate objects have feelings and emotions, exhibit perceptual inconsistencies, have very weird senses of humor, tend to be self-centered, and have little regard for personal appearance or hygiene. Third, with children, one does not usually have any stable history to look back on, as one has with adults. Children generally change, typically at a relatively rapid rate, and go through a number of different qualitative cognitive and physical changes during the developmental process. Therefore, it is often unclear whether behavioral changes that accompany drug treatment are due to the drug or to natural maturational processes. Finally, information about a treatment's effectiveness comes less from the patient being treated and more from the observers of the patient—that is, parents, teachers and clinicians—who often disagree on the outcome of the drug trial.

Although the psychotropics used in children are the same ones used in adults, special considerations for the pharmacokinetics of children and adolescents must be made (Geller, 1991). Children, for their size, have a greater hepatic capacity than adults and, therefore, more rapidly eliminate drugs that utilize hepatic pathways—for example, antipsychotics, tricyclic antidepressants, pemoline, and methylphenidate. Compared with adults, children have relatively less adipose tissue and, therefore may have less ability for long-term storage of parent drugs and their metabolites. Finally, because of relatively greater total body water and more efficient renal mechanisms, children may more rapidly eliminate drugs that use primarily renal pathways, such as lithium. The functional significance of all this is that the mean plasma half-lives of most psychotropic drugs will be considerably shorter in children and adolescents and that young people will be able to tolerate higher dosages—per unit of body weight—than adults.

Attention Deficit Disorder

The most common childhood disorder for which medication is most likely to be used is *attention deficit disorder (ADD)*, also called *attention deficit hyperactivity disorder (ADHD)* because excessive motor activity is one of the more common characteristics of children with the disorder. Over the years it has been known as *hyperactivity,* the *hyperkinetic syndrome,* and *minimal brain dysfunction,* among other terms. ADD may be evidenced in 1.7 percent to

17.8 percent of the school-age population (the wide range is indicative of the difficulties in diagnosis and the differences in criteria used in diagnosis of the disorder), with boy-to-girl estimates ranging from 2:1 in community surveys of school-age children to 3:1 to 9:1 in children referred to child psychiatrists or psychologists (Elia et al., 1999).

The primary symptoms are lack of investment, organization, and maintenance of attention and effort in completing tasks; inability to delay gratification; and impulsive responding without attention to relevant stimuli in the environment (Dulcan, 1986). Excessive levels of motor activity and fidgetiness are common but not always present in ADD. Neurological signs are sometimes evidenced along with these behavioral symptoms. These may include abnormal EEG patterns; mild visual or auditory impairments; crossed eyes; fine, jerky, lateral eye movements; poor visual-motor coordination; or handedness confusion.

Since ADD symptoms present a number of difficulties in learning situations, the disorder is of considerable concern in classroom settings. Other characteristics that may be evidenced are extreme aggressiveness and rapid mood swings. These are most often seen in times of stress or in groups, but they may be absent in some calm situations. The children generally show little evidence of fear, and their behavior is refractory to punishment involving aversive stimulation (that is, pain). Many symptoms of ADD tend to induce dominating and negative controlling responses on the part of teachers, parents, and peers (that is, they yell and scold a lot). These in turn may compound the ADD child's difficulties (Cunningham et al., 1985).

The etiology of the disorder (if indeed it is one disorder) is unclear, although there is sometimes evidence of notable birth trauma or abnormalities during pregnancy. Genetic factors have been implicated in ADD, and there is often a family history of the disorder (Biederman et al., 1995; Faraone et al., 1995). Long-time speculations that there is insufficient catecholamine activity in the brains of individuals with ADHD have been supported recently with the observation that adults diagnosed with ADHD have a higher density of dopamine transporters (the proteins responsible for dopamine reuptake) (Dougherty et al., 1999; Krause et al., 2000). Theoretically, higher dopamine transporter availability would result in insufficient levels of dopamine to act on receptors. Not surprisingly, dopamine reuptake inhibition is a prominent pharmacodynamic property of the medications shown to have the highest efficacy in the treatment of ADHD, and recently, treatment with one of these drugs (methylphenidate) was shown to decrease dopamine transporter availability in adults diagnosed with ADHD (Krause et al., 2000). Associations of both the dopamine D_4 receptor gene and the dopamine transporter gene with ADHD have also been reported (Cook et al., 1995; Faraone et al., 1999). Despite the common popular belief that sugar worsens hyperactive behavior in children, the majority of well-controlled experimental studies have failed to provide any support for this belief (Spring et al., 1987). A largely carbohydrate meal does tend to disrupt children's concentration, but that effect is common with just about everybody.

Before drug intervention is resorted to, a complete physical and neurological examination of the child should be conducted to establish that he or she is not suffering from hypoxia (insufficient blood supply to the brain), low calcium levels, low blood sugar levels, or hyperthyroidism, all of which can result in hyperactive symptoms. It is also important to determine whether or not the child is actually hyperactive. Surprisingly, this is not always easy because the term is broadly defined and no norms for child activity levels exist. For example, in a 1958 report based on questionnaires submitted to parents, approximately half of the children were noted to be overactive. A similar rate of distractibility and hyperactive symptoms in children was noted in a 1971 report based on questionnaires submitted to teachers. These reports suggest that parents and teachers may have unrealistic views as to what normal behavior in children is (Weiss & Hechtman, 1979).

The most common drugs used in the treatment of ADD or ADHD are the psycho-stimulants methylphenidate (Ritalin), amphetamine and dextroamphetamine (Adderall, Dexedrine), and pemoline (Cylert). Methylphenidate is, by far, the most often prescribed, although no well-controlled, head-to-head comparisons, using appropriate dosages, have found reliable differences in the overall efficacy of these drugs (Elia et al., 1999). They do differ in terms of potency—with dextroamphetamine being most potent and pemoline being least potent—but as discussed in Chapter 2, this is not generally relevant in terms of clinical efficacy. As discussed in Chapter 9, methylphenidate and dextroamphetamine are virtually indistinguishable in terms of their pharmacodynamic properties—that is, both act by enhancing the release of NE and DA and inhibiting their reuptake. While there hasn't been much research on the pharmacodynamic properties of pemoline, there is some evidence that it acts primarily by enhancing DA release and inhibiting its reuptake (Sallee et al., 1992).

Although methyphenidate, amphetamine, and pemoline are virtually indistinguishable from each other in terms of efficacy in reducing ADD symptoms and side-effect profile (Elia et al., 1999), pemoline has the least abuse liability (it is a Schedule IV controlled substance as opposed to the Schedule II designation for the other two drugs). For example, unlike methyphenidate and dextroamphetamine, pemoline is not self-administered in either naïve or cocaine-dependent animals (Langer et al., 1986). This decreases the likelihood of its being diverted to illicit use, as is sometimes the case with the other two drugs. Pemoline is also more slowly absorbed and exerts effects a few hours longer—pharmacokinetic properties similar to those of sustained-release forms of methylphenidate (SR-20 Ritalin) and dextroamphetamine (Dexedrine Spansule) (Pelham et al., 1990, 1995; Sallee et al., 1992). Unfortunately, pemoline has been linked to increased risk of liver toxicity, which is usually mild and reversible, and acute liver failure, which, while extremely rare, can be lethal (Shevell & Schreiber, 1997). Thus, pemoline is likely to be considered an alternative treatment for ADD only if other drugs fail to produce satisfactory results, and its use would require vigilant monitoring of liver function. A once-daily tablet of methylphenidate (marketed as Concerta) has recently been approved by the FDA for the treatment of ADHD. The tablet employs an advanced form of technology, different from previous sustained-release preparations, to deliver medication at a more controlled rate, which should minimize the peak and trough blood fluctuations associated with repeated dosing of immediate-release methylphenidate products.

While there is no compelling empirical evidence to support the wide disparity in the use of methylphenidate and amphetamine in the treatment of ADD, some studies have indicated that perhaps as many as 20 percent of ADD children who do not respond to one type of psychostimulant may respond to another (Dulcan, 1986). On the other hand, the psychostimulant caffeine, often preferred by laypersons who do not believe in giving a "drug" to children, has virtually no efficacy but does have side effects. Barbiturate-like sedative–hypnotics also induce no beneficial effects with respect to any of the target symptoms of ADD and oftentimes prove to be worse than placebo.

For nonresponders to psychostimulants, a number of alternative drugs are sometimes beneficial. Tricyclic antidepressant drugs such as imipramine and desipramine often are effective, in some cases inducing a very rapid symptom remission, but these effects may disappear with time. Their long-term safety in children, especially with respect to growth and development, is not well established. Some tricyclics may have a less burdensome profile of side effects and may result in better treatment compliance (Levin, 1995). The most frequent adverse events of tricyclic therapy are associated with the anticholinergic activity of these agents, but the most common serious adverse events are associated with tricyclic overdose. Concern has been expressed because of case reports describing an association between antidepressant therapy for ADD and sudden death (Fox & Rieder, 1993).

MAO inhibitors have been shown to possess efficacy comparable to methylphenidate and amphetamine, but because of the precautions required of MAO inhibitors regarding diet and use of other drugs, they would only be clinically useful in children with idiosyncratic negative responses to these other stimulants or in cases in which stimulant abuse might be of concern (Zametkin et al., 1985).

Clonidine (Catapres), an alpha-2-adrenergic receptor agonist, has been shown in several studies to be effective in reducing the symptoms of ADD, particularly in children with comorbid tic disorders such as Tourette's syndrome (Hunt et al., 1986; Steingard et al., 1993). Similar improvements have been found with guanfacine (Tenex), also an alpha-2-adrenergic receptor agonist, but without clonidine's sedative effects (Chappell et al., 1995; Hunt et al., 1995). (Both Catapres and Tenex are FDA-approved for treatment of hypertension.) Clonidine has also been shown to induce clinical improvement in children with comorbid ADHD and conduct disorder who failed trials of conventional psychostimulant drug therapy (Schvehla et al., 1994). These findings add considerable confusion to the pursuit of understanding the pathophysiology of ADD. Whereas psychostimulants predominantly amplify noradrenergic activity (by enhancing NE release and blocking its reuptake), alpha-2-adrenergic receptor agonists (which supposedly activate noradrenergic autoreceptors) should reduce the release of NE. Thus, we have a most curious paradox: Drugs that amplify and drugs that reduce noradrenergic functioning have both been shown to be beneficial in reducing ADD symptoms.

Approximately 60 percent to 80 percent of the children diagnosed with ADD respond favorably to psychostimulants—in some cases dramatically—with significant increases in attention span and significant decreases in motor activity and restlessness. However, if one tries both methylphenidate and dextroamphetamine and uses a wide range of doses, some degree of behavioral improvement almost always occurs in ADD children (Elia et al., 1999; Rapport et al., 1994). This is reflected in better learning of rote material and improved performance of fine motor tasks like handwriting. Also, aggression and impulsivity are decreased. The amount and quality of the child's interpersonal relationships with both peers and teachers are generally improved, thus increasing the child's self-esteem and normalizing student–teacher interactions (Cunningham et al., 1985).

It should be pointed out that few children with ADD respond favorably to psychostimulants across all behavioral dimensions. Thus, depending on the parameters of the study and the characteristics of the children involved, the efficacy rate reported in studies of psychostimulant treatment of ADD has varied widely—anywhere from 33 percent to 100 percent (Swanson et al., 1991). For example, if one is using multiple measures of response, multiple psychostimulant drugs, and different doses of the drugs, the favorable response rate on at least one measure approaches 100 percent; in contrast, if the requirement is a favorable response on all measures, almost all individuals would be identified as nonresponders. ADD children most likely to respond favorably to methylphenidate are those with high I.Q., considerable inattentiveness, young age, low severity of disorder, low rates of anxiety, and a positive response to their first dose of methylphenidate (Buitelaar et al., 1995; Tannock et al., 1995).

Psychostimulant intervention should be accompanied by elimination of disturbing influences in the family or classroom through counseling and psychotherapy, implementation of behavior modification and cognitive training programs, and possibly enrollment of the child in learning disabilities classrooms (to help restore the confidence of the child, whose experiences are typically failures). In some cases these interventions alone may be sufficient to ameliorate the condition, or they may interact synergistically with psychostimulant treatment (Ajibola & Clement, 1995). However, in general, the benefits of nondrug interventions have been less substantial than those of drug treatment (Brown et al., 1985; Pelham et al., 1993). There is also evidence that the positive reinforcers used in behavior modification programs may actually take the ADD child's attention away from the task at hand and direct it toward the reinforcing agent. Finally, there are economic factors that must be considered. Unfortunately, most psychological treatments are rather arduous and costly to implement, particularly in comparison to the few cents a day it costs for *d*-amphetamine.

If improvement with psychostimulants is going to occur, it will be apparent immediately. If these drugs produce only doubtful benefits in a few days (or, at most, a couple of weeks), their use should be terminated. Unfortunately, determining whether benefits occur may sometimes be difficult, because not all ADD children respond to the same dose and not all of the different target symptoms may respond equally to the same doses of these drugs. In fact, the effects of methylphenidate (the most commonly studied psychostimulant) on cognitive function in ADD children interact with and are interdependent on a host of variables—for example, dose, time course following administration, child characteristics, type of information processing required, task factors, and prevailing social and environmental conditions (Rapport & Kelly, 1991). In general, children's performance on tasks requiring primarily vigilance appears most benefited with low (0.1–0.4 mg/kg) doses (or shortly after the drug is administered). For highly effortful tasks that require greater behavioral inhibition, optimal benefits are most likely with high (0.6–0.9 mg/kg) doses (or 3 to 4 hours after the drug is administered). For tasks requiring nearly equal degrees of vigilance and inhibition, such as learning tasks, optimal performance is most likely with intermediate (0.3–0.7 mg/kg) doses (or 2 to 4 hours after drug administration). Thus, whether one observes benefits or not may depend on what the observer is looking for, what dose has been given, and the time after the drug is given.

Perhaps for these reasons, there has been no resolution to the 20-year debate over whether higher doses of methylphenidate (those in the 1.0 mg/kg range) induce cognitive toxicity—that is, detrimental effects on high-level cognitive processes necessary for learning. See, for example, Sprague and Sleator (1977), who reported an inverted U-shaped dose–response function on learning with disruption of learning occurring at a 1.0 mg/kg dose; Swanson et al. (1991), who reviewed the literature on this issue up to 1990; and Douglas et al. (1995), who found linear improvement on measures of mental flexibility (for example, divergent thinking, ability to shift mental set) and other cognitive processes in ADHD children with doses of methyphenidate up to 0.9 mg/kg.

Unfortunately, routine monitoring of the plasma concentrations of any of the drugs used to treat ADD does not appear to be clinically useful, because of wide variations in optimum plasma concentration as well as a poor correlation between behavioral improvement and plasma levels (Elia, 1991), although several studies have found reliable correlations between psychostimulant plasma levels and clinical improvement during the first 1 to 4 hours of the absorption phase (Geller, 1991). Fortunately, there is a lack of effect of food on psychostimulant absorption in ADD children, which eliminates the need for a fasting state for drug efficacy.

It has long been believed that the response to psychostimulants of ADD children with hyperactivity is different from that of "normal" children and adults, or that it is paradoxical because hyperactive children appear to be calmer, rather than more excited, under their influence. However, studies have found that normal children and hyperactive children respond in a qualitatively similar way to psychostimulants; the effect may just be more apparent in hyperactive children (Rapoport et al., 1980). In a variety of measures, both types of children respond to psychostimulants as adults do, with the exception of mood. Adults tend to report mood elevation or euphoria with psychostimulants, whereas children tend to say that these drugs make them feel "funny" or "strange." Finally, ADD children without hyperactivity benefit as much with psychostimulant treatment as those children with hyperactivity, although the latter children may require somewhat higher doses because they have greater difficulty in the area of behavioral inhibition (Barkley et al., 1991).

The paradoxical reduction in motor activity with psychostimulants may be resolved by noting that sustained attention and high motor activity are incompatible; when attention increases, activity is most likely going to decrease. (Have you ever noticed how "zombie-like" children look when they are watching their favorite Saturday morning cartoon?) Another possibility is that hyperactive children may actually be physiologically underaroused, and that psychostimulants bring arousal up to normal, while sedative–hypnotics decrease arousal even further and worsen the symptoms. (You may notice that many of the characteristics of the hyperactive child are analogous to those of a moderately drunken adult—that is, inattentiveness, belligerence, and unresponsiveness to normal social controls).

Studies attempting to determine whether activity in the brains of ADD children differs from that of normal children have not yielded definitive answers. For example, the results of studies examining cerebral glucose metabolism (a measure of the level of brain activity) with PET scan techniques have been inconclusive; low cerebral glucose metabolism has been found in adolescent girls and adults with ADHD but not adolescent boys with ADHD (Ernst et al., 1994; Zametkin et al., 1990, 1993). Also, no robust effects of psychostimulants on cerebral glucose metabolism have been demonstrated, although they may produce differential patterns of increases and decreases in metabolism in certain regions of the brain (Matochik et al., 1993, 1994). Other studies have found that the amplitudes of a particular type of brain wave pattern (called the P3 wave of event-related potentials), which tends to reflect the impact of information processing, such as attention and decision making, are abnormally small in ADHD children, but can be normalized by psychostimulants (Verbaten et al., 1994).

Despite the consistent improvement in the symptoms of the disorder, which should theoretically allow the children to learn more efficiently, there seems to be no clear evidence that long-term learning and academic achievement are benefited by psychostimulants (Dulcan, 1986), although a modest improvement in I.Q. was found after 15 months of amphetamine treatment (a mean of 4.5 I.Q. points versus 0.7 I.Q. points with placebo) in ADHD children in a recent randomized, double-blind, placebo-controlled study (Gillberg et al., 1997). This paradox has not been resolved, but it may be due in part to the practice of using doses that most facilitate classroom behavior but have the least effectiveness with respect to learning. It is also possible, because of the long duration of exposure to these drugs, that much of the learning accomplished under the drug was state-dependent (Swanson & Kinsbourne, 1976). If such is the case, then it is not surprising that individuals who were treated with drugs do not show any long-term gains from the treatment when they are later tested as adolescents or adults without the drugs. Although there has been no definitive study of this possibility, as discussed below, adults who were hyperactive as children (and treated with psychostimulants) do respond favorably in some psychomotor tasks with psychostimulants.

Some long-term benefits of psychostimulant treatment in ADHD have been suggested. One study compared young adults who had been treated for hyperactivity with psychostimulants during childhood with a similar group of unmedicated individuals and a control group (Hechtman et al., 1984). They found that the adults who had been hyperactive as youths differed greatly from the control group, regardless of their therapy as children. However, the adults who had been treated with psychostimulants as youths differed from the untreated adults on only a few variables. It seemed that the treated young adults had fewer car accidents, viewed their childhood more positively, stole less in elementary school, and generally had better social skills and self-esteem. The authors suggested that the medicated individuals may have suffered less from early social ostracism and subsequently developed better feelings toward themselves and others.

It is generally believed that ADD is eventually outgrown in puberty and that the effectiveness of psychostimulant medication ceases at this time. Therefore, some experts suggest that these medications should be withdrawn at puberty. However, neither belief is supported by empirical evidence (Faraone et al., 2000). Although the symptoms do tend to dissipate at puberty, many ADD symptoms, such as impulsivity, poor social skills, learning disabilities, and lower educational achievement, often continue into adulthood in 30 percent to 70 percent of childhood-onset cases. Furthermore, several studies have indicated that adolescents and adults diagnosed with ADD can benefit markedly from psychostimulant drug therapy. It is possible that the decreased positive response to psychostimulants over time in some individuals is due to tolerance.

The most common side effects associated with psychostimulant treatment of ADD are decreased appetite, which may result in small, temporary effects on normal weight gain, and insomnia (Fine & Johnston, 1993). However, some studies have questioned whether insomnia or related sleep disturbances are a direct result of psychostimulant treatment or are a result of the disorder itself, as they found essentially the same degree of sleep disturbances with placebo as with methylphenidate in ADD children (Fine & Johnston, 1993; Kent et al., 1995). Less common, but more problematic, side effects are symptoms of social withdrawal (as noted, interpersonal relationships are generally improved with psychostimulant treatment) or acute psychotic reactions. Also, psychostimulants may exacerbate or induce motor and phonic tics in individuals predisposed to multiple-tics Tourette's syndrome (to be described shortly), although these adverse effects occur rarely and are reversible (Castellanos et al., 1997; Gadow et al., 1999). Nevertheless, clinicians and people who deal with children should be particularly aware of this possibility because early signs of Tourette's syndrome may be difficult to distinguish from hyperactivity and would only get worse with psycho-stimulants (Caine et al., 1984).

Psychostimulant treatment in hyperactive children does not appear to increase their risk for drug dependency later on. Clinical experience has not revealed any association between the use of these drugs in preadolescents and their later drug abuse (Pelham, 1993). In fact, while it has long been recognized that individuals with ADHD have a significantly higher risk for substance abuse (Clure et al., 1999; Milberger et al., 1997), recent research suggests that pharmacotherapy of ADHD dramatically reduces the risk for substance abuse disorders (Biederman et al., 1999). These findings may be due to the fact that ADD children do not experience any pleasurable effects from these drugs and are quite willing to terminate this therapy when the suggestion to do so is made. The fact that ADD children dislike taking these medications can lead to noncompliance, which some authorities have suggested may be partially responsible for the variable and conflicting results from drug studies and the lack of long-term efficacy of psychostimulants in this disorder. Therefore, children should not be given sole responsibility for taking their medication and should not be allowed to take it to school with them, since they may "forget" to take it or succumb to pressure from peers to "share" their medication. For example, in a recent survey of ADD children being treated with Ritalin, 16 percent of the children reported that they had been approached to sell, give, or trade their medication (Musser et al., 1998).

Over the past two decades there has been considerable discussion about the benefits of nutritional interventions for the treatment of hyperactivity, such as elimination of foods containing artificial colors and flavors, natural and artificial salicylates (aspirin-like substances), preservatives, and sugar. This is sometimes referred to as the Feingold diet, named after Ben Feingold, the allergist who initially proposed the association between these substances and many cases of hyperactivity. Although empirical studies have not supported Feingold's contention that as many as 50 percent of hyperactive children may benefit from such dietary restrictions, they have indicated that some hyperactive children, perhaps between 5 percent and 10 percent, show behavioral improvements from them (Kolata, 1982).

Infantile Autism

Infantile autism is currently diagnosed by the presence of severe disturbances that are generally noted during the first 30 months of life. The primary symptoms are failure to develop interpersonal relationships, inability to use communicative speech, the presence of bizarre motor behaviors such as rocking and head banging, and an anxious desire for sameness in the child's surroundings. There is an absence of delusions, hallucinations, and loosening of associations common to schizophrenia. Some autistic children show evidence of a very high level of cognitive functioning in a specific area, such as rote memory, but in general, intellectual functioning is significantly below average. I.Q.s are below 50 in 60 percent of autistic children, between 50 and 70 in 20 percent, and above 70 in only 20 percent. Approximately 5 out of 10,000 children are diagnosed with the disorder, and it is four to five times more prevalent in males than in females (Ritvo & Freeman, 1984).

Divergent lines of evidence indicate that autism is a syndrome of heterogeneous origins with similar behavioral manifestations, although research consistently favors neurological abnormalities with a strong genetic inheritance pattern (Hunsinger et al., 2000). A number of electrophysiological and neurochemical findings have suggested that autistic patients are in a state of chronic hyperarousal (Ritvo & Freeman, 1984). Unfortunately, the procedures used in determining these results may be sufficiently fear-arousing in these patients to create the abnormalities found. There is no evidence that the symptoms and developmental delays of autism are due to psychological trauma, physical abuse, bad parenting, or separation (Hunsinger et al., 2000).

The primary goals of intervention with autistic children are to promote development of rudimentary or nonexistent functions such as language and adaptive social and self-care skills, and to decrease behavioral symptoms such as stereotypies, withdrawal, hyperactivity, self-mutilation, and aggressiveness directed toward others. Structured educational programs, designed to systematically teach the child higher and wider skills in developmental problem areas, are the preferred mode of treatment (Campbell et al., 1996). Most pharmacological interventions are used to control behaviors such as assaultiveness, self-mutilation, and unmanageable hyperactivity. However, more recently, chemicals have been used in attempts to correct presumed neurological deficits underlying the symptoms.

Antipsychotics have been used for many years in treating this disorder and have been shown to effectively reduce the symptoms of hyperactivity, stereotypy, and aggressiveness. However, the higher-potency antipsychotics, such as haloperidol (Haldol), thiothixene (Navane), and trifluoperazine (Stelazine), are more effective than the low potency drugs like chlorpromazine (Thorazine), since the latter drugs' strong sedative properties can interfere with performance and learning (Campbell, 1978). The use of antipsychotics in this disorder may also lead to what has been called an *akathisia frenzy* (what might appear to be a severe case of "ants in the pants"), which begins a cycle in which behavioral disturbances are exacerbated. This may lead to escalating the dose of the antipsychotic, which can produce an increase in akathisia-induced impulsive behavior.

Studies with haloperidol have found it to be significantly superior to a placebo in reducing withdrawal and stereotypies in autistic children and, combined with contingent reinforcement, to be an effective method of facilitating the acquisition of imitative speech (Anderson et al., 1984). In addition, lithium may have some value in the treatment of aggression, explosive affect (emotion/mood), and hyperactivity. However, the potentially severe side effects of these drugs, noted in Chapters 12 and 13, make their long-term use a questionable practice. Several recent preliminary studies on the efficacy of atypical antipsychotics, primarily risperidone, have reported clinical improvements in children with autism in several behavioral domains, for example, aggression, self-injury, social relatedness, and poor sleep hygiene (Hunsinger et al., 20000). Since no unexpected adverse reactions were reported, further more controlled clinical trials of these drugs in autistic children are warranted.

A wide variety of drugs have been tried with autistic children, with mixed, mostly negative, results. Back in the days when LSD was being used in psychotherapeutic contexts, LSD was suggested to have some beneficial effects, in that it seemed to assist the child in retaining eye contact and to prolong the child's attention span (Campbell, 1978). Amphetamines have been shown to slightly increase attention span and verbal production and to decrease hyperactivity in some autistic children, but numerous and common side effects of these drugs (such as worsening of withdrawal and stereotypies and loss of appetite) are such that these drugs should not be used as a treatment in this disorder (Gadow, 1992). On the other hand, antagonists at adrenergic beta receptors—for example, propranolol (Inderal)—have been shown to significantly reduce impulsive, aggressive, and self-abusive behaviors, as well as the need for sameness, in adult autistics (Ratey et al., 1987). These findings support the notion that some autistics are in a chronic state of hyperarousal. However, sedative–hypnotics have not been found to be any better than placebo in controlling autistic symptoms. Administrations of L-dopa, the precursor to dopamine, and 5-hydroxytryptophan, the precursor to serotonin, have been shown to have no beneficial effects in autistic children (Sloman, 1991).

Stimulated by Linus Pauling's orthomolecular hypothesis of mental illness, which proposed that some forms of mental illness are related to biochemical imbalances in the body that may be correctable with large doses of vitamins, approximately a dozen studies have been published assessing the efficacy of vitamin supplements, primarily vitamins B3 and B6 (niacin and pyridoxine) and magnesium, in the treatment of autism. While the majority of these studies report a favorable response to vitamin treatment, interpretation of these positive findings needs to be tempered because of methodological problems in many of the studies (Pfeiffer et al., 1995). As is typical of many studies investigating chemical interventions for autism, a number of these studies employed imprecise outcome and were based on small samples. Some possibly repeated use of the same subjects in more than one study, did not adjust for regression to the mean effects in measuring improvement, and omitted collecting long-term follow-up data. Thus, better controlled studies of this type of treatment for autism are needed.

In the early 1980s, the use of the nonamphetamine appetite suppressant fenfluramine (Pondimin) in the treatment of autism created a great deal of excitement. This drug, which reduces the levels of serotonin in the brains of animals, was reported in several studies to have both long-lasting and reversible effects in autistic children. Its use was suggested from research indicating that perhaps a third of autistic children have abnormally high levels of blood serotonin (you might recall that this is a primary neurotransmitter in the reticular activating system, which modulates sensory input, activity level, attention, and arousal) (Hashino et al., 1984). Initial studies conducted with autistic children indicated that fenfluramine treatment for several weeks or months was accompanied by notable improvements in both intellectual and social functioning (Gadow, 1992).

Unfortunately, subsequent investigations of fenfluramine on severely and profoundly developmentally disabled autistic children and adults did not support these earlier observations. In addition to finding no significant clinical improvements in autistic symptoms, several side effects (weight loss, moderate tension and agitation, and insomnia) were observed both during and shortly after fenfluramine treatment (Sloman, 1991; Leventhal et al., 1993). Concerns over potential cardiac damage associated with fenfluramine's use in obesity treatment led to its withdrawal from the market, so the issue over whether it may have efficacy in the treatment of autism appears to be a moot point at this time.

Interestingly, fluoxetine, an SSRI antidepressant with pharmacodynamic actions that are believed to enhance serotonergic system functioning, has been shown in several uncontrolled trials to have some efficacy in the treatment of autism. For example, improvement in inappropriate speech, ritualistic behaviors, motor stereotypies, and social functioning and increased interest in the environment have been reported (Cook et al., 1992; DeLong et al., 1998; Fatemi et al., 1998; Peral et al., 1999). Whether these benefits will be evidenced under more controlled conditions (i.e., double-blind, placebo-controlled trials) remains to be determined.

As enthusiasm for fenfluramine in the treatment of autism began to decline, enthusiasm for the use of naltrexone, a long-acting opiate receptor antagonist, began to grow—based on the premise that elevated endogenous opioids were a factor in the etiology of the disorder (Goldberg, 1987; Sahley & Panksepp, 1987). It was theorized that parental warmth or contact may stimulate opioid activity as a way of strengthening the bond between parent and child. However, some autistic children who already have elevated opioid levels may not need the surge of opioids induced by parental contact. Therefore, these children may avoid attachment and parental warmth. This may also be the reason why these children do not appear to experience normal pain, which would stop them from engaging in self-injurious behaviors. Another possibility is that these behaviors stimulate abnormally high levels of endorphin activity, inducing a pleasurable reaction that reinforces these behaviors.

In tests of the endorphin hypothesis, early studies looked for elevated levels of endorphins in autistic individuals or attempted to determine whether naltrexone would reduce autistic symptoms. In both cases, results were inconclusive, with some positive findings and some negative findings (Gadow, 1992; Gillberg, 1995). These conflicting results are not surprising considering that in most cases the studies used small sample sizes, lacked placebo controls, involved short drug trials, or were susceptible to experimenter bias effects. Unfortunately, more recent studies employing larger sample sizes and using placebo-controlled, double-blind procedures appear to be just as contradictory and perplexing as the early ones (Bouvard et al., 1995; Cazzullo et al., 1999; Feldman et al., 1999; Gonzelez et al., 1994; Kolmen et al., 1997; Willemsen-Swinkels et al., 1995). However, despite the inconsistent and inconclusive nature of the current state of research, enough evidence has accumulated to support the potential efficacy of naltrexone treatment in at least a small subgroup of autistic individuals.

Recently, the potential therapeutic value of secretin, a peptide hormone that stimulates pancreatic secretion, in the treatment of autism was suggested by a report about three children with autism whose conditions appeared to improve markedly after a single intravenous (I.V.) dose of secretin (which was given as part of a diagnostic test for the children's gastrointestinal complaints) (Horvath et al., 1998). Although this case study reported a dramatic improvement in the children's behavior, manifested by improved eye contact, alertness, and expansion of expressive language, two subsequent double-blind, placebo-controlled studies did not find any benefit of a single dose of secretin in the treatment of autism and pervasive developmental disorder (Owley et al., 1999; Sandler et al., 1999). Thus, further controlled studies are needed to determine whether this hormone exerts benefits beyond those found with a placebo.

Childhood Schizophrenia

Pharmacological interventions for the symptoms of schizophrenia in childhood are essentially the same as those for adults (Campbell & Cueva, 1995). With the antipsychotics there is maximal improvement in 2 to 4 weeks, and the degree of improvement is comparable to that of adult improvement. Following cessation of drug treatment, most children, unlike adults, relapse into schizophrenic symptoms in 1 to 2 weeks. As is the case with adults, children in the early stages of the illness are generally more responsive to these medications. Children seem to tolerate many of the adverse effects of these drugs better than adults do (Engelhardt & Polizos, 1978). Drowsiness is more likely to occur with the lower-potency antipsychotics, while extrapyramidal effects are more likely with the higher-potency drugs. Weight gain is generally above normal. After several months of exposure to antipsychotics, withdrawal effects involving involuntary movements, ataxia, or oral dyskinesia may occasionally be evident upon abrupt drug cessation, but these dissipate within a week or two. Tardive dyskinesia may also occur; based on findings with adolescents treated with typical antipsychotics, its incidence appears to be on the same order as with adults (Hendren, 1996).

Due to concerns over extrapyramidal symptoms, such as tardive dyskinesia, that are associated with typical antipsychotics, the atypical antipsychotics are currently being assessed for their efficacy in the treatment of childhood-onset schizophrenia. Use of the atypical antipsychotic clozapine (Clozaril) in children under 16 years of age is considered investigational, but a number of reports on clozapine therapy in children and adolescents have suggested beneficial effects, perhaps superior to those achieved with typical antipsychotics (Hendren, 1996). For example, clozapine has produced good response in adolescents resistant to typical antipsychotics and those with negative symptoms, and a 2.5-year follow-up on these patients has not found a significant reduction in white blood cell count (Gordon et al., 1994). However, the possibility of agranulocytosis, and potential side effects of seizure induction and excessive weight gain, limit the use of clozapine in this population. One particularly interesting finding from one of these studies, should it be replicable, is that enlargement of the caudate (a nucleus of the basal ganglia) in patients with childhood-onset schizophrenia may occur secondary to their exposure to typical antipsychotics, but with long-term treatment with clozapine, their caudate volume may decrease to normal levels (Frazier et al., 1996). The newer atypical antipsychotics have not been adequately studied in this population to determine their efficacy, but it would be surprising if they were not at least as effective as typical antipsychotics, with, of course, a lower incidence of extrapyramidal side effects.

Some children with schizophrenic symptoms also show signs of hyperactivity. Unfortunately, the symptoms of these children get worse when treated with psychostimulants. There is some evidence that aggressive psychotic children, with or without periodicity, may respond favorably to lithium (Campbell et al., 1984).

Mental Retardation

Mentally retarded children, roughly defined as those having I.Q.s of 75 or less, often evidence symptoms of impulsivity, hostility, aggressiveness, hyperactivity, poor manageability, and self-mutilation. No chemical interventions have been shown to enhance cognitive functioning in mentally retarded individuals, but a number of drugs may be useful in reducing some of the negative behaviors in these individuals or reducing symptoms of comorbid disorders (Gadow, 1992). Antipsychotics are capable of suppressing aggressive behaviors, stereotypies, and self-injurious behavior. In cases in which these drugs do appear to induce socially appropriate behavior, one should be careful that the effects are not simply due to a general reduction of behavior to meet the demands of the institutional environment. All too often drugs are used to control patients rather than to enhance their capabilities. Furthermore, antipsychotics are likely to interfere with the already minimal performance and learning skills of these children. Also, considering the numerous side effects of antipsychotics (such as extrapyramidal effects, drowsiness, and tardive dyskinesia), it is unlikely that a severely mentally retarded child will benefit from antipsychotic intervention.

Drugs without the motor-disturbance side effects of antipsychotics that may be effective in reducing aggressive behaviors in mentally retarded persons include the beta-adrenergic blocking drugs (for example, propranolol), lithium, fenfluramine, and buspirone (Gadow, 1992). The selective serotonin reuptake inhibitors (SSRIs) (for example, clomipramine, fluoxetine) have been shown to reduce stereotypies, disabling compulsive behaviors, and self-injurious behaviors in mentally retarded persons (Barak et al., 1995; Lewis et al., 1995; Markowitz, 1992; Sovner et al., 1993). On the other hand, fluoxetine may increase aggressive behavior in mentally retarded adults with epilepsy and a history of aggressive behavior (Troisi et al., 1995). Although some case reports suggest that naltrexone may also be useful in reducing self-injurious behavior, it has not been shown to be effective in double-blind, placebo-controlled studies (Willemsen-Swinkels et al., 1995a).

The psychostimulants, such as amphetamine and methylphenidate, have not been found to improve the target symptoms associated with mental retardation. However, there is fairly strong evidence that psychostimulants are a safe and effective treatment for hyperactivity in some mildly to moderately retarded children and adolescents (Gadow, 1992).

Affective Disorders in Adolescents

It has only fairly recently been appreciated that adolescents may exhibit affective disorders (mainly depression) and that drug therapy may be warranted. Drug treatments for affective disorders in adolescents are essentially the same as those for adults (Biederman, 1988). Unfortunately, the efficacy of these treatments in adolescents is much less apparent than with adults (Campbell & Cueva, 1995), partially because the rate of placebo response in these individuals is quite high. It has also been suggested that the dramatic changes in sex and growth hormones and differences in neurotransmitter activity that accompany adolescence may account for the less than satisfactory response to antidepressant drugs (Gadow, 1992).

Most studies with depressed adolescents have utilized tricyclic antidepressants. There is some evidence, however, that monoamine oxidase inhibitors (MAOIs) may be effective in adolescents who do not respond to tricyclics (Gadow, 1992). There is limited evidence for efficacy of the SSRIs in the treatment of depressed adolescents, but double-blind, placebo-controlled studies have failed to demonstrate that the response to active drugs is significantly greater than that obtained with placebos (DeVane & Sallee, 1996). Unfortunately, establishing the actual efficacy of antidepressant medications in the pediatric population is very difficult because the vast majority of studies in this area are methodologically flawed, partly due to reasons discussed at the beginning of this chapter. A meta-analysis of these studies concluded that the greater the methodological rigor of a study—that is, utilization of double-blind, placebo-controlled procedures with adequate sample size—the lower the magnitude or likelihood of a therapeutic response to antidepressant drugs (Thurber et al., 1995).

Parkinson's Disease

Parkinson's disease (PD) is a degenerative brain disorder that afflicts nearly one million people in the United States. The main symptoms are difficulty in initiating voluntary movements, slowness of movement, muscular rigidity, tremors, and inability to maintain an upright posture while standing or walking. In addition, approximately a third of the cases have accompanying dementia. In 90 percent of the cases, the symptoms develop after the age of 55.

Properly controlled family studies have failed to document a family concentration of PD, and the concordance rates for the disease among identical twins are no higher than those among fraternal twins (Duvoisin, 1986; Plomin et al., 1994). These findings would indicate that heredity has little to do with developing this disease; however, the discovery that a gene mutation may be involved in the disease raises questions about the potential role of genetics in its induction (Polymeropoulos et al., 1996).

The discovery that a metabolite of the compound MPTP (MPP+, discussed in Chapter 10) is capable of inducing both CNS lesions and symptoms that are almost indistinguishable from PD (Kopin & Markey, 1988) has focused attention on environmental pollutants with similar structures, such as industrial chemicals. The environmental-cause hypothesis has been bolstered by studies showing a high correspondence between area use of insecticides and the incidence of PD (Lewin, 1985). Also, studies have indicated that more patients are developing PD at a young age and that in many families in which more than one member develops the disease, the onset occurs at roughly the same time within the family, but at very different ages for parents and offspring. Both of these phenomena are inconsistent with a pure genetic mechanism (Lewin, 1987).

For reasons unknown, epidemiological studies have repeatedly shown that PD occurs less frequently among chronic cigarette smokers than among nonsmokers (Yong & Perry, 1986); these results suggest that there may be a compound in tobacco smoke that somehow protects the individual. Animal studies have indicated that nicotine and other nicotinic receptor agonists can have neuroprotective actions in neurodegenerative processes (Mihailescu & Drucker-Colin, 2000). In addition, there is an unidentified ingredient in tobacco smoke that reduces the levels of MAO-B (the enzyme that breaks down dopamine) in the brains of smokers (Fowler et al., 1996). Theoretically this should allow higher levels of dopamine to accumulate in the brain and, in turn, potentially compensate for the diminished dopaminergic functioning that leads to the symptoms of PD. On the other hand, this phenomenon may simply be due to the fact that smokers die sooner than nonsmokers, so that they don't live long enough to develop the neurological and behavioral manifestations of PD (Riggs, 1992).

Coffee drinking may also be a protective factor in developing PD. Although early studies suggesting such a phenomenon were equivocal in their results, a recent 30-year prospective study has found a dramatic inverse relationship between coffee and caffeine exposure and the development of PD in Japanese American men (Ross et al., 2000). In fact, nondrinkers of coffee had a risk of PD more than five times that of men who consumed the equivalent of seven or more cups of coffee a day—an effect that was independent of the individuals' tobacco smoking, which was also associated with lower risk for developing the disease. What the mechanism behind this phenomenon might be and whether this relationship is causal are still undetermined.

Whatever the cause, it has been well established that the symptoms are due to the destruction of nigrostriatal dopaminergic neurons providing input to the basal ganglia. The symptoms generally appear when approximately 80 percent of these neurons have been lost (Dakof & Mendelsohn, 1986). It is believed that tracts in this region of the brain, important for the initiation of and smooth control of voluntary movements, normally contain balanced dopaminergic (inhibitory) and cholinergic (excitatory) inputs and that any imbalance in these two systems results in specific movement disorders. Therefore, most of the chemical interventions in the treatment of PD involve attempts to balance these by either inhibiting the cholinergic system or enhancing the dopaminergic system (Quinn, 1995).

Drugs with anticholinergic properties were among the first to be used in the treatment of PD, and until the 1960s they were the most effective drugs available for the disorder. However, more effective drugs have relegated them to a supportive role. They may still be very useful in patients with minimal symptoms, patients who do not respond to the newer drugs, or those who cannot tolerate their side effects. Anticholinergic side effects, such as mental confusion, sleepiness, and delirium, have also limited their usefulness. Antihistamines with anticholinergic properties may also be used, since they produce fewer side effects, but they are less effective than anticholinergics.

Almost immediately after the discovery of the association between dopamine deficiency and PD, attention turned to the use of L-dopa as a treatment for the disorder. L-dopa (for levodihydroxyphenylalanine) is the immediate precursor to dopamine and, once it enters the brain, it is enzymatically converted into dopamine (administering dopamine itself is not of value because it cannot pass through the blood–brain barrier). Theoretically, this provides for higher levels of this neurotransmitter for use by the remaining dopaminergic neurons. In approximately 80 percent of the patients, this treatment induces dramatic reductions in all symptoms of the disorder, except for the symptoms of dementia (Quinn, 1995). In addition, L-dopa partially relieves the changes in mood characteristic of PD, and feelings of apathy are replaced by increased vigor and a sense of well-being. Lost sexual potency may be regained.

L-dopa was clearly the miracle drug of the 1960s and 1970s. Unfortunately, though, as its use became more and more widespread, more and more problems with its use emerged. Although the majority of patients respond well to L-dopa initially, after about 3 to 5 years on L-dopa therapy the drug begins to lose its effectiveness and patients return to pretreatment levels of functioning. There is no evidence that long-term results are markedly improved when low-dose L-dopa regimens are used (Poewe et al., 1986). Therefore, it seems rational to adjust the L-dopa dosage to the individual patient's needs rather than to adhere to a policy that assumes the lowest dose is the best dose. Sometimes the responses of patients fluctuate abruptly between symptom control and no control; this pattern is often referred to as the on–off phenomenon because the control is switched on and off like a light.

In addition, patients often develop distressing and incapacitating problems with chronic L-dopa therapy, including abnormal involuntary movements, and may exhibit psychiatric symptoms such as hallucinations, paranoia, mania, insomnia, anxiety, nightmares, and emotional depression (Quinn, 1995). Whether the psychiatric disturbances and intellectual decline are the result of the continued progression of the disease or are the result of long-term L-dopa exposure is not clear (Lewin, 1987), although most of the side effects are reversible by a reduction in dosage. Also, a number of these symptoms (for instance, psychosis, abnormal movements) can be reduced with the atypical antipsychotic clozapine, which unlike typical antipsyphotics does not induce parkinsonian-like motor disturbances (Pfeiffer & Wagner, 1994). In any event, some clinicians are now suggesting that individuals who can function adequately in their occupations and social interactions should not be treated with L-dopa until their condition begins to deteriorate (Quinn, 1995). Until this time, drugs that are less effective than L-dopa can be given, so that the beneficial effects of L-dopa may be saved until they are truly necessary.

L-dopa's optimal effect comes from keeping concentrations of the drug within a therapeutic window that becomes increasingly narrow with time; thus, pharmacokinetic factors are critical for its efficacy (LeWitt, 1992). The most commonly used formulation of L-dopa is Sinemet, a combination of L-dopa and carbidopa, which prevents the peripheral conversion of L-dopa to dopamine. This formulation produces more reliable brain concentrations, but even with multiple daily doses, plasma concentrations may increase too fast, producing motor disturbances and adverse psychic effects, or fall off too quickly, allowing the disease symptoms to appear suddenly. This problem has been reduced considerably by putting Sinemet in an erodible matrix (called Sinemet CR) that retards gastric tablet dissolution and allows plasma level concentrations to be maintained longer and more smoothly.

L-dopa's efficacy is also influenced by when it is taken and what types of food it is taken with. If taken with meals, this drug's peak plasma levels take longer to be achieved and are reduced. Also, large amounts of amino acids following high-protein meals can interfere with its absorption from the gut as well as into the brain, because the amino acids compete with L-dopa for the transport system that allows it to cross the blood–brain barrier (Montgomery, 1992).

Recently, the potential therapeutic use of catechol-*O*-methyltransferase (COMT) inhibitors in PD has been explored with some success (Kaakkola, 2000). Although peripheral metabolism of L-dopa can be blocked by carbidopa, it may still be metabolically inactivated by COMT. Thus, inhibiting the COMT activity should improve the bioavailability and decrease the elimination of L-dopa and improve its efficacy. Entacapone (Comtan) and tolcapone are new potent, selective, and reversible COMT inhibitors that have been shown to enhance and extend the therapeutic effect of L-dopa in patients with advanced and fluctuating PD. Clinical studies show that they increase the daily *on* time by an average 1 to 3 hours, improve the activities of daily living, and allow daily L-dopa dosage to be decreased. Correspondingly, they significantly reduce the daily *off* time. Tolcapone also appears to have a beneficial effect in patients with nonfluctuating PD. These COMT inhibitors may also be combined with other antiparkinsonian drugs, such as dopamine agonists, selegiline, and anticholinergics, without adverse interactions.

The main adverse effects of the COMT inhibitors are related to their dopaminergic and gastrointestinal effects. Enhancement of dopaminergic activity may cause an initial worsening of L-dopa–induced adverse effects, such as dyskinesia, nausea, vomiting, orthostatic hypotension, sleep disorders, and hallucinations, which may be avoided through L-dopa dose adjustment. Diarrhea occurs in a minority of patients treated with tolcapone and entacapone, with a lower incidence occurring with entacapone. Unfortunately, tolcapone has been associated with acute, fatal hepatitis and potentially fatal neurological reactions, such as neuroleptic malignant syndrome, and degeneration of skeletal muscle, which has led to the suspension of its marketing authorization in the European community and Canada. In many other countries, the use of tolcapone is restricted to patients who are not responding satisfactorily to other therapies, and regular monitoring of liver enzymes is required. No such adverse reactions have so far been described for entacapone, and no laboratory monitoring has been proposed.

Because of the restricted efficacy of L-dopa therapy, researchers have been searching for ways to decrease the amount of L-dopa needed to control symptoms as well as for more direct means of amplifying dopamine activity. Several drugs have been investigated for this purpose (Quinn, 1995). Anticholinergic drugs act synergistically with L-dopa, thereby lowering the dosage needed, but they can decrease the absorption of L-dopa to the point that it is no longer therapeutically beneficial. Amantadine (Symmetrel), which is believed to release dopamine from intact terminals, has been found to be somewhat more effective than anticholinergics but considerably less effective than L-dopa. It is sometimes used for short periods as a supplement to L-dopa therapy. Bromocriptine (Parlodel) is one of several ergot derivatives with demonstrated dopaminergic activity that may be useful in the control of PD symptoms. It appears to be equivalent to L-dopa in therapeutic efficacy, and it may manage the on–off phenomenon more smoothly than L-dopa and induce less dyskinesia. However, visual and auditory hallucinations, hypotension, and purplish discolorations of the skin are more common with bromocriptine. Other adverse effects of bromocriptine may occur with short- or long-term treatment.

Over the past several years, a great deal of interest has been generated by selegiline (also called L-deprenyl and marketed as Eldepryl) in the treatment of PD in terms of not only reducing the disabling symptoms but perhaps altering the course of its development. Selegiline is a selective, irreversible inhibitor of MAO-B, which is an enzyme that inactivates dopamine. Inhibition of MAO-B should lead to a diminished metabolism of dopamine in the nigrostriatal system and significantly increase its concentration (Knoll, 1995). Selegiline also inhibits the reuptake of catecholamines and has other actions that facilitate catecholamine activity in the brain. However, it does not interact with tyramine to produce sympathomimetic effects, such as the hypertensive crises common to other MAOIs. Selegiline has been shown to significantly postpone the need for L-dopa and allows a significant saving in the patient's subsequent L-dopa dosage (Myllyla et al., 1995). Randomized, placebo-controlled, double-blind, 5-year trials evaluating the possible advantages of combining selegiline and levodopa in the early treatment of PD have indicated that patients treated with the combination of selegiline and levodopa developed markedly less severe parkinsonism and required lower doses of levodopa during the 5-year study periods than patients treated with levodopa and placebo (Larsen et al., 1999; Przuntek et al, 1999).

Unfortunately, with further degeneration of the dopaminergic tracts responsible, eventually no drugs exert beneficial effects, or they exert side effects that cannot be tolerated. Thus, research has focused on ways of lessening the progression of PD using two primary strategies: inhibition of MAO-B with selegiline and the use of general antioxidant drugs, such as vitamin E (LeWitt, 1994). The reasoning behind this approach comes from the previously mentioned hypothesis concerning environmental toxins in the lesioning process, which might well be speeded up by the oxidation enzyme MAO or the presence of harmful oxidative molecules. For example, selegiline has been shown to protect nigrostriatal dopaminergic neurons against several selective neurotoxins, including MPTP (Knoll, 1995). Unfortunately, studies comparing the effectiveness of L-dopa–carbidopa treatment alone or combined with selegiline in patients with early, mild PD have failed to find neuroprotective effects of selegiline (Brannan & Yahr, 1995; Lees, 1995). Therefore, at this point selegiline's primary usefulness appears to be one of reducing the dose of L-dopa needed to produce a therapeutic response in PD patients. Whether this is a significant improvement in their treatment remains to be seen. In fact, in one study, mortality was actually higher in patients treated with selegiline, plus L-dopa–carbidopa than it was in patients treated with L-dopa–carbidopa alone, casting doubts on its chronic use in PD (Lees, 1995). Studies have also failed to show evidence of neuroprotection with vitamin E treatment (LeWitt, 1994).

Tourette's Syndrome

The symptoms of *Tourette's syndrome (TS)* are, to some extent, opposite to those of PD. Rather than reflecting an inability to voluntarily initiate motor activities, they reflect an inability to suppress unwanted motor activities (Shapiro & Shapiro, 1980). The syndrome is characterized by involuntary motor and verbal tics; the former involve the head, torso, and limbs, and the latter involve grunts, sounds, words, or phrases, often of a vulgar or obscene nature (known as coprolalia). (In earlier times, it was thought that persons with these symptoms were victims of demonic possession, as depicted in the movie *The Exorcist.*) Its onset is generally noted in childhood and early adolescence, and the symptoms persist throughout the person's lifetime, with spontaneous remissions and exacerbations. The symptoms of obsessive–compulsive disorder (discussed shortly) and attention deficit disorder often accompany TS (Cohen et al., 1992).

As with PD, the basal ganglia have been implicated in the etiology of TS, but with dopaminergic overactivity being involved (Wolf et al., 1996), rather than underactivity. Thus, the pharmacological modes of treatment for TS are essentially the opposite of those for PD. The antipsychotics, such as phenothiazines and haloperidol (Haldol), reduce the symptoms of the disorder. The most recent of these is pimozide (Orap), which some studies have indicated may induce fewer side effects (Regeur et al., 1986). Anxiolytics do not appear to be any more effective than placebos. Although there are no clear data supporting one antipsychotic over the other in efficacy, the most stable long-term effects have been found with haloperidol or pimozide. Either of these is the drug of choice in the vast majority of cases.

Drugs that lower dopamine synthesis (such as alpha-methyl-p-tyrosine) or dopamine depletors (for example, tetrabenazine) have produced beneficial effects in the disorder, but they exert troublesome side effects and are not believed to be as useful as haloperidol or pimozide. However, these may be combined with an antipsychotic because of their synergistic effects. Several studies have also indicated that the administration of nicotine by way of the patch or gum can significantly augment the effectiveness of antipsychotic treatments in reducing the symptoms of TS (Mihailescu & Drucker-Colin, 2000). The atypical antipsychotic risperidone has been found to be efficacious in reducing the motor tics in the majority of Tourette's patients who failed to respond adequately to conventional drug treatments (for example, haloperidol, clonidine) (Bruun & Budman, 1996), whereas the frequency of tics in Tourette's patients does not appear to be significantly reduced by the atypical antipsychotic clozapine (Pfeiffer & Wagner, 1994).

As many as 50 percent of patients with TS also meet diagnostic criteria for ADHD (Spencer et al., 1993). Because antipsychotic drugs are of limited value in controlling the symptoms of ADHD and psychostimulants can exacerbate the symptoms of TS, alternative treatments that have been shown to be efficacious in reducing the ADHD symptoms and motor/verbal tics are the alpha-2-adrenergic agonists clonidine and guanfacine (discussed earlier in this chapter) and the tricyclic antidepressants (such as desipramine, nortriptyline) (Chappell et al., 1995; Singer et al., 1995; Spencer et al., 1993). In most cases, these drugs are more effective in reducing the symptoms of ADHD than in suppressing motor tics. Clonidine does not appear to be as efficacious as haloperidol or pimozide in the treatment of core TS symptoms, but many clinicians prefer it as the initial drug in treatment because of its lower incidence of serious side effects.

Approximately 7 percent of TS patients also exhibit obsessive–compulsive symptoms (Steingard & Dillon-Stout, 1992). In these cases, the SSRIs appear to be effective in reducing these symptoms (Cohen et al., 1992; Silvestri et al., 1994), but some case reports have suggested that SSRIs may exacerbate or bring out tic disturbances (Fennig et al., 1994; Hauser & Zesiewicz, 1995).

Epilepsy

Epilepsy is a term used to categorize a number of diverse chronic disorders characterized by sudden attacks of brain dysfunction (seizures) that are usually associated with some alteration of consciousness. The seizures are almost always correlated with abnormal and excessive discharges in the EEG and are often accompanied by violent muscle spasms (convulsions). (By now you are probably aware that essentially the same symptoms may accompany withdrawal from sedative–hypnotics after chronic exposure.) In the past, people with epilepsy were considered demonically possessed, keepers of mystical powers, or mentally ill. We now know the symptoms of epilepsy are the result of a sudden change in behavior and mental activity caused by abnormal neuronal discharge in the brain. The epilepsies—there are over 40 distinct forms—are common and frequently devastating disorders, affecting approximately 2.5 million people in the United States alone (McNamara, 1996).

Several lines of evidence suggest that in most of these disorders the seizure begins with and is sustained by the synchronous firing at high frequency of a relatively localized group of neurons, which then spreads to adjacent neurons. A reduction in inhibitory components of neuronal circuits (such as GABA activity) is a likely mechanism for this action (Dichter & Ayala, 1987). For example, a reduction in GABA levels because of a diet deficient in pyridoxine (vitamin B_6), which is required for GABA synthesis, can result in seizures; the problem can be successfully reversed by adding pyridoxine to the diet (Cooper et al., 1996). Modulatory substances such as norepinephrine and opioid peptides may also play a role.

Since there are a variety of disorders involved, the etiology varies considerably, with suspected causes ranging from hereditary factors to head injuries, infectious diseases, allergies, and nutritional abnormalities, among others. As is the case with numerous brain disorders, neurotoxicity resulting from overactivity of the excitatory amino acid neurotransmitters at NMDA receptors has been proposed as a mechanism for promoting seizure activity (Olney, 1990). However, in many cases, no cause for the seizures can be identified (idiopathic epilepsy). In approximately three-fourths of the cases, the symptoms are evidenced prior to adulthood.

The most common types of epileptic seizures are classified into *partial seizures* (sometimes called *focal* seizures)—that is, those beginning in a fairly localized cortical site—and *generalized seizures*—that is, those that involve both hemispheres widely from the outset (McNamara, 1996). These can be further subdivided into more detailed descriptions of the symptoms—for example, *simple partial, complex partial,* and *partial with secondarily generalized tonic–clonic seizure* (partial seizures) and *absence seizure, myoclonic seizure,* and *tonic–clonic seizure* (generalized seizures). Tonic–clonic seizures (also termed *grand mal seizures*)—a sequence of maximal tonic spasms of all body musculature, followed by synchronous clonic jerking movements—are characterized by generalized convulsions of the entire body, accompanied by the loss of consciousness. Peripheral manifestations may consist of bluing of the lips, face, and fingernails (resulting from deficient oxygenation of the blood), drooling, discharge of urine and feces, and tongue biting. Before the convulsions begin, many grand mal patients often describe an aura, which may consist of an unexplainable fear, an unpleasant or unusual odor, peculiar sounds, tingling of the skin, or spots before the eyes. After the episode, the person is in a weakened and confused state.

Absence (petit mal) seizures may not be accompanied by clear motor disturbances and are associated with periods of blank stares—indicative of a loss of conscious awareness. They are most prevalent in children and are often mistaken for daydreaming. Rapid eye blinking and twitching movements sometimes accompany the seizures. There is no aura associated with the seizures, and the person is able to resume normal activity immediately following them. Although they are of short duration (approximately 5 to 20 seconds), several dozen may occur daily.

Simple partial seizures involve either disturbances in motor function or loss of sensory function for approximately 20 to 60 seconds, with preservation of consciousness. Partial with secondarily general tonic–clonic seizures begin with simple or complex partial seizures and evolve into tonic–clonic seizures. Complex partial seizures (sometimes called *psychomotor* seizures) generally stem from temporal lobe dysfunction, and their manifestations take on various forms. They are characterized by an aura, a duration of 1 to 2 minutes, and postseizure confusion and amnesia. During a seizure, the person may make purposeless movements, such as lip smacking, chewing, fumbling with clothing, or rubbing of the hands or legs.

Since seizures appear to involve a hyperexcitability of neuronal tissue, it is not surprising that most sedative–hypnotic drugs are anticonvulsants and that most anticonvulsants have sedative–hypnotic properties. However, since the sedative–hypnotic properties are not necessary for antiseizure efficacy and are viewed as undesirable, drugs that are most effective in the treatment of epilepsy are those that can reduce or eliminate seizure activity without inducing sedation or sleep. Furthermore, the efficacy and type of drug treatment is heavily dependent upon the type of seizure experienced; that is, a drug effective with one type of seizure may not be effective with another (McNamara, 1996).

From 1857 to 1912 sodium bromide was used to control epilepsy. However, the bromide salts cause mental sluggishness, and prolonged treatment may cause chronic toxicity, which is manifested by sedation, psychotic disturbances, increased glandular secretion, and gastric distress. In 1912 the barbiturate phenobarbital was discovered to be useful in reducing seizures without inducing as many side effects as sodium bromide. To this day it remains a cheap and effective treatment for many forms of epilepsy.

In 1938 phenytoin (or diphenylhydantoin [Dilantin]), which is structurally related to the barbiturates (the initial basis for its use in epilepsy), was found to be effective for both grand mal and psychomotor seizures without inducing sedation (refuting the then-current hypothesis that an effective anticonvulsant had to have sedative properties). It is still one of the most commonly used drugs for these types of seizures.

In 1954 primidone (Mysoline), structurally related to phenobarbital (one of its metabolites in the body is phenobarbital), was found to be an effective treatment for epilepsy. Ethosuximide (Zarontin), which has a relatively low incidence of toxicity, came into use in 1960 as one of the more effective treatments of petit mal epilepsy. Carbamazepine (Tegretol), related chemically to the tricyclic antidepressants, was approved for use in the United States as an antiepileptic agent in 1974. The efficacy of valproic acid (Depakene), approved for use in the United States in 1978, was discovered accidentally when it was used as a vehicle for other compounds that were being screened for antiepileptic activity.

After 15 years with no new drugs being approved for use in the treatment of epilepsy, several new antiepileptic drugs have been introduced for clinical use in the United States since 1993—felbamate (Felbatol), gabapentin (Neurontin), topiramate (Topamax), oxycarbazepine (Trileptal), zonisamide (Zonegran), tiagabine (Gabitril), and lamotrigine (Lamictal). Although studies indicate that most of these drugs may be effective in a wide range of seizure disorders and may be used in monotherapy for patients who don't respond adequately to older anticonvulsant drugs, it is likely that most of these new drugs will be used initially as additives in a polydrug regimen (Gatti et al., 2000; Wilder, 1995). Because these new drugs interact with established antiepileptic drugs, such as phenytoin, phenobarbital, carbamazepine, and valproic acid, they will need more frequent monitoring during polydrug therapy (Fraser, 1996).

Several mechanisms have been suggested that contribute to the ability of anticonvulsants to either enhance inhibitory or reduce excitatory control over neuronal firing, which is believed to be responsible for seizure activity. Drugs effective against the most common forms of seizures, partial and secondarily generalized tonic–clonic seizures, appear to work by one of three mechanisms to limit the sustained repetitive firing of a neuron (McNamara, 1996). Following depolarization-triggered opening of Na^+ channels during the action potential, the Na^+ channels spontaneously close, a process termed *inactivation*. Drugs that reduce the recovery rate of Na^+ channels from inactivation would limit the ability of a neuron to fire at high frequencies, an effect that appears to underlie the effects of carbamazepine, phenytoin, and valproic acid. Lamotrigine appears to block Na^+ channels and prevent depolarization. A third mechanism would be to reduce neuronal excitability by enhancing GABA-mediated inhibition either postsynaptically at $GABA_A$ receptors—for example, with benzodiazepines or barbiturates—or presynaptically by enhancing the amount of GABA released—for example, with gabapentin.

A low-threshold, voltage-regulated Ca^{++} current in thalamic neurons appears to be pivotally involved in the generation of the three-per-second generalized spike and wave discharges in the EEG that occur during absence seizures. Drugs effective in absence seizures, such as ethosuximide and valproic acid, appear to work by inhibiting this type of Ca^{++} current. Note that some drugs, such as valproic acid, work through more than one mechanism, thus making them effective in the treatment of more than one type of epilepsy. Felbamate appears to be the most novel of the new antiepileptic drugs, in that it appears to have the dual actions of both inhibiting NMDA-evoked (excitatory) responses and potentiating GABA-evoked (inhibitory) responses (McNamara, 1996).

Overall, the drugs we have discussed abolish seizure activity in approximately half of the cases, and significantly reduce seizure frequency in another quarter of patients. It is important to realize that seizure disorders are due to a variety of mechanisms and thus are effectively treated by different groups of anticonvulsant drugs (McNamara, 1996). For example, most drugs that are effective in the treatment of partial seizure disorders and tonic–clonic seizures (that is, carbamazepine, phenytoin, phenobarbital, primidone) are not effective in absence seizures. Conversely, most drugs effective in reducing absence seizures (such as clonazepam, ethosuximide) are not effective in the treatment of partial and tonic–clonic seizures. However, valproate appears to be effective in virtually all types of epilepsy. While there is no clear difference among drugs within a group in terms of overall efficacy, some patients refractory to one compound within a group may respond to another in that group. Each anticonvulsant has its own spectrum of side effects—which range from minimal CNS disturbances to death from aplastic anemia (blood cell suppression) or liver failure—and these must be considered in selecting an appropriate drug or combination of drugs. Lower-than-effective dosages of drugs within a group may be combined to decrease the relative incidence or degree of side effects induced by larger doses of the individual drugs. Multiple drug therapy may also be required in cases in which more than one type of seizure activity occurs in the same patient.

Felbamate is not only effective in some seizure disorders that are refractory to earlier anticonvulsants, but is the first antiepileptic with specific efficacy in *Lennox-Gastaut syndrome* (a disorder of childhood characterized by multiple seizure types, mental retardation, and refractoriness to antiseizure medication). Unfortunately, a year after it was introduced, cases were reported of aplastic anemia and liver failure associated with felbamate therapy, so rigorous liver function and blood controls are required of patients treated with it (Perez-Miranda et al., 1995).

In cases of *status epilepticus* (a condition in which one major attack of epilepsy succeeds another with little or no intermission), a rapid-onset benzodiazepine such as diazepam is generally given intravenously (in conjunction with mechanical supports for preventing asphyxiation).

All of the drugs used in the treatment of epilepsy have a number of potential side effects that may limit their usefulness in certain patients. Many of these, such as dizziness, loss of balance, slurred speech, and visual difficulties, may be attributable to their sedative–hypnotic properties. Other reactions may involve gum enlargement, rashes, allergic reactions, endocrine alterations, and gastrointestinal complaints. Some of these drugs may cause liver damage or blood cell deficiencies, which can have lethal consequences. The type and degree of reaction vary considerably among these drugs, and the particular drugs administered often depend on these, rather than the relative efficacy with respect to antiseizure activity.

Although epilepsy is viewed as a chronic disorder requiring continuous drug treatment, it may be desirable at some point to withdraw medication (very gradually over a period of months, since the risk of status epilepticus is great with abrupt cessation). Medication may be withdrawn because of evidence of unacceptable side effects or to prevent potential side effects from occurring or if the patient has been seizure-free for a considerable length of time. Studies have indicated that the majority of patients who have been free of seizures for several years with medication will not show a recurrence of symptoms when the medications are withdrawn (McNamara, 1996). However, since a history of a single recent seizure may be detrimental to one's employment or access to a driver's license, the decision to withdraw medication must be made with some deliberation.

Geriatric Psychopharmacology

Although I would like to emphasize that growing old is not considered a disease in and of itself, the fact remains that as we grow older a number of drugs are often used to treat cognitive, emotional, or behavioral deficits that are alleged to be caused by the normal aging process. Also, drugs may be used to treat a disease or condition that is found solely, or at least more frequently, among the elderly. Although most persons over the age of 65 are in good mental health, close to a quarter of this population suffer from disorders ranging from depression (which is reflected in a high suicide rate within this group) to *dementia,* that is, CNS changes that lead to memory deficits, confusion, irritability, apathy, or disturbed behavior (Domino et al., 1978; Finch, 1982).

Reduction in blood flow to the brain as a result of cerebral arteriosclerosis may cause progressive mental impairment. Specific neurological lesions in the brain can cause such disorders as Parkinson's disease and *Alzheimer's disease.* The latter condition is characterized by loss of intellectual abilities, including memory, judgment, abstract thought, and higher cortical functions, as well as changes in personality and behavior. Although senile onset occurs after age 65 and presenile onset usually occurs between the ages of 50 and 65, these two conditions are indistinguishable forms of dementia with respect to cellular pathology. Mental depression is also common among the elderly (Ban, 1984). Some of the symptoms of these disorders respond well to drug therapy, but in many cases drugs do little good and may even make psychogeriatric illnesses worse.

There are special problems in treating the elderly with drugs. The first of these centers on diagnoses (Ban, 1984). For example, the treatment of dementia is likely to include psychotropic medication. However, dementia is defined by changes in behavior, not by laboratory tests or CAT or PET scans. Since mental capacities tend to decline with age, it is difficult to decide when normal aging ends and dementia begins. Furthermore, virtually every type of disease and medication can induce symptoms of dementia: antihypertensive and antiulcer drugs, depression, altered thyroid function and kidney failure, isolation, vascular disease, AIDS and other viral infections, brain tumors, vitamin deficiencies, alcoholism and other drug abuse—the list is endless (Kolata, 1987). Diagnosing other behaviors or emotional problems amenable to psychotropic drug treatment is equally difficult. To compound this problem, because of numerous health problems, geriatric patients often take many drugs (prescription, over-the-counter, and social), a practice that not only makes diagnosis difficult, but also puts the elderly at a much higher risk for complex and harmful drug interactions than younger patients.

Another problem, or set of problems, is related to the alteration of pharmacokinetics that occurs with aging (Friedel, 1978). The increase in percentage of body fat means that psychotropic drugs, which for the most part are lipid-soluble, are more widely distributed throughout the body and may have a larger volume of distribution. There is the possibility that psychotropics may accumulate in adipose tissue in older persons, which could result in a longer duration of action and an increased sensitivity to the drugs. Decreased plasma proteins may lead to less plasma binding and an increased possibility of toxicity. The potential for reaching toxicity is further enhanced by the decreased efficiency of metabolism of drugs in the liver and reduced filtration of drugs by the kidneys. Thus, higher levels of a drug may be present in the body for a longer period of time than would be the case in younger subjects. For these reasons, it is generally recommended that pharmacological treatment should commence with one-third to one-half the recommended adult dosage with most drugs, and the dosage should be increased only very gradually (Ban, 1984)—start low and go slow.

A classic example of these difficulties can be seen in the treatment of depression—the most commonly diagnosed psychological disorder in the elderly (Ban, 1984). The anticholinergic side effects of many antidepressants, which may be merely troublesome to most younger individuals, can be very annoying and possibly life-endangering in the elderly. Examples would be aggravation of prostate hypertrophy, precipitation of glaucoma, or bowel impaction. Antidepressants may cause delirium or confusional states in geriatric patients whose symptoms are misdiagnosed (and dismissed) as symptoms of dementia. Reduced cardiovascular functioning of the elderly person, in combination with antidepressant medication, can lead to bradycardia (abnormally low heart rate), orthostatic hypotension, severe cardiac arrhythmias, or complete disruption of cardiac conduction. The coexistence of chronic medical illness with depression or mental disturbances in many geriatric persons makes psychotropic treatment particularly complex.

Fortunately, and in spite of the potential hazards and discomforts of using antidepressants in elderly patients, they can be just as effective in elderly patients as in non-elderly patients (Ban, 1984; Volz et al., 1995). If the drug is cautiously selected and the initial dosage is one-third to one-half the amount given to younger patients, and plasma levels are carefully monitored, then antidepressant treatment can be safe and effective. Antidepressants may also reduce symptoms similar to those of early senile dementia, which occur secondary to depression (for example, pseudodementia). At this point, the SSRIs, because of their low toxicity, absence of anticholinergic side effects, and lack of detrimental effects on cognitive functioning appear to be the best antidepressants for the elderly (Knegtering et al., 1994). If they become approved for use (assuming clinical trials don't reveal any new adverse reactions), the reversible inhibitors of monoamine oxidase A (RIMAs) appear to be a good second choice. They have minimal influence on cognitive performance, are void of hypotensive effects, including orthostatic hypotension, and do not interact with foods to induce a hypertensive crisis (Norman & Burrows, 1995). This class of antidepressant also appears to be effective in the treatment of depression that accompanies dementia, and may improve cognitive ability as well (Priest et al., 1995).

For those psychiatric or psychological dysfunctions common to both younger and older individuals (such as anxiety, sleep disturbances, psychotic reactions, and manic depression), as long as the pharmacokinetic considerations that we have noted are taken into account, pharmacological interventions are essentially the same for both groups (Ban, 1984). For example, benzodiazepines are recommended for anxiety-related symptoms, but the shorter-acting benzodiazepines, such as oxazepam, should be used to prevent excessive accumulation of these compounds. Buspirone and the SSRIs would also be appropriate for many of these symptoms.

Drug intervention for sleep disturbances in the elderly should take into consideration the fact that the need for sleep normally decreases with age. Hypnotic doses of chloral hydrate are less likely to cause persistent effects in the elderly than other hypnotic agents, and drug "hangover" may be less common with chloral hydrate than with most barbiturates and some benzodiazepines. However, chloral hydrate may exert both peripheral side effects (gastric distress, vomiting, and flatulence) and undesirable CNS effects (malaise, light-headedness, ataxia, and nightmares). It should definitely be avoided in patients with marked liver or kidney impairment and should probably be avoided in patients with severe cardiac disease.

Antipsychotics are legitimately used in cases in which there is a recurrence of a psychotic episode or in patients with dementia who are extremely agitated to the point of hurting themselves or others (Katz et al., 1999; Salzman, 1988). However, unless there is evidence of symptoms specific to psychosis, antipsychotics are likely to overly sedate the patients. Unfortunately, antipsychotics tend to be overused in most nursing homes and institutions, and they are more likely given for the benefit of the staff than of the patients. Lithium treatment for manic depression symptoms is just as effective in elderly patients as it is in younger patients, although with considerably lower doses (approximately 15 percent to 20 percent of normal).

With respect to the primary sources of the cognitive and memory dysfunctions common to the geriatric population, most drug interventions have yet to produce clear successes in clinical trials. Psychostimulants such as amphetamines, methylphenidate, pemoline, and pipradol have not been found to benefit cognitive functioning in geriatric patients (Galizia, 1984). Furthermore, while psychostimulants may be useful in the treatment of apathetic, withdrawn, disheartened, or demoralized older people (Salzman, 1985), these drugs may produce an increase in agitation and psychotic thinking and behavior when the demented states are severe (Salzman, 1988). At one time it was believed that cerebrovasodilators might be beneficial by increasing blood flow; however, such interventions have not produced reliable results (Ban, 1978). For example, a popular drug of this type, Hydergine (ergoloid mesylates), has been touted as having vasodilating and cerebral metabolic activity with concomitant cognitive improvement, but several studies have found contrary results. There is some evidence that Hydergine may improve a subset of cognitive functions (such as short-term memory) in elderly patients with mild dementia (Thienhaus et al., 1987). The issue of efficacy is clouded by the possibility that Hydergine acts as a mood elevator, such that improvement in cognitive function may be secondary to the antidepressant effects.

Neuropeptides have been investigated but are generally ineffective in reducing mild cognitive impairment resulting from age, dementia, or other trauma (Galizia, 1984). ACTH 4-10 (a fragment of adrenocorticotropic hormone) may increase arousal and improve cognitive functioning in some areas in the elderly (Koob, 1987). Vasopressin (a peptide found in the pituitary gland) has resulted in improvement in tests of concentration, attention, and memory, including storage and retrieval of information in humans (Crook, 1988). However, it is not clear whether these effects are directly linked to memory or are simply due to improvements in mood, attentiveness, or some other aspect of performance. For example, vasopressin causes hypertension via its action at peripheral blood vessel receptors. It has been argued that, because the behavioral effects of vasopressin can be blocked by antagonists of these receptors, the apparent CNS effect of vasopressin is indirectly mediated by an arousal secondary to the inappropriate hypertension induced by peripheral receptor activation (Cooper et al., 1996).

Piracetam, a GABA derivative that was one of the first drugs to be referred to as a **nootropic** (a term coined to describe drugs that specifically enhance cognitive functioning), has a considerable popular lore regarding its ability to enhance cognitive functions such as memory and learning, without having any sedative, analgesic, stimulant, neuroleptic, or autonomic effects. Despite over 100 studies conducted around the world over the past three decades, many of which report positive results with piracetam (or its analogues), its efficacy in enhancing cognitive functions in a variety of subjects, including the elderly, is still elusive.

In summary, a wide variety of different classes of drugs have been tested for the treatment of dementia, specifically Alzheimer's disease, including psychostimulants, anticoagulants, vasodilators, hyperbaric oxygen, hormones, nootropics, monoaminergics, and neuropeptides, without conclusive evidence of any of these being beneficial for the treatment of this condition (Soares & Gershon, 1994). Based on the consistent finding that there is a deterioration in cholinergic neurotransmitter systems in Alzheimer's patients (although there are a number of other systems that deteriorate as well), clinical trials attempted to compensate pharmacologically for the cholinergic disturbance by increasing the availability of acetylcholine precursors (that is, by administering choline or lecithin), reducing acetylcholine metabolic degradation with drugs that inhibit the enzyme cholinesterase, or administering nicotine or muscarinic agonists (Emilien et al., 2000).

Of these treatments, the cholinesterase inhibitor tacrine (Cognex) emerged with the most empirical support, and it was the first drug to be approved (in 1993) specifically for the treatment of Alzheimer's disease. Research indicates that a definite subpopulation of patients does benefit from therapy with tacrine, in terms of enhancing cognitive functioning and adaptive living skills (Madden et al., 1995). Tacrine is associated with large interindividual pharmacokinetic variation in patients after oral, intravenous, or rectal administration (Parnetti, 1995), which may influence both the efficacy and incidence of symptomatic adverse effects in individual patients. The benefits of tacrine are most apparent at doses that, unfortunately, induce significant adverse reactions in two-thirds of the patients (Soares & Gershon, 1994). One of the most problematic adverse effects is the induction of high levels of enzymes that can lead to liver damage.

The primary benefit of tacrine over physostigmine, a widely used cholinesterase inhibitor with a long history, appeared to be primarily pharmacokinetic. Physostigmine has an extremely short half-life (approximately 30 minutes), whereas tacrine's duration of action is five to six times longer. However, it appears that tacrine's efficacy may also be due to differences in pharmacodynamics, since it has a wide variety of other actions unrelated to its cholinesterase inhibition.

Donepezil (Aricept) and rivastigmine (Exelon) are other cholinesterase inhibitors that have been approved for the treatment of mild to moderately severe cases of Alzheimer's. These drugs have greater specificity than tacrine in augmenting cholinergic functioning in the brain, as opposed to affecting cholinergic activity in other parts of the body. They do not appear to induce serious liver abnormalities, although they may cause diarrhea and nausea. Another advantage is that they only need to be taken once a day—in contrast to tacrine, which must be taken four times a day.

The benefits of cholinesterase inhibitors in reducing the symptoms of Alzheimer's disease or preventing further deterioration are modest at best. The percentage of patients obtaining a clinically relevant benefit from treatment with these drugs ranges from 25 percent to 54 percent versus 7 percent to 27 percent with placebo for cognitive improvement, and ranges from 25 percent to 32 percent versus 11 percent to 19 percent with placebo for improvement in global measures of functioning (Wettstein, 2000; Wilcock, 2000). Interestingly, in a recent review comparing these cholinesterase inhibitors and gingko extracts (Gingko special extract EGb 761) in placebo-controlled studies of at least 6 months' duration, it was determined that there were no major differences in efficacy (expressed as the delay in symptom progression or the difference in response rate between active substance and placebo) between the cholinesterase inhibitors and the gingko extracts in the treatment of mild to moderate Alzheimer's dementia (Wettstein, 2000). Only tacrine exhibited a high dropout rate due to adverse drug reactions.

The reason for the failure of most drug treatments to reverse Alzheimer's disease symptoms may be that neuronal death is so severe that the affected systems are incapable of responding to pharmacologic manipulation. As a result, it has been suggested that pharmacological strategies designed to slow neuronal death rate may have therapeutic value. Estrogen, the predominantly female hormone widely used for the treatment of a variety of disorders, has been suggested in a number of studies to have protective effects against Alzheimer's disease and to enhance mood and specific aspects of cognitive functioning in postmenopausal women. Unfortunately, a recently completed randomized, double-blind, placebo-controlled clinical trial found that estrogen replacement therapy for one year did not slow progression of the disease, nor did it improve global, cognitive, or functional outcomes in women with mild to moderate Alzheimer's disease (Mulnard et al., 2000). Thus, the potential efficacy of estrogen in the prevention of Alzheimer's disease remains unclear.

Although neuronal cell death may occur because of a wide variety of pathological and toxicological processes (for example, insufficient oxygen or low blood glucose levels), as well as normal gene-programmed processes, in most of them the final common pathway for the activation involves a sustained elevation of free intracellular Ca^{++} concentration (Branconnier et al., 1992). Thus, chronic treatment with calcium-channel blockers or antagonists of NMDA receptors (which mediate Ca^{++} flow into cells) may have therapeutic value in preventing or delaying the onset of the disease. (This is a tricky procedure because NMDA receptor activity plays a vital role in a variety of CNS functions [e.g., memory formation], so, for example, blocking NMDA receptor activity with phencyclidine [PCP] would not be useful for this purpose because it has psychotomimetic effects.) Memantine is a blocker of glutamate-gated NMDA receptor channels that allows the physiological activation of NMDA channels during memory formation while blocking their pathological activation. For over 10 years, it has been approved for the treatment of dementias in Germany. In a recent double-blind, placebo-controlled trial in care-dependent patients with severe dementia, memantine was shown to reduce care dependence and produce global behavioral improvements, relative to placebo controls, after 4 weeks of treatment, and the improvements became even greater after 12 weeks of treatment (73 percent improved with memantine versus 45 percent with placebo) (Winblad & Poritis, 1999). Clinical trials in the United States have also shown that memantine significantly slows the progression of Alzheimer's symptoms in patients with moderately severe symptoms while producing few, if any, side effects.

Other approaches in preclinical and clinical phases that are attempting to decrease the cellular reaction to neurodegeneration involve the use of drugs that mimic nerve growth factor (which is heavily involved in the maintenance of function of the cholinergic forebrain system), antiinflammatory drugs (based on reports that individuals using nonsteroidal anti-inflammatory drugs are less likely to develop Alzheimer's disease), and drugs that reduce oxidative stress (e.g., vitamin E, estrogen). Perhaps the greatest focus is in developing inhibitors of the enzymes that are believed to be responsible for the formation of β-amyloid and its plaques, which are the hallmarks of Alzheimer's disease and the primary causes of the neurodegeneration (Emilien et al., 2000).

Sexual Dysfunction

It has often been said that the major sex organ in humans is the brain (Taberner, 1985). Thus, it is not surprising that many human sexual difficulties may be psychological in origin, or that they may respond favorably to everything from ground-up rhinoceros horns to Tabasco sauce or oysters. Belief is a powerful drug. Unfortunately, the vast majority of substances taken to alleviate sexual dysfunctions have no direct effects on sexual potency or the ability to achieve orgasm. Other than testosterone, which enhances sexual motivation in both men and women (Sherwin, 1988), there are very few, if any, true **aphrodisiacs**—that is, substances that generally enhance libido and sexual performance. In fact, more often than not, drugs that humans take tend to inhibit the sex drive and sexual performance (Morgentaler, 1999).

Alcohol is perhaps the drug most frequently used by people to try to enhance the sex drive. However, as Shakespeare stated long ago, "Lechery, sir, it provokes, and unprovokes; it provokes the desire, but it takes away the performance" (*Macbeth,* Act 2, scene 3). Modern science has verified this hypothesis. Although alcohol's ability to disrupt our cortical control over our inhibitions may lead to increased psychological sexual arousal (at low doses), it tends to decrease physiological measures of sexual arousal (that is, vaginal and penile vasocongestion) in both males and females in a dose-dependent fashion (Leavitt, 1982). With chronic use, a variety of sexual difficulties often occur. These may include impotence, atrophy of the testicles, lower testosterone levels, and impaired sperm production.

Spanish fly, a general term for several species of beetles, has long been renowned for its aphrodisiac qualities. At best, it irritates the urethra (and a variety of other organs) and leads to inflammation of the bladder; at worst, it causes death by shock from bleeding (Taberner, 1985).

Other drugs commonly attributed with sexual-enhancing properties include the P/P/H drugs discussed in Chapter 11, particularly marijuana (Leavitt, 1982). Again, however, most of this enhancement comes from belief and expectation (Taberner, 1985). Most concerns have been over marijuana's potential to suppress testosterone, the primary hormone involved in sexual arousal—despite the absence of any clear empirical evidence that marijuana exposure, either acutely or chronically, alters testosterone levels in humans outside of normal variations (Block et al., 1991; Cone et al., 1986). However, because marijuana is often used along with alcohol, which, as discussed above, may affect testosterone levels, the possibility of their interacting to induce effects on behavior cannot be discounted.

Cocaine was the aphrodisiac of the 1980s. By itself, if injected or smoked, it can elicit a reaction described as a whole-body orgasm and can induce spontaneous ejaculation without genital stimulation. It also has the reputation of enhancing sexual pleasure and "staying power" (Leavitt, 1982). However, because of its vasoconstrictive properties, it, like amphetamine, may decrease the ability to achieve erection in males and orgasm in females. With chronic use, it often leads to impotence and frigidity (Taberner, 1985).

Nonrecreational drugs are also a common source of sexual difficulties. Many medications used to treat cardiac dysfunctions and high blood pressure can cause loss of sexual desire and/or potency. In the aged, who commonly take such medications, this loss can be construed as one of the consequences of aging. Antidepressants (particularly the SSRIs) and antipsychotics may decrease sexual desire in some individuals, although the mood elevation with antidepressants may allow some individuals to enjoy sexual activities again. On the other hand, for men suffering from problems with premature ejaculation, some of the SSRIs have been suggested to be effective in delaying ejaculation (Wise, 1994).

In conclusion, when there is evidence of sexual dysfunction, the person's drug-taking practices should be assessed. If he or she is taking a drug, it may be the culprit, and ceasing taking the drug or shifting to an alternative may very well clear up the problem.

Under some circumstances and in some individuals, there are drugs that can enhance sexual desire and reduce impotence. In patients with Parkinson's disease, the use of L-dopa often restores sexual potency (Taberner, 1985). When this effect was first observed, many individuals concluded that L-dopa was an aphrodisiac. But it does not work with normal individuals, and even if it did, the potential negative side effects would outweigh the benefits.

Research with yohimbine (Yocon, Yohimex), a substance derived from the bark of an African tree, has revealed what West African witch doctors have known for centuries—that yohimbine can be effective in the treatment of certain cases of impotence (Reid et al., 1987). Yohimbine is an alpha-2-adrenergic (noradrenergic autoreceptor) antagonist. Its primary effect is to block the inhibitory feedback system via noradrenergic autoreceptors and allow more norepinephrine synthesis and/or release. Whether the problem was psychological or physiological in origin, almost half the male subjects given yohimbine overcame difficulties in erection and regained the ability to perform sexually. Curiously, the beneficial effects were noted 2 to 3 weeks after the start of therapy; this response latency is not compatible with the rapid onset of yohimbine's known pharmacological properties or autonomic effects. Potential side effects include a significant elevation in blood pressure, which could be fatal, and sweating, nausea, and vomiting.

At the present time, the most successful drug treatment for impotence (or, more technically, erectile dysfunction), which has changed the sexual behavior of millions of men, is a drug without psychoactive properties. Viagra (sildenafil), approved for the treatment of sexual dysfunction in 1998, works by blocking the action of an enzyme called phosphodiesterase, which normally inhibits the action of neurotransmitters that cause muscles surrounding penile arteries to relax. In turn, that allows the arteries to expand and become engorged with blood. Over 60 percent of men with erectile dysfunction resulting from a variety of causes have been shown to benefit from the drug, with over 40 percent having ideal outcomes (Pallas et al., 2000). Viagra's side effects are usually mild to moderate and usually do not last longer than a few hours. The most common side effects are headache, flushing of the face, and upset stomach. Less common side effects that may occur are temporary changes in color vision, eyes being more sensitive to light, and blurred vision. In rare instances, men have reported a painful erection that lasts many hours (priapism), which, if not treated right away, could produce permanent damage to the penis.

Eating Disorders

Obesity is a major problem in many cultures. In some cases, it has psychological consequences in terms of the obese person's self-esteem and social interaction. In extreme cases, it can lead to severe physiological consequences, such as inability to regulate glucose plasma levels and high blood pressure. Thus, a multitude of treatments for obesity have been developed, and often these treatments include psychotropic drugs.

Appetite-control medications, both prescription and nonprescription, are big business. Unfortunately, most of these are amphetamines or are related structurally to amphetamine, and these are easily abused. Furthermore, most do not do much for weight control (perhaps they enhance the person's mood temporarily), or if they do, tolerance develops fairly rapidly. Most studies that have investigated weight losses with these drugs have found the average weight loss to be rather modest, and in most cases, the losses are not maintained for very long. These drugs also have side effects, such as elevated blood pressure. Thus, the consensus is that these drugs are of limited value in the area of weight control.

The difficulties in developing an effective appetite-suppressant drug without adverse side effects are illustrated by the withdrawal (1997) of Redux (dexfenfluramine) from the market only 14 months after its approval by the FDA. Both Redux and its chemical relative Pondamin (fenfluramine) were withdrawn at the FDA's request after an abnormally high incidence of damaged heart valves was found in users, even though they were asymptomatic. Ironically, the fenfluramines by themselves may not have caused the heart lesions, as well as another side effect associated with their use, pulmonary hypertension. These effects may well have been the result of their being combined with the appetite-suppressant phentermine (the popular "fen-phen" combination). It turns out that one of phentermine's little known properties is to inhibit MAO (the enzyme that metabolizes serotonin). This property, combined with the fenfluramines' serotonin reuptake blockade and releasing properties, can elevate serotonin plasma concentrations to toxic levels (Ulus et al., 2000).

More recently, Meridia (sibutramine), a serotonin and norepinephrine reuptake inhibitor, has been approved for weight control. While it has been shown to be moderately effective at helping obese patients shed pounds—in studies, they lost 7 percent to 8 percent more body weight than patients given placebo—and lacks amphetamine-type abuse liability, it can cause increases in blood pressure and pulse rate that may endanger some patients (Ryan, 2000; Schuh et al., 2000). There is no evidence at this point that Meridia poses the risk of heart valve damage that was exhibited with the fen-phen drug combination. Other nonpsychoactive drugs that may be useful in weight control consist of "thermogenic agents," which produce weight loss by increasing energy expenditure; "digestion inhibitors," which interfere with the breakdown and digestion of dietary fat; and "fat substitutes," which mimic some of the roles of fat and allow people to reduce their intake of high-fat foods (Ryan, 2000).

Although a reasonably effective and safe drug is not yet available for the treatment of obesity, recent advances in identifying some of the specific ligands and receptors that control body weight and appetite suggest that, within a few years, such a drug may be available. For example, a ligand called "leptin" is a protein that controls body weight, and at least two of its receptors have been identified. As already mentioned, appetite-control medications are big business; a pharmaceutical company has already paid $20 million for exclusive license to develop leptin-based products—despite the fact that there is no guarantee such drugs will be found (Barinaga, 1996).

On the other side of the coin, there has been focus on eating disorders that may result in persons becoming severely underweight. The two disorders receiving the most attention are *anorexia nervosa* and *bulimia nervosa*. While individuals with these disorders may share certain characteristics, they are viewed by most experts as separate disorders. In both disorders, the individuals are predominantly females who fear becoming obese and believe that one must be thin in order to be physically attractive. Depression and anxiety are common symptoms, but they may not be clearly evident. In most cases their weights are below what is considered normal for their age group.

Anorexics are generally severely underweight (as much as 50 percent below normal), whereas the weight of bulimics may be in the normal range. Despite their extreme thinness, anorexics may actually perceive themselves as overweight or gaining weight. Bulimics commonly experience food binges, eating everything in sight, but then purge themselves by self-induced vomiting or by taking laxatives. This is rarely the case with anorexics, who generally are on a self-starvation diet. Because of malnutrition-induced disruption in metabolism and hypothalamic functions, anorexics may actually not feel hungry at all.

In addition to the direct problems associated with malnutrition (such as lowered resistance to disease, death by starvation, and absence of menstruation), there are a number of other consequences of these disorders, such as deterioration of the teeth and esophagus (due to stomach acid upon vomiting), constipation, and drug dependence. (One study indicated that one-third of the cocaine abusers who called a cocaine hot line met the criteria for anorexia or bulimia [Jonas et al., 1987].) Thus, although these disorders are not very common, some kind of intervention is definitely called for when they occur.

A variety of psychological and physiological etiologies and treatments have been explored (the discussion of which is beyond the scope of this text) with, as yet, no consensus as to how these disorders come about or how they should be treated. Many pharmacological interventions have been tried, with very limited success. Most studies in this area have not been methodologically sound; for example, they used small samples, did not use a control group, used inconsistent criteria for symptoms, or mixed a variety of psychological and drug treatments.

In both illnesses, it is important to diagnose and treat any comorbid conditions, including mood and anxiety disorders; this may involve the use of anxiolytics or mood-stabilizing drugs. Numerous studies have reported that antidepressants are effective in the treatment of bulimia, especially if there are clear signs of concomitant depression (Advokat & Kutlesic, 1995; Crow & Mitchell, 1994). However, the tricyclics may induce weight gain and carbohydrate craving, which can exacerbate the individual's fear of losing control over eating behavior, and drug regimens using the older MAOIs must be closely monitored because of the dietary restrictions that are involved. Perhaps for these reasons, the SSRIs have become the most commonly used type of antidepressant in the treatment of bulimia. They not only are effective antidepressants, but also tend to suppress appetite in many individuals, which may lessen the urge to binge. Opiate antagonists have been shown to reduce binge eating in bulimics (Mitchell et al., 1986), but further trials are necessary for determining their overall efficacy in this disorder. Basically, there is, as yet, no drug treatment regimen that carries a promise for a sustained and speedy recovery from eating disorders. Although no differential effect regarding efficacy and tolerability among the various classes of antidepressants has been demonstrated in bulimic patients (Bacaltchuk et al., 2000), numerous lines of research indicate that abnormal serotonergic regulation in bulimic patients may contribute to recurrent binge eating, depressed mood, and impulsivity (Kaye et al., 2000; Wolfe et al., 2000).

For anorexia, the consensus in the field is that drug therapy has little to offer and that supportive psychotherapy and behavioral intervention used in inpatient programs are the best methods for producing weight gain (Vitiello & Lederhendler, 2000). A similar belief is held for the treatment of bulimia. Although antidepressant drugs have been shown to reduce patients' frequency of binging significantly, only a small minority of bulimic patients treated with drugs alone are viewed as cured of the disorder.

Websites for Further Information

Site providing general information on psychiatric disorders and pharmacotherapy:

http://uhs.bsd.uchicago.edu/~bhsiung/tips/tips.html

Bibliography

Advokat, C., & Kutlesic, V. (1995). Pharmacotherapy of the eating disorders: A commentary. *Neuroscience & Biobehavioral Reviews, 19,* 59–66.

Ajibola, O., & Clement, P. W. (1995). Differential effects of methylphenidate and self-reinforcement on attention-deficit hyperactivity disorder. *Behavior Modification, 19,* 211–233.

Anderson, L. T., Campbell, M., Grega, D. M., et al. (1984). Haloperidol in the treatment of infantile autism: Effects on learning and behavioral symptoms. *American Journal of Psychiatry, 141,* 1195–1202.

Arnold, L. E. (1993). A comparative overview of treatment research methodology: Adult vs. child and adolescent, psychopharmacological vs. psychosocial treatments. *Psychopharmacology Bulletin, 29,* 5–18.

Bacaltchuk, J., Hay, P., & Mari, J. J. (2000). Antidepressants versus placebo for the treatment of bulimia nervosa: A systematic review. *Australian and New Zealand Journal of Psychiatry, 34,* 310–317.

Ban, T. A. (1978). Vasodilators, stimulants and anabolic agents in the treatment of geropsychiatric patients. In M. A. Lipton, A. DiMascio, & K. F. Killman (Eds.), *Psychopharmacology* (pp. 1525–1534). New York: Raven Press.

Ban, T. (1984). Chronic disease and depression in the geriatric population. *Journal of Clinical Psychiatry, 45,* 18–23.

Barak, Y., Ring, A., Levy, D., et al. (1995). Disabling compulsion in 11 mentally retarded adults: An open trial of clomipramine SR. *Journal of Clinical Psychiatry, 56,* 459–461.

Barinaga, M. (1996). Obesity: Leptin receptor weighs in. *Science, 271,* 29.

Barkley, R. A., DuPaul, G. J., & McMurray, M. B. (1991). Attention deficit disorder with and without hyperactivity: Clinical response to three dose levels of methylphenidate. *Pediatrics, 87,* 519–531.

Biederman, J. (1988). Pharmacological treatment of adolescents with affective disorders and attention deficit disorder. *Psychopharmacology Bulletin, 24,* 81–87.

Biederman, J., Faraone, S. V., Mick, E., et al. (1995). High risk for attention-deficit hyperactivity disorder among children of parents with childhood onset of the disorder: A pilot study. *American Journal of Psychiatry, 152,* 431–435.

Biederman, J., Wilens, T., Mick, E., et al. (1999). Pharmacotherapy of attention-deficit/hyperactivity disorder reduces risk for substance use disorder. *Pediatrics, 104,* e20.

Block, R. I., Farinpour, R., & Schlechte, J. A. (1991). Effects of chronic marijuana use on testosterone, luteinizing hormone, follicle stimulating hormone, prolactin and cortisol in men and women. *Drug & Alcohol Dependence, 28,* 121–128.

Bouvard, M. P., Leboyer M., Launay, J. M., et al. (1995). Low-dose naltrexone effects on plasma chemistries and clinical symptoms in autism: A double-blind, placebo-controlled study. *Psychiatry Research, 58,* 191–201.

Branconnier, R. J., Branconnier, M. E., Walshe, T. M., et al. (1992). Blocking the Ca^{2+}-activated cytotoxic mechanisms of cholinergic neuronal death: A novel treatment strategy for Alzheimer's disease. *Psychopharmacology Bulletin, 28,* 175–182.

Brannan, T., & Yahr, M. D. (1995). Comparative study of selegiline plus L-dopa-carbidopa versus L-dopa-carbidopa alone in the treatment of Parkinson's disease. *Annals of Neurology, 37,* 95–98.

Brown, R. T., Borden, K. A., & Clingerman, S. R. (1985). Pharmacotherapy in ADD adolescents with special attention to multimodality treatments. *Psychopharmacology Bulletin, 21,* 192–211.

Bruun, R. D., Budman, C. L. (1996). Risperidone as a treatment for Tourette's syndrome. *Journal of Clinical Psychiatry, 57,* 29–31.

Buitelaar, J. K., Van der Gaag, R. J., Swaab-Barneveld, H., & Kuiper, M. (1995). Prediction of clinical response to methylphenidate in children with attention-deficit hyperactivity disorder. *Journal of the American Academy of Child and Adolescent Psychiatry, 34,* 1025–1032.

Caine, E. C., Ludlow, C. L., Polinsky, R. J., & Ebert, M. H. (1984). Provocative drug testing in Tourette's syndrome: *d-* and *l-*amphetamine and haloperidol. *Journal of the American Academy of Child Psychiatry, 23,* 147–152.

Campbell, M. (1978). Use of drug treatment in infantile autism and childhood schizophrenia: A review. In M. A. Lipton, A. DiMascio, & K. F. Killman (Eds.), *Psychopharmacology* (pp. 1451–1462). New York: Raven Press.

Campbell, M., & Cueva, J. E. (1995). Psychopharmacology in child and adolescent psychiatry: A review of the past seven years. Part II. *Journal of the American Academy of Child and Adolescent Psychiatry, 34,* 1262–1272.

Campbell, M., Perry, R., & Green, W. H. (1984). Use of lithium in children and adolescents. *Psychosomatics, 25,* 95–106.

Campbell, M., Schopler, E., Cueva, J. E., & Hallin A. (1996). Treatment of autistic disorder. *Journal of the American Academy of Child and Adolescent Psychiatry, 35,* 134–143.

Castellanos, F. X., Giedd, J.N, Elia, J., et al. (1997). Controlled stimulant treatment of ADHD and comorbid Tourette's syndrome: Effects of stimulant and dose. *Journal of the American Academy of Child and Adolescent Psychiatry, 36,* 589–596.

Cazzullo, A. G., Musetti, M. C., Musetti, L., et al. (1999). β-Endorphin levels in peripheral blood mononuclear cells and long-term naltrexone treatment in autistic children. *European Neuropsychopharmacology, 9,* 361–366.

Chappell, P. B., Riddle, M. A., Scahill, L., et al. (1995). Guanfacine treatment of comorbid attention-deficit hyperactivity disorder and Tourette's syndrome: Preliminary clinical experience. *Journal of the American Academy of Child and Adolescent Psychiatry, 34,* 1140–1146.

Clure, C., Brady, K. T., Saladin, M. E., et al. (1999). Attention-deficit/hyperactivity disorder and substance use: Symptom pattern and drug choice. *American Journal of Drug and Alcohol Abuse, 25,* 441–448.

Cohen, D. J., Riddle, M. A., & Leckman, J. F. (1992). Pharmacotherapy of Tourette's syndrome and associated disorders. *Psychiatric Clinics of North America, 15,* 109–129.

Cone, E. J., Johnson, R. E., Moore, J. D., & Roache, J. D. (1986). Acute effects of smoking marijuana on hormones, subjective effects and performance in male human subjects. *Pharmacology, Biochemistry & Behavior, 24,* 1749–1754.

Cook, E. H., Jr., Rowlett, R., Jaselskis, C., et al. (1992). Fluoxetine treatment of children and adults with autistic disorder and mental retardation. *Journal of American Academy of Child and Adolescent Psychiatry, 31,* 739–745.

Cook, E. H., Jr., Stein, M. A., Krasowski, M. D., et al. (1995). Association of attention-deficit disorder and the dopamine transporter gene. *American Journal of Human Genetics, 56,* 993–998.

Cooper, J. R., Bloom, F. E., & Roth, R. H. (1996). *The biochemical basis of neuropharmacology,* 7th ed. New York: Oxford University Press.

Crook, T. (1988). Pharmacotherapy of cognitive deficits in Alzheimer's disease and age-associated memory impairment. *Psychopharmacology Bulletin, 24,* 31–38.

Crow, S. J., & Mitchell, J. E. (1994). Rational therapy of eating disorders. *Drugs, 48,* 372–379.

Cunningham, C. E., Siegel, L. S., & Offord, D. R. (1985). A developmental dose-response analysis of the effects of methylphenidate on the peer interactions of attention deficit disordered boys. *Journal of Child Psychology and Psychiatry, 26,* 955–971.

Dakof, G. A., & Mendelsohn, G. A. (1986). Parkinson's disease: The psychological aspects of a chronic illness. *Psychological Bulletin, 99,* 375–387.

DeLong, G. R., Teague, L. A., & McSwain, K. M. (1998). Effects of fluoxetine treatment in young children with idiopathic autism. *Developmental Medicine and Child Neurology, 40,* 551–562.

Devane, C. L., & Sallee, F. R. (1996). Serotonin selective reuptake inhibitors in child and adolescent psychopharmacology: A review of published experience. *Journal of Clinical Psychiatry, 57,* 55–66.

Dichter, M. A., & Ayala, G. F. (1987). Cellular mechanisms of epilepsy: A status report. *Science, 237,* 157–164.

Domino, E. F., Dren, A. T., & Giardina, W. J. (1978). Biochemical and neurotransmitter changes in the aging brain. In M. A. Lipton, A. DiMascio, & K. F. Killman (Eds.), *Psychopharmacology* (pp. 1507–1516). New York: Raven Press.

Dougherty, D. D., Bonab, A. A., Spencer, T. J., et al. (1999). Dopamine transporter density in patients with attention deficit hyperactivity disorder. *The Lancet, 354,* 2132–2133.

Douglas, V. I., Barr, R. G., Desilets, J., & Sherman, E. (1995). Do high doses of stimulants impair flexible thinking in attention-deficit hyperactivity disorder? *Journal of the American Academy of Child and Adolescent Psychiatry, 34,* 877–885.

Dulcan, M. K. (1986). Comprehensive treatment of children and adolescents with attention deficit disorders: The state of the art. *Clinical Psychology Review, 6,* 539–569.

Duvoisin, R. C. (1986). Etiology of Parkinson's disease: Current concepts. *Clinical Neuropharmacology, 9,* S3–S11.

Elia, J. (1991). Stimulants and antidepressant pharmacokinetics in hyperactive children. *Psychopharmacology Bulletin, 27,* 411–416.

Elia, J., Ambrosini, P. J., & Rapoport, J. L. (1999). Treatment of attention-deficit-hyperactivity disorder. *New England Journal of Medicine, 340,* 780–788.

Emilien, G., Beyreuther, K., Masters, C. L., et al. (2000). Prospects for pharmacological intervention in Alzheimer disease. *Archives of Neurology, 57,* 454–459.

Engelhardt, D. M., & Polizos, P. (1978). Adverse effects of pharmacotherapy in childhood psychosis. In M. A. Lipton, A. DiMascio, & K. F. Killman (Eds.), *Psychopharmacology* (pp. 1463–1471). New York: Raven Press.

Ernst, M., Liebernauer, L. L., King, A. C., et al. (1994). Reduced brain metabolism in hyperactive girls. *Journal of the American Academy of Child and Adolescent Psychiatry, 33,* 858–868.

Faraone, S. V., Biederman, J., Chen, W. J., et al. (1995). Genetic heterogeneity in attention-deficit hyperactivity disorder (ADHD): Gender, psychiatric comorbidity, and maternal ADHD. *Journal of Abnormal Psychology, 104,* 334–345.

Faraone, S. V., Biederman, J., Spencer, T., et al. (2000). Attention-deficit/hyperactivity disorder in adults: An overview. *Biological Psychiatry, 48,* 9–20.

Faraone, S. V., Biederman, J., Weiffenbach, B., et al. (1999). Dopamine D4 gene 7-repeat allele and attention deficit hyperactivity disorder. *American Journal of Psychiatry, 156,* 768–770.

Fatemi, S. H., Realmuto, G. M., Khan, L., et al. (1998). Fluoxetine in treatment of adolescent patients with autism: A longitudinal open trial. *Journal of Autism and Developmental Disorders, 28,* 303–307.

Feldman, H. M., Kolmen, B. K., & Gonzaga, A. M. (1999). Naltrexone and communication skills in young children with autism. *Journal of the American Academy of Child and Adolescent Psychiatry, 38,* 587–593.

Fennig, S., Fennig, S. N., Pato, M., & Weitzman, A. (1994). Emergence of symptoms of Tourette's syndrome during fluvoxamine treatment of obsessive-compulsive disorder. *British Journal of Psychiatry, 164,* 839–841.

Finch, C. E. (1982). The neurobiology of aging. *Science, 216,* 49–50.

Fine, S., & Johnston, C. (1993). Drug and placebo side effects in methylphenidate-placebo trial for attention-deficit hyperactivity disorder. *Child Psychiatry & Human Development, 24,* 25–30.

Fowler, J. S., Volkow, N. D., Wang, G. J., et al. (1996). Inhibition of monoamine oxidase B in the brains of smokers. *Nature, 379,* 733–736.

Fox, A. M., & Rieder, M. J. (1993). Risks and benefits of drugs used in the management of the hyperactive child. *Drug Safety, 9,* 38–50.

Fraser, A. D. (1996). New drugs for the treatment of epilepsy. *Clinical Biochemistry, 29,* 97–110.

Frazier, J. A., Giedd, J. N., Kaysen, D., et al. (1996). Childhood-onset schizophrenia: Brain MRI rescan after 2 years of clozapine maintenance treatment. *American Journal of Psychiatry, 153,* 564–566.

Friedel, R. O. (1978). Pharmacokinetics in the geropsychiatric patient. In M. A. Lipton, A. DiMascio, & K. F. Killman (Eds.), *Psychopharmacology* (pp. 1499–1506). New York: Raven Press.

Gadow, K. D. (1992). Pediatric psychopharmacotherapy: A review of recent research. *Journal of Child Psychology and Psychiatry, 33,* 153–195.

Gadow, K. D., Sverd, J., Sprafkin, J., et al. (1999). Long-term methylphenidate therapy in children with comorbid attention-deficit hyperactivity disorder and chronic multiple tic disorder. *Archives of General Psychiatry, 56,* 330–336.

Galizia, V. J. (1984). Pharmacotherapy of memory loss in the geriatric patient. *Drug Intelligence and Clinical Pharmacy, 18,* 784–791.

Gatti, G., Bonomi, I., Jannuzzi, G., & Perucca, E. (2000). The new antiepileptic drugs: Pharmacological and clinical aspects. *Current Pharmaceutical Design, 6,* 839–860.

Geller, B. (1991). Psychopharmacology of children and adolescents: Pharmacokinetics and relationships of plasma/serum levels to response. *Psychopharmacology Bulletin, 27,* 401–410.

Gillberg, C. (1995). Endogenous opioids and opiate antagonists in autism: Brief review of empirical findings and implications for clinicians. *Developmental Medicine & Child Neurology, 37,* 239–245.

Gillberg, C., Melander, H., von Knorring, A. L., et al. (1997). Long-term stimulant treatment of children with attention-deficit hyperactivity disorder symptoms. A randomized, double-blind, placebo-controlled trial. *Archives of General Psychiatry, 54,* 857–864.

Goldberg, J. R. (1987). Healthy addiction. *Health, 19(8),* 18.

Gonzalez, N. M., Campbell, M., Small, A. M., et al., (1994). Naltrexone plasma levels, clinical response and effect on weight in autistic children. *Psychopharmacology Bulletin, 30,* 203–208.

Gordon, C. T., Frazier, J. A., McKenna, K., et al. (1994). Childhood-onset schizophrenia: An NIMH study in progress. *Schizophrenia Bulletin, 20,* 697–712.

Hakansson, L. (1993). Mechanism of action of cholinesterase inhibitors in Alzheimer's disease. *Acta Neurologica Scandinavica, 194,* 7–9.

Hashino, Y., Yamamoto, T., Kaneko, M., et al. (1984). Blood serotonin and free tryptophan concentration in autistic children. *Neuropsychobiology, 11,* 22–27.

Hauser, R. A., & Zesiewicz, T. A. (1995). Sertraline-induced exacerbation of tics in Tourette's syndrome. *Movement Disorders, 10,* 682–684.

Hechtman, L., Weiss, G., & Perlman, T. (1984). Young adult outcome of hyperactive children who received long-term stimulant treatment. *Journal of the American Academy of Child Psychiatry, 23,* 261–269.

Hendren, R. L. (1996). Management of psychosis in adolescents suffering from schizophrenia and bipolar disorder. *Essential Psychopharmacology, 1,* 38–53.

Horvath, K., Stefanatos, G., Sokolski, K. N., et al. (1998). Improved social and language skills after secretin administration in patients with autistic spectrum disorders. *Journal of the Association for Academic Minority Physicians, 9,* 9–15.

Hunsinger, D. M., Nguyen, T., Zebraski, S. E., & Raffa, R. B. (2000). Is there a basis for novel pharmacotherapy of autism? *Life Sciences, 67,* 1667–1682.

Hunt, R. D., Arnsten, A. F., & Asbell, M. D. (1995). An open trial of guanfacine in the treatment of attention-deficit hyperactivity disorder. *Journal of the American Academy of Child and Adolescent Psychiatry, 34,* 50–54.

Hunt, R. D., Minderaa, R. B., & Cohen, D. J. (1986). The therapeutic effect of clonidine in attention deficit disorder with hyperactivity: A comparison with placebo and methylphenidate. *Psychopharmacology Bulletin, 22,* 229–236.

Jonas, J. M., Gold, M. S., Sweeney, D., & Pottash, A. L. C. (1987). Eating disorders and cocaine abuse: A survey of 259 cocaine abusers. *Journal of Clinical Psychiatry, 48,* 47–50.

Kaakkola, S. (2000). Clinical pharmacology, therapeutic use and potential of COMT inhibitors in Parkinson's disease. *Drugs, 59,* 1233–1250.

Katz, I. R., Jeste, D. V., Mintzer, J. E., et al. (1999). Comparison of risperidone and placebo for psychosis and behavioral disturbances associated with dementia: A randomized, double-blind trial. *Journal of Clinical Psychiatry, 60,* 107–115.

Kaye, W. H., Gendall, K. A., Fernstrom, M. H., et al. (2000). Effects of acute tryptophan depletion on mood in bulimia nervosa. *Biological Psychiatry, 47,* 151–157.

Kent, J. D., Blader, J. C., Koplewicz, H. S., et al. (1995). Effects of late-afternoon methylphenidate administration on behavior and sleep in attention-deficit hyperactivity disorder. *Pediatrics, 96,* 320–325.

Knegtering, H., Eijck, M., & Huijsman, A. (1994). Effects of antidepressants on cognitive functioning of elderly patients. A review. *Drugs and Aging, 5,* 192–199.

Knoll, J. (1995). Rationale for (-)deprenyl (selegiline) medication in Parkinson's disease and in prevention of age-related nigral changes. *Biomedicine and Pharmacotherapy, 49,* 187–195.

Kolata, G. (1982). Consensus on diets and hyperactivity. *Science, 215,* 958.

Kolata, G. (1987). Panel urges dementia be diagnosed with care. *Science, 237,* 725.

Kolmen, B. K., Feldman, H. M., Handen, B. L., et al. (1997). Naltrexone in young autistic children: Replication study and learning measures. *Journal of the American Academy of Child and Adolescent Psychiatry, 36,* 1570–1578.

Koob, G. F. (1987). Neuropeptides and memory. In L. Iverson, S. Iverson, & S. Snyder (Eds.), *New directions in behavioral pharmacology* (pp. 531–573). New York: Plenum Press.

Kopin, I. J., & Markey, S. P. (1988). MPTP toxicity: Implications for research in Parkinson's disease. *Annual Review of Neuroscience, 11,* 81–96.

Krause, K-H., Dresel, S. H., Krause, J., et al. (2000). Increased striatal dopamine transporter in adult patients with attention deficit hyperactivity disorder: Effects of methylphenidate as measured by single photon emission computed tomography. *Neuroscience Letters, 285,* 107–110.

Langer, D. H., Sweeney, K. P., Bartenbach, et al. (1986). Evidence of lack of abuse or dependence following pemoline treatment: Results of a retrospective survey. *Drug and Alcohol Dependence, 17,* 213–227.

Larsen, J. P., Boas, J., & Erdal, J. E. (1999). Does selegiline modify the progression of early Parkinson's disease? Results from a five-year study. The Norwegian-Danish Study Group. *European Journal of Neurology, 6,* 539–547.

Leavitt, F. (1982). *Drugs and behavior,* 2nd ed. New York: John Wiley & Sons.

Lees, A. J. (1995). Comparison of therapeutic effects and mortality data of levodopa and levodopa combined with selegiline in patients with early, mild Parkinson's disease. Parkinson's Disease Research Group of the United Kingdom. *BMJ, 311,* 1602–1607.

Leventhal, B. L., Cook, E. H., Jr., Morford, M., et al. (1993). Clinical and neurochemical effects of fenfluramine in children with autism. *Journal of Neuropsychiatry and Clinical Neurosciences, 5,* 307–315.

Levin, G. M. (1995). Attention-deficit hyperactivity disorder: The pharmacist's role. *American Pharmacy, 35,* 10–20.

Lewin, R. (1985). Parkinson's disease: An environmental cause. *Science, 228,* 257–258.

Lewin, R. (1987). More clues to the cause of Parkinson's disease. *Science, 237,* 978.

Lewis, M. H., Bodfish, J. W., Powell, S. B., & Golden, R. N. (1995). Clomipramine treatment for stereotype and related repetitive movement disorders associated with mental retardation. *American Journal of Mental Retardation, 100,* 299–312.

LeWitt, P. A. (1992). Clinical studies with and pharmacokinetic considerations of sustained-release levodopa. *Neurology, 42* (suppl. 1), 29–32.

LeWitt, P. A. (1994). Clinical trials of neuroprotection in Parkinson's disease: Long-term selegiline and alpha-tocopherol treatment. *Journal of Neural Transmission, 43,* 171–181.

Madden, S., Spaldin, V., & Park, B. K. (1995). Clinical pharmacokinetics of tacrine. *Clinical Pharmacokinetics, 28,* 449–457.

Markowitz, P. I. (1992). Effect of fluoxetine on self-injurious behavior in the developmentally disabled: A preliminary study. *Journal of Clinical Psychopharmacology, 12,* 27–31.

Matochik, J. A., Liebenaur, L. L., King, A. C., et al. (1994). Cerebral glucose metabolism in adults with attention-deficit hyperactivity disorder after chronic stimulant treatment. *American Journal of Psychiatry, 151,* 658–664.

Matochik, J. A., Nordahl, T. E., Gross, M., et al. (1993). Effects of acute stimulant medication on cerebral metabolism in adults with hyperactivity. *Neuropsychopharmacology, 8,* 377–386.

McNamara, J. O. (1996). Drugs effective in the treatment of the epilepsies. In A. G. Gilman, L. S. Goodman, J. G. Hardman, L. E. Limbard, P. B.

Molinoff, & R. W. Ruddon (Eds.), *The pharmacological basis of therapeutics* (pp. 461–486). New York: McGraw-Hill.

Mihailescu, S., & Drucker-Colin, R. (2000). Nicotine, brain nicotinic receptors, and neuropsychiatric disorders. *Archives of Medical Research, 31,* 131–144.

Milberger, S., Biederman, J., Faraone, S. V., et al. (1997). Associations between ADHD and psychoactive substance use disorders. Findings from a longitudinal study of high-risk siblings of ADHD children. *American Journal of Addictions, 6,* 318–329.

Montgomery, E. B. (1992). Pharmacokinetics and pharmacodynamics of levodopa. *Neurology, 42* (Suppl 1), 17–22.

Morgentaler, A. (1999). Male impotence. *The Lancet, 354,* 1713–1718.

Mulnard, R. A., Cotman, C. W., Kawas, C., et al. (2000). Estrogen replacement therapy for treatment of mild to moderate Alzheimer disease: A randomized controlled trial. *JAMA, 283,* 1007–1015.

Musser, C. J., Ahmann, P. A., Theye, F. W., et al. (1998). Stimulant use and the potential for abuse in Wisconsin as reported by school administrators and longitudinally followed children. *Journal of Developmental and Behavioral Pediatrics, 19,* 187–192.

Myllyla, V. V., Heinonen, E. H., Vuorinen, J. A. et al. (1995). Early selegiline therapy reduces levodopa dose requirement in Parkinson's disease. *Acta Neurologica Scandinavica, 91,* 177–182.

Norman, T. R., & Burrows, G. D. (1995). A risk-benefit assessment of moclobemide in the treatment of depressive disorders. *Drug Safety, 12,* 46–54.

Olney, J. W. (1990). Excitotoxic amino acids and neuropsychiatric disorders. *Annual Review of Pharmacology and Toxicology, 30,* 47–71.

Owley, T., Steele, E., Corsello, C., et al. (1999). A double-blind, placebo-controlled trial of secretin for the treatment of autistic disorder. *Medscape General Medicine.* <http://hiv.medscape.com/Medscape/General Medicine/journal/1999;v01.n10/mgm1006.owle/mgm1006.owle-01.html>

Pallas, J., Levine, S. B., Althof, S. E., et al. (2000). A study using Viagra in a mental health practice. *Journal of Sex and Marital Therapy, 26,* 41–50.

Parnetti, L. (1995). Clinical pharmacokinetics of drugs for Alzheimer's disease. *Clinical Pharmacokinetics, 29,* 110–129.

Pelham, W. E., Jr. (1993). Pharmacotherapy of children with attention-deficit hyperactivity disorder. *School Psychology Review, 22,* 199–227.

Pelham, W. E., Jr., Carlson, C., Sams, S. E., et al. (1993). Separate and combined effects of methylphenidate and behavior modification on boys with attention-deficit hyperactivity disorder in the classroom. *Journal of Consulting & Clinical Psychology, 61,* 506–515.

Pelham, W. E., Jr., Greenslade, K. E., Vodde-Hamilton, M., et al. (1990). Relative efficacy of long-acting stimulants on children with attention deficit-hyperactivity disorder: A comparison of standard methylphenidate, sustained-release methylphenidate, sustained-release dextroamphetamine, and pemoline. *Pediatrics, 86,* 226–237.

Pelham, W. E., Jr., Swanson, J. M., Furman, M. B., & Schwindt, H. (1995). Pemoline effects on children with ADHD: A time-response by dose-response analysis on classroom measures. *Journal of the American Academy of Child and Adolescent Psychiatry, 34,* 1504–1513.

Peral, M., Alcami, M., & Gilaberte, I. (1999). Fluoxetine in children with autism. *Journal of American Academy of Child and Adolescent Psychiatry, 38,* 1472–1473.

Perez-Miranda, J., Aguirre, J., Parrilla, J. L., & Perez-Miranda, M. (1995). Felbamate: Perspectives for new antiepileptic treatment. *Revista de Neurologia, 23,* 1220–1225.

Pfeiffer, C., & Wagner, M. L. (1994). Clozapine therapy for Parkinson's disease and other movement disorders. *American Journal of Hospital Pharmacy, 51,* 3047–3053.

Pfeiffer, S. I., Norton, J., Nelson, L., & Shott, S. (1995). Efficacy of vitamin B6 and magnesium in the treatment of autism: A methodology review and summary of outcomes. *Journal of Autism & Developmental Disorders, 25,* 481–493.

Plomin, R., Owen, M. J., & McGuffin, P. (1994). The genetic basis of complex human behaviors. *Science, 264,* 1733–1739.

Poewe, W. H., Lees, A. J., & Stern, G. M. (1986). Low-dose L-dopa therapy in Parkinson's disease: A 6-year follow-up study. *Neurology, 36,* 1528–1530.

Polymeropoulos, M. H., Higgins, J. J., Golbe, L. I., et al. (1996). Mapping of a gene for Parkinson's disease to chromosome 4q21–q23. *Science, 274,* 1197–1199.

Priest, R. G., Gimbrett, R., Roberts, M., & Steinert, J. (1995). Reversible and selective inhibitors of monoamine oxidase A in mental and other disorders. *Acta Psychiatrica Scandinavica, 386,* 40–43.

Przuntek, H., Conrad, B., Dichgans, J., et al. (1999). SELEDO: A 5-year long-term trial on the effect of selegiline in early Parkinsonian patients treated with levodopa. *European Journal of Neurology, 6,* 141–150.

Quinn, N. (1995). Drug treatment of Parkinson's disease. *BMJ, 310,* 575–579.

Rapoport, J. L., Buchsbaum, M. S., Weingartner, H., et al. (1980). Dextroamphetamine: Its cognitive and behavioral effects in normal and hyperactive boys and normal men. *Archives of General Psychiatry, 37,* 933–943.

Rapport, M. D., Denney, C., DuPaul, G. J., & Gardner, M. J. (1994). Attention-deficit disorder and methylphenidate: Normalization rates, clinical effectiveness, and response prediction in 76 children. *Journal of the American Academy of Child and Adolescent Psychiatry, 33,* 882–893.

Rapport, M. D., & Kelly, K. L. (1991). Psychostimulant effects on learning and cognitive function: Findings and implications for children with attention deficit hyperactivity disorder. *Clinical Psychology, 11,* 61–92.

Ratey, J. J., Mikkelsen, E., Sorgi, P., et al. (1987). Autism: The treatment of aggressive behaviors. *Journal of Clinical Psychopharmacology, 7,* 35–41.

Regeur, L., Pakkenberg, B., Fog, R., & Pakkenburg, H. (1986). Clinical features and long-term treatment with pimozide in 65 patients with Gilles de la Tourette's syndrome. *Journal of Neurology, Neurosurgery, and Psychiatry, 49,* 791–795.

Reid, K., Surridge, D. H. C., Morales, A., et al. (1987). Double-blind trial of yohimbine in treatment of psychogenic impotence. *The Lancet, 8556,* 421–423.

Riggs, J. E. (1992). Cigarette smoking and Parkinson disease: The illusion of a neuroprotective effect. *Clinical Neuropharmacology, 15,* 88–99.

Ritvo, E. R., & Freeman, B. S. (1984). A medical model of autism: Etiology, pathology and treatment. *Pediatric Annals, 13,* 298–305.

Ross, G. W., Abbott, R. D., Petrovitch, H., et al. (2000). Association of coffee and caffeine intake with the risk of Parkinson disease. *JAMA, 283,* 2674–2679.

Ryan, D. H. (2000). Recent progress in obesity pharmacotherapy. *Current Opinion in Gastroenterology, 16,* 166–172.

Sahley, T. L., & Panksepp, J. (1987). Brain opioids and autism: An updated analysis of possible linkages. *Journal of Autism and Developmental Disorders, 17,* 201–216.

Sallee, F. R., Stiller, R. L., & Perel, J. M. (1992). Pharmacodynamics of pemoline in attention deficit disorder hyperactivity. *Journal of the American Academy of Child and Adolescent Psychiatry, 31,* 244–251.

Salzman, C. (1985). Geriatric psychopharmacology. *Annual Review of Medicine, 36,* 217–228.

Salzman, C. (1988). Treatment of agitation, anxiety, and depression. *Psychopharmacology Bulletin, 24,* 39–42.

Sandler, A. D., Sutton, K. W., DeWeese, J., et al. (1999). Lack of benefit of a single dose of synthetic human secretin in the treatment of autism and pervasive developmental disorder. *New England Journal of Medicine, 341,* 1801–1806.

Schuh, L. M., Schuster, C. R., Hopper, J. A., et al. (2000). Abuse liability assessment of sibutramine, a novel weight control agent. *Psychopharmacology, 147,* 339–346.

Schvehla, T. J., Mandoki, M. W., & Sumner, G. S. (1994). Clonidine therapy for comorbid attention deficit hyperactivity disorder and conduct disorder: Preliminary findings in a children's inpatient unit. *Southern Medical Journal, 87,* 692–695.

Shapiro, A. K., & Shapiro, E. S. (1980). *Tics, Tourette syndrome and other movement disorders.* New York: Tourette Syndrome Association, Inc.

Sherwin, B. B. (1988). A comparative analysis of the role of androgen in human male and female sexual behavior: Behavioral specificity, critical thresholds, and sensitivity. *Psychobiology, 16,* 416–425.

Shevell, M., & Schreiber, R. (1997). Pemoline-associated hepatic failure: A critical analysis of the literature. *Pediatric Neurology, 16,* 14–16.

Silvestri, R., Raffaele, M., De Dominico, P., et al. (1994). Serotoninergic agents in the treatment of Gilles de la Tourette's syndrome. *Acta Neurologica, 16,* 58–63.

Singer, H. S., Brown, J., Quaskey, S., et al. (1995). The treatment of attention-deficit hyperactivity disorder in Tourette's syndrome: A double-blind placebo-controlled study with clonidine and desipramine. *Pediatrics, 95,* 74–81.

Sloman, L. (1991). Use of medication in pervasive developmental disorders. *Psychiatric Clinics of North America, 14,* 165–182.

Soares, J. C., & Gershon, S. (1994). Advances in the pharmacotherapy of Alzheimer's disease. *European Archives of Psychiatry & Clinical Neuroscience, 244,* 261–271.

Sovner, R., Fox, C. J., Lowry, M. J., & Lowry, M. A. (1993). Fluoxetine treatment of depression and associated self-injury in two adults with mental retardation. *Journal of Intellectual Disability Research, 37,* 301–311.

Spencer, T., Biederman, J., Wilens, T., et al. (1993). Nortriptyline treatment of children with attention-deficit hyperactivity disorder and tic disorder or Tourette's syndrome. *Journal of the American Academy of Child and Adolescent Psychiatry, 32,* 205–210.

Sprague, R. L., & Sleator, E. K. (1977). Methylphenidate in hyperkinetic children: Differences in dose effects on learning and social behavior. *Science, 198,* 1274–1276.

Spring, B., Chiodo, J., & Bowen, D. J. (1987). Carbohydrates, tryptophan, and behavior: A methodological review. *Psychological Bulletin, 102,* 234–256.

Steingard, R., Biederman, J., Spencer, T., et al. (1993). Comparison of clonidine in the treatment of attention-deficit hyperactivity diorder with and without comorbid tic disorders. *Journal of the American Academy of Child and Adolescent Psychiatry, 32,* 350–353.

Steingard, R., & Dillon-Stout, D. (1992). Tourette's syndrome and obsessive compulsive disorder. Clinical aspects. *Psychiatric Clinics of North America, 15,* 849–860.

Swanson, J. M., Cantwell, D., Lerner, M., et al. (1991). Effects of stimulant medication on learning in children with ADHD. *Journal of Learning Disabilities, 24,* 219–230.

Swanson, J. M., & Kinsbourne, M. (1976). Stimulant-related state-dependent learning in hyperactive children. *Science, 192,* 1354–1356.

Taberner, P. V. (1985). Sex and drugs—Aphrodite's legacy. *Trends in the Pharmacological Sciences, 6,* 49–54.

Tannock, R., Ickowicz, A., & Schachar, R. (1995). Differential effects of methylphenidate on working memory in ADHD children with and without comorbid anxiety. *Journal of the American Academy of Child and Adolescent Psychiatry, 34,* 886–896.

Thienhaus, O. J., Wheeler, B. G., Simon, S., et al. (1987). A controlled double-blind study of high-dose dihydroergotoxine mesylate (Hydergine) in mild dementia. *Journal of the American Geriatrics Society, 35,* 219–223.

Thurber, S., Ensign, J., Punnet, A. F., & Welter, K. (1995). A meta-analysis of antidepressant outcome studies that involved children and adolescents. *Journal of Clinical Psychology, 51,* 340–345.

Troisi, A., Vicario, E., Nuccetelli, F., et al. (1995). Effects of fluoxetine on aggressive behavior of adult inpatients with mental retardation and epilepsy. *Pharmacopsychiatry, 28,* 73–76.

Ulus, I. H., Maher, T. J., & Wurtman, R. J. (2000). Characterization of phentermine and related compounds as monoamine oxidase (MAO) inhibitors. *Biochemical Pharmacology, 59,* 1611–1621.

Verbaten, M. N., Overtoom, C. C., Koelega, H. S., et al. (1994). Methylphenidate influences on both early and late ERP waves of ADHD children in a continuous performance test. *Journal of Abnormal Child Psychology, 22,* 561–578.

Vitiello, B., & Lederhendler, I. (2000). Research on eating disorders: Current status and future prospects. *Biological Psychiatry, 47,* 777–786.

Volz, H. P., Müller, H., & Möller, H.-J. (1995). Are there any differences in the safety and efficacy of brofaromine and imipramine between non-elderly and elderly patients with major depression? *Neuropsychobiology, 32,* 23–30.

Weiss, G., & Hechtman, L. (1979). The hyperactive child syndrome. *Science, 205,* 1348–1354.

Wettstein, A. (2000). Cholinesterase inhibitors and Gingko extracts—are they comparable in the treatment of dementia? Comparison of published placebo-controlled efficacy studies of at least six months' duration. *Phytomedicine, 6,* 393–401.

Wilcock, G. K. (2000). Treatment for Alzheimer's disease. *International Journal of Geriatric Psychiatry, 15,* 562–565.

Wilder, B. J. (1995). The treatment of epilepsy: An overview of clinical practices. *Neurology, 45,* S7–S11.

Will a pill take your pounds off? (1996, August). *Consumer Reports, 61,* 15–17.

Willemsen-Swinkels, S. H., Buitelaar, J. K., Nijhof, G. J., & van Engeland, H. (1995a). Failure of naltrexone hydrochloride to reduce self-injurious and autistic behavior in mentally retarded adults. Double-blind placebo-controlled studies. *Archives of General Psychiatry, 52,* 766–773.

Willemsen-Swinkels, S. H., Buitelaar, J. K., Weijnen, F. G., & van Engeland, H. (1995b). Placebo-controlled acute dosage naltrexone study in young autistic children. *Psychiatry Research, 58,* 203–215.

Winblad, B., & Poritis, N. (1999). Memantine in severe dementia: Results of the 9M-Best Study (Benefit and efficacy in severely demented patients during treatment with memantine). *Journal of Geriatric Psychiatry, 14,* 135–146.

Wise, T. N. (1994). Sertraline as a treatment for premature ejaculation. *Journal of Clinical Psychiatry, 55,* 417.

Wolf, S. S., Jones, D. W., Knable, M. B., et al. (1996). Tourette syndrome prediction of phenotypic variation in monozygotic twins by caudate nucleus D2 receptor binding. *Science, 273,* 1225–1227.

Wolfe, B. E., Metzger, E. D., Levine, J. M., et al. (2000). Serotonin function following remission from bulimia nervosa. *Neuropsychopharmacology, 22,* 257–263.

Yong, V. W., & Perry, T. L. (1986). Monoamine oxidase B, smoking, and Parkinson's disease. *Journal of the Neurological Sciences, 72,* 265–272.

Zametkin, A. J., Liebenauer, L. L., Fitzgerald, G. A., et al. (1993). Brain metabolism in teenagers with attention-deficit hyperactivity disorder. *Archives of General Psychiatry, 50,* 333–340.

Zametkin, A. J., Nordahl, T. E., Gross, M., et al. (1990). Cerebral glucose metabolism in adults with hyperactivity of childhood onset. *New England Journal of Medicine, 323,* 1361–1366.

Zametkin, A. J., Rapoport, J. L., Murphy, D. L., et al. (1985). Treatment of hyperactive children with monoamine oxidase inhibitors. I. Clinical efficacy. *Archives of General Psychiatry, 42,* 962–966.

Zito, J. M., Safer, D. J., dosReis, S., et al. (2000). Trends in the prescribing of psychotropic medications to preschoolers. *JAMA, 283,* 1025–1030.

Drug Name Index

Brand Name	Generic Name	Brand Name	Generic Name
Actiq	fentanyl	**Exelon**	rivastigmine
Adderall	amphetamine	**Felbatol**	felbamate
Ambien	zolpidem	**Gabitril**	tiagabine
Anafranil	clomipramine	**Halcion**	triazolam
Antabuse	disulfiram	**Haldol**	haloperidol
Aricept	donepezil	**Hydergine**	ergoloid mesylates
Artane	trihexyphenidyl	**Inderal**	propranolol
Asendin	amoxapine	**Ionamin**	phentermine
Ativan	lorazepam	**Ketalar**	ketamine
Benadryl	diphenhydramine	**Klonopin**	clonazepam
Benzedrine	amphetamine	**Lamictal**	lamotrigine
Buprenex	buprenorphine	**Librium**	chlordiazepoxide
BuSpar	buspirone	**Loxitane**	loxapine
Catapres	clonidine	**Ludiomil**	maprotiline
Celexa	citalopram	**Luvox**	fluvoxamine
Clozaril	clozapine	**Marinol**	dronabinol
Cogentin	benztropine	**Mellaril**	thioridazine
Cognex	tacrine	**Meridia**	sibutramine
Comtan	entacapone	**Miltown**	meprobamate
Concerta	methylphenidate	**Moban**	molindone
Cylert	pemoline	**Mysoline**	primidone
Dalmane	flurazepam	**Narcan**	naloxone
Darvon	propoxyphene	**Nardil**	phenelzine
Demerol	meperidine	**Navane**	thiothixene
Depokene	valproic acid	**Neurontin**	gabapentin
Desoxyn	methamphetamine	**Norpramin**	desipramine
Desyrel	trazodone	**Novocain**	procaine
Dexedrine	*d*-amphetamine	**Orap**	pimozide
Dilantin	phenytoin	**Orlamm**	levo-alpha-acetyl-methadol
Dilaudid	hydromorphone	**Pamelor**	nortriptyline
Dolophine	methadone	**Parlodel**	bromocriptine
Edronax	reboxetine	**Parnate**	tranylcypromine
Effexor	venlafaxine	**Paxil**	paroxetine
Elavil	amitriptyline	**Paxipam**	halazepam
Eldepryl	selegiline	**Pondimin**	fenfluramine

407

Brand Name	Generic Name	Brand Name	Generic Name
Prolixin Decanoate	fluphenazine decanoate	**Symmetrel**	amantadine
Provigil	modafinil	**Talwin**	pentazocine
Prozac	fluoxetine	**Tegretol**	carbamazepine
Quaalude	methaqualone	**Tenex**	guanfacine
Redux	dexfenfluramine	**Thorazine**	chlorpromazine
Remeron	mirtazapine	**Tofranil**	imipramine
Restoril	temazepam	**Topamax**	topiramate
Revex	nalmefene	**Tranxene**	chlorazepate
ReVia	naltrexone	**Trilafon**	perphenazine
Risperdal	risperidone	**Trileptal**	oxcarbazepine
Ritalin	methylphenidate	**Valium**	diazepam
Rohypnol	flunitrazepam	**Viagra**	sildenafil
Romazicon	flumazenil	**Vivactil**	protriptyline
Serax	oxazepam	**Wellbutrin**	bupropion
Serentil	mesoridazine	**Xanax**	alprazolam
Seroquel	quetiapine	**Zarontin**	ethosuximide
Serzone	nefazodone	**Zeldox**	ziprasidone
Sinequan	doxepin	**Zoloft**	sertraline
Stelazine	trifluoperazine	**Zonegran**	zonisamide
Sublimaze	fentanyl	**Zyprexa**	olanzapine
Surmontil	trimipramine		

Note: Most of the drugs in this list are those cited in this book that have been approved (or were approved at one time) by the Food and Drug Administration (FDA) for marketing in the United States. Some of these drugs are only marketed outside the United States. Other drugs that have been cited in this text, but for which a brand name has not been provided, are under investigation or have not been approved by the FDA.

Index

Boldface page numbers indicate definition, *f* indicates figure, *t* indicates table.

409